THE FUTURE OF WORK IN DEVELOPING COUNTRIES

INITIATIVE FOR POLICY DIALOGUE AT COLUMBIA:
CHALLENGES IN DEVELOPMENT AND GLOBALIZATION

INITIATIVE FOR POLICY DIALOGUE AT COLUMBIA: CHALLENGES IN DEVELOPMENT AND GLOBALIZATION

JOSÉ ANTONIO OCAMPO AND JOSEPH E. STIGLITZ, SERIES EDITORS

The Great Polarization: How Ideas, Power, and Policies Drive Inequality, Rudiger L. von Arnim and Joseph E. Stiglitz, eds.

The Quality of Growth in Africa, Ravi Kanbur, Akbar Noman, and Joseph E. Stiglitz, eds.

International Policy Rules and Inequality: Implications for Global Economic Governance, José Antonio Ocampo, ed.

The Welfare State Revisited, José Antonio Ocampo and Joseph E. Stiglitz, eds.

Efficiency, Finance, and Varieties of Industrial Policy: Guiding Resources, Learning, and Technology for Sustained Growth, Akbar Noman and Joseph Stiglitz, eds.

Too Little, Too Late: The Quest to Resolve Sovereign Debt Crises, Martin Guzman, José Antonio Ocampo, and Joseph E. Stiglitz, eds.

Macroeconomics and Development: Roberto Frenkel and the Economics of Latin America, Mario Damill, Martín Rapetti, and Guillermo Rozenwurcel, eds.

Industrial Policy and Economic Transformation in Africa, Akbar Noman and Joseph E. Stiglitz, eds.

New Perspectives on International Migration and Development, Jeronimo Cortina and Enrique Ochoa-Reza, eds.

Development Cooperation in Times of Crisis, José Antonio Ocampo and José Antonio Alonso, eds.

Reforming the International Financial System for Development, Jomo Kwame Sundaram, ed.

Taxation in Developing Countries, Roger Gordon, ed.

Growth and Policy in Developing Countries: A Structuralist Approach, José Antonio Ocampo, Codrina Rada, and Lance Taylor

Privatization: Successes and Failures, Gérard Roland, ed.

The Right to Know, Ann Florini, ed.

Escaping the Resource Curse, Macartan Humphreys, Jeffrey D. Sachs, and Joseph E. Stiglitz, eds.

For a complete list of books in the series, please see the Columbia University Press website.

THE FUTURE OF WORK IN DEVELOPING COUNTRIES

EDITED BY

Arjun Jayadev, Akbar Noman, and Joseph E. Stiglitz

COLUMBIA UNIVERSITY PRESS
NEW YORK

Columbia University Press
Publishers Since 1893
New York   Chichester, West Sussex
cup.columbia.edu

Library of Congress Cataloging-in-Publication Data

Names: Jayadev, Arjun editor | Noman, Akbar editor |
Stiglitz, Joseph E. editor
Title: The future of work in developing countries /
edited by Arjun Jayadev, Akbar Noman, Joseph E Stiglitz.
Description: New York : Columbia University Press, [2026] |
Series: Initiative for policy dialogue at Columbia:
challenges in development and globalization |
Includes bibliographical references.
Identifiers: LCCN 2025025844 | ISBN 9780231220330
hardback | ISBN 9780231563185 epub | 9780231565240 PDF
Subjects: LCSH: Labor—Developing countries |
Labor market—Developing countries | Labor policy—
Developing countries
Classification: LCC HD8943 .F87 2026 |
DDC 331.091724—dc23/eng/20251120
LC record available at https://lccn.loc.gov/2025025844

Cover design: Noah Arlow
Cover image: Shutterstock

GPSR Authorized Representative: Easy Access System Europe,
Mustamäe tee 50, 10621 Tallinn, Estonia,
gpsr.requests@easproject.com

INITIATIVE FOR POLICY DIALOGUE AT COLUMBIA: CHALLENGES IN DEVELOPMENT AND GLOBALIZATION

JOSÉ ANTONIO OCAMPO AND JOSEPH E. STIGLITZ, SERIES EDITORS

The Initiative for Policy Dialogue (IPD) at Columbia University brings together academics, policy makers, and practitioners from developed and developing countries to address the most pressing issues in economic policy today. IPD is an important part of Columbia's broad program on development and globalization. The Initiative for Policy Dialogue at Columbia: Challenges in Development and Globalization presents the latest academic thinking on a wide range of development topics and lays out alternative policy options and tradeoffs. Written in a language accessible to policy makers and students alike, this series is unique in that it both shapes the academic research agenda and furthers the economic policy debate, facilitating a more democratic discussion of development policies.

This volume was only made possible through a generous grant
from the Japan International Cooperation Agency.

CONTENTS

INTRODUCTION AND OVERVIEW OF THE BOOK

The Challenges of Employment in the Twenty-First Century

Arjun Jayadev, Akbar Noman, and Joseph E. Stiglitz

1. INTRODUCTION

Policymakers concerned with generating employment and growth in their economies are faced with at least four overlapping crises that threaten both short-term stabilization and the long-term structural transformation that are key to economic development and welfare. These crises are affected by five (partially related) megatrends whose impacts are likely to be particularly significant in developing countries.

FOUR CRISES

First, there is the immediate aftermath of the pandemic and the dislocations to employment wrought both by labor market adjustments within the country and the reorganization of global output and supply chains outside it.

Second, there are the consequences wrought by geopolitical upheavals and their consequences. The Ukraine War and the ripple effects from energy prices exacerbated the supply-side price shocks of COVID-19, which took several years to work out. The lack of resilience of supply chains is having profound implications for economic globalization. The global economic and political consequences of the sharp intensification of the conflict in Israel and Palestine creates additional uncertainties.

Third is the climate crisis, the impact of which will be particularly significant in the Global South. Governments will have to devote considerable resources to mitigation and adaptation, as well as repairing the damage caused by climate change. This seriously constrains the policy space of developing countries.

Fourth, much of the world faces an inequality crisis—and while the fraction living in poverty has been reduced in Africa, the total number living in poverty in that region has increased.[1]

FIVE MEGATRENDS

The challenges posed by these crises are even more pronounced in developing countries. Moreover, while shocks and uncertainties are inevitable, some emerging longer-term trends raise particular concerns for developing countries.

First, several countries, but especially those in the Middle East, sub-Saharan Africa, and South Asia, excluding Sri Lanka and Bangladesh, are at key junctures in their demographic evolution. For these countries, the bulge of those in the working age population—the so-called demographic dividend—is well under way, but job availability is not keeping pace. Fertility and youth dependency rates in sub-Saharan Africa remain very high, as they do in the other parts of the world, notably Pakistan.

The youth bulge in many African countries means an increasing population that has to be educated and for whom jobs will have to be created over the decades to come. Most of the world's population increase will be in Africa (Paice 2021). By 2050, the continent is likely to have a fourth of the world's citizens and a third of the world's working-age population. The UN's medium-case population projections see an increase of 2 billion people in the world's labor force between 2010 and 2100, and in Africa (including North Africa), a rise of 2.1 billion—that is, the labor force outside of Africa will be shrinking. Clearly, there is a particular urgency in addressing employment generation for the region.

Other regions, such as Latin America and the Caribbean, East Asia, and Europe, face different difficulties—while population growth rates are declining or have turned negative, the population is aging and is therefore less capable of bearing shocks to employment patterns that may arise from global dislocations. Young people are more flexible in choosing, for instance, the sector in which they work; mobility becomes harder for those in later decades of their lives.

Second, there is increasing concern about the possibilities for an economic development transition arising from manufacturing-led employment. Most historical experiences, especially the successes in East Asia, suggest that a sustained rise in per capita incomes and improvement in employment conditions are attainable only with the movement away from a dual economy, and by dint of the profound structural transformation that reallocates surplus labor toward higher productivity activities, typically in manufacturing and oriented toward exports. In recent decades, the viability of this model is increasingly coming under question because of the headwinds from automation, "premature deindustrialization" (Rodrik 2016), and the declining role of manufacturing in the global economy (Stiglitz 2021). While the fact that the share of Africa in global manufacturing has remained stagnant and tiny (less than 1 percent) (see Balchin et al. 2016) might suggest ample scope for expansion of that sector in Africa, the magnitude of the increase in the labor force is simply too large, particularly given technological trends to be absorbed by a growth in manufacturing: Even if a large fraction of global employment in the sector were to shift to Africa, there would be a gap that would somehow have to be filled.

Third, broader emerging trends in technology, such as artificial intelligence (AI) and robotization, while global in nature, have a particular impact on the prospects for developing countries, especially sub-Saharan Africa. The reasons are clear: Much of Asia is at higher levels of per capita income and is moving to more complex technologies. For those countries (including China), the traditional escalator to development is not entirely broken. In addition, because of relatively high income, domestic markets and internal growth therein can work to absorb labor. Latin America, too, is at a higher level of income and faces less of an immediate demographic challenge than does sub-Saharan Africa.

For the poorest countries, one of their main assets is their unskilled labor—and these changes in technology imply a decline in the relative value of unskilled labor. In the absence of strong government policies to increase employment and skills, increasing poverty is an almost inevitable consequence.

Fourthly, the dominant model of economic policymaking—neoliberalism—is increasingly being questioned, and rightly so: Because these policies have failed to deliver broad-based prosperity and employment, neoliberalism no longer affords a politically viable model. But there is not yet a widely accepted alternative.

And fifthly, there are seismic changes in the global geo-economic and geo-political order, with Donald Trump's destruction of the already frail rules-based international trade regime. A rising tide of nationalism across the world, a more fragmented world order, and increasing polarization have made the nature of the future global economic system substantially more uncertain.

Any of these concerns by themselves provides a daunting set of challenges, but taken together, they present a global landscape that is possibly the most difficult in decades.

We begin this book by outlining the current and near-term challenges of employment in the twenty-first century. We start with the immediate aftermath of COVID and its dislocations. We then turn to the question of structural transformation. In the third part, we turn to policy considerations before concluding in part four with some reflections on the issues and a sketch of the contributions in this book.

2. THE CHALLENGES OF EMPLOYMENT IN THE TWENTY-FIRST CENTURY

2.1 COVID AND ITS AFTERMATH

In late 2023, the dominant ongoing macroeconomic debate in the global economy was centered on the issue of the resurgence of inflation. The remarkably strong labor market recovery of the northern economies, and the United States in particular, has led to disputes about whether the fiscal response to the pandemic has led to a demand-driven inflation or whether, in fact, this is primarily a supply-side phenomenon, driven by lingering effects of Covid-19 disruptions and the Ukraine War (on this, see Stiglitz and Regmi 2023). The rapid fall in the inflation rate in the second half of 2023 reinforced the compelling evidence that the post-pandemic recession was largely the result of pandemic- and war-related supply-side interruptions and demand shifts.

Given the intensity of these debates, it is easy to forget that labor market recovery was initially slower in developing economies. While employment in richer economies rebounded to a significant extent, lower and slower vaccination rates, weaker social protection in terms of Covid-related government support, and fewer macroeconomic policy levers have meant that employment growth was substantially lower in developing economies.

In addition, but not surprisingly, the costs of Covid were concentrated among vulnerable populations such as youth and lower-skilled workers. Women in particular were disproportionately affected: Kugler et al. (2021) find that they were the first to leave the job force and are the last to rejoin. Kugler et al. also find evidence of more informalization and self-employment, which has persisted through the recovery. The concern with such long-term persistence is that of hysteresis—that there will be no return to trend for particularly badly affected workers who have lost out, or who have joined the ranks of the discouraged. With already high levels of informalization, such processes lead to increasing precarity and rising inequality (evidence from earlier crises suggests that recovery between worker types is uneven, with low-skilled workers sometimes seeing a decade of lower earnings, in contrast to high-skilled workers, who can be redeployed much more quickly (Silva et al. 2020). In some developing countries without a very diversified economy, there could be significant, potential long-term concentrated job losses. At the same time, developing economies faced the same cost spirals seen in developed economies, with particularly critical problems arising from fuel and food price escalations that are further reducing economic and social welfare. Spending more abroad to purchase food and energy means spending less on domestic nontraded goods, leading to lower employment in the short run.

All these problems have well-discussed policy solutions that may be effective. These solutions include substantial job- and income-protection schemes, rapid and widespread reskilling programs, and other forms of targeted labor market interventions. In developing countries, however, these approaches are far more circumscribed, especially given the limited fiscal means of these countries. Even when such support was available, the presence of a large informal economy in many developing countries impairs the efficacy of some policy instruments, such as providing lines of credit. In any case, fiscal support provided after the crisis was far lower in developing economies, especially for labor. For a great many countries, the crisis saw the ballooning of indebtedness and an inability to maintain support policies.

Moreover, the rise in global inflation meant that most countries have switched to a considerably more contractionary macroeconomic stance. As the US Federal Reserve raised rates, many countries were compelled to increase interest rates to prevent sharp capital outflows and a depreciation of their currency, which (given that so much of the debt is denominated in foreign exchange) forced them to pay more in debt servicing in domestic terms. (2023 saw inflation come down from the 2022 peak, with global price pressures moderating substantially by year-end. However, contrary to earlier expectations, many central banks maintained high interest rates well into 2024, adopting a "higher for longer" stance due to above-target inflation and strong economic data. The US Federal reserve cuts were gradual, and further cuts into 2025 were postponed until the second half of the year with the expanding trade wars). As a result, in many economies, the scope for continued attempts to improve employment and working conditions were severely curtailed. Without tailored and consistent policy, the scars from the pandemic and other crises noted above will continue to exact a heavy toll.[2]

2.2 EMPLOYMENT, GROWTH, AND STRUCTURAL TRANSFORMATION

The strong labor market in the United States, at least at the macroeconomic level and in the period immediately following Covid, resulted in reduced anxiety about technological unemployment, although it did not allay concerns about the implications of AI for inequality. While AI and automation have continued apace, running a high-pressure economy has meant that the much-feared jobs crisis arising out of labor substitution has not come to pass as yet as this book goes to press in late 2025. While there has been a reallocation of labor away from low- to high-productivity jobs (Mason and Jayadev 2023), most measures of real wages show a marked decrease—the opposite of what one would have expected in a truly tight labor market. It is possible that, in some areas, technological advance is complementary to high-skilled labor. It is also possible that the decline in real wages is little more than a result of short-run wage-price dynamics and the short-run monopoly/monopsony resulting from supply chain and other pandemic-related disturbances. With weak unions, wages respond slowly to price rises—the decline in real wages confuses the feeling of being in a tight labor market. There is more recent evidence that some of these effects are temporary, with real wages on some measures (adjusting for composition) showing an increase.

However, there is a reasonable set of questions about whether the same can be said for the workforces of developing economies. Specifically, there is increasing evidence that automation can limit low-skill jobs (see Rodrik 2018) in, say, manufacturing, which might have otherwise absorbed the kind of labor that is available in abundance during the process of structural transformation.

At the macroeconomic level, there is yet little evidence of a generalized decrease in the elasticity of employment with respect to output. Some countries (e.g., India and China) certainly experienced this, but it is not universally the case. Basole (2022) details the growth elasticity of employment for selected countries at roughly the same level of income as India at the start of the 1990s. In the decades since then, there is no discernible pattern in changing decadal elasticities. Of course, such an exercise needs to account for the fact that employment itself depends heavily on issues such as demographics, informality, and so on. Employment in informal activities often reflects the supply of, rather than the demand for, labor. Thus, the elasticity is, in general, an endogenous variable, not just a technology parameter, which might have been the case in the absence of sectoral, demographic or technological changes.

What is most important for developing economies is not the sum of jobs but the moving of labor from relatively low-productivity jobs (such as in the subsistence agriculture sector) to higher-productivity formal employment. Development involves structural transformation. For almost every country that has entered the ranks of the Organisation for Economic Co-operation and Development (OECD), a profound change led by manufacturing has been central. Most recently and famously, the East Asian model was predicated fundamentally on the ability of manufacturing-led exports to absorb surplus labor and generate other follow-on benefits. While the contours of this success are reasonably well known, it is worthwhile to outline them briefly here.

The manufacturing export sectors generated jobs for new entrants into the labor force and those leaving agriculture without requiring high levels of initial skills. Given that manufacturing is tradable, there was always an external market, which meant that it was not constrained by domestic demand and allowed for scaling up even if productivity (and therefore demand) was low in the rest of the economy. Sectors such as textiles and light manufacturing were relatively labor-intensive and required little retraining. The higher wages in manufacturing in turn led to increasing demand for nontraded goods and higher standards of living. The benefits of manufacturing-led exports did not end there. Exports generated much-needed foreign exchange and tax revenue, and did away with the need for material balances. Perhaps it was most critical that it led to increased learning by doing. As Stiglitz (2021) notes, "Those engaging in trade had to interact with others, and those seeking to compete in export markets had to learn about manufacturing technology and international standards. Manufacturing is particularly well suited for learning, because it occurs in large and long-lived institutions (in contrast to, say, agriculture, where, especially in developing countries, the unit of production is a small farm). There are large economies of scale in the production and absorption of knowledge, and greater incentives for large institutions to engage in learning."

Given the centrality of manufacturing in this process, there is naturally concern about whether this path is still available for developing countries. Rodrik (2016) identified and raised the alarm about the phenomenon of premature deindustrialization, whereby countries experience their peak industrialization (in terms of value added and employment) at much lower incomes than the historical norm. Latin American countries and sub-Saharan Africa have been affected most significantly (Asia and in particular East Asia has been less affected by this pattern). The reason for this process is distinct from the deindustrialization observed in higher-income countries. In the United States and Europe, decades-long deindustrialization has been driven by relentless productivity increases whereby manufacturing has been the victim of its own success, with productivity rising faster than demand (see table I.1) In those economies, this has been relatively benign because labor has, by and large, been absorbed by high-productivity services, and per capita incomes have risen. (This process has had distinctly adverse effects, however, on the distribution of income.)

In low- and lower-middle-income countries, by contrast, there are at least two effects driving the phenomenon. First, most developing economies are exposed both to competition from China and other East Asian countries producing at low-unit labor costs—with the lower wages being more than offset in many cases by even lower productivity—and in other sectors, countries are competing with the low relative prices of

Table I.1 Manufacturing share of gross domestic product (GDP) (%)

	2000	2015	2019
World	19	15	15
East Asia and the Pacific (EAP)	25	23	23
Eastern Europe and Central Asia	19	16	14
Latin American Countries	17	14	13
North America	16	12	
South Asia	15	16	14
Sub-Saharan Africa (SSA)	11	11	11
Low-Income Countries	10	8	. . .
Lower-Middle-Income Countries	17	16	15
Upper-Middle-Income Countries	24	21	20
High-Income Countries	18	15	13

Note: EAP data in the last column refer to 2018. The year 2019 was as latest year because of COVID-19 impacts in 2020 and 2021and also the unavailability of data for those years for some of the regions and categories.

Source: World Bank, World Development Indicators

manufactured goods from advanced economies. Many industries that were protected and moderately large have therefore shrunk in size as these countries have opened up. In addition, state-led or supported manufacturing industries, which were often labor-intensive, were retrenched, leading to further reduction in employment opportunities in manufacturing.

China's dominance in manufacturing has led some to suggest that, as the country's per capita income rises and it goes through the Lewisian transition, moving from lower value-added to higher value-added manufacturing and services, there will be new space opening for other developing countries to pursue manufacturing-led export growth strategies once again.

There is one more important positive prospect: the new geopolitics and geoeconomics—what some have called the new Cold War. This has led to a new demand for supply chain diversification (though friend-shoring and nearshoring may limit the benefits; and Trump's tariffs were especially high on some African countries. There are several caveats, however, to these notes of optimism.

First, as several authors have noted, there is a declining labor share in manufacturing globally (see Baldwin and Forslid 2020; Dauth et al. 2018; Dinlersoz and Wolf 2018). Around the world, manufacturing is absorbing less labor than it did earlier. Cali et al. (2016) find that the job intensity of manufacturing exports has steadily declined in both developing and developed economies. While manufacturing exports are relatively more labor-intensive in developing economies, the trend of lower job creation is common across all regions. With the declining importance of labor in manufactured goods, the competitive advantage provided by low wages in developing countries is diminishing. Manufacturing becomes less of an advantage, both as a basis of comparative advantage (seizing demand from the rest of the world), and even when demand is garnered, of generating jobs.

Second, until very recently, China continued to maintain and expand its share of lower value-added manufacturing exports (Stapleton 2019). Only after Covid rearranged supply chains and China continued with its Covid-restricting policy longer than elsewhere has evidence suggested that there has been a significant relocation of manufacturing employment.[3] Here, too, it should be emphasized that the bulk of manufacturing exports that have relocated have been very concentrated in a few countries, even while China continues to be the single largest producer in the sector. Thus, for example, Vietnam (especially) but also Malaysia and Bangladesh have seen their shares of low value-added manufacturing exports (such as textiles and garments) rise. And in each case, these countries had preexisting capacity built to take advantage of this opportunity. Thus, a shift of manufacturing out of China has been and may continue to be of little benefit to sub-Saharan Africa.

Third, the nature of new technologies and the requirements of global value chains, and compliance requirements makes it more difficult for developing countries to use low-skilled workers easily in the production process. In terms of the traditional terminology, the new technologies are "unskilled labor saving" and will result in more inequality and lower, or at least stagnant, wages and higher unemployment among the unskilled everywhere—but this will have especially adverse effects on developing countries. Rodrik (2018) notes that the trends in the technology of production in manufacturing have resulted in a new complementarity between new production processes and skilled labor, and the demand for unskilled labor will be reduced. This is consistent with the view that today's technological change is more (unskilled) labor replacing than labor augmenting, as suggested by Korinek et al. (2019, 2022). Similarly, as Autor and Dorn (2013) note, new technologies in manufacturing do away with routinization, precisely those jobs that may be done most easily by relatively unskilled labor in developing economies.[4] To the extent that global value chains have built-in demands for certification and compliance and high standards of quality control, this is unlikely to be achievable with low-skilled labor or without scale. See Goger et al. (2014) for a study on the limitations of horticultural exports from sub-Saharan Africa based on strict compliance needs.

A contrary line of thinking, however, suggests that digitalization and associated new technologies may actually serve to enhance job creation. In countries that have had very little internet and digital penetration, there may be very large productivity gains to be had from the adoption of these technologies that could in turn result in an expansion of employment opportunities. Banga and te Velde (2018) examine several cases, particularly that of Kenya, to suggest that if the digital divide is lessened, then there is a pathway, even if temporary, for sub-Saharan African economies to increase their share of global manufacturing jobs. Other changes in the global economy may have similar effects: Sub-Saharan Africa is rich in solar energy, which enables the provision of energy more easily and more cheaply than with older technologies, and there are encouraging signs of enhanced investment in solar energy in the region. While it is not clear the force of these countertrends is strong enough, countries in sub-Saharan Africa should clearly work hard to take advantage of such opportunities.

The trend has been a reduction in the labor component of manufacturing. The effective use of such technologies requires a substantial number of relatively high-skilled workers who work as complements to technology. Here again, there is little to suggest a positive effect on the comparative advantage of developing economies.

Put another way, while digitization and access to international markets may make manufacturing output rise in developing economies even outside Asia, there is not much evidence that it can do so in a way that aids structural transformation in the labor market and instead may entrench a divide between workers with higher levels of training who can be absorbed into the new production processes and the substantially larger mass of workers who do not have these complementary skills.

2.3 SERVICES

Outside Asia, the manufacturing-led export development strategy therefore faces serious headwinds. In addition, the process of reshoring is accelerating, which means that the space for manufacturing exports may become even smaller as a fraction of total manufacturing in the future. With the onset of the fourth industrial revolution, the prospects for manufacturing as the development escalator and the sector that will lead structural transformation seem substantially curtailed.

This leaves the options of agriculture and services. While there is scope for increased productivity in agriculture, greater diversification and access to international markets, and so on, all of which may lead to more remunerative jobs in agriculture and a corresponding reduction in the pace of exit from the agricultural labor force, room for the sector to be a net absorber of labor is limited in most countries. (But see Cramer and Sender (2019) on the blurring of sectoral distinctions and the possibilities of industrializing agriculture in Africa.) In countries with large agricultural markets and well-developed supply chains, like India, there has been a slow but steady secular decline in the share of the labor force in agriculture. It is only in times of economic distress, as with Covid, that one observes a reabsorption of labor into agriculture. At the same time, the disparity between incomes in agriculture and manufacturing has remained large, and there are real questions about the ability of small-scale agriculture to compete against the large-scale, capital- and knowledge-intensive agriculture of the North. While it is important and critical to focus on agricultural productivity and policy to enhance the quality and pay of jobs in the sector, development almost inevitably entails the creation of relatively more productive jobs outside it (except to the extent that agriculture can be industrialized). Countries with natural resources may be able to generate employment in their extraction and processing, but these opportunities have tended to be limited and constrained by the resource curse. Botswana is a promising candidate for taking this route because the country has been moving from exporting rough, undifferentiated diamonds to sorting and classifying them and is aiming for the next stage of cutting and polishing the stones. The raw materials needed for meeting the increasing demand for green energy and batteries may well offer similar opportunities for moving up the value chain elsewhere in Africa.

If manufacturing is unlikely to absorb unskilled labor, and the scope for industrializing agriculture and moving up on the value chain of minerals and metals is limited for most countries, services sectors become critical in structural transformation. In many countries which have seen slow growth in manufacturing, the services sector has absorbed labor that is shed from agriculture. The issue, of course, is that services is a catchall term that includes both high-productivity formal jobs and low-productivity precarious and informal jobs. Here it is useful to make the distinction, as Basole (2022) does, between the linked but analytically distinct Kuznets and Lewisian transformations. The first refers to the transition between agriculture and manufacturing; the second refers to the absorption of surplus labor from low-productivity sectors. A sound structural transformation would require both these processes to occur together—although in the twenty-first century, the transformation out of agriculture may be to high-productivity service sector jobs. The risk is that labor shed from agriculture moves to low-productivity services, which do not generate the demand for follow-on goods and services. In turn, wages remain low and working conditions of the entire workforce are depressed, and demand is concentrated more narrowly. All of which hinder the kind of virtuous cycle of development that characterized the success stories of structural transformation in the past. Such transformation now calls for a lesser focus on sectors and more on the kind of firms and technologies within sectors that will facilitate a shift of labor from low- to high-productivity jobs.

Thus, it is important to emphasize that, for services to be able to generate the kind of development path that is desirable, the right kind of services sector jobs needs to be created. Because services are less tradable, some of the collateral benefits that were part of the manufacturing growth model (foreign exchange, a large external market, and learning and institutional development) may be less available, although some countries have done a reasonable job of managing well a limited structural transformation from agriculture to modern services, with Rwanda being a notable example of using industrial policy to take advantage of information technology (IT) and tourism to boost service exports and employment.

Ghani and O'Connell (2014) argue, however, that the potential for services-led development is severely underestimated. They suggest that, contrary to previously held positions, new technologies allow services to be traded just like manufactures. Given that the global trade in services is rising faster than trade in manufacturing, the benefits of scale and the ease of near costless transport make the sector much more accessible to developing countries. The kind of foreign exchange benefits and advantages from a large external source of demand applies to services, too. In addition, they argue, services can be high productivity and remunerative. While manufacturing often needs large and costly capital investment and thus financing, it is easier for developing economies to develop the infrastructure for services for which the main input is simply available and trained workers. This infrastructure can allow for greener and more gender-friendly growth.

The optimistic scenario pictured here, however, requires that the structural transition occurs so that labor can be absorbed by the right kind of sectors and subsectors. For example, one would want labor to move into sectors such as IT services or tourism (or industrialized agriculture) that may generate high productivity and are also tradable. But it is not clear that these sectors can absorb sufficiently the large amounts of relatively unskilled labor that may be shed from low-productivity activities.

There is considerable evidence that such labor often enters personal and retail services and wholesale trade, largely non-tradeable sectors that are typically fragmented, informal, and with low productivity. Rodrik (2018) and Diao et al. (2019) provide compelling evidence that across countries and in African economies in particular, labor moving out of agriculture is employed most easily in the low-productivity subsectors within services. India is another case. While the IT services sector in the country is globally lauded for its spectacular rise over the last three decades, the Ministry of Electronics and IT estimates that it directly employs 5 million people, with indirect employment of about 12 million people.[6] This corresponds to about 1 to 2 percent of the labor force, less if one counts only the high-productivity formal jobs. Instead, most of the growth in services is in the informal sector. While manufacturing has remained steady as a fraction of gross domestic product (GDP) and agriculture has declined, most people have moved to informal services. In India, for example, over 75 percent of workers are in informal employment, perhaps not surprising because services have grown sharply as a percentage of GDP and employment, and much of the services sector is informal. While India may be an extreme case, this is likely to be the case in many, if not most, low-income countries.

Banga et al. (2023),[7] however, find that the digital and related technologies, such as robots and AI, have troubling implications for employment in low- and middle-income countries. They assess the impact of such technological change and global value chains on structural transformation for fifty-one economies, using a cross-country panel data set for the period 1990–2018. They find a positive impact on structural change in output and labor productivity in manufacturing but a negative impact on the share of manufacturing employment, with labor moving from agriculture to nonbusiness services, which echoes the findings of Sen (2019).[8]

A SHORT OVERVIEW

Around the world, the combination of the rapid obsolescence of jobs and a high pace of labor shedding is creating an economic situation that is marked by declining labor productivity for large portions of the workforce, and greater precarity and vulnerability for large portions of the population. This describes the current situation, but this situation may not be inevitable.

3. POLICY

The employment landscape presents a rather challenging if not bleak set of prospects in the decades to come, especially for regions such as sub-Saharan Africa and other countries behind in their demographic transition, such as Pakistan and some countries in the Middle East.

But such pessimism is perhaps unwarranted when one takes a longer view. Barely seventy years ago, the first wave of decolonization occurred, and the development story, by and large, has been one of substantial success. East Asia and China saw perhaps the most rapid improvement in living standards in global history in this period. To a lesser but still substantial degree, growth in South Asia and some Latin American economies in this period has led to sharp declines in poverty, a burgeoning middle class, and higher standards of living. In the 1960s and 1970s, such outcomes could not have been predicted, and economists such as Gunnar Myrdal predicted dismal prospects for decades (Myrdal 1968).

The reasons that East Asia and China in particular defied these expectations have been written about extensively, but what is clear is that it required every one of the countries to undertake policies that were somewhat unorthodox, including, in Alice Amsden's memorable phrasing, "getting prices wrong" (Amsden 1989). At the time, the prospects for sustained growth and development in these countries seemed unpromising, but policymakers experimented with approaches that allowed for economic integration, structural transformation, and growth on their own terms, with Ethiopia (until its tragic civil conflict) and Rwanda being examples in Africa of success (Kanbur, Noman, and Stiglitz 2019).

While one need not be entirely pessimistic about the potential of technological unemployment in developing economies, it is also clear that older paths (manufacturing-based, export-led growth) are narrowing, and much of the breathless anticipation of new technologies (digitalization) has yet to bear fruit. And even when they bear fruit, it seems that they are just as likely to exacerbate the problems of jobs and inequality as alleviate them. Thus, developing countries need to be able to explore creative new paths (Rodrik and Stiglitz 2025). In the rest of this section, we explore some policies that seem necessary and central to this exercise.[9] Even if they don't "solve" the problem, these policies may make things better.

3.1 DOMESTIC POLICY

The East Asian experience suggested that sustained growth and structural transformation needed a range of interventions and policies that supported long-term learning and upgrading. As Stiglitz (2021) notes, "All successful development has entailed government playing an important role—the development state. It has a multiplicity of jobs to do: providing enabling conditions for markets to work, including good physical and institutional infrastructure and an educated labor force; regulating markets—preventing negative externalities, including exploitation and excessive volatility; promoting development more directly, including through industrial policies ... understanding the 'big picture,' including the problems posed by excessively rapid population growth; and coordinating more broadly developmental strategies among the many different participants in a country's development process."

The hope that "leaving it to the market" could generate these changes was belied by the many policies chosen that *used* the market, but within strict confines, and simultaneously went *beyond* markets alone. The reasons are clear—markets by themselves don't manage transformation well. Critical impediments to the functioning of markets arising from asymmetries of information, incompleteness of markets, and imperfections of competition, the need for extended coordination, the inability to take the short-term losses that typically arise when technologies are marked by increasing returns and learning-by-doing, and the fact of pervasive externalities mean that there has always been a need for government and collective action. To varying degrees and in varying ways, government has guided and coordinated successful developmental processes, and it has aided, assisted, and abetted private agents in a wide variety of ways. This was at one time the clear logic of development thinking, with the big push hypotheses and other comprehensive approaches, such as the comprehensive development framework articulated by the World Bank toward the end of the last century, albeit not followed in practice in a sustained and systematic manner that sought to intervene effectively to create virtuous cycles of growth, inclusion, employment, and productivity increases.

The dominance of the Washington Consensus (WC) for more than three decades meant that these earlier approaches were discarded. More recent insights from development economics as well as the manifest failures of the WC have given rise to a rethinking of development policy—moving from a critique of the WC to the creation of an alternative. Consider, as an example, macroeconomic stabilization. Under WC, stabilization too often focused on price stabilization rather than on real stabilization. Now there is openness to new objectives going beyond the control of inflation, with an awareness of how monetary and credit policy can affect structural transformation, and new instruments (Stiglitz 2001). Even in developed economies, the Great Recession of 2008–2009 allowed for a panoply of instruments (quantitative easing, fiscal expansion, capital controls, and the like) that were considered verboten up to that time.

There can now be openness to more instruments for developmental transformation, including in particular industrial policies, more appropriately labeled as learning, industrial and technology (LIT) policies,[10] that can generate employment as a central plank of the development strategy.

LIT policies, in spite of the name, should not be seen as limited to industry proper but rather as a set of strategies that aim to transform all sectors toward a process whereby they can scale up the productivity ladder more effectively. LIT policies and active labor markets should aim, too, to moving resources to more productive sectors and places (see Noman and Stiglitz 2012, 2015).[11]

Central to this task is ensuring that learning and new technologies are embedded in production processes. This entails not just increasing average education levels, although that will certainly help. One should think instead about all policy decisions (on trade, labor, competition, and law) in light of how they will affect individual and firm behavior, and both current and future productivity and resource allocations.

A frequent criticism of LIT policy is that it would result in governments picking winners, with the accompanying rent-seeking issues. While this can (and has) often been the case, it should also be noted that virtually all countries that have had success over the medium to long run have employed such policies. Examples of such successes abound—whether it is with the preferential credit system that supported East Asian corporates or horticulture and leather products in Ethiopia; intellectual property rights (IPRs) regimes that promoted domestic capacity in India, especially in pharmaceuticals; or specific kinds of support in export marketing provided in developing economies. Many countries have used procurement policies, domestic content policies, and even restrictions on the export of natural resources.

For all of these, the key was the acceptance that governments needed to reorient rules and regulations to promote sectors that had the best chance of growing and learning by doing, not only generating in that process both foreign exchange and employment but also leading to other kinds of spillovers in terms of learning and upgrading. This typically involves choosing sectors where a country can perceive further pathways on which to build. This can arise not just from learning—with technologies and skills in one subsector being relevant for others—but also from institutional development. Stiglitz and Greenwald (2014), in *Creating a Learning Society*, describe the multiple ways that this can occur. Hausmann et al. (2011) describe a scale of complexity and suggest that development involves moving up this complexity ladder in different ways.

Finding and stimulating production in the appropriate sectors that can maximize learning and learning spillovers, and find deeper backward and forward linkages, is key therefore to a more holistic strategy. Which of these are priorities and what form they take is highly dependent on the particular country, but the overall strategy of maximizing learning and spillovers is common.

For governments of each country, the specific choice of policy mixes will depend on the circumstances. For example, in several African economies, natural resources can play a significant part in the economy. To ensure that the source of wealth does not give rise to the well-known resource curse, countries will have to rely on public ownership and/or well-designed competitive auctions and contracts. Where services appear to provide opportunities for absorbing labor, putting in place training and retraining programs could help quickly yield employment outcomes that can generate spillovers. In many economies with large agricultural sectors, providing modern agricultural innovations such as better crop mixes, planting patterns, fertilizers, irrigation, and extension services can lead to higher productivity, knowledge spillovers, and crop diversification, and can even limit the speed at which agriculture sheds labor.

With respect to direct employment policy, Bandiera et al. (2022) provide several instances of both demand- and supply-side policies that can support growth in employment. Some are large-scale programs aimed at supporting firm growth; these include large credit expansion (see Burgess and Pande 2005) or large-scale investment. Moneke (2020) and Noman and Stiglitz (2015) show that in Ethiopia, for example, investment in infrastructure and LIT policies helped the reallocation of workers from agriculture to secondary and tertiary sectors. Supply-side efforts, such as public provision of vocational training and government subsidies to firms for training have shown mixed results but could also be part of the package of policies adopted.

But there needs to be broader thinking about restructuring of the economy and each of the sectors within it. For instance, what is taught in the schools today in developing countries is hardly linked to the needs of today's economy. The financial sector in many developing countries is ill-suited for providing finance to those sectors and firms whose prospects of enhancing jobs is the greatest.

The need for stronger LIT policies and active labor policies is particularly evident today but so is the opportunity. Even advanced countries have recognized the need for industrial policies and that one simply can't leave it to the market. The United States has now adopted industrial policies to promote the development of a domestic chips industry and to help transform the economy toward a green economy. (And under Trump, there is a massive attempt to use old fashioned trade policy as an instrument of industrial policy; whether the way that policy is being implement will be successful given the chaotic and unprincipled way in which it is being implemented remains questionable.)

3.2 THE GLOBAL ENVIRONMENT

One underappreciated factor in the development of East Asia was the fact that the global economic order placed much fewer constraints on its experimenting in policy than may be possible today. For example, it was possible for countries to erect trade barriers, impose capital controls, circumscribe IPRs to support learning in domestic industry, or subsidize specific firms either by direct subsidies or by allowing preferential credit. Even if those policies were desirable today, for much of the world they are not feasible without running afoul of World Trade Organization (WTO) rules. (Or at least that was the case before the arrival of Trump, who totally flaunted WTO rules. As this goes to press, it remains an open question whether the rules-based system, constructed over more than four decades, is effectively a matter of the past; or whether there will remain a vestige among the remaining countries.) These rules are sometimes not just restrictive but antithetical to development. Stiglitz and Charlton (2005) note how the structure of tariffs inhibit developing countries from moving up the value-added chain into manufacturing. As Baker et al. (2017) show, IPRs work in some cases to close off development opportunities that were enjoyed by industrialized countries earlier—a point emphasized incisively by Ha-Joon Chang (2002).[12] Additional bilateral agreements between developing countries and developed ones, such as some so-called free trade agreements, partnership agreements, tax agreements, and investment agreements, further limit policy space beyond WTO rules.

Several new approaches can be and are being promoted and adopted to make the global environment more conducive to supporting development and structural transformation, especially given current global realities. For instance, the above discussion suggests that one important factor in supporting domestic employment generation is to expand policy space in such agreements.

One key area that reaps global benefits is to support a transition away from fossil fuels to renewables and other green technology as the primary source of energy. This is an area that will require global cooperation and investment in new green technologies on a massive scale. One advantage that later developers will have is the possibility of skipping over infrastructure that is carbon intensive and instead investing in cleaner technology from the outset. Many of these new technologies allow for smaller scale and greater decentralization and are therefore likely to be more supportive of the developmental process.

However, this will involve the need for substantial technology transfer. At a minimum, all technologies that support the transition away from fossil fuel consumption should be easily accessible to developing countries (for instance, through compulsory licenses) and not locked up in intellectual property restrictions.

There is a need for globally coordinated programs of investment and technology transfers, the costs of which must be borne partly by developed economies. To date, this has not happened, and developed countries haven't even lived up to what they have committed to. As Greenwald and Stiglitz (2010) note, however, there is a clear way in which assistance targeted at climate change adaptation and mitigation can be resourced while simultaneously supporting global stability and growth: by creating a global reserve system (an expanding of the IMF's system of special drawing rights, SDR's)—where the reserve countries agree to allow the conversion of the global reserve currency into their own currency and the advanced countries commit to allow the global reserves allocated to them to be transferred to developing economies to support their efforts at clean and environmentally friendly structural transformation.

No matter how successful the policies discussed in this section are, the disparity in income between the richest countries and the poorest will likely increase, and one should expect that, in the medium term, there will be strong pressure of outmigration from developing countries, especially from sub-Saharan Africa, if job prospects are dim. This is likely to create a humanitarian and moral crisis that will need to be addressed, although the politically charged issue of migration in rich countries is generating politics that makes migration difficult. The developed world must find a way to adopt humane and effective migration policies that protect the most vulnerable and maintain peace and stability going forward. This would include help to generate jobs and reduce labor market pressures in developing countries where migrants originate. Many countries have well-designed guest worker programs, but finding a way to scale these effectively may be necessary (Milanovic 2018; Weyl 2018). External assistance, including technology transfers for alleviating labor market pressures, remains scant and fragmented, even as the political tensions in rich countries generated by migration are becoming more salient.

3.3. SOCIAL AND WELFARE POLICY

The first best outcome for any country is for it to be able to generate good jobs, maintain high levels of employment, and move up the productivity ladder as labor is reallocated across sectors. Both currently and in the future, however, this transition appears to be harder to achieve and may be less smooth and self-sustaining than in the past. In the meantime, given the so-called demographic dividend and imperative to support youth employment, it is essential for the safety net to expand and for active labor market policies to be designed to match workers to jobs.

One essential and broad-based policy would be to promote universal appropriate and high-quality education to all. This is especially critical to ensuring a smoother transition from schooling to the labor force. In this regard, the excellent report of the international Education Commission chaired by Gordon Brown that called for much greater efforts to raise access to, increase the quality of, and support financing for education needs to be revisited. In the words of that report, "Today's generation of young people faces a radically changing world. Up to half of the world's jobs—around 2 billion—are at high risk of disappearing due to automation in the coming decades. In contrast to the impact of innovation in previous generations, new technologies risk not creating new jobs at anything like the scale they are eradicating them. Due to shifts between industries and the changing nature of work within industries, demand for high-level skills will grow, and many low- and medium-skilled jobs will become obsolete. Jobs open to those without high-level skills will often be insecure and poorly paid. Only quality education for all children can generate the needed skills, prevent worsening inequality and provide a prosperous future for all."[13]

Second, if services become the sector that absorbs labor, it is likely that there will be increased inequality, with a large chunk of workers stuck in low-productivity jobs and a small elite group of workers who have access to the small number of high-wage, high-productivity jobs generated. In such situations, direct transfers and other forms of income support may be necessary, notwithstanding the fiscal constraints.

A third approach might be to intervene directly in the labor market to provide employment opportunities where the private sector is unable to do so. Here, for example, the Indian national rural employment guarantee scheme (NREGS) provides some instructive evidence. Despite early skepticism, it has been a very popular program, supporting workers in slack periods and simultaneously building valuable rural infrastructure, reducing poverty, and creating pressures for rising wages (see Muralidharan et al. 2021). As a result, the Indian government and various state governments have evinced interest in expanding the program to urban areas to absorb surplus labor and provide critical resources for key needs such as urban environmental management and health care.

In principle, given the enormous needs posed by development and the green transition, there *should* be a huge demand for labor, enough to absorb all. This is especially so in a world that Ben Bernanke characterized as having a savings glut. We have simultaneously surplus labor and capital but a deficiency of resources needed to meet basic social needs. In some fundamental ways, the market system is not working.

4. THE OUTLINE OF THIS BOOK AND PROSPECTIVES

The chapters in this book all speak to the major challenges we have outlined. The authors include scholars who are situated in universities around the world, as well as others who have worked extensively on these concerns in multilateral organizations such as the International Labor Organization (ILO), the World Bank, and the International Monetary Fund (IMF). They bring their considerable expertise to bear on various aspects of the issues we have described.

Part I comprises two chapters that provide basic theoretical grounding for labor market analyses in developing country contexts. In chapter 1, Nancy H. Chau, Ravi Kanbur, and Vidhya Soundararajan explore the evidence for monopsony in developing country labor markets. They find that the default model of competitive markets is a misleading one and that there is growing empirical and theoretical evidence suggesting a considerable role for employer power. This obviously has major implications for the conduct of policy, especially around wage setting and worker welfare.

Chapter 2, by Zico Dasgupta and Amit Basole, explores the issue of the decoupling of output growth and employment growth. This so-called jobless growth has been a concern in the literature and among policymakers, especially in developing economies that are also undergoing structural change. They develop a theoretical model that clarifies the relative roles of labor demand and labor supply in determining the output-employment relationship, showing a variety of possible trajectories, and explore these with a special focus on the Indian case, where there has been close to jobless growth in the formal sector.

Part II comprises five chapters that address structural changes in regional and global labor markets over medium-term horizons and, in some cases, policy responses to these. Africa is, of course, much of the focus of the book because it is the continent for which these concerns are most pertinent; however, we also include a chapter on Argentina, and another on Bangladesh and India. The purpose is to have a comparative perspective of two regions that are in a different stage of development and that are struggling with different concerns in employment that can help illuminate some of the same issues.

Chapter 3 assesses the performance of the Middle East and North Africa (MENA) region in terms of employment generation, particularly in light of the challenges arising from automation. Sidra Rehman and Agustin Velasquez describe trends in employment generation in the region, an area in which output creation has been linked weakly to robust employment generation. They look in particular at the ways in which automation and other new features such as remote work may affect different sections of the working population.

Chapter 4 turns the focus to another region of the world—Latin America—where questions of employment generation and jobless growth abound, especially in the formal sector. Claudio Moroni et al. examine the Argentinian case as an example of a middle-income country struggling with establishing the right labor market regulations and schemes to support inclusive growth and employment.

Chapter 5, by Karishma Banga, continues the exploration of the impact of automation, this time with an in-depth case study of the apparel sector in India and Bangladesh. In both countries, textiles are a major potential and actual source of employment. Banga finds that there are significant impacts on skill segmentation of the labor market and, in particular, she finds substantial differences between firms connected to global value chains and those that are not, with the former being more successful at adapting to technological trends.

In chapter 6, Ryosuke Nakata uses the insufficiently explored Global Trade Analysis Project (GTAP) database to demonstrate how industrial structures in different low-income countries contribute to generating income and to the eventual distribution of this income across the population. In particular, he is interested in the difference between sub-Saharan African economies and other low-income economies. His analysis suggests that the possibility of growth leading to remunerative manufacturing employment and income in the region, compared to East Asia, is low. The import of his analysis is that the East Asian model may have limited applicability in Africa; in particular, manufacturing exports are unlikely to provide the central engine for structural transformation.

In chapter 7, Ozlem Onaran and Cem Oyvat develop a post-Keynesian model (that is, a model focusing especially on government policies centered on increasing aggregate demand) and undertake vector autoregression analysis aiming to project employment possibilities arising from expansionary and targeted public spending. Examining data from six emerging economies, they find a hopeful conclusion—that public spending aimed at green (environmentally friendly) sectors and purple (care economy) sectors can have substantial positive employment effects.

Part III comprises four chapters that lay out key features of sub-Saharan African economies that need to be considered in any policy formulation. In chapter 8, David Lam and Murray Leibbrandt describe the changes in demographics in the region, the impacts for growth in the working-age population, and the consequent need for employment policy. They show that, between 2020 and 2100, almost all the additional working-age people in the world will be located in sub-Saharan Africa and that, by 2050, Africa will be the only region in the world with a growing working-age population. (Demographics are complicated. One cannot simply extrapolate population growth rates. On the other hand, there are long lags in adjustment in both fertility and mortality, and demographic models have been able to give us a good picture of overall population changes. As noted, the changes anticipated for Africa and the world are dramatic and should be a first-order concern for policymakers around the world, as we suggested earlier in this introduction.) This has important implications for supply-side policies such as improving education but also demand-side management to meet the challenge of job generation in the region.

In chapter 9, Tetsuya Harada builds on these concerns by examining how structural change has not been sufficiently robust in creating job opportunities. He shows that labor productivity continues to be low in manufacturing, and while employment has shifted from agriculture to manufacturing, labor productivity has risen in agriculture, fallen in manufacturing, and remained the same in nontradable sectors. Taken as a whole, this provides an even more dismal picture of growth *alone* as providing the solution to modernization and the increase in standards of living in sub-Saharan Africa—along the lines of the East Asia model—unless more active intervention is taken to shape that growth. In East Asia and elsewhere, large and sustained differences in productivity between manufacturing and agriculture have meant that continued shifting of labor from the latter to the former has continued to have substantial effects in raising average productivity and wages. Simply following the old East Asia model may not have as much of a transformational effect in Africa—even were it possible to follow that model.

In chapter 10, Caitlin Whitehead et al. analyze the South African manufacturing sector to determine to what extent automation technologies may act as a constraint on the creation of manufacturing-led growth for the country. The authors use South African labor force data to look at the content of various jobs, using techniques and categories developed by, among others, Autor and Acemoglu (2011), to identify those that are under threat of being automated. Overall, they find that (1) the South African labor market is particularly polarized in terms of occupation, and (2) that it remains fairly vulnerable to automation.

Chapter 11, the final chapter in the book, is an exercise aimed at understanding the prospects for structural transformation and employment generation while simultaneously aiming at environmentally responsible policies. Antonio Andreoni and Simon Roberts examine the scope for a green transition and the ways in which the particular natural resources of Africa may be developed and regulated to achieve such a transformation. The authors are clear that, while there are opportunities in sectors such as critical minerals, green hydrogen, and the like, it will require policymakers to invest effectively and strategically to ensure that such growth has the maximal benefit in terms of welfare and employment. As such, it will involve considerable strategic planning and policy and considerable resources. The United States and Europe have, at last, adopted green industrial policies, and, at least in the United States, they seem to be working—not so much because of fine-tuning in the design (there is a consensus that they were far from optimally designed) but because of their massive scale. (The green industrial policies were largely reversed by President Trump.) The United States has had and explicit objective of getting the green jobs of the future—explicitly recapturing them from China and implicitly diverting them from the rest of the world. But developing countries don't have the resources to respond—presenting now a new challenge to clean job creation in the South.

5. CONCLUSION

Taken as a whole, the chapters that comprise this book suggest that the prospects for employment and effective development seem significantly less promising than at other points in the post–World War II period, especially for sub-Saharan Africa. The limits of the export-led growth strategy are far starker: a combination of technological change; demographic pressures; a relatively hostile international landscape; and pressures coming from the need for alternative, greener paths to development all serve to limit degrees of freedom for policy makers, although the green transition also presents opportunities for technological catch-up and employment generation.

The challenge is that almost all countries that have made it to industrialized status have relied on the traditional escalator of manufacturing for their modernization. This path looks increasingly inaccessible. In the case of sub-Saharan Africa in particular, technological change may continue to further erode any competitive advantage arising from cheap unskilled labor and an abundance of natural resources.

This situation suggests a need to create different and potentially more complex development strategies. The particular needs of Africa, however, are also areas of opportunity, as many of the chapters underline. The green transition, the need for infrastructure, and improving productivity in key areas such as agriculture could all support employment, but, if this strategy is to work, it will be necessary to have several enabling factors in place. Good domestic policies (along the lines described in this introduction and the various chapters of this book) and changed international policy that promotes fairer global agreements, combined with foreign assistance, compensation for costs of climate change, and support for new technologies are essential.

From our perspective, this is not simply an economic issue but a moral and humanitarian one. But it should be remembered that the world has faced such situations before. Decades ago, developing countries, especially in East Asia but elsewhere too, embarked on a series of experiments after they threw off the yoke of colonial rule. And while the picture is certainly not uniformly one of progress, many, many countries have defied expectations and emerged as growing, successful economies. Even more than manufacturing, what probably is common across the successful experiences is a willingness to get the balance right between the market and government intervention, to experiment, and to create the possibility of learning societies in which knowledge and know-how were valorized and knowledge spillovers were maximized. "Catching up" itself provides enormous opportunities for increases in standards of living. There are still likely to be many ways in which a fundamental commitment to shared prosperity can be maintained to face the challenges to come, even if the particular elements and strategies to forge these paths are not yet fully known. And in that, there continues to be hope for global development and employment in the twenty-first century.

NOTES

1. One World Bank study suggested that extreme poverty increased by 149 million in the thirty-eight years between 1990 and 2018. See Marta Schoch and Christoph Lakner, *World Bank Blogs*, December 16, 2020, https://blogs.worldbank.org/en/opendata/number-poor-people-continues-rise-sub-saharan-africa-despite-slow-decline-poverty-rate.

2. Even in developed countries, there is a discussion of scarring effects from the interruption of education. The return by the end of 2023 of the usual macroeconomic relations like the Phillips curve and the Beveridge curve suggests that, at least in some dimensions, hysteresis effects may be smaller than was once feared.

3. The new geopolitics may have played a role, especially with respect to manufactured exports to the United States. The United States has raised tariffs against Chinese goods in both the Trump and the Biden administrations, and there appears to be bipartisan support to policies that are variously called friend-shoring, near-shoring, onshoring, or just derisking.

4. Although there are also routine skilled jobs, like radiologists.

5. See https://www.pib.gov.in/PressReleaseIframePage.aspx?PRID=2097125.

6. Karishma Banga, P. Harbansh, and S. Singh, "Digital De-industrialization, Global Value Chains, and Structural Transformation: Empirical Evidence from Low-and-Middle Income Countries," United Nations University, WIDER Working Paper 2023/65.

7. Kunal Sen, 2019.

8. Much of the following discussion draws from Stiglitz (2021).

9. See Noman and Stiglitz (2015).

10. Noman and Stiglitz, 2012

11. Chang, 2002.

12. The International Commission on Financing Global Education Opportunity, (2002), p. 12.

REFERENCES

Acemoglu, Daron, and David Autor. 2011. "Skills, Tasks and Technologies: Implications for Employment and Earnings." In *Handbook of Labor Economics*, volume 4B, edited by Orley Ashenfelter and David Card. Elsevier. https://doi.org/10.1016/S0169-7218(11)02410-5.

Amsden, Alice. 1989. *Asia's Next Giant.* Oxford University Press.

Autor, David H., and David Dorn. 2013. "The Growth of Low-Skill Service Jobs and the Polarization of the US Labor Market: Dataset." *American Economic Review* 103(5): 1553-1597.

Bahal, Girish, and Anand Shrivastava, 2022. "Fiscal Transfers and Inflation: Evidence from India." *Empirical Economics* 63 (4): 1837–58.

Baker, D., A. Jayadev, and J. E. Stiglitz. 2017. "Innovation, Intellectual Property, and Development: A Better Set of Approaches for the 21st Century." AccessIBSA: Innovation & Access to Medicines in India, Brazil & South Africa.

Balchin, Neil, Stephen Gelb, Jane Kennan, Hope Martin, Dirk Willem te Velde, and Carolin Williams. 2016. "Developing Export-Based Manufacturing in Sub-Saharan Africa." *London: Overseas Development Institute.* https://odi.org/en/publications/developing-export-based-manufacturing-in-sub-saharan-africa/

Baldwin, R., and R. Forslid. 2020. "Globotics and Development: When Manufacturing Is Jobless and Services Are Tradable. Working Paper No. 26731, Working Paper Series. National Bureau of Economic Research. https://doi.org/10.3386/w26731.

Bandiera, Oriana Ahmed Elsayed, Andrea Smurra, and Céline Zipfel. 2022. "Young adults and labor markets in Africa". *Journal of Economic Perspectives*, 36 (1): 81-100.

Banga, Karishma, and Dirk Willem te Velde. 2018. *Digitalisation and the Future of Manufacturing in Africa.* Overseas Development Institute, Supporting Economic Transformation Programme. https://set.odi.org/wp-content/uploads/2018/03/SET_Digitalisation-and-future-of-African-manufacturing_Final.pdf

Banga, K., Harbansh, P., & Singh, S. 2023. "Digital deindustrialization, global value chains, and structural transformation: Empirical evidence from low and middle-income countries." WIDER Working Paper No. 2023/65, United Nations University World Institute for Development Economic Research (UNUWIDER). doi:10.35188/UNU-WIDER/2023/373-4.

Basole, A. 2022. "Structural Transformation and Employment Generation in India: Past Performance and the Way Forward." *The Indian Journal of Labour Economics* 65: 295–320. https://doi.org/10.1007/s41027-022-00380-y.

Burgess, Robin, and Rohini Pande. 2005. "Do Rural Banks Matter? Evidence from the Indian Social Banking Experiment." *American Economic Review* 95 (3): 780–95.

Cali, Massimiliano, Francois, Joseph, Claire H. Hollweg, Miriam Manchin, Doris Anita Oberdabernig, Hugo Rojas-Romagosa, Stela Rubinova, and Patrick Tomberger. 2016. "The Labor Content of Exports Database." Policy Research Working Paper No. 7615. World Bank. https://openknowledge.worldbank.org/handle/10986/24156.

Chang, Ha-Joon. 2002. *Kicking Away the Ladder: Development Strategies in Historical Perspective.* Anthem Press.

Cramer, C., and J. Sender. 2019. "Oranges Are Not Only Fruit: The Industrialization of Freshness and the Quality of Growth." In *The Quality of Growth in Africa*, edited by A. Noman, J. E. Stiglitz, and R. Kanbur. Columbia University Press.

Dauth, W., S. Findeisen, J. Suedekum, and N. Woessner. 2018. "Adjusting to Robots: Worker Level Evidence." Working Paper 13. Federal Reserve Bank of Minneapolis, Opportunity and Inclusive Growth Institute.

Diao, Xinshen, Margaret McMillan, and Dani Rodrik. 2019. "The Recent Growth Boom in Developing Economies: A StructuralChange Perspective." In *The Palgrave Handbook of Development Economics*, edited by. M. Nissanke and J. A. Ocampo. Palgrave Macmillan. https://doi.org/10.1007/978-3-030-14000-7_9.

Dinlersoz, E., and Z. Wolf. 2018. "Automation, Labour Share, and Productivity: Plant-Level Evidence from US Manufacturing." *Economics of Innovation and New Technology*, 33: 604–626.

Ghani, Ejaz, and Stephen D. O'Connell. 2014, July. "Can Service Be a Growth Escalator in Low Income Countries?" Policy Research Working Paper 6971, World Bank.

Goger, Annelies, Andy Hull, Stephanie Barrientos, Gary Gereffi, and Shane Godfrey. 2014. "Capturing the Gains in Africa: Making the Most of Global Value Chain Participation." Duke Center on Globalization, Governance, and Competitiveness.

Greenwald, B., and J. E. Stiglitz. 2010. "A Modest Proposal for International Monetary Reform." In *Time for a Visible Hand*, edited by S. Griffith-Jones, J.A. Ocampo, and J. E. Stiglitz. Oxford University Press.

Greenwald, B., and J. E. Stiglitz. 2013. "Learning and Industrial Policy: Implications for Africa." In *The Industrial Policy Revolution II*, edited by J. E. Stiglitz, J. Yifu Lin, and E. Patel. Palgrave Macmillan.

Greenwald, B., and J. E. Stiglitz. 2014. "Industrial Policies, the Creation of a Learning Society, and Economic Development." In *The Industrial Policy Revolution I.*, edited by J. E. Stiglitz and J. Yifu Lin. Palgrave Macmillan.

Hausmann, R., C. A. Hidalgo, S. Bustos, M. Coscia, A. Simoes, and M. A. Yildirim. 2011. *The Atlas of Economic Complexity*. MIT Press.

International Labour Organization. 2022. *World Employment and Social Outlook: Trends 2022*. International Labour Organization. https://www.ilo.org/publications/flagship-reports/world-employment-and-social-outlook-trends-2022

Jayadev, A., and J. E. Stiglitz. 2010. "Medicine for Tomorrow." *Journal of Generic Medicines* 7 (3): 217–26.

Kanbur, R., Noman, A., and Stiglitz, J. E. 2019. *The Quality of Growth in Africa*. Columbia University Press.

Korinek, A., Martin Schindler, and J. E. Stiglitz. 2022. "Technical Progress and Artificial Intelligence," *How to Achieve Inclusive Growth*, edited by Valerie Cerra, Barry Eichengreen, Asmaa El-Ganainy, and Martin Schindle. Oxford University Press. http://fdslive.oup.com/www.oup.com/academic/pdf/openaccess/9780192846938.pdf.

Korinek, A., and J. E. Stiglitz. 2019. "Artificial Intelligence and Its Implications for Income Distribution and Unemployment." In *The Economics of Artificial Intelligence: An Agenda*, edited by Ajay Agrawal, Joshua Gans, and Avi Goldfarb. NBER/University of Chicago Press.

Kugler, Maurice, Mariana Viollaz, Daniel Duque, Isis Gaddis, David Newhouse, Amparo Palacios-Lopez, and Michael Weber. 2021. "How Did the COVID-19 Crisis Affect Different Types of Workers in the Developing World?" *World Development* 170: 106331.

Milanovic, Branko. 2018. "Migration Into Europe: A Long-Term Solution?" *Social Europe.* https://www.socialeurope.eu/migration-into-europe-a-long-term-solution

Moneke, Niclas. 2020. "Can Big Push Infrastructure Unlock Economic Development? Evidence from Ethiopia." Thesis, University of Oxford, 2020. https://niclasmoneke.com/wp-content/uploads/Moneke-JMP-Big_Push_Infrastructure.pdf

Muralidharan, Karthik, Paul Niehaus, and Sandip Sukhtankar. 2023. "General equilibrium effects of (improving) public employment programs: Experimental evidence from India." *Econometrica* 91 (4): 1261–1295.

Myrdal, G. 1968. *Asian Drama: An Inquiry into the Poverty of Nations (Volumes, I, II and III).* Pantheon.

Noman, Akbar, and Joseph E. Stiglitz. 2012. "Strategies for African Development." In *Good Growth and Governance in Africa: Rethinking Development Strategies,* edited by Akbar Noman, Kwesi Botchwey, Howard Stein, and Joseph E. Stiglitz, 3–47. Oxford: Oxford University Press.

Noman, Akbar, and Stiglitz, J. E., eds. 2015. *Industrial policy and Economic Transformation in Africa.* Columbia University Press.

Noman, Akbar, Kwesi Botchwey, Howard Stein, and Joseph E. Stiglitz, eds. 2012. *Good Growth and Governance in Africa: Rethinking Development Strategies.* Oxford University Press.

Paice, Edward. 2021. *Youthquake: Why African Demography Should Matter to the World.* Head of Zeus.

Rodrik, D. 2016, March. "Premature Deindustrialization." *Journal of Economic Growth* 21 (1): 1–33.

Rodrik, D. "New Technologies, Global Value Chains, and the Developing Economies." NBER Working Paper No. 25164, National Bureau of Economic Research, 2018. http://www.nber.org/papers/w25164

Rodrik, Dani and J. E. Stiglitz, 2025, "A New Growth Strategy for Developing Nations," in *The New Global Economic Order* (eds. Lili Yan Ing and Dani Rodrik), London: Routledge.

Schoch, Marta, and Christoph Lakner. December 16, 2020. "The number of poor people continues to rise in Sub-Saharan Africa, despite a slow decline in the poverty rate." *World Bank Blogs.* Retrieved from https://blogs.worldbank.org/en/opendata/number-poor-people-continues-rise-sub-saharan-africa-despite-slow-decline-poverty-rate

Sen, K. 2019. "Structural Transformation around the World: Patterns and Drivers." *Asian Development Review* 36: 1–31. https://doi.org/10.1162/adev_a_00130

Silva, Joana, Liliana Sousa, Truman Packard, and Raymond Robertson. 2020, June 17. *Employment in Crisis: The Path to Better Jobs in a Post-COVID-19 Latin America.* World Bank Latin American and Caribbean Studies. World Bank.

Stapleton, K. 2019. *Automation, Global Value Chains and Development: What Do We Know So Far?* Pathways for Prosperity Commission Background Paper Series. no. 26. Pathways for Prosperity Commission.

Stiglitz, J. E. 2001. *Joseph Stiglitz and the World Bank: the Rebel Within.* Anthem Press.

Stiglitz, Joseph E. 2021. "From Manufacturing-Led Export Growth to a Twenty-First Century Inclusive Growth Strategy: Explaining the Demise of a Successful Growth Model and What to Do About It." In *Inequality in the Developing World.*, edited by Carlos Gradín, Murray Leibbrandt, and Finn Tarp. Oxford University Press.

Stiglitz, J. E., and A. Charlton. 2005. *Fair Trade for All.* Oxford University Press.

Stiglitz, J. E., and B. Greenwald. 2010. "Towards a New Global Reserve System." *Journal of Globalization and Development* 1 (2): 0000102202194818371126. https://doi.org/10.2202/1948-1837.1126

Stiglitz, J.E. and B. Greenwald. 2014. *Creating a Learning Society: A New Approach to Growth, Development, and Social Progress.* Columbia University Press.

Stiglitz, Joseph E., and Ira Regmi. 2023, April. "The Causes of and Responses to Today's Inflation." *Industrial and Corporate Change* 32 (2): 336–85.

The International Commission on Financing Global Education Opportunity, T he Learning Generation (2022), https://report.educationcommission.org/wp-content/uploads/2016/09/Learning_Generation_Full_Report.pdf

Weyl, Glen E. 2018. "The Openness-Equality Trade-Off in Global Redistribution." *The Economic Journal* 128 (612): F1–F36. https://doi.org/10.1111/ecoj.12469.

PART I

Developing Economy Labor Markets

THEORETICAL PERSPECTIVES

CHAPTER 1

Employer Power and Employment in Developing Countries*

Nancy H. Chau, Ravi Kanbur, and Vidhya Soundararajan

Abstract: The issue of employer power is underemphasized in the development literature. The default model is usually one of competitive labor markets. This assumption matters for analysis and policy prescription. There is growing evidence that the competitive labor markets assumption is not valid for developing countries. Our objective in this chapter is to review this evidence, to present theoretical and policy perspectives which follow from it, and to highlight areas for further research.

JEL Classification: J42, O15

Keywords: employer power, employment, developing countries

1. INTRODUCTION

The issue of market power is underemphasized in the development economics literature. Concerning employment in particular, the default model is one of competitive labor markets. But this assumption matters for analysis and policy prescription. And there is growing evidence that

*This chapter has been prepared for the JICA-IPD Task Force on Employment, directed by Joseph Stiglitz, Arjun Jayadev, and Akbar Noman. We thank them and participants in task force meetings for their helpful comments. Chau: Charles H. Dyson School of Applied Economics and Management, Cornell University, Ithaca, NY 14853, and the Institute for the Study of Labor (IZA) (email: hyc3@cornell.edu); Kanbur: Department of Economics and Charles H. Dyson School of Applied Economics and Management, Cornell University, Ithaca, NY 14853 (email: sk145@cornell.edu); Soundararajan: Centre for Advanced Financial Research and Learning (CAFRAL) (email: vidhya.srajan@cafral.org.in).

the competitive assumption is not valid. Our objective in this chapter is to review this evidence, present theoretical and policy perspectives that follow from it, and highlight areas for further research.

The idea that employers can have market power over workers is not new in economics. In book 1, chapter 8, of *An Inquiry into the Nature and Causes of the Wealth of Nations* (usually abbreviated as *The Wealth of Nations*), Adam Smith highlights such power and the effect it has on wages:

> What are the common wages of labour, depends everywhere upon the contract usually made between those two parties, whose interests are by no means the same. The workmen desire to get as much, the masters to give as little as possible. . . . It is not, however, difficult to foresee which of the two parties must, upon all ordinary occasions, have the advantage in the dispute, and force the other into a compliance with their terms. The masters, being fewer in number, can combine much more easily . . . In all such disputes the masters can hold out much longer. . . . Masters are always and everywhere in a sort of tacit, but constant and uniform combination, not to raise the wages of labour above their actual rate.

Economic theorizing about employer power took a giant leap forward with Joan Robinson's classic *The Economics of Imperfect Competition* (Robinson 1932). She famously coined the term "monopsony" for the case of a labor market with a single employer and developed the formula linking the elasticity of the labor supply to the wage markdown when compared to the competitive equilibrium outcome. We will return to this formula many times in this chapter.

Adam Smith also notes that "the law, besides, authorizes, or at least does not prohibit their combinations, while it prohibits those of the workmen." In the history of developing countries, the legal backing from colonial powers to employers strengthening their bargaining power is well recorded. Indentured labor from India was effectively captive labor on plantations throughout the British Empire, in Mauritius, South Africa, Fiji, the West Indies, Ceylon, and do on. The draconian laws that increased employer power in these colonies is well recorded by Hugh Tinker (1974). Within India, the state notoriously supported European indigo plantation owners against the poor workers and sharecroppers, leading to Mahatma Gandhi's first major agitation, the Champaran Satyagraha in April 1917 (Remesh, 2006). Even without state backing, the burden of debt reduced the bargaining power of peasants against landlords who, in many cases, were also their creditors, as documented by Sir Malcolm Darling (1928). These concerns on asymmetry in market power between landlords and peasant workers is also present in the history of Latin America and the role of large latifundia estates and landed elites in the political economy of development.

With this background, the literature on labor markets and employer power in developing countries seems to have developed in two directions. One direction continued the focus on the power of landlords as employers through mainly micro-level studies in rural areas. For India, studies in this vein by authors like Beteille (1974) and Srinivas (1987) in sociology and anthropology, and Bardhan (1984), Datt (1996), and Rudra (1982) in economics are among the best known. The empirical economic investigations were accompanied by theoretical understandings of the nature of power relations and the role of interlinkages across credit and labor markets in sustaining asymmetric market power (Bardhan 1980; Basu 1990; Bell and Srinivasan 1989). These types of studies in development economics went hand in hand with, and sometimes underpinned, policy interventions in credit markets and in land markets.

The second strand of literature in development economics is remarkable for being somewhat separate from, and seemingly uninformed by, the above literature on the nature of labor markets in developing countries. Two classic works illustrate this strand: Lewis's (1954) "Economic Development with Unlimited Supplies of Labour", for which Lewis was awarded a Nobel Prize in Economics. Harris and Todaro's (1970) "Migration, Unemployment and Development: A Two-Sector Analysis." garnered more than 10,000 citations on Google Scholar and was chosen as one of the top twenty articles published in the *American Economic Review* for its centenary edition in 2011.

Both works present two sector models, and it is instructive to consider the labor market specifications in each. In the Lewis model, the rural or agricultural sector is famously the source of unlimited supplies of labor. Either because the marginal productivity of labor is zero and there is simply a socially determined wage or, as in subsequent literature, because of household adjustments (Sen 1966), withdrawal of a unit of labor from the rural sector does not change the supply price of labor to the urban/industrial sector. There is thus no modeling of and certainly no emphasis on the rural labor market and market power asymmetries in this market. The modeling of industry is in term of firms facing an infinitely elastic supply curve of labor. There is thus no market power modeled in this sector either. Profits are reinvested, and demand for labor increases without an increase in the wage. The process continues until the surplus labor is exhausted and this phase of "dualistic development" comes to an end.

In the Harris-Todaro model, the labor market is standard competitive with wage equal to the marginal product of labor with a standard production function. The action is in the urban market, where there is a formal sector with a minimum wage above the marginal product of labor so that there is urban unemployment. Thus, the market power in this model is in the hands of urban formal sector workers. Firms are wage takers with no market power. The focus of the model is famously on the migration equilibrium between the rural and urban sector, where migrants compare the rural wage to the expected wage in the urban sector, allowing for the probability of securing a high-paying formal sector job.

The informal sector, where the urban unemployed congregate, is not modeled in detail in Harris and Todaro (1970), but subsequent studies essentially treat the urban informal sector in a competitive frame with no market power on either side, even when they model the transition from unemployment to employment in a more sophisticated fashion (Fields 1975; Basu et. al. 2019). The idea of the informal sector being competitive has become deeply ingrained, and the wage being above marginal product in the formal sector is then seen as a distortion that leads to inefficiency. But this notion of perfect competition in the informal labor market does not sit well with those who work at the ground level with these workers, especially women. The experience of organizations like SEWA (www.sewa.org) is that these workers need to be protected from employer power in their labor markets. Basu et al. (2015) provide a theoretical analysis where contracting difficulties in the informal sector labor market place market power in the hands of employers, in the very sector in which it is thought competition reigns supreme.

Thus, in contrast to the tradition of microeconomic analysis of rural sector labor markets, in which the market power of employers is emphasized, such asymmetry in market power is largely missing in the broad macro-level multisector analysis literature in development economics, following the lead of its classic progenitors. Indeed, in one of these, departures from competition are identified as being in the direction of worker power. This tradition leads naturally to a policy stance of deregulation of labor markets, starting from the removal of minimum wage laws, as the basis of a vibrant employment and development strategy. A competitive view of developing country labor markets also leads to a corresponding stance on the distributional consequences of trade liberalization. A standard Stolper-Samuelson perspective says that trade liberalization will benefit the abundant factor of production, which, in developing countries, would be labor, so that the distributional consequences would be egalitarian on standard assumptions. But the Stolper-Samuelson theorem depends on competitive factor markets and, in particular, on competitive labor markets. Thus, it becomes important to establish whether labor markets in developing countries are indeed competitive.

Recent years have seen an increase in research on questions of employer power in developed country labor markets and in economics in general (see, for example, the review by Manning 2021). There has been a reawakening of research interest in the topic in developing countries, where policy issues such as the minimum wage have been and are being hotly debated (see, for example, Bhorat et al. 2021; Bhorat et al. 2016).

Section 2 of this chapter provides a review of the growing but still limited empirical literature on employer power in developing countries. Section 3 builds on this evidence to present some theoretical perspectives on labor markets in developing countries. Section 4 considers the policy implications, and section 5 concludes with policy and analytical implications.

2. EMPIRICAL EVIDENCE ON EMPLOYER POWER IN DEVELOPING COUNTRIES

The basic theory, as developed by Robinson (1932), says that the wage markdown in monopsony is inversely related to the elasticity of labor supply. The empirical studies investigating monopsony power follow two broad methods. First, studies directly measure the labor supply elasticity. The lower (higher) the elasticity, the higher (lower) the monopsony power. The main challenge in estimating elasticity is in overcoming the problem of wages being endogenously determined through both supply and demand changes. An exogenous variation in wages is required to elicit supply elasticities, separately from demand elasticities. Second, without necessarily estimating the supply elasticity, studies indirectly illustrate the presence of market power, for example, using rent pass-through to wages, measuring differences between wages and marginal revenue product, and understanding changes in wages as a result of mergers and acquisitions. We present in this chapter an overview of both type of studies, with a focus on developing markets but also covering key insights from developed countries.

2.1 DIRECT MEASURES

In developed country settings, monopsony has been traditionally measured by exploiting changes in wage and employment regulation. For example, studies exploit exogenous wage changes among schoolteachers (Falch 2010; Ransom and Sims 2010) or nurses (Staiger et al., 2010) and exploit minimum employment requirement restrictions for nurses (Matsudaira 2014) to obtain labor supply elasticities. Other studies utilize randomized control trial designs in online labor markets (Dube et al. 2020) or instrumental variables regressions for faculty hiring (Goolsbee and Syverson 2019). The estimated elasticities in these studies range from 1.4 to 5. Studies show that supply elasticities for women are smaller than for men, indicating that employers exert higher market power on female workers (Ransom and Oaxaca 2010; Hirsch et al., 2010).[1]

For developing countries, a variety of methodologies have been used to estimate labor supply elasticities. Amodio and De Roux (2021) exploit predetermined variation across plants in sales export destination combined with exchange rates variation to generate plant-specific shocks in Colombian manufacturing. Because of a positive marginal revenue shock, employment would increase under all types of labor markets, but wages would increase under perfect competition but not under monopsony. Following this approach, they demonstrate the presence of monopsony and estimate a firm-level labor supply elasticity of around 2.5. Dal Bó et al. (2013) randomize wages through a public program in Mexico called the Regional Development Program (RDP). Different salaries were announced randomly across recruitment sites, with the following job offers also subsequently randomized. Experimental estimates of labor supply elasticity were measured to be around 2.15. Brummund (2011) uses the production function approach to compute labor supply elasticities in Indonesian manufacturing plants and finds that over half of the manufacturing establishments have a significant amount of market power, with the median firm facing a labor supply elasticity of 0.52. Tortarolo and Z'arate (2020) estimate combined market power for labor and product market in Colombia using the production function approach. The authors then disentangle the combined market power into firm markups and wage markdowns using their estimates of labor supply elasticity. They found that, on average, Colombian manufacturing firms pay wages 11 percent less than marginal revenue productivity of labor, and they estimate a median labor supply elasticity to the individual firm of 2.74.

2.2 INDIRECT MEASURES

Studies have also tested the presence and extent of monopsony power using indirect means without necessarily measuring labor supply elasticity. In developed country markets, for example, studies understand the deviation between wages and marginal revenue product (Isen 2013; Yeh et al. 2022), find the effect of patent rents on additional earnings (Kline et al. 2019), and use fiscal stimulus shocks from American Recovery and Reinvestment Act (ARRA) contracts to examine wage changes (Cho 2019). Others explore the relationship between employer concentration and wages, and show a negative relationship. Higher concentration is associated with lower wages (Azar et al., 2022), and the relationship between productivity and wage levels is weaker when labor markets are more concentrated (Abel et al., 2018; Benmelech et al. 2022). If mergers increase local labor market concentration, earnings, and wage growth fall for workers in affected establishments (Arnold 2019; Prager and Schmitt 2021).

In developing country contexts, Naidu et al. (2016) exploit relaxation of visa restrictions of migrant worker movements across employers in the United Arab Emirates (UAE). Before the reform, workers needed to obtain permission from employers to switch to new contracts once current contract expired. The reform allowed workers to transition to new employers without approval. The results indicate that real earnings and labor retention improved for incumbent workers after the reform and that firms paid workers 51 percent of the marginal product before the reform, but they paid workers 72 percent afterward. Brooks et al. (2021) find that building transportation infrastructure, specifically the Golden Quadrilateral highway in India, disrupted local monopsony power. Labor markdowns were reduced among firms near newly constructed highways relative to firms that remain far from highways. Highway construction increased the labor share of income by 1.8 to 2.3 percentage points. Using firm-level data and variations in tariff reductions across industries in China, Kondo et al. (2021) find that input tariff liberalization is associated with lower labor markdowns across firms. The decline in labor markdown after trade liberalization is more pronounced for skill-intensive firms compared to non-skill-intensive firms.

Felix (2022) exploits the trade liberalization in the 1990s Brazil and finds that a higher import competition ratio increased the payroll HHI by 0.03 points. The estimated impact of this rise in labor market power on wages was small, however. The study finds that the decline in wages was primarily from changes in the marginal revenue product of labor. Sharma (2022) exploits the end of the Multi-Fiber Arrangement that ended export quotas from China to Western countries and consequently delivered a negative shock to Brazilian textile and clothing firms. The results indicate that the shock reduced both men's and women's wages by 6 percent, but men were significantly more likely to switch jobs to help recover their wages, unlike women, who did not switch jobs and whose wages remained persistently lower. Of the observed 42 percent gender wage gap, 18 percent is explained by differential monopsony power. Likely explanations for monopsony include women's stronger affinity for their present employer (10 percent) and the higher concentration of good jobs for women in the textile industry (8 percent).

Szerman (2024) explores a regulation in Brazil requiring firms with one hundred or more workers to employ at least 2 percent with disabilities or individuals enrolled in vocational rehabilitation programs. Results indicate that higher enforcement of these quotas increases employment among people with disabilities following inspections, without decreasing the employment of people without disabilities. Overall, these results point out that firms may be inefficiently small because of imperfect labor market competition, and enforcing reasonable quotas can improve outcomes for those with disability.

Muralidharan et al. (2022) use the randomized rollout of biometric smartcards in the payment of work for the national rural employment guarantee scheme (NREGS) in India. They find better implementation of NREGS substantially increased real incomes, of which 80 percent came from non-NREGS private labor market earnings. With higher wages, employment rose. The authors pose oligopsony power as one potential explanation. They find that positive employment effects are consistently larger in markets with higher concentration of land market power. The study also calculates an aggregate elasticity of 3.07 based on the moments in their data.

2.3 MONOPSONY AND THE MINIMUM WAGE

Textbook theories indicate that an introduction of the minimum wage or an increase in the minimum wage has a negative effect on employment. These results presuppose that labor markets are competitive. If the labor markets are monopsonistic, however, minimum wage does not adversely affect employment, and in some cases also improves employment outcomes (Stigler 1946). In the presence of imperfect enforcement and imperfect competition, Basu et al. (2010) predict that employment responses to introducing a minimum wage can be negative, positive, or muted depending on the level of enforcement and the minimum wage.

Because of these clear predictions and the popularity of minimum wage laws, plenty of studies empirically investigate the effect of minimum wage on employment. In developed countries, there is emerging evidence in favor of monopsony (Card and Krueger, 1994; Dube et al., 2010), but studies also continue to show negative employment effects, illustrating that labor markets are competitive (Machin et al., 2003; Burkhauser et al., 2000), especially among very low-skilled workers—in particular for teens (Neumark et al. 2014).

In developing countries, null employment effects were observed by Hohberg and Lay (2015) in the case of Indonesia and by El-Hamidi and Terrell (2002) in the case of Costa Rica across both formal and informal workers. No adverse employment effects were observed in South Africa, except in the case of agriculture (see Dinkleman and Ranchhod [2012] for domestic workers, Bhorat et al. [2013] for a variety of sectors). The effect of minimum wage on construction workers in India suggests evidence in favor of monopsonistic labor markets (Soundararajan, 2019). The study explores variation in enforcement, and hence the probability of the prevailing minimum wage being enforced. Results indicate that higher enforcement of minimum wage laws increases both market wages and employment. Null or positive employment effects are observed in districts with higher employer concentration.

Bhorat et al. (2017) provide an overview of the results in the minimum wage literature on developing countries. Their work examines ninety-eight studies reviewed in Neumark and Wascher (2007), along with seventeen recent studies focused on lower-middle-income (LMI) countries. They find that 55 percent of the employment elasticities are not significantly different from zero and that the median elasticity is –0.08. This meta study suggests that the minimum wage has either benign or slightly negative employment effects across many settings. Broecke et al. (2017) review evidence on minimum wage effects in fourteen major emerging economies (Argentina, Brazil, Chile, China, Colombia, India, Indonesia, Mexico, Poland, the Philippines, the Russian Federation, South Africa, Thailand, and Turkey) and find minimal impact on employment. Vulnerable groups, such as youth and the low-skilled, are more negatively affected.

3. THEORY FROM THE PERSPECTIVE OF A DEVELOPING COUNTRY

Monopsony power and wage markdowns are inextricably interwoven via a simple elasticity formula in this fast-growing literature on employer power. The canonical model features a profit-maximizing producer faced with an upward-sloping labor supply schedule. Profit maximization prescribes a markdown on wages—a proportionate wage shortfall relative to the marginal value of the product of labor—to equal the elasticity of the inverse labor supply schedule as the employer internalizes the wage consequences of hiring at the margin. The competitive case, at the limit, optimally sets the markdown at zero as the elasticity goes to zero. The intermediate case of Cournot labor market competition yields predictions that are consistent with developed country evidence as well—the higher the Herfindahl Index of labor market concentration, the steeper the wage markdown (e.g., Azar et al. 2020; Azar et al. 2022).

Naidu and Posner (2022) and Manning (2021) expand on the definition of the wage elasticity of labor supply and observe that high labor supply elasticities and steep wage markdowns are associated with concentration and nonconcentration drivers. Drawing an analog from a product market power model driven by random utility (Gabaix et al. 2016), Naidu and Posner (2022) point out that wage markdowns can persist even in labor markets with many employers, for example, in multinomial choice models with heterogeneous worker preferences (e.g., Card et al. 2018). Another alternative is that search friction can give rise to wage markdown in the presence of many competing firms, particularly when job offer arrival rates to job destruction rates are low (e.g., Burdett and Mortensen 1998; Manning 2003).

This elasticity-centric story of the wage markdown glosses over many labor market characteristics in developing countries, leaving important questions unanswered. For example, how appropriate are standard prescriptions of antitrust actions as a cure for steep wage markdowns in developing country labor markets?[2] Beyond the perceived labor supply schedule, are there worker-level, institution-specific, and policy-related drivers of the wage markdown? In this section, we present insights from three models that showcase three respective sets of often-noted features of developing country labor markets:

> Formal sector wages are often regulated via minimum wage laws, although full enforcement of the minimum wage is the exception rather than the rule (Basu, Chau, and Kanbur 2015); even when a formal wage anchor (e.g., minimum wage) is absent, workers may nonetheless harbor

fair wage concerns and penalize employers by undercutting effort when fair wage demands are not met (Basu, Chau, and Soundararajan 2019); when wage contracts are not fully enforced by a third party to different extents depending, for example, on the formality of the job, self-enforcement of open-ended employment relationships are subject to nonreneging constraints (Basu, Chau, and Kanbur 2015).

Next, we describe the three models briefly. We then show the corresponding revision in wage markdown formulas in relation to the canonical prescription, discuss potential causes that drive compression or magnification in the markdown, and point out the role of labor market policies in the determination of the markdown.

3.1 WAGE MARKDOWN, IMPERFECT ENFORCEMENT, AND THE MINIMUM WAGE

We present a simple setup in which wage markdowns are outcomes of (1) monopsony power, (2) minimum wage, and (3) imperfect enforcement of the minimum wage. The variable $aR(\ell)$ denotes a downward-sloping and continuously differentiable revenue schedule of an monopsonistic employer hiring ℓ workers, and $aR_\ell(\ell)$ is the associated marginal revenue product of ℓ. The parameter a denotes a Hicks neutral parameter of monopsony productivity. Let $w(\ell)$ denote an upward-sloping and continuously differentiable inverse labor supply schedule with elasticity $d\log w(\ell)/d\log \ell \equiv \varepsilon$.

Let a minimum wage policy be a wage, enforcement intensity combination $\{\overline{w},\lambda\}$, where $\lambda \varepsilon [0,1]$ denotes the probability of inspection. In response, the employer has three options: overcompliance, exact compliance, and noncompliance. An overcomplying employer sets the wage at $w > \overline{w}$. Total cost of employing ℓ workers is just

$$W(\ell) = w(\ell)\ell,\ w(\ell) > \overline{w}.$$

For an employer in exact compliance, the total cost is

$$W(\ell) = \overline{w}\ell.$$

Finally, for a noncomplying employer, the total wage cost is:

$$\begin{aligned} W(\ell) &= (1-\lambda)w(\ell)\ell + \lambda\left[\overline{w} + \delta\left(\overline{w} - w(\ell)\right)\right]\ell,\ w(\ell) < \overline{w} \\ &= w(\ell)\ell + \lambda(1+\delta)\left(\overline{w} - w(\ell)\right)\ell \end{aligned}$$

where δ is the transaction cost of transferring back wages amounting to $(\overline{w}-w(\ell))\ell$ to workers when noncomplying employers are discovered. The marginal labor cost schedule is piecewise continuously differentiable, and given by:

$$W_\ell(\ell)=\begin{cases} w(\ell)(1+\varepsilon), & l>\overline{\ell} \\ w(\ell)(1+\varepsilon)+\lambda(1+\delta)(\overline{w}-w(\ell)(1+\varepsilon)), & l<\overline{\ell} \end{cases} \quad (1)$$

where $\overline{\ell}=\{\ell|w(\ell)=\overline{w}\}$ is the level of labor supply consistent with full payment of the minimum wage.

Figure 1.1 illustrates this upward-sloping marginal labor cost schedule in bold as $W_\ell(\ell)$, and the standard marginal labor cost equaling $w(\ell)(1+\varepsilon)$ for overcompliers. For noncompliers, the marginal labor cost curve is a weighted average of the minimum wage $\overline{w}$ and the original marginal labor

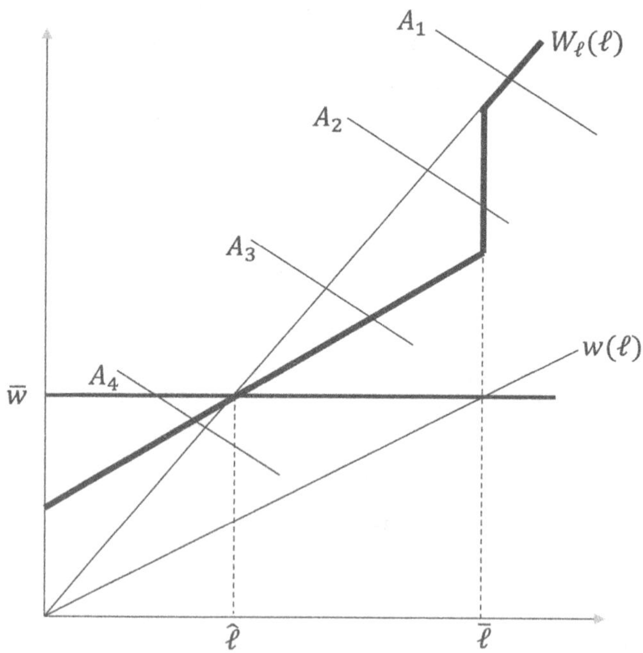

Figure 1.1 The analytics of a minimum wage with monopsony power and imperfect enforcement

cost $w(\ell)(1+\varepsilon)$ in the absence of the minimum wage policy. As a weighted average, this revised marginal labor cost pivots at $\hat{\ell}$—the level of employment at which the original marginal labor cost $w(\ell)(1+\epsilon)$ intersects the minimum wage. In particular, $W_\ell(\ell)$ lies below the original marginal labor cost curve whenever $\bar{w}$ is less than $w(\ell)(1+\varepsilon)$ or when $\ell > \hat{\ell}$, and above the original marginal labor cost curve whenever $\bar{w}$ is greater than $w(\ell)(1+\varepsilon)$ or when $\ell < \hat{\ell}$. Finally, at $\bar{\ell}$, the level of employment consistent with the minimum wage, there is a sharp drop in the marginal labor cost schedule to reflect a sharp drop in the marginal labor cost in the transition from overcompliance to noncompliance:

$$w(\bar{\ell})(1+\varepsilon)+\lambda(1+\delta)\left(\bar{w}-w(\bar{\ell})(1+\varepsilon)\right)<w(\bar{\ell})(1+\varepsilon)$$

because $\bar{\ell} > \hat{\ell}$.

Consider therefore a profit-maximizing monopoly that sets employment ℓ^* at a level that implicitly solves $aR_\ell(\ell^*) = W_\ell(\ell^*)$. We make the following observations:

CHANGES IN THE WAGE MARKDOWN FORMULA

Because the marginal labor cost schedules contain three distinctive segments, the markdown formula changes depending on the productivity of the firm. For sufficiently high-productivity monopsonies (e.g., A_1), the minimum wage is nonbinding, and thus the markdown is independent of the minimum wage policy. The corresponding wage markdown consistent with profit maximization is given by

$$\frac{aR_\ell(\ell)-w(\ell)}{w(\ell)}=\varepsilon$$

for employers that operate in this range.

For the next range of productivities (e.g., A_2), there is a clustering of employers who comply exactly with the minimum wage policy. These are employers that find it profit maximizing to pay the minimum wage, hiring exactly $\bar{\ell}$. The wage markdown consistent with profit maximization is given by

$$\frac{aR_\ell(\ell)-w(\ell)}{w(\ell)}=\frac{aR_\ell(\bar{\ell})-w(\bar{\ell})}{w(\bar{\ell})}$$

for the cluster of employer productivity types with exact compliance, and $\ell = \bar{\ell}$ is labor supply consistent with the minimum wage. This markdown is higher with higher firm-level productivity. The markdown is also strictly decreasing in the minimum wage $\bar{w}$, but it is completely independent of the enforcement intensity λ.

For productivity levels that are lower, the employer is still a noncomplier (e.g., A_3). The equilibrium wage markdown can be written as[3]

$$\frac{aR_\ell(\ell^*) - w(\ell^*)}{w(\ell^*)} = \varepsilon - \lambda(1+\delta)(1+\varepsilon)\frac{aR_\ell(\ell^*) - w(\ell^*)}{w(\ell^*)}$$

The wage markdown once again depends evidently on the elasticity of labor supply, but with an adjustment that depends on firm-level productivity, the minimum wage, along with the enforcement intensity λ, and the transaction cost associated with being fined for incurring back pay.

MARKDOWN COMPRESSION OR MAGNIFICATION

A natural question at this point is whether an imperfectly enforced minimum wage can compress the wage markdown to achieve a more equitable division of surplus between employer and workers. The answer to this question is nuanced and highly nonuniform depending specifically on the productivity of the monopsony.

Note that the wage markdown for each level of employment ℓ in the end depends on the marginal labor cost, for profit maximization:

$$\frac{aR_\ell(\ell) - \bar{w}}{\bar{w}} = \frac{W_\ell(\ell) - \bar{w}}{\bar{w}}$$

Figure 1.1, which displays the marginal labor cost curve before and after the minimum wage policy, shows that the minimum wage policy clearly has no effect on the wage markdown for overcompliers because both employment and wages are independent of the policy for this group of employers. The minimum wage policy does indeed compress the wage markdown for intermediate-productivity employers, however, who hire $\ell^* > \hat{\ell}$ but less than $\bar{\ell}$ for the minimum wage policy $W_\ell(\ell)$ around $\hat{\ell}$. The minimum wage policy has the opposite effect of magnifying the wage markdown among the lowest productivity producers, for whom $\ell^* < \hat{\ell}$.

Thus, the effect of the minimum wage policy on wage markdown runs the gamut, from unchanging to a compression, and then further to a magnification effect across firm types.

INTERPLAY BETWEEN WAGE MARKDOWN AND LABOR MARKET POLICIES

The case of an imperfectly enforced minimum wage offers a particularly nuanced view on how labor market policies can affect the markdown. The lesson is simple—any policy combinations that give rise to a reduction in the marginal labor cost will compress the equilibrium wage markdown. What remains underappreciated in the literature, however, is that observed wage markdowns should be understood case-by-case as the joint outcome of the interaction between labor market policy and firm-level characteristics. To give two examples based on our simple model, a gradual magnification of the wage markdown can be a symptom of rising monopsony wage-setting power or of changes in labor market policies that consistently increase the marginal labor cost at a constant labor supply schedule $w(\ell)$. An increase in enforcement intensity may reduce markdown among some employers (higher productivity) but increase it among others (lower productivity).

3.2 WAGE MARKDOWN AND FAIR WAGE CONSIDERATIONS

When enforcement of wage contracts cannot be ensured, what options do workers have to guarantee a living wage? In a seminal article, Akerlof and Yellen (1990) posits the fair-wage-effort hypothesis, in which worker reprisal in the form of a reduction in work effort takes place in the event wages are below a level that workers deem fair—the fair wage. There is emerging empirical evidence supporting this hypothesis. For example, see Breza et al. (2018) for India, and Verhoogen et al. (2014) and Dube et al. (2019) for the United States.[4] The proportional reduction in work effort is taken to be equal to the wage shortfall relative to the fair wage so that the employer is naturally incentivized to pay just the fair wage to reap the full effort from worker. Worker reprisal implies an upward-sloping labor supply at the worker level, where the effort of each worker e is a function of the wage received w relative to the fair wage w^f:

$$e(w) = \min\left\{\frac{w}{w^f}, 1\right\}.$$

As shown, effort is bounded above at the maximal effort level per worker at unity.

Given this incentive structure associated with the fair wage-effort relationship where employers are incentivized to pay exactly w^f, the associated wage markdown naturally departs from the canonical formula, depending instead only on the determinants of the fair wage. In this regard, Akerlof and Yellen (1990) furthermore posit a fair wage to be given by the weighted average of the marginal value product of a worker at full effort, p, and the wage the worker can expect if she opts out of the fair wage contract, w_o.[5]

$$w^f = \beta p + (1-\beta) w_o \tag{2}$$

where $\beta \in [0,1]$ is a fairness preference parameter indicating workers' desire for pay commensurate with productivity p. The wage markdown is thus simply

$$\frac{p - w^f}{w^f} = (1-\beta)\left(\beta + \frac{w_o}{p - w_o}\right)^{-1}.$$

The wage markdown is strictly decreasing with respect to the fairness preference parameter β. Furthermore, the wage markdown reflects the gap between the marginal value product of labor p and the opt-out wage w_o.

Basu et al. (2019) introduce more structure to the model to consider the profit maximization problem of the employer. Assume that the relationship between labor input and output is one-for-one. The employer in question selects a price p, equivalently the marginal value product of labor, to maximize profits subject to a weakly downward-sloping demand curve $x(p)$ with elasticity of demand $-d\log x(p)/d\log p = \rho$:

$$\pi = \max_{p,w}\left(p - \frac{w}{e(w)}\right)x(p). \tag{3}$$

subject to the fair wage-effort relationship

$$e(w) = \min\left\{\frac{w}{w^f}, 1\right\}.$$

CHANGES IN THE WAGE MARKDOWN FORMULA

The solution to equation (3) reiterates the familiar output pricing solution to the firm's maximization problem as

$$p^* = w_o / \rho > w_o,$$

which implies that the fair wage in equilibrium is ultimately determined by the opt-out wage w_o, the preference parameter β, in addition to the product market power of the employer parameterized by the demand elasticity ρ. Substituting this solution to p^* into the fair wage markdown, we have

$$w^* = \beta p^* + (1-\beta)w_o = w_o\left(1+\beta(1-\rho)/\rho\right).$$

The corresponding wage markdown can be expressed simply as a function of two parameters of the model β and ρ:

$$\frac{p^* - w^*}{w^*} = (1-\beta)\left(\beta + \frac{\rho}{1-\rho}\right)^{-1}.$$

MARKDOWN COMPRESSION OR MAGNIFICATION

Contrary to the canonical prescription that the wage markdown is a function only of labor market power, the current setup presents an alternative view when wage contracts are enforced by threat of worker reprisal. The drivers of the corresponding wage markdown are the fairness preference parameter β, and the monopoly power of the employer given by ρ. Markdown compression occurs when the fairness preference parameter swings in favor of giving a higher share of the workers' marginal product as wages. The more potent the monopoly power (a lower ρ), the more magnified the wage markdown will be.

INTERPLAY BETWEEN WAGE MARKDOWN AND LABOR MARKET INSTITUTIONS

An important takeaway is that, in the absence of third-party enforcement of wage contracts, the wage markdown is held in check by workers' fairness preference, conditional on employers' ability to manipulate the value of workers' effort. This form of tacit agreement is not universal, and indeed there are multiple ways to further extend this path of reasoning. Basu et al. (2019) make the argument that employers are incentivized to pay more if they are sure that the workers are direct beneficiaries of the higher wage. This direct employment relationship can be severed when workers are hired indirectly through subcontractors. Basu et al. (2019) ascertain the determinant of the wage markdown for subcontracted workers, who are paid by contractors and not employers. The payment of the fair wage to subcontracted workers is no longer guaranteed. This gives rise to effort and wage cost implications that employers must then take into account when making subcontracting decisions. What is important is that labor market institutions enter the markdown debate through a composition effect—in this case, the share of regular versus contract workers—that can shed potentially new light in the research on the drivers of the economy-wide labor share.

An alternative extension can involve endogenizing the opt-out wage w_0 as a function of the labor demand of the employer. This takes us back, of course, to the canonical territory of wage markdown in the presence of monopsony power. The precise ways in which the elasticity of labor supply through w_0 interacts with fairness preference in the determination of a wage markdown is an interesting question for future research.

3.3 WAGE MARKDOWN AND THE SELF-ENFORCEMENT CONSTRAINT

Beyond the threat of worker reprisal, credibility in labor contracting can also be achieved by ensuring that any wage promise made will be kept via a self-enforcing constraint. Basu, Chau and Kanbur (2015) examine the nature of self-enforcing wage contracts in the formal and the informal sectors, where minimum wage enforcement differ in intensity. A nonreneging constraint in this context gives the maximal wage that workers can demand such that employers are incentivized to pay as promised in order to maintain a long-term employment relationship with the same worker. The alternative is to terminate employment after reneging on the contract. The extent to which employers can expect to get away with the practice is assumed to depend on the extent to which minimum wages are enforced. Assume henceforth that workers can find employment either in the formal (*f*) or the informal (*i*) sector, where minimum wage enforcement intensities are q_f and q_i, respectively, and where $1 \geq q_f > q_i \geq 0$.

A self-enforcing wage contract in this context is the maximal wage satisfying a nonreneging constraint. Let $V_k(w^*, a)$ denote the value function of an employer who hires a worker with marginal value product a and who promises to pay w every period in sector $k = f, i$ in an open-ended employment relationship. Contracts are terminated at an exogenous rate δ every period.

Thus, in a steady state at discount factor $\beta \varepsilon (0,1)$:

$$V_k(w^*,a) = a - w - b(1-\delta)V_k(w^*,a) = \frac{a - w^*}{1 - b(1-\delta)}, \quad k = f,i.$$

As an alternative, the expected profits of a reneging employer in sector k is

$$V_k^o(w^*,a) = a - q_k \overline{w}.$$

The nonreneging constraint in k requires that paying the promised wage ω^* is the better option:

$$V_k(w^*,a) = \frac{a - w^*}{1 - b(1-\delta)} > a - q_k \overline{w}.$$

The highest possible wage consistent with the nonreneging constraints implies strictly positive wage markdowns, with

$$\begin{aligned} w_k^{NR}(a,\overline{w}) &= \max\{w \mid V_i(w,a) \geq q - q_k \overline{w}\} \\ &= b(1-\delta)a + (1 - b(1-\delta))q_k \overline{w}. \end{aligned} \quad (4)$$

The application of a minimum wage raises w_f^{NR} disproportionately more than w_i^{NR} because the lowest expected wage that a reneging employer will be forced by law to pay is $q_f \overline{w}$ in the formal sector and $q_i \overline{w}$ otherwise. The key observation here is that the potential wage savings from reneging, all else being equal, is strictly less severe in the formal sector thanks to government enforcement of the minimum wage for the same promised wage.

CHANGES IN THE WAGE MARKDOWN FORMULAS

Using equation (4), the wage markdown formulas are:

$$\frac{a - w_f^{NR}}{w_f^{NR}} = (1 - b(1-\delta))\left(b(1-\delta) + \frac{q_f \overline{w}}{a - q_f \overline{w}}\right)^{-1}, \tag{5}$$

$$\frac{a - w_i^{NR}}{w_i^{NR}} = (1 - b(1-\delta))\left(b(1-\delta) + \frac{q_i \overline{w}}{a - q_f \overline{w}}\right)^{-1}. \tag{6}$$

Thus, in the context of a self-enforcing constraint, the wage markdown offers the employer just enough surplus to reject reneging on the wage contract. These prescriptions closely resemble that of the fair wage setting in our earlier discussion. Here, the contract termination risk-adjusted discount rate, $b(1-\delta)$, takes the place of the fairness preference parameter in the fair wage setting. The variable $q_k \overline{w}$ is, of course, just the expected level of third-party enforced wage payment, which now takes the place of the opt-out wage in the fair wage setting.

MARKDOWN COMPRESSION OR MAGNIFICATION

The rationale behind a wage markdown in the current context is to set wages low enough so that employers choose voluntarily to maintain an open-ended employment relationship. As long as formal sector employers are faced with a better-enforced minimum wage, their wage savings from reneging is restricted relative to an informal employer promising the same wage. One would thus expect that the self-enforcing wage markdown in the formal sector is a compressed version of the wage markdown in the informal sector, and this is exactly what we find in equations (5) and (6), all else being equal.

The wage markdowns are driven by firm- and worker-level considerations as well. Uncertainty in operating a formal establishment, as parameterized by δ, has the effect of magnifying the wage markdown by making open-ended employment relationships less attractive, while an increase in the productivity of the worker a increases the wage markdown by raising the profitability of a fly-by-night employer. These considerations once again depart from the canonical elasticity-based markdown formula, bringing together policy-, firm- and worker-level considerations.

INTERPLAY BETWEEN WAGE MARKDOWN AND LABOR MARKET INSTITUTIONS

Informal employment is a ubiquitous feature of labor markets in developing countries. Yet our understanding of the determinants of wage markdown here is notably scant. The current model is a first step in this direction, and many directions for extension remain. Suppose that informal employment feeds into formal production by acting as an intermediate input supplier (e.g., Chen 2007). What then is the nature of the link between wage markdowns in the two sectors when employers can cross-substitute between labor input providers? In addition, workers self-select into formal and informal sector employment (Basu et al. 2015) because their productivity naturally feeds into wages in the two sectors, as we saw in equations (5) and (6). Worker productivity thus gives rise to another systematic driver of observed wage markdowns in the formal and the informal sectors. The informal wage markdown falls with minimum wage enforcement, but the same markdown increases if relatively high-productivity workers simultaneously self-select to work in the informal sector because better enforcement of formal wages gives rise to formal job rationing. These two drivers have opposite effects on the informal sector wage markdown. Which one of these tendencies dominates in aggregate wage markdown observations? These and other related questions related to composition effects are promising areas for future research.

4. CONCLUSION: POLICY AND ANALYTICAL IMPLICATIONS FOR DEVELOPING COUNTRIES

Conceptual and analytical perspectives matter for policy. A worldview based on the assumption of competition everywhere will be inclined against intervention and regulation. When empirical evidence stacks up against such a position, it prompts questions on appropriate public policy to enhance social welfare. It also prompts analytical perspectives founded on features of the real world, including constraints on policy implementation.

We have already alluded to the profound influence of the Harris-Todaro (1970) perspective where the departure from competitive labor markets is assumed to occur in the formal sector through the power of labor unions, in other words, employee power. This reduces employment in the formal sector and displaces labor to the informal labor market, which is assumed to be competitive, with no market power on either side. The policy conclusion is straightforward. Because the distortion away from perfect competition lies in the power of labor unions, this power needs to be dismantled—a policy that has indeed been followed in recent years. From a competitive worldview, an inappropriately instituted minimum wage in the formal labor market leads to a reduction in employment and the displacement of labor toward the informal sector, a worldview found in critiques of the minimum wage policies that are widespread in developing countries.

But what if labor markets are not competitive and, far from labor unions having power, it is employers who have such power? As reviewed in this chapter, the evidence is certainly accumulating that employers have power. The case against regulation and the case for intervention then need to be revised. Specifically for the minimum wage, employer power justifies its use as a device to increase efficiency and equity. The argument now turns on the context and detail of the labor market structure, and on the level and structure of minimum wages. Nothing said so far precludes a critique of actual minimum wages as set—they may be too high or not well structured—but a blanket negation of this policy instrument is no longer warranted (Bhorat et al. 2021). Detailed economic analysis is needed and necessary.

Let us then accept that the need for state intervention cannot be blocked out a priori by the assumption that labor markets are competitive. But this still leaves open the question of implementation of interventions when state enforcement capacity is weak, as it is generally recognized to be in developing countries. The intensity of enforcement is a key factor in determining the efficacy of a minimum wage in delivering its efficiency and equity gains (Basu et al. 2010). At one extreme, zero enforcement means that there is in effect no intervention. But intermediate levels of enforcement interact with different levels of enforcement in intricate ways. Apart from the empirical difficulties in making inferences from the variation in employment as minimum wage varies, when enforcement can vary as well, this raises the conceptual question, How is the enforcement intensity chosen and why? And how does the ability or inability to commit to enforcement (rather than to turn a blind eye) play into the choice of the minimum wage? Such issues are highlighted in section 3.

Thus, while the competitive labor markets presumption is too simple and empirically invalid, so is the presumption of easily implemented policy correctives to employer power in labor markets. The difficulty of enforcing minimum wages is but one example. There is no easy transference of an antitrust frame, which is very well developed for product markets in developed countries, to labor markets in developing countries. Defining the boundaries of a labor market with the prevalence of informality and then identifying measures and limits to concentration in the way it is done in conventional antitrust regulation for product markets in developed countries will be extremely difficult in developing countries.

If directly addressing employer power in developing country labor markets can be only a partial answer, is there an alternative or a supplement? We get a clue from the basic wage markdown formula in the elasticity-centric framework. The lower the elasticity, the greater the markdown. In simple terms, the more workers are bound to supply labor no matter the wage, the greater the power that employers have over them. Thus, raising the elasticity lowers the markdown. The attention then shifts analytically to the factors underlying the elasticity of labor supply and, from a policy perspective, to interventions that can raise this elasticity. What might such interventions look like?

In section 2 of this chapter, we have already alluded to the role of transport infrastructure. As developed in Basu et al. (2010) for example, transportation costs are a key determinant of the responsiveness of labor supply to changes in wage. And the empirical evidence reviewed in section 2 suggests that the development of transport infrastructure can lower the degree of employer power. But transportation is just a start. Other economic, social, cultural, and institutional barriers to labor force participation can have the same effect, and these barriers prompt us to investigate these features of developing countries more closely as underpinnings of employer power. The specific models of section 3 of this chapter are a start on such an exercise.

In sum, employer power is a feature of labor markets in developing countries. This feature changes our policy perspective on labor market interventions significantly, and it opens up interesting and important areas of empirical and theoretical research.

NOTES

1. See Naidu and Posner (2022) and Card (2022) for an overview of the literature of monopsony in developed country labor markets, and Sokolova and Sorensen (2021) for a meta-analysis based on various studies around the world but primarily focused on the United States, Canada, and Australia.

2. A host of other policies studied in the developed country context continues to be open questions in the context of developing countries (Naidu and Posner 2022). These include means-tested transfers (Posner and Weyl 2018), tacit agreements on no-poaching rules and noncompete contracts (Ashenfelter et al. 2021), and mergers and acquisition policies (Benmelech et al. 2018).

3. Note that we have taken the $w(\ell^*)$ at equilibrium employment ℓ^* as the baseline wage in the markdown formula to capture wage markdown among workers receiving subminimum wages.

4. Wage disparity is important in both developed and developing country labor markets. See Duman (2019) for a review of the literature and estimates from various studies. This disparity presents a departure from the canonical labor market model of monopsony power on a homogeneous workforce.

5. There are alternative specifications as well, including specifications that put weight on the wages of others, for example, in the same establishment in the definition of fairness.

REFERENCES

Abel, W., S. Tenreyro, and G. Thwaites. 2018. "Monopsony in the UK." Discussion Paper CFM-DP2018-27. Centre for Macroeconomics.

Akerlof, G. A., and J. L. Yellen. 1990. "The Fair Wage–Effort Hypothesis and Unemployment." *Quarterly Journal of Economics* 105 (2): 255–83. https://doi.org/10.2307/2937787.

Amodio, F., and N. De Roux. 2021. "Labor Market Power in Developing Countries: Evidence from Colombian Plants." Discussion Paper 14390. IZA. Institute for the Study of Labor. https://doi.org/10.2139/ssrn.3855954

Arnold, D. 2019. "Mergers and Acquisitions, Local Labor Market Concentration, and Worker Outcomes." Working Paper. Princeton University Press. http://dx.doi.org/10.2139/ssrn.3476369.

Ashenfelter, O., D. Card, H. S. Farber, and M. Ransom. 2021. "Monopsony in the Labor Market: New Empirical Results and New Public Policies." Princeton University Industrial Relations Section, Working Paper 652. Princeton University Press.

Azar, J., I. Marinescu, M. I. Steinbaum, and B. Taska. 2020. "Concentration in U.S. Labor Markets: Evidence from Online Vacancy Data." *Labour Economics* 66. https://doi.org/10.1016/j.labeco.2020.101886

Azar, J., I. Marinescu, and M. Steinbaum. 2022. "Labor Market Concentration." *Journal of Human Resources* 57 (S): S167–99. https://doi.org/10.3368/jhr.monopsony.1218-9914R1.

Bardhan, P. K. 1980. "Interlocking Markets and Agrarian Development: A Review of the Issues." *Oxford Economic Papers* 32: 82–98. https://doi.org/10.1093/oxfordjournals.oep.a041472.

Bardhan, P. K. 1984. *Land, Labour and Poverty: Essays in Development Economics.* Oxford University Press.

Basu, A. K., N. H. Chau, and R. Kanbur. 2010. "Turning a Blind Eye: Costly Enforcement, Credible Commitment and Minimum Wage Laws." *The Economic Journal* 120 (543): 244–69. https://doi.org/10.1111/j.1468-0297.2009.02298.x.

Basu, A., N. Chau, and R. Kanbur. 2015. "Contractual Dualism, Market Power and Informality." *The Economic Journal* 125: 1534–73. https://doi.org/10.1111/ecoj.12222.

Basu, A., N. Chau, G. Fields, and R. Kanbur. 2019. "Job Creation in a Multi-Sector Labour Market Model for Developing Economies." *Oxford Economic Papers* 71 (1): 119–44. https://doi.org/10.1093/oep/gpy029.

Basu, A.K., N. Chau, and V. Soundararajan. 2019. "Wage fairness in a subcontracted labor market," *Journal of Economic Behavior & Organization* 168 (2019): 24–42. https://doi.org/10.1016/j.jebo.2019.09.022.

Basu, K. 1990. *Agrarian Structure and Economic Development*. Harwood Academic.

Bell, C., and T. N. Srinivasan. 1989. "Interlinked Transactions in Rural Markets." *Oxford Bulletin of Economics and Statistics* 51: 73–83. https://doi.org/10.1111/j.1468-0084.1989.mp51001005.x.

Benmelech, E., N. Bergman, and H. Kim. 2018. "Strong Employers and Weak Employees: How Does Employment Concentration Affect Wages?" Working Paper 24307. National Bureau of Economic Research (NBER). https://doi.org/10.3386/w24307.

Benmelech, E., N. K. Bergman, and H. Kim. 2022. "Strong Employers and Weak Employees: How Does Employer Concentration Affect Wages?" *Journal of Human Resources* 57 (S): S200–50. https://doi.org/10.3368/jhr.monopsony.0119-10007R1.

Beteille, A. (1974). *Studies in Agrarian Structure*. Oxford University Press.

Bhorat, H., R. Kanbur, and N. Mayet. 2013. "The Impact of Sectoral Minimum Wage Laws on Employment, Wages, and Hours of Work in South Africa." *IZA Journal of Labor & Development* 2 (1): 1–27. https://doi.org/10.1186/2193-9020-2-1.

Bhorat, H., R. Kanbur, and L. Shi. 2016. "Thematic Series on Reforming Minimum Wage and Labor Regulation Policies in Developing Economies." *IZA Journal of Labor and Development*. https://izajold.springeropen.com/rmwl.

Bhorat, H., R. Kanbur, and B. Stanwix. 2017. "Minimum Wages in Sub-Saharan Africa: A Primer." *World Bank Research Observer* 32 (1): 21–74. https://doi.org/10.1596/30139.

Bhorat, H., R. Kanbur, and B. Stanwix. 2021. "An Empirical Assessment of the National Minimum Wage in South Africa." In *Ethics, Politics, Inequality: New Directions.*, ed. N. Bohler-Muller, V. Reddy, and C. Soudien. HSRC Press.

Breza, E., K. Supreet, and S. Yogita. 2018. "The Morale Effects of Pay Inequality." *Quarterly Journal of Economics* 133: 611–63. https://doi.org/10.1093/qje/qjx041.

Broecke, S., A. Forti, and M. Vandeweyer. 2017. "The Effect of Minimum Wages on Employment in Emerging Economies: A Survey and Meta-Analysis." *Oxford Development Studies* 45 (3): 366–91. https://doi.org/10. 1080/13600818.2017.1279134.

Brooks, W. J., J. P. Kaboski, I. O. Kondo, Y. A. Li, and W. Qian. 2021. "Infrastructure Investment and Labor Monopsony Power." *IMF Economic Review* 69 (3): 470–504.

Brummund, P. 2011. "Variation in Monopsonistic Behavior across Establishments: Evidence from the Indonesian Labor Market." PhD diss., Cornell University. https://ecommons.cornell.edu/server/api/core/bitstreams/bde6825a-2656-4d5d-96fc-8691530f96e7/content.

Burdett, K., and D. T. Mortensen. 1998. "Wage Differentials, Employer Size, and Unemployment." *International Economic Review* 39 (2): 257–73. https://doi.org/10.2307/2527292.

Burkhauser, R. V., K. A. Couch, and D. C. Wittenburg. 2000. "A Reassessment of the New Economics of the Minimum Wage Literature with Monthly Data from the Current Population Survey." *Journal of Labor Economics* 18 (4): 653–80. https://doi.org/10.1086/209972.

Card, D. 2022. "Who Set Your Wage?" *American Economic Review* 112(4): 1075–90.

Card, D., A. R. Cardoso, J. Heining, and P. Kline. 2018. "Firms and Labor Market Inequality: Evidence and Some Theory." *Journal of Labor Economics* 36 (S1): S13–70. https://doi.org/10.1086/694153.

Card, D., and A. B. Krueger. 1994. "Minimum Wages and Employment: A Case Study of the New Jersey and Pennsylvania Fast Food Industries." *American Economic Review* 84 (4): 772–93.

Chen, M. A. 2007. "Rethinking the Informal Economy: Linkages with the Formal Economy and the Formal Regulatory Environment." DESA Working Paper 46. UN Department of Economic and Social Affairs.

Cho, D. 2019. "Essays on the Determination of Employment and Wages." PhD diss., Princeton University. https://dataspace.princeton.edu/jspui/bitstream/88435/dsp01xs55mf94k/1/Cho_princeton_0181D_13042.pdf.

Dal Bó, E., F. Finan, and M. A. Rossi. 2013. "Strengthening State Capabilities: The Role of Financial Incentives in the Call to Public Service." *Quarterly Journal of Economics* 128 (3): 1169–1218. https://doi.org/10.1093/qje/qjt008.

Darling, M. 1928. *The Punjab Peasant in Prosperity and Debt.* Oxford University Press.

Datt, G. 1996. *Bargaining Power, Wages and Employment: An Analysis of Agricultural Labor Markets in India.* Sage.

Dinkelman, T., and V. Ranchhod. 2012. "Evidence on the Impact of Minimum Wage Laws in an Informal Sector: Domestic Workers in South Africa." *Journal of Development Economics* 99 (1): 27–45. https://doi.org/10. 1016/j.jdeveco.2011.12.006.

Dube A., L. Giuliano, and J. Leonard. 2019. "Fairness and Frictions: The Impact of Unequal Raises on Quit Behavior." *American Economic Review* 109 (2): 620–63. https://doi.org/10.1257/aer.20160232.

Dube, A., J. Jacobs, S. Naidu, and S. Suri. 2020. "Monopsony in Online Labor Markets." *American Economic Review: Insights* 2 (1): 33–46. https://doi.org/10.1257/aeri.20180150.

Dube, A., T. W. Lester, and M. Reich. 2010. "Minimum Wage Effects Across State Borders: Estimates Using Contiguous Counties." *Review of Economics and Statistics* 92 (4): 945–64. https://doi.org/10.1162/REST_a_00039.

Duman, A. 2019. "Wage Penalty for Temporary Workers in Turkey: Evidence from Quantile Regressions." *The Developing Economies* 57 (4): 283–310. https://doi.org/10.1111/deve.12206.

El Hamidi, F., and K. Terrell. 2002. "The Impact of Minimum Wages on Wage Inequality and Employment in the Formal and Informal Sector in Costa Rica." In *Inequality around the World*, ed. R. B. Freeman. Springer. https://doi.org/10.1007/978-1-137-09971-6_8.

Falch, T. 2010. "The Elasticity of Labor Supply at the Establishment Level." *Journal of Labor Economics* 28 (2): 237–66. https://doi.org/10.1086/649905.

Felix, Mayara. 2022. "Trade, Labor Market Concentration, and Wages." Working Paper. https://www.mayarafelix.com/papers/Felix_JMP.pdf.

Fields, G. S. 1975. "Rural–Urban Migration, Urban Unemployment and Underemployment, and Job Search Activity in LDCs." *Journal of Development Economics* 2: 165–88. https://doi.org/10.1016/0304-3878(75)90014-0.

Gabaix, X., D. Laibson, D. Li, H. Li, S. Resnick, and C. G. de Vries. 2016. "The Impact of Competition on Prices with Numerous Firms." *Journal of Economic Theory* 165: 1–24. https://doi.org/10.1016/j.jet.2016.04.001.

Goolsbee, A., and C. Syverson. (2019). "Monopsony Power in Higher Education: A Tale of Two Tracks." Working Paper 26070. NBER. https://doi.org/10.3386/w26070.

Harris, J. R., and M. P. Todaro. 1970. "Migration, Unemployment and Development: A Two-Sector Analysis." *American Economic Review* 60 (1): 126–42.

Hirsch, B., T. Schank, and C. Schnabel. 2010. "Differences in Labor Supply to Monopsonistic Firms and the Gender Pay Gap: An Empirical Analysis Using Linked Employer–Employee Data from Germany." *Journal of Labor Economics* 28 (2): 291–330. https://doi.org/10.1086/651208.

Hohberg, M., and J. Lay. 2015. "The Impact of Minimum Wages on Informal and Formal Labor Market Outcomes: Evidence from Indonesia." *IZA Journal of Labor & Development* 4 (1): 1–25. https://doi.org/10.1186/s40175-015-0036-4.

Isen, A. 2013. "Essays on Labor and Public Economics." PhD diss., University of Pennsylvania. https://repository.upenn.edu/dissertations/AAI3566393.

Kline, P., N. Petkova, H. Williams, and O. Zidar. 2019. "Who Profits from Patents? Rent-Sharing at Innovative Firms." *Quarterly Journal of Economics* 134 (3): 1343–1404. https://doi.org/10.1093/qje/qjz011.

Kondo, I., Y. A. Li, and W. Qian. 2024. "Trade Liberalization and Labor Monopsony: Evidence from Chinese Firms." http://dx.doi.org/10.2139/ssrn.4088005.

Lewis, W. A. 1954. "Economic Development with Unlimited Supplies of Labour." *Manchester School* 22 (2): 139–91. https://doi.org/10.1111/j.1467-9957.1954.tb00021.x.

Machin, S., A. Manning, and L. Rahman. 2003. "Where the Minimum Wage Bites Hard: Introduction of Minimum Wages to a Low Wage Sector." *Journal of the European Economic Association* 1 (1): 154–80. https://doi.org/10.1162/154247603322256792.

Manning, A. 2003. *Monopsony in Motion: Imperfect Competition in Labor Markets.* Princeton University Press.

Manning, A. 2021. "Monopsony in Labor Markets: A Review." *ILR Review* 74 (1): 3–26. https://doi.org/10.1177/0019793920922499.

Matsudaira, Jordan D. "Monopsony in the Low-Wage Labor Market? Evidence from Minimum Nurse Staffing Regulations." *The Review of Economics and Statistics* 96, no. 1 (2014): 92–102. http://www.jstor.org/stable/43554915.

Naidu, S., Y. Nyarko, and S.-Y. Wang. 2016. "Monopsony Power in Migrant Labor Markets: Evidence from the United Arab Emirates." *Journal of Political Economy* 124 (6): 1735–92. https://doi.org/10.1086/688877.

Naidu, S., and E. A. Posner. 2022. "Labor Monopsony and the Limits of the Law." *Journal of Human Resources* 57 (S): S284–323. https://doi.org/10.3368/jhr.monopsony.0219-10030R1.

Neumark, D., J. I. Salas, and W. Wascher. 2014. "More on Recent Evidence on the Effects of Minimum Wages in the United States." *IZA Journal of Labor Policy* 3 (1): 1–26. https://doi.org/10.1186/2193-9004-3-24.

Neumark, D., and W. Wascher. 2007. "Minimum Wages and Employment." Discussion Paper 2570. Institute for the Study of Labor. https://doi.org/10.2139/ssrn.961374.

Posner, E. A., and E. G. Weyl. 2018. *Radical Markets: Uprooting Capitalism and Democracy for a Just Society*. Princeton University Press. https://doi.org/10.23943/9781400889457.

Prager, E., and M. Schmitt. 2021. "Employer Consolidation and Wages: Evidence from Hospitals." *American Economic Review* 111 (2): 397–427. https://doi.org/10.1257/aer.20190690.

Ransom, M. R., and R. L. Oaxaca. 2010. "New Market Power Models and Sex Differences in Pay." *Journal of Labor Economics* 28 (2): 267–89. https://doi.org/10.1086/651245.

Ransom, M. R., and D. P. Sims. 2010. "Estimating the Firm's Labor Supply Curve in a 'New Monopsony' Frame-Work: Schoolteachers in Missouri." *Journal of Labor Economics* 28 (2): 331–55. https://doi.org/10.1086/649904.

Remesh, B. P. 2006. "Champaran Satyagraha for Indigo Workers: A Memorable April in the Mahatma's Diary." *Labour File* 4 (2). https://www.labourfile.com/section-detail.php?aid=328.

Robinson, J. 1932. *The Economics of Imperfect Competition*. Macmillan.

Rudra, A. 1982. *Indian Agricultural Economics: Myths and Realities*. Oxford University Press.

Sen, A. 1966. "Peasants and Dualism with and Without Surplus Labor." *Journal of Political Economy* 74 (5): 425–50. https://doi.org/10.1086/259198.

Sharma, Garima. 2022. "Monopsony and Gender," Working Paper. https://garimasharma.com/files/monopsony_gender_gsharma.pdf

Smith, A. 1776. *An Inquiry into the Nature and Causes of the Wealth of Nations*. W. Strahan and T. Cadell.

Sokolova, Anna and Todd Sorensen. "Monopsony in Labor Markets: A Meta-Analysis". *ILR Review* 74 (1): 27–55.

Soundararajan, V. 2019. "Heterogeneous Effects of Imperfectly Enforced Minimum Wages in Low-Wage Labor Markets." *Journal of Development Economics* 140: 355–74. https://www.sciencedirect.com/science/article/pii/S0304387818305972.

Srinivas, M. N. 1987. *The Dominant Caste and Other Essays*. Oxford University Press.

Staiger, D. O., J. Spetz, and C. S. Phibbs. 2010. "Is There Monopsony in the Labor Market? Evidence from a Natural Experiment." *Journal of Labor Economics* 28 (2): 211–36. https://doi.org/10.1086/652734.

Stigler, G. J. 1946. "The Economics of Minimum Wage Legislation." *American Economic Review* 36 (3): 358–65.

Szerman, Christiane. 2024. "The Labor Market Effects of Disability hiring Quotas." Working Paper. https://chriszerman.github.io/cszerman/JMP_Szerman.pdf.

Tinker, H. 1974. *A New System of Slavery: The Export of Indian Labour Overseas, 1830–1920*. Oxford University Press.

Tortarolo, Dario and Zarate, Roman D. 2020. "Imperfect competition in product and labour markets. A quantitative analysis," Nottingham Interdisciplinary Centre for Economic and Political Research (NICEP) Discussion Papers No. 2020-05.

Verhoogen, E. A., S. V. Burks, and J. P. Carpenter. 2014. "Fairness and Freight-Handlers: Local Labor Market Conditions and Wage-Fairness Perceptions in a Trucking Firm." *ILR Review* 60 (4): 477–98. https://doi.org/10.1177/001979390706000402.

Yeh, Chen, Claudia Macaluso, and Brad Hershbein. 2022. "Monopsony in the US Labor Market." *American Economic Review* 112 (7): 2099–2138.

CHAPTER 2

Jobless Growth and Structural Transformation

SOME THEORETICAL CONSIDERATIONS AND EMPIRICAL EVIDENCE FROM INDIA

Zico Dasgupta and Amit Basole
Azim Premji University

Abstract: The decoupling of output growth and employment growth, known popularly as jobless growth, has been a problem plaguing many countries. Using cross-country data from 1990 to 2018, we show that India has underperformed significantly on job creation compared to the average developing country, with lower-than-average employment elasticities at both the aggregate level and for the nonagricultural sector. We find a striking one-for-one relationship between output growth and productivity growth in India's nonagricultural sector, that is, a Kaldor-Verdoorn (KV) coefficient of 1. Despite this joblessness of growth, the Indian economy has experienced some structural transformation, with the share of the nonagricultural sector and the share of regular wage employment rising at the expense of agriculture and self-employment. We develop a theoretical model that clarifies the relative roles of labor demand and labor supply in determining the output-employment relationship. In this model, the Indian case of some structural transformation, even with jobless growth, emerges as one case among four possible cases (growth with or without jobs/structural change or no structural change). We conclude with some policy implications.

1. INTRODUCTION

The challenge of jobless growth facing many developing countries today needs urgent attention because it has not only economic but also social and political consequences. Alongside this problem, where output growth seems to be decoupled from employment growth, developing countries also face the challenge of structural transformation—how to grow the share of relatively higher productivity and of formal employment, and reduce the share of workers engaged in agriculture as well as informal work. In this chapter, we present evidence on the Indian experience regarding these two challenges. We also develop a model that clarifies the conditions under which growth will deliver jobs as well as structural transformation, either jobs or structural transformation, or neither.

Since the 1980s, the Indian economy has shown two features. The first feature is that, while the Indian economy was able to attain a higher output growth rate, the responsiveness of the employment growth rate has remained weak (Basole et al. 2018; Kannan and Raveendran 2009; Tejani 2016). The second feature is that the share of regular wage employment in the nonagricultural sector has risen. If such a rising share of employment is considered as an indicator of structural transformation, then the phenomenon of jobless growth would appear to coincide with the phenomenon of structural transformation.[1]

While the theoretical discussions on these two issues have been conducted in the literature separately and independently of each other, this chapter attempts to understand the mechanism that creates the two phenomena simultaneously in the Indian context. Structural transformation depends on the relative strength of labor demand in the modern sector with respect to labor supply; thus, we attempt to analyze the dynamics of the two variables in the case of the nonagricultural sector along with their relationship to output growth.

With the growth rate of employment or labor demand determined by the difference between output and productivity growth rates, the nature of the relationship between employment growth rate and output growth rate depends on the manner in which productivity growth rate responds to output growth rate. While post-Keynesian theories can be argued to provide a more general framework than neoclassical theories to analyze employment constraints, there have been limited analyses of the employment constraints in the specific context of a developing country like India.

The productivity function has been analyzed in post-Keynesian literature through two different routes. The first route involves an exogenously given labor productivity growth rate. At any given productivity growth rate, changes in output growth rate would bring about proportional changes in employment growth rate in this route. Arrow (a) in figure 2.1 reflects the channel through which growth affects employment. Any exogenous rise in productivity growth rate, however, adversely affects employment growth rate via arrow (b). The growth regime can be characterized as jobless if the adverse effect of higher productivity growth rate offsets the positive effect of output growth rate on employment growth rate. The phenomenon of jobless growth emerges *despite* higher output growth rate.

In the second route, productivity growth rate is endogenous and affected by output growth rate. The magnitude of impact is given by the Kaldor-Verdoorn (KV) coefficient. Output growth rate affects employment growth rate through two channels, arrow (a) and a combination of arrows (b) and (c) (figure 2.1). The phenomenon of jobless growth within the second route pertains to the case where the KV coefficient attains a high value of 1 or higher (Rada and Arnim 2012). The phenomenon of jobless growth emerges because of higher output growth rate that brings about a sharp rise in productivity growth rate.

In the case of labor supply, its dynamics can be argued to depend on at least three sets of factors. The first includes demographic and cultural factors that are exogenous to the changes in employment opportunities and output growth rate of the formal capitalist sector. The second factor comprises the positive effect of the employment opportunities created in this sector, which in turn encourages a greater number of out-of-labor-force workers to participate in the labor force. The third set of factors involve outflow and inflow regarding the nonagricultural sector on account of higher output growth rate in the formal sector. Higher output growth rate can be associated with a negative income effect on labor supply, where rising household incomes lead to some workers withdrawing from the labor force, typically women in the case of India, but also, in an earlier phase of development, a reduction in child labor.

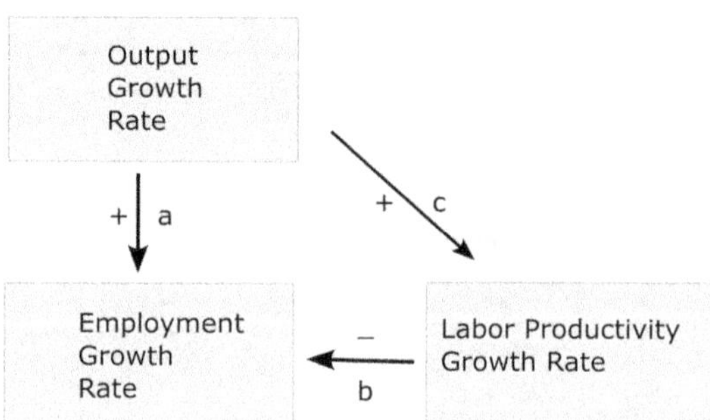

Figure 2.1 Possible causal mechanisms for jobless growth

Note that workers leaving the agricultural sector and the labor force completely because of the same income effect, as occurred in the case of women during the period 2004 to 2017, does not have an impact on the supply of labor to the nonagricultural sector. On the other hand, the expansion of the formal sector may bring about forcible displacement of labor from agriculture, either by primitive accumulation (Sanyal 2007; Patnaik 2011; Bhaduri 2018) or by changing the terms of trade against agriculture (Sadhu and Chakrabarti 2021). If a fraction of such displaced workers happens to seek jobs in the nonagricultural sector, then higher output growth rate in the formal sector can increase labor supply to the nonagricultural sector.

The mutual relationship among growth, employment and structural transformation depends on the relative strength of all these factors. The model presented in section 4 formalizes these ideas. The key aspects of the model are: first, the possibility of involuntary unemployment and existence of informality in the long run; second, the possibility of jobless growth and its two variants mentioned above; and third, the possibility of jobless growth accompanied by structural transformation. By endogenizing the labor supply to the nonagricultural sector, we make the standard post-Keynesian model more relevant to the case of developing countries such as India.

The main policy implication of our analysis is that setting targets for output growth by itself cannot solve the employment problem in the presence of jobless growth. An independent employment policy is needed. While a detailed discussion of what such a policy looks like is not the focus of this chapter, we discuss a few aspects in the last section.

The rest of the chapter is organized as follows. Section 2 presents the key output and employment trends in the Indian economy since the 1980s. Section 3 outlines the theoretical approaches that have been used to understand the growth-employment relationship and develops the model. In section 4, we discuss policy implications and conclude.

2. THE INDIAN EXPERIENCE

We now discuss some key empirical relationships between output growth, employment growth, labor supply, and structural transformation observed in the Indian economy over the past forty years. We start with an overview of India's performance, then we place India in a cross-country perspective with respect to the long-run relationship between output and employment over a three-decade period (1990 to 2018). Finally, we dive deeper into the Indian data over a longer period of time (from 1983 to 2018). In both cases, our analysis ends before the growth slowdown of 2019 and the COVID-19 pandemic of 2020. We do not discuss pandemic-induced disemployment effects or distortions to the structural transformation process.

2.1 KEY STYLIZED FACTS

The first thing to appreciate when discussing the Indian economy is the size of the total workforce as well as various main sectors of the economy. Figure 2.2 shows the key compartments as far as the workforce is concerned, along with the approximate number of individuals in each as of 2018.[2] The entire working-age population of around 985 million can be divided into those in the workforce and those outside it. In a dual economy such as India, the workforce is in turn divided into the agricultural (175 million) and the nonagricultural (261 million) sectors. The nonagricultural sector itself is dual, consisting of a subsistence sector and a capitalist sector. The former, also called the informal sector, comprises self-employment (own-account work) as well as casual labor, and constitutes the major part of this sector. The hallmark of the informal sector is that labor demand automatically adjusts to labor supply, either via income sharing (in the case of self-employment) or via work sharing (in the case of casual labor). The formal sector, employs regular wage labor (typically on weekly or monthly salaries).

Table 2.1 shows important indicators for three subperiods within the overall period of analysis. These correspond roughly to the pre-reform (1983 to 1993), early reform (1993 to 2004), and later reform (2004

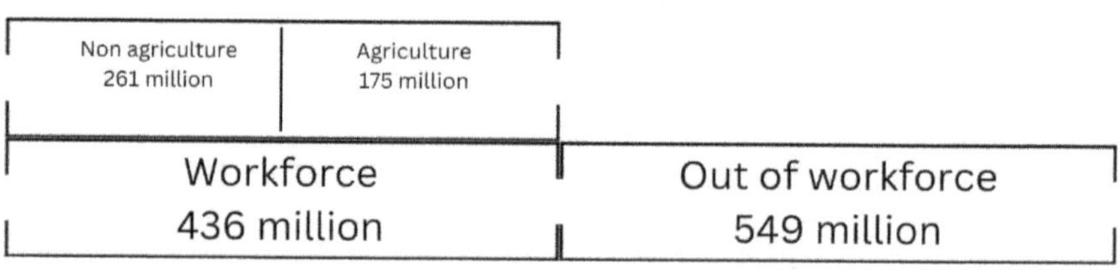

Figure 2.2 Absolute size and structure of India's workforce

Source: Periodic Labour Force Survey (2018–2019).

Table 2.1 Key indicators of the Indian economy

Indicator (%)	1983 to 1993	1993 to 2004	2004 to 2018
Gross domestic product (GDP) growth	5.2	6.2	7.0
Nonagricultural value-added growth	6.5	6.9	7.6
Investment-GDP ratio	25.6	28.1	36.5
Export-GDP ratio	6.9	12.3	21.7
Working-age population growth	3.2	2.3	2.3
Workforce growth	3.6	2.2	0.2
Nonagricultural employment growth	4.2	3.2	2.3
Nonagricultural salaried growth	3.3	3.0	3.9

Sources: Reserve Bank of India and Ministry of Statistics and Programme Implementation.

to 2018) periods. The choice of start and end points is dictated by the availability of employment data from the quinquennial employment-unemployment surveys of the National Sample Survey Office (NSSO).

A few points are worth noting. The Indian economy registered a healthy rate of overall as well as nonagricultural output growth above 6 percent per annum over the entire period, increasing to more than 7 percent in the most recent subperiod. Other macroeconomic indicators, such as the investment to GDP ratio as well as the export to GDP ratio, also showed an increasing trend over the period. Regarding the employment indicators, note that since the 1990s, until just before the pandemic the workforce consistently grew more slowly than the working-age population, indicating that the workforce participation rate has dropped. This happened because of an absolute decline in the number of agricultural workers (a desirable feature of structural transformation) and a withdrawal of women from the labor force (Lahoti and Swaminathan 2016). In the recent (high growth) subperiod, it appears that the decrease in agricultural employment was barely met with a commensurate increase in the nonagricultural workforce, resulting in near zero growth of the workforce. Note that regular wage or salaried employment in the high-growth period grew faster than overall nonagricultural employment, indicating that the share of salaried workers in the nonagricultural workforce increased in this period. We take this as a sign of structural change occurring in India. We return to this point later.

2.2 JOBLESS GROWTH AND STRUCTURAL TRANSFORMATION IN INDIA IN CROSS-COUNTRY PERSPECTIVE

We start with a commonly used indicator of the job-creating nature of economic growth—the growth elasticity of employment. Figure 2.3 shows the distribution of elasticities obtained in a cross-country, fixed effects, log-log regression between aggregate output (value added) and aggregate employment as well as nonagricultural output and nonagricultural employment.[3] The elasticities for India are indicated by red lines. The aggregate employment elasticity is lower at 0.2 than the elasticity of nonagricultural employment at 0.47. This is expected because agriculture was shedding labor over a significant part of the period under analysis. India's values for both elasticities are significantly lower than the mean across fifty developing countries in the ETD data set.[4] This shows that, even as most developing countries have been facing headwinds that make employment generation difficult, the pattern of growth in India has been less job-intensive than the developing country average.

In this chapter, however, our main concern is with the relationship between output *growth* and employment *growth* rather than the level changes captured by the elasticity numbers. There are two reasons for this. First, the KV relationship that describes the role of automation or technical change is understood in growth terms. Second, with respect to policy, stimulating growth is commonly understood to be a solution to increasing employment growth, once again making the relationship

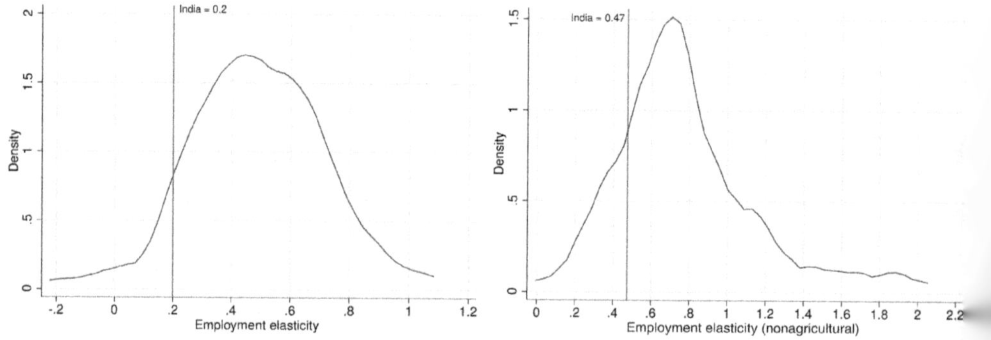

Figure 2.3 Cross-country distribution of aggregate (left) and nonagricultural (right) employment elasticities (1991–2018)

Source: Groningen ETD.

between output growth and employment growth the key relationship of interest. In this framework, the term "jobless growth" can be interpreted more precisely to mean a lack of responsiveness of employment growth rate to changes in output growth rate. Because employment growth rate is the difference between output growth rate and the growth rate of labor productivity, it follows that the nature of the relationship between employment growth rate and output growth rate depends on how productivity growth rate responds to output growth rate. The causal relationship between productivity growth and output growth depends, as discussed earlier, on the theoretical perspective one adopts.

We estimate the contemporaneous relationship between output growth rate and employment growth rate as well as output growth rate and labor productivity growth rate in a cross-country regression framework using ETD data. Figure 2.4 shows the distribution of the coefficients obtained from these two regressions. There is a weak negative relationship between output growth and employment growth for India (coefficient = –0.11), and the corresponding KV coefficient is slightly greater than 1.[5] The corresponding mean values for the coefficient across all the countries in the sample are 0.3 and 0.7. Note that the KV coefficient is expected to be around 0.7. That is, productivity growth does not rise one-for-one with output growth, allowing some correlation between the latter and employment growth. But this has clearly not been the case for India over the period in question. To understand this lack of relationship better, we need to look at India-specific data sources, which we do in the next section.

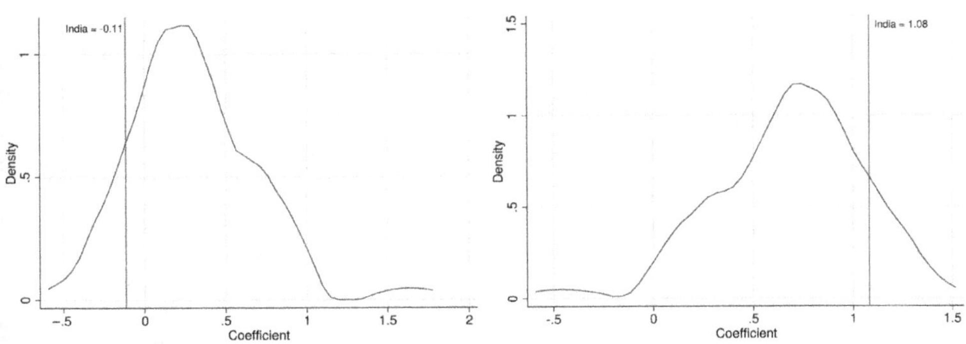

Figure 2.4 Cross-country distribution of coefficients—output growth and employment growth (left) and output growth and productivity growth (right) in the nonagricultural sector

Source: Groningen ETD.

Before leaving the cross-country framework, we show how India has performed in comparison to other developing countries with regard to structural change. In this context, it is important to note that a key sign that structural transformation is occurring is the rise in the share of formal employment and not just a rise in the share of nonagricultural employment. Following Ghose (2016), we may label these two distinct processes that are part of structural transformation as the Lewis process and the Kuznets process. The former is the process of moving workers from subsistence to the modern or capitalist economy. The latter is the process of moving workers from the agricultural to the nonagricultural sector. Available data usually enable us to estimate the pace of the Kuznets process without much difficulty. For the Lewis process, however, we need to resort to proxies because data on "modern economy" are not directly available. In this chapter, we use two proxies: The share of regular wage employment in the nonagricultural sector and the share of employment accounted for by establishments that employ ten or more workers (known in India as the organized sector).

Figure 2.5 plots agricultural as well as informal share of employment as a function of gross domestic product (GDP) per capita for the year 2018. As expected, there is a strong negative relationship seen in both plots. The thing to note however, is that India (encircled) lies much closer to the regression line for the agricultural share and is a significant outlier in the case of informal share.[6]

This point can be substantiated by looking at detailed labor force data from India from the quinquennial NSSO employment surveys as well the more recent annual Periodic Labour Force Surveys. Figure 2.6 shows that the share of agriculture in total employment has been steadily declining in India, and it has picked up pace since the early 2000s. The share of nonagricultural employment rose from 37 percent in 1983 to 60 percent in 2018. However, the pace of rise in nonagricultural employment was not matched by the rise in the share of formal employment within the nonagricultural sector. Only in the most recent high-growth period do we see a small increase in the share of regular wage workers in the nonagricultural sector, as well as a small increase in the share of workers employed in establishments having ten or more workers. This means that workers leaving agriculture were much more likely to end up in the informal nonagricultural sector. As pointed out by Ghose (2016) and Basole (2022), this points to a weakening of the link between the Lewis and Kuznets processes.

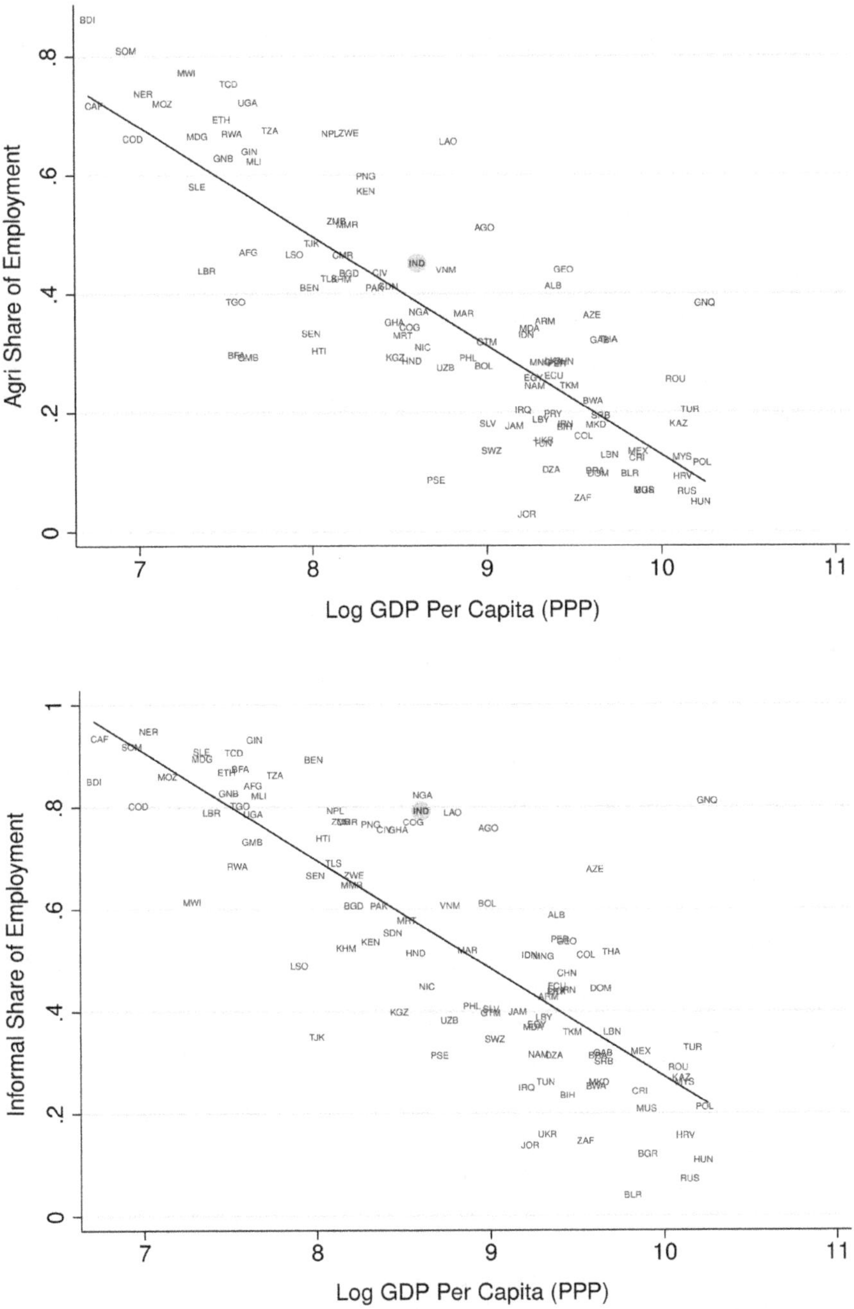

Figure 2.5 Agricultural (top) and informal (bottom) share across developing countries as a function of GDP per capita

Source: WDI database. India is circled.

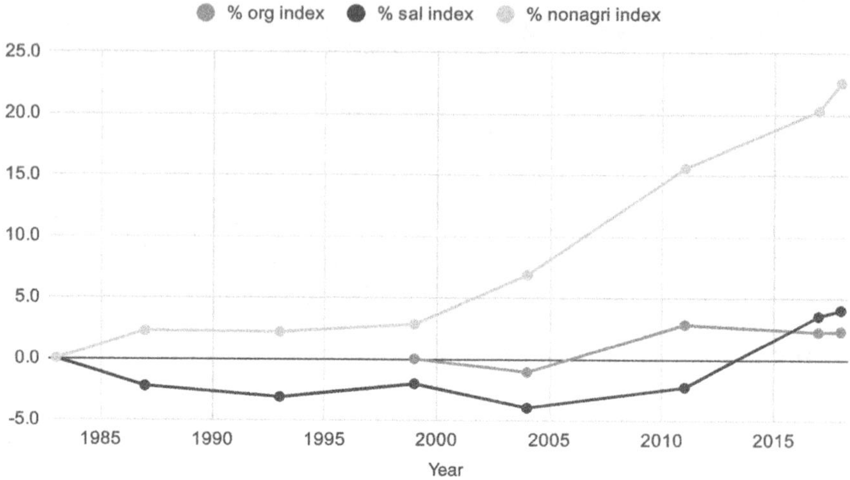

Figure 2.6 Share of nonagricultural (light), organized (medium), and regular wage (dark) employment in total nonagricultural employment

Source: NSSO surveys, various years.

2.3 TRENDS IN EMPLOYMENT AND OUTPUT GROWTH

We use two main data sources, the KLEMS database and the NSSO employment survey database, to dive deeper into the relationship between output growth and employment growth in India. KLEMS gives us value-added and employment at the aggregate level as well as the sectoral level since the 1980s. But it does not distinguish between formal and informal employment or output. The labor force data from the quinquennial employment-unemployment surveys conducted by the NSSO give us more detailed information on movements into and out of the labor force as well as the distribution of employment type since the 1980s.

As expected from the cross-country analysis presented earlier, the KLEMS data show that annual growth rates of output were weakly negatively correlated with employment growth rates (beta = –0.16) and strongly correlated one-for-one with labor productivity growth (beta = 1.13). This relationship is even clearer at the sectoral level (figure 2.7). It is worth noting that the overall relationship shown here does hide some variation in the correlation between output and productivity growth rate at the level of individual industries. While the KV coefficient is close to 1 for several industries in both manufacturing and services, it

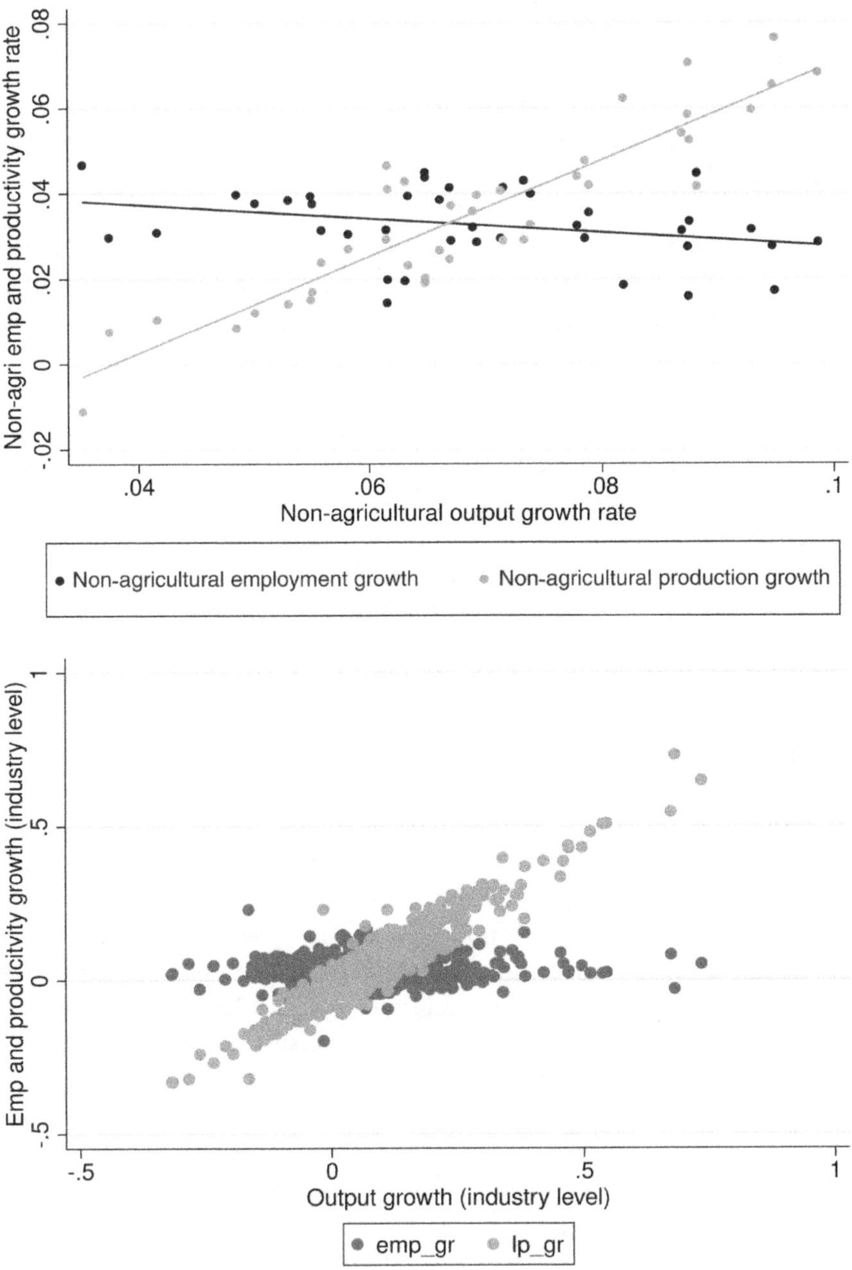

Figure 2.7 Relationship between employment growth and output growth (light) as well as productivity growth and output growth (dark) at the aggregate and industry level from 1980 to 2019.

Source: India KLEMS.

is 0.77 for construction and 0.66 for miscellaneous services (such as personal services). Naturally, these, by definition, tend to be the labor-absorbing sectors.

The heterogeneity with respect to the output-productivity relationship within manufacturing is also worth noting. The manufacturing sector includes both a formal or registered as well as an informal or unregistered part. Using data from the Annual Survey of Industries (ASI), which provides data for formal manufacturing, we find the KV coefficient to be significantly lower, at 0.54. This value is closer to (and lower than) the cross-country average that was shown earlier. We discuss possible reasons for this discrepancy in section 4.

Moving beyond KLEMS data and drawing on the NSSO surveys, we can look at the output-employment relationship in more detail by type of employment. The survey points are only available every five years or so until 2017 and then on an annual basis after that. Our analysis ends in 2018–2019, a year prior to the COVID-19 pandemic.

We find that employment growth and output growth move roughly out of phase with each other over the entire period from 1983 to 2018. This is the case for both the aggregate economy and the nonagricultural sector (figure 2.8). Note that the growth rates presented here are CAGRs for the period between two survey years. The period of notably high output growth in the Indian economy, from 2004 to 2017, was accompanied by a decline in employment growth. At the aggregate level, employment growth turned negative during the period 2011 to 2017 (figure 2.8[a]). This was because the fall in agricultural employment was not met by adequate employment generation in the nonagricultural sector. Note that during this period, the compound annual growth rate (CAGR) for employment in the nonagricultural sector was a mere 1 percent compared to 5 percent in the period 1999 to 2004 (Figure 2.8[b]).

As noted earlier, from a structural change perspective, it is not only the movement of workers out of agriculture that matters but also their movement into the capitalist part of the nonagricultural sector rather than the subsistence part. We now focus on the former, proxied here by two variables—salaried employment and employment in firms in the organized sector. We find again that there is no clear relationship between nonagricultural output growth and the growth of salaried or organized sector employment (figure 2.9). Employment growth in the organized sector correlated positively with output growth during the first part of the high-growth period, rising from 4.2 percent to 5.8 percent CAGR

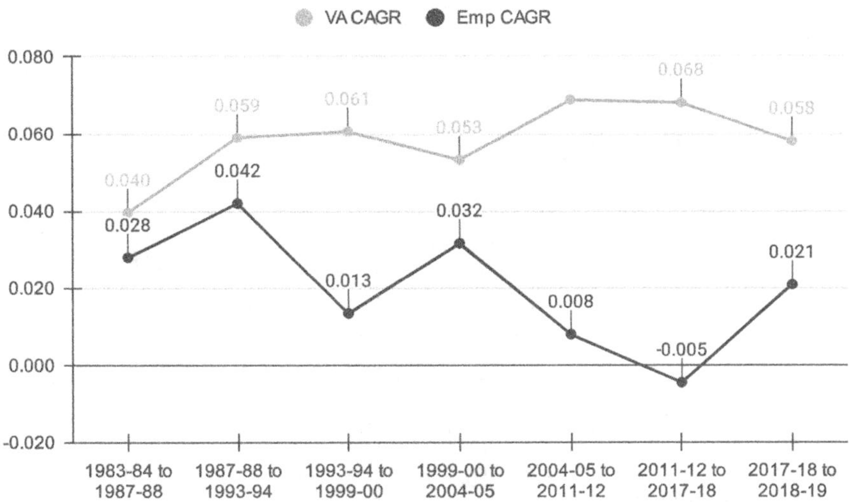

Figure 2.8a Trends in aggregate output growth and employment growth

Source: NSSO surveys various years.

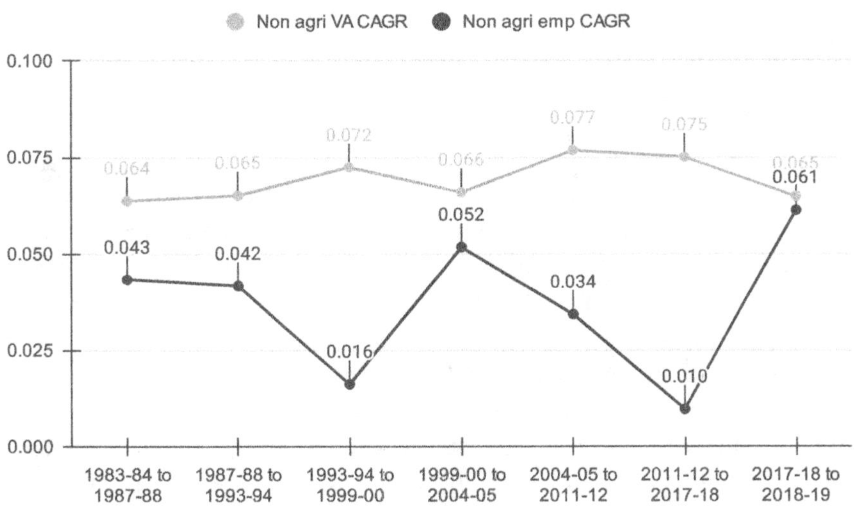

Figure 2.8b Trends in nonagricultural output growth and employment growth

Source: NSSO surveys various years.

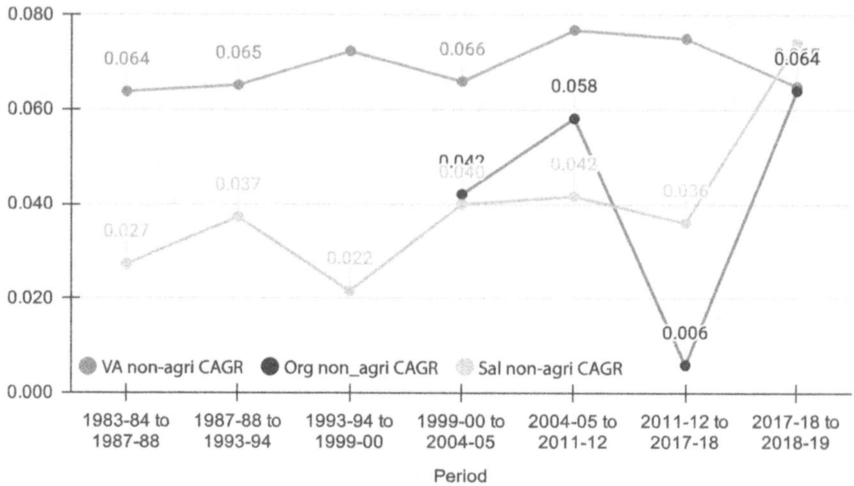

Figure 2.9 Nonagricultural output growth and salaried/organized sector employment growth

Source: NSSO surveys, various years.

between 1999–2004 and 2004–2011. But then it plummeted to less than 1 percent in the 2011–2017 period. In the most recent period after 2017, when growth was beginning to slow down, there was an uptick in both indicators.

2.4 MOVEMENTS INTO AND OUT OF VARIOUS SECTORS

As outlined in the introduction to this chapter, the lack of relationship between output growth and employment growth can be the result of two distinct channels: first, with the modern or capitalist economy, the KV channel, and second, the labor supply dynamics or movements into and out of the capitalist economy.

To get a better handle on the latter, we start by looking at how the working-age population has moved into either the workforce (employment), education, or domestic duties (care work and other household work). The way to read figures 2.10 to 2.12 is that we show what fraction of the change in the working-age population or the workforce between two survey years is accounted for by different components mentioned in the figure. For example, if the working-age population increased by one hundred individuals between two time points and twenty-five of them

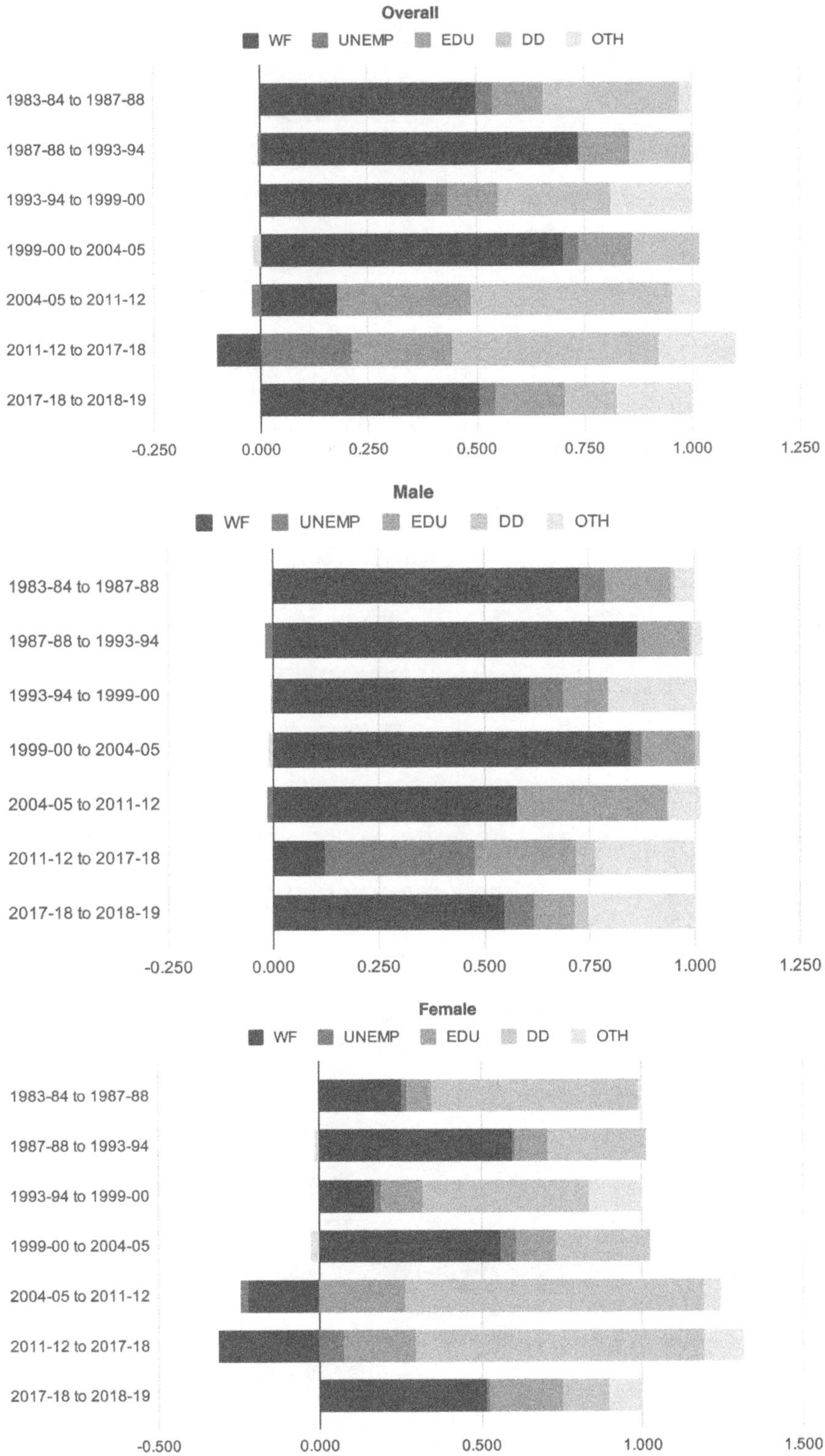

Figure 2.10 Where did the additional working-age individuals go in each period?

Source: NSSO surveys, various years. Working age = 15 years or older. WF = workforce, UNEMP = unemployed, EDU = in education, DD = domestic duties.

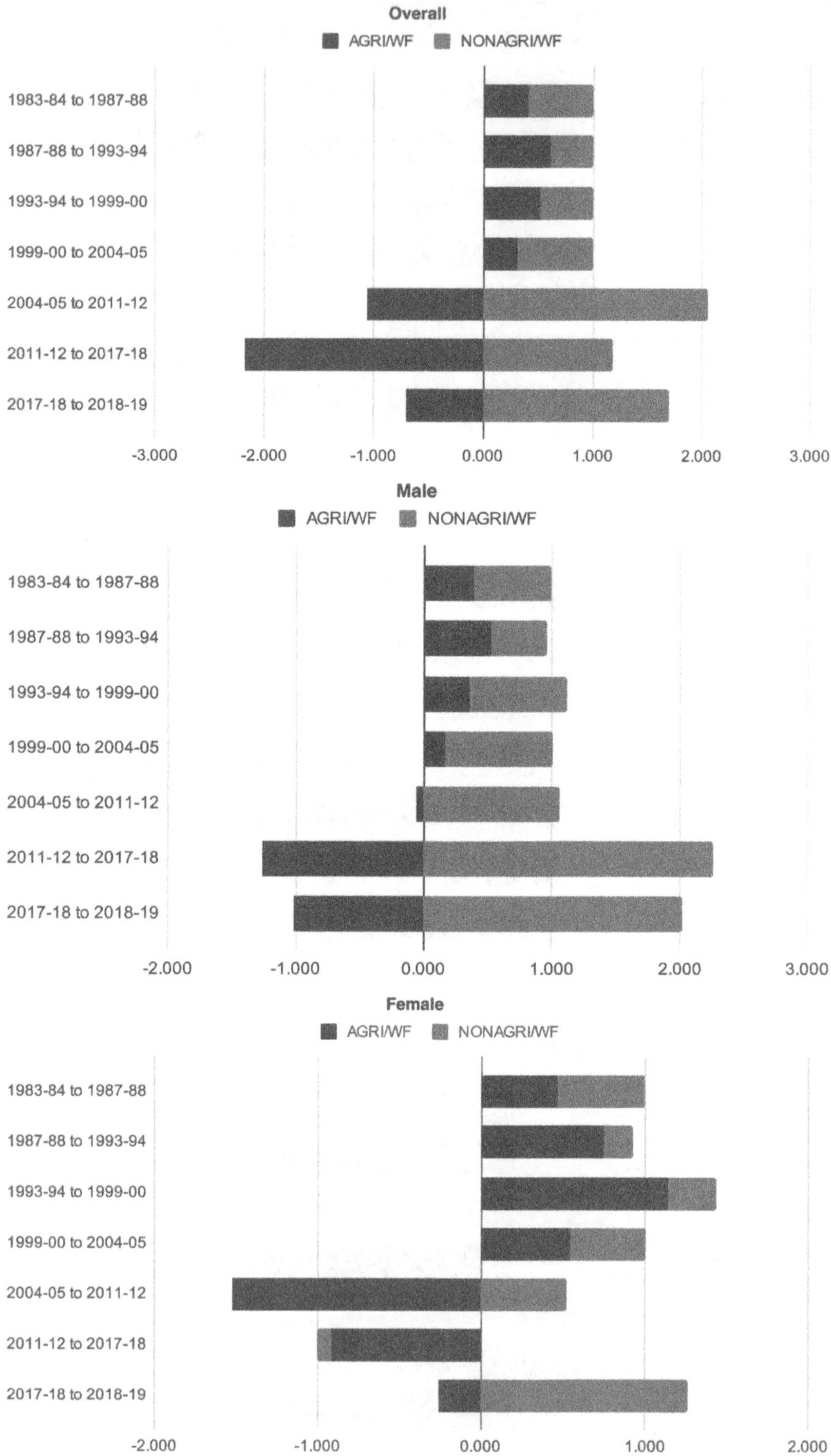

Figure 2.11 Changes in the workforce broken down by changes in agricultural and nonagricultural components

Source: NSSO surveys, various years.

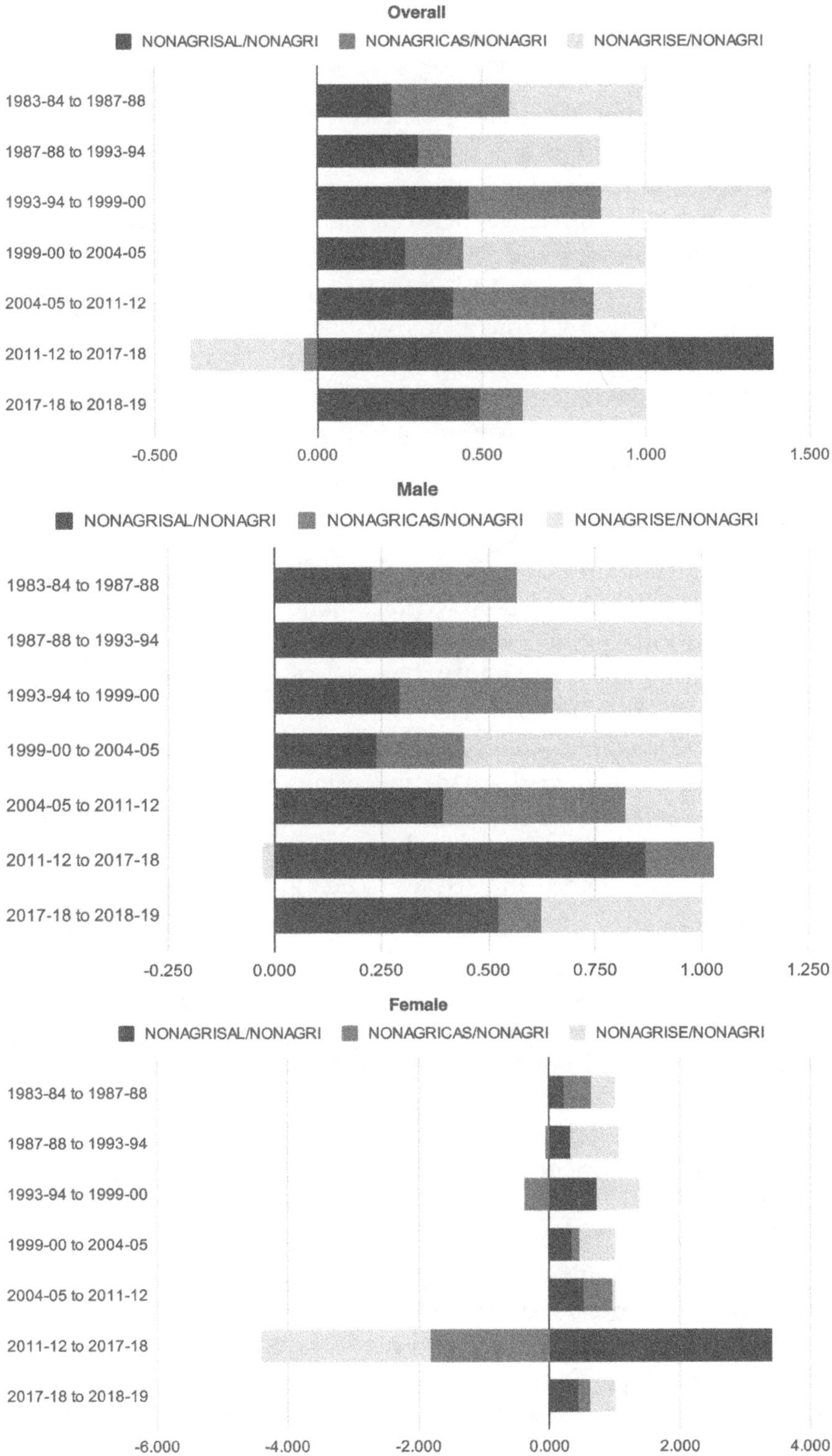

Figure 2.12 Changes in nonagricultural workforce broken down by type of employment

Source: NSSO surveys, various years.

went into education, the value of education will be 0.25. Keep in mind that there may sometimes be a decrease in a particular component even as the denominator increases.

We focus on the differences between male and female workers rather than looking at the aggregate numbers, which hide substantial gender-based heterogeneity. Several features are worth noting. As expected, domestic (unpaid) work forms a large destination for new women entering working age. In contrast, this is negligible for men. Pertinent to our current story, note that during the high-growth years (2004 to 2017), the share of women in the workforce turned negative. This means that there was an absolute fall in the size of the female workforce in this period. No such decline is seen for men. It appears that at least some of the lack of relationship between output growth and employment growth could be explained by falling women's employment during the high-growth period. Much has been written about India's declining (rural) female labor force participation rate (LFPR; Lahoti and Swaminathan 2016; Mehrotra and Parida 2017). We do not enter that debate here except to note that two major factors have been identified for the falling LFPR in rural areas—a displacement of women workers because of mechanization (Afridi et al. 2023) and rising household income combined with social norms that value women's unpaid work more than paid work. Our interest lies in exploring the implications of movements into and out of the labor force as well as within the labor force across different sectors, for the aggregate relationship between output growth and employment growth.

The most striking decline in female employment has been in agriculture. Figure 2.11 shows what part of the change in the workforce between each survey year is accounted for by changes in agricultural versus nonagricultural employment. Once again, it is more instructive to look at the gender-disaggregated data. For men, in each period after 2004, agricultural employment fell in absolute terms, while nonagricultural employment rose. The rise in the latter more than compensated for the fall in the former. But for women, between 2004 and 2011, the rise in nonfarm work did not compensate for the decline in farm work, and in the 2011–2017 period, there was an absolute decline in both kinds of employment. It is only in the most recent period, after 2017, that we see a rise in women's nonfarm employment more than compensating for the loss of farm work. As a result, after 2018, there has been a recovery in the female labor force participation rate.

These movements, especially of women workers, from agriculture to leaving the workforce during the high-growth period can explain the converse relationship between growth and aggregate employment, but they cannot explain the lack of relationship between nonfarm output and employment. For this, we look at the change in just the nonagricultural part of the labor force. Here, we hope to see a decline in the share of informal employment (self-employed and casual wage work) and a rise in regular wage work. Overall (for both men and women), we see this only for the period 2011–2017 (figure 2.12), and this is driven largely by women workers. In this period, even though overall nonfarm employment for women fell (see figure 2.11[c]), we see a significant increase in salaried or regular wages nonfarm employment (figure 2.12[c]). However, it is more than compensated for by a fall in self-employment and casual wage work, resulting in an overall decline in nonfarm work for women in this period. Thus, it seems that the income effect dominates the pace of employment generation in the formal sector. However, this increase in salaried work for women, taken together with the fact that the same period saw the largest increase in salaried work for men as well (figure 2.12[b]), meant that the proportion of regular wage or salaried workers in the workforce increased sharply during this period (see figure 2.6).

The empirical evidence presented in this section highlights two aspects of the Indian story: first, a strikingly high KV coefficient implying jobless growth, and second, significant labor supply flows into and out of the nonagricultural sector, along with some structural transformation. We now turn to some theoretical considerations that link growth, employment, and structural change, and develop a model that can account for the observed features. In the model, the Indian case emerges as one possibility out of four different cases.

3. GROWTH, EMPLOYMENT, AND STRUCTURAL CHANGE: THEORETICAL APPROACHES AND MODEL

Developing countries have historically confronted the dual challenge of maintaining a high-output growth rate as well as an increasing employment growth rate in the modern and high-productive sectors. The latter objective is closely related to the issue of structural transformation, which involves increasing the share of employment in favor of the modern or capitalist part of the nonagricultural sector. The pace of structural transformation depends on the extent to which employment opportunities in this sector expand in relation to the labor supply. Because employment opportunities depend on output and labor productivity, the pace of structural transformation can be argued to depend on output growth rate, productivity growth rate, and labor supply growth rate. The mutual relationship among these variables can be analyzed in two distinct and contesting theoretical frameworks.

3.1 GROWTH, EMPLOYMENT AND LABOR SUPPLY: CONTESTING THEORETICAL CONSIDERATIONS

The neoclassical framework is characterized by at least two distinguishing features. The first feature relates to how employment is determined in the short run. Under the assumption of flexible wages and prices, any gap between labor demand and labor supply brings about a necessary adjustment in the real wage rate via which the economy necessarily settles to full employment output. The second feature involves the manner in which output and employment growth rate are determined in the long run. The issue of long-run growth has been analyzed within the neoclassical framework in terms of either exogenous or endogenous theories. The former (Solow 1956) took productivity growth rate as exogenously given, whereas the latter, following Romer (1986, 1990) and Lucas (1988), endogenized productivity growth rate in terms of knowledge spillovers and accumulation of human capital. Notwithstanding such differences, all neoclassical growth theories presume wage-price flexibility in the long run and assign a one-way causal relationship from the natural growth rate to the actual output growth rate and from the labor supply growth rate to the employment growth rate.[7] Such a causal relationship is based on the proposition that any rise in labor productivity growth rate or labor supply growth rate compared to output growth rate brings about an increase in technological output-capital ratio (fall in capital-labor ratio), which in turn leads to an increase in savings-capital ratio, investment rate, and steady-state output growth rate.

There are at least three theoretical implications that follow from this mechanism. First, involuntary unemployment ceases to exist when wages and prices become flexible in the long run. Second, with employment growth rate being determined by labor supply, the explanation for low employment growth rate can be sought in terms of low growth rate of labor supply. Third, labor-saving technological progress per se does not exert any adverse impact on employment growth rate because higher labor productivity keeps the latter unchanged by bringing about proportional change in output growth rate.

In the specific context of long-run growth, there are *at least* two criticisms that have been leveled against neoclassical theories from two different theoretical traditions. The first criticism emerges from the Keynesian tradition that points out the limitation of the assumption of investment necessarily adjusting to ex ante savings. This is because investment decisions are based on subjective expectations of capitalists, and the latter remain analytically distinct from savings decisions. The short-run implication of acknowledging the role of subjective expectations and exogenous investment decisions in Keynes (1936) was the emergence of the possibility of involuntary unemployment.[8] In the long run, as pointed out by Sen (1970), investment rate and output growth rate would cease to adjust to natural growth rate once an analytically distinct investment function is included within an otherwise neoclassical growth model.

The second strand of criticism comes from the Kaleckian and classical framework, which highlights the unrealistic assumption of wage-price flexibility on account of institutional factors. The capitalist economy is perceived as a terrain of conflicting interests, where antagonistic classes contest over distributional shares through wage bargaining and cost-plus pricing (Bhaduri 1986).

Post-Keynesian theories provide an alternative analytical framework to the neoclassical growth theories. While there are multiple and contesting theories within this tradition that vary widely in terms of their analysis of investment behavior or binding constraint on growth, there are at least two common features that make them distinct from neoclassical theories. First, it is only by chance that output happens to be at full employment. investment plays a key role in determining output growth rate, employment growth rate, and unemployment rate (Blecker and Setterfield 2019; Palley 2019). Second, the steady-state output growth rate gets determined by factors that can be independent of productivity growth rate and labor supply growth rate. The steady-state output growth rate is determined by autonomous components of demand in Kaleckian, Harrodian, and neo-Keynesian models, whereas it is determined by exports and capital flows in the balance of payment constrained growth model (Kaldor 1966; Thirlwall 1979). Third, a causal relation runs from actual to natural growth rate and from growth rate of labor demand to labor supply. There are two routes through which this mechanism operates. The first mechanism involves endogenizing technological progress in terms of output growth rate on account of increasing returns to scale (IRS) and firms engaging in learning by doing (Kaldor 1961, 1966; Verdoorn 2002). The second mechanism involves labor supply growth rate adjusting to output growth rate (Patnaik 1997; Nah and Lavoie, 2019).

There are three implications of this analytical framework. First, the possibility of involuntary unemployment within this framework exists both in the short run and the long run. Such a notion of involuntary unemployment has been used to understand the phenomenon of disguised unemployment in a developing country. Similar to involuntary unemployment, disguised unemployment has been perceived as a symptom of demand constraint in the nonagricultural sector (Robinson, 1937).[9] Second, the employment growth rate is determined by the difference between output growth rate and productivity growth rate. In other words, the growth rate of the labor supply does not *necessarily* affect the employment growth rate. By implication, the phenomenon of low employment growth rate cannot be explained exclusively in terms of constraints in labor supply. Third, in the absence of any adjustment mechanism where productivity growth rate leads to a proportional change in output growth rate, technological progress can have an adverse impact on the employment growth rate.

3.2 THE MODEL

This section attempts to outline the mutual relationship among output growth rate, employment growth rate, and the degree of structural transformation in a dual economy, as indicated by the share of the modern or capitalist sector employment in the nonagricultural sector. For simplicity, we use the term "formal" to describe this sector, although it should be clear that the regulatory or legal aspects of formality are not the concern here. To simplify the existing complexity of employment relations, analytically the "formal" is synonymous with "capitalist," and "informal" is synonymous with subsistence. To highlight the key arguments, we develop a simple dual economy model comprising the nonagricultural formal and informal sector. The role of the agricultural sector is limited to supplying labor to the nonagricultural sector. For the sake of simplicity, all relative prices are assumed to be constant. The model abstracts away from the agricultural sector.

3.2.1 THE BASIC EQUATIONS

The basic equations are divided into two analytical blocks—the short run and the long run. In the short run, labor productivity, labor supply, and autonomous component of demand are exogenously given. The long run is defined as a period when all these variables change and register a positive growth rate.

Short Run: The nonagricultural output (Y) is defined as the sum of formal sector (Y_f) and informal sector output (Y_n). The terms of trade between the formal and informal sector are assumed to be constant and normalized at the value 1. The relationship between nonagricultural, formal and informal sector output is shown in equation (1).

$$Y = Y_f + Y_n \qquad (1)$$

The formal and the informal sector engage in trade. The informal sector output is given by its consumption demand and the trade balance between the informal and formal sector. The consumption demand of the informal sector equals the product of consumption propensity (c_n) and output of the informal sector. While exports to the formal sector are assumed to be proportional to output of the formal sector ($f\,Y_f$), imports from the formal sector are assumed to be a product of import propensity of informal sector and output of informal sector ($m_n Y_n$). The informal sector output is given by equation (2).

$$Y_n = (c_n - m_n)Y_n + fY_f \qquad (2)$$

where

$$0 < c_n < 1; 0 < m_n < 1; 0 < f < 1$$

The short-run relationship between output in the formal sector and nonagricultural sector as a whole are given by equations (3a) and (3b), respectively. Because the formal sector acts as an external market for informal sector output, any rise in formal sector output brings about an expansion in output in the informal sector via equation (3a). By implication, the nonagricultural output in equation (3b) responds positively to the formal sector output through the trade multiplier.

$$\left(1 + \frac{f}{1 - c_n + m_n}\right)$$

$$Y_n = \frac{fY_f}{1 - c_n + m_n} \qquad (3a)$$

$$Y = Y_f\left[1 + \frac{f}{1 - c_n + m_n}\right] \qquad (3b)$$

The labor force (N) seeking jobs in the nonagricultural sector is disaggregated into two components: workers employed by the formal sector (L) and workers who are absorbed into the informal sector (S). For the sake of simplicity, open unemployment is assumed to be zero. In the absence of open unemployment, labor supply to the nonagricultural sector equals total employment in the nonagricultural sector and is given by the sum of formal and informal sector employment, as shown in equation (4).

$$L + S = N \tag{4}$$

The level of employment in the formal sector is determined by labor demand in the formal sector, as described by equation (5). Higher output (Y_f) increases labor demand, whereas higher labor productivity (q) reduces labor demand at a given level of output.

$$L = \frac{Y_f}{q} \tag{5}$$

The employment rate in the formal sector (v) is defined as the ratio between formal sector employment and labor force in the nonagricultural sector, as described in equation (6a). The ratio v can be interpreted as an indicator of the extent of structural transformation, the value of which is bounded between 0 and 1. The informal employment ratio is a residual (equation 6b).

$$\frac{L}{N} = v \tag{6a}$$

$$\frac{S}{N} = 1 - v \tag{6b}$$

From equations (3a), (5), and (6a), the short-run equilibrium employment rate in the formal sector is given by equation (7). At the given level of labor productivity and labor supply, a higher level of autonomous demand is associated with higher-level short-run employment rate in the formal sector.

$$v_s = \frac{Y_f^*}{qN} = \frac{A}{(1-b)qN} \tag{7}$$

Long Run: In the long run, output, labor productivity, and labor supply register positive growth rate. The employment rate (v) responds to the changes in these variables, and its long-run value depends on the relative strength of these variables.

Taking derivatives and making necessary adjustments in equations (3a) and (3b), the output growth rates of the formal, informal, and nonagricultural sector as a whole become equal. Long-run growth rate of output is denoted as g and is described by equation (8).

$$\widehat{Y_n} = \widehat{Y_f} = \widehat{Y} = g \tag{8}$$

Technological progress in the nonagricultural sector is assumed to be Harrod-neutral and is associated with higher growth rate of labor productivity. The labor productivity function is given by equation (9), where labor productivity growth rate in the formal sector ($\hat{q}$) is assumed to be a positive function of output growth rate of nonagricultural sector and an exogenous component (λ_0). The positive coefficient λ_1 can be termed as the KV coefficient. Canonical Kaldorian models have emphasized the technological aspect exclusively, with the positive KV coefficient reflecting increasing returns to scale. We see this coefficient as being sensitive to both technological as well as historically given institutional and socioeconomic factors of a country because the latter affects the ease at which new (labor-saving) technology can be introduced. The lower the bargaining power of workers in resisting being displaced by new machines, the greater is the KV coefficient in our framework, all other things remaining unchanged.

$$\hat{q} = \lambda_0 + \lambda_1 g \tag{9}$$

where

$$\lambda_1 > 0$$

By definition, the growth rate of labor demand in the formal sector ($\hat{L}$) is given by the difference between the growth rate of output and the labor productivity growth rate in the formal sector. Thus, the employment growth rate in the formal sector is given by equation (10).

$$\hat{L} = g - \hat{q} \tag{10}$$

The dynamics of labor supply growth rate ($\widehat{N}$) is given by equation (11). The autonomous component n_o includes all factors that affect labor supply growth rate at given employment opportunities and output growth rate. The second term of the Right hand side (RHS) reflects the relationship between labor supply growth rate and formal employment rate (v), with v indicating the extent of job opportunities in the formal sector. The positive coefficient n_1 indicates the positive responsiveness of labor supply growth rate to changes in employment opportunities. It includes the possibility of a discouraged-worker effect whereby reduction in the employment opportunities leads workers to withdraw from the labor force. The third term of the RHS captures the effect of output growth rate on labor supply at any given employment rate in the formal sector. Output growth rate in the formal sector affects labor supply through two distinct mechanisms—the income effect and the dispossession effect.

The possibility of a negative income effect on labor supply emerges as higher output growth rate in the formal sector increases income growth rate in the informal sector through equation (8), leading workers (generally women but also children and young adults) to withdraw from the labor force. The coefficient n_n captures the negative income effect of formal sector output growth rate on labor supply. The dispossession effect is similar to the mechanism described in Sanyal (2007) and Bhaduri (2018), where the expansion of formal sector output brings about forcible displacement of workers from the agricultural sector to the nonagricultural informal sector. The positive responsiveness on the nonagricultural workforce because of changes in formal sector output growth rate is captured by the coefficient n_a. The net effect of output growth rate in the nonagricultural sector on labor supply ($n_n - n_a$) depends on the relative strength of the income effect compared to the dispossession effect. The coefficient ($n_n - n_a$) plays a key role in our model and can be termed as the growth elasticity of labor supply (ε_N). Depending on the relative strength of income and dispossession effects, the sign of growth elasticity of labor supply can be positive, negative, or zero.

$$\begin{aligned}\widehat{N} &= n_o + n_1 v - (n_n - n_a) g \\ &= n_o + n_1 v - \varepsilon_N g \qquad (11)\end{aligned}$$

$$n_1 > 0; n_a > 0; n_n > 0; \varepsilon_N = n_n - n_a$$

3.2.2 LONG RUN EQUILIBRIUM AND COMPARATIVE STATICS

Steady State Equilibrium: The growth rate of the share of employment in the formal sector in the long run is given by $\hat{v} = \hat{L} - \widehat{N}$. Plugging in equations (8) to (11), we get equation (12a):

$$\hat{v} = (1 - \lambda_1)g - \lambda_0 - n_o - n_1 v - \varepsilon_N g \tag{12a}$$

The long-run equilibrium condition is given by $\hat{v} = 0$. Setting equation (12a) to 0, we get equation (12b):

$$n_o + n_1 v - \varepsilon_N g = (1 - \lambda_1)g - \lambda_0 \tag{12b}$$

Solving for the endogenous variable v in equation (12b), the long-run equilibrium employment rate in the formal sector can be derived as equation (13). Taking the partial derivative of equation (12a) w.r.t 'v', the stability condition is described as condition (C.1). The steady-state equilibrium in equation (12b) is stable because $\frac{\partial \hat{v}}{\partial v}$.

$$v^* = \frac{(1 - \lambda_1 + \varepsilon_N)g}{n_1} - \frac{(\lambda_0 + n_o)}{n_1} \tag{13}$$

$$\frac{\partial \hat{v}}{\partial v} = -n_1 < 0 \tag{C.1}$$

The steady-state employment growth rate in the formal sector and the nonagricultural sector can be derived as equation (14) by plugging in the value of v^* in equation (11) and using equations (9) and (10).

$$\hat{L}^* = \widehat{N}^* = (1 - \lambda_1)g$$

Figure 2.13 depicts the mechanism by which output growth rate, productivity growth rate, and labor supply growth rate determine the long-run equilibrium level of formal sector employment rate (v) and employment growth rate.

The right panel in the figure plots the employment rate of formal sector (v) on the horizontal axis and the output growth rate (g) and sum of productivity and labor supply growth rate ($g_n = \lambda + \widehat{N}$) on the vertical axis. The output growth rate is exogenously given, and the growth line (G_0) is horizontal in the g-v space. The sum of productivity and labor supply growth rate is described by $g_n = \lambda_0 + n_o + (\lambda_1 - \varepsilon_N)g + n_1 v$ and

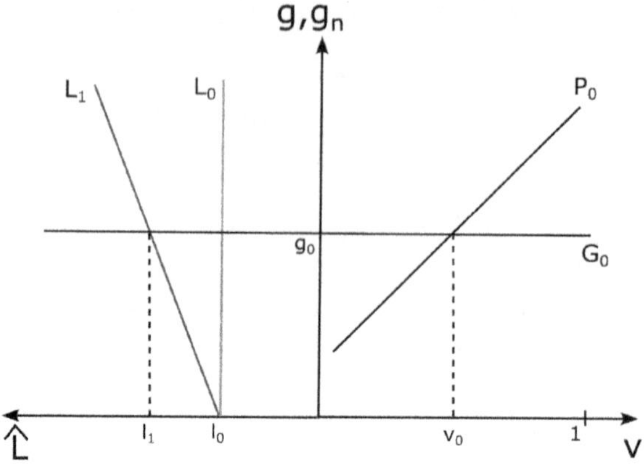

Figure 2.13 Long-run equilibrium

depicted by a positively sloped line (P_0), with slope $n_1 > 0$ and intercept term $\lambda_0 + n_o + (\lambda_1 - \varepsilon_N)g$. At any point to the left (right) of v_0, employment growth rate is greater (lower) than the growth rate of the labor supply because of output growth rate is greater (lower) than the sum of productivity and labor supply growth rate. Starting from any point to the left of equilibrium, the employment rate increases (falls) until it settles at v_0. The steady-state employment rate (v_0) is one where $\hat{v} = 0$ or output growth rate is equal to the sum of productivity and labor supply growth rate. The share of surplus labor in the nonagricultural workforce is given by the segment 1 - v_0.

The left panel in figure 2.13 describes the relationship between formal sector employment growth rate ($\hat{L}$) and output growth rate, as described by $\hat{L} = (1 - \lambda_1)g - \lambda_0$. The two lines L_0 and L_1 have slopes $1 - \lambda_1$ and intercept terms $-\lambda_0$. The two lines depict two different values of KV coefficients, with the KV coefficient $\lambda_1 = 1$ for line L_0, and the KV coefficient $\lambda_1 < 1$ for line L_1. The two lines intersect with the growth line (G_0) to provide equilibrium employment growth rate l_0 and l_1, respectively. The figure shows that, depending on the value of the KV coefficients, the same amount of output growth rate (g_o) and employment rate in the formal sector (v_o) can be associated with different levels of employment growth rate in the formal and nonagricultural sector (l_0 and l_1).

Comparative Dynamics: The effect of exogenous change in output growth rate on employment growth rate in formal and nonagricultural sector is described by equation (15). The sign of the partial derivative depends on the value of the KV coefficient λ_1. The partial derivatives are $\frac{\partial \hat{L}^*}{\partial g} > 0$ and $\frac{\partial \widehat{N}^*}{\partial g} > 0$ if $\lambda_1 < 1$. The partial derivatives are $\frac{\partial \hat{L}^*}{\partial g} \leq 0$ and $\frac{\partial \widehat{N}^*}{\partial g} \leq 0$ if $\lambda_1 \geq 1$. The absence of a positive relationship between formal sector output growth rate on the one hand and the employment growth rate in formal and nonagricultural sector on the other can be described as a phenomenon of jobless growth.

$$\frac{\partial \hat{L}^*}{\partial g} = \frac{\partial \widehat{N}^*}{\partial g} = 1 - \lambda_1 \tag{14}$$

The effect of exogenous change in output growth rate on the employment rate in the formal sector is described by equation (16). The sign of the partial derivative depends on the relative strength of two factors: the value of the KV coefficient (λ_1) and the growth elasticity of the labor supply (ε_N). The higher the KV coefficient, the lower is the responsiveness of the employment rate to changes in output growth. At any given KV coefficient, high (low) value of growth elasticity of the labor supply (ε_N) is associated with strong responsiveness of the employment rate to changes in the output growth rate. Because $\varepsilon_N = n_n - n_a$, a strong dispossession effect (n_a) is associated with low elasticity values, and a strong income effect (n_n) is associated with high elasticity values. The partial derivative is $\frac{\partial v^*}{\partial g} > 0$ if $1 - \lambda_1 + \varepsilon_N > 0$. The partial derivative is $\frac{\partial v^*}{\partial g} \leq 0$ if $1 - \lambda_1 + \varepsilon_N \leq 0$.

$$\frac{\partial v^*}{\partial g} = \frac{1 - \lambda_1 + \varepsilon_N}{n_1} \tag{15}$$

Combining the four possibilities, the relationship between output growth rate, employment growth rate, and structural transformation can be categorized into four distinct cases.These cases are described in table 2.2.

The common feature in cases 1 and 2 is that both are job-creating growth regimes where employment growth rate responds positively to output growth rate $\left(\frac{\partial \hat{L}^*}{\partial g} > 0\right)$ with $0 < \lambda_1 < 1$. The difference between the two cases lies in the magnitude of the effect of output growth rate on structural transformation or the employment share of the formal sector. For case 1, higher output growth rate leads to structural transformation $\left(\frac{\partial v^*}{\partial g} > 0\right)$, with $1 - \lambda_1 + \varepsilon_N > 0$. For case 2, higher output growth rate is associated with the absence of structural transformation $\left(\frac{\partial v^*}{\partial g} \leq 0\right)$, with

Table 2.2 The four cases of structural transformation

Cases	$1-\lambda_1$ (how labor demand responds to output growth)	$1-\lambda_1+\varepsilon_N$ (how formal share responds to labor demand and labor supply)	Nature of growth regime
Case 1	+	+	Job-creating growth *with* structural transformation
Case 2	+	–/0	Job-creating growth *without* structural transformation
Case 3	–/0	+	Jobless growth *with* structural transformation
Case 4	–/0	–/0	Jobless growth *without* structural transformation

$1-\lambda_1+\varepsilon_N \leq 0$. This is because, at any given value of KV coefficient, the value of ε_N is lower for case 2 compared to case 1, reflecting a relatively strong dispossession effect (n_a) or weak income effect (n_n). That is, the influx of workers into the nonagricultural sector because of dispossession exceeds the withdrawal of workers from the nonagricultural sector because of rising incomes. It can be noted that the necessary (but not sufficient) condition for case 2 is that $\varepsilon_N < 0$.

The mechanisms that bring about these two cases, 1 and 2, can be illustrated in figure 2.14 by considering different values of growth elasticity of labor supply. In both cases, the KV coefficient is sufficiently low, with $0 < \lambda_1 < 1$. Case 1 can be depicted by considering a scenario where the income effect is sufficiently high with respect to the dispossession effect such that growth elasticity of labor supply is $\varepsilon_N = \lambda_1 > 0$. These examples are consistent with the conditions that bring about case 1 because they guarantee $1-\lambda_1 > 0$ and $1-\lambda_1+\varepsilon_N > 0$. Case 2 can be illustrated by considering a scenario where the dispossession effect is sufficiently high with respect to the income effect such that growth elasticity of labor supply is negative, with $\varepsilon_N < 0 < \lambda_1 < 1$ and $1-\lambda_1+\varepsilon_N = 0$.

The P_0 and G_0 lines in figure 2.14 correspond to the baseline scenarios for both cases. Any rise in the output growth rate leads to an upward shift of the growth line from G_0 to G_1, leading to higher employment growth rate from l_1 to l_2. For case 1, the P_0 line remains unchanged because the

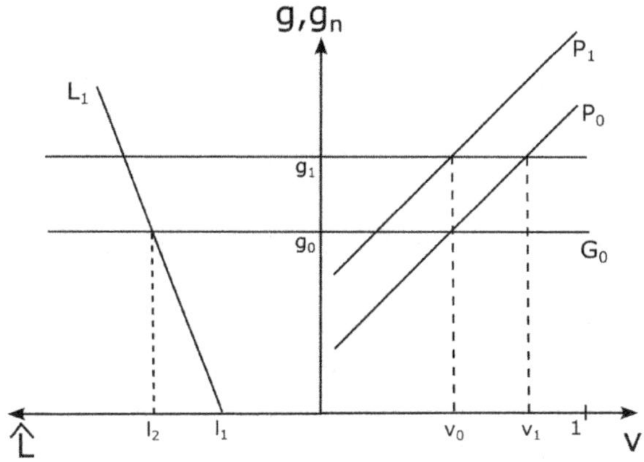

Figure 2.14 Job-creating growth regime with and without structural transformation (cases 1 and 2)

intercept term remains unchanged in response to higher output growth rate, with $\varepsilon_N = \lambda_1$. The long-run equilibrium is attained by the intersection of G_1 and P_0 because the steady-state employment share rises from v_0 to v_1. For case 2, the intercept term of the P_0 line increases (because $\lambda_1 - \varepsilon_N > 0$) in response to higher output growth rate, bringing about an upward shift of the line to P_1. The steady-state employment share is attained by the intersection of G_1 and P_1 line at v_0. The formal sector employment share in this case remains unchanged despite higher output growth rate and employment growth rate because of high dispossession effect (low-income effect).

The common feature in cases 3 and 4 is that both are jobless growth regimes where employment growth rate remains unresponsive or responds negatively to output growth rate $\left(\frac{\partial \hat{L}^*}{\partial g} \leq 0\right)$, with $\lambda_1 \geq 1$. While both these cases indicate weak employment elasticity because of a high KV coefficient, the difference between the two cases pertains to the effect of output growth rate on structural transformation. For case 3, a higher output growth rate leads to structural transformation $\left(\frac{\partial v^*}{\partial g} > 0\right)$, with $1 - \lambda_1 + \varepsilon_N > 0$. For case 4, a higher output growth rate is associated with the absence of structural transformation $\left(\frac{\partial v^*}{\partial g} \leq 0\right)$, with $1 - \lambda_1 + \varepsilon_N \leq 0$. The specificity of case 3 lies in a high positive value of growth elasticity of the labor supply such that the condition of $1 - \lambda_1 + \varepsilon_N > 0$ is satisfied despite $1 - \lambda_1 \leq 0$. It indicates a stronger income effect with respect to the dispossession effect. That is, the outflow of workers from the nonagricultural sector because of rising household incomes far exceeds the influx because of dispossession from the agricultural sector. Note that the case 3 way of achieving a rising share of formal employment relies primarily on a falling denominator rather than on a rising numerator. Thus, from a larger perspective, it is not the desirable way to achieve structural transformation. From the evidence presented in section 2, this appears to be the situation in India. The mechanisms that bring about cases 3 and 4 can be illustrated in figure 2.15.

In both cases, the KV coefficient is high and can be illustrated by setting $\lambda_1 = 1$. The key difference between case 3 and case 4 again lies in the values of growth elasticity of labor supply. Case 3 has a high income effect with respect to dispossession effect and can be illustrated by setting $\varepsilon_N = \lambda_1 \geq 1$. These examples are consistent with the conditions that bring about case 3 because they guarantee $1 - \lambda_1 = 0$ and $1 - \lambda_1 + \varepsilon_N > 0$. Case 4 has a high dispossession effect with respect to income effect and can be illustrated by setting the value of growth elasticity of labor supply negative with $\varepsilon_N < 0 < \lambda_1 < 1$ such that $1 - \lambda_1 = 0$ and $1 - \lambda_1 + \varepsilon_N = 0$. The effect of higher output growth rate on employment growth rate and employment share is shown in figure 2.15. The employment line *L*1 in figure 2.15 is vertical for cases 3 and 4 because the employment growth rate remains unaffected by output growth rate, with $\lambda_1 = 1$. For reasons that are similar to what is shown in figure 2.14, higher output growth rate increases employment share from *v*0 to *v*1 in case 3, while employment share remains unchanged for case 4.

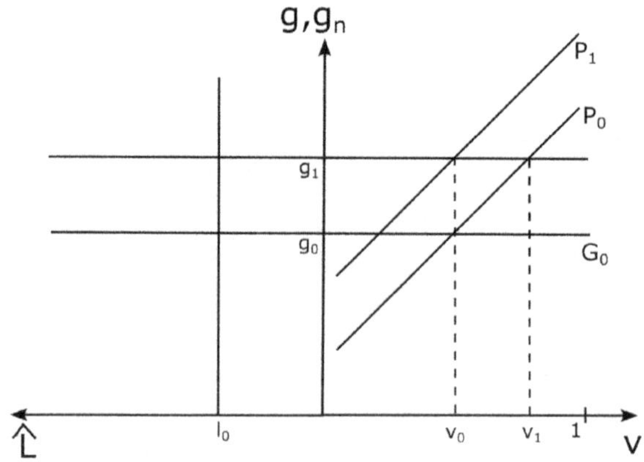

Figure 2.15 Jobless growth regime with and without structural transformation (cases 3 and 4)

4. DISCUSSION AND CONCLUSION

This chapter outlines the key features of India's structural transformation process since the 1980s and attempts to provide a theoretical framework to understand their underlying mechanisms. Challenging dual economy theories, where the binding constraint on employment growth rate and structural transformation is the output growth rate, the Indian experience has been different in at least two ways. First, its employment growth rate remained unresponsive despite a higher output growth rate. Second, it registered a higher share of regular wage and organized sector employment without any improvement in the overall employment growth rate. We locate the explanation for such a dual phenomenon of jobless growth and structural transformation in a dual economy framework by analyzing the mutual interactions between growth, labor demand, and labor supply.

The model presented in this chapter produces four distinct cases depending on how the employment growth rate and employment share of the formal sector respond to the output growth rate. The Indian experience is a specific case based on different theoretical possibilities because of a high KV coefficient and income effect on labor supply.

Unlike many post-Keynesian models, labor supply plays an important role in our analytical framework in explaining employment share or the pace of structural transformation. At any given labor demand, employment share of the formal sector is adversely affected by labor supply growth rate. The latter responds to output growth rate, the direction of which depends on the relative strength of the income and dispossession effects. In contrast to neoclassical models, the growth rate of the labor supply does not affect employment growth rate in this analysis. Similar to post-Keynesian theories, employment growth rate depends on labor demand and is derived as a difference between output and productivity growth rate. The constraint on employment growth rate and the phenomenon of jobless growth is explained through the productivity channel, which reflects the real-world phenomenon of automation and rapid introduction of labor-saving technology.

The phenomenon of jobless growth has been argued to emerge from two distinct routes, which were described as routes 1 and 2 in the introduction. While jobless growth in route 1 emerges *despite* higher output growth rate because of proportional and exogenous changes in labor productivity growth rate, jobless growth in route 2 emerges because of higher output growth rate involving a high KV coefficient. This chapter highlighted the problem of India's jobless growth particularly in terms of route 2. If the KV coefficient is interpreted in a broader sense to include historically given socioeconomic factors, then a plausible explanation for its high value can be located in the presence of large surplus labor that India inherited during the time of independence and the nature of social institutions that emerged since the introduction of liberalization policies. In this context, it is worth returning to the observation that the KV coefficient is far lower for the organized manufacturing sector (as measured in the ASI data) than for the manufacturing sector as a whole (as measured in KLEMS). This can happen if the informal part of the manufacturing sector absorbs more of the negative shock from labor-displacing technical change. It can also happen if this sector is more prone to labor supply changes arising from the income or dispossession effects. Both these factors will serve to weaken the relationship between output growth and employment growth.

This specific nature of jobless growth has key policy implications for employment generation. In route 1, the employment growth rate can be increased by implementing policies that increase the output growth rate over and above the labor productivity growth rate. For example, if the output growth rate at a specific level is unable to increase the employment growth rate in the midst of automation and rapid introduction of labor-saving technology, policymakers can aim for an even higher output growth rate that sufficiently counters the adverse effect of the labor productivity growth rate. The policy target of increasing the output growth rate remains analytically the same as increasing the employment growth rate when the KV coefficient is adequately low.

In route 2, employment constraints cannot be relaxed exclusively through the output channel. This is reflected in the case of India, which was unable to relax its employment constraint despite registering a higher output growth rate since 2004. This is because a higher output growth rate in itself pushes up the labor productivity growth rate proportionately involving the KV channel. The policy targets of increasing output growth rate and employment growth rate are analytically distinct in this case. Additional policy instruments are needed to increase the employment growth rate over and above the ones that increase the output growth rate.

Regarding structural transformation, the model produces a scenario where, even in the case of jobless growth, the share of formal employment rises because of the dominance of the income effect over the dispossession effect. That is, higher output growth pushes some workers (mostly women) out of the nonagricultural workforce, thereby lowering the denominator and raising the share of formal employment. This describes the Indian case but is obviously not a desirable route to structural transformation. We wish instead to see a scenario where the KV coefficient is small enough that even if there is a net positive flow of workers into the nonagricultural sector, we still obtain a rising share of formal employment. This remains the clear policy challenge.

We end with two observations in this regard. First, if fiscal policy is seen as one possible instrument for addressing the employment constraint, then the nature of such policy can be changed in keeping with the nature of jobless growth. If an economy is characterized by route 1 jobless growth, then capital expenditures that typically have high multiplier values compared to revenue expenditures can be a preferred instrument for job creation. But if an economy is confronting the jobless growth of route 2, then implementing such an expenditure may not be sufficient to relax employment constraints. The objective of employment generation may require undertaking expenditures in the form of employment guarantee programs, despite them having relatively lower multiplier values compared to capital expenditures.

Second, there is likely to be significant heterogeneity in the KV coefficient across the firm-size spectrum, with smaller firms showing lower coefficients. In other words, the composition of output growth also matters for employment growth. If most of the output growth comes from large firms that have high KV coefficients, growth will be much more jobless than if growth comes from smaller firms. This, of course, is the commonly advanced argument in favor of industrial policy that promotes smaller firms.

In this chapter, we have abstracted away from income distribution impacts of growth and the implications of changes in the former for the structure of demand as well as employment intensity of growth. This remains a topic for future research.

NOTES

1. "Regular wage," as opposed to casual/daily wage and self-employment, is admittedly a liberal definition of "formality." Stricter definitions, such as the presence of social security, protection under labor laws, and so on, will change the nature of the trends, but for our purposes, the key analytical difference is between employment that is created via labor demand in the capitalist economy and does not display income-sharing or work-sharing properties. Regular wage employment fulfils this criterion.

2. We ignore the openly unemployed, who constituted less than 2 percent of the total labor force until the increase to 6 percent reported in the 2017–18 Periodic Labour Force Survey (PLFS) data. The numbers here are estimates derived by multiplying sample-survey-derived ratios with census projections.

3. The complete regression results are provided in the appendix to this chapter.

4. The results are not substantially different in the World Development Indicators (WDI) database. We present analysis using Economic Transformation Database (ETD) here because it gives more detailed sector-wise data on output and employment than does the WDI database. We have also verified that the aggregate and nonagricultural employment elasticities obtained here match those obtained from the India-specific KLEMS database.

5. As before, the full regression results are displayed in the appendix to this chapter. And once again, we have verified that the Kaldor-Verdoorn (KV) coefficient obtained in ETD is the same as that obtained in KLEMS.

6. A more detailed discussion on these graphs is available in Basole (2022).

7. The natural growth rate is defined as the sum of labor productivity growth rate and labor supply growth rate. Because the employment growth rate is the difference between the output and productivity growth rate, the growth rate of employment (labor demand) is equal to the growth rate of labor supply when the actual and natural growth rate are equal.

8. While the assumption of rigid nominal wage rate in Keynes (1936) acts as a stability condition, the possibility of involuntary unemployment in this framework emerges independent of the assumption of wage-price flexibility (Marglin 2020).

9. As noted by Joan Robinson (1937), "decline in demand for product of the general run of industries leads to a diversion of labour from occupations in which productivity is higher to others where it is lower. The cause of this diversion, a decline in effective demand, is exactly the same as the cause of unemployment in the ordinary sense, and it is natural to describe the adoption of inferior occupations by dismissed workers as *disguised unemployment*."

REFERENCES

Afridi, F., M. Bishnu, and K. Mahajan. 2023. "Gender and Mechanization: Evidence from Indian Agriculture." *American Journal of Agricultural Economics* 105 (1): 52–75.

Basole, A. 2022. "Structural Transformation and Employment Generation in India: Past Performance and the Way Forward." *Indian Journal of Labour Economics* 65: 295–320.

Basole, A., R. Abraham, A. Shrivastava, and A. Jayadev. 2018. *State of Working India* (Technical Report). Centre for Sustainable Employment, Azim Premji University.

Bhaduri, A. 1986. *Macroeconomic: The Dynamics of Commodity Production*. Macmillan.

Bhaduri, A. 2018. "A Study in Development by Dispossession." *Cambridge Journal of Economics* 42 (1): 19–31.

Blecker, R. A., and M Setterfield. 2019. *Heterodox Macroeconomics: Models of Demand, Distribution and Growth*. Edward Elgar Publishing.

Ghose, A. K. 2016. "Globalization, Growth and Employment in India." *Indian Journal of Human Development* 10 (2): 127–56.

Kaldor, N. 1961. "Capital Accumulation and Economic Growth." In *The Theory of Capital*, ed. F. H. Lutz. Macmillan.

Kaldor, N. 1966. *Causes of the Slow Rate of Economic Growth in the United Kingdom.* Cambridge University Press.

Kannan, K. P., and G. Raveendran. 2009. "Growth Sans Employment: A Quarter Century of Jobless Growth in India's Organised Manufacturing." *Economic and Political Weekly*, 80–91.

Keynes, J. 1936. *The General Theory Employment, Interest and Money*. Macmillan.

Lahoti, R., and H. Swaminathan. 2016. "Economic Development and Women's Labor Force Participation in India." *Feminist Economics* 22 (2): 168–95.

Lavoie, M. 2022. *Post-Keynesian Economics: New Foundations*. Edward Elgar Publishing.

Lucas, R. 1988. "On the Mechanics of Economic Development." *Journal of Monetary Economics* 22 (1): 3–42.

Marglin, S. A. 2020). *Raising Keynes: A Twenty-First-Century General Theory*. Harvard University Press.

McCombie, J., and T. Thirlwall. 1995. "Economic Growth and the Balance-of-Payments Constraint Revisited." In *Markets, Unemployment and Economic Policy: Essays in Honour of Geoff Harcourt*, ed. P. Arestis, J. Sawyer, and M. Palma. Routledge.

Mehrotra, S., and J. K. Parida. 2017. "Why Is the Labour Force Participation of Women Declining in India?" *World Development* 98: 360–80.

Nah, W. J., and M. Lavoie. (2019b). "The Role of Autonomous Demand Growth in a Neo-kaleckian Conflicting-claims Framework." *Structural Change and Economic Dynamics* 51: 427–444.

Palley, T. 2019. "Unemployment and Growth: Putting Unemployment into Post Keynesian Growth Theory." *Review of Political Economy* 31 (2): 194–215.

Patnaik, P. (1997). *Accumulation and Stability Under Capitalism*. Oxford University Press.

Patnaik, P. (2011). "Economic Growth and Employment." *Economic and Political Weekly* 46 (26): 172–76.

Rada, C., and R. Arnim. 2012. "Structural Transformation in China and India: A Note on Macroeconomic Policies." *Structural Change and Economic Dynamics* 23 (3): 264–75.

Robinson, J. 1937. "Disguised Unemployment." *Economic Journal* 46 (182), 225–37.

Romer, P. 1986. "Increasing Returns and Long-Run Growth. *Journal of Political Economy* 94 (5): 1002–1037.

Romer, P. 1990. "Endogenous Technological Change." *Journal of Political Economy* 98 (5): 71–102.

Sadhu, K., and S. Chakrabarti. 2021. Neo-Dualism: Accumulation, Distress, and Proliferation of a Fissured Informality. *Review of Radical Political Economics* 53 (4): 694–724.

Sanyal, K. 2007. *Rethinking Capitalist Development: Primitive Accumulation, Governmentality and Post-Colonial Capitalism*. Routledge.

Sen, A. 1970. "Interest, Investment and Growth." In *Growth Economics*, ed. A. Sen. Penguin.

Solow, R. M. 1956. "A Contribution to the Theory of Economic Growth. *Quarterly Journal of Economics* 70 (1): 65–94.

Tejani, S. 2016. "Jobless Growth in India: An Investigation. *Cambridge Journal of Economics* 40 (3): 843–70.

Thirlwall, A. P. 1979. "The Balance of Payments Constraint as an Explanation of International Growth Rate Differences. *BNL Quarterly Review* 32 (128): 45–53.

Verdoorn, P. 2002. "Factors That Determine the Growth of Labour Productivity." In *Productivity Growth and Economic Performance: Essays on Verdoorn's Law*, ed. J. P. McCombie. Palgrave Macmillan.

Appendix 2.1 Elasticities and Kaldor-Verdoorn coefficients for countries in the ETD database

		Aggregate		Nonagricultural						
WDI Code	Country	Coefficient	Elasticity	Coefficient	Elasticity	Country	Coefficient	Emp KV	Coefficient	Productivity KV
110	India	—	0.20	—	0.47	India	—	-0.11	—	1.08
10	Argentina	0.55	0.74	0.36	0.83	Argentina	0.40	0.29	-0.38	0.70
20	Burkina Faso	0.07	0.27	0.82	1.29	Burkina Faso	0.46	0.35	-0.43	0.65
21	Bangladesh	0.11	0.30	0.20	0.68	Bangladesh	1.75	1.64	-1.54	-0.46
29	Bolivia	0.32	0.52	0.58	1.06	Bolivia	-0.34	-0.46	0.31	1.39
30	Brazil	0.45	0.65	0.56	1.04	Brazil	0.63	0.51	-0.60	0.48
34	Botswana	0.46	0.65	0.23	0.71	Botswana	-0.07	-0.18	0.09	1.17
40	Chile	0.31	0.51	0.12	0.59	Chile	0.60	0.48	-0.59	0.49
41	China	-0.13	0.07	-0.18	0.29	China	0.45	0.34	-0.46	0.62
43	Cameroon	0.58	0.78	1.30	1.78	Cameroon	0.20	0.08	-0.18	0.90
46	Colombia	0.53	0.73	0.41	0.88	Colombia	0.65	0.53	-0.61	0.47
49	Costa Rica	0.41	0.60	0.31	0.79	Costa Rica	0.55	0.44	-0.54	0.54
67	Ecuador	0.80	1.00	0.72	1.19	Ecuador	0.90	0.79	-0.86	0.22
68	Egypt, Arab Rep.	0.40	0.59	0.17	0.64	Egypt, Arab Rep.	0.21	0.09	-0.20	0.88
73	Ethiopia	0.24	0.44	0.34	0.81	Ethiopia	0.89	0.77	-0.88	0.21

(*continued*)

Appendix 2.1 *(continued)*

		Aggregate		Nonagricultural						
WDI Code	Country	Coefficient	Elasticity	Coefficient	Elasticity	Country	Coefficient	Emp KV	Coefficient	Productivity KV
84	Ghana	0.34	0.54	0.32	0.79	Ghana	0.99	0.87	−0.99	0.10
97	Hong Kong SAR, China	0.14	0.34	-0.11	0.36	Hong Kong SAR, China	0.26	0.15	−0.24	0.84
107	Indonesia	0.21	0.41	0.24	0.71	Indonesia	0.48	0.37	−0.43	0.65
116	Israel	0.51	0.71	0.35	0.82	Israel	0.80	0.69	−0.79	0.29
120	Japan	−0.33	-0.13	-0.39	0.08	Japan	0.37	0.26	−0.34	0.75
122	Kenya	0.47	0.67	1.49	1.96	Kenya	-0.20	-0.31	0.18	1.27
124	Cambodia	0.20	0.40	0.27	0.74	Cambodia	0.22	0.11	−0.24	0.85
127	Korea, Rep.	0.07	0.27	-0.10	0.38	Korea, Rep.	0.76	0.65	−0.75	0.33
130	Lao PDR	0.13	0.33	0.18	0.66	Lao PDR	0.16	0.04	−0.03	1.05
139	Sri Lanka	0.16	0.36	0.00	0.47	Sri Lanka	-0.01	-0.12	0.07	1.15
142	Lesotho	0.44	0.63	-0.09	0.38	Lesotho	-0.10	-0.21	0.13	1.21
149	Morocco	0.14	0.33	-0.04	0.43	Morocco	0.28	0.17	−0.26	0.82
155	Mexico	0.75	0.95	0.62	1.09	Mexico	0.38	0.27	−0.36	0.72
161	Myanmar	-0.07	0.13	-0.21	0.26	Myanmar	0.01	-0.11	-0.01	1.07
166	Mozambique	0.14	0.34	0.20	0.67	Mozambique	0.38	0.26	−0.39	0.70
168	Mauritius	0.07	0.27	-0.13	0.34	Mauritius	-0.01	-0.12	0.04	1.12

169	Malawi	0.11	0.31	1.11	1.58	Malawi	0.89	0.77	-0.81	0.27
170	Malaysia	0.36	0.56	0.15	0.62	Malaysia	0.43	0.31	-0.42	0.66
172	Namibia	0.40	0.60	0.41	0.89	Namibia	0.19	0.08	-0.19	0.89
175	Nigeria	0.41	0.61	0.64	1.11	Nigeria	0.95	0.84	-0.92	0.16
179	Nepal	0.39	0.58	0.34	0.81	Nepal	0.14	0.02	-0.15	0.93
185	Pakistan	0.56	0.76	0.31	0.79	Pakistan	0.32	0.21	-0.33	0.76
187	Peru	0.36	0.56	0.16	0.63	Peru	0.37	0.26	-0.38	0.71
188	Philippines	0.30	0.50	0.18	0.65	Philippines	0.28	0.17	-0.28	0.81
204	Rwanda	0.11	0.31	0.70	1.17	Rwanda	0.63	0.51	-0.56	0.52
208	Senegal	0.62	0.82	0.97	1.44	Senegal	0.93	0.82	-0.89	0.20
209	Singapore	0.44	0.64	0.13	0.61	Singapore	0.32	0.21	-0.31	0.77
234	Thailand	0.11	0.31	0.21	0.68	Thailand	0.49	0.38	-0.47	0.61
244	Tunisia	0.27	0.47	0.04	0.51	Tunisia	0.17	0.06	-0.17	0.91
245	Turkiye	0.23	0.43	0.19	0.67	Turkiye	0.39	0.28	-0.38	0.70
247	Tanzania	0.32	0.52	0.50	0.97	Tanzania	0.96	0.84	-0.91	0.17
248	Uganda	0.25	0.44	0.04	0.52	Uganda	0.03	-0.08	-0.04	1.04
258	Viet Nam	0.15	0.35	0.41	0.88	Viet Nam	0.07	-0.04	-0.11	0.97
264	South Africa	0.18	0.38	0.11	0.59	South Africa	0.39	0.28	-0.35	0.73
265	Zambia	0.32	0.52	0.17	0.65	Zambia	0.71	0.60	-0.70	0.38

PART II

Employment Trends and Patterns Across Countries and Regions

CHAPTER 3

The Changing Nature of Work

IMPROVING THE FUNCTIONING OF LABOR MARKETS

Sidra Rehman and Agustin Velasquez

Abstract: This chapter examines how automation, artificial intelligence (AI), and remote work are transforming labor markets in the Middle East and North Africa (MENA) region. While job creation has not kept pace with economic growth, especially for youth and women, the region is also presented with new avenues for inclusion and productivity. Using recent literature and newly developed indices of job vulnerability to automation and remote work amenability, the authors evaluate how MENA economies can navigate these evolving trends. The findings show that while many MENA countries remain relatively exposed to automation—particularly in routine, male-dominated sectors—there are growing opportunities for high-skilled, flexible employment through remote work. Encouragingly, remote work may improve access to jobs for women and young professionals, especially in countries investing in digital infrastructure. The chapter emphasizes the need for proactive policies—such as improving education systems, boosting digital access, aupdating labor market regulations—to help the region adapt to change and harness the potential of the future of work.

1. INTRODUCTION

While annual gross domestic product (GDP) growth has accelerated in the Middle East and North Africa (MENA) region by about 5 percentage points since 2000, job creation has been limited and unemployment remains high. In the MENA region, the elasticity of employment to growth is estimated to be lower than in high-income countries and below levels that would be required to employ the region's growing young population (International Monetary Fund [IMF] 2021a; Crivelli et al. 2012).

A rich and growing literature (Crivelli et al. 2012; IMF 2018, 2021a, 2021b; ElGanainy et al. 2022) has attributed limited job creation in the MENA region to a host of structural and macroeconomic factors, including (1) skills mismatches; (2) widespread rigidities in labor markets, mainly from restrictive labor legislations for the hiring and dismissal of workers; and (3) a large government sector. A confluence of these factors has resulted in stagnant employment and unemployment rates in the region, with segmented labor markets, characterized by low levels of female and youth labor force participation rates and a large informal sector.

Emerging global trends could change the MENA region's labor markets over the next few decades in directions that are difficult to fully gauge. On the one hand, working-age population in the MENA region will increase by 15 percent over the next two decades (equivalent to 30.8 million people), further raising pressures on economies in the region to generate employment.[1] On the other hand, the MENA region will not be immune to the transformation drivers that started in advanced economies a few years ago and were accelerated by the COVID-19 pandemic, in particular:

- *Advances in automation technologies and artificial intelligence (AI)* have led to growing fears about job losses, especially for unskilled labor. While economic theory suggests that technological progress is likely to create both winners and losers, a disproportionate impact on low-skilled workers could, at least temporarily, increase labor market segmentation and income inequality.
- The pandemic is likely to have permanently changed the nature of work, with a widespread adoption of *remote work arrangements* and persistent reallocation of jobs across sectors, including from hospitality and high-contact sectors to information technology (IT) and e-commerce. The nature of these changes will likely vary across countries depending on the distributions of jobs and occupations, the possibility to work from home, and the quality of internet access.

Automation, AI, and remote work are likely to present challenges to MENA economies but also provide opportunities, especially to some excluded groups like youth and women. AI will increase the demand for high-skill workers to support automation, while remote work will reduce location and mobility impediments and allow for more flexible work schemes in jobs that do not require physical proximity. While jobs affected by AI, automation, and remote work do not necessarily overlap one-to-one, one factor is clear: upskilling the labor force is key to adapting to creating jobs in this new labor market landscape and mitigating long-lasting job deficits in the MENA region.

Against this background, this chapter addresses a few key questions: How will these trends affect the nature of work and labor market outcomes in MENA countries? Will they lead to further polarization in regional labor markets and further entrench inequality, or will they provide an opportunity for more inclusion? To shed some light on these questions, we first review recent academic literature on the future of jobs globally and in the MENA region. Then, leveraging this literature, we build indexes that measure the degree to which employment in MENA economies is exposed to changes related to both automation and remote working, and discuss the implications for different demographic groups and countries in the region. We conclude by discussing the policy implications to help navigate the changing landscape so that the MENA region is poised to take advantage of the trends that could change the future of work.

2. AUTOMATION

We first look at the potential impact of advances in AI and related forms of automation technologies on the MENA region's labor markets. According to many economists—although by no means all, advances in AI and related technologies will allow machines to substitute for human labor across a much wider range of tasks than earlier waves of automation. Autor and Price (2003) and Autor (2013) suggest that automation tends to hurt workers by substituting humans in performing noncognitive and routine tasks. Technological progress has been skill-biased, disproportionately favoring high-skilled over low-skilled workers, leading to a polarization of the labor market and income gains at the global level (Berg et al. 2018; Jaumotte et al. 2013; Korinek et al. 2021). Sachs (2019) and Yusuf (2017) suggest profound implications of automation on development pathways and strategies as well as the prospect of premature deindustrialization, along with reductions in demand for unskilled labor. Nedelkoska and Quintini (2018) find that developing countries are more vulnerable to automation based on differences in industrial structure and, more important, in the way work is organized in these countries (notably, a greater dependence on unskilled labor).

The overall impact of automation trends on employment, however, is likely to be both complex and ambiguous—with creative and destructive forces that affect the demand for labor, and the distribution and the reallocation of tasks across factors of production. Acemoglu and Restrepo (2019) identify two effects: (1) a *displacement effect*, where automation results in job losses, and (2) a *reinstatement effect*, which has a positive effect on job creation whereby new technologies create new employment opportunities. It remains to be seen if the nature of automation will be employment reducing or employment enhancing on balance.

In general, the impact of automation on jobs is likely to be greater in (1) manufacturing, a sector characterized by many occupations involving manual and routine tasks, and (2) administration and middle management, which tends to involve many cognitive but routine tasks. In contrast, employment in sectors with many occupations involving cognitive and nonroutine work, like education and health-care sectors, is likely to be less affected by technological change. There could also be at least a few forms of manual employment that would be difficult to computerize, such as those in agriculture, and are thus less likely to be affected by automation.

Based on the skill composition of its labor force, employment in the MENA region could be relatively more susceptible to automation given its large concentration of employment in low-skill occupations. The share of the workforce in high- and medium-skill occupations continues to be lower in the MENA region than in the rest of the world. This has been worsened by limited employment creation in these types of occupations (figure 3.1).[2] As of 2020, only 19 percent of the region's workers were in high-skill

Figure 3.1 Change in the share of employment by skill level, in percentage points (2000–2020)

Source: Authors' calculations based on International Labor Organization (ILO) data.

Figure 3.2 Share of employment by skill level, as a percentage (2020)

Source: Authors calculations based on ILO data.

occupations, compared to 21 percent in non-MENA economies, 44 percent were in medium-skill occupations (41 percent in non-MENA economies) and 37 percent were in low-skills occupations (38 percent in non-MENA economies). Over the past two decades, high-income countries in MENA (e.g., oil-reliant economies in the Gulf Cooperation Council) have lagged in creating high-skill jobs, continuing to rely on medium-skill occupations in a dominant public sector (figure 3.2) (World Bank 2022).

Next, we examine if countries in the MENA region have employment concentrated in occupations that are more vulnerable to automation. Viollaz and Winkler (2020) show that a few MENA countries—Egypt, Jordan, and Tunisia, for which detailed survey data are available—are characterized by an occupational structure with significantly fewer tasks requiring nonroutine (both interpersonal and analytical) skills, the so-called jobs of the future that are less vulnerable to automation, compared to Germany, Turkey, and Chile (figure 3.3). The difference is even greater in these countries' private sector, which seems to require less nonroutine cognitive tasks than the public sector—a finding that underscores the relative underdevelopment of the private sector in MENA economies.

We gauge the vulnerability of employment to automation across MENA countries by building an employment vulnerability index for all countries in the region. The index is based on measures of the automatability of occupations that have been suggested in the literature by Frey and Osborne (2017) and used in recent research (Abdychev et al. 2018).

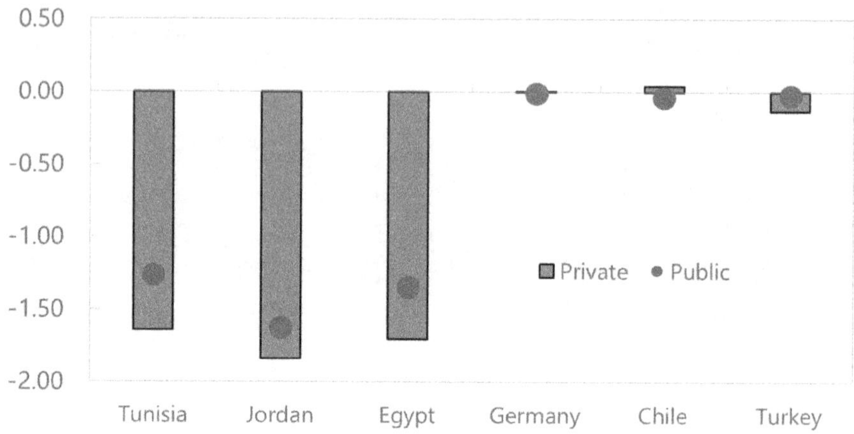

Figure 3.3a Nonroutine interpersonal tasks, in standard deviations with respect to Germany's mean

Source: Authors estimates based on data from Viollaz and Winkler (2020).

Using data from the Occupational Information Network (O*NET) database, a comprehensive system developed by the US Department of Labor that provides information for over 1,100 occupations within the US economy, Frey and Osborne estimate indexes that measure the degree

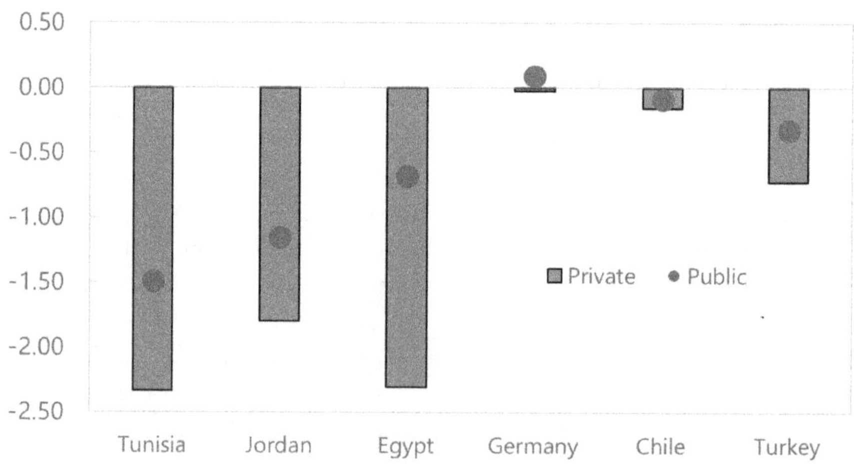

Figure 3.3b Nonroutine analytical tasks, in standard deviations with respect to Germany's mean

Source: Authors estimates based on data from Viollaz and Winkler (2020).

by which an occupation can be automated.[3] Combining these indexes by the share of occupations in sectors yields an index of vulnerability to automation by sector:

$$AV_i = \sum_{o} sh_{o,i} AV_o$$

where
AV_o = the automation vulnerability index of occupation o
$sh_{o,i}$ = the share of workers with occupation o employed in industry i

By doing this, Frey and Osborne (2107) show that the sectors with the greatest vulnerability to automation in the United States are a few service sectors that may be affected by disruptive trends, including driverless cars and self-checkout counters (accommodation and food, retail trade, real estate, transportation), followed by manufacturing, mining, and construction given advances in robots and machinery used in these sectors (figure 3.4).

To assess the vulnerability to automation in different countries in the MENA region, we combine these industry level indexes (AV_i) to MENA country-specific industry-employment shares $shl_{c,i}$ (with subscript c referring to "country"):

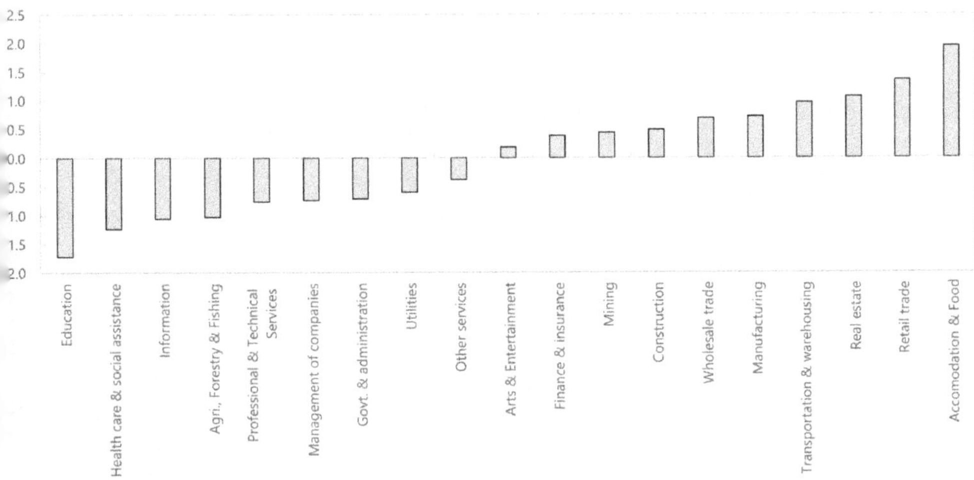

Figure 3.4 Employment vulnerability by economic activity: *z*-score

Source: Authors estimates based on data from Frey and Osborne (2017) and the US Bureau of Labor Statistics (BLS).

$$AV_c^E = \sum_i shl_{c,i} AV_i$$

While in principle the same industry in different countries could employ a different combination of occupations, in the absence of detailed country-specific data, we assume that all countries in the MENA region use the same mix of occupations employed in US industries (thus implicitly that the technology is the same within industries).

We also create an index that measures the overall vulnerability of employment to automation by gender. The index is constructed for male and female employment where the weights of total employment for each industry are replaced by the share of male and female employment, captured by the subscript g as follows:

$$AV_c^{Eg} = \sum_i she_{c,i}^g AV_i.$$

Based on our index, employment tends to be more exposed to automation in advanced MENA economies (figure 3.5), where employment is relatively more concentrated in industries with a high density of largely

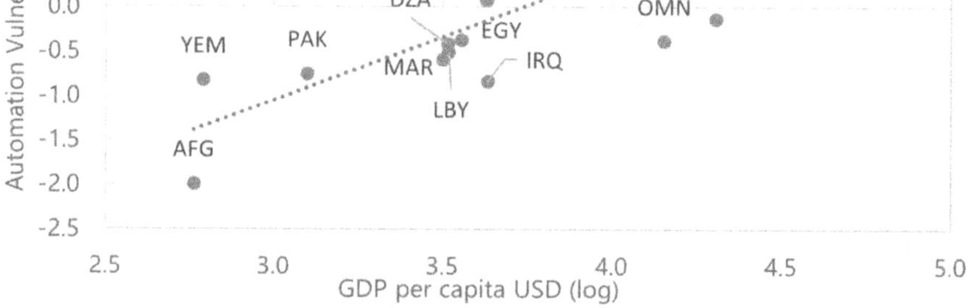

Figure 3.5 Employment vulnerability and gross domestic product (GDP) per capita

Source: Authors' estimates based on data from Frey and Osborne (2017), BLS, and Occupational Information Network (O*NET).

Note: The figure uses International Organization for Standardization (ISO) country codes.

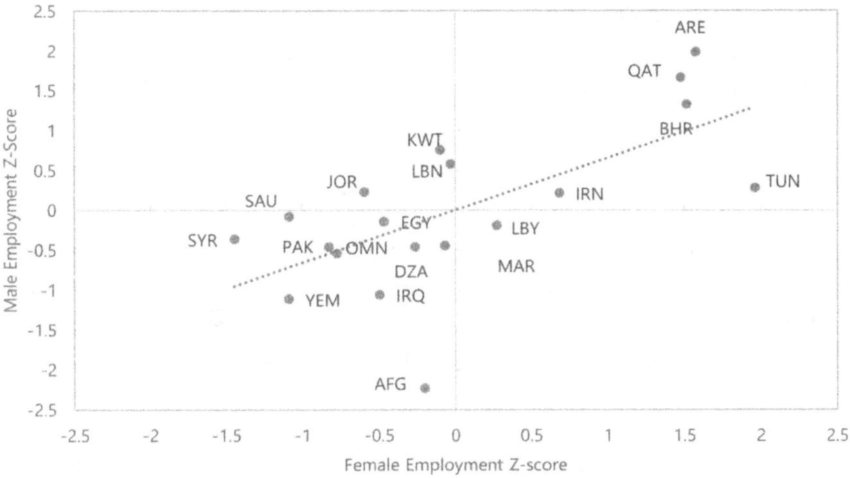

Figure 3.6 Employment vulnerability by gender, *z*-scores

Source: Frey and Osborne (2007), BLS, O*NET, authors' calculations.

routine and noncognitive tasks, such as construction, manufacturing, accommodation, and food services.

The employment vulnerability index by gender shows that employment for male workers is relatively more susceptible than female employment across the MENA region (figure 3.6). This is driven by the fact that male employment tends to be higher in more automatable sectors across the MENA region, such as construction, transportation, and warehousing, whereas females tend to be employed in less automatable sectors, such as agriculture and education.

3. REMOTE WORK

The pandemic has affected labor markets in an unprecedented way. In response to the lockdowns and other social-distancing measures to curb the spread of COVID-19, many firms turned to remote working arrangements and relied on information and communication technologies (ICTs) to carry out tasks that previously required workers' physical presence. This unparalleled and synchronized work reorganization has helped mitigate the impact of COVID-19 on output, job losses, and productivity, especially for occupations that do not require close physical proximity.

Even after the pandemic subsides, remote work setups are likely to remain in place and shape the future of work in many occupations.

Remote work setups depend largely on two key factors: (1) the nature and the task content of jobs and (2) the availability of proper ICT infrastructure:

- High-skilled jobs that require high degrees of cognitive nonroutine and/or interpersonal tasks are more likely to be performed remotely through ICT (World Bank 2019). In contrast, jobs intensive in routine and/or manual tasks, often performed by low-skilled workers, are less likely to be performed remotely (World Economic Forum [WEF] 2020).
- Even if the content of certain jobs can be performed remotely, the actual possibility to work remotely depends crucially on the availability of infrastructure such as computing power and high-quality internet access that allows adequate telecommunication.

These two factors explain the dual labor market outcomes through the pandemic across countries. In advanced economies, during the first year of the pandemic, close to half of the workers were able to work from their homes (WEF 2020), and the demand for analytical and nonroutine jobs, as well as the supply of labor, increased sharply (Baldwin 2019). In contrast, it is estimated that only 10 to 20 percent of urban jobs in developing countries could be performed remotely (Gottlieb et al. 2020; Gottlieb et al. 2021) because of the relatively larger share of workers engaged in noncognitive and routine jobs and relatively less developed ICT infrastructure.

Remote work could also bring new opportunities for (high-skilled) women and the young, who have generally found it more difficult to find (formal) jobs in the MENA region. The reduced need to commute from home to work could mitigate the issues associated with the lack of efficient transportation infrastructure, which has been shown to hinder women's participation to the labor market in many MENA countries (Fogli and Veldkamp 2011). In addition, working from home could allow workers to rely on more flexible work schedules, something that can be particularly useful for women, who may need to balance paid work with household duties and family care, and young people, who may need to balance work with studying (International Labor [ILO] 2021). However, remote work could forestall the building of formal and informal professional and social networks that could be useful to find (formal) jobs (IMF 2021b).

Recent literature has measured the extent to which jobs can be done remotely and has identified the sectors and countries that are more likely to be affected by the widening use of remote work. Using the O*NET database and detailed labor surveys, Dingel and Neiman (2020) reviewed the characteristics of almost one thousand occupations in the US economy to assess whether they can be performed remotely. For example, the authors examined whether the job requires physical activity, outdoor location(s), and/or specific equipment or involves frequent contact with the public. Using this information, they built an index of tele-workability for each occupation. They found that occupations that rely on cognitive skills and carry a wage premium are more adaptable to remote settings (figure 3.7). Using the share of occupations within economic sectors, Dingel and Neiman (2020) built indexes of tele-workability for US sectors and used them to determine the extent to which a country has jobs that can be performed remotely.[4] Their sample covers eighty-five countries, including four MENA countries (Afghanistan, Egypt,

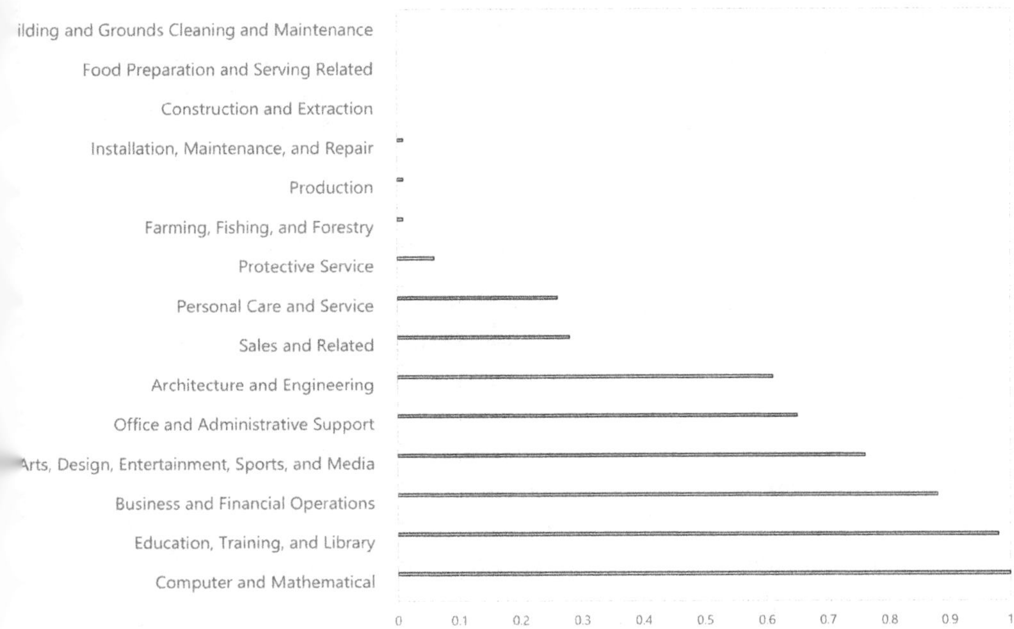

Figure 3.7 Share of jobs that can be done remotely by major occupations group, selected sectors

Source: Authors' estimates based on Dingel and Neiman (2020).

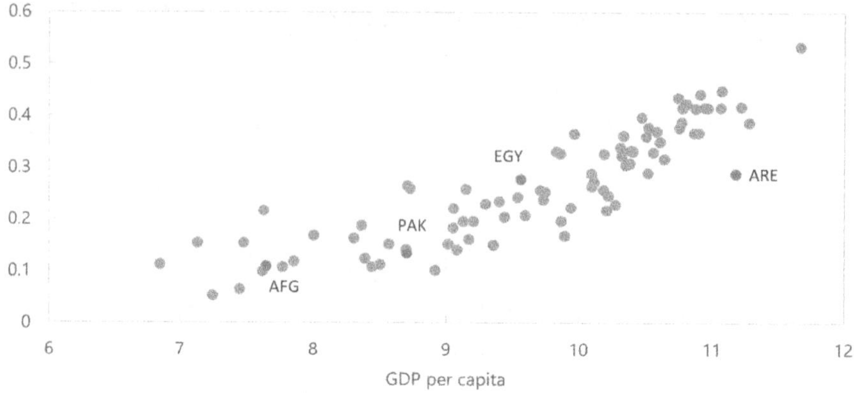

Figure 3.8 Work from Home (WFH) potential: range from 0–1

Source: Authors' estimates based on Dingel and Neiman (2020).

Pakistan, and United Arab Emirates [UAE]). They found that there is a strong positive correlation between the share of jobs that can be performed remotely and a country's GDP per capita (figure 3.8).[5] MENA countries fit within this general correlation pattern, with the exception of the UAE, that show a lower value of the index relative to what is predicted by the level of income, possibly reflecting the importance of the oil sector in value added and the fact that few jobs in that sector can be performed remotely.

One limitation of Dingel and Neiman's (2020) study is that they utilize US sector-specific indexes of tele-workability, while technological differences across countries may lead to very different job characteristics compared to the United States, especially for low-income countries. To mitigate this problem, many studies have relied on country-specific labor surveys (see Garrote Sanchez et al. 2021). In particular, Hatayama et al. (2020) build an index of remote work amenability for Egypt, Jordan, and Tunisia that is based on the specific characteristics of occupations in these three countries, controlling for internet access both at work and at home.[6] They find that on average for these MENA countries:

- *Tasks performed by professionals and clerical workers* are more likely to be done remotely than those by crafters and elementary workers, for which in-person routine tasks requiring some degree of physical activity are more prevalent (figure 3.9).

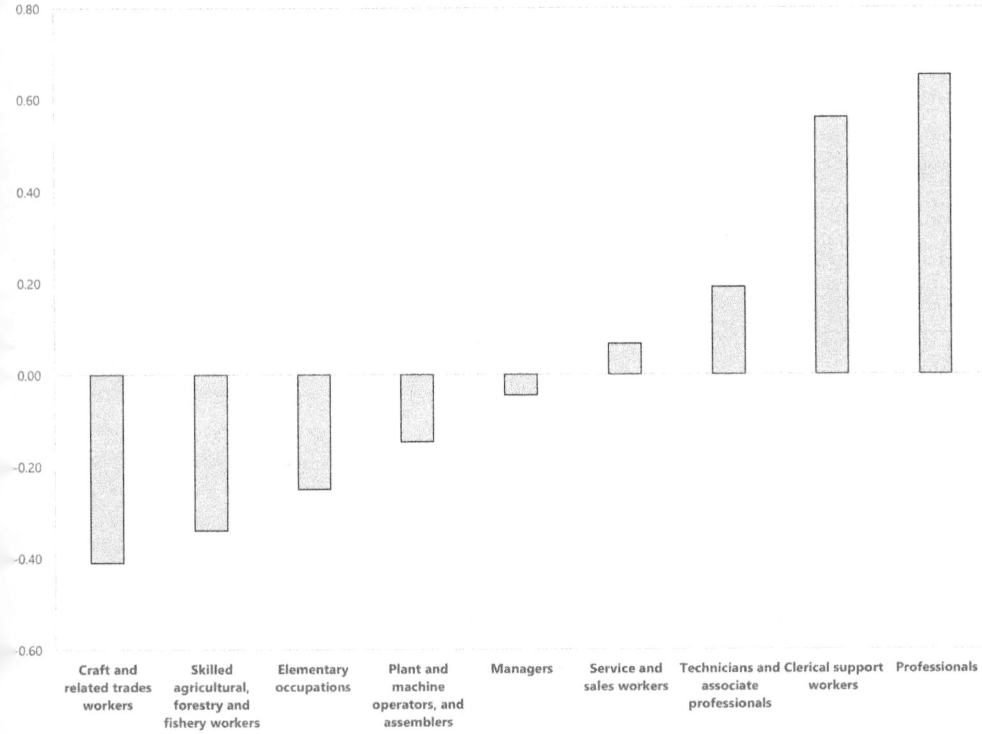

Figure 3.9 WFH amenability for MENA by occupation, *z*-score

Source: Authors' estimates based on Hatayama, Viollaz, and Winkler (2020).

- *IT, finance, professional services, and education* are more amenable to remote work than sectors such as construction, agriculture, and manufacturing (figure 3.10).
- *Women* are more likely to have jobs amenable to remote work because they are less likely to work in physical/manual jobs than men (figure 3.11).[7]
- *Workers with higher (college) education* are more likely to work remotely given the more cognitive tasks performed at their jobs, especially compared to noncollege workers, who are more likely to perform more manual and routine tasks.
- *Older workers* are less likely to have jobs amenable to remote work. This finding is the result of counteracting forces. On the one hand, physical/manual tasks tend to decline with age, while supervision roles tend to increase with age, making the jobs of older workers easier to be

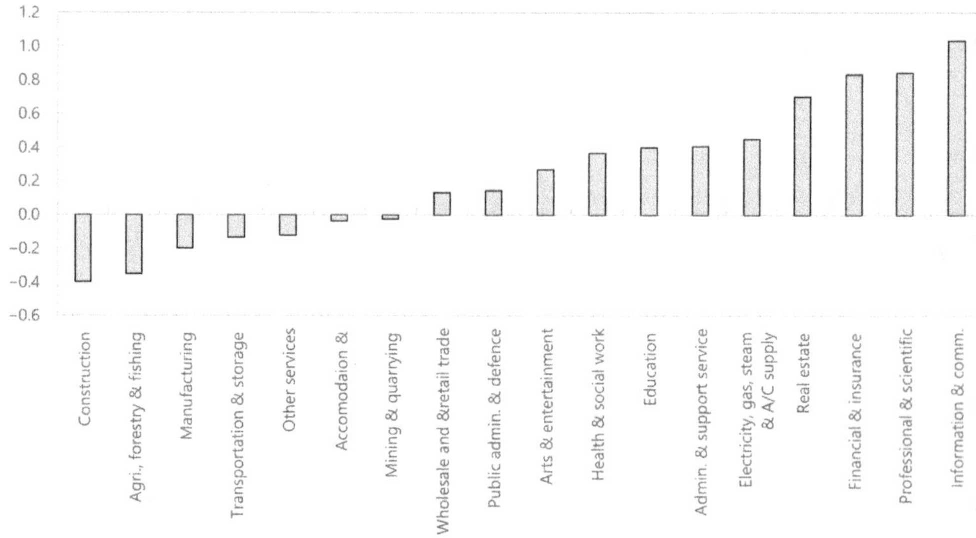

Figure 3.10 WFH amenability in MENA by economic activity, *z*-score

Source: Authors' estimates based on Hatayama, Viollaz, and Winkler (2020).

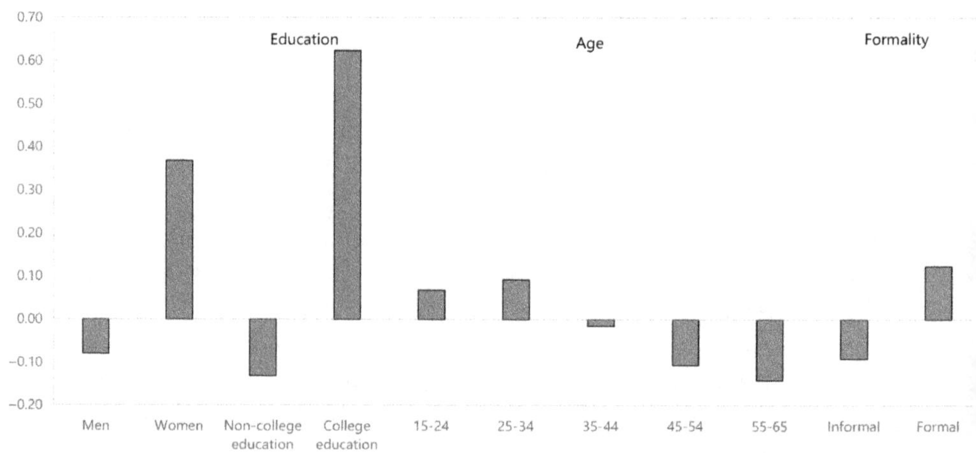

Figure 3.11 Remote work amenability by worker characteristics, *z*-score

Source: Source: Authors' estimates based on Hatayama, Viollaz, and Winkler (2020).

performed remotely. On the other hand, ICT adoption declines with age, which tends to reduce older workers' remote work amenability. For the MENA countries in the sample, the second effect seems to dominate.[8]

- *Workers in formal jobs* are more likely to be amenable to remote work than those in informal jobs because they tend to have less manual-intensive tasks and higher ICT usage (also thanks to appropriate training from their employers).

To gauge which MENA country is more amenable to adopt remote work, we followed a similar strategy as with the automation indexes; that is, we combined the indexes of remote work amenability by sectors built by Hatayama et al. (2020) (as the average for Egypt, Jordan, and Tunisia) with MENA country-specific sector employment shares.[9]

As in Dingel and Neiman (2020), we find that high-income MENA countries are more amenable to set up remote work because a relatively larger share of their workforce is employed in professional services sectors (figure 3.12).[10] Among middle-income MENA countries, Jordan and Lebanon also stand out as displaying high remote work amenability. Morocco, Pakistan, and Afghanistan present the least opportunities for remote work, consistent with their relatively larger concentration of employment in the agricultural sector.

As mentioned above, remote work may offer greater opportunities for women in the MENA region to join the labor market. Which countries

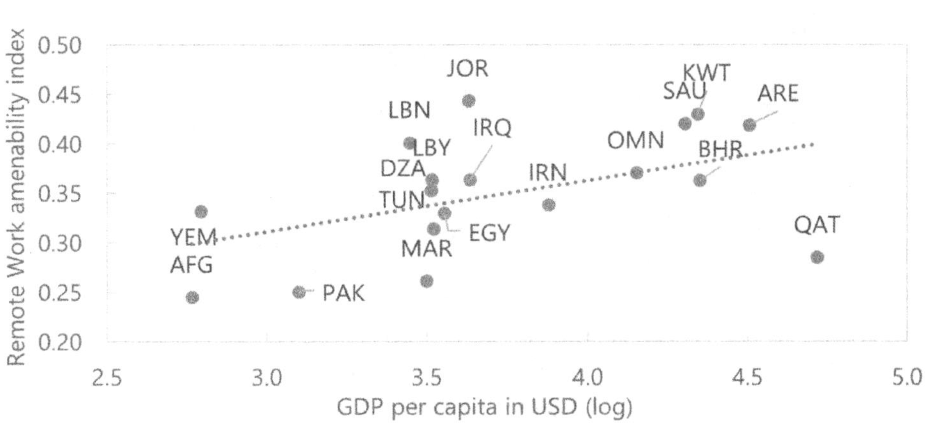

Figure 3.12 Remote work amenability index and GDP per capita

Source: Authors estimates based on ILO data.

in the region are more likely to experience greater female labor force participation by adopting remote work? To answer this question, we built a national remote work female inclusion index (described in box 3.1) based on three indicators: (1) female labor force participation, (2) internet access, and (3) female human capital index. Countries in the MENA region with lower female labor participation, greater internet access, and a higher estimated female human capital are the ones that could experience a greater increase in female participation in the labor market thanks to the extension of remote work.

This seems to be the case mainly for Saudi Arabia, Iran, and Jordan (figure 3.13). In contrast, countries with low connectivity and/or educational scores, such as Iraq or Egypt, are less likely to benefit from remote

Box 3.1 Remote Work: Female Inclusion Index

The composite index is built as the geometric average of three indexes, each scaled between 0 and 1, with a higher value pointing to greater potential benefit from remote work:

- *Female labor participation index*, from the International Labor Organization, defined as $FLFP_{index} = 1 - (I_{actual} - I_{min}) / (I_{max} - I_{min})$, where I refers to female labor force participation in the country in 2019. I_{max} is defined as 60 percent, a high participation rate often found in advanced economies and emerging markets in other regions, and I_{min} is defined at 6 percent, the lowest female participation rate in our country sample. The index provides higher scores to countries that have lower female labor force participation rates (because they stand to benefit the most from remote work, holding everything else constant).
- *Internet access* (from the World Bank and the International Telecommunication Union) is the percentage of the population that had access to the internet (through computer, mobile phone, digital television, and so on) in the past three months.
- The *female human capital index* combines indicators of a country's education and health into a metric of the human capital that a female newborn can expect to accumulate by her eighteenth birthday in 2020 (for more details, see World Bank 2020).

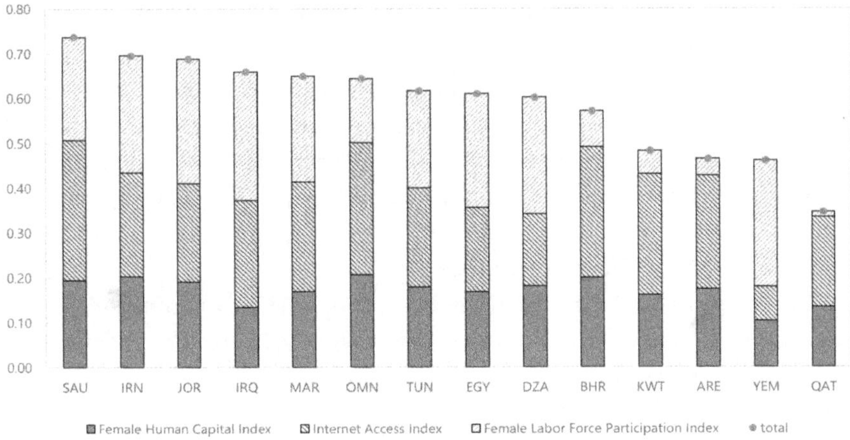

Figure 3.13 Remote work female inclusion index: total and relative contribution of each subcomponent

Source: Authors' estimates based on World Bank, International Telecommunications Union (ITU), and ILO (2020) data.

job opportunities for women. Several high-income MENA countries, such as the UAE, Kuwait, and Qatar, have relatively high internet access and human capital indicators but score low in the overall index because they have already relatively higher female labor participation rates, although mainly because of the significant number of female expatriate workers.

4. CONCLUSIONS

The acceleration in automation and remote work presents both challenges and opportunities for the MENA region in the years to come. We find that the labor force in this region is relatively more vulnerable to automation compared to other regions, but with differences varying across skill, gender, and sector. The overall vulnerability is attributable to the dominance of sectors such as construction and manufacturing, which mostly include occupations that tend to be routine and noncognitive. The MENA region has not pivoted away from high levels of employment in low- and medium-skill occupations, which tend to be routine and nonanalytical. This reliance is even more prominent in the private sector—a feature that may limit the region's dynamism. On a positive note, our analysis suggests that female employment is relatively less vulnerable to automation.

Remote work has undergone a rapid expansion following the COVID-19 pandemic and may be here to stay for years. Establishing remote work environments can be logistically challenging, but doing so may provide opportunities to some excluded demographics, such as women. In general, countries that tend to have more employment in professional areas (like countries from the Gulf Cooperation Council) or that have invested more in ICT infrastructure (like Jordan) are more likely to leverage remote work opportunities.

These trends, which are already shaping the job landscape in the region, make it even more imperative to remove existing barriers in regional labor markets and prepare the labor market for the future, thus ensuring that the MENA region can tap into its demographic dividend and growing labor force. This requires a well-sequenced policy agenda with a focus on the following pillars:

- Strengthen and improve the education system to remove skills gaps and mismatches. This can be achieved by upskilling and/or reskilling the current workforce and better aligning educational programs with employer needs. In addition, improving the quantity and quality of education at all levels, including vocational training for middle-aged workers, will create a more productive workforce.
- Boost public investments in digitalization and internet connectivity, both in urban and rural areas, to ensure broad access and adequate connectivity to the whole population.
- Reform labor market codes and regulations to cater to the shifting attitudes and changing makeup of the workforce. This would require not only removing obstacles to more flexible work arrangements at the firm level but also introducing measures that better regulate and protect the jobs of the future.

NOTES

1. Based on UN population prospects projections based on the medium-fertility variant for Middle East and North Africa (MENA) countries.

2. Following the International Labor Organization's (ILO) definition, high-skill occupations include managers, professionals, technicians, and associate professionals. Medium-skill occupations include clerical support workers, service and sales workers, skilled agriculture, forestry and fishery workers, craft and related trades workers, plant and machine operators, and assemblers. Low-skill workers are those in elementary occupations such as selling goods in streets and public places, or from door to

door; providing various street services; cleaning, washing, pressing; taking care of apartment houses, hotels, offices, and other buildings; and washing windows.

3. The database contains an accurate description of the mix of knowledge, skills, and abilities required as well as the activities and tasks performed by each occupation in its taxonomy.

4. The country indexes are estimated by first building an index of tele-workability for US sectors, using the share of occupations *o* in sector *i* in the US economy. Once the sector indexes are obtained, country indexes are obtained by using the shares of employment by sector in the eighty-five countries considered in the study.

5. Gottlieb et al. (2020), Mongey et al. (2021), Garrote Sanchez et al. (2021), and Brussevich et al. (2020) extend Dingel and Neiman's (2020) influential study and find that high-income countries have a higher share of jobs that can be performed remotely compared to low-income countries.

6. Based on data from Labor Market Panel Surveys (LMPS).

7. This finding has also been documented in other regions of the world. See Garrote Sanchez et al. (2021).

8. Garrote Sanchez et al. (2021) find that first effect seems to dominate in other regions of the world as remote work amenability increases with age in Turkey, Brazil, Mexico, India, and the European Union.

9. The remote work amenability index for the MENA region is built based on the relative values in figure 3.10.

10. One exception is Qatar, which, despite having a high gross domestic product (GDP) per capita, displays low levels of remote work amenability because a large share of its workforce is concentrated in the construction sector.

REFERENCES

Abdychev, A., C. Alonso, E. Alper, et al. 2018. "The Future of Work in Sub-Saharan Africa." IMF Departmental Paper 18/18, International Monetary Fund.

Acemoglu, D., and P. Restrepo. 2019. "Automation and New Tasks: How Technology Displaces and Reinstates Labor." *Journal of Economic Perspectives* 33 (2): 3–30.

Alonso, C., A. Berg, S. Kothari, C. Papageorgiou, and S. Rehman. 2020. "Will the AI Revolution Cause a Great Divergence?" IMF Working Paper 20/184, International Monetary Fund.

Autor, D. 2013. "The 'Task Approach' to Labor Markets: An Overview." *Journal for Labour Market Research* 46 (3): 185–99.

Autor, D., and B. Price. 2003. "The Changing Task Composition of the US Labor Market: An Update of Autor, Levy, and Murnane." MIT Working Paper, MIT.

Baldwin, R. 2019. *The Globotics Upheaval: Globalization, Robotics, and the Future of Work.* Oxford University Press.

Berg, A., E. F. Buffie, and L. Zanna. 2018, August. "Should We Fear the Robot Revolution? (The Correct Answer Is Yes)." *Journal of Monetary Economics* 97: 117–48.

Brussevich, M., E. Dabla-Norris, and S. Khalid. 2020. "Who Will Bear the Brunt of Lockdown Policies? Evidence from Tele-Workability Measures Across Countries." IMF Working Paper 20/88, International Monetary Fund.

Crivelli, E., D. Furceri, and J. Toujas-Bernate. 2012. "Can Policies Affect Employment Intensity of Growth? A Cross-Country Analysis." IMF Working Paper 12/218, International Monetary Fund.

Dingel, J. I., and B. Neiman. 2020. "How Many Jobs Can Be Done at Home?" NBER Working Paper 26948, National Bureau of Economic Research.

ElGanainy, A., E. Ernst, R. Merola, R. Rogerson, and M. Schindler. 2022, February 16. "Chapter 3: Inclusive Labor Markets." In *How to Achieve Inclusive Growth*, edited by Valerie Cerra, Barry Eichengreen, Asmaa El-Ganainy, and Martin Schindler. Oxford University Press.

Fogli, A., and L. Veldkamp. 2011. "Nature or Nurture? Learning and the Geography of Female Labor Force Participation." *Econometrica* 79 (4): 1103–38.

Frey, C. B., and M. A. Osborne. 2017. "The Future of Employment: How Susceptible Are Jobs to Computerisation?" *Technological Forecasting and Social Change* 114 (C): 254–80.

Garrote Sanchez, D., N. G. Parra, C. Ozden, B. Rijkers, M. Viollaz, and H. Winkler. 2021. "Who on Earth Can Work from Home?" *World Bank Research Observer* 36 (1): 67–100.

Gottlieb, C., J. Grobovšek, and M. Poschke. 2020. "Working from Home Across Countries." CIREQ Working Paper Cahier 07–2020, Centre Interuniversitaire de Recherche en Économie Quantitative.

Gottlieb, C., J. Grobovšek, M. Poschke, and F. Saltiel. 2021. "Working from Home in Developing Countries." *European Economic Review* 133 (S1): 103679.

Hatayama, M., M. Viollaz, and H. Winkler. 2020. "Jobs' Amenability to Working from Home: Evidence from Skills Surveys for 53 Countries." World Bank Policy Research Paper 9241, World Bank.

International Labour Organization (ILO). 2021. Teleworking Arrangements During the COVID-19 Crisis and Beyond." International Labour Organization.

International Monetary Fund (IMF). 2018. "Opportunity for All: Promoting Growth and Inclusiveness in the Middle East and North Africa." Departmental 18/11, International Monetary Fund.

International Monetary Fund (IMF). 2021a. "Economic Governance Reforms to Support Inclusive Growth in the Middle East, North Africa, and Central Asia." International Monetary Fund.

International Monetary Fund (IMF). 2021b. "Recessions and Recoveries in Labor Markets: Patterns, Policies, and Responses." In *World Economic Outlook 2021.* International Monetary Fund.

Jaumotte, F., S. Lall, and C. Papageorgiou. 2013. "Rising Income Inequality: Technology, or Trade and Financial Globalization?" *IMF Economic Review* 61 (2): 271–309.

Korinek, A., M. Schindler, and J. E. Stiglitz. 2021. "Technological Progress, Artificial Intelligence, and Inclusive Growth." IMF Working Paper 21/166, International Monetary Fund.

Mongey, S., L. Pilossoph, and A. Weinberg. 2021. "Which Workers Bear the Burden of Social Distancing Policies?" *Journal of Economic Inequality* 13: 509–526

Nedelkoska, L., and G. Quintini. 2018. "Automation, Skills Use and Training." OECD Technical Report 202, Organisation for Economic Co-operation and Development.

Sachs, J. D., 2019. "Some Brief Reflections on Digital Technologies and Economic Development." *Ethics & International Affairs* 33 (2): 159–67.

Viollaz, M. and H. Winkler. 2020. "The Task Content of Jobs in MENA." The World Bank. Mimeo.

World Bank. 2019. *The Changing Nature of Work.* The World Bank.

World Bank. 2020. *The Human capital Index Update: Human Capital in the Time of COVID-19.* World Bank Group.

World Bank. 2022. "Jobs Undone: How the Middle East and North Africa Region Can Recover its Lost Decades." World Bank Report. The World Bank.

World Economic Forum (WEF). 2020. *The Future of Jobs Report 2020.* World Economic Forum.

Yusuf, S., 2017, September 13. "Automation, AI, and the Emerging Economies. Technical Report. Center for Global Development." Center for Global Development. https://www.cgdev.org/publication/automation-ai-and-emerging-economies.

CHAPTER 4

Employment in Argentina

DIAGNOSIS AND PROPOSED SOLUTIONS

Claudio Omar Moroni, Eduardo Óscar Álvarez, Alejandro Raul Ferrari, Diego Schleser, Pablo Arnaldo Topet, and David Trajtemberg

Abstract: This paper analyzes the structural and regulatory characteristics of Argentina's labor market, focusing on key challenges to achieving sustained improvements in job quality and working conditions. Grounded in three core premises—the centrality of work for social integration, the notion of transition as a historical constant, and the imperative to update labor regulations without eroding rights—it examines obstacles stemming from the country's productive structure and sluggish productivity growth. This context sustains persistently high levels of labor informality, affecting both salaried and self-employed workers, particularly in low-productivity, poorly formalized sectors.

The diagnosis reveals a deeply segmented labor market, shaped by inequalities related to gender, firm size, and educational attainment. The paper proposes public policies to strengthen vocational training, support the development of formal productive units, and adapt regulations to new forms of work such as telework and the platform economy. It emphasizes collective bargaining as a key mechanism for reconciling productive flexibility with labor protections. The study also includes specific proposals for self-employment and the popular economy, promoting formalization through tax incentives, expanded labor rights, and institutional recognition.

Keywords: labor market, labor informality, productivity, economic development, labor regulation, vocational training, collective bargaining.

1. INTRODUCTION

The purpose of this chapter is to analyze the characteristics and problems of the labor market in Argentina and to describe the challenges faced in the short and medium term to improve the working conditions of the

Figure 4.1 Modern Times

Source: Charles Chaplin Productions

population. This analysis is approached from two distinct perspectives: one from an economic standpoint and the other from the perspective of labor regulations. Before delving into the analysis at hand, it is important to establish the underlying premises upon which this chapter is built.

The first premise is that true social integration is only possible if there is work with labor rights, whether dependent or independent. There are consequences resulting from this premise in terms of policy decisions, especially in those cases where the community faces the dilemma of having to bear the costs of an activity with low productivity but a high level of employment or also bearing the costs of generating income replacement mechanisms for workers who become unemployed—and have no possibility of reintegration—if such activity is abandoned.

Discussions on the creation of a universal basic income have been ongoing since the 1980s. Proposals for its implementation are recurring either in times of employment crisis or as a solution to the predicted disappearance of work as we know it. However, no country has implemented such a scheme to date and the theoretical debate does not provide an answer to the fundamental question: Is it possible to be truly integrated into the community without a job? The history of human evolution does not seem to be moving in that direction, and although there are current debates on whether this principle will continue to be present in the future, the times in which this may happen make it necessary to continue to place work at the core of the discussion.

A second premise is that transition is the only constant. It has been argued that social changes, even during the so-called revolutionary periods, do not involve completely new constructions but rather a process of transformation that combines elements of the old and the new.

The idea that nothing changes suddenly for everyone at the same time remains true, as the concept of "coetaneity of the noncoetaneous" suggests. With the acceleration of changes in production methods, we are in a state of constant transition. There is no ultimate goal where everything stabilizes, providing a static environment for a certain period, such as an entire working life. Therefore, it is crucial to have a comprehensive understanding of this phenomenon of transition and of how individuals, knowledge, and production modes from different periods coexist.

This situation generates tensions: What do we do with the modes of production and their workers that have not advanced at the speed of other sectors? "Internal development gaps" are a reality to live with, especially in Latin America. While policy mistakes in our region have certainly contributed to this issue, it is important to recognize that such coexistences are typical in any period of transition and represent one of its central points. Acknowledging the perpetual nature of transition raises the question of how to make inherent tensions at least manageable and, based on this premise, to make use of the source of rules that best suits this situation.

The third premise is that the acknowledgment of the need for certain changes in labor regulations does not involve, in any form of work, a regression in the resulting rights. The aim is to uphold those rights while recognizing the existence of modes of production that differ from those prevalent in the 1960s and 1970s, which served as the basis for current regulations. The approach and expectations of some of the new generations in relation to Fordist dependent work should also be considered. One of the challenges is how to ensure that this change in the way of working does not end in precariousness. Simply resisting any form of change does not seem to be working.

This chapter first focuses on the limitations imposed on the labor conditions of workers by the productive structure of the Argentine economy. The third section provides a diagnosis of the Argentine labor market situation, where aspects such as the labor participation of the population and the structure of employment are investigated. In the following sections, we delve into the issue of labor institutions, and we ask ourselves how labor regulations shape the functioning of the labor market and what are the requirements that they demand in an uncertain economic and social context, affected by challenges imposed by the productive structure, the emergence of new technologies that raise questions about present and future employment, and the demands of international economic integration with respect to the competitiveness of companies and the qualifications of workers.

2. PRODUCTION STRUCTURE AND PROBLEMS DERIVED FROM THE LABOR MARKET

In Argentina and Latin America generally, the production structure has created severe obstacles to the possibility of sustaining and deepening the processes of expanding formal employment and improving labor income, especially when the international situation becomes restrictive. One of the main obstacles to the creation of formal employment is the manifest inability of Argentina and the region to build a long-term path of productivity growth. There cannot be any experience of economic development and social progress without a long-term framework for productivity growth that expands the capabilities and skills of both companies and workers to produce more quality goods and services under better employment conditions.

In this scenario, productivity should be understood as a systemic and multidimensional concept that includes, inter alia, the technology used, the technical and scientific knowledge available in the economy, the tacit knowledge of workers and companies, the quality of the goods and services produced, credit policies, tax and foreign trade regulations, the socioterritorial environment of companies (inter alia, the density of the local production system, infrastructure, specific production development policies), and relations with supplier companies and clients. From the perspective of labor, productivity depends on the development of skills and qualifications; formal and informal acknowledgment; professional training; work organization; and improved wage, health, and safety conditions.

Productivity growth makes it possible to expand the level of activity and productive investment and increase the profitability of companies. Although it is not a guarantee, it is a condition for the generation of formal employment and an increase in workers' income.

In Argentina, the evolution of productivity in the last fifty years shows a clear stagnation, which contrasts with the dynamics observed in developed and other emerging countries. The result of this process is that, not only did productivity in Argentina not grow sufficiently, but the gap between the country's productivity and that of the most industrialized nation-states as a whole has progressively widened.

Figure 4.2 shows the comparative evolution of labor productivity between 1970 and 2021 between Argentina and three countries (Australia, Germany, and Norway) that, despite having very different economic characteristics, have experienced significant productivity growth in the last fifty years. While in Argentina productivity grew by 26 percent between 1970 and 2021, in the other three countries evaluated, it did not increase by less than 83 percent (in Australia by 83 percent, in Germany by 87 percent, and in Norway by 133 percent).

One of the consequences of insufficient productivity growth is the spread of the informal economy and informal labor. According to the approach developed by the Programa Regional del Empleo para América Latina y el Caribe (PREALC, Regional Employment Program for Latin America and the Caribbean) of the International Labour Organization (ILO), since the early 1970s in Latin America, informality is a phenomenon resulting from the inability of the formal sector to absorb surplus

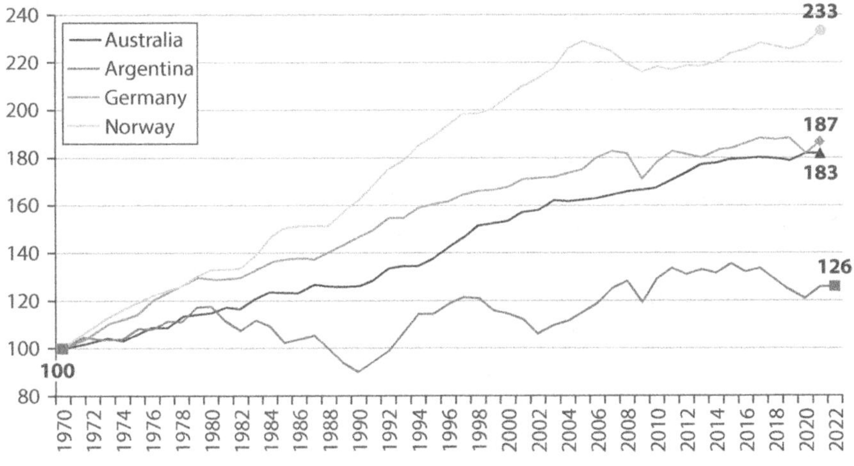

Figure 4.2 Labor Productivity in Australia, Argentina, Germany, and Norway since 1970

labor. Because of technological and training requirements, self-employment and salaried employment in small establishments are a source of attraction for people excluded from the formal sector of the economy. Indeed, the informal sector includes a set of economic units that operate in competitive markets characterized by easy entry, few capital requirements, low productivity, and small size (Tokman 2001).

The heterogeneity of the production of goods and services and the inability to sustain prolonged productivity growth processes in the Argentine economy place a limit on the possibility of expanding the size of the formal sector. One of the characteristics of the informal sector (composed of low-skilled self-employment and unregistered salaried employment) is its low level of productivity. Thus, an economy that finds it difficult to grow and generate highly productive jobs in the formal sector must resort to the informal sector to incorporate workers into productive activity.

Argentina's growing productivity gap in relation to developed and even emerging countries creates a problem of a lack of competitiveness and puts pressure on the design of economic policy. This external gap has consequences for the national labor market because any process of opening and international economic integration affects the sectors with lower relative productivity, causing unemployment and worse working conditions for those who remain employed. This also highlights the internal gap that is expressed in the intra- and intersectoral productive heterogeneity and that causes a relatively low result in the national economy.

Some of the most severe consequences of the presence of internal and external gaps in the production system are seen in the labor market (Porta 2015, 132). The relationship between structural heterogeneity, expressed in the aforementioned gaps, and the labor market is significant because, as Bárcena and Prado highlight, "productivity gaps translate into segmented labor markets, both in terms of access to jobs and salary and work income" (Bárcena and Prado 2015, 132).

As a result of the processes described above, the Argentine labor market presents a dual structure in which part of the employed population works in labor relations in which the institutions of both individual and collective labor law operate. In addition to protection against arbitrary dismissal, these workers have their rights and working conditions established through collective bargaining. Another part of the population has an informal labor insertion that, although it assumes different modalities and characteristics, has as a common factor the complete absence of contributory benefits from the social security system.

To measure the extent of informality in the Argentine labor market, the recommendations of the International Conference of Labour Statisticians (ICLS) organized by the ILO are used, which were prepared for the measurement of this problem. As a starting point, these recommendations define informal work as "a productive labor activity that is not registered in the internal, tax, and/or social security systems."

According to the information collected by the Encuesta nacional a trabajadores sobre Condiciones de Empleo, Trabajo, Salud y Seguridad (ECETSS, National Survey of Workers on Employment, Labor, Health and Safety Conditions) of Argentina, in 2018 (latest available data), labor informality affected 42.8 percent of the employed population. It should be noted that the impact of this problem varies considerably depending on the occupational category and the sector in which the worker is categorized.

In the case of salaried employment in productive units, informality reaches 28.5 percent. In the case of domestic labor in private homes (which in Argentina is rendered under a regular employment contract), the problem amounts to 76.8 percent.

The rate of informality in self-employment reaches 68.3 percent, while it amounts to 23 percent among employers. It should be noted that the largest proportion of the informally employed population is represented by self-employment, which accounts for 36 percent of employment in such situations. Thus, labor informality affects all modalities of work, including salaried employment in formal companies.

The second most important group is salaried work in informal production units, which represents 27 percent of the total unregistered work. These establishments are characterized by their small size, limited use of technology or outdated infrastructure, and productivity levels well below the average for the sector and/or the economy.

In third place, we find salaried employment in formal companies, which accounts for 23 percent of the total informal working population. In this case, unlawful work is the result of employers' circumvention of labor regulations.

Thirteen percent of the informally employed population is concentrated in domestic labor for family households. This is a segment with particular characteristics, where the employer is not a productive unit but a family, and where most of the workers in this sector are women.

Although labor informality is a cross-cutting issue involving the entire economy, the most significant volume of informal salaried employment is concentrated in a few branches of activity: the aforementioned work in private homes (19 percent), commerce (17 percent), construction (15 percent), and manufacturing industry (9 percent). In total, these four sectors of activity account for 60 percent of informal salaried employment. Among salaried employment in productive units, there is a heterogeneous range regarding the importance of informality, and the size of the establishment is one of the variables that best explains the presence of unregistered employment. Seventy-six percent of workers in establishments with up to five employees are unregistered. This figure drops to forty percent in establishments with six to forty employees, and to twelve percent in companies with more than forty workers.

Nonetheless, this situation cannot be fully explained without recognizing that informality often constitutes a temporary phase of workers involved in precarious employment trajectories. Such individuals frequently combine informal employment with unemployment and/or inactivity. In other words, informal work, because of its unstable and precarious nature, is closely linked to overt and covert unemployment or simply to inactivity, which means that informal workers have a high probability of becoming unemployed or inactive.

The information gathered by the Encuesta Permanente de Hogares (EPH, Permanent Household Survey) conducted by the Instituto

Nacional de Estadística y Censos (INDEC, Argentine Institute of Statistics and Census) reveals that 40 percent of the workers who occupy informal salaried positions in a given quarter change their occupational situation in the following quarter. Of the total number of workers with informal jobs who change their occupational status between two consecutive quarters, 46 percent become unemployed or inactive.

3. EMPLOYMENT IN ARGENTINA: DIAGNOSIS AND ACTIONS PROPOSED

As Table 4.1 shows, in the third quarter of 2022, 46.4 percent of the urban population was part of the Economically Active Population (EAP). In the working-age population (sixteen to sixty-five years old), the percentage of the employed and unemployed population reached 70.5 percent of the total urban population. The activity rate by sex shows the gender gap that exists between men and women in the labor market. Although we have witnessed an increase in female activity rate in recent years, the difference in labor participation between men and women continues to be considerable. In fact, for the third quarter of 2022, the activity rate of the male labor force was 54.3 percent; for the female labor force, it was 38.9 percent. Ninety-three percent of the EAP was employed in the labor market and the remaining 7 percent was unemployed.

With respect to the unemployment rate, it can be observed that, throughout the 1990s, in the framework of an open economy and deregulated markets, such an indicator was in the double digits. After the convertibility experience, the index was reduced to single digits from the second five-year period of the first decade of this century, which was caused by the growth of production and the incorporation of workers into formal employment. The contractionary effect caused by the abrupt devaluations of the exchange rate in the 2016–2019 period and the effects of the pandemic in 2020 and 2021 raised the unemployment rate again to double-digit levels. Economic growth in the last two years brought unemployment back down to levels close to 7 percent.

Among the employed population, 72 percent were employed under regular employment contracts, 24 percent were selfemployed, and 4 percent represented the category of employers. Furthermore, 81 percent of the employed population worked in privatesector establishments, and the remaining 19 percent worked in the state sector. If we refer exclusively to workers under regular employment contracts, the proportions in which employment is divided between the private and state sectors are 74 percent and 26 percent, respectively.

Table 4.1 Key indicators of the urban labor market in Argentina, as of the third quarter of 2022

Indicator	Value
Activity rate	46.4
Men	54.3
Women	38.9
Employment rate	43.3
Unemployment rate	6.7
Total number of people employed	**100%**
Occupational category	
Salaried	72%
Self-employed	24%
Employer	4%
Institutional area	
Private	81%
Public	19%
Activity branch	
Commerce	19%
Industry	12%
Construction	10%
Public administration	9%
Education	8%
Domestic work	7%
Health	6%
Transportation	5%
Other	26%
Qualification of occupation	
Operational	55%
Unskilled	19%
Technical	17%
Professional	8%

Source: Author, drawing on data from the Encuesta Permanente de Hogares (EPH, Permanent Household Survey), Instituto Nacional de Estadística y Censos (INDEC, Argentine Institute of Statistics and Census).

Regarding the distribution with respect to each branch of activity, 41 percent of the urban population's employment is concentrated in three sectors: commerce (19 percent), industry (12 percent), and construction (10 percent). In addition, public administration (9 percent), education (8 percent), and health (6 percent) account for another 22 percent of employment, with a marked prevalence of the state in the hiring of these workers. Salaried household workers, responsible for domestic and care tasks in households, represent 7 percent of employment. Finally, there is a less prominent presence in the work structure represented by employment in transportation (5 percent), restaurants and hotels (3 percent), and the agriculture (3 percent).

Regarding the professional qualification(s) required for the positions covered in the third quarter of 2022, it is observed that 55 percent are skilled workers, 19 percent are unskilled workers, 17 percent are workers with technical qualifications, and 8 percent are workers with professional qualifications. Skilled workers are overrepresented (they represent a number that is higher than the employment of the sector in the total number of employed), mainly in the industry, construction, commerce, and transportation sectors. In addition, jobs with technical qualifications are overrepresented in the education and health branches, while jobs with professional qualifications are overrepresented in public administration; health; and professional, scientific, and technical activities. Finally, household workers account for 33 percent of unskilled employment, although they constitute 6 percent of total employment in the economy.

The composition of employment by educational level shows that 41.7 percent of the employed have a secondary education (complete or incomplete), and 31.4 percent have a primary education (also complete or incomplete). If we add to these populations the number of employed persons with no education, we conclude that 77.6 percent of employed persons have attained, at most, a secondary level of education. The employed individuals with higher education (complete or incomplete university) represent the remaining 22.4 percent.

In summary, the Argentine labor market exhibits a behavior that results in a relatively low unemployment rate. The activity rate in the working-age population is not low if compared to others of the region, although the low female participation in the labor market prevents the expansion of this indicator. A significant segment of the population works in sectors with low productivity or where productivity growth is less likely to expand, and where the occupations in demand are mainly skilled and/or unskilled. In addition, the occupational structure still includes a considerable proportion of selfemployment and lowskilled jobs, and there is a precarious integration of a segment of salaried employment.

4. THE CRITICAL ISSUE OF INFORMALITY AS A LABOR PROBLEM

Given the current state of the labor market in Argentina, it is imperative to acknowledge the critical issue of informality. The current labor regulations have their roots in a production system from the 1960s and 1970s. While these regulations have proven to be effective—and continue to be effective—in certain sectors of production, they have not been adapted to the changes that have occurred in modern modes of production.

Something similar happens with other regulations (tax, environment, and health and safety conditions) that have an impact on such activities. This disparity in development stages causes tensions that must be addressed because our countries cannot afford to leave people and activities behind by excluding them from the system.

This might be one of the main points that should be considered when designing public policies aimed at achieving greater formalization. If the goal is to achieve inclusion through work in any of its forms (independent or dependent), it is important to explore ways to foster the creation of productive units that promote real development within legal frameworks.

This situation is especially concerning in our region, which has already been marked by internal development gaps. Rather than improving in recent years, this phenomenon has tended to increase, resulting in a growing differentiation between economic activities and sectors of the population. Informality has reached concerning and chronic levels, which may have even greater impacts on our communities' ability to integrate and to reap the benefits of inclusion fully.

As stated above, informality (lack of registration) and its consequences in terms of productivity have a significant role in the problems affecting the labor market. A key determinant of informality is the insufficient level of productivity of the economy. In Argentina, however, the problem is multicausal because the conditions for its appearance and permanence include the distribution of the tax burden, the inefficiency of state control and labor inspection services, deep-rooted cultural patterns, short economic cycles, and a negative perception of the state's role. Each of these causes also has various origins, which makes it impossible to try to cover the whole spectrum with only a couple of policies. The search for a single perfect solution to the problem may become a hindrance to the adoption of a series of measures that will limit the phenomenon and generate a path with a certain stability that will make it possible to address, one by one, those issues that were not addressed in the first attempt.

This chapter focuses on the regulatory changes and the state's practices (especially in the auditing area) that should be implemented to reduce the impact of informality. The actions that will be proposed should be carried out within the framework of a consistent program aimed at the systematic growth of productivity. In Argentina, unfortunately, this issue has been wrongly associated with the reduction of workers' rights or the simple intensification of their tasks. In the 1990s, the proposals for the flexibility and deregulation of labor standards gained popularity as a means of increasing productivity. Such proposals closed the door, however, to any debate regarding the benefits of discussing this issue, both for workers and the wider community.

In contrast, an increase in productivity, as we understand it, is associated, inter alia, with improvements in working conditions, the participation of workers in the design and adjustment of production systems, and the equitable distribution of the results of this increase in productivity, in line both with the relevant constitutional norm in force in Argentina and the professional training we mentioned before. These are the essential factors that could mark a trend toward an improvement of the productive unit.

Both the current situation of the labor market in Argentina and the map of informal labor constitute the necessary starting point to identify the groups and problems that require attention. According to the data presented in the second section of this chapter, the analysis of this information reveals that informal labor has a high impact on both dependent and independent work and is present in both formal and informal productive units. The relevance of these data lies in the fact that informal work is often treated as a problem involving only dependent workers who are not duly registered.

Another relevant aspect is the existence of a strong presence of informal productive units. Thus, not only is there a lack of registration of workers, but the productive unit itself is informal; that is, it does not comply with current labor, tax, or licensing regulations.

Selfemployed workers present major challenges. The impact of informality on this sector is greater than in the dependent sector, and its importance in the labor force is growing. In addition, because of the importance that dependent work has historically had in terms of value, the situation of the self-employed has not been adequately addressed.

As for salaried workers, what determines the major point is their distribution according to the size of the company: Approximately 55 percent of them are found in productive units with up to five workers.

5. PROFESSIONAL TRAINING

There is broad consensus that the set of competencies, knowledge, and skills of workers determines a country's productive capacity. At present, this tends to be an increasingly predominant factor to explain the economic development of nations compared to more traditional productive factors, such as natural resources and capital goods. In this sense, it can be affirmed that labor training and education policies can play an important role in the growth of productivity in the economy and thus will be a relevant instrument for reducing informality.

The professional training of workers that provide their services in any of the forms we have mentioned is a fundamental aspect. If the formal education system does not provide adequate responses, either because it does not reach reasonable percentages or because its contents are inadequate, it is necessary to establish alternative channels that meet this need in a way that is in line with the demands of the production system, in addition to promoting measures that tend to fill the gaps. Strictly speaking, all possible modes of knowledge transmission should be used, without privileging some over others. The recognition of knowledge acquired through any of these channels must conclude with the due certification by the administrative labor authorities in a decentralized manner.

We understand that professional training should be part of employment policies. It should be used as a fundamental mechanism to socialize parts of the so-called cultural capital in the universe of those who work in the informal economy in order to improve their technological and productive capacity.

This concept makes it possible to value the encounter between informal segments and their spontaneous productive knowledge, built on their work experience, with other knowledge of actors in the modern, specialized, or scientific-technological sectors. Therefore, two things are both possible and desirable: to link the formal and modern sectors of the economy with the informal sector by means of programs to transfer cultural capital in processes of mutual positive influences, and to implement professional training policies to address the different logics (educational, productive, and social) that have been developing in our country. The implementation of this professional training should not only increase qualifications but also allow their progressive development and their adaptation according to changes in the production system and, at the same time, individual growth.

6. SMALL EMPLOYERS

The growth of a productive unit makes the lack of registration of both the unit and its workers unsustainable. Therefore, a sustained development program is, in itself, a path toward formalization. The situation of these productive units requires analyzing several factors that encourage informality.

In some cases, the lack of registration is not directly related to the consequences of labor regulations but to taxation in general. Certain production chains are highly informal almost throughout their entire length, which makes it difficult to find a solution that does not consider the particularities of that chain.

In cases where this situation does not occur, the results of some experiences should be reviewed to establish which alternatives are more likely to be successful.

In Argentina, a series of decreases in employer contributions were introduced for one region of the country. The boost to job creation and formalization was really low, as was the case with several previous initiatives in that sense.

It seems that the mere reduction of stable and predictable costs such as contributions, albeit important, is not enough to boost formalization. Two reasons seem to be the most relevant. The first is the instability of the company. As already mentioned, short cycles of growth followed by large downturns generate a sort of culture of informality; small companies are not sure that they will continue to exist in the coming years. The second is that the very situation of informality in employment necessarily generates workers' claims, compensation, and fines that have a financial impact on small units that is very difficult to assume, putting the very continuity of the productive unit at risk.

A possible way forward for small companies with up to five workers would be the combination of all these factors: A development model that allows temporary stability, lower costs, and a plan regarding the consequences of termination that, without leaving the worker unprotected, does not generate such strong impacts on their finances. Because foreseeable fixed costs do not seem to generate a problem, a scheme of monthly deposits in a worker's account whose balance is available regardless of the form of termination appears as a possible way forward. In a regime of this type, the scope of the protection against arbitrary dismissal provided by the Argentine constitution must be evaluated according to the current judicial interpretation to cover such a requirement without leaving the scheme of cost predictability. A generalization of a similar scheme is not advisable because the situation in large productive units is quite different.

As in other aspects where labor regulation comes into play, modifications must be generated through collective bargaining. This issue will be discussed specifically in section 10.

7. DECENTRALIZATION OF PRODUCTION AND NEW FORMS OF WORK

Technological evolution, especially, digitalization, information technology, and robotics, has been key to transforming the production model. The change brought about what might be called the fall of Fordism, a system that is now in crisis. As is well known, Fordism was a production system in which the entire process of manufacturing goods took place in a given space (the company), which integrated all the functions necessary for manufacturing the product. Subcontracting, outsourcing, or externalization were limited to activities that may be called peripheral (surveillance, cleaning, or food services).

This production system entailed a clear identification of the employer and constituted the factual foundation of a regulatory regime, which was based on the premise of the classic labor contract with a vocation of permanence and gave birth to centralized collective bargaining, which was activity based, with a vertical union. The traditional mode of production was based on equipment, systems, and workers and involved a rigid repetition of the tasks or the process itself.

Today, however, the new production design has replaced the manufacture of standardized products. Instead, a kind of dynamic and changing production has become widespread, which is typical of a postindustrial society with fluctuating and variable markets. The classic Fordist assembly line has now been replaced by computer-assisted design and manufacturing systems and digital media, which make it possible to outperform previous production standards.

The demand for competitiveness and productivity, as well as the requirement of adaptability to market fluctuations, gave rise to profound transformations in the model of labor relations. New technologies and modern patterns of production organization (diffuse factory, just in time, outsourcing) and their management methods had an impact on the labor market, causing job losses and, above all, a very high turnover that affected the homogeneity of the labor sector.

In line with the changes described above, there was a spread of contracting modalities consisting essentially of contractual types without a vocation of permanence. In addition, legal subordination, which is a key aspect of the employment contract in the classic doctrine, becomes less important in such contracting modalities and raises doubts about its existence, even though there is a clear economic dependence. New aspects, such as working at home (and no longer only teleworking, which was another typical work modality of the legal regimes), have generated controversy regarding their inclusion in the rules of protection, especially when they allow internal delegation.

Despite irrelevant differences, "decentralization," "outsourcing," and "externalization" are words that describe the new ways of organizing the production process. These are based on a management technique that involves contracting external business entities (which act as a kind of supplier) to take on multiple facets or activities of the company that exceed the concept of mere periphery (such as security or cleaning services).

A system is thus configured in which companies retain only what has been called core competence and delegate to other companies certain aspects of production that complete the final result. The computer metaphor of networked production is then used. The final product is no longer the epilogue of an organized activity with management unity in a given space but the result of the interrelation of several lean companies. In some activities, decentralization has been so intense that the existence of dependent companies has been maintained, which a classical conception of labor law considers an inadmissible contradiction.

The new production model highlights the outdated nature of the rules on subcontracting. It shows a crisis of adaptability, especially in Argentine law, which is based on the premise of an outdated concept of "main activity" or "essential activity" in order to extend financial liabilities to companies that were not the original employers. Therefore, the legal system must undergo a general revision in this respect.

The situation described above has produced a sort of atomization of the employer, who appears as a somewhat elusive figure, especially regarding interemployer contracts for specific works. In many cases, this generates a certain lack of definition among the collective partners that must be remedied to strengthen collective bargaining as the most suitable means of achieving adaptability and efficiency in the labor relations model.

There is also a very prominent change in the conception of working time and availability on the part of the workers themselves. They opt for modalities in which the autonomy of the will acquires relevance, and there is a tendency to negotiate the working day for fixed amounts, which calculate the payment without computing overtime and offer freedom of distribution and attendance. In reality, there are contracting typologies that could collide with the regulations and that should be analyzed with caution because they may constitute cases of fraud or avoidance of labor law.

The rapid spread of teleworking, whose intensity grew with the COVID-19 pandemic, is another phenomenon that deserves to be analyzed with a broad perspective, devoid of dogmatism. In Argentina, teleworking has been regulated by a specific legal norm that included it—as we have already pointed out—as a particular labor modality. It should be noted with particular emphasis that, beyond teleworking itself, there is a way of carrying out a task that is favored by the computer and relativizes the workplace, making it no longer essential both for the employer and for the worker. It is common to set objectives and deliveries that are made by computer, regardless of where they are carried out, in a sort of virtual piecework. An employer can contract a task under a dependency relationship and relative temporary permanence, and the worker can carry it out satisfactorily and efficiently in different places, either in Argentina or in other countries to which they may travel for any given reason. In a globalized economy, this specific aspect is not minor because it could generate debate on the applicable law. Both the Argentine law and Mercosur clearly establish that employment contracts are governed by the rules of the place where the work is performed. Thus, indifference to the place of work involves rethinking the rules of safety and even working time given the impossibility of control by the employer. What has been described above reveals the importance that must be given to collective autonomy in light of the insufficiency and ineffectiveness of heteronomous law, which lacks the adaptability to the multiple differing situations that reality imposes.

8. WORK PROVIDED THROUGH THE USE OF PLATFORMS

The so-called platform economy has given rise to a strong debate about the relationship between those who provide a service and the company that administers the platform. While the business sector argues that they only intermediate between those who provide and those who receive the service (use of the digital environment to bring supply and demand closer together), the workers' sector perceives a service that lacks the protection received by dependent employees that perform similar tasks. The workers consider that it is not possible to regard this work as independent because the possibility of autonomy is reduced to the workers' choice of the days and times of service.

This discussion has had different solutions worldwide (generally derived from court rulings rather than legislative decisions) that are difficult to extrapolate because of the marked differences in the regulation of employment contracts among the countries. Thus, Argentine legislation has little to do with its counterpart norm in the state of California or the United Kingdom, to cite only two examples where the issue has been raised.

Working through digital platforms is becoming increasingly important. The worker has no obligation to report to a workplace, and the employer has no monopoly in terms of setting the workday. Legally speaking, it is the worker who decides when and for how long to provide services. However, the platform administrator can decisively influence this choice through various mechanisms of rewards and punishments.

None of these situations fit easily within the provisions of the Argentine labor contract law. Workers in this situation lack any real protection during the term of the relationship. They may receive compensation at the time of termination of the relationship if they file a legal claim and obtain a favorable judgment. However, this delayed response of a favorable judicial decision fails to consider that the worker lacked the minimum protections during the entire term of the relationship, both in terms of economic rights and in terms of safety, health, and other benefits that characterize dependent work. The delayed response also does not consider that the percentage of workers who file claims upon termination is low, in addition to the fact that none of this has the slightest influence on the hiring of new workers under the same situation of labor precariousness.

Another aspect to consider regarding this form of work that is increasing rapidly and with no modification of this trend in sight refers to its strong implementation in tasks that require low qualifications on the part of the worker, and it continues to be a way of obtaining a first job. In countries with high unemployment rates for long periods of time, a particular phenomenon occurs in which young individuals with low qualification rates come from homes where their elders have not achieved integration through a formal job either.

An appropriate solution could be to recognize that there is a real employment contract, with an employer and a worker bound by a relationship with characteristics that require specific legislation. A contractual type in which some nonattendance does not result in the worker's breach could be helpful.

On the other hand, this sort of time sovereignty on the part of the worker would be limited. The employer would have the power to establish quotas and minimum working hours during which those who voluntarily log in under these conditions could not refuse the request for service.

In return, the worker would be entitled to a guaranteed salary for that workday, to receive payment for each service rendered; to the employer's duty of safety; to protection against occupational diseases and accidents; and to the remaining rights (sick leave, vacations, breaks, etc.) proportionate to the time of service rendered. Thus, the same categories of rights provided for in the labor contract law would be recognized, but the scope of the protection would be determined by the scope of the services rendered.

Of course, the enforcement of the worker's collective rights should be expressly included. Being part of a union with the right to bargain collectively and the right to strike are basic elements to achieve the protection and improvement of working conditions.

9. SELF-EMPLOYMENT AND POPULAR ECONOMY ORGANIZATIONS

Current regulations focus on salaried workers, while attention to self-employed workers has been relegated to the background. There are even certain public qualifications of this type of work as low quality, as something to overcome, even though the local and global trend is toward its growth. This is a demonstration of the mismatch between the mode of development of the production system and the regulations on the provision of work.

The issue to be resolved is how to ensure that these jobs are provided in a formal manner, with a certain degree of tax equity. In turn, consideration must also be given to how these workers may access certain social goods at a level similar to their dependent peers, as well as how they can access the institutionalization of their organizations.

To provide an idea of the importance of undertaking such a program, note that the number of informal selfemployed workers is twice the number of their formal counterparts: 3.3 million are unregistered while 1.6 million are registered.

Without pretending to have a detailed answer to this problem, we will indicate those points that should be considered in the attempt to mitigate this problem:

- Lack of enjoyment by the worker of the benefits of registration or of the disadvantages resulting from the lack of registration.
- Income instability.
- Welfare payment mechanisms that expire at a certain income level.
- Lack of interest on the part of the recipient of the services to have documents proving the payment made.

In Argentina, health and education services are free of charge for every inhabitant. For this reason, the lack of registration does not prevent inhabitants from having this social good; that is, there are no incentives in relation to such services. However, with the idea of generating an attraction for the formalization of these sectors, it was originally established that those registered in the simplified regime could have access to the health services of dependent workers (*obras sociales*, that is, union-managed health insurance). After several decades, this does not seem to have been a successful solution in terms of promoting formalization. In addition, it seems to have generated complex issues in terms of equity because the contribution made by the self-employed to the system is much lower than the average contribution made by the dependent workers, thus burdening the latter with financing the system.

Access to pension benefits also seems to be delayed, and the lack of registration does not deprive inhabitants of Argentina from accessing benefits. At least, they have access to the Pensión Universal para el Adulto Mayor (PUAM, Universal Benefit for the Elderly) or manage to enter the general regime with one of the repeated moratoriums. The benefit for those persons related to the worker with pension rights in case of the death of the worker, or for the workers themselves in case of disability, does not seem to act as a sufficient incentive.

As for the different social assistance mechanisms, the regime provides for their expiration at a certain level of income, which ends up being linked to the lack of registration or to income understatements. As for the recipient of the services, in the case of services rendered to the individual (basically, in the home) there is no interest in documenting the payment because it does not have an impact on reducing the tax burden.

Organizations representing this type of worker suggest that one way of providing an incentive is to allow registration without payment for an initial period, a mechanism that is already provided for in a couple of categories (mainly, the so-called *Monotributo social*, a special tax regime for small taxpayers) but without a term of validity; that is, those who enter this category may remain in it as long as they do not exceed a certain level of income.

An attempt to solve these limitations would basically include the following:

- Modifications to the simplified regime to eliminate some of these distortions: During the year 2021, the Administración Federal de Ingresos Públicos (AFIP, Federal Administration of Public Revenue) drafted a bill that is on the right track. One of the objectives proposed was to achieve the integration of small taxpayers who are informal workers whether they have been inactive for a long period, have just started activities, or are included in the Monotributo social. It provides for an initial stage exempt from payments or with reduced payments—with respect to both taxes and social security, the elimination of the current promoted categories (Monotributo social), and a progressive integration plan (inclusion bridge) to the simplified regime that also has modifications to achieve greater equity in terms of contribution. Regarding tax obligations, there should be a plan compatible with the instability of the income of these workers, with the required regulatory caution to avoid plain and simple noncompliance.
- Establishment of an impact on the tax burden of the person receiving the service, in the case of services not related to the generation of income, in which case such payments are deductible for income tax purposes: The deductions and nontaxable minimums of the so-called fourth category, which do not require proof of the expense, could be gradually limited in exchange for an increase in the deductible expenses for certain services received, basically made by means of bank transfers or other similar means of payment that allow them to be traced. While this may add complexity to the tax administration process, it could ultimately contribute to achieving the intended goals. The number of individuals subject to income tax has ranged in the last decade between 2,000,000 and 3,000,000. An increase in the size of this group, together with an equal extension of deductible expenses for services received, would improve the functioning of a control network if we consider that this

is the population with the highest consumption capacity of the services that are intended to be provided in a formal way. A scheme similar to the one applied to domestic work could be an appropriate tool.

- Changes in tax administration: The importance of this sector in terms of tax collection is not high; thus, the relationship between the administrative work required for its control and the benefit in terms of tax collection is not good. Therefore, this issue does not usually receive much attention; however, there should be a change of focus to value formalization itself as a way of closing the gap. As an initial step, a requirement could be set for every adult not registered in any tax category to answer a simple question: What do you do for a living? In some cases, the incentive, or rather the imposition, of a traceable means of payment is another way that has proven to be effective.
- Expansion of the benefits available to the registered self-employed worker: We have already indicated which benefits are already available or could be made available by being formally registered. A point that could generate some interest is to establish some type of income replacement benefit for the periods in which the worker is temporarily unable to perform their work because of a temporary disability. Although a design of this type presents great difficulties (inter alia, financing and requirements to avoid fraud), it appears to be a relatively uncomplicated means of promoting social welfare, particularly for individuals who rely solely on their own work, and it should be easy to implement.
- Access to professional training and certification of the knowledge acquired under the condition of formalizing the work of the self-employed: In this regard, unions representing salaried workers in trades similar to the self-employed should also participate, thus bringing this sector of workers closer to collective representation. For the user of these services, a practice of this type would provide some form of support to the service provider's technical capacity, while the service provider would incorporate a differential factor into their offer and the possibility of being part of a group dedicated to the defense and expansion of their rights as a worker.
- Technical assistance: The informal selfemployed worker requires assistance both with regard to their own trade or profession and with respect to their duties vis-à-vis the public sector.
- Access to credit: To be valued, this important social good requires certain macroeconomic conditions that are not always met. Formalization

alone clearly fails to achieve this goal, so there could be a form of incentive from the state to credit givers or directly through the use of public funds.

- Changes to the social welfare system regarding individuals in a situation of unemployment or labor informality: To prevent them from becoming an incentive for nonregistration, benefits of this type should be targeted and temporary with respect to the working-age population and with adequate conditions to perform productive tasks. A special point of discussion is the indigent population with low probabilities of insertion into the labor market in any of its forms. The Argentine experience shows that detecting specific cases through the use of state registries is very difficult. The prevalence of informality makes it difficult to distinguish between those who are truly indigent and those who are simply not registered but engaged in profitable activities. The design of a welfare mechanism for these cases should include the provision of some verifiable service or training for their insertion. The expiration modes should provide for the assumption of the rejection of job offers made through public systems. In short, these welfare plans should move closer to unemployment insurance with the characteristics that they have, to a greater or lesser extent, in most of the developed world.
- Workers in the popular economy: Workers in the popular economy and basic subsistence are considered to be those who work individually or collectively to generate personal and family income, whether they are selfemployed workers; workers who perform casual or occasional tasks; street vendors; occupants of street stalls; individuals engaged in waste recovery or care work in community places, such as kindergartens and canteens; sellers at small fairs; family farmers; sellers of handicrafts; (informal) car minders; shoeshine workers; workers in cooperatives; small entrepreneurs promoted by social programs and all those individuals who, under simislar contractual types and without any relationship that would characterize the link as an employment contract, participate in the process of the production of goods and services in asymmetrical relationships in order to subsist.

Within the scope of the obligations assumed by Argentina in the International Covenant on Economic, Social and Cultural Rights and in the Additional Protocol to the American Convention on Human Rights in the Area of Economic, Social and Cultural Rights (aka the Protocol of San Salvador), and with the objective of preserving social peace, it is possible to adopt specific measures to guarantee the right of every person to have the opportunity to earn a living by means that ensure them decent living conditions and to form associations that represent them. Thus, in Argentina, a legal framework has been given to these new subjects that act as interlocutors and exercise their collective representation, allowing the channeling of petitions and initiatives for development in a legal environment. This is in line with the Social Protection Floors Recommendation, 2012 (No. 202), adopted by the 101st International Labour Conference of the ILO, which suggests that member states carry out suitable measures to assist the most vulnerable sectors, expressly including those of the informal economy.

Therefore, a system has been designed to make it possible to exercise the right of these sectors to form associations for the achievement of the purposes discussed in this chapter. These associations conceptualize them as interlocutors, reaffirming their belonging to the world of work in its broadest sense and under all the forms it may assume, in view of the need for a general approach to all those activities whose purpose is to obtain basic income for subsistence.

10. COLLECTIVE AUTONOMY AS AN APPROPRIATE RESPONSE

In Argentina, collective bargaining has historically provided adequate solutions to complex problems and continues to do so today. In 2022, about 6 million jobs were covered by a collective labor regulation for the determination of working conditions (collective bargaining agreements or other collective regulations), which amounts to 92 percent of the total number of registered private sector jobs (6.5 million jobs).

In an ever-changing situation, as described above, it is necessary to have an agile tool that allows for adequate harmony between the preservation and extension of workers' rights and the needs of the different production systems. The regulation of labor relations by heteronomous means alone may not be sufficient to achieve this ability of mutation. However, it should determine the framework within which bargaining is possible, both in its formal aspects (subjects, requirements) and in its substance, that is, which workers' rights cannot be negotiated.

In contrast, collective autonomy meets all the conditions to fulfill this role. As a consequence of the economic framework and the existence of high inflation, most of the discussions are focused unfortunately on the wage issue. This does not invalidate the tool of collective bargaining, however, which is useful to address other aspects, as has indeed been the case in many activities.

In this regard, the following aspects should be emphasized:

- Wider availability to favor collective bargaining agreements in terms of work organization (working hours, leave, remote work, temporary and casual employment, trial periods): The emergence of teleworking, which has already been legally regulated in Argentina, and the advance of digital tools in all branches of activity are radically changing the way work is organized. The idea of having a single uniform regulation for all sectors on these points does not seem appropriate under these new conditions. Of course, aspects related to psychophysical health and the physical and emotional effects on the workers must be preserved. The same applies to the issue of occupational health and safety. It is unlikely that any one piece of legislation will accurately cover all the needs in every sector of the economy. A clear general framework and a greater capacity for agreement by sector or collective instances of confederations by sector are more appropriate to achieve an effective result.
- The regulation of relations in small companies with up to five workers: As already pointed out, the agreement is key to ensure that any changes in terms of the consequences of the termination of the employment contract or other contractual elements be done within the framework of negotiation. This is the only way for such a change to generate adequate protection and social legitimacy.
- Productivity as a central objective of bargaining: In Argentina, "productivity" has become associated—as we warned above—with the simple intensification of tasks and a flexible approach to workers' rights when in fact what could be achieved is exactly the opposite. The correct approach to this concept involves a discussion of the best working conditions and environment, workers' participation in the organization of the production system, sectoral professional training, and an equitable distribution of the economic result of productivity growth.

REFERENCES

Tokman, V. 2001. "De la informalidad a la modernidad." *Economia*, 24(48): 153–178. https://doi.org/10.18800/economia.200102.005.

Porta, F. 2015. "Trayectorias de cambio estructural y enfoques de política industrial: una propuesta a partir del caso argentino." In *Neoestructuralismo y corrientes heterodoxas en América Latina y el Caribe a inicios del siglo XXI*, edited by A. Bárcena and A. Prado. Libros de la CEPAL.

Bárcena, A. and A. Prado. 2015. *Neoestructuralismo y corrientes heterodoxas en América Latina y el Caribe a inicios del siglo XXI*. Libros de la CEPAL. https://repositorio.cepal.org/entities/publication/e4cc9753-9cf2-4441-97ee-6822d73552b7.

CHAPTER 5

Digital Technologies, Global Value Chains, and Skill-Segmentation of the Workforce

EVIDENCE FROM THE APPAREL SECTOR IN INDIA AND BANGLADESH

Karisma Banga[1]

Abstract: This chapter examines how digitalization and international trade are shaping the skill structure of the apparels manufacturing workforce in emerging economies. Using data from the World Bank Enterprise Survey (WBES) on 1,381 firms from India and Bangladesh, the chapter empirically examines the impact of firm digitalization and trade linkages on the share of middle-skilled workers in employment and the share of middle-skilled workers relative to other skill categories. Digitalization is captured using the share of digital sales in total sales, while trade linkages are captured using the participation of firms in global value chains (GVCs) and their exposure to global end-markets. To address issues of endogeneity, an instrumental variable approach with two-stage least squares is used. Empirical results reveal a contrasting effect: firms linked into GVCs are found to have a significantly higher share of middle-skilled workers relative to high-skilled workers than non-GVC firms, while digitalization is found to have a negative impact on the ratio of the share of middle-skilled to high-skilled workers. This contrasting effect highlights the need for emerging economies to develop coherent digital industrial policies.

1. INTRODUCTION

The apparel manufacturing sector has been critical for job creation in many emerging economies, with developing country firms embedded in apparel global value chains (GVCs) predominantly as suppliers. These GVCs have traditionally been set up, coordinated, and controlled by large branded manufacturers and retailers with headquarters in the

Global North—known as the lead firms. Higher value-added processes of research and development (R&D), design, and retail tend to be kept in-house with the lead firms, while the lower value-added, labor-intensive manufacturing processes are offshored to developing countries in the Global South (López 2023). However, new geo-economic and geo-political dynamics are rapidly challenging the GVC-led manufacturing growth model in the garment industry for emerging economies. After 2015, there has been a slowdown in global trade, in part because of rising automation of production in developed economies, rising wages in Asian economies, increasing US-China tensions, and the shift within China from export-driven manufacturing to domestic markets. The last few years have further exposed the vulnerabilities of GVC apparel trade to pandemic-induced supply- and demand-side economic shocks. Some lead firms responded by fast-automating their supply-chains to increase resilience to economic shocks (Winkler and Seric 2020), while others took to alternative strategies for maintaining flexibility, including near-sourcing, friend-shoring, or even reshoring of production (Berg et al. 2020). This has increased concerns among scholars over the comparative advantage of developing economies in labor-intensive apparel manufacturing, especially given with the rise of new technologies (Rodrik 2018; Banga and Faith 2021).

Albeit low compared to the other sectors, the growing digitalization of apparel production will have important employment implications for emerging country supplier firms. These are likely to be both direct effects (supplier firm digitalization and automation) and indirect effects (through lead firm digitalization and automation) on employment outcomes. While the literature on digitalization and its impact on employment in developing economies is growing, the evidence on how digitalization is changing the skill structure of the workforce remains scant. In this chapter, I address this gap by using the newly released World Bank Enterprise Survey (WBES 2023) data to examine digitalization and skill segmentation in the apparel manufacturing sector of India and Bangladesh. These countries make for interesting case studies: the apparel sector accounts for a significant share in total employment in both India and Bangladesh and forms the backbone of employment for micro-small and medium enterprises (MSMEs), women workers, and informal employment. Yet the two economies differ in terms of their engagement in garment manufacturing GVCs and digital capabilities. Bangladesh is closely linked to the apparel value chains, with growth driven by ready-made garments

(RMGs) (Swazan and Das 2022). Much of the success of its RMG sector lies in a vast labor force pool, lower wages compared to other countries, suitable locations, and targeted export interventions by the government of Bangladesh (Zaman 2021; Hasan et al. 2020; Swazan and Das 2022). Despite being one of the largest exporters of RMG and despite its digital prowess, India remains less linked into apparel GVCs, in part because of low ability to attract Foreign Direct Investment (FDI) in this sector, greater orientation toward the domestic market, and archaic labor laws (Banga 2022b).

Section 2 reviews the broad literature on digitalization, employment, and skill structure. Section 3 presents the data and methodology used in this chapter. Section 4 presents empirical results, and Section 5 concludes by comparing the results with other studies.

2. DIGITALIZATION, EMPLOYMENT, AND WORKFORCE SEGMENTATION IN EMERGING ECONOMIES

Studies analyzing the employment implications of digitalization are largely based on developed economy contexts and reveal a lack of consensus. Some studies find a job creation effect (Gregory et al. 2016; Aghion et al., 2020), while others indicate a labor substitution effect (Acemoglu and Restrepo 2017; Dauth et al. 2017; Mann and Püttmann 2018). Firm-level evidence from the apparel sector in Kenya and South Africa, both developing countries, suggests some increases in employment linked to productivity gains through digitalization of supplier firms (Banga and te Velde 2018; Parschau and Hauge 2020). Digital technologies can lead to job losses in some manufacturing tasks but create new jobs in others. For example, the deployment of modern cutting lasers in the A-Z garment factory in Tanzania displaced workers engaged in cutting, but the resultant productivity gains in this area of operations led to greater output and created jobs in the next stage, that is, stitching, and created overall net employment gains in the factory (Banga and te Velde 2018). Interviews with apparel manufacturing firms in Bangladesh revealed that automation increased productivity and growth, and subsequently employment in clothing firms (Hoque et al. 2022). However, unskilled employment is expected to decrease in the long run when automation is well adopted within the system (Hoque et al. 2022). Given the required dexterity in handling and stitching fabrics, the sewing jobs in garment manufacturing—largely dominated by women workers (Bamber and Staritz 2016;

Barrientos 2019)—have been relatively protected from automation thus far. Experts predict, however, that the window of opportunity in garment manufacturing is about fifteen to twenty years, after which digital automation in sewing could also become relevant for a significant portion of the clothing industry (Altenburg et al. 2020). Successful trials of Sewbots indicate that robots could soon eliminate the roles of tailors and sewing machine operators, which account for as much as 65 percent of the garment industry's workforce in India (Vashisht and Rani 2020).

Employment in garment supplier firms will also be affected through digital-led reconfiguration of GVCs. First, lead companies in developed economies are rapidly investing in digital production technologies, which could bring down their own costs of production and kick-start reshoring. It is anticipated that the use of robotics will reduce the unit labor cost of producing a cotton shirt in the United States and Europe to around 40 to 50 cents (Vashisht and Rani 2020), the same as India (at 50 cents) but still higher than Bangladesh (20 cents). However, the average monthly incomes in Bangladeshi manufacturing have been on the rise, increasing by 3.1 percent in 2018 from 2013 (Gu et al. 2021). With rising wages and a persistent digital divide with lead firms, India, Bangladesh, and several other developing economies could lose their competitive edge in labor-intensive manufacturing, leading to reshoring or limited future offshoring of garment manufacturing (Vashisht and Rani 2020). While significant reshoring has not yet occurred (Mattos et al 2020) because of factors such as the geographic proximity of clothing manufacturing countries and the input material supply chain (Parschau and Hauge 2020), data from the Reshoring Initiative 2020 shows that the number of apparel manufacturing jobs being reshored to the United States more than quadrupled between 2015 and 2020, with the number of job losses per company engaged in reshoring jumping from fifty-four to eighty-eight workers in just five years (Banga and Faith 2021). The potential reconfiguring of garment value chains is likely to disproportionately affect women workers who tend to be concentrated in low-skill and routine tasks (Banga and Faith 2021).

Second, lead firms are also investing in digitalization of tasks traditionally done in-house, such as apparel designing and product development, which in turn could affect suppliers down the value chain. For example, Levi Strauss has invested in digital imaging and automation of the finishing tasks in its jeans. Designers in its San Francisco factory send digital files to the depot, where lasers mass-produce customized jeans within minutes, which can then be delivered to nearby customers. While automation of finishing tasks does not directly take away jobs from developing countries, the subsequent increase in cost competitiveness and the growing demand for mass customizable production could lead to Levi's bringing other manufacturing tasks that have been offshored closer to home (Banga and te Velde 2018). Jeonologia, a Spanish tech company, reshored some of Levi's production facilities to the United States while reducing resource consumption and lead time (Martínez-Mora and Merino 2020). The use of collaborative robots could lead to significant job displacement and reduction in working hours in garment manufacturing (Mattos et al. 2020).

Third, in many cases, the motivation or pressure on the supplier to digitalize comes from the lead firm itself. In the era of digital capitalism, traditional lead firms such as H&M and Zara are facing competition from ultra-fast born-digital firms such as BooHoo and Oh Polly, which have digitally integrated, highly demand-driven, and cost-efficient supply chains (Brun et al. 2019). This has created incentives for Zara and H&M to integrate their offline and online sales to enhance the speed, flexibility, and cost efficiency of their supply chains (López et al. 2022). This pressure is transferred onto suppliers in terms of a push toward digital technologies in production and coordination (Brun et al. 2019) and a pressure to keep wages down to retain competitiveness.

In terms of the impact of digitalization and automation on the skill composition of the workforce, there appears to be a consensus that developed economies have hollowed out. At the country level, digitalization has contributed to a decline in the demand of middle-skilled workers relative to low- and high-skilled workers (see Autor et al. 2006; Goos and Manning 2007; Autor and Dorn 2013; Goos et al. 2014; Beaudry et al. 2016). The key explanation for this polarization is routinization; middle-skilled workers such as machine operators and assembly line workers are engaged in occupations that consist of routine tasks that can be automated more easily. In contrast, high-skilled workers perform nonroutine tasks that can complement technology—for instance, research and development and professional services (Beaudry et al. 2016), while low-skilled workers perform nonroutine manual tasks that are harder to automate.

Much less is known about job polarization in the context of developing economies. At a macro level, Banga et al. (2023) find that digitalization has reduced the overall share of the manufacturing sector in total employment, contributing to deindustrialization in low- and middle-income countries. Several scholars find evidence of skill-biased technological change in developing economies. For example, the adoption of information and communication technology (ICT) in Argentinian manufacturing between 2010 and 2012 increased employment levels across all skills categories, with the effect being largest for skilled workers (Brambilla and Tortarolo 2018). Similarly, in African countries, broadband increased the share of skilled jobs (Hjort and Poulsen 2019). For a panel of forty-two countries in the period 2001–2017, including developing countries like India, South Africa, Thailand, Malaysia, Mexico, Indonesia, China and others, Jung and Lim (2020) found that extensive use of industrial robots suppressed employment growth, disproportionately affecting low-skilled labor. In Chilean manufacturing, Almeida et al. (2018) find digital-induced deskilling between 2007 and 2013, but in the case of China, mechanization of agriculture led to a rise in routine employment (World Bank 2016). In some cases, job polarization has also been observed, such as in Brazil, Mexico, and Chile (Maloney and Molina 2016; Messina et al. 2016). Banga and te Velde (2019) conclude that the impact of automation on the skill structure of the labor market will depend on several factors, including globalization, relative price of investment goods, labor frictions, and institutional differences affecting relative wages.

3. DATA CONSTRUCTION AND EMPIRICAL STRATEGY

Analysis of digitalization and skill segmentation in this chapter is based on data from the textile and garment manufacturing firms in India and Bangladesh, captured in the latest round of WBES (2023). Firm-level data across the two countries are coded, merged, and cleaned. We are left with a cross-sectional data set of 1,381 firms, reporting on key variables for the year 2022. Of these, 668 firms are in the garment sector, and 713 engaged in the manufacturing of textiles. The summary statistics of the data set is provided in the appendix to this chapter, and the construction of key variables is given below.

3.1 DEPENDENT VARIABLE

Skill segmentation at the firm level is captured using (1) the share of middle-skilled workers in total full-time employment; (2) the ratio of the share of middle-skilled workers to the share of low-skilled workers; and (3) the ratio of the share of middle-skilled workers to the share of high-skilled workers. From the appendix, it is noted that, on an average, a firm in textile and manufacturing has 15 percent of low-skilled workers (in tasks that require no specialized knowledge), 22 percent of semi-skilled or middle-skilled workers (in tasks requiring some level of mechanical or technical knowledge), and 43 percent of high-skilled workers (in tasks requiring extensive theoretical and technical knowledge).

3.2 FIRM-LEVEL DIGITALIZATION

Firm digitalization is captured by the share of internet/ digital sales in total sales. This involves the use of internet and digital platforms to conduct business-to-business (B2B) transactions (e.g., sourcing cheaper fabrics) and business-to-consumer (B2C) transactions (e.g., e-commerce). The use of online platforms is a key form of digital integration and captures new models of value creation and capture. Some firms in garment GVCs use enhanced data collection and data sharing, processing, and analysis to build highly flexible and integrated online and offline retail supply chains (Azevedo and Carvalho 2012; Yip and Huang 2016). In the appendix, 53.5 percent of firms in the sample have basic digital capabilities; that is, they have their own website and/or use social media, and 17 percent of sales, on average, are conducted digitally. Almost 60 percent of the Indian garment manufacturing firms have basic digital capabilities compared to 42 percent of Bangladeshi garments firms (figure 5.1).

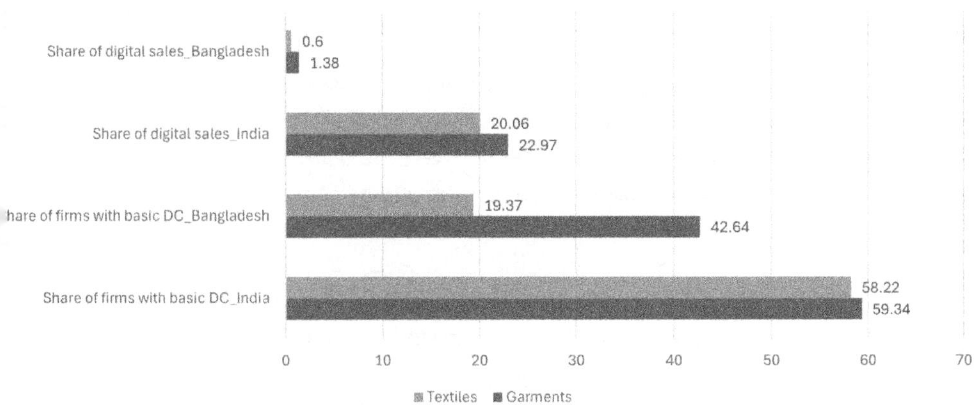

Figure 5.1 Distribution of digital capabilities across stages of apparel global value chains (GVCs, in %)

Source: Author, data set constructed from World Bank Enterprise Survey (WBES, 2023)

The gap is even more stark in the case of textile firms, where 58 percent of Indian firms report basic digital capabilities compared to less than 20 percent of Bangladeshi firms. On average, 20 to 22 percent of sales are conducted online in Indian textile and garment firms compared to less than 2 percent in Bangladeshi firms.

3.3 TRADE LINKAGES

A firm's participation in GVCs is used to capture its exposure to international pressures and dynamics, which can influence it's skill structure. The WBES reports information on direct and indirect export shares of total sales, which are added to arrive at total export shares of each textile and garment manufacturing firm. The survey also reports on the percentage of material inputs or suppliers of the firm that are of foreign origin, which refers to imports of intermediate goods by the firms as a share in total intermediate purchases. From this, a new dummy variable called GVC firm is created to identify firms participating in textile and manufacturing GVCs. Following the approach of Baldwin and Yan (2014) and Banga (2022a 2023), the GVC firm dummy = 1 for firms that are simultaneously importing intermediates and exporting. It is noted that only 10 percent of firms are classified as GVC firms.

The WBES also allows us to identify the primary end-markets of the firm, which can further account for the exposure of Indian and Bangladeshi firms to global lead firms. Using this information, a categorical variable called Type of trader is created, which is 0 for domestic firms that are not engaged in any international trade (or minimally engaged, i.e., less than 0.1 percent of sales are exported); 1 for one-way traders, whose main product primarily serves the global market; 2 for one-way traders, whose main product primarily serves the local/national market; 3 for GVC firms, whose main product primarily serves the global market; and 4 for GVC whose main product primarily serves the local/national market. Analyzing digital capabilities across these traders, it is noted that, in the case of Indian GVC firms with the international market as the main market for main product, 32 percent of sales, on average, are conducted online compared to only 19 percent of sales in Indian domestic firms (table 5.1).

Table 5.1 Average share of digital sales, across type of trader (%)

	Indian firms	Bangladeshi firms
Domestic firms	19.90	0.85
One-way traders, supplying main product primarily globally	23.45	1.96
One-way traders, supplying main product primarily locally and/or nationally	23.21	0.29
GVC firms, supplying main product primarily globally	32.18	1.09
GVC firms, supplying main product primarily locally and/or nationally	22.57	3.00

3.4 ECONOMETRIC MODEL AND EMPIRICAL STRATEGY

To examine the impact of digitalization empirically on skill segmentation at the firm level, the following baseline econometric models are estimated:

$$MS\_share_i = a_1 Share\_digital\, sales_i + a_2 Trade\, linkages_i + a_3 foreign\, equity_i + X_i + u_y + u_c + u_s \ldots \quad (1)$$

$$MS\_share\, /\, HS\_share_i = a_1 Share\, digital\, sales_i + a_2 Trade\, linkages_i + a_3 foreign\, equity_i + X_i + u_y + u_c + u_s \ldots \quad (2)$$

$$MS\_share\, /\, LS\_share_i = a_1 Share\, digital\, sales_i + a_2 Trade\, linkages_i + a_3 foreign\, equity_i + X_i + u_y + u_c + u_s \ldots \quad (3)$$

where

MS_share = the share of middle-skilled workers in total full-time employment

MS_share/LS_share = the ratio of share of middle-skilled workers to low-skilled workers

MS_share/HS_share = the ratio of share of middle-skilled workers to high-skilled workers. An increase in the main explanatory variable *Share_ digital sales* indicates a higher use of digital platforms and higher digital capabilities at the firm level. Trade linkages are captured by different variables, such as participation in GVCs, and types of traders. X_i is a vector of firm-level control variables, such as firm size, innovation status, sales basket concentration, and machinery upgrades. We further control for industry, country, and state effects.

In analyzing the causal relationship between digital sales and skill structures, we face the problem of endogeneity because of reverse causality. Firms with a higher share of skilled workers are more likely to adopt digital technologies and build digital capabilities. To reduce endogeneity in our model, we run equation 1 using a dummy variable called 'Predominantly digital firm' to capture digitalization. Predominantly digital firm = 1 for firms in which the majority of sales (more than 50 percent) are through online channels, and 0 otherwise. While this is expected to reduce endogeneity, we further check the robustness of results for equations 1 to 3 using instrumental variable regressions with two-stage least squares (IV-2SLS). We exploit external instruments in our data set, which we expect to be correlated with the level of digitalization in the firm (the endogenous variable) but not with the skill structure (dependent variable), except through the endogenous variable.

The first instrument we test is the share of digitalized firms in the state to which the firm belongs, that is, the share of firms having a web presence or using social media in the state. The second instrument is the average share of digital sales in the state to which the firm belongs. Both these variables capture the relative level of digitalization of the state to which the firm belongs. Third, we use information on internet issues in the WBES and construct a state-level variable measuring the average incidences of insufficient internet access in a typical month. This captures the overall quality of digital infrastructure at the state level and is expected to be negatively and significantly correlated with share of digital sales at the firm level but uncorrelated with the skill structure across firms. The fourth instrument is the average share of digital sales in the industry to which the firm belongs. We exploit information on four-digit International Standard Industrial Classification of All Economic Activities (ISIC) codes in the enterprise survey to construct the average share of digital sales across subindustries within textile and manufacturing. Firms belonging to more digitalized states and sub-industries are likely to have spillovers in terms of technology, knowledge, and learning effects, and therefore these instruments are expected to be correlated to a firm's digitalization level. However, these instruments are measured at the state/industry level and are therefore not expected to be affected by the skill structure at the firm-level.

The tests for endogeneity of variables, overidentifying restrictions, and exogeneity of instruments are conducted to ensure the validity of instruments. A *p* value on Sargan's (1958) and Basmann's (1960) χ 2 test statistic above 0.05 indicates that the null hypothesis of the instruments being valid cannot be rejected at 5 percent. For excluded exogenous variables to be valid instruments, they should be sufficiently correlated with the included endogenous regressors but uncorrelated with the error term. In the case of weak instruments, the 2SLS estimators are biased and therefore inferences could be misleading. The postestimation command "estat firststage" produces several statistics for judging the explanatory power of the instruments. An *F* statistic above 10 with a significant *p* value (less than 0.05) confirms the joint significance of external instruments (Stock et al. 2002, 109–120). The *F* statistic is then compared to the critical values obtained for the 2SLS size of nominal 5 percent Wald test (Stock and Yogo 2005). If the test statistic exceeds the critical value, we can conclude that the set of instruments is not weak.

4. EMPIRICAL RESULTS

Table 5.2 presents results from equation 1, with the dependent variable capturing the share of middle-skilled workers in total firm employment. Model 1 finds that the share of digital sales is negatively and significantly related to the middle-skill share, implying that more digitalized firms have a significantly lower share of middle-skilled workers in total employment. This result is robust to the addition of control variables in models 2 and 3. Model 4 replaces the continuous endogenous variable with a dummy variable. Note that predominantly digital firms (with over 50 percent of sales being digital) have a significantly lower share of middle-skilled workers in total employment than other firms. Models 5–7 present results of IV-2SLS regressions, in which the endogenous variable—Sh_digital sales—is correlated with the instrument "share of digital firms in the industry" and the instrument "average internet failure incidents" in the state to which the firm belongs. Even after accounting for the endogenous variable, it is noted that the coefficient on Sh_digital sales is significant and negative. The coefficient on foreign equity is also negative, implying that firms with a higher share of foreign equity tend to have a lower share of middle-skilled workers.

The coefficients on both variables linking into GVCs and machinery upgrades indicate a positive and significant effect on middle-skilled

Table 5.2 Dependent variable: Medium-skilled workers, share in total employment (%)

Variables	Model 1	Model 2	Model 3	Model 4	Model 5 IV-2SLS	Model 6 IV-2SLS	Model 7 IV-2SLS
Sh_digital sales	−0.0336*	−0.0326*	−0.0361*		−0.493***	−0.310***	−0.310***
	(0.0196)	(0.0194)	(0.0200)		(0.174)	(0.0823)	(0.0804)
GVC firm	5.563***						
	(1.683)						
Predominantly digital firm				-3.065*			
				(1.564)			
One-way, global market		7.111***	4.910**	7.099***	7.337**	6.511**	6.511**
		(1.993)	(2.180)	(1.986)	(3.560)	(2.966)	(2.965)
One-way, local market		0.834	0.531	0.738	−0.107	0.403	0.401
		(1.277)	(1.295)	(1.283)	(2.263)	(2.023)	(2.031)
GVC, global market		13.97***	11.95***	13.95***	16.39***	12.34***	12.34***
		(2.506)	(2.664)	(2.507)	(3.770)	(3.170)	(3.171)
GVC, local market		1.282	1.426	1.125	1.325	0.243	0.241
		(1.994)	(2.221)	(2.018)	(2.347)	(2.467)	(2.482)
Machinery upgrade		1.886*	1.729*	1.911*	4.108***	3.241***	3.241***
		(1.000)	(1.048)	(1.000)	(1.356)	(1.250)	(1.249)
Innovative firm		0.404	1.312	0.536	1.336	2.172	2.170
		(1.792)	(1.879)	(1.802)	(3.494)	(3.929)	(3.922)
Medium firm	-1.418	−0.239	−0.0995	−0.235	−2.066	−2.406	-2.403
	(1.048)	(1.055)	(1.080)	(1.053)	(2.007)	(1.736)	(1.716)

Small firm	0.259	1.950*	1.294	1.896	1.585	–2.571	–2.565
	(1.165)	(1.174)	(1.218)	(1.181)	(2.380)	(2.005)	(1.950)
Foreign equity	–0.0539	–0.0815	–0.0855*	–0.0835	–0.203***	–0.145**	–0.145**
	(0.0650)	(0.0612)	(0.0437)	(0.0606)	(0.0621)	(0.0629)	(0.0629)
Wage rate	–0.0187	–0.0204	–0.00338	–0.0241	–0.0295	0.00568	0.00568
	(0.0258)	(0.0270)	(0.0277)	(0.0272)	(0.0293)	(0.0940)	(0.0938)
Firm age							0.000800
							(0.0469)
i. Indian firm	12.37**	10.61*	17.74**	9.992*	15.13***	24.90	24.90
	(5.981)	(6.025)	(7.595)	(6.005)	(3.721)	(53.39)	(41.48)
State FE	Yes	Yes	Yes	Yes	No	Yes	Yes
Subindustry FE	No	No	Yes	No	Yes	Yes	Yes
Broad sector FE	Yes	Yes	No	Yes	No	No	No
Constant	8.084	4.555	4.774	4.826	13.82**	7.170	7.143
	(5.203)	(5.832)	(6.045)	(5.820)	(5.390)	(6.422)	(6.658)
Observations	1,320	1,235	1,235	1,235	897	897	897

Notes: Robust standard errors in parentheses *** $p < 0.01$, ** $p < 0.05$, * $p < 0.1$. FE refers to fixed effects. The variable i.Indian firm refers to a dummy variable =1 for firms in India. Results from the endogeneity test confirm that we cannot rule out that the variable Sh_digital sales is endogenous, and therefore there is a need to use instruments. The result of the overidentification test in model 5 shows a p value above 0.05, which means that we fail to reject the H0 of overidentifying restrictions. The F statistic is significant, greater than 10 and greater than the LIML size of nominal 5 percent Wald statistics at all levels, and greater than 2SLS size of nominal 5 percent Wald test at 15 percent, 20 percent, and 25 percent.

employment shares. The coefficient on the GVC firm dummy in model 1 indicates that, on an average, the share of middle-skilled workers in total employment is 5.5 percent higher in GVC firms than non-GVC firms. Models 2–4 disaggregate across type of traders and end-markets and find that the share of middle-skilled workers is significantly higher in both one-way traders and GVC firms that supply their main product primarily to the global market, compared to domestic firms that are not engaged in international trade. These results hold in the IV-2SLS regressions.

Table 5.3 presents results of middle-skilled employment shares relative to other skill categories. The dependent variable in models 1–3 is ratio *MS_share/HS_share (hereon MS/HS)*, and the dependent variable in models 4–6 is *MS_share/LS_share (hereon MS/LS)*. In the IV-2SLS regressions, the variable firm-level Sh_digital sales is instrumented by the average level of digital sales in the industry and the average level of digital sales in the state to which the firm belongs. While we find weak evidence of a negative effect of digitalization on *MS/LS* in the OLS regression, the coefficient on Sh_digital sales is negative and significant for *MS/HS* across models 1–3, indicating that more digitalized firms have a significantly lower share of medium-skilled workers relative to high-skilled workers. This indicates a skill bias of digitalization in garment manufacturing; high-skilled workers perform nonroutine tasks that can complement technology—for instance, research and development and professional services—while middle-skilled workers perform routine tasks that are easier to automate (Beaudry et al. 2016).

While no significant effect of trade linkages is observed for the *MS/LS* ratio, both one-way traders and GVC firms supplying their main product primarily to the global market have a significantly higher *MS/HS* ratio compared to domestic firms, indicating that exposure to global markets have increased the share of middle-skilled work in textile and manufacturing factories relative to high-skilled work. Together, these findings could be indicative of a shift in skill structure driven by functional specialization. Developing country firms typically integrate into the lower value-added stages, such as cut-and-trim, assembly, and finishing. GVC linkages drive the demand for middle-skilled workers—such as machine operators and production planners—in developing countries to meet international standards and ensure production efficiency. There could also be a potential functional de-skilling of work, where middle-skilled workers are performing roles previously done by high-skilled staff, due to the modularized and standardized task structures in GVCs. A similar

Table 5.3 Dependent variable: Share of MS workers to other skill categories

Dependent variable	Model 1 OLS MS/HS	Model 2 IV-2SLS MS/HS	Model 3 IV-2SLS MS/HS	Model 4 OLS MS/LS	Model 5 IV-2SLS MS/LS	Model 6 IV-2SLS MS/LS
Sh_digital sales	−0.00700***	−0.0584**	−0.0203***	−0.00904***	0.0140	0.0154
	(0.00254)	(0.0264)	(0.00417)	(0.00260)	(0.0139)	(0.0142)
GVC firm			1.305***			0.0203
			(0.487)			(0.192)
One-way, global market	1.475***	1.432***		0.256	0.310	
	(0.550)	(0.556)		(0.234)	(0.247)	
One-way, local market	0.149	0.0826		−0.236	−0.147	
	(0.175)	(0.230)		(0.155)	(0.180)	
GVC, global market	3.217***	2.997***		0.277	0.344	
	(0.789)	(0.812)		(0.233)	(0.283)	
GVC, local market	−0.0836	−0.210		−0.260	−0.174	
	(0.252)	(0.375)		(0.238)	(0.271)	
Innovative firm	−0.460**	−0.612**	−0.640***	0.142	0.124	0.0569
	(0.226)	(0.286)	(0.245)	(0.335)	(0.336)	(0.317)
Percentage sales of main product		0.0173***	0.0129**		−0.00259	−0.00251
		(0.00602)	(0.00508)		(0.00354)	(0.00363)
Machinery upgrades		0.506***	0.606***		0.0994	0.116
		(0.181)	(0.189)		(0.149)	(0.149)
Medium firm	−0.625***	−0.700***	−0.728***	−0.246*	−0.198	−0.216
	(0.193)	(0.241)	(0.220)	(0.147)	(0.152)	(0.150)

(*continued*)

Table 5.3 (*continued*)

Dependent variable	Model 1 OLS MS/HS	Model 2 IV-2SLS MS/HS	Model 3 IV-2SLS MS/HS	Model 4 OLS MS/LS	Model 5 IV-2SLS MS/LS	Model 6 IV-2SLS MS/LS
Small firm	-0.582***	-0.981***	-0.869***	-0.338**	-0.0322	-0.0406
	(0.201)	(0.373)	(0.237)	(0.155)	(0.220)	(0.208)
Age		0.00854	0.00505		-0.00225	-0.00471
		(0.00658)	(0.00529)		(0.00477)	(0.00533)
Foreign equity	-0.0302*	-0.0312*	-0.0207	-0.00547	-0.00403	-0.00271
	(0.0155)	(0.0177)	(0.0140)	(0.00770)	(0.00737)	(0.00742)
Wage rate	-0.00670*	-0.00172	-0.00640	-0.00196	-0.00572*	-0.00600*
	(0.00386)	(0.00509)	(0.00794)	(0.00259)	(0.00319)	(0.00311)
i. Indian firm	Yes	Yes	Yes	Yes	Yes	Yes
Sub-industry FE	No	No	Yes	No	No	No
State FE	Yes	Yes	Yes	Yes	Yes	Yes
Broad sector FE	Yes	Yes	No	Yes	Yes	Yes
Constant	1.439***	-0.144	0.822	1.472***	1.365***	1.564***
	(0.377)	(0.755)	(0.870)	(0.308)	(0.420)	(0.436)
Observations	1,257	1,215	1,251	986	959	989

Notes: Robust standard errors in parentheses *** $p < 0.01$, ** $p < 0.05$, * $p < 0.1$. FE refers to fixed effects. The variable i.Indian firm refers to a dummy variable =1 for firms belonging to India. For model 2 and model 6, the F statistic is significant, greater than 10, and greater than the 2SLS and the LIML size of nominal 5 percent Wald test at all levels, indicating that the H0 of weak instruments can be rejected. The p values on both the Sargan and Basmann test statistic is above 0.5, indicating that the H0 of overidentifying restrictions cannot be rejected. The p values on Durban and Wu-Hausman test statistics are below 0.05, indicating that the H0 of Share_digital sales being exogenous can be rejected at 5 percent.

finding was noted by Machacek and Hess (2019) in the case of Chinese automotive parts manufacturing. Codification of tasks and tacit information in GVCs limited some Chinese workers to performing routine tasks and removed them from any innovative collaboration, which resulted in a relative deskilling of workers in automotive GVCs. In India, while skilled workers are needed for handling computer-aided technologies, customized garment production has moved from artisanal tailored production to customized assembly-line production (Nathan and Ahmed, 2018), in which the largest share of the workforce is now classified as unskilled or semiskilled (López 2023).

It is further noted from table 5.3 that, as the sales concentration of a firm increases (percentage of sales attributed to its main product), the share of middle-skilled work relative to high-skilled work increases. Firms that report upgrading their machinery in the past three years also tend to have a higher share of middle-skilled workers relative to the share of high-skilled workers. In contrast, the coefficients on the innovation firm dummy and foreign equity are negative and significant for *MS/HS* but insignificant for *MS/LS*, implying that foreign ownership and innovation reduce the share of middle-skilled work in favor of high-skilled work.

5. CONCLUSION

Using data from India and Bangladesh textile and manufacturing firms, this chapter empirically examined the impact of firm digitalization and trade linkages on skill segmentation. Results show that firm digitalization—captured by the share of digital sales—is negatively related to the middle-skilled employment share and the ratio of the share of middle-skilled employment to the share of high-skilled employment. Taken together, these findings indicate that, in textile and garment manufacturing in India and Bangladesh, digitalization is associated with a reduced share of middle-skilled work (known to be intensive in routine tasks) in favor of high-skilled work. A similar effect is also noted for foreign equity. This indicates that national policies on building digital capabilities and foreign direct investment should be complemented with sector-specific skills development strategies to equip employees in the garment workforce with the changing skill needs.

In contrast to firm digitalization, trade linkages have a positive effect on middle-skilled employment share. Firms that are linked into GVCs are found to have a significantly higher share of middle-skilled workers relative to high-skilled workers than non-GVC firms. One-way traders and GVC traders that supply primarily to the global garment manufacturing market have a significantly higher ratio of middle-skilled workers to high-skilled workers compared to domestic firms. This is indicative of GVCs changing the skill composition of work in garment manufacturing in the case of India and Bangladesh. The contrasting effects of digitalization and trade linkages on the skill structure of the workforce highlight the urgent need for emerging economies to develop coherent digital industrial policies.

NOTE

1. Dr. Karishma Banga, Assistant Professor in Digital Economy, Department of Digital Humanities, King's College London, London. Contact: karishma.banga@kcl.ac.uk

REFERENCES

Acemoglu, D., and P. Restrepo. 2017. "Robots and Lobs: Evidence from US Labor Markets." National Bureau of Economic Research (NBER) working paper no. w23285. NBER. http://www.nber.org/papers/w23285.

Aghion, P., Antonin, C., Bunel, S. and Jaravel, X., 2020. What are the labor and product market effects of automation? New evidence from France. Available at https://sciencespo.hal.science/hal-03403062v1.

Almeida, R. K., Fernandes, A. M., & Viollaz, M. 2018. Software Adoption, Employment Composition, and the Skill Content of Occupations in Chilean Firms. *The Journal of Development Studies*, *56*(1), 169–185. https://doi.org/10.1080/00220388.2018.1546847

Altenburg, T., X. Chen, W. Lütkenhorst, C. Staritz, and L. Whitfield. 2020. *Exporting out of China or out of Africa?: Automation Versus Relocation in the Global Clothing. Industry Discussion Paper 1/2020.* Deutsches Institut für Entwicklungspolitik. https://www.idos-research.de/uploads/media/DP_1.2020.pdf.

Autor, D. H., and D. Dorn. 2013. "The Growth of Low-Skill Service Jobs and the Polarization of the US Labor Market." *American Economic Review* 103 (5): 1553–97.

Autor, D., L. F. Katz, and M. Kearney. 2006, May. "Measuring and Interpreting Trends in Economic Inequality." *AEA Papers and Proceedings* 96 (2): 189–94.

Azevedo, S. G., and H. Carvalho. 2012. "Contribution of RFID Technology to Better Management of Fashion Supply Chains." *International Journal of Retail & Distribution Management* 40 (2): 128–56.

Baldwin, J. R., and B. Yan. 2014. *Global Value Chains and the Productivity of Canadian Manufacturing Firms.* Canadian Electronic Library. https://coilink.org/20.500.12592/8pzrcg.

Bamber, P., and C. Staritz. 2016. *The Gender Dimensions of Global Value Chains.* International Center for Trade and Sustainable Development.

Banga, K., 2022a. "Impact of Global Value Chains on Total Factor Productivity: The Case of Indian Manufacturing." *Review of Development Economics* 26 (2):.704–35.

Banga, K. 2022b. "Opportunities, Risks and Realities of India's Participation in Global Value Chains." Ideas for India. https://www.ideasforindia.in/topics/trade/opportunities-risks-and-realities-of-india-s-participation-in-global-value-chains.html.

Banga, K., 2023. "Global Value Chains and Product Sophistication in Developing Countries: The Case of Indian Manufacturing." *Journal of International Trade & Economic Development* 32 (4): 509–36.

Banga, K., and B. Faith. 2021. "How Digitally Restructured Value Chains Are Reshaping Labor Futures for Women in the Global South." IT for Change. https://opendocs.ids.ac.uk/opendocs/handle/20.500.12413/17064.

Banga, K., P. Harbansh, and S. Singh. "Digital De-Industrialization, Global Value Chains, and Structural Transformation." Wider Working Paper 2023/65. United Nations University World Institute for Development Economics Research, May 2023. https://www.wider.unu.edu/sites/default/files/Publications/Working-paper/PDF/wp2023-65-digital-de-industrialization-global-value-chains-structural-transformation.pdf.

Banga, K., and D. W. te Velde. 2018. *Digitalization and the Future of Manufacturing in Africa.* ODI.B

Banga, K., and D. W. te Velde. 2019. "Preparing Developing Countries for the Future of Work: Understanding Skills-Ecosystem in a Digital Era." Background Paper 29. Pathways for Prosperity Commission, October 2019. https://pathwayscommission.bsg.ox.ac.uk/sites/default/files/2019-11/preparing_developing_countries.pdf.

Bárcia de Mattos, F., S. Dasgupta, X. Jiang, D. Kucera, and A. F. Schiavone. 2020. *Robotics and Reshoring: Employment Implications for Developing Countries.* International Labour Organization.

Barrientos, S. 2019. *Gender and Work in Global Value Chains: Capturing the Gains?* Cambridge University Press.

Basmann, R. L. 1960. "On Finite Sample Distributions of Generalized Classical Linear Identifiability Test Statistics." *Journal of the American Statistical Association* 55 (292): 650–59.

Beaudry, P., D. A. Green, and B. M. Sand. 2016. "The Great Reversal in the Demand for Skill and Cognitive Tasks." *Journal of Labor Economics* 34 (S1): .S199–S247.

Berg, A., L. Haug, S. Hedrich, and K. H. Magnus. 2020. "Time for Change. How to Use the Crisis to Make Fashion Sourcing More Agile and Sustainable." McKinsey and Company. https://www.mckinsey.com/~/media/McKinsey/Industries/Retail/Our%20Insights/Time%20for%20change%20How%20to%20use%20the%20crisis%20to%20make%20fashion%20sourcing%20more%20agile%20and%20sustainable/Time-for-change-How-to-use-the-crisis-to-make-fashion-sourcing-more-agile-and-sustainable.pdf.

Brambilla, I. and D.Tortarolo, D. 2018. "Investment in ICT, productivity, and labor demand: the case of Argentina." Policy Research Working Paper Series 8325, The World Bank.

Brun, L., G. Gereffi, and Zhan, J. 2019. "The 'Lightness' of Industry 4.0 Lead Firms: Implications for Global Value Chains." In Transforming Industrial Policy for the Digital Age, edited by P. Bianchi, C. Durán, and S. Labory. Edward Elgar Publishing.

Dauth, W., S. Findeisen, J. Südekum, and N. Woessner. "German Robots: The Impact of Industrial Robots on Workers." IAB-discussion Paper Number 30, Institute for Employment Research, 2017.

Goos, M., and A. Manning. 2007. "Lousy and Lovely Lobs: The Rising Polarization of Work in Britain." *Review of Economics and Statistics* 89 (1): 118–33.

Goos, M., A. Manning, and A. Salomons. 2014. "Explaining Job Polarization: Routine-Biased Technological Change and Offshoring. *American Economic Review* 104 (8): 2509–26.

Gregory, T., A. Salomons, and U. Zierahn, U. "Racing with or against the machine? Evidence from Europe." Centre for European Economic Research Discussion Paper No. 16-053, Centre for European Economic Research, 2016.

Gu, Y., G. Nayyar, and S. Sharma. 2021. "Gearing Up for the Future of Manufacturing in Bangladesh." World Bank. https://documents1.worldbank.org/curated/en/702731624306432211/pdf/Gearing-Up-for-the-Future-of-Manufacturing-in-Bangladesh.pdf

Hasan, I., M. N. Islam, and S. R. Khan. 2020. "Ready-Made Garment Industry Attractiveness: The Case of Bangladesh Garments' Blue-Collar Employees." *International Journal of Emerging Markets.* https://doi.org/10.1108/IJOEM-03-2019-0232

Hjort, J. and J. Poulsen. 2019. "The arrival of fast internet and employment in Africa." *American Economic Review*, 109(3):1032-1079.

Hoque, M. A., R. Rasiah, F. Furuoka, and S. Kumar. 2022. "Linkages Among Automation, Job Displacement and Reshoring: Evidence from the Bangladeshi Apparel Industry." *Research Journal of Textile and Apparel* 26 (4): 515–31.

Jung, J. H., and D. G. Lim. 2020. "Industrial Robots, Employment Growth, and Labor Cost: A Simultaneous Equation Analysis." *Technological Forecasting and Social Change* 159: 120202.

López, T. 2023. "Situating the Bangalore Export-garment Cluster Within the Garment GPN." In *Labour Control and Union Agency in Global Production Networks.* Springer. https://doi.org/10.1007/978-3-031-27387-2_5

López, T., T. Riedler, H. Köhnen, and M. Fütterer. 2022. "Digital Value Chain Restructuring and Labor Process Transformations in the Fast-Fashion Sector: Evidence from the Value Chains of Zara & H&M." *Global Networks* 22 (4): 684–700.

Machacek, E., and M. Hess. 2019. "Whither 'High-Tech' Labor? Codification and (De)skilling in Automotive Components Value Chains." *Geoforum* 99: 287–95.

Maloney, W., and C. Molina. 2016. "Are Automation and Trade Polarizing Developing Country Labor Markets, Too?" World Bank Policy Research Working Paper 7922. World Bank.

Mann, K., and L. Püttmann. 2018. "Benign Effects of Automation: New Evidence from Patent Texts." SSRN 2959584. https://doi.org/10.2139/ssrn.2959584.

Martínez-Mora, C., and F. Merino. 2020. "Consequences of Sustainable Innovations on the Reshoring Drivers' Framework." *Journal of Manufacturing Technology Management* 31 (7): 1373–90.

Messina, J., A. M. Oviedo, and G. Pica. 2016. "Job Polarization in Latin America." Mimeo. World Bank.

Nathan, D., and N. Ahmed. 2018. "Technological Change and Employment: Creative Destruction." *Indian Journal of Labor Economics* 61: 281–98.

Parschau, C., and J. Hauge. 2020. "Is Automation Stealing Manufacturing Jobs?: Evidence from South Africa's Apparel Industry." *Geoforum* 115: 120–31.

Rodrik, D. 2018. "New Technologies, Global Value Chains, and Developing Economies." NBER Working Paper No. w25164. National Bureau of Economic Research.

Sargan, J. D. 1958. "The Estimation of Economic Relationships Using Instrumental Variables." *Econometrica: Journal of the Econometric Society* 26 (3): 393–415.

Stock, J. H., J. H. Wright, and M. Yogo. 2002. "A Survey of Weak Instruments and Weak Identification in Generalized Method of Moments." *Journal of Business & Economic Statistics* 20 (4): 518–29.

Stock, J., and M. Yogo. 2005. "Asymptotic Distributions of Instrumental Variables Statistics with Many Instruments." In *Identification and inference for econometric models: Essays in honor of Thomas Rothenberg*, edited by Donald W. K. Andrews.

Swazan, I. S., and D. Das. 2022. "Bangladesh's Emergence as a Ready-Made Garment Export Leader: An Examination of the Competitive Advantages of the Garment Industry. *International Journal of Global Business and Competitiveness* 17 (2): 162–74.

Vashisht, P., and N. Rani. 2020. "Automation and the Future of Garment Sector Jobs in India." *Indian Journal of Labor Economics* 63: 225–46.

Winkler, D., and A. Seric. 2020. "COVID-19 Could Spur Automation and Reverse Globalisation—To Some Extent." *Voxeu*, April 28. https://cepr.org/voxeu/columns/covid-19-could-spur-automation-and-reverse-globalisation-some-extent

World Bank Enterprise Surveys (WBES). "Enterprise Surveys." Dataset for 2023. World Bank Publications. https://www.enterprisesurveys.org/en/enterprisesurveys.

World Bank Group. 2016. *World Development Report 2016: Digital Dividends*. World Bank Publications.

Yip, A. C., and M. Huang. 2016. "Strategic Values of Technology-Driven Innovation in Inventory Management: A Case Study of Zara's RFID Implementation." *International Journal of Inventory Research* 3 (4): 318.

Zaman, S. 2021. *Researching the Garment Sector in Bangladesh: Fieldwork Challenges and Responses: Field Guide for Research in Community Settings*. Edward Elgar Publishing. https://doi.org/10.4337/9781800376328.00013

FUNDING

This chapter is drawn from a project on technology transformation in Asian countries, funded by the Asian Development Bank.

Appendix 5.1 Summary statistics

	Number of observations	Construction of variables	Mean	Standard deviation (SD)	Minimum	Maximum
Trade variables						
Importer	1,377	1 if total imports > 0.1 percent of sales	0.15	0.35	0.00	1.00
Exporter	1,381	1 total exports > 0.1 percent of sales	0.25	0.43	0.00	1.00
Global value chain (GVC) firm	1,377	1 if a firm is an importer and exporter	0.10	0.30	0.00	1.00
Digitalization Variables						
Share of digital sales	1,379	Digital sales as a percentage of total sales in the firm	17.41	24.59	0.00	100.00
Predominantly digital	1,381	1 if share of digital sales > 50 percent of total sales in the firm	0.09	0.29	0.00	1.00
Industry digitalization	1,381	Average share of digital sales in industry	17.46	6.56	0	95
State digitalization	1,373	Average share of digital sales in state	17.35	13.07	0.16	58.07
Internet failure state	1,021	Number of incidents of insufficient internet connection in a typical month in the state	9.24	9.48	1.50	31.67
State share of digital firms	1,315	Percentage of firms with basic digital capability in state	52.01	22.16	12.5	86.36
Skill Variables						
Share of high-skilled workers	1,381	Percentage of high-skilled workers in employment	43.83	25.57	0.00	100.00
Share of low-skilled workers	1,381	Percentage of low-skilled workers in employment	15.37	16.42	0.00	100.00
Share of middle-skilled workers	1,381	Percentage of middle-skilled workers in employment	22.09	17.11	0.00	100.00
Share of middle-skilled workers relative to the share of low-skilled workers	1,065	Share of middle-skilled workers divided by share of low-skilled workers	1.88	2.03	0.00	19.00
Share of middle-skilled workers relative to the share of high-skilled workers	1,351	Share of middle-skilled workers divided by share of high-skilled workers	1.32	2.92	0	34

Controls						
Age	1,381	2022 - year of incorporation	21.47	13.55	2.00	110.00
Wage rate	1,325	Total real annual cost of labor in USD (including wages, salaries, bonuses)/ number of full-time permanent employees	18.00	16.63	0.00	187.00
Basic digital capabilities	1,379	1 if firm uses its own website/social media	0.54	0.50	0.00	1.00
Employees	1,381	Number of full-time employees	166.86	500.83	2.00	10000.00
Foreign equity	1,381	Percentage of foreign-owned shares	0.46	5.77	0.00	100.00
Innovative firm	1,381	1 if a firm undertakes R&D or has introduced a new product/service	0.07	0.26	0.00	1.00
Ln (real sales USD)	1,337	Natural log of manufacturing sales, normalized using GDP deflator and converted to USD using official exchange rate obtained from WDI	8.52	2.06	4.11	16.19
Machinery upgrade	1,364	1 if a firm upgraded machinery in last 3 years	2.48	0.55	1.00	3.00
Sales concentration	1,346	Share of main product in total sales	88.61	19.54	5.00	100.00

CHAPTER 6

Industrial Development, Sectoral Linkages, and Factor Income

A MULTIPLIER AND CLUSTERING ANALYSIS

Ryosuke Nakata

1. INTRODUCTION

To achieve the goal of poverty reduction, developing countries need not only to develop their domestic industries but also to ensure that the fruits of development are equitably distributed among the population. The growth of East Asian emerging economies was driven primarily by the development of the manufacturing sectors through participation in global value chains (GVCs). But more important, their industrialization processes absorbed the surplus labor and, through adequate wage payments, generated a large middle class whose increased domestic demand created a further virtuous economic cycle. If the generated profits had been disproportionally distributed to capital or a small group in the population, such a virtuous cycle would not have been possible. In other words, the leading sectors may not have to be the manufacturing sectors.

In the case of East Asia, the presence of investment source countries such as Japan, South Korea, and Taiwan—and the European Union (EU) in the case of Eastern Europe—made it possible to build GVCs in the regions. In the case of Africa, however, such partners have yet to emerge in sufficient numbers. With the enormous growth in the supply capacity of the manufacturing sectors in recent years and the stagnation in the progress of GVCs, it is debatable whether the same model of development that is occurring in East Asia and Eastern Europe can be transferred directly to Africa.

Do agriculture, the extractive industries, and/or the service sectors play a similar role to that of the manufacturing industries in East Asia or Eastern Europe? In this chapter, we try to analyze industrial structure, especially in low-income countries, from the viewpoint of their capacity to generate income for different factors of production.

2. DATA AND APPROACH

This study uses the Global Trade Analysis Project (GTAP) database, which was created for the multilateral computable general equilibrium (CGE) models. It records the annual value of transactions in goods and services for the entire world in a given base year. The Social Accounting Matrix (SAM) system, which consists of an input-output table; imports and exports with foreign countries; and incomes and expenditures of households, government, and so on, can be derived for individual countries. The system is slightly different from the multiregion input-output table but can be reorganized into a similar system.

The GTAP version 10 consists of 121 countries and twenty aggregate regions,[1] sixty-five economic sectors, and eight production factors (land, natural resources, capital, officials and managers, technicians and associate professionals, clerks, service and market sales workers, and agricultural and unskilled workers)[2] with base years for 2004, 2007, 2011, and 2014. However, especially because the primary sectors are narrowly split in the GTAP database, these sixty-five sectors are aggregated into thirty-two sectors in this study.

This study does not run the GTAP model but performs a Leontief-type multiplier analysis. In running the GTAP/CGE model, the "closures" of the model need to be set by the analyst, and this choice often results in very different outcomes.[3] For our purposes, we simply calculate the impact of the increased production in each sector and analyze, assuming shocks equivalent of 5 percent of final demand, how it induces increased compensation to the eight production factors through the additional production of intermediate goods and services domestically and abroad.

3. CHARACTERISTICS OF THE FACTOR INCOME MULTIPLIERS

3.1 CLUSTERING

Because the above calculation generates a large amount of data (the changes in remuneration of thirty-two sectors (after aggregation) times eight production factors for 121 countries), it is not easy to scrutinize them individually. Therefore, clustering is performed. Clustering is a type of machine-learning technique that groups samples based on the similarity of data. It is a method of unsupervised learning in which the analyst does not impose any classification criteria in advance. After calculating all the *distances* between the elements, this method classifies countries into groups by minimizing the distances within the same cluster and maximizing the average distances between the different clusters to capture the most evident characteristics of the groups.[4]

This exercise grouped 121 countries, each having 256 data points by sectors and production factors, into four clusters (hereinafter denoted as C1 to C4) (table 6.1). By income levels, most high-income countries (HICs) belong to C1, while most low-income countries (LICs) belong to C3. Upper-middle-income countries (UMCs) are almost equally divided into C1 and C2, and many of the lower middle-income countries (LMCs) belong to C2. The rest are separated into C1 or C3. C4 is a special cluster consisting mainly of Middle East oil-producing countries (Saudi Arabia, United Arab Emirates [UAE], Kuwait, etc.). Looking at the cluster distribution by developing country regions, more than half of the countries in Africa belong to C3. The European and Central Asian regions saw some shift from C2 to C1, while the opposite is observed for the Latin American region.

We may summarize that C1 is a cluster of mainly developed countries and some middle-income countries, C2 is mostly a middle-income country cluster almost equally shared by UMC and LMC, C3 is mainly an African country cluster, and C4 is the Middle East oil-producer cluster.[5] Cluster results are stable, with forty-six of the sixty countries classified as C1 in 2004 and belonging to the same cluster in 2007, 2011, and 2014. Twenty of the thirty-nine countries in C2 also belong to the same cluster throughout the period.

The clustering results are stable, and the distribution of regions and income levels is generally consistent. Therefore, the clusters for each year are considered representative of the structural characteristics of each country rather than of the temporary effects of occasional economic trends or business cycles. Hence, the clustering results for 2014 are used hereafter. C4 is a special cluster and therefore is not the main subject of the analysis below.

Table 6.1 Number of countries in each cluster

	High income				Upper middle income				Lower middle income				Low income			
	2004	2007	2011	2014	2004	2007	2011	2014	2004	2007	2011	2014	2004	2007	2011	2014
c1	40	39	42	43	13	14	13	14	6	7	5	4	1	1	—	—
c2	3	4	—	—	17	16	18	17	17	15	17	18	2	1	1	1
c3	—	—	1	—	—	—	—	—	9	10	9	9	6	7	8	8
c4	6	6	6	6	1	1	—	—	—	—	1	1	—	—	—	—

By region (developing countries only)

	East Asia and Pacific				South Asia				Middle East and North Africa			
	2004	2007	2011	2014	2004	2007	2011	2014	2004	2007	2011	2014
c1	4	5	3	2	1	1	—	—	1	—	1	1
c2	4	4	6	7	4	4	5	5	4	4	4	4
c3	1	—	—	—	—	—	—	—	—	1	—	—
c4	—	—	—	—	—	—	—	—	—	—	—	—

	Europe and Central Asia				Latin America				Sub-Sahara Africa			
	2004	2007	2011	2014	2004	2007	2011	2014	2004	2007	2011	2014
c1	2	3	7	7	10	10	5	6	—	3	2	2
c2	9	8	4	4	6	5	11	10	9	7	6	6
c3	1	1	1	1	1	2	1	1	12	13	15	15
c4	1	1	1	1	—	—	—	—	—	—	—	—

3.2 CHARACTERISTICS OF EACH CLUSTER

First, we examine the general overview of the multiplier effects for each cluster (figure 6.1). The box plot in the figure shows the distribution of the cluster members, with the box indicating the second to fourth quintile and the whiskers indicating the maximum and minimum values excluding outliers. It may not be appropriate to use box plots for C3, which consists of only seventeen countries, but the same diagram is used for the purpose of side-by-side comparison. The multiplier effects for land and natural resources are extremely large in agriculture, livestock, and fuel sectors. Hence, these two factors are omitted in the figure.

The first noticeable feature of C3 is very large effect on unskilled labor in the agriculture sector, both relative to other sectors and relative to other factors of production. Note that the scales of the *y*-axis are different for visualization purpose. Growth of the agriculture sector is clearly effective in raising the income of unskilled labor, of which a high proportion is poor households.

Skilled workers in C3, such as managers and technicians, can gain the highest benefits from the agriculture sector, too. They also enjoy high benefits throughout the service sectors. The recreation and trade sectors are most beneficial for sales workers, while clerks enjoy relatively high benefits in business-to-business (B2B) service sectors like utility and transport.[6]

In the case of C1, the trade sector delivers the highest returns for all types of labor except unskilled workers, who benefit the most from the food sector, followed by trade, and hotels and restaurants. In the case of C2, the effects in the food sector are similarly high, but relatively high effects are expected throughout the service sectors in general. But the unskilled laborers benefit a great deal only from the food, agriculture, and livestock sectors.

The effects from the manufacturing sectors are low across the clusters. This possibly reflects the fact that the manufacturing sectors need more intermediate inputs, which lowers the ratio of value added (factor payments) to sales values (figure 6.2). The value-added ratios of the manufacturing sectors in C3 tend to be even lower than other clusters. A detailed look at the intermediate inputs by C3 manufacturing sectors shows that the majority of inputs come from the trade sector (the graph is omitted). The median ratios of inputs from the trade sector are 5 to 6 percent for C1 manufacturing sectors, and 3 to 7 percent for C2. But

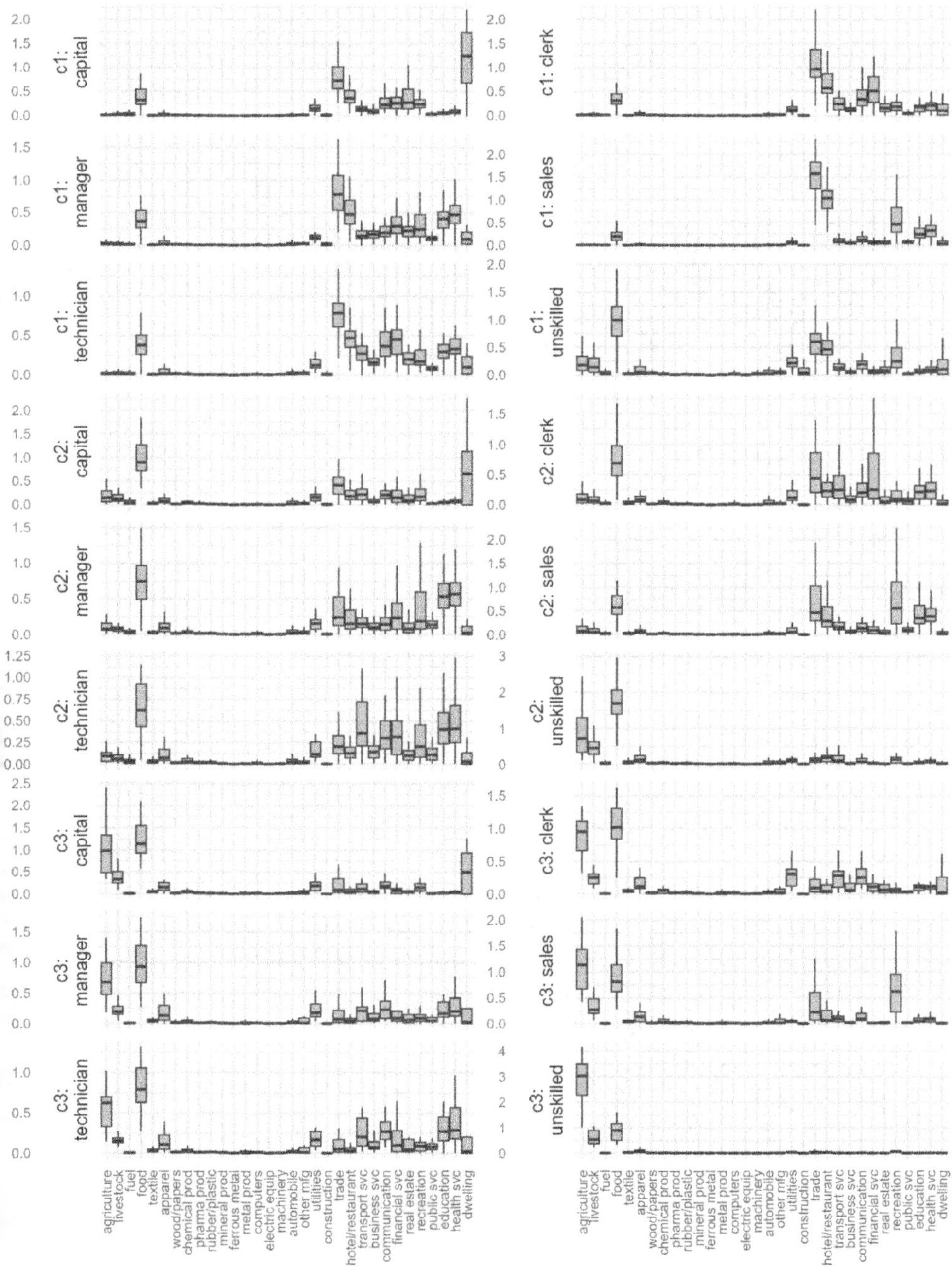

Figure 6.1 Multiplier effects by sector and cluster

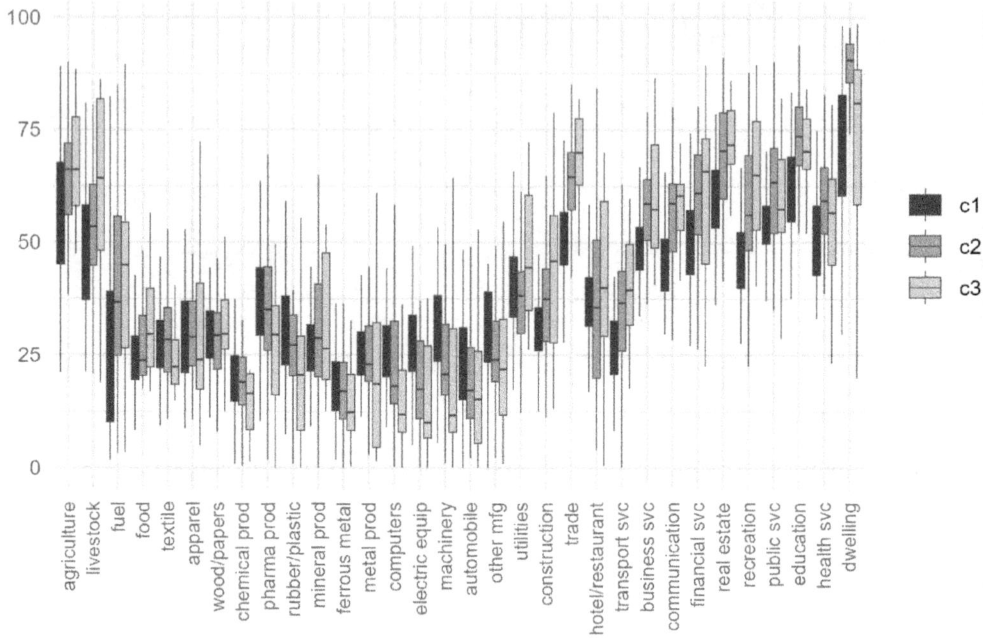

Figure 6.2 Share of factor payments to total value (%)

for C3, the ratios for complex manufacturing, such as automobile, computers, electrical equipment, and machinery, are between 35 and 42 percent, and even for light industries such as apparel or textiles, the ratios are 12 to 16 percent. Only for ferrous metal and metal products are the median ratios are around 10 percent. In other words, some of the manufacturing sectors in C3 are considered to have a dealer nature, acting as intermediaries for manufactured products, including imported goods, rather than as manufacturers of these products. The manufacturing sectors may currently not be well positioned for broad-based growth and a poverty reduction strategy in C3.

The multiplier effects by SAM (or the input-output table) are influenced by the production size of each sector because the spillover effects to other sectors are larger for the large sectors.[7] The multiplier effect is obtained by multiplying the Leontief inverse matrix by the scale of production expansion in each sector. The effects, independent of the production size, can be observed by examining each element of the Leontief matrix. The figures 6.3 through 6.5 compare the medians of matrix elements between the clusters. For example, figure 6.3 shows the median

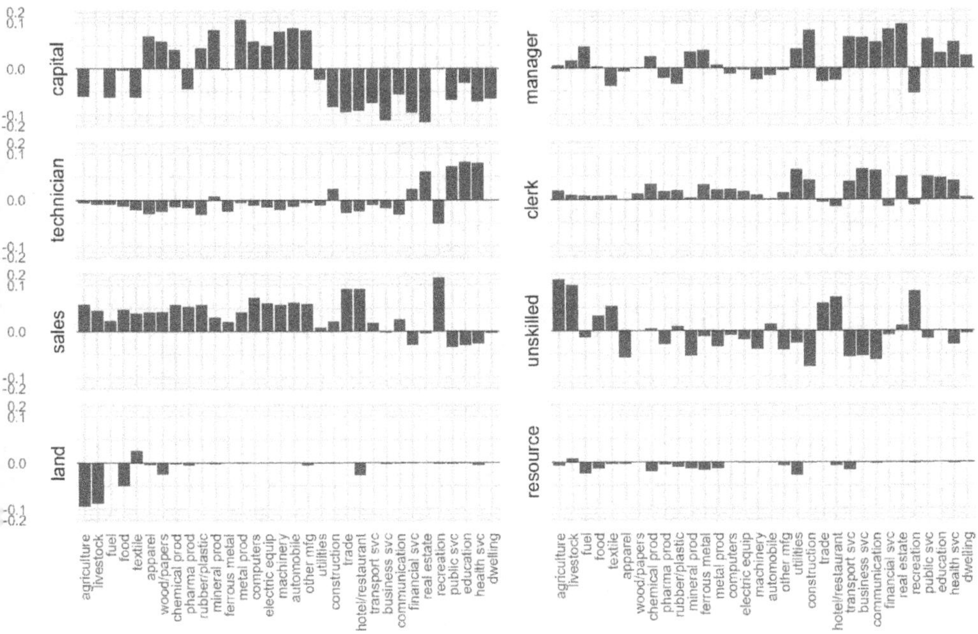

Figure 6.3 Difference of median coefficients (cluster 3 from cluster 2)

matrix element of C3 minus C2. The negative value means that the effect of this sector in C3 is less than C2, while the positive value means that the effect in C3 is greater. Of course, the multiplier itself is always positive, so even if the value is negative, it does not mean that sector expansion lowers the factor income. Even if an element of some sector in C3 is smaller than in C2, the multiplier effect of this sector in C3 can be higher than in C2 if the production scale of this sector in C3 is large enough.

The greatest concern is that the coefficients on unskilled labor in C3 are inferior to C2 in most of the sectors, although the agriculture and livestock sectors are more beneficial to unskilled labor in this criterion. Negative magnitudes are relatively mild, but the coefficients on land and natural resources are inferior, too, in almost all sectors. While it is true that relatively abundant resources theoretically draw lower prices, the low impacts of these abundant resource endowments are not desirable for low-income African countries. Middle-skilled workers such as clerks and shop workers generally perform better, including in the manufacturing sectors. The coefficients on the capital are higher, too, in most manufacturing sectors. Although it is encouraging that middle-skilled workers

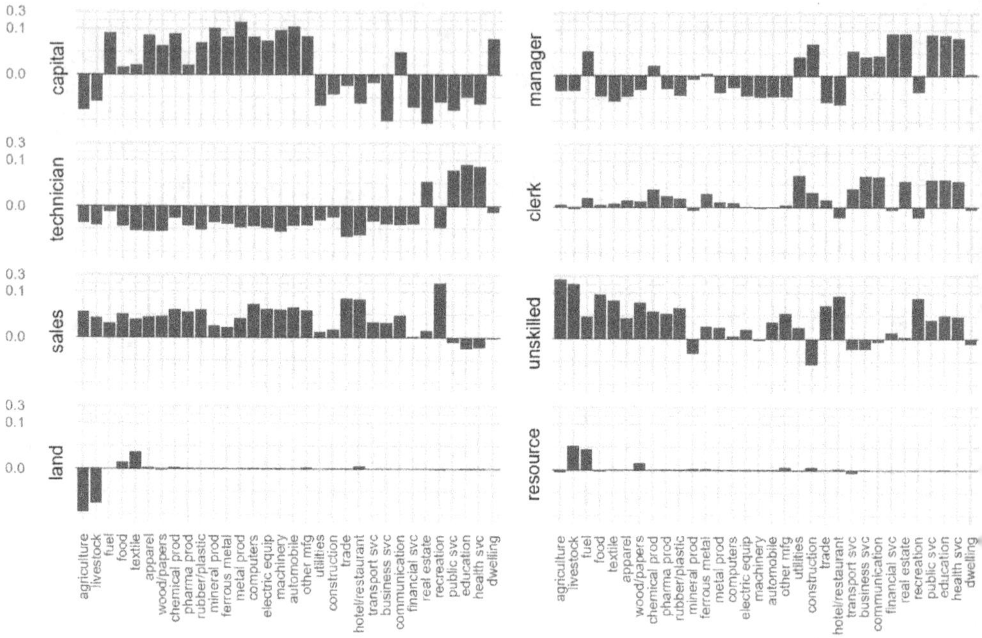

Figure 6.4 Difference of median coefficients (cluster 3 from cluster 1)

tend to benefit more from the expansion of these sectors in C3, it would be misleading to assume that manufacturing sectors show higher returns than in other clusters because of there is a concern about the dealer nature of these sectors. Among high-skilled workers, too, the general underperformance of technicians against the high performance of managers may indicate a lack of need for the former, who are typically needed more in the manufacturing sectors.

The comparison with C1 shows a similar picture, while unskilled workers in C3 perform better in almost all the sectors in this case (figure 6.4). The coefficients of the agriculture and livestock sectors on the land and natural resources are inferior in C3 to those in C1. High return on the land in C1 primary sectors may reflect the high value added of the products because of income levels in these sectors. As we will see later, however, the agriculture and livestock sectors in C1 may receive large government subsidies, potentially distorting the economic structure.

When comparing C1 and C2, some diversion is observed between high-skilled workers, that is, managers and technicians, and other factors (figure 6.5). A major trend is that the coefficients for C1 on the former

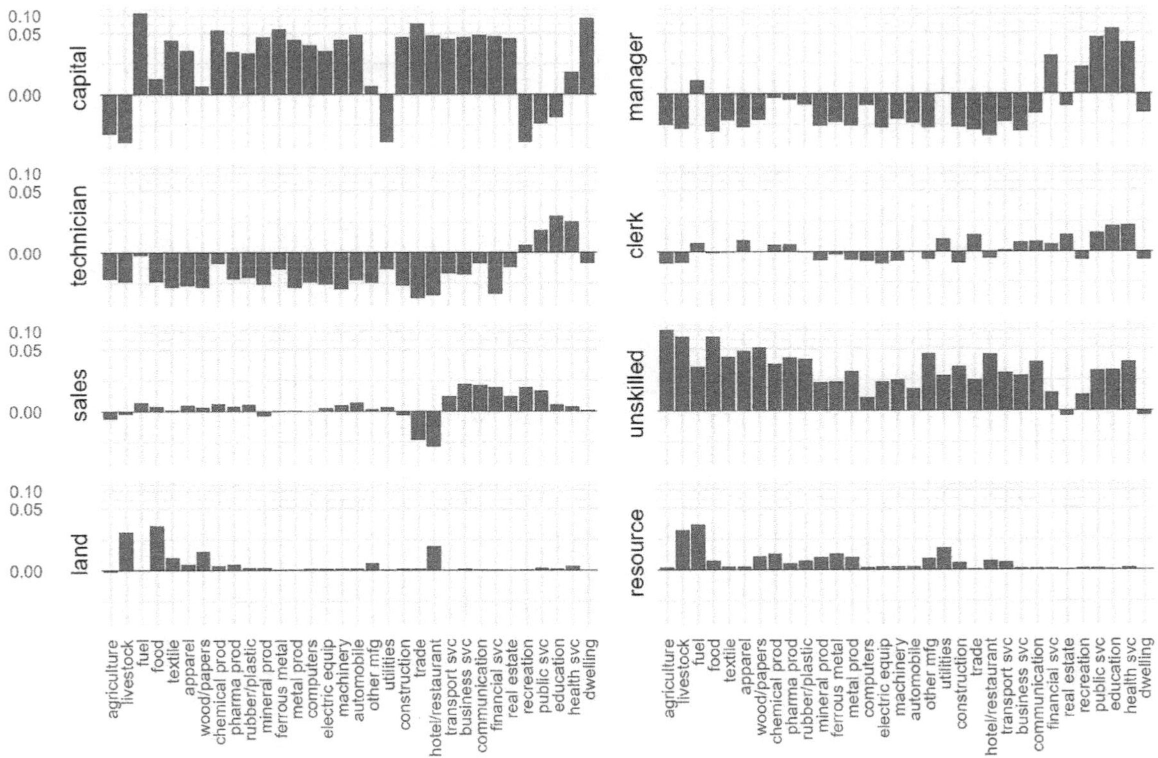

Figure 6.5 Difference of median coefficients (cluster 2 from cluster 1)

group are better in most sectors, except for some business-to-consumer (B2C) service sectors, while C2 shows better results for the latter group in almost all the sectors. This pattern may have caused the loss of the middle-class in the advanced economies in the past decades.

An overall concern in C3, which mainly consists of low-income African countries, is the underperformance of unskilled labor, land, and natural resources compared with C2. Capital and middle-skilled workers, that is, clerks and shop workers, perform better in the manufacturing sector, which is encouraging for the income generation of these segments of the population. But we also have to note the possibility that C3 manufacturing sectors show a dealer nature. With the global manufacturing market saturated and new opportunities to enter the GVCs not readily available, income-generating measures that make the most use of endowed resources, such as the agriculture and the natural resource industries, is needed in addition to further promote the sectors benefitting the middle-class population. It is encouraging that the unskilled workers in C3 benefit highly from the agriculture and the livestock sectors, even after discarding the scale effects. But these sectors are unlikely to have developed a modern production system with inputs from other sectors that would add more value.

4. FACTORS BEHIND THE DIFFERENCES BETWEEN THE CLUSTERS[8]

4.1 FACTOR PAYMENT PATTERNS

Figure 6.6 shows the share of each factor of production in the total factor payments (land and natural resources are omitted). Note that the *y*-axis is adjusted because of the very small shares of sales workers, particularly in the manufacturing sector. Care should be taken when comparing across the factors.

First, it is clear that the share of payments to capital is highest across the clusters in almost all the sectors (except agriculture, livestock, and some service sectors). The allocations to the managers, technicians, and clerks are generally higher in C1 than in other clusters, while sales and unskilled workers are paid less. One concern is that the manufacturing sectors in C3 tend to have a larger share of payments to capital, while the payments for labor compensation tend to be lower, regardless of the skill levels, except in some service sectors. As already discussed, the manufacturing sectors in C3 are considered to have a dealer character

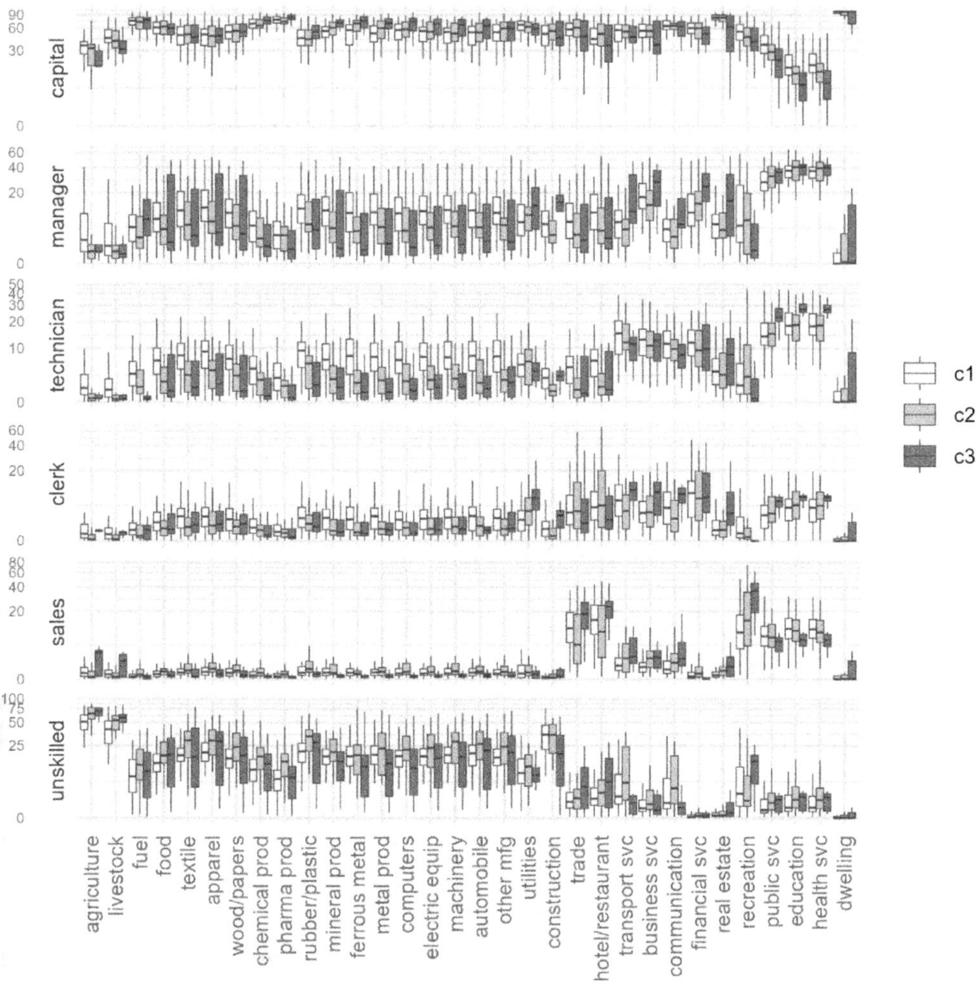

Figure 6.6 Share of factor payments by sector (%)

and, in addition the value-added ratios themselves are lower than in other clusters. The pattern to achieve inclusive economic growth seen in East Asia—employment absorption through labor-intensive production processes—is not strong at present. In addition, the upper quintiles of managers generally receive more than in other clusters in almost all the sectors, while the lower quintiles of unskilled laborers receive less, which raises a concern about income inequality in C3.

The payments to unskilled labors are high in the agriculture and livestock sectors in all the clusters, and especially in C3, while the payments to sales workers are high only in the trade, hotels and restaurants, and recreation sectors. This conforms with the pattern of the multiplier effects we saw in figure 6.1.

4.2 COST BURDENS

Next, we compare the cost factors that are likely to be burdens for low-income countries, that is, transport costs, utility charges, and taxes. Transport costs and utilities in figure 6.7 represent the ratio of these intermediate input purchases to total sales, while the tax burden represents the ratio of taxes and tariffs paid by the production sector to total sales. However, taxes also include negative taxes (subsidies).

When we look at domestic transportation costs, we generally see a high burden for C3, except for B2B services—although differences are not large for the median levels. Delays in the development of public transport and road networks may result in such higher cost burdens, which in turn put pressure on factor compensation. In contrast, when we look at overseas transportation costs, the overall burden is much lower than in domestic transportation. In addition, the differences between clusters are not necessarily large, except for a few sectors. The burden looks generally higher in C1, which may indicate the heavy use of imported intermediate goods in this cluster.

The burden on C2 and C3 from utility bills (payments to the electricity, gas, and water sectors) are relatively large in the manufacturing sectors. Combined with the burden of high domestic transportation costs, this may be an obstacle to the development of manufacturing sectors in C3. On the other hand, the burden is extremely low in the agriculture, livestock, and food sectors of C3. Although the graph is omitted, inputs from the fuel and the chemical sectors (such as chemical fertilizers) are also very low for these sectors compared to other clusters, with most inputs coming from the trade sector. This indicates that the C3 agriculture sector is still dominated by simple farming with little advanced intermediate inputs.

Regarding taxes, the burden on C1 is relatively high for the service sectors, while differences between clusters are not large for the manufacturing sectors. The burdens for C1 agriculture and livestock sectors are generally low. The median levels are not negative but only slightly

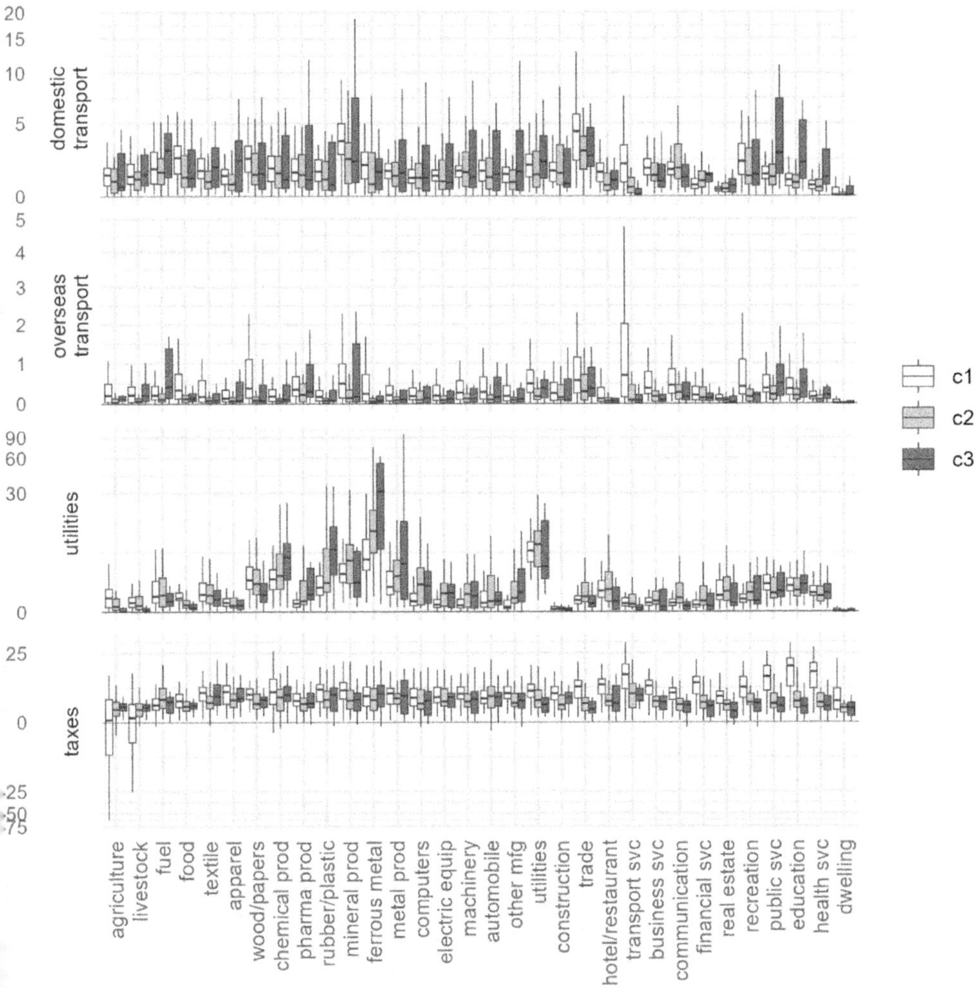

Figure 6.7 Share of transport, utility, and tax burden (%)

positive. This could be because subsidies are largely given to factors such as land in C1. As a result, and as we saw previously, the Leontief matrix coefficients to land and natural resources are higher in C1 than in C3 for the agriculture and livestock sectors, which theoretically should be less competitive. Without this, the factor compensation in these sectors of C3 could be higher because of higher exports, helping their economic growth and poverty reduction.

4.3 SALES STRUCTURES

Are there any differences between clusters in terms of where goods are sold? We compare the sales ratios of four types of transactions: intermediate goods or final goods, and domestic or overseas sales destinations (figure 6.8). The service sectors, except transport and business services, have very low ratios of overseas transactions and thus are excluded.

C3 is characterized by high ratios of domestic sales of final goods and very low export ratios for both final and intermediate goods, except for fuel, ferrous metal, and metal products. C1 has high ratios of intermediate goods, especially export ratios. For example, in the case of agriculture, the share of domestic sales of final goods is 60.9 percent of total output in C3, while it is only 21.6 percent in C1 and 34.2 percent in C2 (all median values). Conversely, domestic intermediate goods account for 37.2 percent and 47.7 percent of the total in C1 and C2, respectively, but only 20.6 percent in C3. In the case of C1, intermediate goods are extensively transacted with domestic and overseas partners, and the products

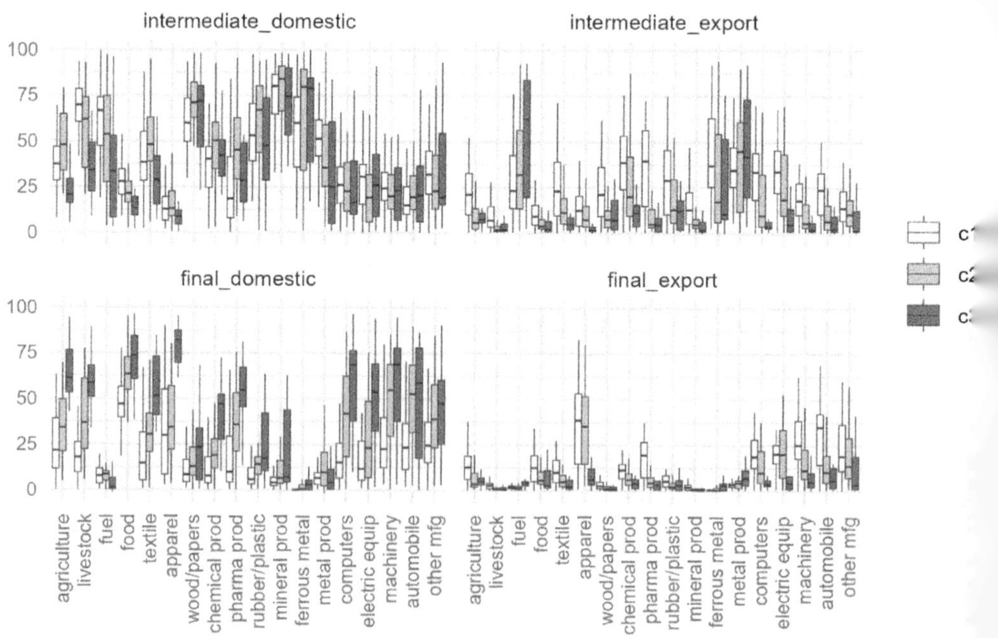

Figure 6.8 Sales structures (%)

become final goods after several stages of processing, whereas in C3, the goods tend to be consumed domestically as final goods without significant processing.

The picture is vastly different in the case of the fuel, ferrous metal, and metal products sectors. In the case of fuel, the ratio of intermediate goods export is 23.1 percent in C1 and 32.1 percent in C2, but it is 62.6 percent in C3. For mineral products, the domestic supply ratio of intermediate goods is 66.5 percent and 53.6 percent in C1 and C2, respectively, while it is low, at 33.6 percent in C3. Metal products show a similar pattern, while ferrous metals are used more as domestic intermediate goods in the case of C2 and C3. This may have been caused by the industrial nature of these sectors in C3, where presumably products are sold to foreign countries in the form of raw materials, without significant processing.

Although information on unit price is not available from the GTAP database, exports from low-income countries (especially African countries) are reportedly subject in many cases to low transfer prices in intercompany transactions with overseas commodity trading firms, and source countries do not retain sufficient benefits, including tax revenues. As a result, the resource and mineral sectors in Africa have not enjoyed high factor compensation comparable to their production scales, which has constrained the economic development of these countries.

Next, we focus on the transactions of intermediate goods but look in more details at the clusters of counterparts. We take the entire transaction value of intermediate goods as one and divide it into domestic and overseas transactions, and further divide the overseas transaction partners into C1 to C4.

First, in terms of destinations (figure 6.9), as we have already seen, domestic sales are overwhelmingly high in C3, except for fuel, ferrous metal, and metal products. The C3 countries have not established their positions internationally as intermediate goods suppliers. If we look at C3 export destinations by cluster, C1 is the largest destination in most cases, with C2 standing out in ferrous metal and C4 standing out in metal products.[9]

In contrast, in the case of C1, the median domestic supply is around 50 to 75 percent, and a large part of the supply goes overseas, with C1 as the main export destination. A similar pattern is observed for C2, but the share of domestic sales is higher than for C1. Major destinations are C1, but in some sectors, the shares of C2 are comparable to C1.

In terms of sources (figure 6.10), C1 countries purchase overwhelmingly from C1, too, while the shares of sources from C2 are closer to

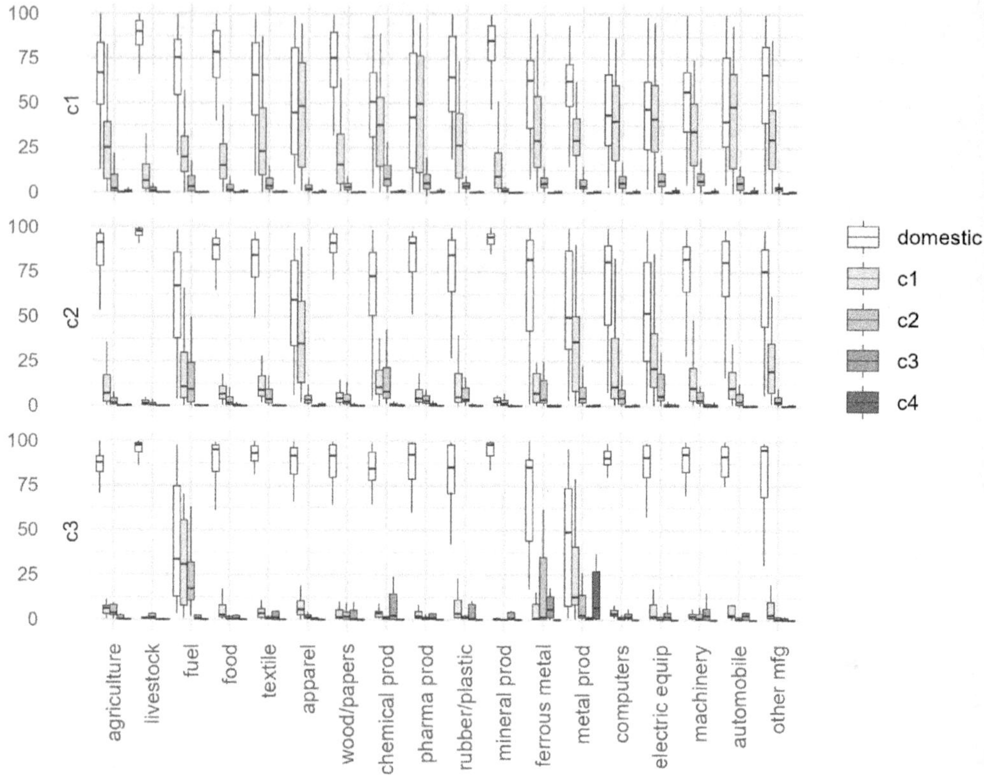

Figure 6.9 Destinations of intermediate goods (%)

C1 in some sectors of the C2 market, and shares from C2 tend to be higher than C1 in the C3 markets. In other words, C1 countries have developed mutual supply-and-demand networks mainly among C1 countries. C2 is connected to both C1 and C2 as suppliers of intermediate goods and mainly with C1 as purchasers of intermediate goods. C3 has established a certain position in the supply of raw materials, such as fuel and metals, but is unable to participate in the network generally.

The pros and cons of GVCs do exist, but the importance of international trade networks cannot be ignored because of the narrow domestic markets of developing countries, the need for foreign currency sources, and the international knowledge spillovers. C3 countries can currently participate in the international markets only for extractive sectors such as

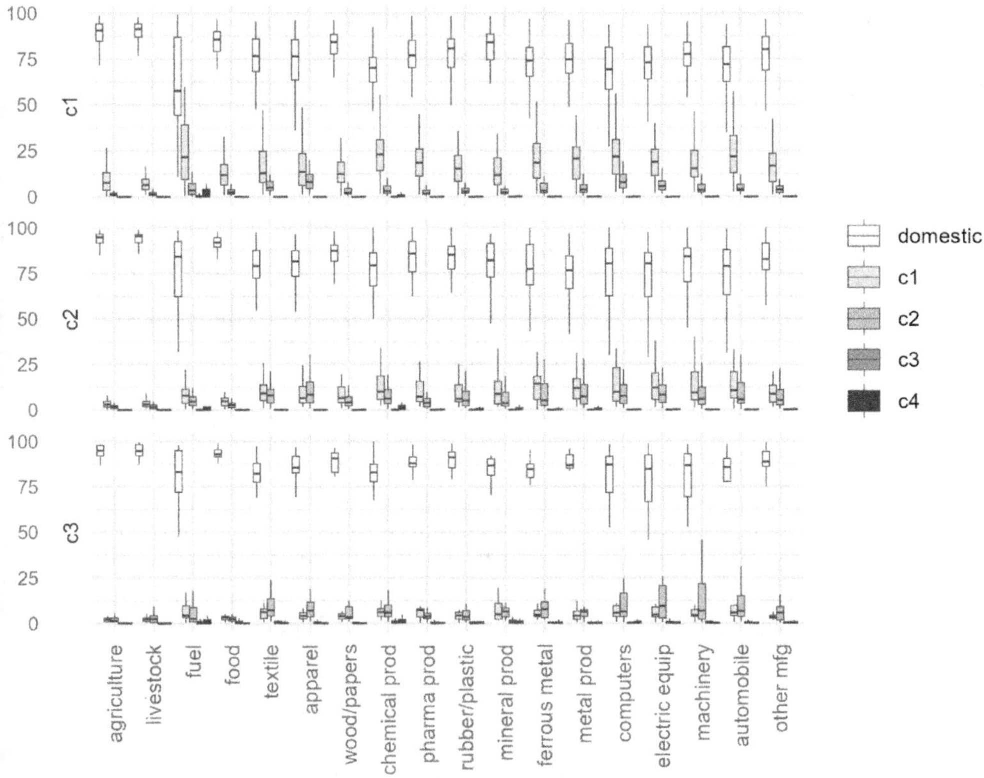

Figure 6.10 Sources of intermediate goods (%)

fuel and metals. Measures to increase values in these sectors, such as more in-country processing rather than simply exporting as raw materials, are needed.

4.4 SPILLOVERS FROM MAJOR FOREIGN COUNTRIES

The clustering exercise was based on the impact of domestic industries on factor payments. We now briefly review the degree of spillovers from major foreign countries (the United States, Japan, Germany, China, India, and South Africa). Figure 6.11 shows the impact of production expansion in the selected sectors on the y-axis from the five countries on factor compensations in each cluster.[10] As we saw, C3 countries are positioned as source countries of raw materials for C1 and C2. The impact on

C3 is thus relatively high in sectors related to raw material production, such as the fuel, food, metal products, and utility sectors.

The spillover effects in C3 from C2 countries (China, India, and South Africa—the latter three countries in each panel group) are

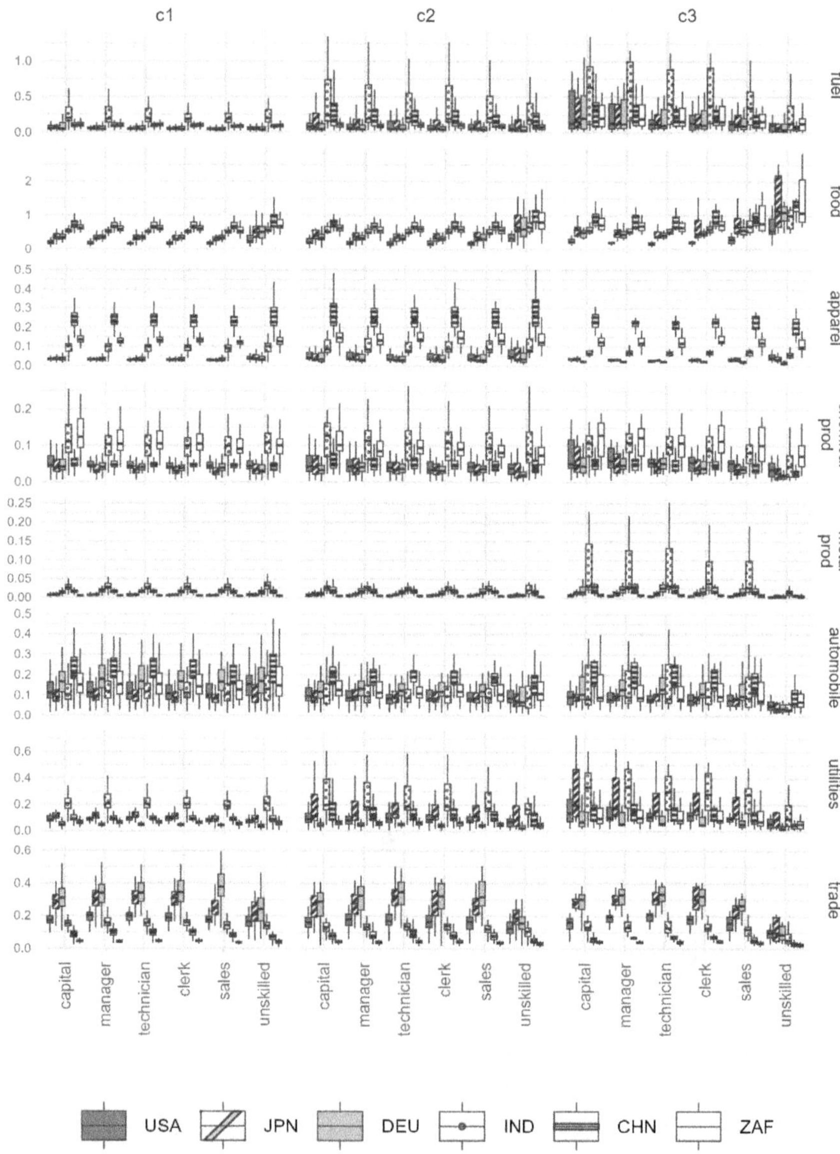

Figure 6.11 Multiplier effects from major foreign countries

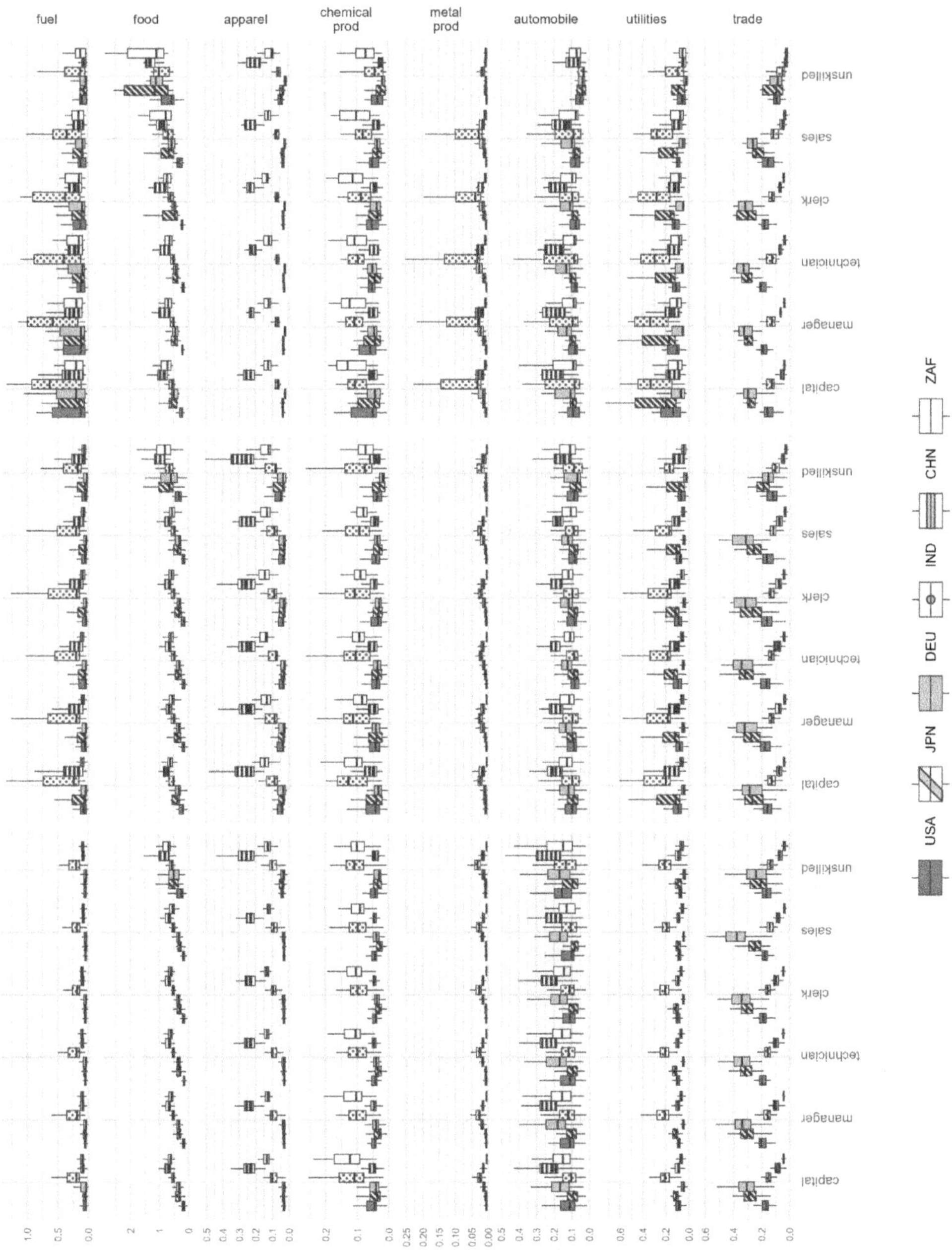

Figure 6.11 *(continued)*

prominent in many sectors and tend to be larger than from C1 countries (the United States, Japan, and Germany—the former three countries in each panel group). C2 countries may have deeper economic connections with African countries. Even in automobiles, the largest spillover in C3 is from China, followed by India, while the spillovers from C1 are surprisingly small.

While all factors of production exhibit similar levels of spillover effects in C1 and C2, only the unskilled labor in C3 receives low spillover impact in most sectors. Even in the sectors that are strongly related to raw material supplies from C3, unskilled workers do not benefit a great deal, except in the food sector where unskilled workers strongly benefit. Although this outcome is a concern in terms of poverty reduction and inequality, international trade—especially with emerging economies and not only with advanced economies, as seen above—looks beneficial in terms of economic growth because C3 middle-skilled workers benefit greatly.

4.5 INDUSTRIAL LINKAGES

To examine the issue of interindustry linkages further, we again observe the elements of the Leontief inverse matrix. Here, we will compare the matrix elements on the degree of production spillovers between industries (not on the factor payments, as we did earlier in this chapter). Each element shows the strength of the production spillover through interindustry linkages, independent of the effect of size on the sector in which the shock occurs. Figure 6.12 shows how production on the vertical axis sector spills over to the horizontal axis sectors in each cluster. For the sake of simplicity, it shows only the median value for each cluster. Figure 6.13 shows the gap between the values of C3 and those of C1 and C2. The negative value means that the element of C3 is smaller than other clusters.

The high coefficients that the C3 trade sector receive from shocks in the nonservice sectors are the first prominent features. As we have already discussed, most C3 manufacturing sectors, with the exception of some metal sectors, are more likely to act as dealers rather than manufacturers of products. Even the agriculture sector procures mostly from the trade sector. As a result, the spillover effects to the trade sector are significantly higher in C3 compared with C1 or C2, as well as compared with other sectors in C3.

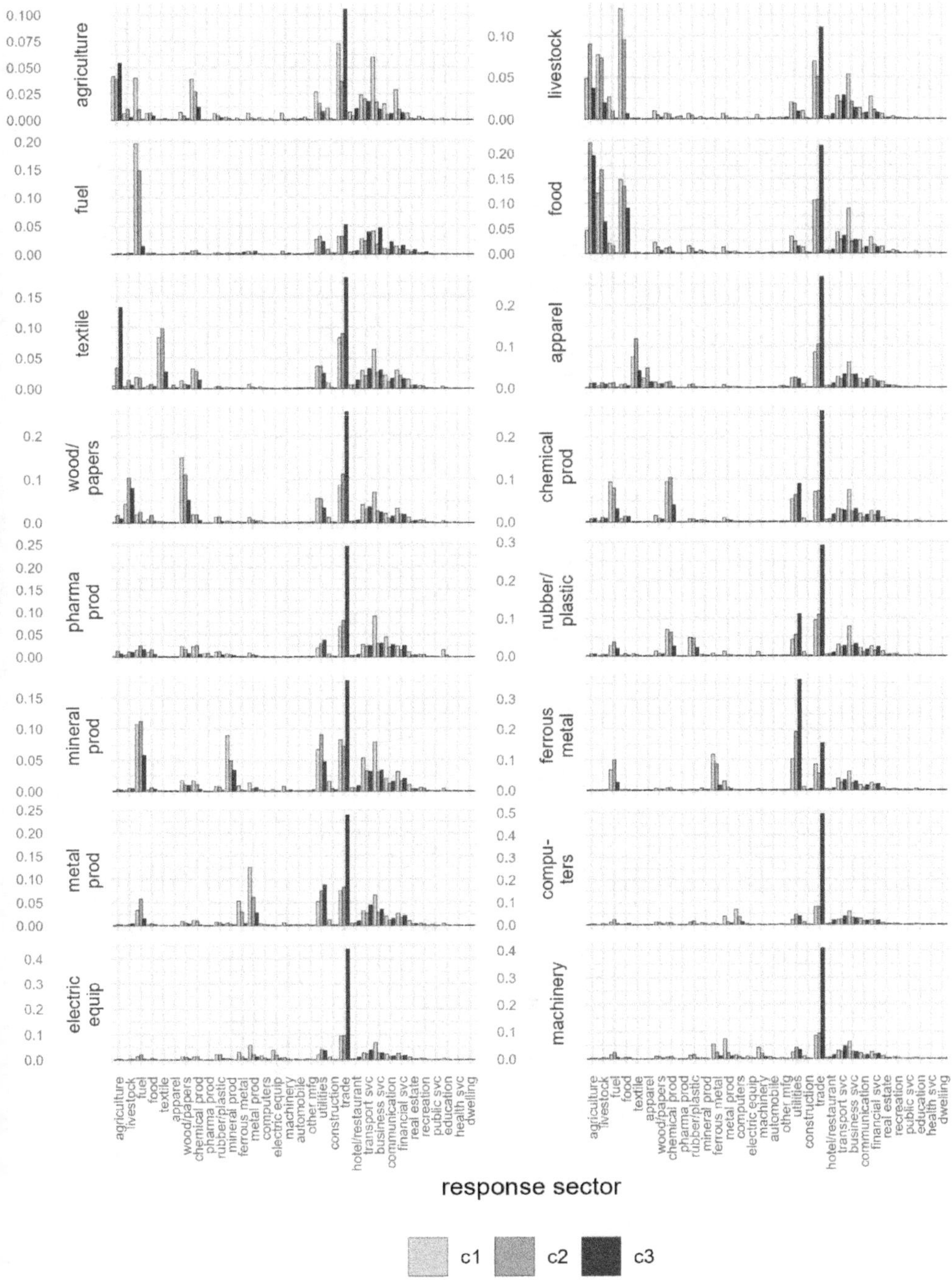

Figure 6.12 Leontief matrix coefficients: median

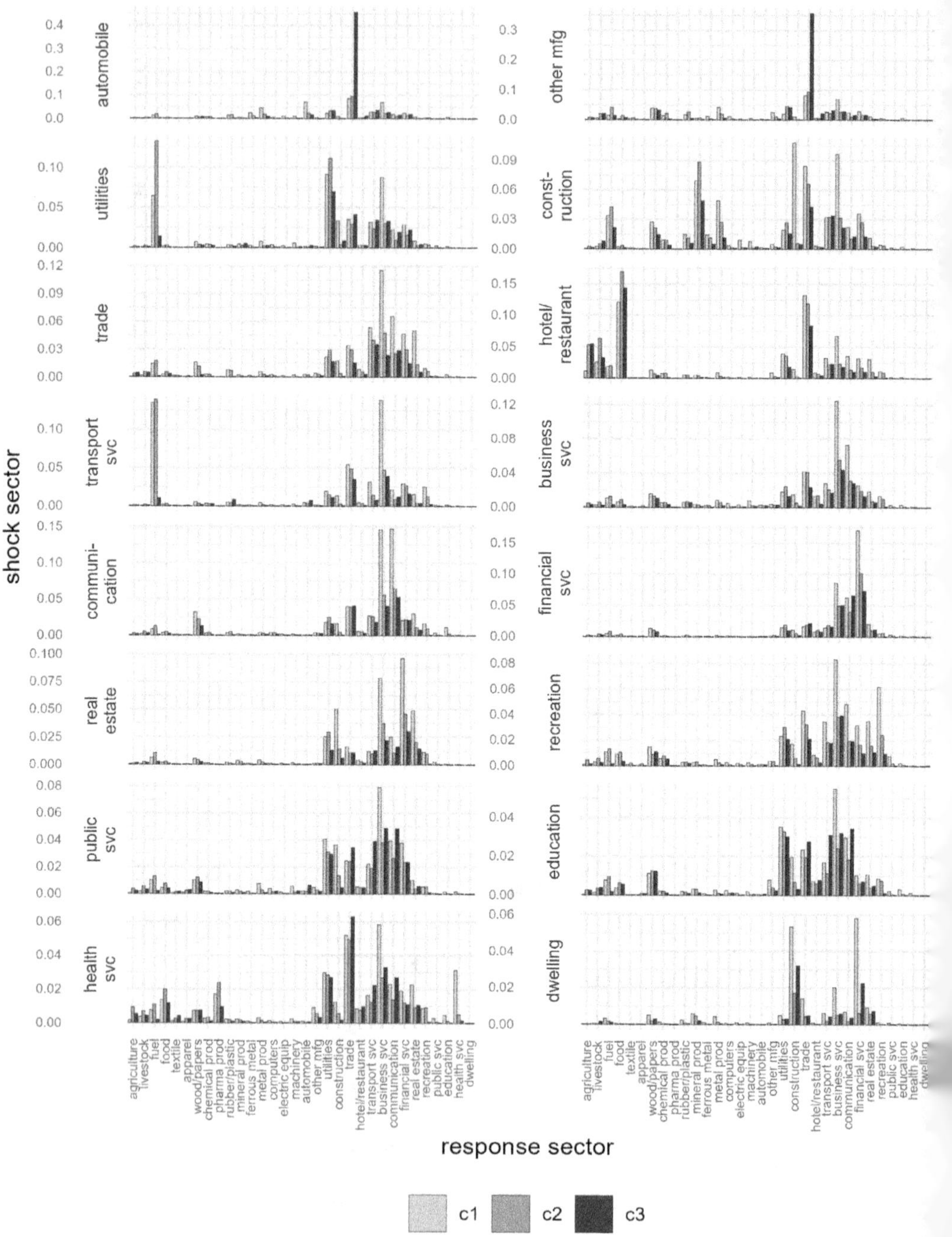

Figure 6.12 (*continued*)

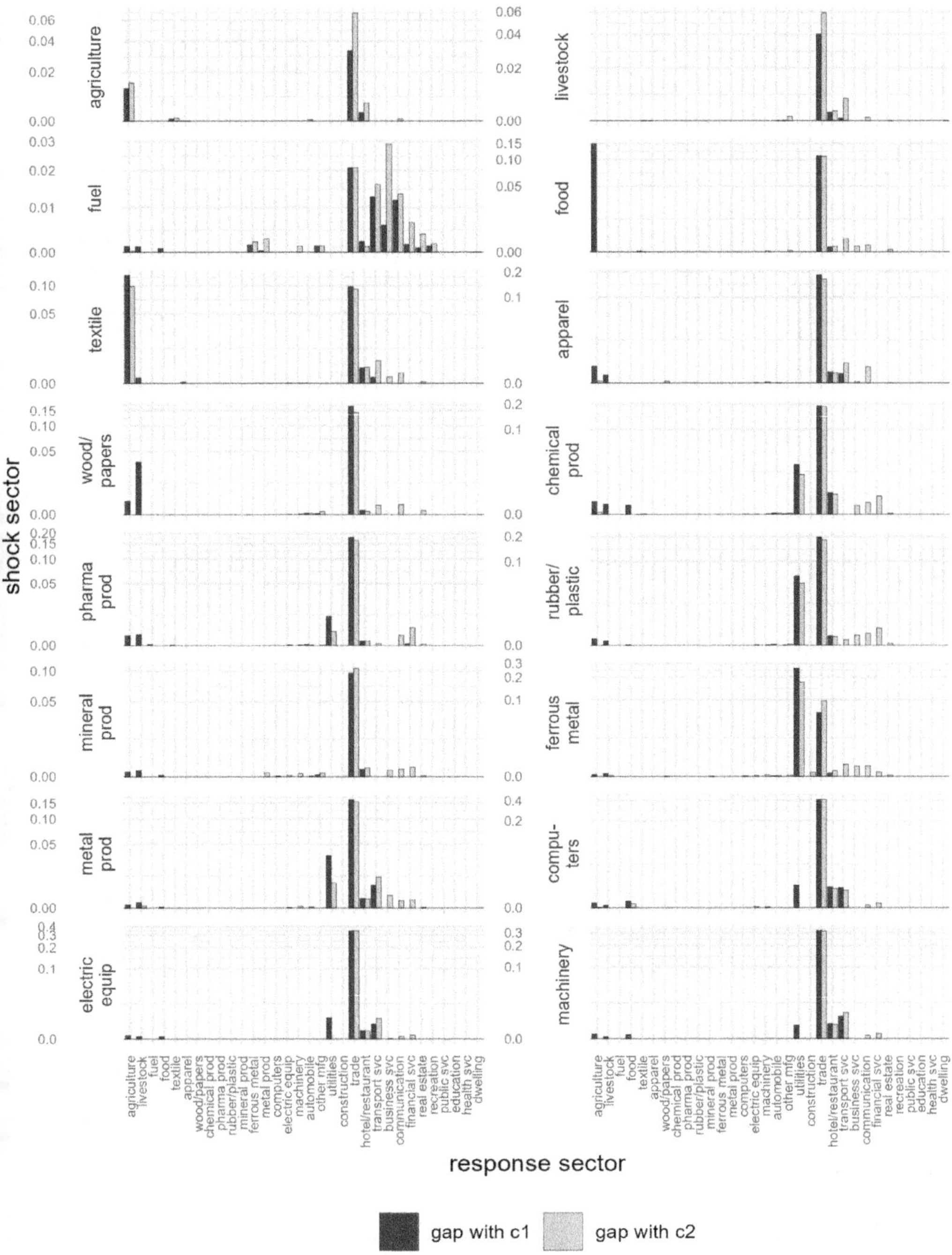

Figure 6.13 Difference of median coefficients

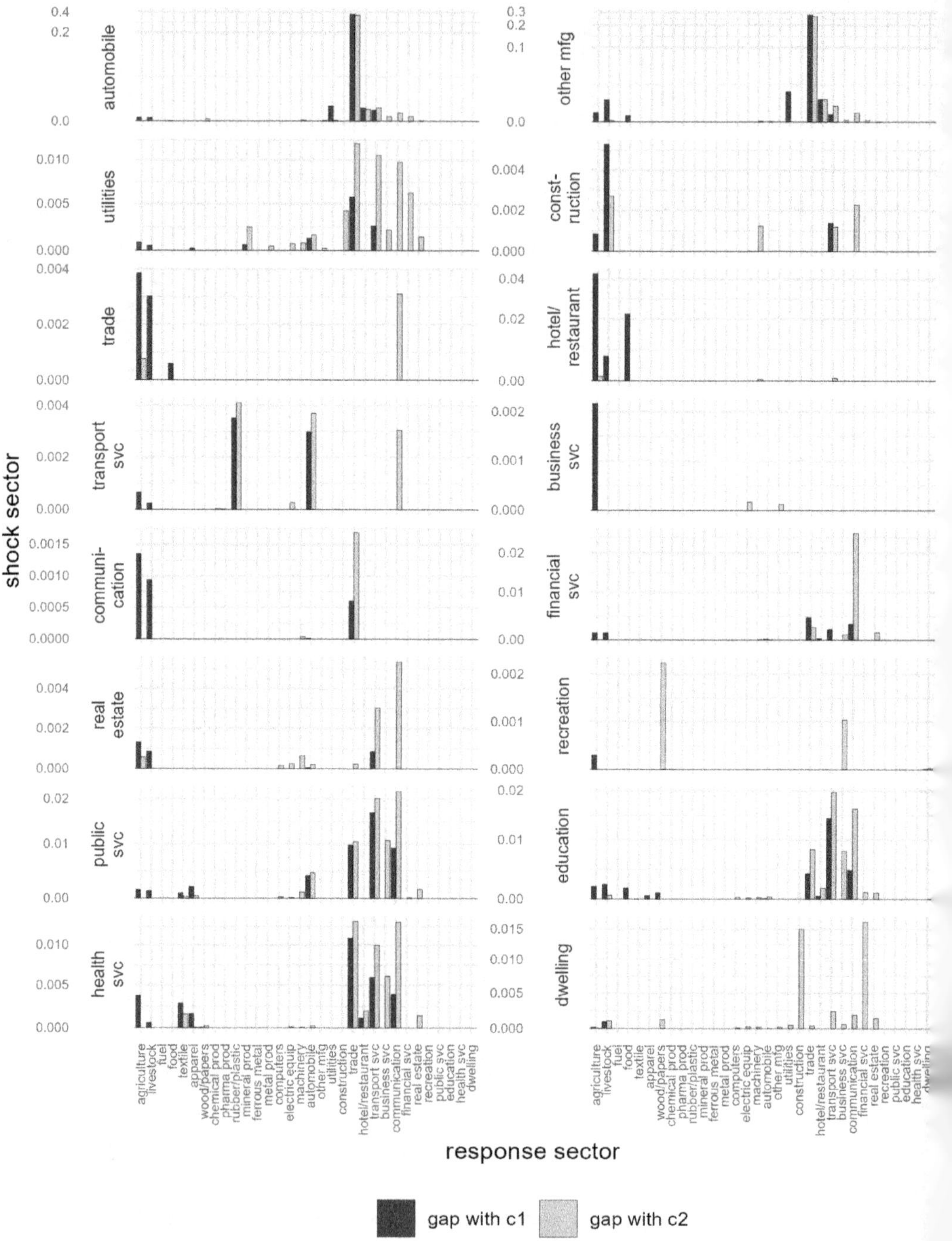

Figure 6.13 (*continued*)

When we look at the source sectors of spillover, there are very few sectors in which C3 is superior to other clusters (except for the spillover to the trade sector). The sectors in which the spillovers to nonservice sectors are superior in C3 to C1 or C2 include agriculture, food, textiles, and hotels and restaurants. These sectors are considered, to a certain extent, as procuring intermediate goods from domestic production sectors—mostly the agriculture and livestock sectors—for their own production. The high impact from hotels and restaurants on the food sector in particular and in turn from food on the agriculture and livestock sectors is potentially a promising form of industry upgrading for more value added. Agricultural products may add more value when supplied to hotels and restaurants, particularly in urban markets, rather than when they are simply sold in rural household markets.

Except for these sectors, there are few linkages among domestic industries in C3. In such an economic structure, even when production in one sector expands and spills over to other sectors, the impact is too weak to benefit the economy as a whole. The trade sector, which receives a high degree of spillover effect from other sectors, has little effect on other sectors. The low spillovers from the trade sector suggest that a certain share of traded goods is imported, leading to backward linkages leaking overseas.

While the importance of intermediary sectors (that is, trade) is obvious in improving the efficiency of flows of goods throughout the economy, overall factor compensations would not increase, especially if many of such goods are imported. An import substitution policy harmed the efficiency of many economies in the past and was not necessarily beneficial to consumers. It is also unlikely that a manufacturing base like that of C2 countries can be established in a relatively short time. The first step that C3 should pursue may be to build strong forward linkages with agriculture or metal industries that use domestic resources to add more value and, in the process, create backward linkages to spread the impact to wider segments of the domestic economy.

5. CONCLUSION

In this chapter, we have clustered countries into four groups according to the impact on factor remuneration and discussed the differences between the clusters. Focusing particularly on C3, which mainly consists of low-income African countries, we examined how the economic structure of these countries differs from other clusters, especially C2, which includes many emerging market countries.

Except for a few sectors, such as agriculture and livestock, unskilled workers in C3 receive less income-generating effect than those in C2 from the production growth of each sector. Technicians also benefit less in almost all sectors. Middle-skilled workers, such as clerks and sales workers, benefit from a higher effect. While this is encouraging because it raises the livelihood of the middle-class population, it also causes concern about income inequality. C3 countries need both to advance industrial development that benefits middle-skill labor and to add more value to the primary sectors and in turn benefit unskilled workers.

One important issue in the economic structure of C3 is its heavy reliance on the trade sector. A large part of C3 manufacturing sectors, except for a few sectors such as ferrous metals, are likely only acting as dealers, or intermediaries, in the distribution of manufactured goods. This may explain the low income-generating effect for technicians. High domestic transportation costs and utility burdens may be among the impediments to the sector's development. The current remuneration structure, tilted more toward capital, is another cause for concern in this respect. It is unlikely that C3 countries are currently in a position to follow a growth model similar to that of East Asia, where the manufacturing sector drives economic growth in a way that benefits a large part of the country's population.

C1 and C2 countries are participating, to varying degrees, in international production networks in addition to displaying a high level of domestic industrial linkages through intermediate goods transactions. In C3, in contrast, the majority of industries primarily supply final goods to domestic consumers rather than intermediate goods to other industries, domestic or abroad. This causes a low level of industrial spillovers domestically and from overseas. In addition, exports of raw materials to C1 countries (especially at low transfer prices) also limit labor remunerations. International spillovers from emerging countries such as India, China, and South Africa are currently larger than those from developed countries such as the United States, Japan, and Germany. Strengthening economic ties with these emerging economies and/or raising domestic interindustry linkages from the current structure that is mainly producing less processed final goods are the main priorities in this respect.

Unskilled workers do not benefit much, however, from nonprimary sector expansion. The coefficients for the service sectors are also low, except for recreation. It is unlikely that the expansion of nonprimary sectors under the current structure will increase the incomes of the poor population and promote equity in income distribution. A certain degree of interindustry linkages among service industries domestically is observed, and some sectors, such as construction and hotels and restaurants, have high spillover effects to a relatively wide range of sectors. The expansion of these sectors needs to be promoted in a way that will improve the profitability of other production sectors. In particular, the agriculture and livestock sectors have ample room to add value through supplying hotels and restaurants. Measures are needed to improve the quality of agriculture and livestock products and also to increase their value added by strengthening the cooperation between the hotels and restaurants sector and the agriculture and livestock sectors where the unskilled labors even currently benefit highly.

In addition, some issues need to be resolved in an international framework, such as agricultural subsidies in C1 countries, and low transfer prices in the resource industries. Needless to say, raising the skill levels of unskilled workers to enable them to be employed in middle-skill sectors should also be pursued, even if it cannot be achieved instantaneously. The problem of factor payment patterns tilted toward capital in C3 cannot be corrected without upgrading unskilled labor.

NOTES

1. Data for some countries, especially low-income countries, are not available. These missing country data are estimated as aggregate regions, such as "the rest of East Asia." The multipliers for the twenty aggregate regions are calculated but not separately analyzed.

2. In this chapter, they are referred to as land, resource, capital, manager, technician, clerk, sales, and unskilled, respectively.

3. *Closures* are additional constraints imposed by the analyst to match the number of variables and equations in the model, for example, whether wages are flexibly adjusted or the volume of employment is adjusted (i.e., unemployment exists). Because the main purpose of this chapter is to look at the impact on factor compensation, it is crucial to select the factor market characteristics for all 121 countries in an uncontroversial manner, which is not an easy task. For this reason, this chapter conducts a simple multiplier analysis.

4. As an alternative, countries could be classified by income levels or regions. However, grouping based on income levels may not be desirable because there are only nine low-income countries in the database. The classification by regions may be a problem in arbitrarily assigning the same structure to countries in the same region.

For this reason, we used a classification method that let the data speak for themselves. The results showed a strong correlation with income levels, but they identify an additional nine to ten countries with a similar multiplier effect structure to that of low-income countries.

5. Almost all Organisation for Economic Co-operation and Development (OECD) countries belong to Cl, except Mexico which is classified as C2. Taiwan, Singapore, and Malaysia are among the non-OECD countries in Cl. C2 includes major emerging economies such as China, India, Indonesia, Brazil, Thailand, and Vietnam. C3 consists mainly of African countries such as Ethiopia, Ghana, Kenya, Mozambique, Nigeria, Rwanda, Uganda, Tanzania, Togo, and Zambia. El Salvador and Tajikistan are non-African countries in C3.

6. Not necessarily an accurate description, but utility, transport service, business services, and so on, are considered to have a business-to-business (B2B) service character, while recreation, public service, education, and so on, are considered to have a business-to-consumer (B2C) service character.

7. In addition, the supply-demand structure of the intermediate goods (that affects spillover effects) and the pattern of payments to each factor are other elements to determine the outcome. These are discussed later in the chapter.

8. Because the number of countries belonging to C3 in the entire sample is relatively small, we did not conduct regression analysis but observed the general trend from the graphs.

9. The large destination countries of C2 for ferrous metals are India and South Africa. For metal products, the destination countries are China, India, and South Africa. The largest destination for metal products in the C4 category is the United Arab Emirates (UAE).

10. The domestic impacts from these countries are excluded from the calculations.

REFERENCES

Aguiar, A., M. Chepeliev, E. Corong, R. McDougall, and D. van der Mensbrugghe. 2019. "The GTAP Data Base: Version 10." *Journal of Global Economic Analysis* 4 (1): 1–27.

Anantsuksomsri, S., N. Pattanapong, and N. Tontisirin. 2017. "Global Backward and Forward Multiplier Analysis: The Case Study of Japanese Automotive Industry." In *Socioeconomic Environmental Policies and Evaluations in Regional Science: Asian Perspectives*, edited by H. Shibusawa, K. Sakurai, T. Mizunoya, and S. Uchida. Springer.

Blanchard, O., and D. Rodrik. 2021. *Combating Inequality: Rethinking Government's Role.* MIT Press.

Breisinger, C., M. Thomas, and J. Thurlow. 2009. *Social Accounting Matrices and Multiplier Analysis: An Introduction with Exercises.* Food Security in Practice Technical Guide 5. International Food Policy Research Institute

Defourny, J., and E. Thorbecke. 1984. "Structural Path Analysis and Multiplier Decomposition within a Social Accounting Matrix Framework" *Economic Journal* 94: 111–36.

Durongkoveroj, W., and R. Osathanunkul. 2013. "Regional Multipliers of Social Accounting Matrix and the Effective Eradication of Poverty." *Empirical Econometrics and Quantitative Economics Letters* 2 (4): 39–52.

McDonald, S. and K. Thierfelder. 2004. "Deriving a Global Social Accounting Matrix from GTAP version 5 Data." Global Trade Analysis Project Technical Paper 23, Center for Global Trade Analysis. Purdue University.

Mondlane, S., and D. van Seventer. 2019. "Agricultural Development, Trade, and Income Distribution." WIDER Working Paper 2019/77. United Nations University World Institute for Development Economic Research.

Noman, A., and J. E. Stiglitz, eds. 2015. *Industrial Policy and Economic Transformation in Africa*. Columbia University Press.

Noman, A., and J. E. Stiglitz, eds. 2017. *Efficiency, Finance, and Varieties of Industrial Policy*. Columbia University Press.

Nseera, E. 2014. "Growth and Distributional Impact of Agriculture, Textiles and Mining Sectors in Lesotho." Working Paper Series No. 206, African Development Bank.

Pyatt, G. 1989. "The Method of Apportionment and Accounting Multipliers." *Journal of Policy Modeling* 11: 111–30.

Pyatt, G., and J. I. Round. 1979. "Accounting and Fixed-Price Multipliers in a Social Accounting Matrix Framework." *Economic Journal* 89 (356): 850–73.

Robbie M. A., and G. P. Peters. 2013. "A Multi-Region Input-Output Table Based on the Global Trade Analysis Project Database (GTAP-MRIO)." *Economic Systems Research* 25 (1): 99–121.

Rodrik, D. 2018. "New Technologies, Global Value Chains, and Developing Economies." NBER Working Paper 25164. National Bureau of Economic Research (NBER).

Sim, B., F. Secretario, and E. Sim. 2007. "Developing an Interregional Input-Output Table for Cross-Border Economies: An Application to Lao People's Democratic Republic and Thailand." ERD Occasional Statistical Paper Series, Asian Development Bank.

Stiglitz, J. E. 2019. *People, Power, and Profits: Progressive Capitalism for an Age of Discontent*. Norton.

Walmsley, T. L., T. Hertel, and D. Hummels. 2014. "Developing a GTAP-Based Multi-Region, Input–Output Framework for Supply Chain Analysis." In *Asia and Global Production Networks Implications for Trade, Incomes and Economic Vulnerability*, edited by Benno Ferrarini and David Hummels. Asian Development Bank.

Whalmsley, T. L., A. H. Aguiar, and B. Narayanan. 2012. "Introduction to the Global Trade Analysis Project and the GTAP Data Base." GTAP Working Paper No. 67. Global Trade Analysis Project (GTAP), Purdue University.

CHAPTER 7

Green and Purple Jobs for Equitable and Sustainable Development

Özlem Onaran* and Cem Oyvat**

Abstract: This chapter analyzes the impact of public spending in the care economy, in the green economy, and on infrastructure on the employment of men and women and on gross domestic product (GDP) in selected emerging economies. Using a vector autoregression (VAR) model for each country, we explore policy scenarios involving a mix of public spending for an equitable green transition to a caring and sustainable economy. The findings indicate the potential for redeployment of brown, high-carbon, and fossil fuel–based sectors to green and care jobs by creating new decent formal jobs with adequate pay, working conditions, rights, and social security while addressing the effects of technological change on employment in emerging economies.

* Corresponding author: University of Greenwich, Institute of Political Economy, Governance, Finance and Accountability, email: o.onaran@greenwich.ac.uk.

** University of Greenwich, Institute of Political Economy, Governance, Finance and Accountability, email: c.oyvat@greenwich.ac.uk.

Acknowledgments: The research grant from the International Trade Union Confederation (ITUC) and Friedrich Ebert Foundation is gratefully acknowledged. The authors are grateful for comments from Evelyn Astor, Bert De Wel, İpek İlkkaracan, Maria Nikolaidi, Rafael Wildauer, Yannis Dafermos and Engelbert Stockhammer at various stages of this research. All errors and omissions are the sole responsibility of the authors.

1. INTRODUCTION

The world is at a crossroad of intersecting crises with inequalities; deficits in the care infrastructure; and ecological breakdown, including climate change, biodiversity loss, deforestation, and plastic pollution at the core. While there has been a mobilization of public spending in response to the COVID-19 crisis, the short-term emergency response fell short of a long-term strategic vision to address these intersecting crises, which requires placing public spending in the green and care economy at the heart of policy.

Reversing the ecological crisis requires a massive and urgent mobilization of large amounts of investment in renewable energy, public transport, and energy efficiency. Public spending in the green economy is the key policy to address both the scale and timing of the investment required for transition to a zero-carbon economy.

The pandemic exacerbated the deficits in the care infrastructure of our societies, and its effects were amplified because of inadequate levels of public provision of health and social care. Unpaid domestic care work increased further during the pandemic because of restrictions such as school closures, and was carried out disproportionately by women, increasing their time poverty, and reversing former gains made toward gender equality.

The pandemic exacerbated multiple dimensions of inequalities, whether based on class, race, gender, region, and/or country. Addressing inequalities is key to tackling both the public health crisis and the economic fallout in the aftermath of the pandemic. Technological change in the age of the fourth industrial revolution, with the increasing use of artificial intelligence (AI) and robotization, is adding to concerns about the balance between job destruction and creation. Meanwhile, there is an urgent need to increase employment in both the green and care economies in an aging population. The public provision of high-quality universal free basic services in social care, health, childcare, and education from early childhood preschool education to higher education tackles both the care deficit and inequalities by creating decent jobs with strong labor market institutions and providing much-needed services.

The scale and the urgency of the spending needs to address inequalities and the deficits in both the green and care economies require a large public spending program, which cannot be substituted by private investment based on profit motive or price signals in a market economy. Private investment in renewable energy has been too little, too late because of the irreversible nature of investment and fundamental uncertainty about the future of innovative green technologies. Private provision of health care, social care, or childcare services has led to an undersupply of these services, which are unaffordable for many, because the private profit maximization motive fails to account for long-term social returns.

The multiple crises of our time requires a paradigm shift toward a full-employment targeting and needs-based approach to macroeconomic policy; in particular, fiscal policy, must avoid competition between urgent social and ecological requirements. Short-term responses such as furlough schemes and flexible short-working time arrangements have helped limit the rise in unemployment during the pandemic, as has the implementation of additional policies such as job guarantee schemes; education grants; retraining schemes; and paid, on-the-job training, but there has never been a more opportune moment, in the aftermath of the pandemic, to make the case for large-scale public spending and employment programs with decent wages and working conditions. A return to fiscal conservatism cannot be a sustainable option at a time when social and environmental needs require a more substantial and urgent mobilization of fiscal policy.

The aim of this chapter is to analyze empirically the impact of public spending in the care economy, in the green economy and on infrastructure on employment of men and women and gross domestic product (GDP) in emerging economies.[1] We empirically estimate a vector autoregression (VAR) model for each country. We then explore policy scenarios involving a mix of public spending for an equitable green transition to a caring and sustainable economy.

The care economy includes health care, social care, education, and childcare. In analyzing public spending in the green economy, we focus on renewable energy, energy efficiency, and public transport. Electricity and heat production, transport, and buildings account for about half of global greenhouse gas (GHG) emissions (Intergovernmental Panel on Climate Change [IPCC] 2014). Energy consumption contributes to around 75 percent of all anthropogenic GHG emissions (Batini et al. 2021). Achieving the international goal of keeping global average temperatures from rising above the 1.5°C threshold relative to the preindustrial era (as recommended by the IPCC and endorsed by the 2015 Paris Agreement on climate change) requires significant and timely reductions in energy-related (and other) emissions (Ferroukhi et al. 2020).

This chapter aims to highlight the employment creation potential of renewable energy, public transport, other infrastructure, and the care economy to facilitate policies that can achieve the transition to a zero-carbon economy. The chapter addresses policy concerns regarding the impact of the transition to a zero-carbon economy on employment and inequalities. The findings clearly indicate the potential for the redeployment of workers from fossil fuel sectors to renewable energy or from the production of private transport vehicles to the production of public transport vehicles. In the context of redeployment, an expansion of the care economy is not only needed in its own right, but it also offers opportunities for redeployment from high-carbon or fossil fuel–based activities. The care economy is a low-carbon sector with a high potential for employment creation given its labor intensity. The transition across sectors also creates new education and training needs, which in turn add to the need for further public spending in the care economy.

We analyze the gendered employment effects of these three types of public spending and emphasize the importance of a policy mix to ensure that a green transition is gender-equitable and both the ecological transition and care needs of the countries are adequately addressed. We estimate the associated fiscal multipliers of public spending in the care and green economies and on infrastructure based on the estimated effects on GDP, analyze the impact of spending on the primary budget balance in the absence of any changes in the tax rates; that is, we analyze what portion of public spending is self-financing. We also discuss further funding possibilities in terms of the use of progressive taxation of income and wealth, national investment banks, or monetary policy to facilitate a needs-based approach to macroeconomic policy.

Combining the effects of public spending on employment and GDP, we analyze the potential for improvements in labor productivity in the medium run. Productivity gains create space for higher wages, better working conditions, and a shorter workweek with wage compensation. They also help to address the concerns regarding the effects of fiscal spending on the balance of payments constraints of the emerging economies.

Existing empirical research indicates that care, green and, infrastructure spending have a strong positive effect on the GDP and employment, in particular because of the labor intensive and domestic input content of the care and green economies. Regarding the effects of public spending in the care economy, empirical research using input-output tables for a variety of emerging and developed economies finds very high effects on the employment of women and, accounting for the indirect effects, also on the employment of men (Antonopoulos et al. 2010; İlkkaracan et al. 2015; İlkkaracan and Kim 2019; De Henau et al. 2016; De Henau et al. 2017; International Labour Organization [ILO] 2018b). Using an econometric analysis, Oyvat and Onaran (2022) estimate that a 1 percent increase in public spending in the care economy contemporaneously increases GDP by 0.5 percent and women's and men's employment by 0.7 percent and 0.1 percent, respectively, and leads to a 2.9 percent increase in GDP, a 2.2 percent increase in women's employment, and a 2.9 percent increase in men's employment, cumulative over ten years (including both direct and indirect effects, thanks to the high multiplier effects on the other sectors of the economy), in South Korea.

Onaran et al. (2019a, 2019b) econometrically estimate that a 1 percentage point increase in public spending in the care economy as a ratio to GDP in the United Kingdom leads, in the medium run, to a 2.7 percent increase in GDP, a 3.2 percent increase in women's employment, a 0.4 percent increase in men's employment, and a 1 percentage point increase in public gross fixed capital formation (GFCF) as a ratio to GDP, which in turn leads to a 2.0 percent increase in GDP, a 1.8 percent increase in women's employment, and a 1.6 percent increase in men's employment. The effects of such spending in the care economy on total employment, as well as on women's employment, is higher because of the care economy being more labor intensive and involving a higher share of women.

The International Monetary Fund (IMF, 2020) estimates that increasing public investment by 1 percentage-point as a ratio to GDP could generate 20 to 33 million new jobs globally, with particularly strong effects in low-income countries. Wildauer et al. (2021) estimate the public investment multipliers to be as high as 5.25 after ten years in the European Union (EU), meaning that an additional €1 billion in public investment may lead to €5 billion in additional GDP after ten years. Both Wildauer et al. (2021) and Obst et al. (2016) find that the effect of fiscal spending is much higher if coordinated across the EU members states.

With respect to the green economy, using multiregional input-output and supply-and-use tables, ILO (2018a) estimates that changes in energy production and use, including a shift toward renewable energy sources and greater efficiency, can create around 18 million jobs (net of some 24 million new jobs and the loss of around 6 million jobs) by 2030 throughout the world economy.[2] This transition is expected to result in a slightly lower share of women in employment given the current gendered sectoral employment patterns while creating more employment for low- and medium-skilled workers (ILO 2018a).

Ferroukhi et al. (2020) presents simulation results based on a macroeconometric, post-Keynesian model, arguing that renewable energy could employ 42 million people worldwide by 2050 (up from about 12 million in 2017), and energy efficiency jobs could reach 21 million as part of a just transition program.[3]

In a recent IMF working paper, Batini et al. (2021) econometrically estimate a stronger and longer-lasting multiplier effect of renewable energy infrastructure on GDP (around 1.1 to 1.5), compared to the non-ecofriendly fossil fuel energy investment (0.5–0.6), using a cross-country VAR analysis for a panel of eleven countries over the period 2003–2019; that is, every dollar (private and public) spent on activities such as zero-emission power plants or the protection of wildlife and ecosystems can generate more than a dollar's worth of economic activity.[4] The results indicate that the cumulative multiplier for green renewable energy spending falls only marginally over the years, which may reflect the fact that the investment includes different types of activities, for example, construction, networks for transmission and distribution, and smart meters. Batini et al. (2021) mention three factors to explain the high multiplier effects: (1) clean energy is more labor intensive than carbon-based fuel spending: in terms of both the direct spending on projects as well as the indirect spending on supplies, clean energy investment spends more on hiring people and relatively less on acquiring land (on- or offshore), machines, supplies, and energy itself; (2) clean energy has a higher domestic content in terms of both direct and indirect spending, such as retrofitting homes or upgrading the electrical grid system locally, and spends less on imports compared to fossil fuel sectors; and (3) clean energy investments produce more jobs at all pay levels, including entry-level jobs, compared to the fossil fuel industry, and include all levels of skills, for example, electricians, carpenters, and plumbers.

Pollin et al. (2015) compare the employment effects of public spending in renewable energy and energy efficiency with spending in fossil fuel sectors using input-output analysis for Brazil, Germany, Indonesia, South Africa, and South Korea, and Pollin et al. (2009) present a similar analysis for the United States. They find that spending in renewable energy and energy efficiency generate more employment than can be generated by spending on fossil fuels. Pollin et al. (2022) focus on South Korea and integrate a more detailed analysis of renewable energy; energy efficiency, including transition in public transport and electric vehicles; reforestation; and phasing out fossil-fuels. Their analysis suggests a pathway for emerging economies to lower their emissions level dramatically by raising both their energy efficiency and reliance on clean energy sources, and they show that clean energy investments can be a major engine supporting long-term development and employment.

With a focus on public transport, the American Public Transport Association (APTA, 2020) estimates that spending $1 billion in the United States could create almost fifty thousand new jobs and a $5 billion increase in GDP, as well as a significant increase in productivity.

Developing a post-Keynesian ecological macroeconomic model, Dafermos and Nikolaidi (2019) found that green subsidies and green public investment can lead to an increase in green capital compared to conventional capital.[5] The greening of public capital also improves the ecological efficiency of private companies. However, Dafermos and Nikolaidi (2019) show that the high level of economic activity, enhanced by increased public spending and subsidies, has an environmental cost. The implementation of green public investment and subsidies together with carbon taxes can reduce some of these adverse environmental effects; however, these policies should be supported with additional measures, such as stricter environmental regulations, changes in consumption patterns, and financial policies. Dafermos et al. (2022) show that public expenditures such as investments in low-carbon public transport could influence consumption patterns.

Section 2 of the chapter presents the theoretical macroeconomic framework of the analysis. Section 3 discusses definitions of the care and the green economy and data issues. Section 4 presents the stylized facts regarding the structure of output and employment in the selected emerging economies. Section 5 analyzes the channels through which public spending affects output and employment of women and men. Section 6 presents the econometric estimation methodology, and section 7 discusses the estimation results. Section 8 concludes with further implications for policy.

2. THEORETICAL FRAMEWORK

In this section, we discuss the theoretical framework for examining the effect of public spending in the care and green economies and on infrastructure on output and employment of men and women. The theoretical framework of the analysis is based on a gendered, structuralist, post-Keynesian, demand-led growth model, building on Onaran et al. (2019a, 2022a, 2022b), Onaran and Oyvat (2023) and Oyvat and Onaran (2022), which synthesize and further the models by Braunstein et al. (2011) and Seguino (2010, 2012), which in turn incorporate explicit analysis of both the components of demand and supply-side analysis, the government, and employment. Our theoretical framework considers (1) demand-side constraints in the economy, which lead to excess capacity and involuntary unemployment; (2) the effects of different types of public spending on demand, income distribution, and employment in both the short run and the medium run, as well as on the supply side on productivity in the medium run; (3) the dual effects of wages on not just production costs but also aggregate demand; (4) the effects of distribution of wealth and income between wages and profits as well as gender gaps in wages and employment on both demand and productivity; and (5) the effects of the structural features of the economy in terms of sectoral composition, oligopolistic price setting, import dependency, gender differences in the distribution of unpaid and paid labor in different sectors, and bargaining power between labor and capital, and between different genders.

Overall, we consider that there are four different types of government spending: (1) current spending in renewable energy, energy efficiency, and public transport; (2) current spending in the care economy, including spending in education, childcare, health care, and social care; (3) capital spending in infrastructure (public sector GFCF); and (4) other government spending. Public sector GFCF includes capital spending in renewable energy, energy efficiency, and public transport as well as buildings for the care economy, for example, hospitals and schools.

We present the structure of the model below. The economy has three sectors: (1) the social sector, which consists of the current expenditure of the government in the care economy, that is, provides public services in education, childcare, health care, and social care (contributing to the development of human capabilities using paid labor, as defined by Braunstein et al. [2011], denoted with a script H in the rest of the chapter); (2) the rest of the market economy (denoted with a script N), and (3) the unpaid care sector. The model introduces two types of workers: women and men. The profits are earned by the employers, who are genderless for simplicity in our model. Aggregate output and income are equivalent to the sum of the wage income of men and women and profits.

The total wage income of women workers is a function of women's wage rate in the social sector, women's employment in the social sector, women's wage rate in the rest of the economy, and women's employment in the rest of the economy. The total wage income of men workers is a function of men's wage rates in the social sector, men's employment in the social sector, men's wage rates in the rest of the economy, and men's employment in the rest of the economy. Gender wage gaps are the ratio of men's wage rate to women's wage rate in each sector.

The aggregate output in the market economy (GDP, excluding unpaid activities) is the is the sum of households' social expenditure; household consumption in the rest of the economy; private investment expenditure; government's social expenditure in the care economy; government's current spending in renewable energy, energy efficiency, and public transport; public investment (gross fixed capital formation); government's other expenditures; and net exports of goods and services.

Government's social expenditure in the care economy constitutes the public social sector output. The rest of the GDP is the market output in the rest of economy, which provides the goods and services to meet both private demand (household consumption, private investment, and exports) and government demand for spending in renewable energy, energy efficiency and public transport (REEEPT), public infrastructure investment (gross fixed capital formation), and other expenditures. Economic activity in the rest of the economy provides output for both spending in the green economy and the rest of the economic activities. The share of government's current expenditure in the care economy, in REEEPT, public infrastructure investment, and other spending are all determined as a fiscal policy decision as a share of aggregate output.

Employment in the rest of the economy is determined by output and labor productivity in the rest of the economy (and is equal to output divided by productivity). The share of women in employment in each sector is socially determined by occupational segregation. The wage paid to men and women workers in the social sector constitutes public social expenditure, and the social sector is not making profits. Any nonlabor inputs used constitute part of other government expenditure. Thus, the public social expenditure is a function of women and men's wage rates and employment in the social sector.

Profits, that is, the operating surplus in the rest of the economy, is income minus wage payments. The profit share is the share of profits in output in the rest of the economy and is a negative function of men's and women's wages and employment, and a positive function of labor productivity in the rest of the economy.

Next, the model introduces the unpaid domestic care labor within the households. For a given demographic structure defining the care needs of a society, higher paid employment by men and women is expected to have some negative impact on the supply of unpaid labor. An increase in government expenditure in the social sector (in education, childcare, health care, and social care) is also expected to reduce the need for care in households; therefore, it leads to lower unpaid labor. The impact of employment and public social expenditure on the time spent on unpaid domestic care might be nonlinear, and this negative impact might be decreasing in absolute values as it gets increasingly more difficult to decrease unpaid care at the lower levels of unpaid care. Unpaid domestic care labor is shared between women and men, and is exogenous and institutionally and socially determined.

On the demand side of the model, components of aggregate demand are defined by behavioral equations.

The household consumption of goods and services other than social expenditure is a function of the after-tax wage income of men and women workers in both sectors and the profit income of capitalists. Households' social expenditure is also a function of after-tax profit and the wage income of women and men workers in the two sectors, albeit with different parameters and government's social expenditure. The marginal propensity to consume goods and services produced in the social sector and the rest of the economy are assumed to be different for men and women workers, who make separate decisions, albeit interdependently and within the same household, reflecting the gender pay gaps as well as gendered differences in behavior.[6] The government's social expenditure can, on the one hand, increase households' social expenditure by providing wage income in the social sector and, on the other hand, decrease households' social expenditure by reducing the need for these expenditures. Government's current or capital spending in REEEPT also affects consumption of the households in two opposite directions; for example, on the one hand, the provision of public transport may reduce demand for private cars, and, on the other hand, government spending leads to indirect rebound effects by increasing household income available for other consumption goods (see Dafermos et al. 2022).

Private investment is expected to increase as a result of higher aggregate output and after-tax profit share in the rest of the economy. Government's infrastructure investment may have further positive direct effects on private investment by improving infrastructure and business expectations or substitute private investment in infrastructure. The model also introduces the effect of public debt to GDP on investment to consider the possible negative crowding out effects of rising public debt on the interest rate and thereby private investment (see Dafermos et al. 2022).

Public debt at a point in time is the public debt accumulated in the previous period plus interest on this debt, plus the total government expenditure in the current period, minus the taxes collected from profits in the current period. Exports are expected to increase with the income of trading partners and the depreciation in currency, and decrease with an increase in relative prices of exports to imports. Imports increase when domestic demand in *N* or domestic prices relative to import prices increase and decrease with the deprecation in currency. For simplicity, we assume that the marginal propensity to import in the social sector is negligible.

Domestic prices and export prices are set as a markup on nominal unit labor costs and other imported input costs, depending on the oligopolistic market power of firms in an imperfectly competitive market. Because nominal unit labor costs are real unit labor costs multiplied by domestic prices, and the wage share is identical to real unit labor costs (corrected for the ratio of GDP at factor cost to GDP at market prices), a fall in the wage share, that is, a rise in the profit share, leads to a fall in relative prices and improves net exports, depending on the labor intensity of exports, the pass-through from labor costs to export prices and domestic prices, and the price elasticity of exports and imports.

On the supply side of the model, labor productivity is constant in the short run and changes endogenously in the medium run in the rest of the economy because we assume that technological change or the adoption of new techniques takes time.[7] In the medium run, the labor productivity is likely to be positively influenced by government's spending in the social sector, REEEPT, and public investment with some time lag. We also expect households' consumption expenditure in marketized social services and domestic unpaid care labor to affect labor productivity positively. Higher output also leads to higher labor productivity because of the Verdoorn effect (Naastepad 2006; Hein and Tarassow 2010), in turn because greater scale can lead to more efficient allocation of sources. We consider that higher wages lead to labor-saving technologies as well as higher effort, which increase labor productivity. Labor productivity is expected to be path dependent and related to its past values because part of the technology from the last period is transferred to the following period. We expect the effects of these to be realized over the medium run. The medium run in the model is a sufficiently long period, for example, five years or more, for these effects on productivity to be realized. The time required for these different factors to affect productivity is an empirical question; for example, the impact of public investment in childcare may take longer than the impact of other types of government spending or higher wages.

Average wages, benefits, social infrastructure increases, and unpaid domestic care labor reduces women's and men's labor force participation rates (labor force as a ratio to population). For simplicity, we assume that the population is exogenously determined as changes in fertility and mortality take a much longer period than our medium-term theoretical and empirical analysis in this chapter. If employment grows faster than the labor force for a particular type of worker, the unemployment rate decreases, and vice versa. An exogenous increase in labor supply because of migration or changing gender norms would help relieve constraints on labor supply if demand for employment for a particular type of worker is not met. A rise in wages in a particular sector is likely to lead to higher labor supply of both men and women, leading also to changes in the sectoral segregation ratios in the social sector and the rest of the economy, as well as a change in social gender norms and the distribution of unpaid domestic labor.

While the wage rates in the social sector are exogenously determined by the government as a policy decision, we allow the wage rates for men and women in the rest of the economy to be determined endogenously as an outcome of a bargaining process between employers and workers. The bargaining power of women and men workers depends on the changes in labor demand in each sector and the labor supply of men and women, as well as exogenous factors determined by labor market institutions and legislation, social wage (determined by public social expenditure on parts of public infrastructure such as public transport or social housing), social norms, and occupational segregation affected by these norms, as well as personal characteristics such as education, which in turn are affected by social norms. For simplicity, we assume that expected prices are equal to actual prices. Hence, the real wage rates in the rest of the economy are functions of employment (or the unemployment rate) for men and women, spillover effects from wages in the social sector and across genders, and a set of exogenous factors affecting bargaining relations. The spillover effects of wage setting in the social sector are twofold: wage setting in the public sector affects the wage norm and negotiations in the rest of the economy too. Public spending in the social sector provides the social wage and improves the bargaining power of the workers in the rest of the economy. The gendered distribution of labor, that is, women's share in labor in both the paid economy in the social sector and the rest of the economy and in the unpaid economy, changes endogenously with changes in wages and employment of men and women and unpaid labor requirement with a lag in the medium run.

3. DEFINITIONS AND DATA

In this section, we present the definitions and data sources for public spending in the care and green economies and on infrastructure. Appendix 7.1 presents the data sources and availability for variables, which we use in the empirical analysis for Chile, Colombia, India, Indonesia, South Africa, and Turkey.[8]

We define public spending in the care economy as the sum of output in the sectors of education, including childcare, health care, and social care (including long-term care).[9] Public spending in education, childcare, health care, and social care is categorized as current spending (government consumption) in national accounts; however, feminist economics literature emphasizes the investment character of this spending given the positive effects on productivity and the positive externalities because of their public good character, and refers to it as social infrastructure investment (Elson 2016, 2017; Women's Budget Group UK and Scottish Women's Budget Group [WBG] 2015; Onaran et al. 2019a, 2019b, 2022a). İlkkaracan (2013) coined the term "purple economy" to identify the care economy.

Public infrastructure spending is defined as public GFCF, as reported in national accounts. Examples of public GFCF are buildings for schools and hospitals, or machinery and equipment used in the care sector, which are not accounted for in the current spending data for the care economy defined above; social housing; transport; and energy infrastructure. The latter two include capital spending in the green economy, for example, in rail transport or in the renewable energy sector, such as investment in wind farms, solar farms, or hydropower plants, or the infrastructure for the distribution of energy.

We define public spending in the green economy as spending in renewable energy (RE, that is, solar, wind, geothermal, and hydro), energy efficiency (EE, that is, weather proofing and installing heat pumps, etc., in public and private buildings; industrial energy efficiency; grid upgrades), and public transport (PT, both infrastructure and current spending to provide the services, excluding air transport, with a larger weight allocated to rail transport infrastructure). We refer to this spending category as public spending in REEEPT. Public spending in the green economy includes the purchase of goods and services produced in various industries such as construction (including construction services) and manufacturing (e.g., based on International Standard Industrial Classification Revision 3 (ISIC Rev. 3) classification) of plastic products (code 2520); glass products (2610); cement and plaster (2694) and concrete products (2695); nonferrous metals (2720); fabricated metal products (all subindustries, i.e., 281, 289); general-purpose machinery (291); special-purpose machinery (292); domestic appliances (2930); electrical machinery and apparatus (31, all subindustries); electronic valves, tubes, and so on (3210); locomotives and rolling stock (3520); other transport equipment (3599); and transport services (excluding air transport).[10] This category combines both current spending and GFCF in terms of the national accounting categories and has an overlap with the public infrastructure. Spending in public transport or energy efficiency includes both infrastructure investment (construction of the railways and manufacture of the rail transport vehicles or investment in the grid) and current spending (in labor compensation or other inputs) to provide public transport or insulation services. Spending in renewable energy includes only capital spending to produce assets (such as wind and/or solar farms, hydropower plants, geothermal plants) but not the labor compensation (or other inputs) to produce energy using renewable energy sources. We discuss further how we address these issues in section 6 on the estimation methodology. We do not have long-term series data on private or public spending in GFCF in renewable energy or energy efficiency and, even in the case of public transport, where there is a long history of investment, data availability does not allow us to disaggregate public GFCF by industry. Therefore, we estimate the effect of an increase in public spending in renewable energy, energy efficiency, and public transport as a ratio to GDP by distributing this spending stimulus across the manufacturing, construction, and transport industries that provide inputs to renewable energy and energy efficiency using the weights described in Pollin et al. (2015), based on input-output data. In the case of public transport, we distribute the spending stimulus across the manufacturing, construction, and transport industries using weights reported in APTA (2020). We summarize these weights in detail in appendix 7.2, tables A7.2.1 and A7.2.2.[11]

In our simulation analysis, we estimate the effect of a policy package that includes public spending in three categories:

1. An increase in spending in the care economy (social sector, i.e., education, childcare, health care, and social care) by 1 percentage-point as a ratio to GDP.
2. An increase in public infrastructure spending (public GFCF) by 1 percentage-point as a ratio to GDP.
3. An increase in public spending in REEEPT by 1 percentage-point as a ratio to GDP.

The latter spending category in REEEPT is split in turn as follows: half of this spending is allocated to renewable energy, which in turn is allocated equally among investments in wind, solar, geothermal. and hydropower.[12] Twenty percent of spending in REEEPT is allocated to energy efficiency, out of which 50 percent is allocated to weather proofing/energy efficiency in public and private buildings, 25 percent is allocated to industrial energy efficiency, and 25 percent is allocated to grid upgrades.[13] Thirty percent of spending in REEEPT is allocated to public transport, out of which 10 percent is allocated to investment in rail transport vehicles, 18 percent is allocated to construction (to build the infrastructure), and 72 percent is allocated to the provision of the transport services. These weights are based on APTA (2020). Appendix 7.2, table A7.2.2, then presents how an increase in spending in REEEPT by 1 percentage point as a ratio to GDP is allocated to manufacturing subindustries (0.458 percentage point), construction (0.327 percentage point), and transport services (0.216 percentage point).

The spending distribution between different types of renewable energy, energy efficiency, and public transport aims to provide an indicative policy simulation and can be adjusted based on the specific needs or resources of each country. The ratios we use for the simulations in this chapter should be regarded as plausible examples.

Next, we repeat the stimuli described above every year, and calculate the cumulative effect of these increases every year for five years.

Appendix 7.3 further presents ILO (2018b; based on İlkkaracan and Kim 2019) estimates regarding the additional spending requirements in the care economy per year, as a ratio to GDP, in the high-road scenario compared to the status quo.[14] Appendix 7.4 presents additional average annual low-carbon energy investment requirements as a ratio to GDP (percent) for the period from 2016 to 2050 to limit global warming to

1.5°C compared to current policies based on Bertram et al. (2021) and McCollum, et al. (2018).[15] The additional average annual low-carbon energy investment requirement as a ratio to GDP ranges between 1.4 percent in Colombia and 3.8 percent in India.[16]

In analyzing public spending in the green economy, we focus on sectors with a public good and/or infrastructure character. In contrast to the ILO (2018a), we do not analyze the spending in private electric vehicles as part of public stimulus to greening transport because we aim to shed light on the role of public spending in realizing the potential to shift from the production of private transport vehicles to the production of public transport vehicles as part of a zero-carbon economy.[17] We also exclude biofuel as part of the renewable energy mix because of the potential strain it would place on global agricultural resources, land use, sustainability, food prices, and poverty.[18] We also did not include energy production using biomass and waste because of concerns about their carbon neutral status.[19] Nuclear energy is excluded from our simulation analysis because of the potentially major public safety concerns and the fact that this form of energy is nonrenewable as a result of the use of uranium.[20]

We define public spending broadly to include spending by municipalities and local authorities and not just central governments, depending on the nature of the sector and the preferences regarding the structure of governance and devolution in the country. The ownership structure in different industries may also take diverse forms, including central government or municipal ownership or cooperatives bringing together producers and/or users. Public spending may take the form of public investment, public employment programs, contracting, or public subsidies, in particular in areas where private capital already exists, and public capital accumulation may take time. For example, in a country where electric utilities are publicly provided, the government can easily use green public investment to decarbonize electricity provision; but in a country where utilities are private, the government may need to rely on green subsidies to reduce the reliance of electricity production on fossil fuels, unless they decide to nationalize the utilities.[21]

4. STYLIZED FACTS OF KEY STRUCTURAL INDICATORS

In this section, we discuss the key structural indicators of the selected countries as of 2019 (the last year before the COVID-19 pandemic). See table 7.1. The emerging country cases in this chapter range from India,

Table 7.1 Key indicators, 2019

	Chile	Colombia	India	Indonesia	South Africa	Turkey
GDP in constant 2015 prices, in USD (1,000)	262,807,032	321,687,569	2,695,611,315	1,049,318,967	358,712,445	997,437,115
GDP per capita in PPP (constant 2017 international $)	24,968	14,585	6,714	11,812	13,710	28,197
Employment rate, total (%)	58.8	60.8	46.7	66.1	40.1	44.5
Employment rate, men (%)	69.3	73.4	71.9	79.7	46.1	62.2
Employment rate, women (%)	48.8	48.9	19.7	52.4	34.5	27.6
Output in the care economy/GDP (%)	11.8	14.8	7.9	4.4	15.6	12.5
Value added in manufacturing sectors providing input to REEEPT/GDP (%) (i)	1.9	1.5	1.8	4.7	3.7	3.5
Value added in construction/GDP (%)	6.9	7.6	6.7	10.7	3.1	5.4
Value added in transport (excluding air transport)/GDP (%)	2.4	3.3	3.5	2.9	7.9 (vii)	0.7
The share of informal employment in total employment (%) (ii)	29.3	62.4	88.6	82.4	35.3	32.0
Public GFCF/GDP (%)	2.3	3.5	6.1	3.6	2.4	3.4
Employment in the care economy/total employment (%) (ii)	14.9	8.4	5.2	6.6	12.2	11.7
Employment in construction/total employment (%) (ii)	8.5	6.9	11.9	6.2	8.2	4.5
Employment in transport (excluding air transport)/total employment (%) (ii)	8.5	7.9	6.2	4.9	6.1	4.5
Employment in manufacturing/total employment (%) (ii)	9.9	11.8	12.1	14.4	10.8	18.4
Women's share in employment in the care economy (%) (ii)	72.9	70.4	45.3	63.1	72.6	61.3
Women's share in employment in construction (%) (ii)	7.4	5.8	7.8	2.1	11.1	4.3
Women's share in employment in transport (excluding air transport) (%) (ii)	19.5	13.7	3.6	6.7	19.1	9.2
Women's share in employment in the manufacturing sector (%) (ii)	32.6	44.9	20.8	43.4	34.7	25.4
Women's share in employment in the manufacturing sectors providing input to REEEPT (%) (iii)	na	25.4	na	36.3	na	na
Imports/value added in the manufacturing sectors providing input to REEEPT (%) (iv)	301.5	192.1	141.5	103.3	261.2	172.7

Imports/value added in the manufacturing sector (%) (v)	162.9	96.4	54.2	47.5	150.7	96.5
Imports/value added in services (%) (v)	8.7	8.1	8.8	7.5	7.4	5.5
Energy imports, net (% of energy use) (v)	65.2	-274.1	34.3	-103.1	-14.5	75.2
CO_2 emissions per capita (tonnes CO_2 per capita) (vi)	4.8	1.5	1.7	2.2	7.4	4.4
CO_2 emissions/GDP constant 2015 USD Power Purchasing Parity (vi)	0.2	0.1	0.3	0.2	0.6	0.2
CO_2 intensity of total energy supply (CO_2/total energy supply; tonnes CO_2/terajoule (vi)	52.3	40.6	58.8	57.8	73.9	59.7
Energy intensity: total energy supply/GDP (PPP) (gigajoule/ thousand 2015 USD PPP) (vi)	4.0	2.7	4.3	3.1	8.3	2.7
Renewable share (modern renewables) in final energy consumption (Sustainable Development Goal 7.2) (%) (vi)	25.3	22.8	15.9	9.7	5.6	14.1

Source: (i) South Africa at two-digit level; 2017 for others 2018, see appendix 7.1. (ii) International Labour Organization Statistics (ILOSTAT) online database, for Turkey informal employment share is proxied by the share of self-employed. (iii) United Nations Industrial Development Organization (UNIDO) database, see appendix 7.1 for details. (iv) UNIDO database, demand-supply balance, 2016, two-digit data for all countries. (v) World Bank World Development Indicators (WDI) database, 2016 for comparability. (vi) International Energy Agency (IEA), https://www.iea.org/data-and-statistics/data-browser, for CO_2 emissions and intensity, energy intensity, renewable share data. See appendix 7.1 for other variables. (vii) Transportation (including air transport) and storage, communication for South Africa.

with the lowest GDP per capita of $6,714 (in purchasing power parity (PPP), constant 2017 international $), to Turkey with a GDP per capita of $28,197 (in PPP). Despite improvements in aggregate income, substantial inequalities persist, with total employment rates still below 70 percent in all six cases, and a very high share of informal employment, reaching above 80 percent in the extreme cases of India and Indonesia. The employment rate of women is below that of men in all cases, with the lowest rate of employment for women at 19.7 percent in India, followed by Turkey at 27.6 percent, and highest rate still below 60 percent in Indonesia (52.4 percent). There are additional issues regarding the lower women's employment rate in urban areas. The employment rate of men ranges between a very low rate of 46.1 percent in South Africa and 79.7 percent in Indonesia.

Both the care economy and the green economy provide important potential for employment as well as just transition, and there are substantial gaps in terms of required investment for a caring and green transition as discussed in section 3. As of 2019, the ratio of output in the care economy to GDP ranges between 4.4 percent in Indonesia and 15.6 percent in South Africa, representing between 5.2 percent of total employment in India and 14.9 percent in Chile. The share of value added in the manufacturing sectors providing input to REEEPT in GDP ranges between 4.7 percent in Indonesia and 1.5 percent in Colombia. The share of construction in GDP is between 3.1 percent (South Africa) and 10.7 percent (Indonesia), and that of transport (excluding air transport) is rather low, at a share between 0.7 percent (Turkey) and 3.5 percent (India).

The employment share of women differs significantly across industries. While the share of women is rather high in the care economy (between 45.3 percent in India and 72.9 percent in Chile), their share is very low in construction (between 2.1 percent in Indonesia and 11.1 percent in South Africa) and transport (3.6 percent in India and 19.5 percent in Chile). In the manufacturing industry, women's share in employment is higher than that in construction and transport; however, in the manufacturing sectors providing input to REEEPT, women's share is lower (between 25.4 percent in Colombia and 36.3 percent in Indonesia) compared to their share in aggregate manufacturing in most countries. These gender differences indicate the importance of investing in both the care and green economies to ensure a gender-equitable just transition.

The share of renewable energy in final energy consumption (modern renewables, as defined by Sustainable Development Goal (SDG) 7.2) ranges between 25.3 percent in Chile and 5.6 percent in South Africa at the low end, indicating the large gap and vast potential for new investment. As in the rest of the world, emerging economies need to reduce the emission intensity of their total energy supply as well as energy intensity (total energy supply/GDP). As of 2019, the CO_2 intensity of total energy supply (tonnes (t) of CO_2 per terajoule (TJ)) ranges between 40.6 in Colombia on the lowest end and 73.9 in South Africa. Energy intensity (gigajoule (GJ)/thousand 2015 USD PPP) is between 2.7 in (Colombia, Turkey) and 8.3in South Africa (again on the high end). There are also important inequalities in terms of global climate justice, with Colombia having the lowest CO_2 emissions per capita (1.5 t CO_2 per capita) and South Africa the highest (7.4 t CO_2 per capita).

Investment in the green economy could have important benefits; however, it also could bring challenges in terms of the balance of payments. It decreases the energy intensity as well as dependence on energy imports, which is an issue particularly for Turkey, Chile, and India, who import (net) between 75.2 percent (Turkey) and 34.3 percent (India) of their energy use. Imports constitute a high share in the value added of manufacturing in general, and even a higher share in the manufacturing sectors providing input to REEEPT in all countries. The decline in the reduction of energy imports through increasing energy self-sufficiency via investing in renewables and energy efficiency could decrease imports in the medium run. In addition, the care economy's positive effects on productivity could reduce the unit labor costs and could further help relax the balance of payment constraints.

5. THE EFFECTS OF PUBLIC SPENDING ON EMPLOYMENT AND GDP

This section examines the impact of public spending on output and employment of women and men, based on the theoretical framework described in section 2. Public expenditure in the care economy can increase through rising employment and/or higher wages in the public social sector.[22] Public spending in REEEPT or infrastructure could be through public sector contracting or subsidizing a private provider to provide the goods and services or direct public employment programs, which would again increase employment and/or wages. Our VAR estimations capture these direct and indirect effects on output and employment.

Public spending has short- and medium-run effects. We first discuss the short-run effects. Public spending on care, REEEPT, and other physical infrastructure has a direct positive effect on output, as well as further multiplier effects, because higher aggregate demand generates employment and stimulates private investments. The magnitude of these multiplier effects will depend on (1) the labor intensity of the sectors receiving the extra spending, (2) the marginal propensity to import out of the new spending, (3) the effects on household consumption by substituting private spending, (4) the effects on private investment by providing public infrastructure, and (5) the gender composition of new employment.

The gender effects of public spending in the care economy are greater compared to REEEPT and other physical infrastructure because women constitute a larger share of employment in the social sector. Expanding the childcare or elder-care sectors also encourages women to participate in labor markets and could improve women's employment. Changing the gender composition of employment in turn affects consumption patterns and average marginal propensity to consume in the economy. Previous research shows that the marginal propensity to consume in education, health care, and social care is larger for women than men, and the marginal propensity to consume for other goods and services is larger for men than women (Onaran et al. 2022a, 2022b; Seguino and Floro 2003; Morrison et al. 2007; Lee and Pocock 2007).

Higher public spending with constant tax rates could increase public indebtedness (public debt/GDP), which might raise interest rates under certain circumstances, particularly if monetary policy does not actively accommodate fiscal policy. Depending on the interest elasticity of investment, there may be negative crowding out effects on private investment. However, this effect might be small if investment is not very sensitive to interest rate and the effect of public borrowing on the interest rate is not very high. Higher public spending could also lead to higher GDP and generate greater tax revenues, which both would alleviate the negative effects on public debt/GDP and private investment.

Rising employment rates of men and women will improve the bargaining power of workers and lead to an increase in the wage rates of men and women. The wage rates of men and women also influence each other. The effects on women's and men's wages would have further impact on output and employment.

Next, we discuss the medium-run effects of public spending on care, REEEPT, and other physical infrastructure. In the case of all three types of public spending, higher output in the economy also leads to higher labor productivity because a growing scale can lead to more efficient allocation of resources. An increase in public social expenditure is expected to have a direct positive impact on labor productivity in the medium run through improving education and health care. Childcare and elder care could improve productivity by unleashing the full productive potential of women. Improvements in physical infrastructure through public spending also increase labor productivity.

The increase in labor productivity affects profit share positively, which in turn encourages private investment. Higher productivity reduces unit labor costs and increases the international competitiveness of the economy, which is expected to affect net exports positively. The change in labor productivity could affect the distribution of income between wages and profits, which would have further effects on consumption as workers and capitalists have different marginal propensities to consume.

An increase in public spending could also change public indebtedness in the medium run, which further influences private investment. However, the positive medium-run productivity effects of public social and physical infrastructure spending could ease or even reverse the possible crowding out effects in the medium run.

The medium-run effect of public spending on employment depends on the relative size of the increase in output and labor productivity. We expect the proportionate increase in output to be larger than that in productivity in response to all three public spending categories, which would lead to a positive medium-run effect on employment, albeit with gender differences.

6. ESTIMATION METHODOLOGY

We estimate the overall impact of public spending, discussed in sections 2 and 5, on output and employment using VAR. In previous studies, Oyvat and Onaran (2022) estimate the effects of public spending in the care economy in South Korea; Batini et al (2021) estimate the effects of public spending in clean renewable energy and alternatives on GDP for a panel of countries, and Wildauer et al. (2021) estimate the effect of public GFCF on GDP in the European Union by using VAR. Onaran and Stockhammer (2005) and Stockhammer and Onaran (2004) estimate the effect of functional income distribution on output and employment using VAR for the cases of Turkey and South Korea, and for the cases of the United States, United Kingdom, and France, respectively. The interaction between public spending, wages, employment, demand, and productivity allows for tracing the effects through an entire system rather than analyzing one equation at a time. VAR is more suitable for dealing with endogeneity issues. Using VAR estimations requires a focus on a subset of the variables in the theoretical model, however, because degrees of freedom in the estimations could quickly erode with extra variables as a result of the use of multiple lags (Enders 2015).

We carry out country-specific estimations using time series data. We determine the estimation period by data availability for each country. We estimate the impact of an increase in public spending in public infrastructure (public GFCF), the care economy, and subindustries providing inputs to REEEPT, on employment of men and women in the nonagricultural sector and GDP. The employment indicator in the econometric estimations is based on the nonagricultural sector to avoid potential biases because of the high share of informal or self-employed or unpaid family workers in agricultural employment.

We estimate alternative specifications with different combinations of public spending variables:

1. Specification 1 exists of five variables in the system with the following order: public GFCF, output in the social sector (education, childcare, health care, and social care), employment of men and women in the nonagricultural sector, and GDP. We do not include REEEPT with public GFCF in the same specification to reduce double counting because most of the infrastructure spending involves construction and inputs from manufacturing. This specification accounts for public spending in REEEPT as part of the total public GFCF and excludes the current spending in REEEPT.
2. Specification 2 includes the subindustries providing input to REEEPT existing of six variables with the following order: value added in construction, public transport services (excluding air transport), the value added of a synthetic sector consisting of the sum of the value added of manufacturing subindustries providing input to REEEPT, employment of men and women in the nonagricultural sector, and GDP.[23] We use the value added in public transport services, construction, and manufacturing subindustries as separate variables rather than using their sum for REEEPT because they are expected to have different multiplier effects as a result of differences in their labor intensity and imported input content.

Based on the estimated cumulative orthogonalized impulse response functions, we first present the effect of an increase in each public spending category as described in section 3 contemporaneously and for the following five years. In specification 1, we analyze the effects of an increase in each of the care economy and public GFCF by 1 percentage point as a ratio to GDP. In specification 2, we analyze the effects of an increase in the sum of the value added in construction by 0.327 percentage point, public transport services by 0.216 percentage point, manufacturing subindustries providing input to REEEPT by 0.458 percentage point, all as a ratio to GDP (based on the weights presented in appendix 7.2, table A7.2.2).

Second, we calculate the cumulative effects of repeating these stimuli for five years.[24] Third, we present an alternative scenario where we multiply the effects of a 1 percentage point increase in the care economy/GDP and the REEEPT/GDP with the required additional investment reported in appendixes 7.3 to 7.4, as discussed in section 3.

Based on these estimations, we calculate the effects of public spending on the employment rate (total as well as for men and women) for the projected rate of growth of the population (applying the rate of growth in nonagricultural employment to total employment).

We calculate the sum of the employment effect of an increase in care, REEEPT, and public GFCF. Alternative specifications (1 and 2) discussed above are used to present the cumulative effects on employment and GDP.

Our RE category does not include current spending for energy production using renewable energy. The VAR methodology partly addresses this issue by accounting for the lagged multiplier effects of capital investment in RE on total employment. We also do not explicitly estimate the effects of reducing brown, fossil fuel–based activities. However, our results show the employment potential of the green economy and care economy, which would open space for policy discussion for redeployment in low-carbon sectors away from the high-carbon sectors.[25]

7. ESTIMATION RESULTS AND POLICY SIMULATIONS

This section presents the estimation results on the impact of public GFCF, the care economy, and the green economy (subindustries providing inputs to REEEPT) on GDP, and women's and men's employment (in the nonagricultural sector), based on VAR analysis. Appendix 7.4 presents the estimated cumulative orthogonalized impulse response functions. Based on the estimated impulse responses for specification 1, we discuss the cumulative percentage change in GDP, and women's and men's employment (and total employment, all in the nonagricultural sector), in response to a one-off 1 percentage point increase in public spending in GFCF, the care economy, and the green economy (REEEPT) as a ratio to GDP.[26] The effects in year zero are the contemporaneous effects of this initial shock, while the effects in year 5 show the cumulative effects in the medium run, over five years, summing the contemporaneous and lagged effects of this one-off shock. The percentage change effect on GDP discussed below is the multiplier effect also illustrating the change in GDP in response to a one-unit change in the public spending category (both measured in local currency).

7.1 THE EFFECTS OF PUBLIC GROSS FIXED CAPITAL FORMATION

In Chile, a one-off increase in public GFCF by 1 percentage point of GDP leads to a 1.8 percent increase in GDP contemporaneously and a 3.7 percent increase in five years, that is, an increase in public spending in public GFCF by one Chilean peso increases the Chilean GDP by 3.7 Chilean pesos at the end of five years. The employment of women and men increases by 1.7 percent and 2 percent, respectively, during the initial year of the stimulus, and by 3.5 percent and 3.2 percent, respectively, in five years.

In Colombia, the contemporaneous increase in GDP is relatively smaller (0.3 percent); however, GDP increases by 1.9 percent in five years. The employment of women and men increases by 2.2 percent and 0.07 percent, respectively, in five years, with total employment increasing by 1.0 percent.

In India, employment of men by year 1 and year 3 increases by 0.4 percent and 0.8 percent, respectively. The effects on women's employment and GDP are insignificant.

In Indonesia, GDP increases by 1 percent contemporaneously, and by 3 percent by the fifth year. The employment of women and men increase contemporaneously by 0.5 percent and 0.6 percent, respectively, and by 2.5 percent and 2.1 percent, respectively, by year 5.

In South Africa, GDP increases by 1.3 percent contemporaneously and by 2.4 percent in five years; the employment of women and men increases by 6.8 percent and 4.1 percent, respectively, in five years. The effect on nonagricultural employment is larger than that on GDP, which could be because of urbanization and/or informality. Public infrastructure spending may have more positive effects on urban output and employment that could attract rural dwellers to urban areas, leading to a higher rate of growth in nonagricultural employment than in the rest of the country. Also, GDP is likely to underestimate the informal economy's output, while employment data based on household labor force surveys are more likely to capture some informal employment. Urbanization itself may contribute to a higher rate of growth in informal employment in the cities. The estimations are based on data for the post-1991 period for South Africa, where the mobility of the Black South African population was severely restricted until 1991, which in turn suppressed the urban share of population at low levels. Thus, our estimations might be capturing the increase in urbanization after the end of migration restrictions during apartheid (Bakker et al. 2020). These results are robust to controlling for urbanization and informal economy share, as discussed in more detail in appendix 7.3.

In Turkey, while the effects are low in the short run, they increase steeply. In five years, GDP increases by 4.1 percent; women's and men's employment increase by 4.5 percent and 2.7 percent, respectively.

To summarize, the multiplier effects of a one-off increase in public physical infrastructure at the end of five years are greater than 1 in five countries and range between 1.9 in Colombia to 4.1 in Turkey; that is, an increase in public spending in physical infrastructure (public GFCF) by one Colombian peso increases the Colombian GDP by 1.9 Colombian pesos at the end of five years. There is one exception: with the multiplier for GFCF below 1 (albeit positive): in India, the multiplier effect of GFCF is insignificant.

Next, we present a simulation of the effects of a five-year-long, repeated annual increase in public spending in GFCF by 1 percentage point as a ratio to GDP every year (repeating the effects of a one-off shock discussed above). Figure 7.1a presents these results. An annual increase in public investment in GFCF by 1 percentage point of GDP at the end of five years creates a cumulative increase in GDP by 8.0 percent in Colombia, 12.4 percent in Turkey, 13.6 percent in Indonesia, 13.9 percent in South Africa, and 21.3 percent in Chile. The consequent cumulative increase in total employment ranges between 1.5 percent in India, 7.5 percent in Colombia, 9.2 percent in Indonesia, 11.0 percent in Turkey, 20.5 percent in Chile, and 31.5 percent in South Africa. In five countries (Chile, Colombia, Indonesia, South Africa, and Turkey), the employment of both men and women increases, and the rate of increase in women's employment is higher, although the number of new jobs for women is

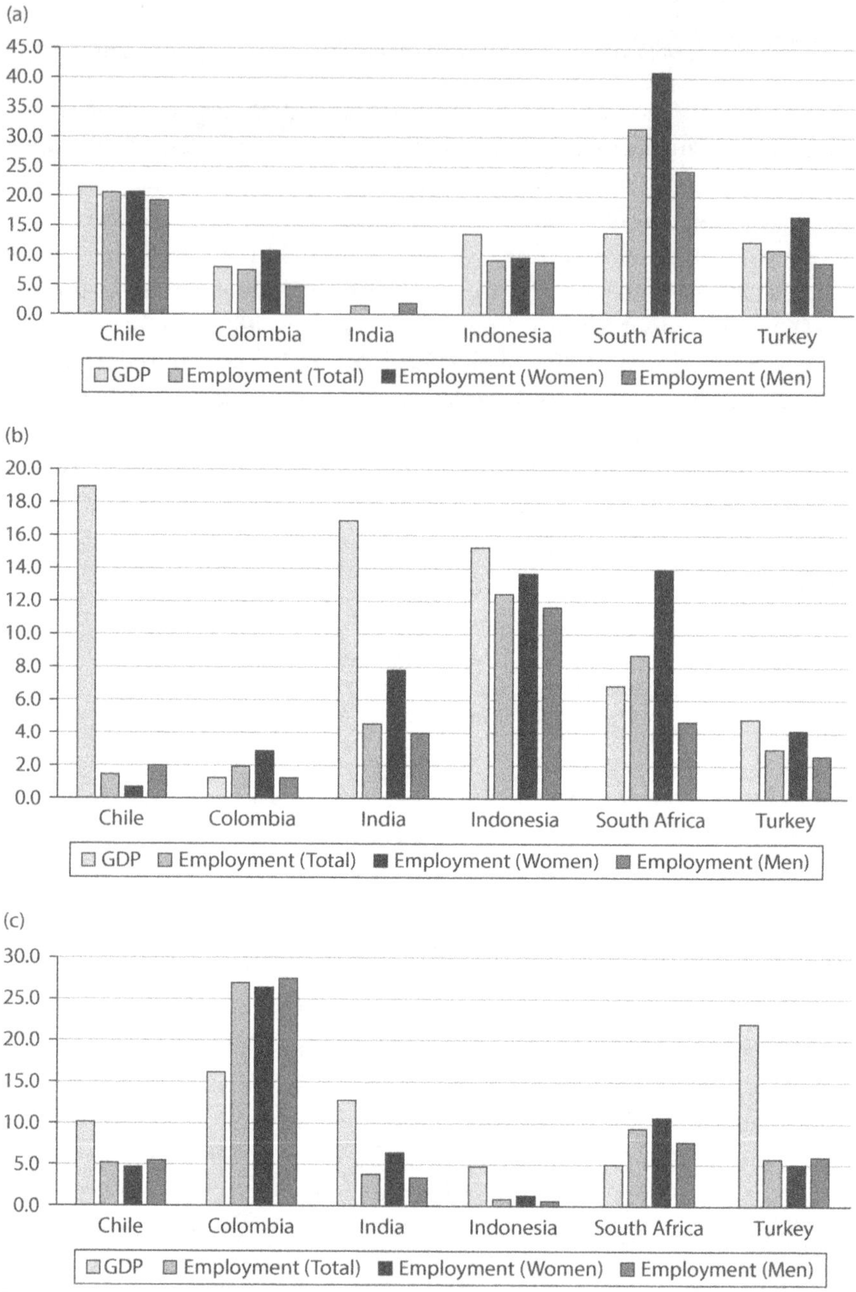

Figure 7.1 The cumulative percentage change in gross domestic product (GDP) and employment (total, women, and men, nonagricultural) and percentage-point change in the employment rate (total, women, and men) at the end of five years in response to a repeated increase in public spending in the care economy, green economy, and public gross fixed capital formation (GFCF) by 1 percentage-point as a ratio to GDP every year. (a) The effects of spending in public gross fixed capital formation. (b) The effects of spending in the care economy. (c) The effects of spending in the green economy (renewable energy, energy efficiency and public transport [REEEPT]).

Note: The employment rate is calculated based on the assumption of projected rate of growth of population.

still lower than that for men because of a low starting point. In India, the employment effect is positive only for men, while the effect on women's employment is insignificant, which illustrates complex movements across urban and rural and formal and informal sectors that put women at a disadvantage, as well as data issues. These differences illustrate the importance of gender mainstreaming in assessing the employment impact of public investment. The employment rate (as a ratio to population aged 15 and over) increases by around 10 percentage points in Chile and South Africa; by about 4 percentage points in Colombia, Indonesia, and Turkey; and by 0.4 percentage point in India.

7.2 THE EFFECTS OF PUBLIC SPENDING IN THE CARE ECONOMY

Based on the estimated impulse responses for specification 1, we report the cumulative percentage change in GDP, and women's and men's employment (and total employment, in the nonagricultural sector) in response to a one-off 1 percentage point increase in public spending in the care economy as a ratio to GDP (the output in the sectors of education, health care, childcare, and social care). The results overall show that growth in the care economy has positive effects on GDP and total employment, with stronger effects on women's employment (with the exception of Chile). This is consistent with the stylized facts discussed in section 4, which show that women's share of employment in the care sector is significantly higher compared to their share in the rest of the economy.

A one-off increase in public spending in the care economy by 1 percentage point of GDP in Chile leads to an increase in GDP by 2.2 percent contemporaneously and by 3.1 percent in five years. The employment of women and men increases contemporaneously by 0.7 percent and 2.1 percent, respectively; however, the effects are insignificant afterward.

In Colombia, GDP increases by 0.3 percent cumulatively over five years, which is rather weak by international standards.[27] The employment of women and men increases contemporaneously by 0.3 percent and 0.2 percent, respectively, and by 0.5 percent and 0.1 percent, respectively, by the fifth year.

In India, GDP increases contemporaneously by 2.0 percent and by 2.8 percent in five years. The employment of women and men increase contemporaneously by 0.4 percent and 0.1 percent, respectively, and by 1.8 percent and 1.0 percent, respectively, in five years.

In Indonesia, the effects are very strong in the medium run, with a 0.8 percent increase in GDP contemporaneously and by a 3.6 percent increase in five years. The employment of women and men increases by 0.3 percent and 0.7 percent, respectively, contemporaneously, and by 3.8 percent and 2.7 percent, respectively, in five years.

In South Africa, at the end of five years, GDP increases by 1.6 percent, and the employment of women and men increases by 2.9 percent and 1.1 percent, respectively. As in the case of GFCF discussed in section 7.1, the effects on employment exceed the effects on GDP, potentially because of urbanization and growing urban informal employment.

Although the effects start slow in Turkey, in five years GDP increases by 1.6 percent. The employment of women and men increases by 1.2 percent and 0.8 percent, respectively.

To summarize the effects of a one-off increase in care spending, the multiplier effects on GDP in five years are larger than 1 in six countries and range between 1.6 in Turkey and South Africa and 3.6 in Indonesia. There is one exception: with the multiplier for care below 1 (albeit positive): In Colombia, the multiplier of care spending is 0.3 in five years.

Next, we present a simulation of the effects of a five-year-long, repeated annual increase in public spending in the care economy by 1 percentage point as a ratio to GDP every year (repeating the effects of the one-off shock discussed above). Figure 7.1b presents these results. An annual increase in public spending in the care economy by 1 percentage point at the end of five years leads to a cumulative increase in GDP by 1.3 percent in Colombia, 4.9 percent in Turkey, 6.9 percent in South Africa, 15.3 percent in Indonesia, 16.9 percent in India, and 18.9 percent in Chile. Total employment increases by 1.5 percent in Chile, 2 percent in Colombia, 3.1 percent in Turkey, 4.6 percent in India, 8.7 percent in South Africa, and 12.5 percent in Indonesia, creating jobs for both women and men, albeit at a faster rate for women. The employment rate (as a ratio to population aged 15 and over) increases by 5.5 percentage points in Indonesia; 3.1 percentage points in South Africa; by around 1 percentage point in Colombia, Turkey, and India; and 0.7 percentage point in Chile.

7.3 THE EFFECTS OF PUBLIC SPENDING IN THE GREEN ECONOMY

Based on the estimated impulse responses for specification 2, we report the cumulative percentage change in GDP, and women's and men's employment (and total employment, all in the nonagricultural sector) in response to a one-off 1 percentage point increase in public spending in the green economy (REEEPT) as a ratio to GDP.

In Chile, GDP increases contemporaneously by 1.9 percent, and by 1.5 percent in five years. Women's and men's employment increase contemporaneously by 1.5 percent and 2.1 percent, respectively. In five years, the cumulative increases in the employment of women and men are only 0.5 percent and 0.6 percent, respectively, illustrating the existence of high positive effects on labor productivity.

In Colombia, GDP increases contemporaneously by 0.9 percent and by 4.1 percent in five years. While the contemporaneous effects on employment are insignificant, the employment of women and men increases substantially by: 7.8 percent and 6.8 percent in five years. Again, the stronger long-run impact of REEEPT on nonagricultural employment compared to GDP could be an outcome of rural to urban migration and the growth of the urban informal sector employment, as discussed in section 7.1 for the case of South Africa and elaborated further in section 7.4.

In India, GDP increases contemporaneously by 3.1 percent and by 1.5 percent in five years. The employment of women and men increases by 1.8 percent and 0.8 percent, respectively, in five years.

In Indonesia, GDP increases contemporaneously by 0.3 percent and by 1.4 percent in five years. While the contemporaneous effects on employment are insignificant, the employment of women and men increases by 0.9 percent and 0.2 percent, respectively, in five years.

In South Africa, GDP increases contemporaneously by 1.0 percent and by 0.7 percent in five years. The employment of women and men increases contemporaneously by 1.6 percent and 1.9 percent, respectively, and by 2.0 percent and 1.5 percent, respectively, in five years. The effect on employment is again higher than that on GDP possibly because of the effects on urbanization and informality as discussed in section 7.1 and elaborated further in section 7.4.

In Turkey, GDP increases contemporaneously by 0.8 percent and by 4.5 percent in five years. There is only a positive contemporaneous effect on men's employment by 0.2 percent but in five years, the employment of women and men increases by 2.2 percent and 1.1 percent, respectively.

To summarize, in response to a one-off increase in spending, the multiplier effects of public spending in the green economy on GDP are greater than 1 in all countries and between 1.3 in South Africa (in year 1) and 4.5 in Turkey (in year 5).

Next, we present a simulation of the effects of a five-year-long, repeated annual increase in public spending in the green economy (REEEPT) by 1 percentage point as a ratio to GDP every year (repeating the effects of a one-off shock discussed above). Figure 7.1c presents these results. An annual repeated increase in public spending in the green economy (REEEPT) by 1 percentage point at the end of five years leads to a cumulative increase in GDP by 4.8 percent in Indonesia, 5.0 percent in South Africa, 10.2 percent in Chile, 12.7 percent in India, 16.1 percent in Colombia, and 22.0 percent in Turkey. The cumulative effect on total employment ranges between 0.9 percent in Indonesia to 3.8 percent in India, 5.2 percent in Chile, 5.7 percent in Turkey, 9.4 percent in South Africa, and 27 percent in Colombia. The employment rate (as a ratio to population aged 15 and over) increases by 13.2 percentage points in Colombia, 3.3 percentage points in South Africa, 2.6 percentage points in Chile, 2.0 percentage points in Turkey, 1.0 percentage point in India, and by 0.3 to 0.4 percentage point in Indonesia.

7.4 SUMMARY AND POLICY SIMULATION

In response to a one-off increase in public spending, the multiplier effects on GDP are, in most countries, substantial in all spending categories and reach greater than 1 in the medium run. However, there are some exceptions, with multipliers for some spending categories below 1 (albeit positive) in some countries: in India, the multiplier effect of GFCF is insignificant. In Colombia, the multiplier of care spending is 0.3 in five years. These exceptional cases against the strong evidence of high multipliers in other countries indicate that not only the amount but also the composition and targeted nature of spending matters. The differences in the import dependency of the industries provide a partial explanation. The degree of informality could be another potential reason: the increase in public spending might be leading to a higher increase in informal economy production not captured by the formal GDP measure in the national accounts compared to other countries; however, controlling for the share of the informal economy in GDP (where significant) only marginally improved the multiplier effects, if at all.[28]

Public spending in all categories has significant effects on productivity (compared to effects on GDP and employment), in particular in the medium run in Chile, Indonesia, and Turkey. There is evidence for productivity effects in Colombia in response to GFCF, and in India to the care economy and REEEPT. In South Africa (in response to all categories) and Colombia (in response to the care economy and REEEPT), potential productivity effects appear to be more than offset by the effects of urbanization and informality, leading to a higher rate of increase in nonagricultural employment compared to GDP.[29] As discussed in section 7.1, public infrastructure spending may have more positive effects on urban output and employment that could attract rural dwellers to urban areas, leading to a higher rate of growth in nonagricultural employment than in the rest of the country. Also, GDP is likely to underestimate the informal economy's output, while employment data based on household labor force surveys are more likely to capture some informal employment. Urbanization itself may contribute to a higher rate of growth in informal employment in the cities.

Given the high multiplier effects of public spending in most cases, public spending is partly self-financing, with the negative effect on primary budget balance/GDP (excluding interest payments, comparing the growth of public spending and GDP based on multiplier effects) around 0.8 percentage point (Turkey, India, Indonesia, South Africa) in the case of the care economy, between 0.8 percentage point (Turkey) and 0.9 percentage point (Chile, Colombia, Indonesia, South Africa) in the case of GFCF, and around 0.9 percentage point in the case of the green economy, based on the cumulative effects of a 1 percentage point increase (one-off) in the public spending category in five years. Care economy spending has a slightly higher rate of self-financing. As we discuss in section 8, however, a substantial mobilization of public spending for a green and caring, just transition with full employment and decent jobs requires more progressive taxation of income and wealth, as well as accommodating monetary policy and borrowing.

Research highlights that required additional spending in the care economy, according to the high-road scenario of the ILO (2018b; İlkkaracan and Kim 2019) for the provision of decent, formal, well-paid care services, and in the green economy, according to the low-carbon investment requirements of the climate models to limit global warming to 1.5°C (Bertram et al. 2021; McCollum et al. 2018), may be higher than 1 percentage point as a ratio to GDP.[30] Our simulations are indicative and provide a tool to estimate the effects of required spending by multiplying the effects of a 1 percentage point increase reported in this section by the desired spending amount.

Figure 7.2 presents the effects of a policy mix combining public spending in the care and green economies, and other infrastructure by

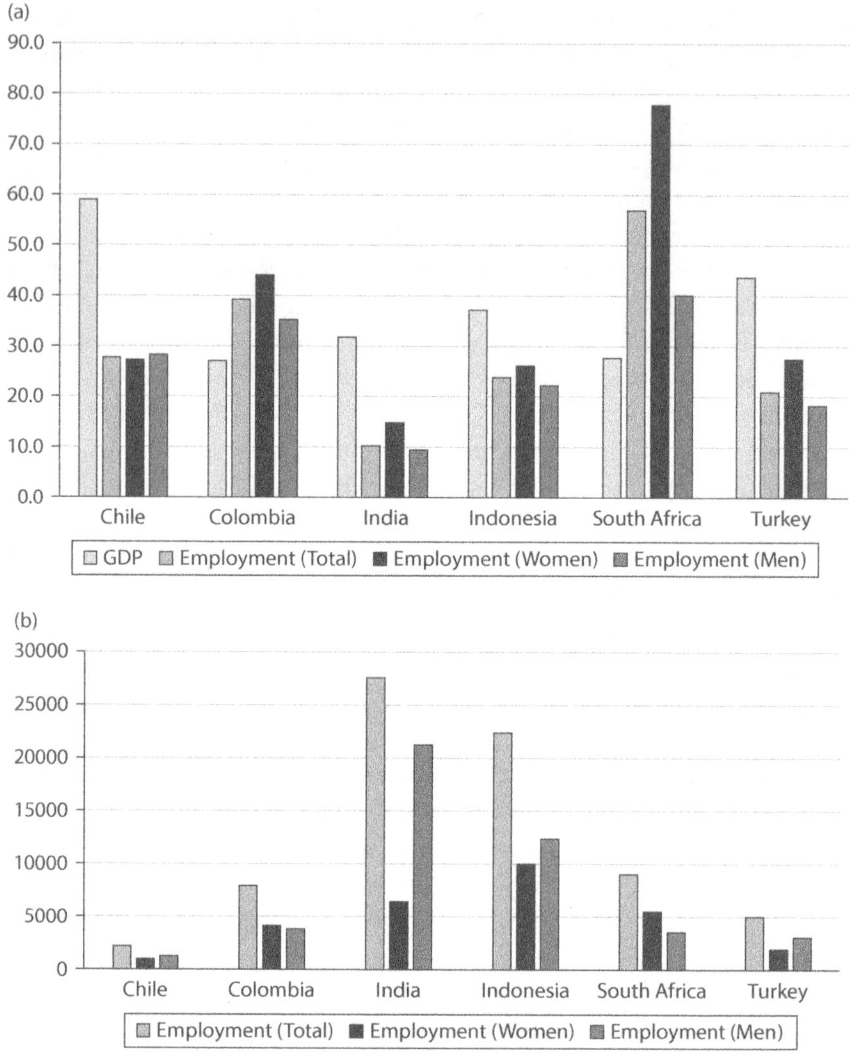

Figure 7.2 Policy mix combining public spending in the care and green economy, and other infrastructure: the sum of the cumulative percentage change in GDP and employment (total, women, and men, nonagricultural) and number of new jobs (total, women, and men, nonagricultural, thousands), at the end of five years in response to a 1 percentage-point annual increase in in the care economy and green economy and public gross fixed capital formation/GDP every year. (a) Percentage change in GDP and employment (total, women, and men, nonagricultural). (b) Number of new jobs (thousands).

1 percent of GDP every year for five years. The creation of a high number of new jobs (2.1 million in Chile, 4.9 million in Turkey, 7.9 million in Colombia, 9 million in South Africa, 27.6 million in India, and 22.4 million in Indonesia) signals the potential of green and care economy jobs for redeployment from the brown, high-carbon, and fossil fuel–based sectors. Starting with high gender gaps in employment, more jobs are created for men than for women (except in South Africa) at the end of this policy stimulus. Despite higher rates of growth in women's employment, the employment rates of women are still significantly lower than that of men. It is important to design hiring and training policies to make sure that the new green and physical infrastructure jobs also benefit women and go beyond the existing occupational segregation patterns, with women concentrating in the care economy and constituting a low share of the green economy.

8. CONCLUSION AND POLICY IMPLICATIONS

Building a caring and sustainable society in the aftermath of the pandemic is possible, and public investment based on a green, purple, and red new deal is the key to such a policy program.

In this chapter, we analyzed the impact of public spending in the care economy, in the green economy, and on infrastructure on employment of men and women and GDP in emerging economies. We examined the effects of these three types of public spending on women's and men's employment and discussed a policy mix that would lead to a green transition that is gender-equitable and would address the ecological transition and care needs of the countries adequately.

We estimated the associated fiscal multiplier effects of public spending in the care and green economies and on infrastructure. The multiplier effects on GDP are always positive and, in most countries, substantial in all spending categories and reach greater than 1 in the medium run. The differences across countries indicate that not only the amount but also the composition and targeted nature of spending matters, in addition to differences in the import dependency or informality.

We presented a policy simulation of the effects of a repeated, annual increase in public spending in physical infrastructure, the care economy, and the green economy for five years. The creation of a high number of new jobs signals the potential of the green and care jobs for redeployment from the brown, high-carbon, and fossil fuel–based sectors. Starting with high gender gaps in employment, more jobs are created for men than for women (except in Colombia and South Africa) at the end of this policy stimulus, despite higher rates of growth in women's employment. These results illustrate the importance of gender mainstreaming in assessing the employment impact of public investment. It is important to design hiring and training policies to make sure the new green and physical infrastructure jobs also benefit women, going beyond the existing occupational segregation patterns with women concentrated in the care economy and constituting a low share of the green economy.

The findings clearly indicate the potential of the green and care jobs for redeployment from the brown, high-carbon, and fossil fuel–based sectors. In the context of redeployment, an expansion of the care economy is not only needed on its own merits, but it also offers opportunities for redeployment from high-carbon or fossil fuel–based activities. The care economy is a low-carbon sector with a high potential for employment creation given its labor intensity. The transition across sectors also creates new education and training needs, which in turn add to the need for further public spending in the care economy.

How to finance such a just green and caring transition? Public spending, even without any increases in the tax rates, is partially self-financing thanks to strong multiplier effects. But the scale and urgency of the social and ecological needs for an effective response to the intersecting crises of inequalities, care, and climate change require the use of all policy tools. Public borrowing to fund some of this spending can be justified given the medium-term effects on productivity and sustainability. An alternative is to focus on the negatives: the expected damage to the ecology, society, and economy if investment needs are not delivered on time means that responsible fiscal policy requires urgent and large public spending funded by all means, including borrowing. Also, in the case of public spending in the care economy, considering the long-term effects on productivity, such spending could be considered as public investment in social infrastructure rather than current expenditure, which justifies borrowing to fund spending if needed. National and regional investment banks working in cooperation with the government and central bank are also crucial for funding large-scale public infrastructure projects.

The large-scale spending needs undeniably require a combination of progressive taxation of both income and wealth eventually. Onaran et al. (2019a) estimate that an increase in the tax rate on wealth has a high positive impact on output, and thereby employment and the budget in the United Kingdom, because it decreases wealth concentration, which in turn reduces the financialization of nonfinancial companies, market concentration, and barriers to entry, and thereby stimulates private investment. Thus, taxation of wealth is a particularly effective policy to fund purple and green public spending while tackling income, gender, and wealth inequalities. Tippet et al. (2021) present the tax revenue potential of a progressive scheme of wealth taxation, aiming at the top 1 percent of the wealthiest households in the United Kingdom. This is particularly important after the pandemic, which is likely to increase wealth inequality substantially.

It is crucial that any policy mix should involve the coordination of fiscal and monetary policies. The strict separation between monetary and fiscal policy is becoming more difficult to justify. Effective monetary policy requires coordination with expansionary fiscal policy targeting long-term public investment in care and green infrastructure, building on a needs-based approach to policy and considering long-term needs to tackle inequalities and social, economic, and ecological sustainability. The lessons of the past decade show that the central banks' mandate should include a dual target of full/high employment and an inflation target high enough to be consistent with the former, moving within a band, with a higher weight for employment. Although unconventional monetary policy (quantitative easing [QE]) carried the heavy lifting in terms of policy since the Great Recession in 2007–2009 and helped to stabilize financial markets and prevented a new Great Depression, monetary policy is less effective than fiscal policy, and one reason for this is that the elasticity (sensitivity) of private corporate investment to interest rates is low and its elasticity to demand is high. QE has further contributed to inequalities, financialization, and higher wealth concentration at the top 1 percent via asset price inflation; and led to lower private corporate investment (Onaran et al. 2019a; Tori and Onaran 2018, 2020, 2022), which in turn leads to low productivity.

International policy coordination can also make a difference, particularly for emerging economies. The effects of public spending are stronger, and negative effects on the current account balance are moderated, if policies are implemented simultaneously in all the countries (Onaran 2016; Obst et al. 2016; Wildauer et al. 2021). If the large, high-income economies lead the way, this creates space for small, import-dependent, balance-of-payments-constrained emerging economies. From the perspective of the emerging economies, public investment as part of a well-designed industrial policy is also key to structural change and productivity gains. Managing the short-run constraints on the balance of payments requires further policies in terms of capital controls and foreign direct investment (FDI) policies. To address global inequalities, which have further deepened with the pandemic, two policies stand out: first, cancellation or restructuring of parts of the debt of developing countries needs to be part of the international development agenda; second, a transfer of technology to support mass nonprofit global production of key public goods, from vaccines and medication to solar panels, turbines, or batteries for storing renewable energy, is the only way to tackle global crises such as the pandemic or climate change in the context of global climate justice.

The coordination of fiscal policies with labor market policies makes the effects of fiscal spending stronger and eases the funding pressures because higher wages lead to higher tax revenues (Onaran 2016; Obst et al. 2016; Onaran et al. 2019a). Strong prolabor institutions—in particular, strong, well-coordinated trade unions, equal pay legislation, increased job security, permanent contracts, higher minimum wages, and an improved and equitable parental leave—are good for an equality-led and sustainable development. Labor-market regulation for a shorter workweek can also promote a rise in gender equality in paid and unpaid work and income while facilitating a green transition as well as higher productivity (Onaran and Calvert Jump 2022). Having more time could facilitate behavioral changes toward greener ways of living with less carbon-intensive activities or commuting to work, and more labor- and time-intensive household work and leisure activities. For example, cooking with fresh and/or local ingredients rather than heating ready-made or frozen food, growing your own food, washing reusable rather than disposable textile goods, walking and/or cycling rather than driving, as well as commuting less, or spending more time on personal education, reading, community interaction, socializing, and exercising rather than on material consumption.[31]

NOTES

1. The empirical analysis covers six selected emerging economies: Chile, Colombia, India, Indonesia, South Africa, Turkey

2. The International Labour Organization (ILO 2018a) simulations are based on the following scenarios: "In terms of electricity, the scenario implies an increased share of renewables for electricity generation (including a 59 percent increase in electricity produced from solar photovoltaic panels in 2030, compared to 2012), a decrease in the use of fossil fuels (a 50 percent reduction in coal-based electricity

production), and a drop in overall demand as a result of greater efficiency. Similarly, under this scenario, energy demand by industry would fall by 20 percent by 2030 as a result of greater efficiency, and the remaining energy needs would be met through greater reliance on biomass and waste, rather than fossil fuel-based energy sources."

3. Ferroukhi et al. (2020) assumes a 50 percent crowding-out effect, that is, the additional investment required for the energy transition drains investment from other sectors with higher employment intensities. It is also assumed that carbon taxation makes it possible to reduce income taxes, leading to higher disposable income and thereby higher consumer spending.

4. The investment made to generate clean renewable energy is directed at building (and operating) the infrastructure, and repowering, which is spending for the refurbishment or upgrading of existing system components with the latest, most advanced equipment. Investment in electricity networks includes investment in new infrastructure to accommodate new demand (increased connections and consumption); investment to replace aging infrastructure; and the investment required to integrate renewables in the power system, including both transmission and distribution; and expenditure on digital equipment for the smart monitoring and operation of the grid (e.g., smart meters, automation, and electrical vehicle fast charging stations). All these data exclude both financing and operational costs.

5. See Dafermos and Nikolaidi (2019) for a comparison of mainstream (integrated assessment models and computable general equilibrium) models based on full-employment assumption and post-Keynesian ecological macroeconomic models.

6. Previous research shows that the marginal propensity to consume social services is larger for women than for men, and the marginal propensity to consume the rest of the goods and services is larger for men than for women (Onaran et al. 2022a, 2022b; Seguino and Floro 2003; Morrison et al. 2007; Lee and Pocock 2007).

7. Increasing productivity in the social sector is less related to the availability of technology because the quality of these services is more important and in many cases requires more nurses, care workers, and teachers per patient or student. Productivity in the social sector is determined simply, by definition, by output per employee.

8. The countries are selected based on data availability and coverage of structurally different emerging economies.

9. Our definition of the output in the care economy is consistent with the ILO (2018b) definition of care sectors, which the ILO define as follows: "Based on ISIC 4, care sectors are: 85. Education; 86. Human health activities; 87. Residential care activities; 88. Social work activities without accommodation. In several cases . . ., health and social work was aggregated at one-digit level." We do not deduct the output produced by the private sector in the care economy because it does not alter our empirical analysis about the effects of an increase in government spending on care. Informal domestic care workers as well as unpaid domestic care work is not part of this analysis, and because of data restrictions in informality, is beyond the scope of this chapter. It is important to note that public investments in formal care services would be expected to decrease the use of informally provided care services and therefore facilitate formalization and better working conditions for care workers. Finally, we do not analyze the effects of tax credits on households to purchase care services separately.

10. We use United Nations Industrial Development Organization (UNIDO) data on value added at four-digit ISIC Rev. 4 classification for the latest periods for which data are available, and link this with the data at four-digit ISICrev3 classification for the earlier years and for the period for which data at four-digit classification are not available. We link this series with the data at two-digit ISICRev3 classification, assuming that the value added for the industry at four-digit classification (e.g., industry 2520) grew at the same rate as the value added of the industry at two-digit classification, which includes the four-digit industry (e.g., industry 25). To make the intuition behind the link between these industries at two-digit versus four-digit classification more comprehensible, we report the industry codes in ISIC Rev. 3 rather than ISIC Rev. 4.

11. The data in the national accounts for the transport industry include both private and public transport services. Because of the lack of data to disaggregate the industry value added by the provider, we need to assume that one unit of stimulus spent in this sector will have the same effect on employment whether the spending is private or public. We excluded air transportation where possible. In the cases of missing data, we used data on total transport services and transportation, communication, and storage and linked them with our original data set. See appendix 7.1 in this chapter.

12. Large-scale hydropower plants may have unsustainable environment effects; the proposed spending in this report prioritizes small-scale hydropower plants. See Batini et al. (2021) and Pollin et al. (2015).

13. The ratios for renewable energy (RE) and energy efficiency (EE) allocation are based on the proposal in Pollin et al. (2015).

14. In the "high road" scenario, care services are expanded by 2030 in terms of the extent of population coverage as well as the quality of services provided and employment created to meet the requirements of Sustainable Development Goals (SDGs) for the provision of public care services, health and well-being, quality education, and full and productive employment and decent work (ILO, 2018b). The "status quo" scenario is the baseline case, which assumes that care services will expand in line with population increases, but with the current coverage rates, quality standards, and working conditions in care sectors remaining constant, the result is that both care deficits and decent employment deficits persist into 2030.

15. Net zero by 2050 is a scenario that limits global warming to 1.5°C through climate policies and innovation, with the planet thus reaching net zero carbon dioxide (CO_2) emissions around 2050, which is compatible with the long-term temperature goal of the Paris Agreement (Bertram et al. 2021). Current policies assumes that only currently implemented policies are preserved, leading to a global warming by up to 3°C by 2100 and high associated climate impacts.

16. Country-specific estimates are provided based on the GCAM5.3_NGFS model in Bertram et al. (2021). McCollum et al. (2018) present estimations for India based on six other models, where additional low-carbon investment ranges between 1 percent and 5.4 percent.

17. See Dafermos and Nikolaidi (2019) for a discussion of the effect of public transport on private car use.

18. Pollin et al. (2015) also argue that "some bioenergy sources such as corn ethanol and woodburning offer little or no improvement on emissions relative to burning coal or oil." They nevertheless explore clean biofuel sources as part of the policy simulation.

19. See Batini et al. (2021) for a discussion.

20. See Pollin et al. (2015), who also exclude nuclear energy in policy simulations.

21. We are grateful to Maria Nikolaidi for this comment.

22. In the short term (within a year contemporaneously), we assume that care employment can be increased with the existing capital stock (e.g., hospitals, care homes, schools, etc.). The model and the estimation methodology allow for growth in the capital stock in the care economy in the following years. We also estimate the combined effects of expanding both care employment (and wages) and public gross fixed capital formation, which includes investment in public buildings such as hospitals, care homes, nurseries, and schools. To overcome labor shortages in this sector, education and training spending is crucial, albeit with potential time lags.

23. For Turkey, Chile, and Colombia, this is the sum of value added in manufacturing subindustries 2520, 2610, 2694, 2695, 2720, 28 (all subindustries, i.e., 281, 289), 291, 292, 293, 31 (all subindustries), 3210, 352, 3599 (codes based on ISIC Rev. 3 classification). For South Africa, India, and Indonesia, this is the sum of value added in manufacturing subindustries 2520, 2610, 2694, 2720, 28 (all subindustries, i.e., 281, 289), 291, 292, 31 (all subindustries), 3210, 352. The names of the industries are listed in section 3 and further details are provided in appendix 7.2 in this chapter. When taking the sum of subindustries, we use value added rather than output to avoid double counting. Because the vector autoregression (VAR) methodology accounts for the effect of an increase in demand in one industry on the others, we also use the value added in construction and public transport services.

24. Five years is realistic as a new term of policy change in the government policies as well as allowing policies to meet the urgency of the required investment by 2030.

25. The effects of renewable energy investment on emissions depend on what happens with high-carbon spending. The emission reduction will be much higher in a case in which the investment in renewables increases and the investment in fossil fuels declines compared to a case in which the investment in renewables increases and the investment in fossil fuels remains unchanged.

26. Henceforth, unless otherwise specified, the employment figures refer to the change in the nonagricultural sector.

27. See section 7.4 for a discussion of potential reasons.

28. As discussed in more detail in section 4, if public spending substitutes private consumption or investment (e.g., by providing alternatives) or crowds out private investment by increasing borrowing cost, the magnitude of the multiplier may get smaller. In the historical data, however, there is less evidence of the former, and previous econometric analysis indicates that investment is not very sensitive to cost of borrowing (Onaran and Galanis 2014, Onaran et al. 2022b). However, the methodology of VAR in this chapter does not provide evidence of these specific channels, and further macro-econometric research utilizing single equation estimations of the

full macroeconomic model is required to shed light on such differences. In addition, further research on country case studies of public spending in different areas could shed light on how the targeted and well-designed features may contribute to a higher multiplier impact of spending.

29. We also estimate the elasticity of employment (total, nonagricultural) to gross domestic product (GDP, based on specification 1 and only significant coefficients), which in the short run (year 1) ranges between 0.03 in Turkey and Indonesia to 0.3 in Chile, and in the medium run (year 5) ranges between 0.1 in Turkey, 0.15 in Indonesia, 0.2 in South Africa and 0.3 in Chile. The elasticity is very low in Colombia (0.01 in year 1). In India, the elasticity is insignificant in years 1 to 5.

30. The required additional annual spending in the care and green economy are presented in tables A7.2.3 and A7.2.4 in appendix 7.2.

31. See Onaran and Calvert Jump (2022), Stronge and Harper (2019), Knight et al. (2013).

32. In Colombia, Indonesia, and Turkey, the effects of the care economy are based on an increase in employment in the care sector because the effects of care output are insignificant in some cases. In our simulations for Colombia, Indonesia, and Turkey, we assume that the percentage change in employment in the care sector and the percentage change in care output will be equal.

33. Because of the short estimation period, we report only the impulse responses for five years after the shock. In specification 1 in the following periods and countries, we take some statistically insignificant effects into account when calculating the cumulative effects where we failed to find statistically significant effects (within a 90 percent confidence interval). In Colombia: in years 4 to 5, the response of GDP and women's employment and in years 3 to 5, the response of men's employment to public gross fixed capital formation (GFCF); in years 0, and 4 to 5, the response of GDP, in year 5 of men's employment, in years 3 to 5 of women's employment to the care sector. In Indonesia: in years 3 to 5 response of GDP, years 0, and 3 to 5 response of women's employment, years 4 to 5 response of men's employment to public GFCF; in year 0, the response of men's employment to care sector. In South Africa: in year 0, the response of women's employment to public GFCF; in year 0, the response of GDP, years 0 to 3 response of women's employment and years 0 to 5 of men's employment to care sector. In Turkey: in years 0 to 2 and 4 to 5 response of GDP, year 0 of men's and women's employment to public GFCF; in year 0, response of GDP, years 2 to 5 of women's employment and year 5 of men's employment to care sector. In India: the response of GDP in all years to the care sector. In India, the effects of GFCF on GDP are negative, albeit insignificant, so we do not consider them as they are economically not plausible.

REFERENCES

American Public Transport Association (APTA). 2020. *Economic Impact of Public Transportation Investment: 2020 Update.* American Public Transportation Association. https://www.apta.com/wp-content/uploads/APTA-econ-impact-transit-investment-2020-ES.pdf.

Antonopoulos, R., K. Kim, T. Masterson, and A. Zacharias. 2010. "Investing in Care: A Strategy for Effective and Equitable Job Creation." Working Paper No.610. Levy Economics Institute.

Bakker, J. D., C. Parsons, and F. Rauch. 2020. "Migration and Urbanization in Post-Apartheid South Africa." *World Bank Economic Review* 34 (2): 509–32.

Barbosa-Filho, N. H., and L. Taylor. 2006. "Distributive and Demand Cycles in the US Economy—A Structuralist Goodwin Model." *Metroeconomica* 57 (3): 389–411.

Batini, N., M. Di Serio, M. Fragetta, G. Melina, and A. Waldron A. 2021 "Building Back Better: How Big Are Green Spending Multipliers?" IMF Working Paper. International Monetary Fund (IMF).

Bertram, C., J. Hilaire, E. Kriegler, et al. 2021. NGFS Climate Scenario Database. Technical Documentation V2.2. NGFS Central Banks and Supervisors Network for Greening the Financial System.

Blanchard, O. J., and D. Leigh. 2013. "Growth Forecast Errors and Fiscal Multipliers." *American Economic Review* 103 (3): 117–20.

Braunstein, E., I. van Staveren, and D. Tavani. 2011. "Embedding Care and Unpaid Work in Macroeconomic Modelling: A Structuralist Approach." *Feminist Economics* 17 (4): 5–31.

Bulutay, T. 1995. *Employment, Unemployment and Wages in Turkey*. International Labour Office and State Institute of Statistics.

Dafermos Y., A. Monserand, and M. Nikolaidi. 2022. "Green Public Investment, Consumption Patterns and the Ecological Transition: A Macroeconomic Analysis." SSRN 4097746. https://papers.ssrn.com/sol3/papers.cfm?abstract_id=4097746

Dafermos, Y., and M. Nikolaidi. 2019. "Fiscal Policy and Ecological Sustainability: A Post-Keynesian Perspective." Greenwich Papers in Political Economy, No. 74. University of Greenwich.

De Henau, J., S. Himmelweit, Z. Lapniewska, and D. Perrons. 2016. *A Gender Analysis of Employment Stimulus in Seven OECD Countries*. International Trade Union Confederation (ITUC).

De Henau, J., S. Himmelweit, and D. Perrons. 2017. *Investing in the Care Economy: Simulating Employment Effects by Gender in Countries in Emerging Economies*. International Trade Union Confederation (ITUC).

Elgin, C., M. A. Kose, F. Ohnsorge, and S. Yu. 2021. "Understanding Informality." CERP Discussion Paper 16497. Centre for Economic Policy Research.

Elson, D., 2016. "Gender Budgeting and Macroeconomic Policy," In *Feminist Economics and Public Policy*, edited by J. Campbell and M. Gillespie. Routledge.

Elson, D., 2017. "A Gender-Equitable Macroeconomic Framework for Europe. In Economics and Austerity in Europe: Gendered Impacts and Sustainable Alternatives, edited by H. Bargawi, G. Cozzi, and S. Himmelweit. Routledge.

Enders, W. 2015. *Applied Econometric Time Series*, 4th ed. Wiley.

Ferroukhi, R., X. G. Casals, and B. Parajuli. 2020 "Measuring the Socio-Economics of Transition: Focus on Jobs." Technical Paper 2/2020. International Renewable Energy Agency (IRENA).

Hein, E., and A. Tarassow. 2010. "Distribution, Aggregate Demand, and Productivity Growth: Theory and Empirical Results for Six OECD Countries Based on a Post-Kaleckian Model." *Cambridge Journal of Economics* 34 (4): 727–54.

Intergovernmental Panel on Climate Change (IPCC). 2014. *Climate Change 2014: Mitigation of Climate Change*. Cambridge University Press.

Intergovernmental Panel on Climate Change (IPCC). 2019. "Climate Change and Land: An IPCC Special Report on Climate Change, Desertification, Land Degradation, Sustainable Land Management, Food Security, and Greenhouse Gas Fluxes in Terrestrial Ecosystems." Intergovernmental Panel on Climate Change.

International Labour Organization (ILO). 2018a. *World Employment Social Outlook 2018: Greening with Jobs*. International Labour Office.

International Labour Organization (ILO). 2018b. *Care Work and Care Jobs for the Future of Work*. International Labour Office.

International Monetary Fund (IMF). 2020. *Fiscal Monitor: Policies for the Recovery*. International Monetary Fund.

İlkkaracan, İ. 2013. "The Purple Economy: A Call for a New Economic Order Beyond the Green." In *Sustainable Economy and Green Growth: Who Cares?*, edited by U. Röhr and C. van Heemstra. LIFE e.V./German Federal Ministry for the Environment.

İlkkaracan, İ., K. Kim, and T. Kaya. 2015. "The Impact of Public Investment in Social Care Services on Employment, Gender Equality, and Poverty: The Turkish Case." Research Project Report, Istanbul Technical University Women's Studies Center in Science, Engineering and Technology and the Levy Economics Institute, in partnership with the International Labour Organization (ILO) and the United Nations Development Programme (UNDP) Turkey, and the UNDP and UN Women Regional Offices for Europe and Central Asia.

İlkkaracan, İ., and K. Kim. 2019. "The Employment Generation Impact of Meeting SDG Targets in Early Childhood Care, Education, Health, and Long-Term Care in 45 Countries." International Labour Organization.

Knight, K. W., E. A. Rosa, and J. B. Schor, 2013 "Could Working Less Reduce Pressures on the Environment? A Cross-National Panel Analysis of OECD Countries, 1970–2007." *Global Environmental Change* 23 (4): 691–700.

Lee, J., and M. L. Pocock. 2007. "Intrahousehold Allocation of Financial Resources: Evidence from South Korean Individual Bank Accounts. *Review of Economics of the Household* 5 (1): 41–58.

McCollum, David L., Wenji Zhou, Christoph Bertram, et al. 2018. "Energy Investment Needs for Fulfilling the Paris Agreement and Achieving the Sustainable Development Goals." *Nature Energy* 3: 589–99.

Morrison, A., D. Raju, and N. Sinha. 2007. "Gender Equality, Poverty and Economic Growth." Policy Research Working Paper 4349. World Bank.

Naastepad, C. W. M. 2006. "Technology, Demand, and Distribution: A Cumulative Growth Model with an Application to the Dutch Productivity Growth Slowdown." *Cambridge Journal of Economics* 30 (3): 403–34.

Obst, T., Ö. Onaran, and M. Nikolaidi. 2020 "The Effects of Income Distribution and Fiscal Policy on Aggregate Demand, Investment and the Budget Balance: The Case of Europe." *Cambridge Journal of Economics* 44 (6): 1221–43.

Onaran, Ö. "The Effects of Structural Adjustment Policies on Labor Market and Income Distribution in Turkey." PhD diss., Doctoral Dissertation. İstanbul Technical University, 1999.

Onaran, Ö. 2016 "Wage- Versus Profit-Led Growth in the Context of Globalization and Public Spending: The Political Aspects of Wage-Led Recovery." *Review of Keynesian Economics* 4 (4): 458–74.

Onaran, Ö., and R. Calvert Jump. 2022. "A Shorter Working Week as Part of a Green, Caring Economy." Women's Budget Group Feminist Green New Deal Policy Paper, Women's Budget Group. https://wbg.org.uk/wp-content/uploads/2022/02/Shorter-Working-Week-Report.pdf

Onaran, Ö., and G. Galanis. 2014. "Income distribution and growth: a global model." *Environment and Planning A*, 46(10): 2489-2513.

Onaran, Ö., and C. Oyvat. 2023. "The Employment Effects of Public Spending for a Green and Caring Economy: The Case of Emerging Economies. International Trade Union Confederation.

Onaran, Ö, C. Oyvat, and E. Fotopoulou. 2019a. "The Effects of Income, Gender and Wealth Inequality and Economic Policies on Macroeconomic Performance in the UK." Greenwich Papers in Political Economy, No. 71. University of Greenwich.

Onaran, Ö., C. Oyvat, and E. Fotopoulou. 2019b. "A Policy Mix for Equitable Sustainable Development in the UK: The Effects of Gender Equality, Wages, Wealth Concentration and Fiscal Policy." GPERC Policy Briefs, University of Greenwich, #PB25-2019.

Onaran, Ö., C. Oyvat, and E. Fotopoulou. 2021. "A Purple, Green and Red New Deal After the COVID-19." Policy Brief for Women's Budget Group, Women's Budget Group.

Onaran, Ö, C. Oyvat, and E. Fotopoulou. 2022a. "Gendering Macroeconomic Analysis and Development Policy: A Theoretical Model." *Feminist Economics* 28(3): 23–55. https://www.tandfonline.com/doi/full/10.1080/13545701.2022.2033294.

Onaran, Ö., C. Oyvat, and E. Fotopoulou. 2022b. "A Macroeconomic Analysis of the Effects of Gender Inequality, Wages, and Public Social Infrastructure: The Case of the UK." *Feminist Economics* 28 (2): 152–88.

Onaran, Ö., and E. Stockhammer. 2005. "Two Different Export-Oriented Growth Strategies: Accumulation and Distribution in Turkey and South Korea." *Emerging Markets Finance and Trade* 41: 65–89.

Oyvat, C., and Ö. Onaran. 2022. "The Effect of Gender Equality and Fiscal Policy on Growth and Employment: The Case of South Korea." *World Development*, 158: 105987.

Oyvat, C., and Ö. Onaran. 2021. "Tax Wealth and Profit Income to Fund Social Care and Healthcare." Policy Brief for Women's Budget Group, Women's Budget Group.

Pollin, R., H. Garrett-Peltier, J. Heintz, and S. Chakraborty. 2015. "Global Green Growth: Clean Energy Industrial Investments and Expanding Job Opportunities." United Nations Industrial Development Organization.

Pollin, R., J. Heintz, and H. Garrett-Peltier. 2009. "The Economic Benefits of Investing in Clean Energy: How the Economic Stimulus Program and New Legislation Can Boost U.S. Economic Growth and Employment." Center for American Progress.

Pollin, R., J. Wicks-Lim, S. Chakraborty, G. Semieniuk, and J. Yoon. 2022. A Green Economy Transition Program for South Korea. Political Economy Research Institute (PERI).

Seguino, S. 2010. "Gender, Distribution, and Balance of Payments Constrained Growth in Developing Countries." *Review of Political Economy* 22 (3): 373–404.

Seguino, S. 2012. "Macroeconomics, Human Development, and Distribution." *Journal of Human Development and Capabilities* 13 (1): 59–81.

Seguino, S., and M.S. Floro. 2003. "Does Gender Have Any Effect on Aggregate Saving?: An Empirical Analysis." *International Review of Applied Economics* 17 (2): 147–66.

Stockhammer, E., W. Qazizada, and S. Gechert. 2019 "Demand Effects of Fiscal Policy Since 2008." *Review of Keynesian Economics* 7 (1): 57–74.

Stockhammer, E., and Ö. Onaran. 2004. "Accumulation, Distribution, and Employment: A Structural VAR Approach to a Kaleckian Macro Model." *Structural Change and Economic Dynamics* 15 (4): 421–47.

Stronge, W. and A. Harper, eds. 2019. *The Shorter Working Week: A Radical And Pragmatic Proposal.* Autonomy.

Tippet, B., R. Wildauer, and Ö. Onaran. 2021. "The Case for a Progressive Annual Wealth Tax in the UK." Greenwich Papers in Political Economy, No: GPERC88. https://gala.gre.ac.uk/id/eprint/33819/.

Tori, D., and Ö. Onaran. 2018. "The Effects of Financialization on Investment: Evidence from Firm-Level Data for the UK." *Cambridge Journal of Economics* 42 (5): 1393–1416.

Tori, D., and Ö. Onaran. 2020. "Financialisation, Financial Development, and Investment: Evidence from European Non-Financial Corporations." *Socio-Economic Review* 18 (3): 681–718.

Tori, D., and Ö. Onaran. 2022. "Financialization and Investment in the Developing Countries." *Cambridge Journal of Economics*, 46(4): 891–919.

Wildauer, R., S. Leitch, and J. Kapeller. 2021. "Is a €10 Trillion European Climate Investment Initiative Fiscally Sustainable?" Greenwich Papers in Political Economy, No. 89. University of Greenwich.

Women's Budget Group UK and Scottish Women's Budget Group (WBG). 2015. "Plan F: A Feminist Economic Strategy for a Caring and Sustainable Economy." Women's Budget Group UK and Scottish Women's Budget Group. http://wbg.org.uk/wp-content/uploads/2015/02/PLAN-F-2015.pdf.

World Bank. 2022. *World Development Indicators.* The World Bank.

APPENDIX 7.1: LIST OF VARIABLES IN THE ECONOMETRIC ESTIMATIONS, DATA SOURCES, AND PERIOD

ariable[†]	Source	Period
are sector output (education, health care, social care) expenditures (constant local currency)	Chile, education: UN data for 2013–2019; OECD education statistics for 2012; UN data for 1974–2011*. Chile, health care, and social care: UN data for 2013–2019; Organisation for Economic Co-operation and Development (OECD) health statistics for 2000–2012; UN data for 1974–1999*. Colombia, education: UN data for 2005–2019.; UN data for 1970–2004*. Colombia, health care, and social care: UN data for 2005–2019; OECD health statistics for 2000–2003; UN data for 1970–1999*. India, education: UN data for 2011–2019; India KLEMS for 1980–2010; UN data for 1970–1980*‡. India, health care, and social care: UN data for 2011–2019; India KLEMS for 1980–2010; UN data for 1970–1980*‡. Indonesia, education, health care, and social care: Statistics Indonesia for 2010–2019.; UN data for 1970–2009*‡. South Africa, public education: World Bank, World Development Indicators for 2000–2019; UN data for 1993–1999*; UN data for 1970–1992*‡. South Africa, health care: WHO Global Health Expenditures for 2000–2019; UN data for 1993–1999*; UN data for 1970–1992*‡. Turkey, education: Turkstat for 2003–2019; UN data for 1998–2002‡, UN data 1970–1997*‡. Turkey, health care: Turkstat for 1999–2019; OECD health statistics (1986–1998); UN data 1970–1985*‡.	Chile: 1974–2019; Colombia: 1970–2019; India: 1970–2019; Indonesia: 1970–2019; South Africa: 1970–2019; Turkey: 1970–2019
re sector (education, health care, social care) employment	ILO for Colombia, Indonesia, Turkey	Colombia, Indonesia, Turkey (1991–2019)
blic gross fixed capital formation (general government, constant local currency)	IMF Investment and Capital Stock Data Set, 1960–2019	All countries (1970–2019)
nstruction value added (constant local currency)	Chile: UN data for 1974–1989, 2018–2019; LA KLEMS for 1990–2017. Colombia: LA KLEMS for 1991–2019; UN data for 1970–1990. India: UN data for 1970–2019. Indonesia: UN data for 1970–2019. South Africa: UN data for 1970–2019. Turkey: UN data for 1970–2019.	Chile: 1974–2019; Colombia: 1970–2019; India: 1970–2019; Indonesia: 1970–2019; South Africa: 1970–2019; Turkey: 1970–2019

(*continued*)

(continued)

Variable[†]	Source	Period
Transportation (air transportation excluded) value added (constant local currency)	Chile: OECD STAN for 2008–2017; UN data for 2005–2007, 2018–2019[§], UN data for 1970–2004[±]. Colombia: OECD STAN for 2005–2019; UN data for 1970–2004[±]. India: Government of India Ministry of Statistics and Programme for 2011–2019; Indian KLEMS for 1980–2010[§]; UN data for 1970–1979[±]. Indonesia: Statistics Indonesia for 2000–2014; Statistics Indonesia for 2015–2019[§]; UN data for 1970–1999[±]. South Africa: UN data for 1970–2019[±]. Turkey: Turkstat for 2003–2019; OECD for 1998–2002[§]; UN data for 1970–1997[±].	All countries (1970–2019)
GDP (constant local currency)	World Bank, World Development Indicators	All countries (1970–2019)
GDP Deflator	World Bank, World Development Indicators	All countries (1970–2019)
Employment (total, men, women)	Chile: Federal Reserve Bank of St. Louis for 1986–2019; ILO for 1975–1983; 1984–1985 data interpolated using Federal Reserve Bank of St. Louis and ILO series. Women's and men's share in total employment in 1976 used for 1975. Colombia: ILO for 1975–2019. The average of women's and men's share in total employment in 1980 and 1982 is used for 1981. India: ILO for 1991–2019; India KLEMS for 1981–1990. Women's and men's share in total employment for 1982–1990 interpolated based on Census of India 1981 and ILO. Indonesia: ILO for 1976–2019. Data for 1981, 1983–1984 are interpolated based on ILO data. South Africa: World Bank, World Development Indicators for 1991–2019. Employment data for 1976–1990 calculated based on registered unemployment data for 1976–1990 and labor force participation data interpolated from World Bank, World Development Indicators data for 1970, 1980, 1985, 1991. Turkey: ILO for 1988–2019; Ministry of Development for 1980–1987; Onaran (1999, based on Bulutay 1995) for 1970–1979. Women's and men's share in total employment in 1985 is used for women's and men's share in 1980–1985	Chile: 1975–2019; Colombia: 1975–2019; India: 1981–2019; Indonesia: 1976–2019; South Afric 1976–2019; Turke 1970–2019
Nonagricultural employment (total, men, women)	Chile: ILO for 1980–2019 Colombia: ILO for 1975–2019 India: India KLEMS for total employment. ILO for women's and men's share in total employment for 1991–2019. Women's and men's share in total employment for 1982–1990 interpolated based on Census of India 1981 and ILO. Women's and men's share in total employment for 1980 is assumed to be the same as in 1981. Indonesia: ILO for 1976–2019. Data for 1981, 1983–1984 are interpolated based on ILO data. South Africa: ILO for 1991–2019	Chile: 1980–2019; Colombia: 1975–2019; India: 1980–2019; Indonesia: 1976–2019; South Afri 1991–2019; Sout Korea: 1970–201 Turkey: 1982–20

	Turkey: ILO for total non-agricultural employment in 1988–2019 and Onaran (1999 based on Bulutay 1995) for total nonagricultural employment in 1982–1987. ILO for share of women's and men's employment in non-agricultural sector in 1982–1985 and 1988–2019. Share of women's and men's employment data for 1986–1987 are interpolated based on ILO data.	
:mployment-to-population ratio (population aged 15 and over, Total, men, women)	Employment (population aged 15 and over; total, men, women)/total population (population aged 15 and over; total, men, women) World Bank, World Development Indicators for total population (population aged 15 and over; total, men, women) for 1970–2019.	Chile: 1975–2019; Colombia: 1975–2019; India: 1981–2019; Indonesia: 1976–2019; South Africa: 1976–2019; Turkey: 1980–2019
opulation (population aged 15 and over; total, men, women)	World Bank, World Development Indicators for total population (population aged 15 and over; Total, men, women) for 1970–2019. UNDESA, World Population Prospects 2019 for population (population aged 15 and over; Total, men, women) projections for 2024.	All countries (1970–2024)
:anufacturing subindustries, value added (constant local currency)	UNIDO-Industrial Statistics Database Manufacturing, four-digit ISIC Rev. 4 data for the latest periods for which data is available, linked with the data at four-digit ISIC Rev. 3 classification for the earlier years and for the period for which data at four-digit classification is not available linked with the data at two-digit ISICRev3 classification, for the following industries (codes according to four-digit ISIC Rev. 3; South Africa has only two-digit ISIC Rev. 3 data): plastic products (code 2520); glass products (2610); cement and plaster (2694) and concrete products (2695); nonferrous metals (2720); fabricated metal products (all subindustries, i.e., 281, 289); general-purpose machinery (291); special-purpose machinery (292); domestic appliances (2930); electrical machinery and apparatus (31, all subindustries), electronic valves, tubes, and so on (3210); railway/tramway locomotives and rolling stock (3520); manufacture of other transport equipment not elsewhere classified (3599)	All countries (1970–2018)

ll nominal variables for value added and output are deflated by GDP deflator.

)utput data including total other community, and social and personal services linked to series on education or health and ial care provided by the database for the later period.

alue-added data linked with the series for the later period.

ata on all transportation and storage industry value added linked with the series for the later period.

ata on all transportation, storage, and communications industry value added linked with the series for the later period.

ata on all transportation value-added data linked with the series for the later period.

Table A7.2.1 The distribution of public spending for the care economy, public infrastructure, and green transition across industries (RE + EE + PT) as a ratio to GDP

			South Africa India, Indonesia				Chile, Colombia, Turkey			
						Ratio to GDP				Ratio to GDP
Care: Health and social care + education and childcare						0.01000				0.01000
Public infrastructure: Public gross fixed capital formation						0.01000				0.01000
			Industry	Manufacturing industry code (ISIC4Rev3 code)	Industry share in RE, EE or PT	Ratio to GDP	Industry	Manufacturing Industry code (ISIC4 Rev3 code)	Industry share in RE, EE or PT	Ratio to GDP
Green (REEEPT)						0.01000				0.01000
	Share in REEEPT	Share in RE								
Renewable energy (RE)	0.50					0.00500				0.00500
Solar		0.25				0.00125				0.00125
			Electrical machinery	31 (total)	0.51	0.00064	Electrical equipment and supplies	31 (total)	0.55	0.00068
			Glass products	2610	0.08	0.00010	Glass products	2610	0.09	0.00011
			Nonferrous metals	2720	0.08	0.00010	Nonferrous metal ingots and primary nonferrous metal	2720	0.09	0.00011

			metal products	[illegible]	[illegible]	0.00015	Fabricated metal products except machinery and furniture	28=281+289	0.12	0.00015
			Engines, turbines	2911	0.07	0.00009	Building construction and repair		0.16	0.00020
			Construction		0.16	0.00020				
Wind		0.25				0.00125				0.00125
			Construction		0.13	0.00016	Building construction and repair		0.26	0.00033
			Construction services		0.13	0.00016	Plastic products	2520	0.13	0.00017
			Plastic products	2520	0.13	0.00017	Fabricated metal products except machinery and furniture	28=281+289	0.13	0.00017
			Other fabricated metal	289	0.13	0.00017	General-purpose machinery and equipment	291	0.38	0.00048
			General machinery	291	0.38	0.00048	Other transportation equipment	359 or 3599	0.04	0.00006
			Lifting equipment	2915	0.04	0.00006	Electronic components and accessories	3210	0.04	0.00006
			Electrical machinery	31 (total)	0.04	0.00006				
Geothermal		0.25				0.00125				0.00125
			Construction		0.60	0.00075	Building construction and repair		0.60	0.00075

Table A7.2.1 (continued)

			Pumps, compressors	2912	0.40	0.00050	Machinery and equipment of general purpose	291	0.40	0.00050
Hydro		0.25				0.00125				0.00125
			Plaster, cement	2694	0.33	0.00041	Cement and concrete products	2694+2695	0.33	0.00041
			Construction		0.18	0.00023	Civil engineering construction		0.18	0.00023
			Engines, turbines	2911	0.21	0.00027	General-purpose machinery and equipment	291	0.21	0.00027
	Share in REEEPT	Share in EE	Electrical machinery	31 (total)	0.28	0.00035	Electrical equipment and supplies	31 (total)	0.28	0.00035
Energy efficiency (EE)	0.20					0.00200				0.00200
Public and private buildings		0.5				0.00100				0.00100
			Construction		0.50	0.00050	Construction		1.00	0.00100
			Construction services		0.50	0.00050				
Industrial energy efficiency		0.25				0.00050				0.00050
			Special machinery	292	0.40	0.00020	General-purpose machinery and equipment	291	0.20	0.00010
			General machinery	291	0.20	0.00010	Special-purpose machinery and equipment	292	0.40	0.00020

			Engines, turbines	2911	0.20	0.00010	Electrical equipment and supplies	31 (total)	0.20	0.00010
			Construction		0.10	0.00005	Building construction and repair		0.20	0.00010
			Construction services		0.10	0.00005				
Grid upgrades		0.25				0.00050				0.00050
			Construction		0.13	0.00006	Building construction and repair		0.25	0.00013
			Construction services		0.13	0.00006	General-purpose machinery and equipment	291	0.25	0.00013
			General machinery	291	0.25	0.00013	Electronic components and accessories	3210	0.25	0.00013
			Electrical machinery	31 (total)	0.50	0.00025	Household electrical appliances	2930	0.125	0.00006
	Share in REEEPT	Share in PT					Electrical equipment and supplies	31 (total)	0.125	0.00006
Public transport (PT)	0.30					0.00300				0.00300
Public transport vehicles: locomotives, rolling stock		0.10			0.10	0.00030			0.10	0.00030
Public transport services		0.72			0.72	0.00216			0.72	0.00216
Construction		0.18			0.18	0.00054			0.18	0.00054

Table A7.2.2 The distribution of green public spending in industries (RE + EE + PT) as a ratio to GDP

South Africa India, Indonesia				Chile, Colombia, Turkey			
Industry	ISIC Rev. 3 Code	ISIC4 Rev. 4 Code	Ratio to GDP	Industry	ISIC Rev. 3 Code	ISIC4 rev4 Code	Ratio to GDP
Plastic products	2520	2220	0.00017	Plastic products	2520	2220	0.00017
Glass products	2610	2310	0.00010	Glass products	2610	2310	0.00011
Plaster, cement	2694	2394	0.00041	Cement and concrete products	2694+2695	2394+2395	0.00041
Nonferrous metals	2720	2420	0.00010	Nonferrous metal ingots and primary nonferrous metal products	2720	2420	0.00011
Structural metal products	281	251	0.00013	Fabricated metal products except machinery and furniture	28=281+289	251+259	0.00031
Other fabricated metal	289	259	0.00017	Machinery and equipment of general purpose	291	281	0.00147
General machinery	291	281	0.00071	Machinery and equipment of special purpose	292	282	0.00020
Engines, turbines	2911	2811	0.00045	Household electrical appliances	2930	2750	0.00006
Pumps, compressors	2912	2813	0.00050	Electrical equipment, and supplies	31 (total)	27	0.00120
Lifting equipment	2915	2816	0.00006	Electronic components and accessories	3210	2610	0.00018
Special machinery	292	282	0.00020	Other transportation equipment	3599	3099	0.00006
Electrical machinery	31 (total)	27	0.00130	Locomotives, rolling stock	352	3020	0.00030
Locomotives, rolling stock	352	3020	0.00030				
Sum of manufacturing subindustries providing input to REEEPT/GDP			0.00458	Sum of manufacturing subindustries providing input to REEEPT/GDP			0.00458
Construction			0.00327	Construction			0.00327
Public transport services			0.00216	Public transport services			0.00216
Total: (manufacturing + consruction + public transport services)/GDP			0.01000	Total: (manufacturing + consruction + public transport services)/GDP			0.01000

Notes: How an increase in spending in REEEPT by 1 percent as a ratio to GDP is allocated to manufacturing subindustries and construction is based on table A.3 in Pollin et al. (2015), which is based on input-output tables for renewable energy and energy efficiency (REEE) spending (excluding biofuel). We use the weights reported in Pollin et al. (2015) for South Africa also for India and Indonesia; and we use the weights reported for South Korea for Chile, Colombia, and Turkey. The allocation of spending in public transport to construction, manufacturing of rail transport vehicles (3520) and transport services is based on APTA (2020). Mining has a weight of 0.10 in the geothermal industry in Pollin et al. (2015), which we allocated to construction to simplify the systems estimation. Research and development (R&D) is distributed to manufacturing to simplify the systems estimation and as a result of a lack of long-time

Table A7.2.3 The cost of expansion of care services under the status quo* versus high-road* scenarios as a ratio to GDP (%)

	Status Quo Scenario	High-Road Scenario	Additional Spending in Care Services Required by 2030 for the High-Road Scenario Compared to Current Policies: High Road—Status Quo
India	3.6	8.6	5
Indonesia	3.9	12.5	8.6
Turkey	8.8	10.9	2.1

Source: İlkkaracan and Kim 2019, also reported in ILO 2018b.

Note:

*In the high-road scenario, care services are expanded by 2030 in terms of the extent of population coverage as well as the quality of services provided and employment created, to meet the requirements of SDGs; in particular, SDG 5, target 5.4, calling for the provision of public care services; SDG 3 on health and well-being; SDG 4 on quality education; and SDG 8 on full and productive employment and decent work.

The status-quo scenario is the baseline case, which assumes that care services will expand in line with population increases but with the current coverage rates, quality standards, and working conditions in care sectors remaining constant, with the result that both care deficits and decent employment deficits persist into 2030.

Table A7.2.4 Average annual low-carbon energy investment requirement as a ratio to GDP (%) for the period 2016–2050 under different scenarios estimated by different models

County/Region	Model	Current Policies	Net Zero 2050 (1.5°C)	Additional Low-Carbon Investment Required to Limit Global Warming to 1.5°C Compared to Current Policies: Net Zero 2050 (1.5°C)—Current Policies
Colombia*	GCAM5.3_NGFS	0.64	2.01	1.37
Indonesia*	GCAM5.3_NGFS	0.30	2.01	1.71
South Africa*	GCAM5.3_NGFS	0.58	2.69	2.11
India*	GCAM5.3_NGFS	1.50	5.27	3.77
India**	AIM/CGE	0.22	3.37	3.15
India**	IMAGE	0.47	1.46	0.99
India**	MESSAGEix-GLOBIOM	0.27	1.52	1.25
India**	POLES	0.79	2.92	2.13
India**	REMIND-MAgPIE	2.29	7.73	5.44
India**	WITCH-GLOBIOM	0.87	5.16	4.29
Asia**	AIM/CGE	0.47	3.38	2.91
	IMAGE	0.33	1.14	0.81
	MESSAGEix-GLOBIOM	0.24	1.06	0.82
	POLES	0.78	2.39	1.61
	REMIND-MAgPIE	1.53	4.88	3.35
	WITCH-GLOBIOM	0.74	4.35	3.61
Middle East and Africa**	AIM/CGE	0.22	4.08	3.86
	IMAGE	0.61	1.57	0.96
	MESSAGEix-GLOBIOM	0.24	1.65	1.41
	POLES	0.52	3.12	2.60
	REMIND-MAgPIE	1.18	5.88	4.70
	WITCH-GLOBIOM	0.66	9.10	8.44
Latin America and the Caribbean**	AIM/CGE	0.52	2.29	1.77
	IMAGE	0.68	1.30	0.62
	MESSAGEix-GLOBIOM	0.27	1.18	0.91
	POLES	0.88	1.84	0.96
	REMIND-MAgPIE	1.34	3.29	1.95
	WITCH-GLOBIOM	0.56	1.91	1.35

Notes: *Ratios to GDP are the authors' calculations based on required investment amount reported in Bertram et al. (2021).

Net-zero 2050 is a scenario that limits global warming to 1.5°C through climate policies and innovation, reaching net-zero CO_2 emissions around 2050, which is compatible with the long-term temperature goal of the Paris Agreement.

Current policies assumes that only currently implemented policies are preserved, leading to a global warming by up to 3°C by 2100 and high associated climate impacts.

Country-specific estimates are provided based on the GCAM5.3_NGFS Model.

**McCollum et al. (2018) supplementary data tables, which provide country estimations only for India among the countries analyzed in this chapter and regional estimates, which we list as an indicative reference.

APPENDIX 7.3: ESTIMATION METHODOLOGY

We estimate the VAR model based on the following specification:

$$AX_t = A_0 + A_1 X_{t-1} + e_t \qquad \text{(A7.3.1)}$$

which can be written in reduced form as

$$X_t = C_0 + C_1 X_{t-1} + u_t \qquad \text{(A7.3.2)}$$

X_t is a vector of endogenous variables consisting of the logarithmic change in the public expenditure items, employment of men and women in the nonagricultural sector (E_t^M *and* E_t^F), and GDP (Y).

X_t for the first specification with five variables is as follows:

$$X_t = \begin{bmatrix} \log(I_t^G) \\ \log Y_t^H \\ \log(Y_t) \\ \log\left(E_t^M\right) \\ \log\left(E_t^F\right) \end{bmatrix} \qquad \text{(A7.3.3)}$$

where I_t^G is public GFCF, Y_t^H is output in the social sector (also referred as the care economy: education, childcare, health carer, and social care), Y_t is GDP, and E_t^M *and* E_t^F is employment of men and women in the nonagricultural sector.[32]

From equations (1) and (2), $Au_t = e_t$:

$$a_{41} \begin{pmatrix} 1 & 0 & 0 & 0 & 0 \\ a_{21} & 1 & 0 & 0 & 0 \\ a_{31} & a_{32} & 1 & 0 & 0 \\ a_{41} & a_{42} & a_{43} & 1 & 0 \\ a_{51} & a_{52} & a_{52} & a_{52} & 1 \end{pmatrix} \begin{pmatrix} u_1 \\ u_2 \\ u_3 \\ u_4 \\ u_5 \end{pmatrix} = \begin{pmatrix} e_1 \\ e_2 \\ e_3 \\ e_4 \\ e_5 \end{pmatrix} \qquad \text{(A7.3.4)}$$

where e_t are structural shocks. Equation (4) defines the contemporaneous effects.

X_t for the second specification with six variables is as follows:

$$X_t = \begin{bmatrix} \log Y_t^C \\ \log Y_t^{PT} \\ \log Y_t^{MRE} \\ \log(Y_t) \\ \log\left(E_t^M\right) \\ \log\left(E_t^F\right) \end{bmatrix} \tag{A7.3.5}$$

where Y_t^C is value added in construction, Y_t^{PT} is the value added of transport services, Y_t^{MRE} is the sum of value added in manufacturing subindustries providing input to REEEPT (see section 3), Y_t is GDP, and E_t^M *and* E_t^F is employment of men and women in the nonagricultural sector.

The contemporaneous effects for specification 2 are defined in equation (A7.3.6):

$$\begin{pmatrix} 1 & 0 & 0 & 0 & 0 & 0 \\ a_{21} & 1 & 0 & 0 & 0 & 0 \\ a_{31} & a_{32} & 1 & 0 & 0 & 0 \\ a_{41} & a_{42} & a_{43} & 1 & 0 & 0 \\ a_{51} & a_{52} & a_{53} & a_{54} & 1 & 0 \\ a_{61} & a_{62} & a_{63} & a_{64} & a_{65} & 1 \end{pmatrix} \begin{pmatrix} u_1 \\ u_2 \\ u_3 \\ u_4 \\ u_5 \\ u_6 \end{pmatrix} = \begin{pmatrix} e_1 \\ e_2 \\ e_3 \\ e_4 \\ e_5 \\ e_6 \end{pmatrix} \tag{A7.3.6}$$

All variables are in logarithms.

We estimate VAR with Cholesky decomposition and impose a triangular structure for the contemporaneous effects for simplicity, given the low number of observations and the relatively high number of variables in the systems. In the VAR estimations, public spending variables are the most exogenous variables because they are part of a policy decision. In specification 1, public GFCF comes at the top of these exogenous public spending variables because of the time lags required to plan and implement these projects. Public spending in the care economy (social sector) is affected by GFCF but is contemporaneously exogenous to GDP and employment. In specification 2, value added in construction comes at the top of these exogenous public spending variables, followed by public transport services, which depends on construction but is otherwise contemporaneously exogenous; value added in manufacturing subindustries are affected by the value added in construction and public transport contemporaneously. In all specifications, an increase in any public expenditure affects aggregate output (GDP) contemporaneously. Public spending categories and aggregate output (GDP) affect employment of men and women contemporaneously. VAR specification allows limited number of contemporaneous effects, so the rest of the interactions in the VAR specification are through lagged effects of all the variables affecting each other.

Both specifications 1 and 2 are estimated, introducing total employment instead of employment of men and women as two separate variables to test for robustness. The results are largely robust.

To test for further robustness or to improve the significance and explanatory power, we also estimate the systems (1) in first differences of the variables; (2) with an estimation period starting in the 1980s (rather than the 1970s); (3) for alternative orders of different public spending categories; (4) with two or three lags; and (5) with a time trend to account for structural change and other variables that we do not account for in the system estimations (e.g., wage rates, labor market institutions, terms of trade, imported input prices) or other exogenous control variables such as population (aged 15 and over), informal economy share in GDP, level of urbanization, real exchange rates, world GDP, trade openness/GDP, and oil rent/GDP in the world, mineral rent/GDP in the world. The details of the specifications chosen as the baseline for simulations are summarized in table A7.3.1–2 for each country.

We calculate the effects of a 1 percentage point increase in GFCF, the care economy output, and the value added of the three subindustries providing input to REEEPT in terms of the percentage change in GDP, and the employment of women and men by using the cumulative impulse response function coefficients, which report the response of GDP, and the employment of women and men (in logarithms) to a one standard deviation increase in changes in public spending categories (all in logarithms, reported in figures 7.A4.1-90) for five periods. Figures 7.1–7.2 in section 7 present these effects.[33] The transformations use data of the last year of the estimation period for GDP, employment, and public spending categories. In the case of REEEPT, in figure 7.1c, we report the sum of the effects in response to an increase in the value added of manufacturing sectors providing input to REEEPT, construction, and transport based on separate estimates of impulse responses to the increase in each sector,

Table A7.3.1 Details of specification 1

	Estimation Period	Lags	Level/ Difference	Control Variables	Order of Variables
Chile	1982–2018	1	Difference	Δ log(population_15); Δ rer; Δ informal; Δ log(world_gdp); Δ rent_gdp_w	Output in the social sector, public GFCF, GDP, E_t^M, E_t^F
Colombia	1994–2018	3	Level	log(population_15); rer; oil_gdp_w; log(world_gdp)	As in Equation (A7.3.3)
India	1982–2018	1	Difference	Δ informal; Δ log(world_gdp); drer; Δ oil_gdp_w; Δ trade_gdp	As in Equation (A7.3.3)
Indonesia	1992–2018	1	Level	log(population_15); log_world_gdp	As in Equation (A7.3.3)
South Africa	1993–2018	1	Difference	Δ urban; Δ informal; Δ rent_gdp_w; Δ log(population_15)	Output in the social sector, public GFCF, GDP, E_t^M, E_t^F
Turkey	1992–2018	1	Level	log(population_15); time trend; informal; rer urban; log(world_gdp)	As in Equation (A7.3.3)

Notes: The definition and data source for the control variables are as follows: "population_15" is population aged 15 and over, "rer" is real exchange rate; "informal" is informal economy's share in GDP; "world_gdp" is total GDP in the world; "rent_gdp_w" is the mineral rent/GDP in the world; "oil_gdp_w" is oil rent/GDP in the world; "trade_gdp" is (exports+imports)/GDP; "urban" is the level of urbanization. population_15, world _gdp; rent_gdp_w; oil_gdp_w; trade_gdp; urban are from World Bank (2022) World Development Indicators. informal is from Elgin et al (2021). We used World Bank (2022) World Development Indicators for real exchange rate (rer) data in Chile, Colombia and estimated rer using official USD exchange rate and GDP deflator in India and Turkey as real exchange rate data is missing for the years of estimation.

that is, the total effects of an increase in the value added in construction by 0.327 percentage point, public transport services by 0.216 percentage point, manufacturing subindustries providing input to REEEPT by 0.458 percentage point, all as a ratio to GDP (based on the weights presented in appendix 7.2, table A7.2.2).

We do not estimate the effects on exports and imports because adding more variables to the system of VAR equations with a short time series is not possible. Estimating import effects would require separate estimations, for example, adding imports while excluding employment.

Table A7.3.2 Details of specification 2

	Estimation Period	Lags	Level/ Difference	Control Variables	Order of Variables
Chile	1982–2018	1	Difference	Δ log_population_15; Δ rer; Δ informal; Δ log_world_gdp; Δ rent_gdp_w	Value added in manufacturing subindustries providing input to REEEPT, construction, transport, GDP, E_t^M *and* E_t^F
Colombia	1978–2018	3	Level	Time trend; log_population_15; rer	As in Equation (A7.3.5)
India	1982–2018	2	Difference	Δ informal; Δ log_world_gdp; Δ rer; Δ urban; time trend	As in Equation (A7.3.5)
Indonesia	1977–2017	1	Level	log_population_15; log_world_gdp; time trend	As in Equation (A7.3.5)
South Africa	1994–2018	2	Difference	Δ rer; Δ log_population_15; Δ rent_gdp_w; Δ informal; durban	As in Equation (A7.3.5)
Turkey	1983–2018	1	Level	log_population_15; time trend; rer; log_world_gdp; urban; informal; rent_gdp_w; oil_gdp_w	Value added in transport, manufacturing subindustries providing input to REEEPT, construction, GDP, E_t^M *and* E_t^F

Notes: See note in table A7.3.1.

However, this is beyond the scope of this chapter. We note the issues of balance of payments constraints in both the theoretical framework and in the descriptive discussion of the stylized facts of the structure of the economy and the green and care economies, and finally in the conclusion. Exchange rates are also not explicitly modeled in the theoretical or empirical analysis, but we check for robustness of our results by controlling for changes in the real exchange rate. Again, further discussions of the exchange rate determination are beyond the scope of this chapter.

APPENDIX 7.4.1: CUMULATIVE ORTHOGONALIZED IMPULSE RESPONSE FUNCTIONS (SPECIFICATION 1)

Figure A7.4.1. Cumulative orthogonalized impulse response functions based on specification 1: the response of GDP and women's and men's employment (employ_w and employ_m) in the nonagricultural sector) to a one standard deviation increase in public gross fixed capital formation and social sector output (care economy).

CHILE

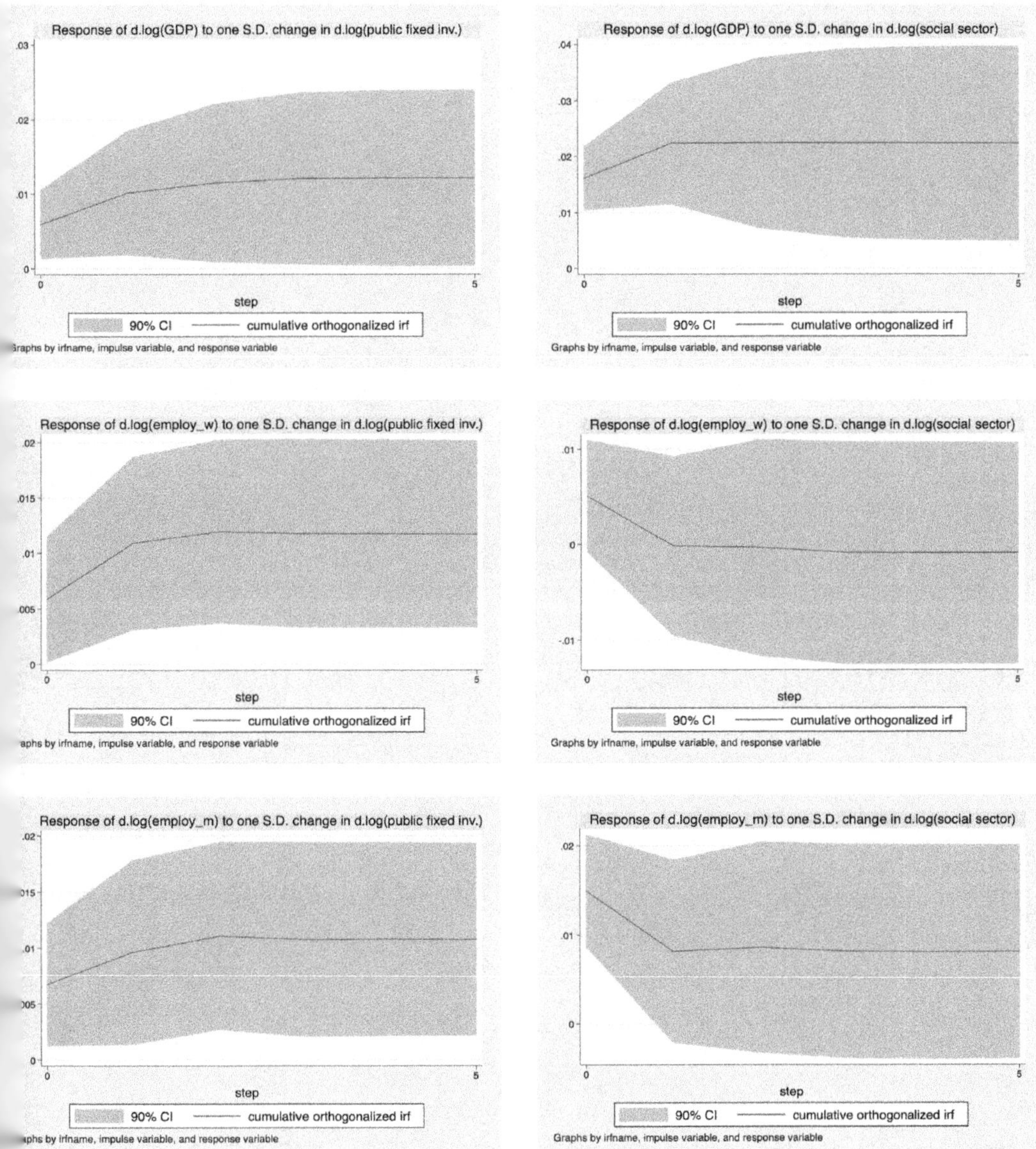
Response of d.log(GDP) to one S.D. change in d.log(public fixed inv.)
.03
.02
.01
0
0
5
step
90% CI
cumulative orthogonalized irf
Response of d.log(GDP) to one S.D. change in d.log(social sector)
.04
.03
.02
.01
0
0
5
step
90% CI
cumulative orthogonalized irf
Graphs by irfname, impulse variable, and response variable
Response of d.log(employ_w) to one S.D. change in d.log(public fixed inv.)
.02
.015
.01
.005
0
0
5
step
90% CI
cumulative orthogonalized irf
Response of d.log(employ_w) to one S.D. change in d.log(social sector)
.01
0
-.01
0
5
step
90% CI
cumulative orthogonalized irf
Graphs by irfname, impulse variable, and response variable
Response of d.log(employ_m) to one S.D. change in d.log(public fixed inv.)
.02
.01
0
0
5
step
90% CI
cumulative orthogonalized irf
Response of d.log(employ_m) to one S.D. change in d.log(social sector)
.02
.01
0
0
5
step
90% CI
cumulative orthogonalized irf
Graphs by irfname, impulse variable, and response variable

COLOMBIA

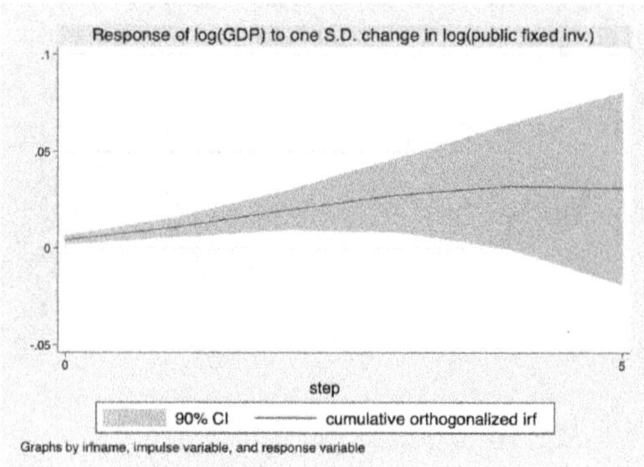
Response of log(GDP) to one S.D. change in log(public fixed inv.)
.1
.05
0
-.05
0
5
step
90% CI
cumulative orthogonalized irf
Graphs by irfname, impulse variable, and response variable

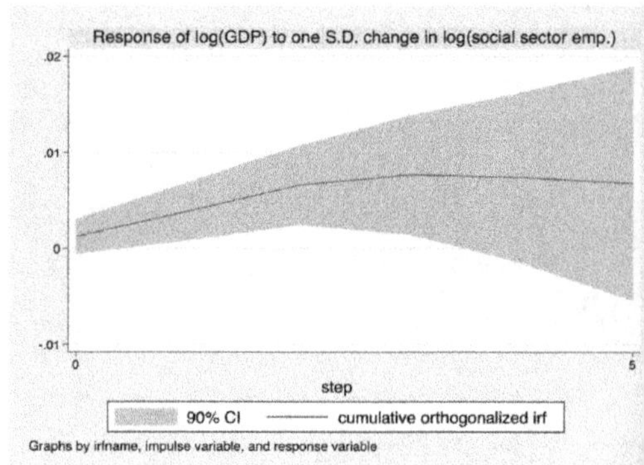
Response of log(GDP) to one S.D. change in log(social sector emp.)
.02
.01
0
-.01
0
5
step
90% CI
cumulative orthogonalized irf
Graphs by irfname, impulse variable, and response variable

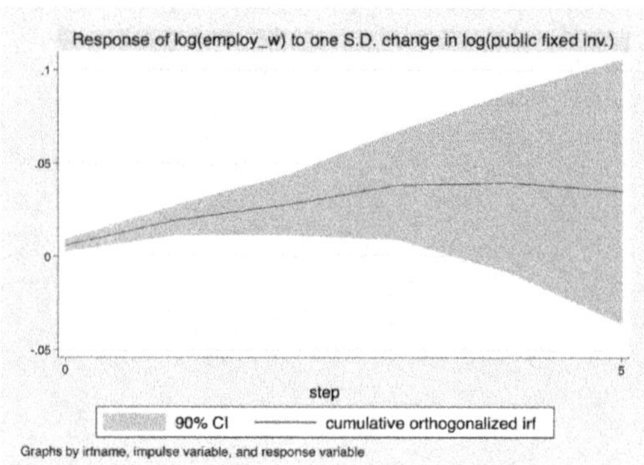
Response of log(employ_w) to one S.D. change in log(public fixed inv.)
.1
.05
0
-.05
0
5
step
90% CI
cumulative orthogonalized irf
Graphs by irfname, impulse variable, and response variable

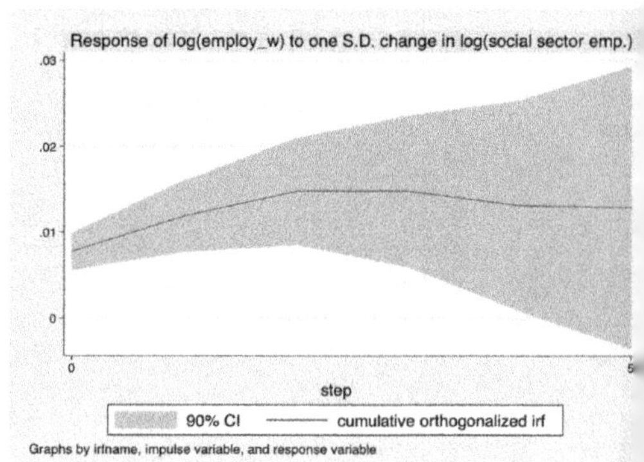
Response of log(employ_w) to one S.D. change in log(social sector emp.)
.03
.02
.01
0
0
step
90% CI
cumulative orthogonalized irf
Graphs by irfname, impulse variable, and response variable

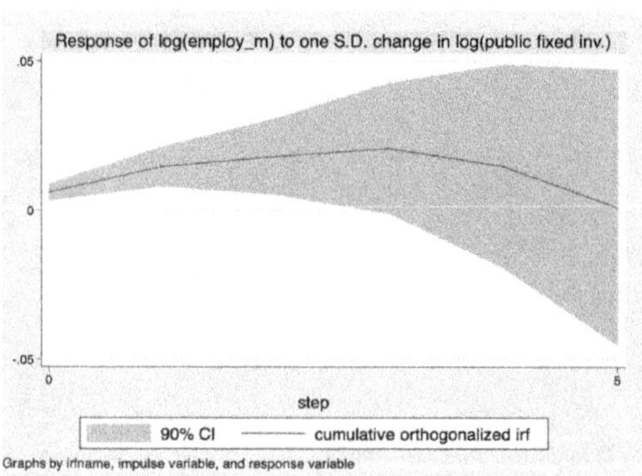
Response of log(employ_m) to one S.D. change in log(public fixed inv.)
.05
0
-.05
0
5
step
90% CI
cumulative orthogonalized irf
Graphs by irfname, impulse variable, and response variable

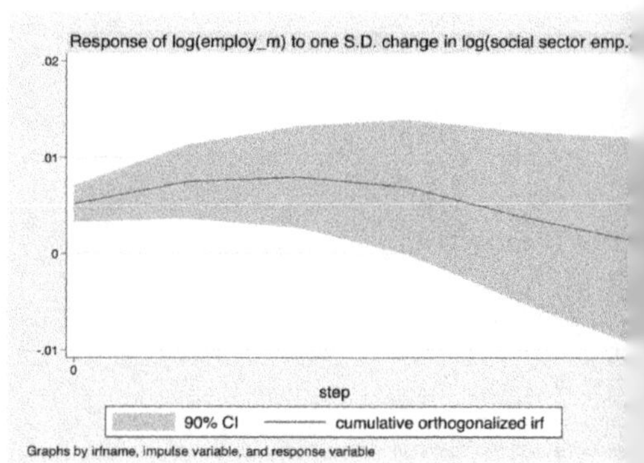
.02
.01
0
-.01
0
step
90% CI
cumulative orthogonalized irf
Graphs by irfname, impulse variable, and response variable

INDIA

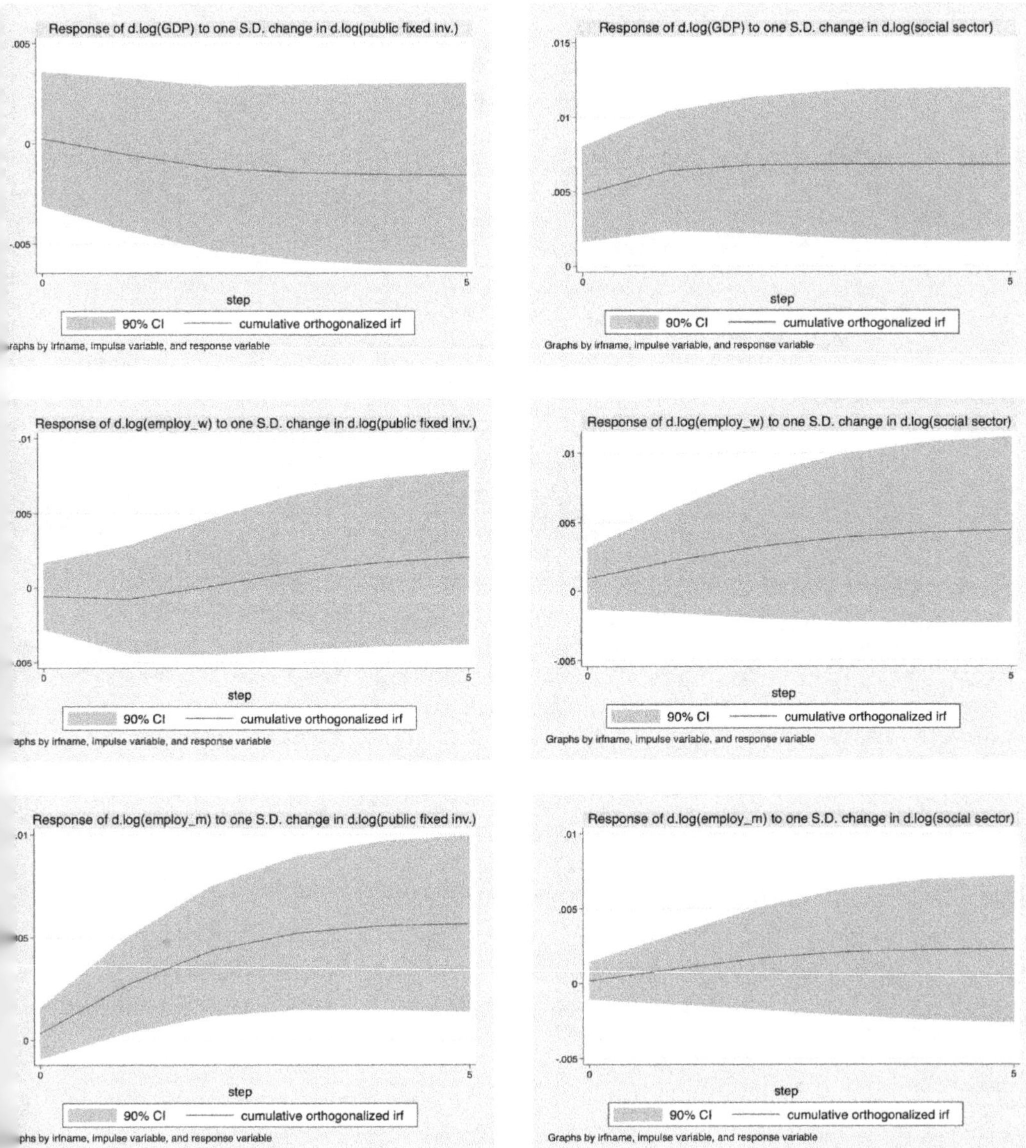
Response of d.log(GDP) to one S.D. change in d.log(public fixed inv.)
.005
0
-.005
0
5
step
90% CI
cumulative orthogonalized irf
Response of d.log(GDP) to one S.D. change in d.log(social sector)
.015
.01
.005
0
0
5
step
90% CI
cumulative orthogonalized irf
Graphs by irfname, impulse variable, and response variable
Response of d.log(employ_w) to one S.D. change in d.log(public fixed inv.)
.01
.005
0
0
5
step
90% CI
cumulative orthogonalized irf
Response of d.log(employ_w) to one S.D. change in d.log(social sector)
.01
.005
0
-.005
0
5
step
90% CI
cumulative orthogonalized irf
Graphs by irfname, impulse variable, and response variable
Response of d.log(employ_m) to one S.D. change in d.log(public fixed inv.)
.01
0
0
5
step
90% CI
cumulative orthogonalized irf
Response of d.log(employ_m) to one S.D. change in d.log(social sector)
.01
.005
0
-.005
0
5
step
90% CI
cumulative orthogonalized irf
Graphs by irfname, impulse variable, and response variable

INDONESIA

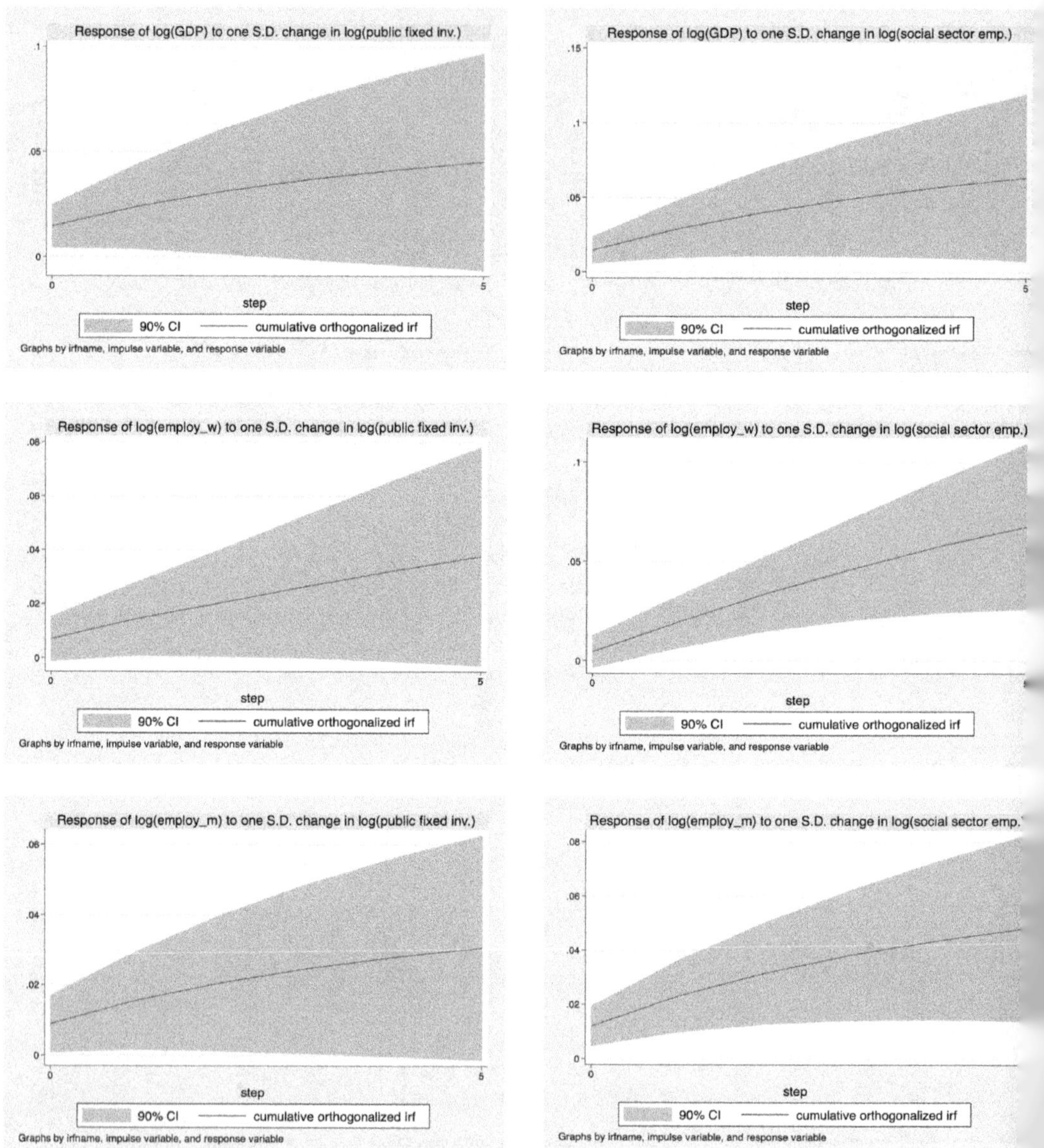
Response of log(GDP) to one S.D. change in log(public fixed inv.)
step
90% CI
cumulative orthogonalized irf
Graphs by irfname, impulse variable, and response variable
Response of log(GDP) to one S.D. change in log(social sector emp.)
step
90% CI
cumulative orthogonalized irf
Graphs by irfname, impulse variable, and response variable
Response of log(employ_w) to one S.D. change in log(public fixed inv.)
step
90% CI
cumulative orthogonalized irf
Graphs by irfname, impulse variable, and response variable
Response of log(employ_w) to one S.D. change in log(social sector emp.)
step
90% CI
cumulative orthogonalized irf
Graphs by irfname, impulse variable, and response variable
Response of log(employ_m) to one S.D. change in log(public fixed inv.)
step
90% CI
cumulative orthogonalized irf
Graphs by irfname, impulse variable, and response variable
Response of log(employ_m) to one S.D. change in log(social sector emp.
step
90% CI
cumulative orthogonalized irf
Graphs by irfname, impulse variable, and response variable

SOUTH AFRICA

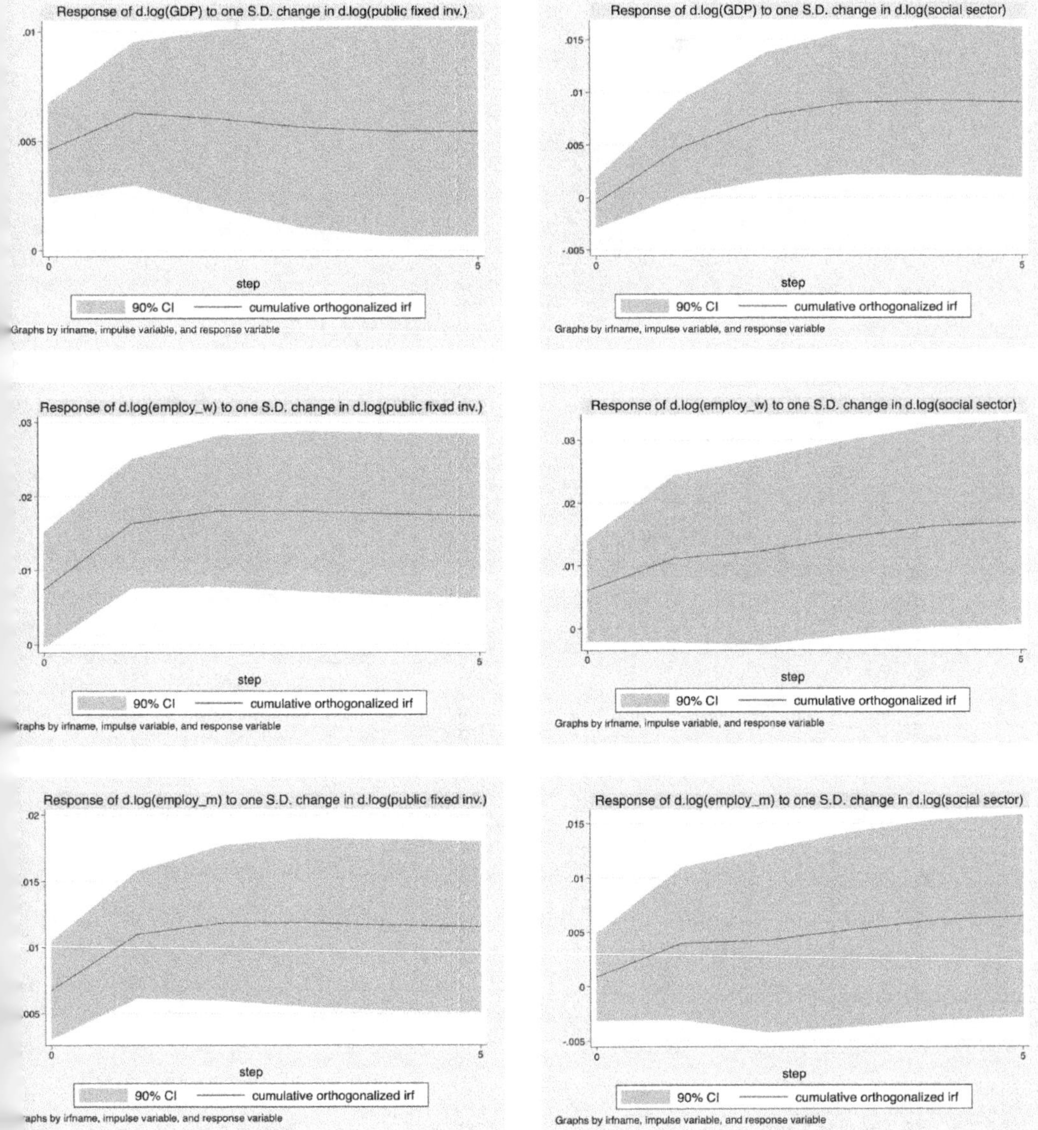

TURKEY

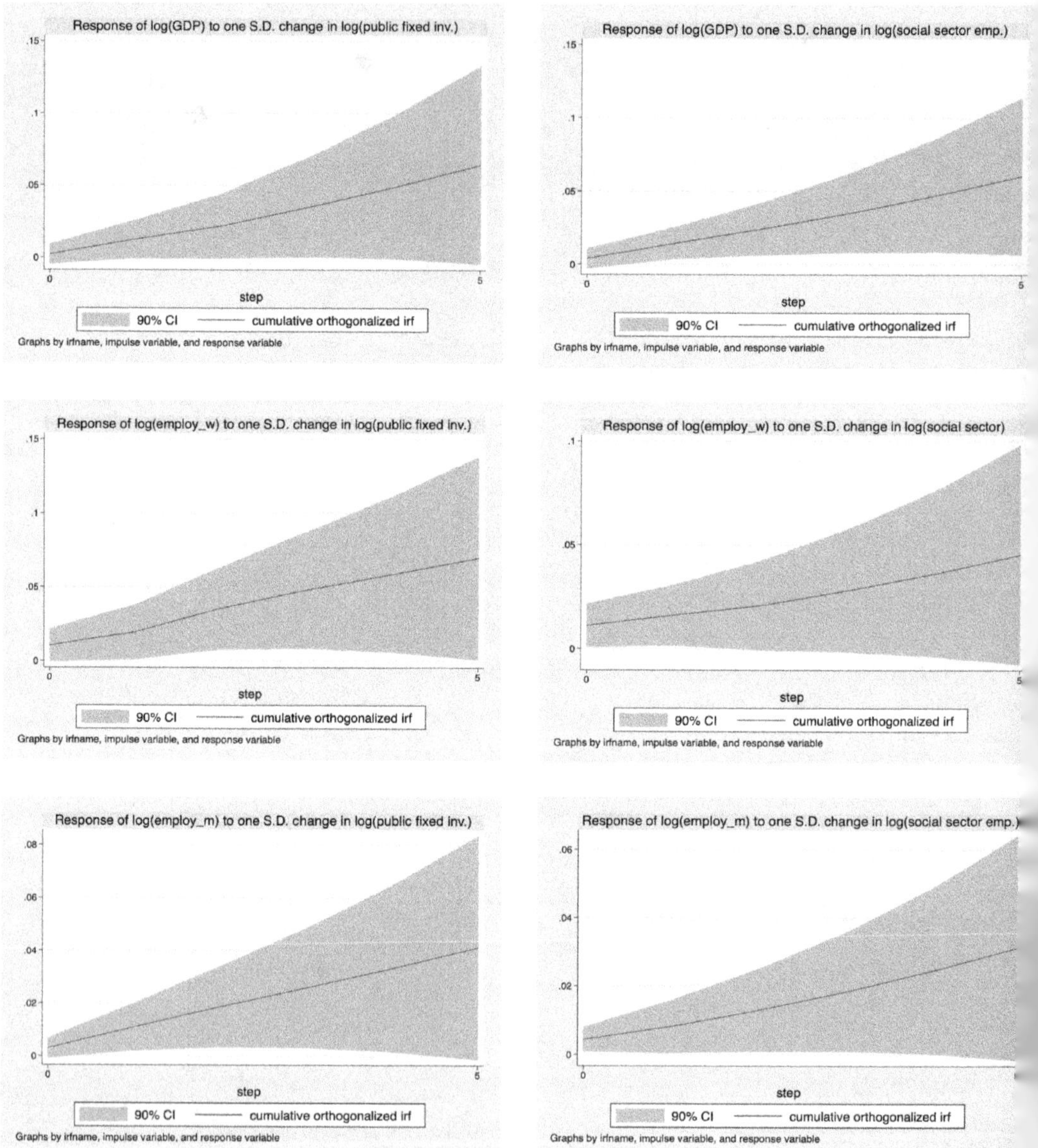
Response of log(GDP) to one S.D. change in log(public fixed inv.)
step
90% CI
cumulative orthogonalized irf
Graphs by irfname, impulse variable, and response variable
Response of log(GDP) to one S.D. change in log(social sector emp.)
step
90% CI
cumulative orthogonalized irf
Graphs by irfname, impulse variable, and response variable
Response of log(employ_w) to one S.D. change in log(public fixed inv.)
step
90% CI
cumulative orthogonalized irf
Graphs by irfname, impulse variable, and response variable
Response of log(employ_w) to one S.D. change in log(social sector)
step
90% CI
cumulative orthogonalized irf
Graphs by irfname, impulse variable, and response variable
Response of log(employ_m) to one S.D. change in log(public fixed inv.)
step
90% CI
cumulative orthogonalized irf
Graphs by irfname, impulse variable, and response variable
Response of log(employ_m) to one S.D. change in log(social sector emp.)
step
90% CI
cumulative orthogonalized irf
Graphs by irfname, impulse variable, and response variable

APPENDIX 7.4.2: CUMULATIVE ORTHOGONALIZED IMPULSE RESPONSE FUNCTIONS (SPECIFICATION 2)

Figure A7.4.2. Cumulative orthogonalized impulse response functions based on specification 2: the response of GDP and women's and men's employment (employ_w and employ_m) in the nonagricultural sector to a one standard deviation increase in value added in the manufacturing sector that supplies inputs to REEEPT (Y^{MRE}; MRE = Manufacturing Renewable Energy), transportation (air transportation excluded, Y^{PT}; PT = Public Transport), construction (Y^{C}; C = Construction)

CHILE

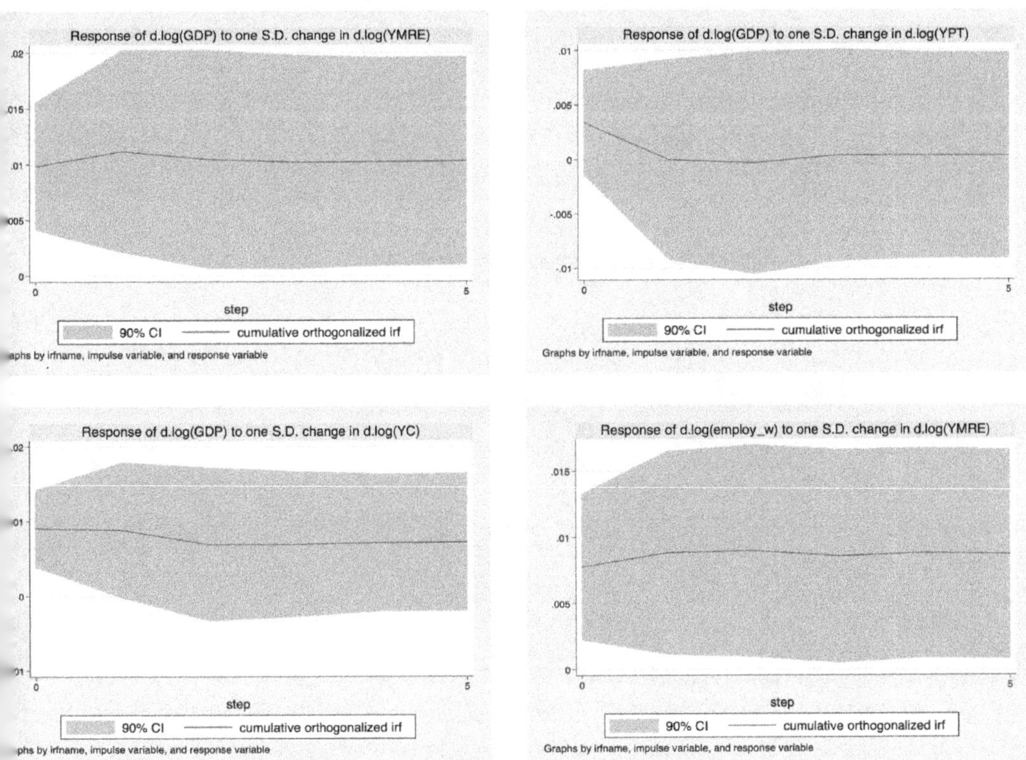

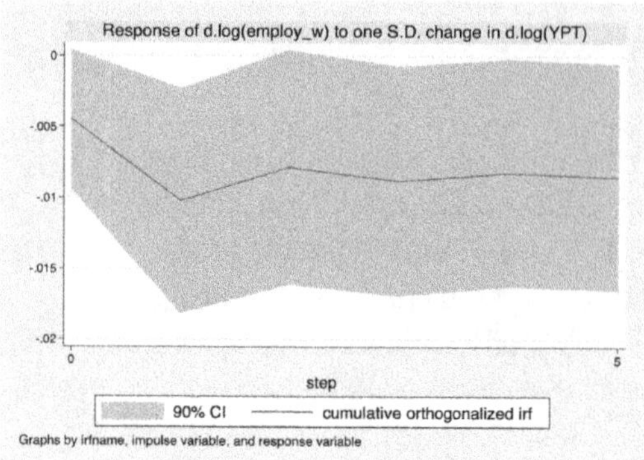
Response of d.log(employ_w) to one S.D. change in d.log(YPT)
0
-.005
-.01
-.015
-.02
0
5
step
90% CI
cumulative orthogonalized irf
Graphs by irfname, impulse variable, and response variable

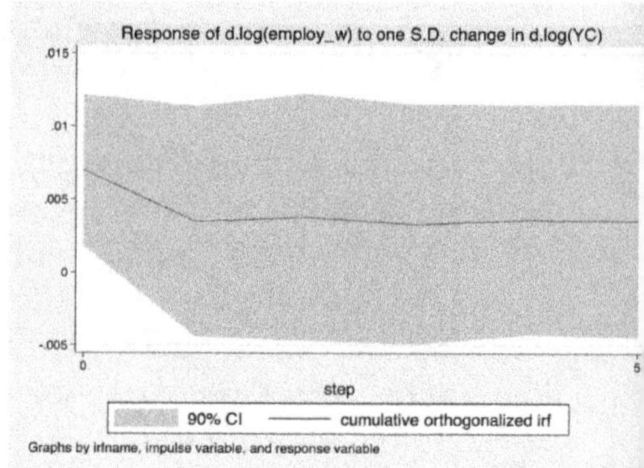
Response of d.log(employ_w) to one S.D. change in d.log(YC)
.015
.01
.005
0
-.005
0
5
step
90% CI
cumulative orthogonalized irf
Graphs by irfname, impulse variable, and response variable

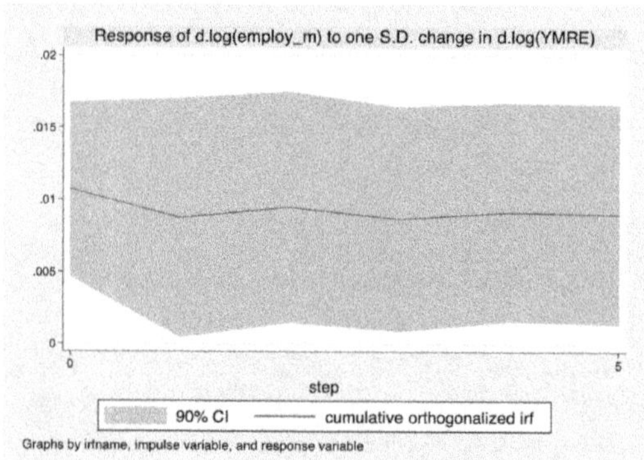
Response of d.log(employ_m) to one S.D. change in d.log(YMRE)
.02
.015
.01
.005
0
0
5
step
90% CI
cumulative orthogonalized irf
Graphs by irfname, impulse variable, and response variable

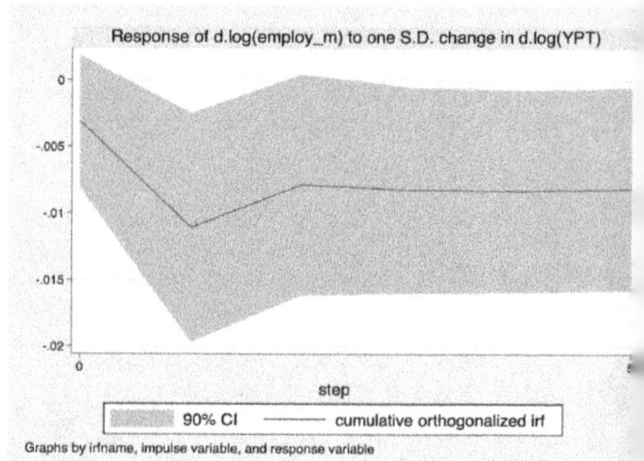
Response of d.log(employ_m) to one S.D. change in d.log(YPT)
0
-.005
-.01
-.015
-.02
0
step
90% CI
cumulative orthogonalized irf
Graphs by irfname, impulse variable, and response variable

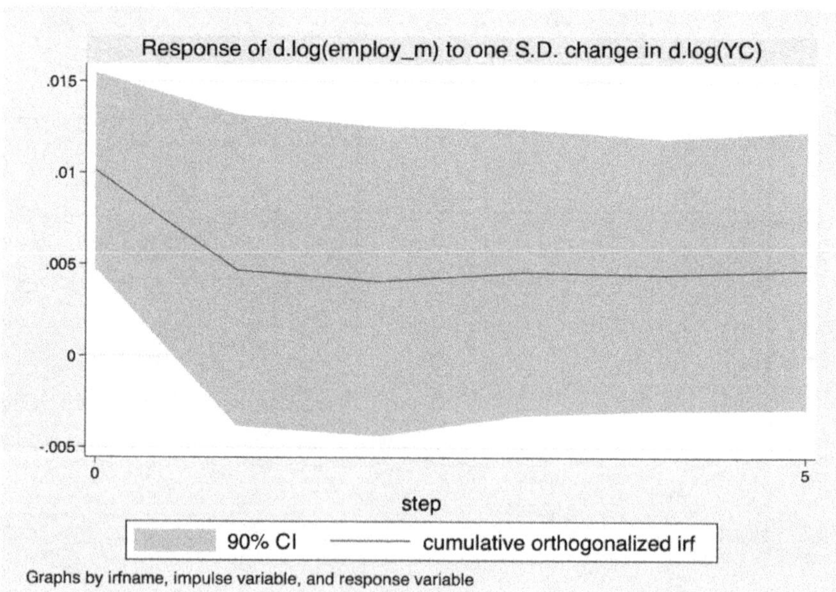
Response of d.log(employ_m) to one S.D. change in d.log(YC)
.015
.01
.005
0
-.005
0
5
step
90% CI
cumulative orthogonalized irf
Graphs by irfname, impulse variable, and response variable

COLOMBIA

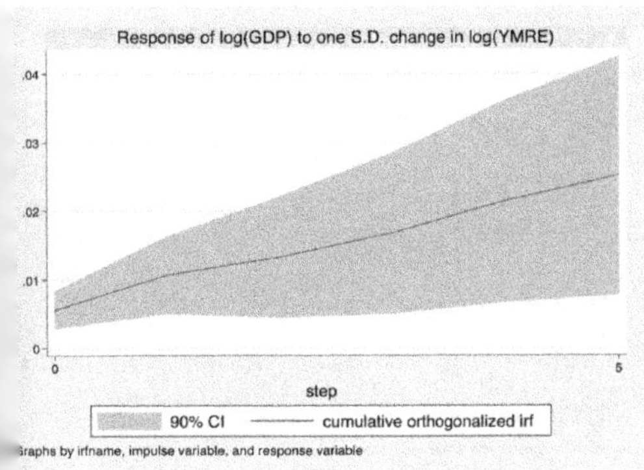
Response of log(GDP) to one S.D. change in log(YMRE)
.04
.03
.02
.01
0
0
5
step
90% CI
cumulative orthogonalized irf
raphs by irfname, impulse variable, and response variable

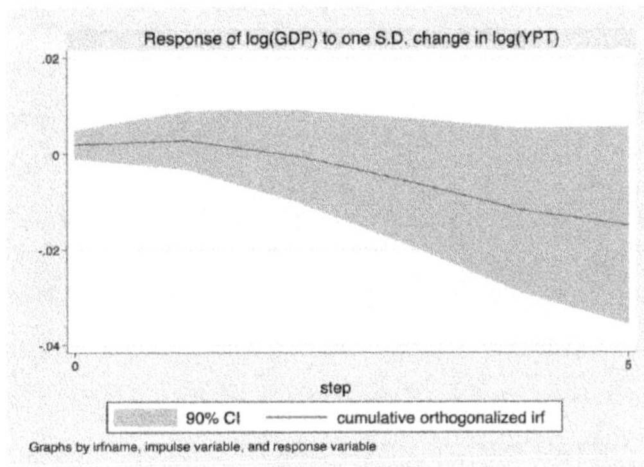
Response of log(GDP) to one S.D. change in log(YPT)
.02
0
-.02
-.04
0
5
step
90% CI
cumulative orthogonalized irf
Graphs by irfname, impulse variable, and response variable

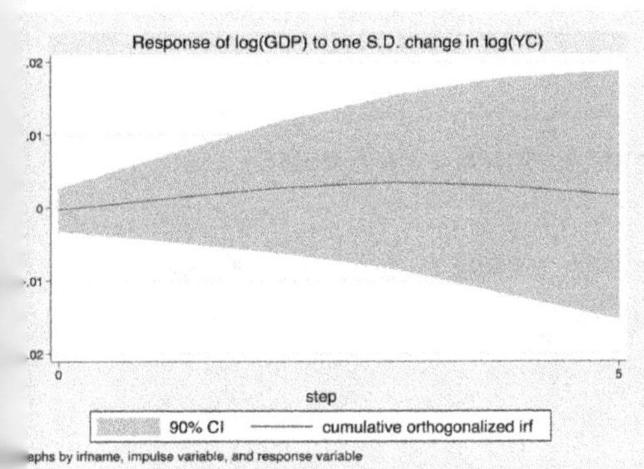
Response of log(GDP) to one S.D. change in log(YC)
.02
.01
0
-.01
0
5
step
90% CI
cumulative orthogonalized irf
aphs by irfname, impulse variable, and response variable

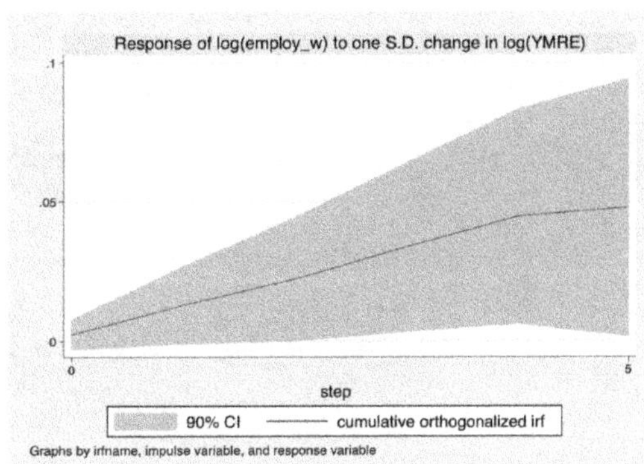
Response of log(employ_w) to one S.D. change in log(YMRE)
.1
.05
0
0
5
step
90% CI
cumulative orthogonalized irf
Graphs by irfname, impulse variable, and response variable

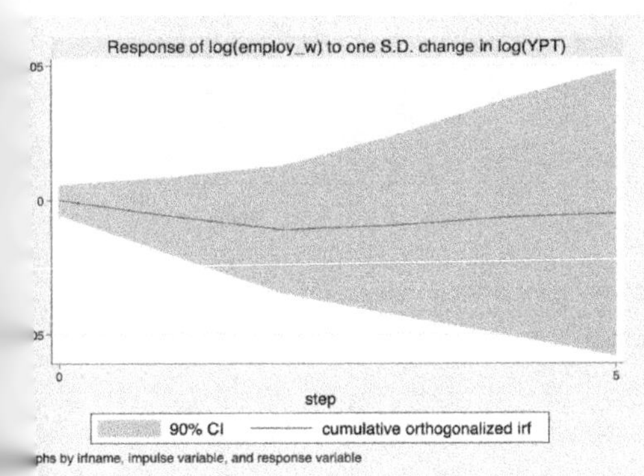
Response of log(employ_w) to one S.D. change in log(YPT)
0
0
5
step
90% CI
cumulative orthogonalized irf
phs by irfname, impulse variable, and response variable

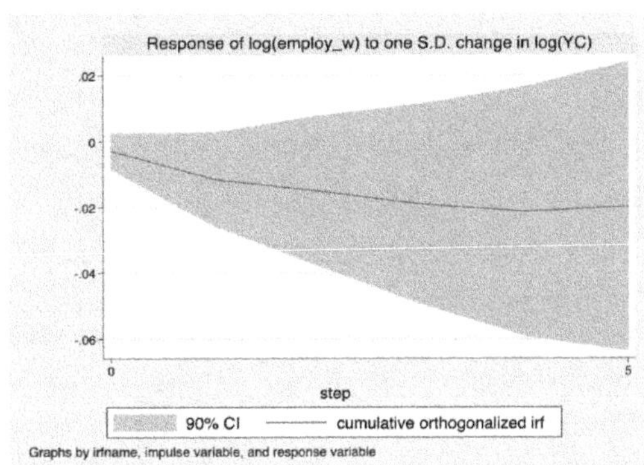
Response of log(employ_w) to one S.D. change in log(YC)
.02
0
-.02
-.04
-.06
0
5
step
90% CI
cumulative orthogonalized irf
Graphs by irfname, impulse variable, and response variable

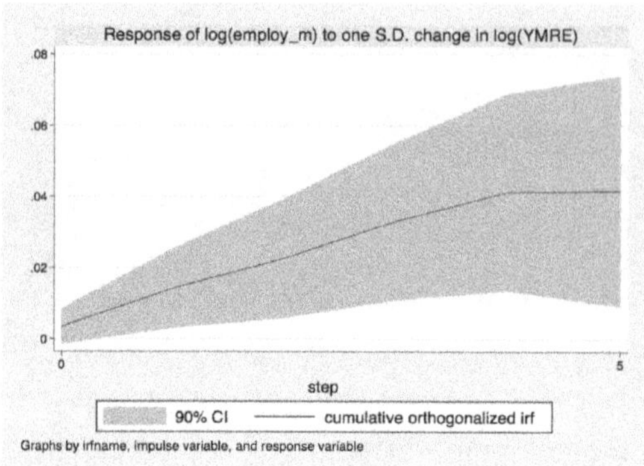
Response of log(employ_m) to one S.D. change in log(YMRE)
.08
.06
.04
.02
0
0
5
step
90% CI
cumulative orthogonalized irf
Graphs by irfname, impulse variable, and response variable

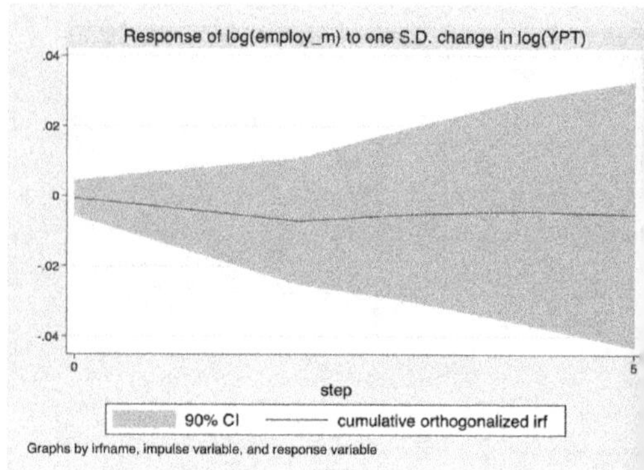
Response of log(employ_m) to one S.D. change in log(YPT)
.04
.02
0
-.02
-.04
0
5
step
90% CI
cumulative orthogonalized irf
Graphs by irfname, impulse variable, and response variable

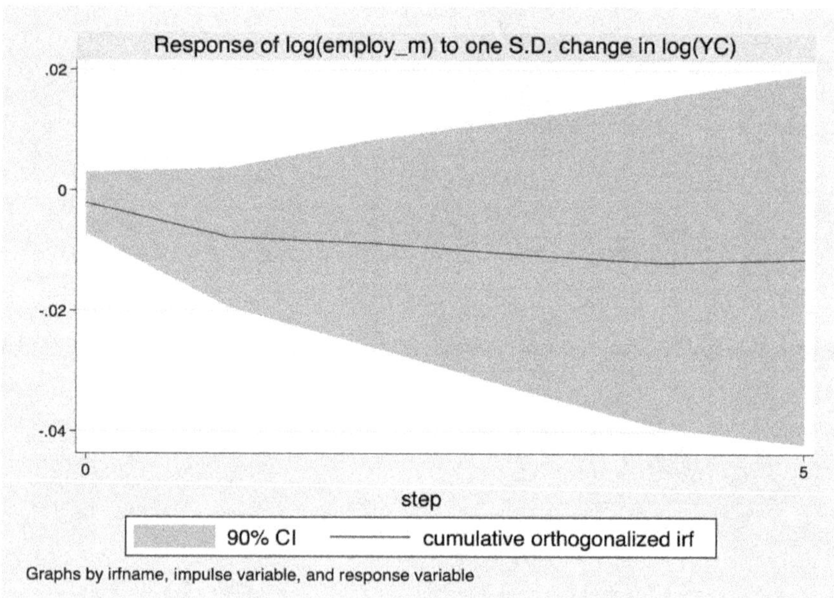
Response of log(employ_m) to one S.D. change in log(YC)
.02
0
-.02
-.04
0
5
step
90% CI
cumulative orthogonalized irf
Graphs by irfname, impulse variable, and response variable

INDIA

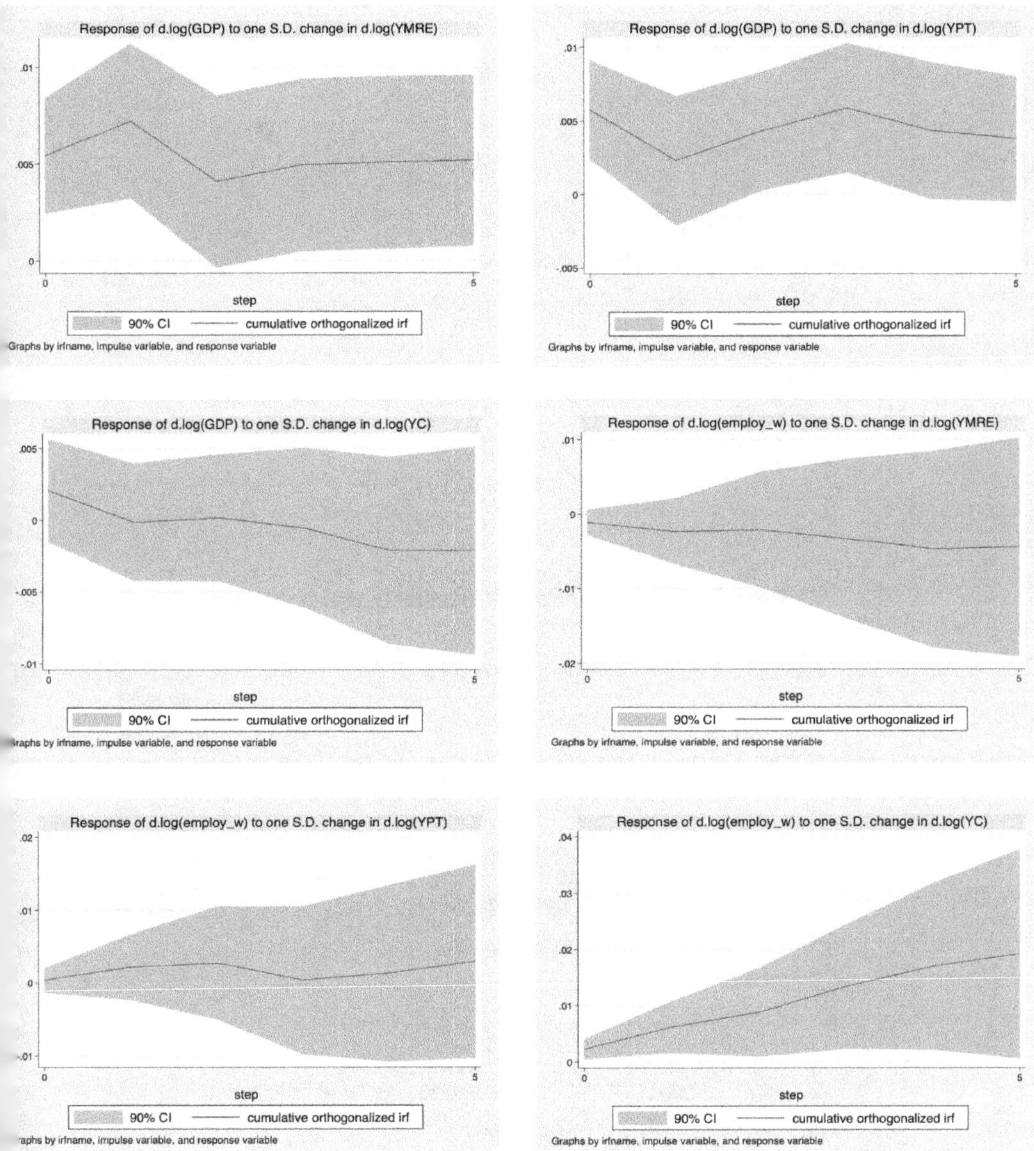
Response of d.log(GDP) to one S.D. change in d.log(YMRE)
step
90% CI
cumulative orthogonalized irf
Graphs by irfname, impulse variable, and response variable
Response of d.log(GDP) to one S.D. change in d.log(YPT)
step
90% CI
cumulative orthogonalized irf
Graphs by irfname, impulse variable, and response variable
Response of d.log(GDP) to one S.D. change in d.log(YC)
step
90% CI
cumulative orthogonalized irf
raphs by irfname, impulse variable, and response variable
Response of d.log(employ_w) to one S.D. change in d.log(YMRE)
step
90% CI
cumulative orthogonalized irf
Graphs by irfname, impulse variable, and response variable
Response of d.log(employ_w) to one S.D. change in d.log(YPT)
step
90% CI
cumulative orthogonalized irf
aphs by irfname, impulse variable, and response variable
Response of d.log(employ_w) to one S.D. change in d.log(YC)
step
90% CI
cumulative orthogonalized irf
Graphs by irfname, impulse variable, and response variable

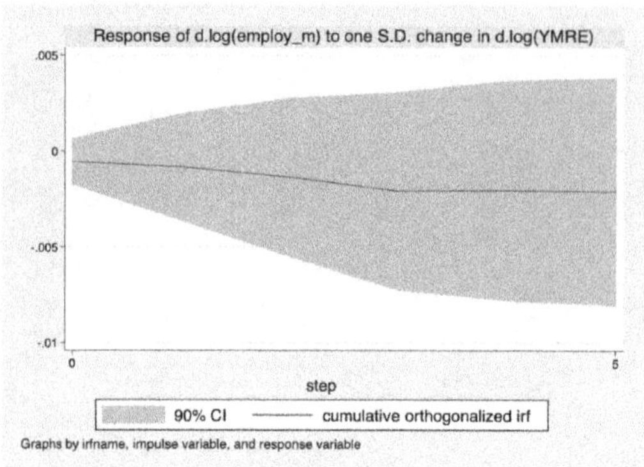
Response of d.log(employ_m) to one S.D. change in d.log(YMRE)
.005
0
-.005
-.01
0
5
step
90% CI
cumulative orthogonalized irf
Graphs by irfname, impulse variable, and response variable

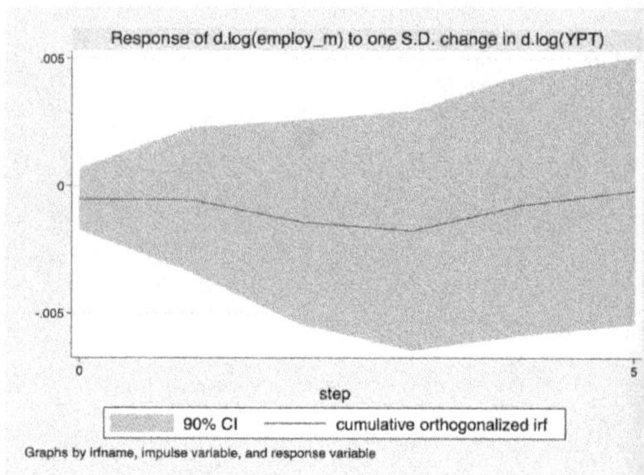
Response of d.log(employ_m) to one S.D. change in d.log(YPT)
.005
0
-.005
0
5
step
90% CI
cumulative orthogonalized irf
Graphs by irfname, impulse variable, and response variable

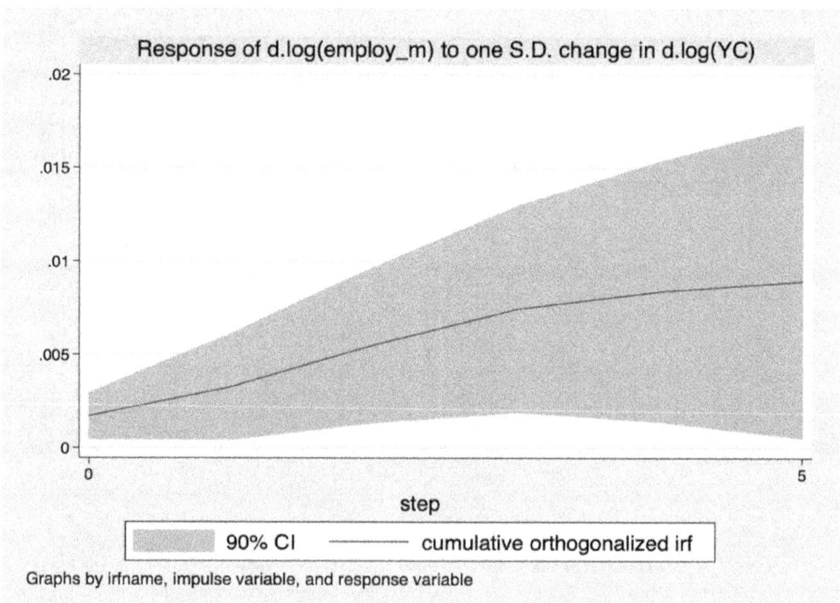
Response of d.log(employ_m) to one S.D. change in d.log(YC)
.02
.015
.01
.005
0
0
5
step
90% CI
cumulative orthogonalized irf
Graphs by irfname, impulse variable, and response variable

INDONESIA

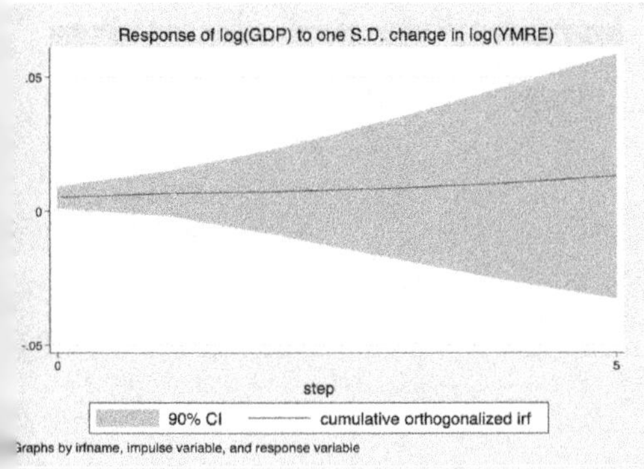
Response of log(GDP) to one S.D. change in log(YMRE)
.05
0
-.05
0
5
step
90% CI
cumulative orthogonalized irf

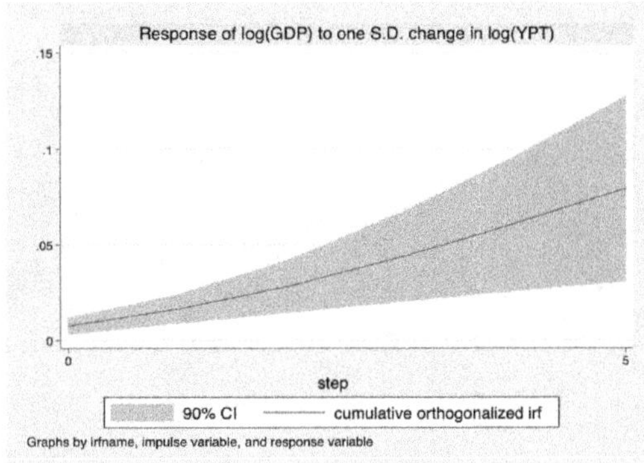
Response of log(GDP) to one S.D. change in log(YPT)
.15
.1
.05
0
0
5
step
90% CI
cumulative orthogonalized irf
Graphs by irfname, impulse variable, and response variable

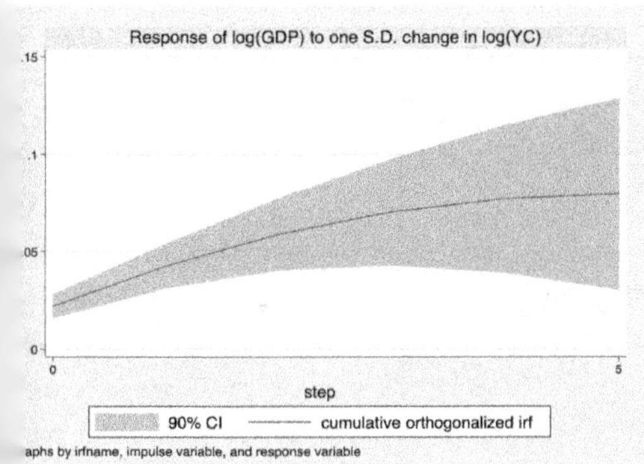
Response of log(GDP) to one S.D. change in log(YC)
.15
.1
.05
0
0
5
step
90% CI
cumulative orthogonalized irf

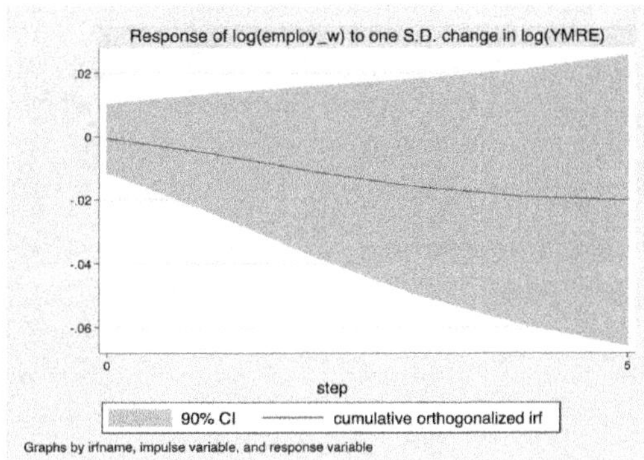
Response of log(employ_w) to one S.D. change in log(YMRE)
.02
0
-.02
-.04
-.06
0
5
step
90% CI
cumulative orthogonalized irf
Graphs by irfname, impulse variable, and response variable

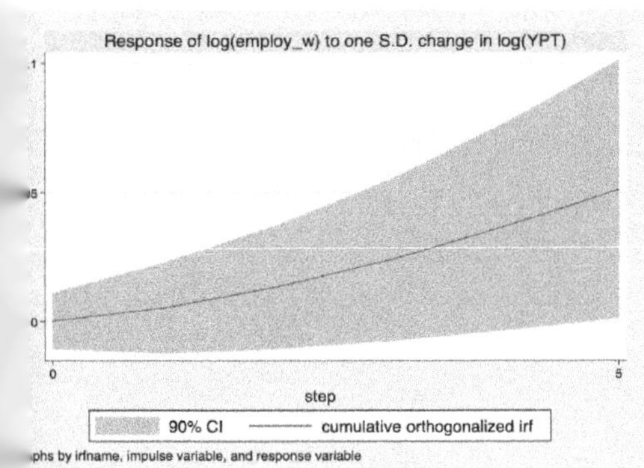
Response of log(employ_w) to one S.D. change in log(YPT)
0
0
5
step
90% CI
cumulative orthogonalized irf

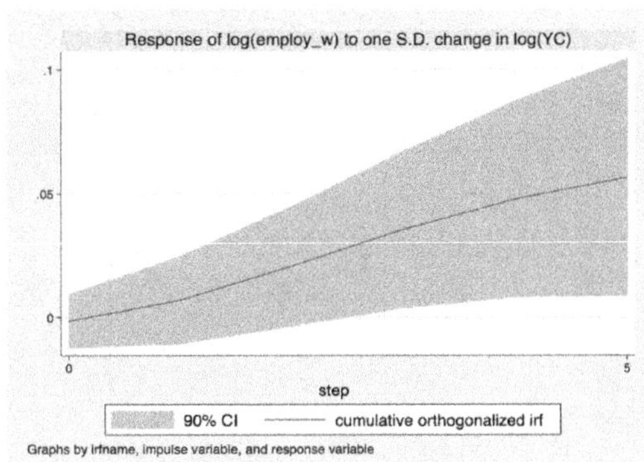
Response of log(employ_w) to one S.D. change in log(YC)
.1
.05
0
0
5
step
90% CI
cumulative orthogonalized irf
Graphs by irfname, impulse variable, and response variable

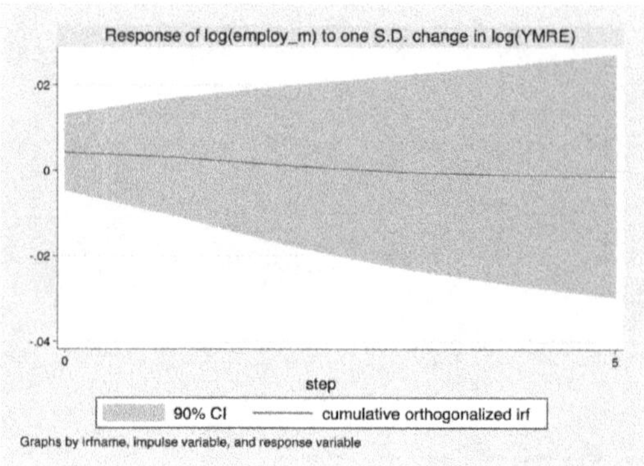

Response of log(employ_m) to one S.D. change in log(YMRE)
.02
0
-.02
-.04
0
5
step
90% CI
cumulative orthogonalized irf
Graphs by irfname, impulse variable, and response variable

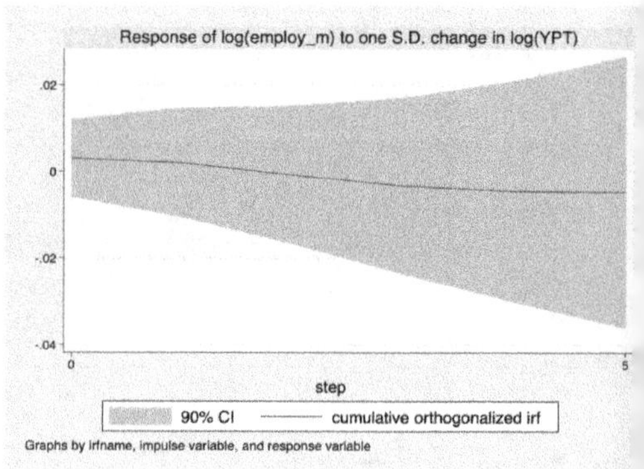

Response of log(employ_m) to one S.D. change in log(YPT)
.02
0
-.02
-.04
0
5
step
90% CI
cumulative orthogonalized irf
Graphs by irfname, impulse variable, and response variable

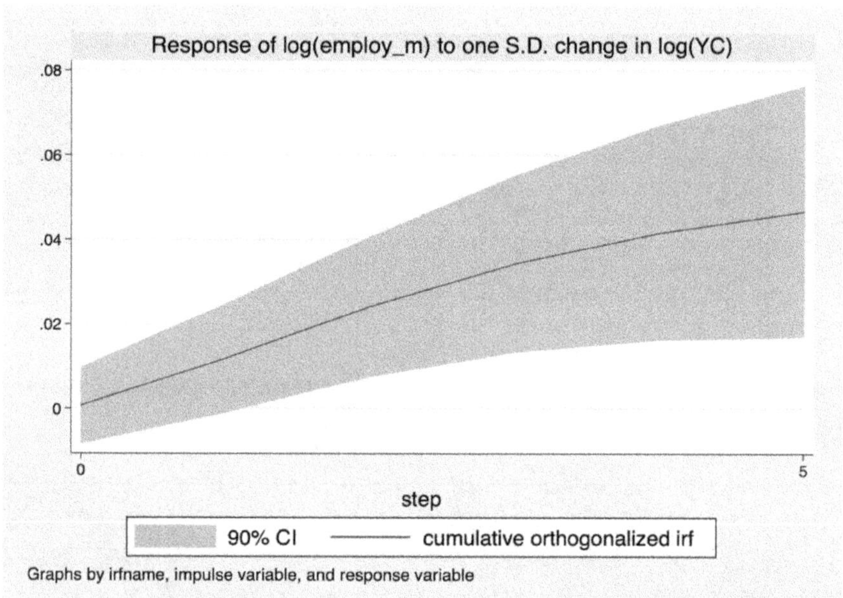

Response of log(employ_m) to one S.D. change in log(YC)
.08
.06
.04
.02
0
0
5
step
90% CI
cumulative orthogonalized irf
Graphs by irfname, impulse variable, and response variable

SOUTH AFRICA

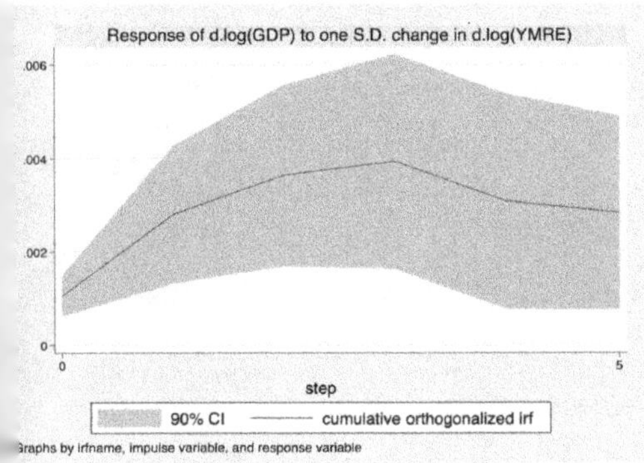

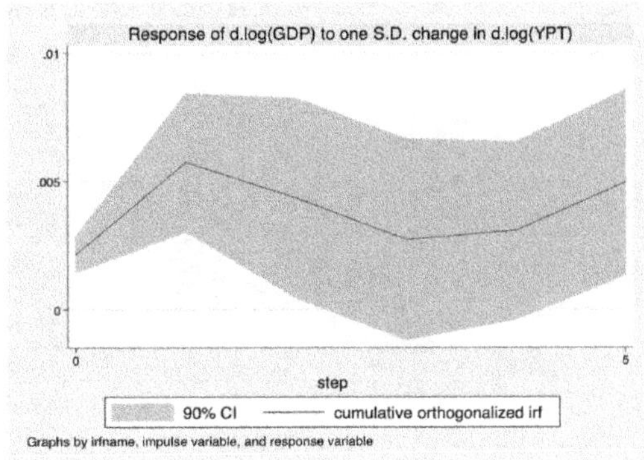

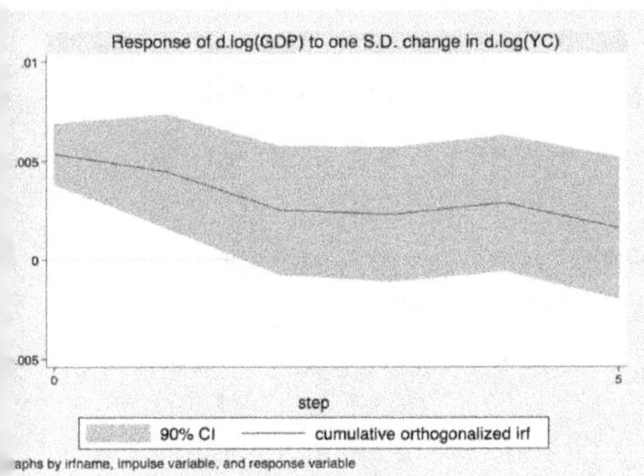

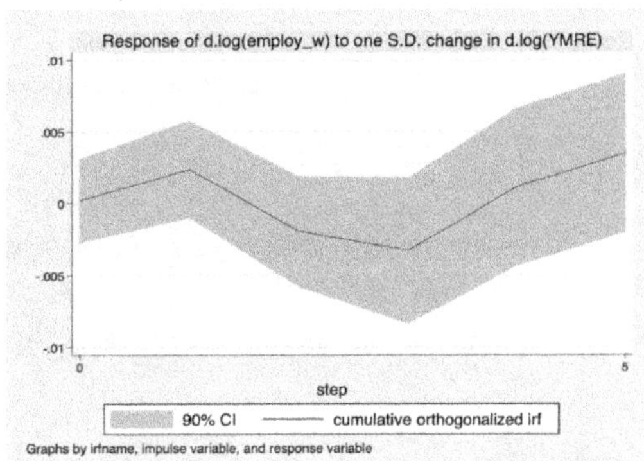

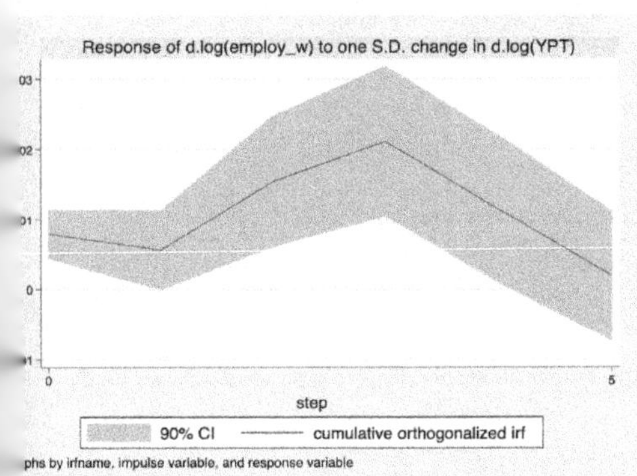

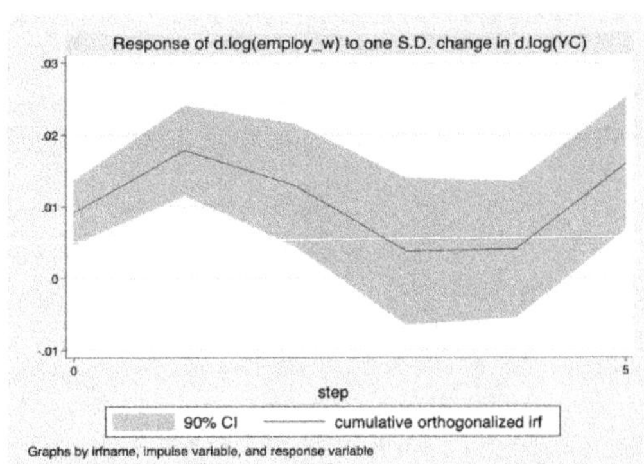

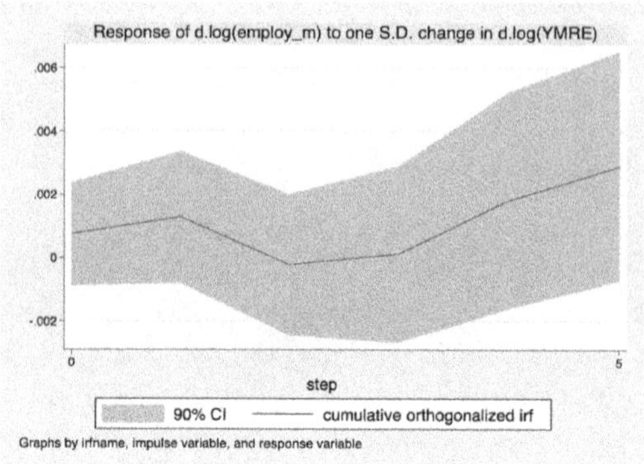
Response of d.log(employ_m) to one S.D. change in d.log(YMRE)
.006
.004
.002
0
-.002
0
5
step
90% CI
cumulative orthogonalized irf
Graphs by irfname, impulse variable, and response variable

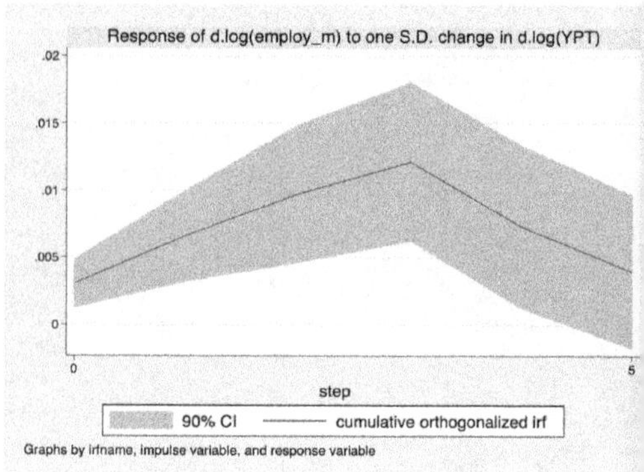
Response of d.log(employ_m) to one S.D. change in d.log(YPT)
.02
.015
.01
.005
0
0
5
step
90% CI
cumulative orthogonalized irf
Graphs by irfname, impulse variable, and response variable

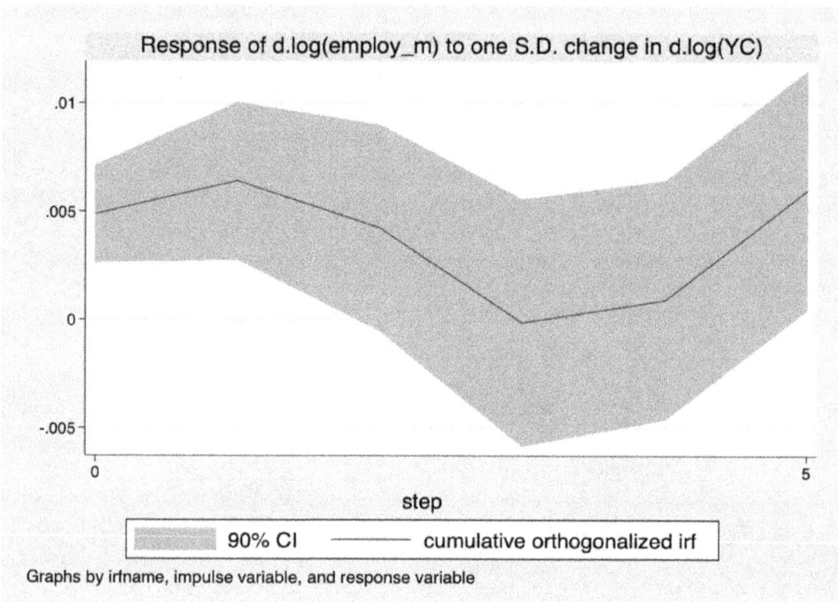
Response of d.log(employ_m) to one S.D. change in d.log(YC)
.01
.005
0
-.005
0
5
step
90% CI
cumulative orthogonalized irf
Graphs by irfname, impulse variable, and response variable

TURKEY

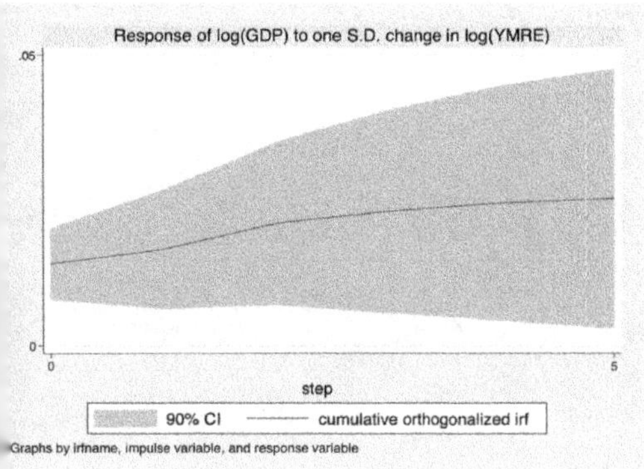
Response of log(GDP) to one S.D. change in log(YMRE)
.05
0
0
5
step
90% CI
cumulative orthogonalized irf
Graphs by irfname, impulse variable, and response variable

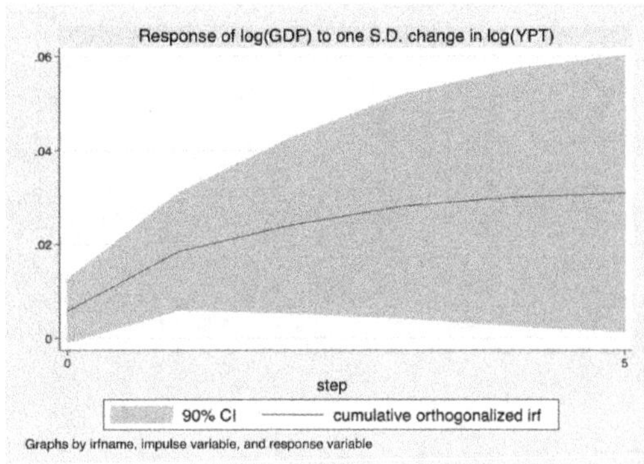
Response of log(GDP) to one S.D. change in log(YPT)
.06
.04
.02
0
0
5
step
90% CI
cumulative orthogonalized irf
Graphs by irfname, impulse variable, and response variable

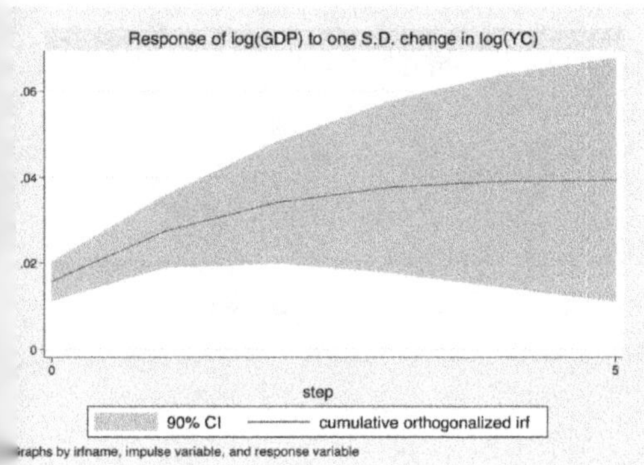
Response of log(GDP) to one S.D. change in log(YC)
.06
.04
.02
0
0
5
step
90% CI
cumulative orthogonalized irf
raphs by irfname, impulse variable, and response variable

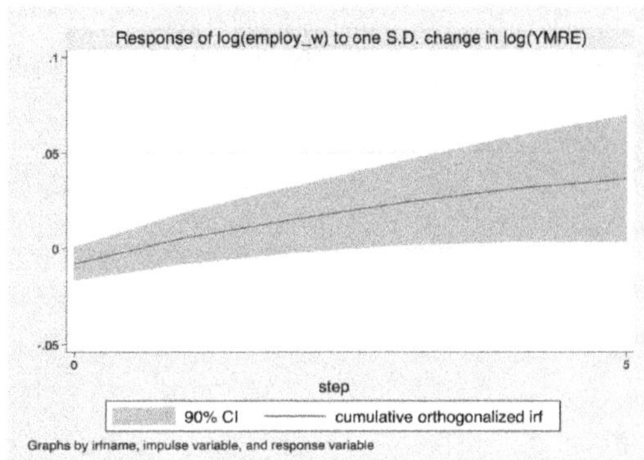
Response of log(employ_w) to one S.D. change in log(YMRE)
.1
.05
0
-.05
0
5
step
90% CI
cumulative orthogonalized irf
Graphs by irfname, impulse variable, and response variable

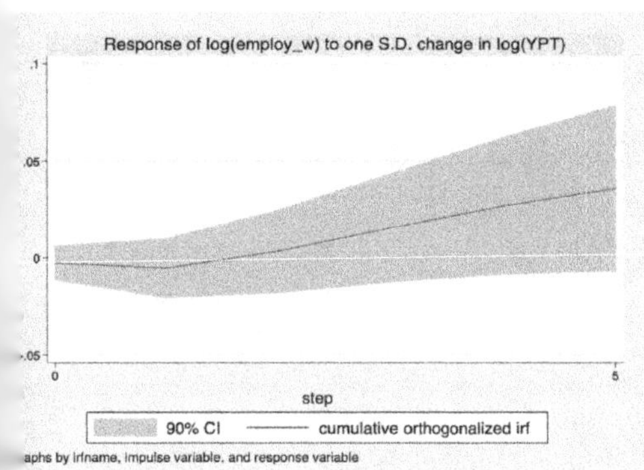
Response of log(employ_w) to one S.D. change in log(YPT)
.1
.05
0
.05
0
5
step
90% CI
cumulative orthogonalized irf
aphs by irfname, impulse variable, and response variable

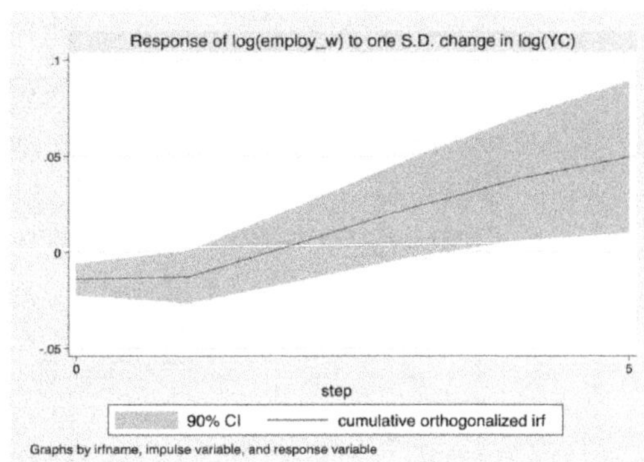
Response of log(employ_w) to one S.D. change in log(YC)
.1
.05
0
-.05
0
5
step
90% CI
cumulative orthogonalized irf
Graphs by irfname, impulse variable, and response variable

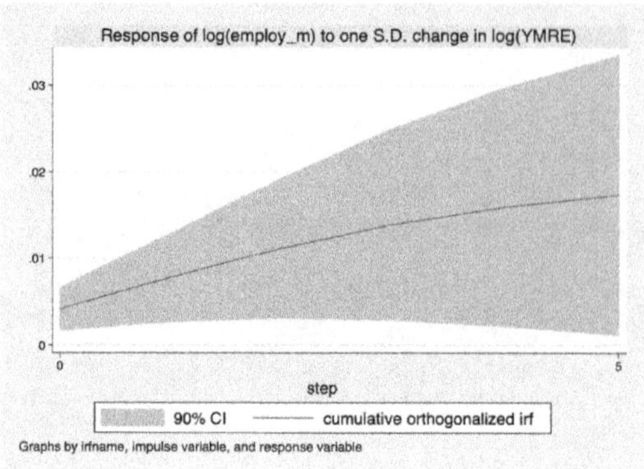
Response of log(employ_m) to one S.D. change in log(YMRE)
.03
.02
.01
0
0
5
step
90% CI
cumulative orthogonalized irf
Graphs by irfname, impulse variable, and response variable

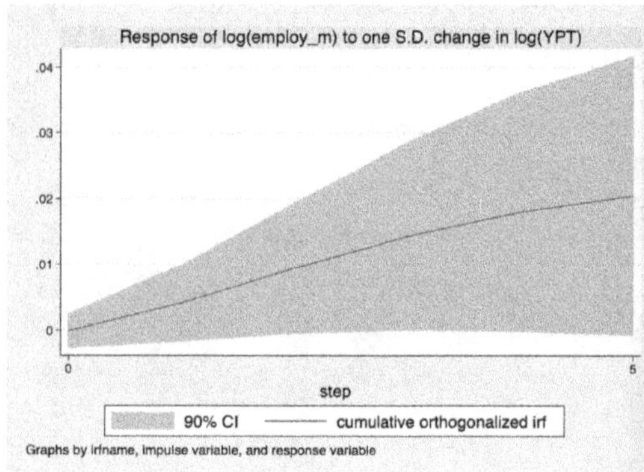
Response of log(employ_m) to one S.D. change in log(YPT)
.04
.03
.02
.01
0
0
5
step
90% CI
cumulative orthogonalized irf
Graphs by irfname, impulse variable, and response variable

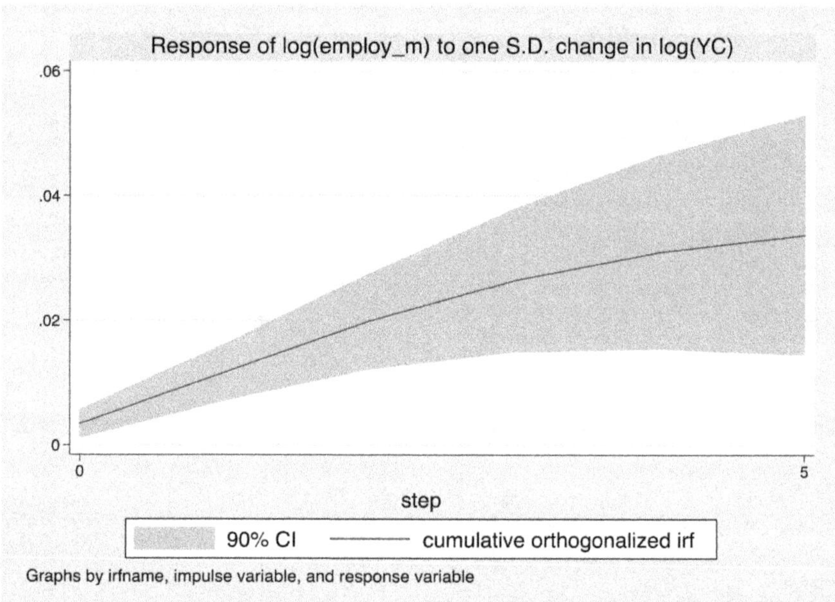
Response of log(employ_m) to one S.D. change in log(YC)
.06
.04
.02
0
0
5
step
90% CI
cumulative orthogonalized irf
Graphs by irfname, impulse variable, and response variable

PART III

Employment in Africa

CHAPTER 8

Demographic Challenges for Global Labor Markets in the Twenty-First Century

AFRICA IN A CHANGING WORLD

David Lam and Murray Leibbrandt

David Lam

Department of Economics and Population Studies Center
University of Michigan
davidl@umich.edu

Murray Leibbrandt

Southern Africa Labour and Development Research Unit (SALDRU)
University of Cape Town
Murray.Leibbrandt@uct.ac.za

Prepared for:
Task Force on Employment
The Initiative for Policy Dialogue
Columbia University[1]

Abstract: The world is projected to add 2.5 billion people to the total population and 1.1 billion people to the working-age population between 2020 and 2100. Almost all the additional working-age people will be added in sub-Saharan Africa, a dramatic change from previous decades, when the growth of the working-age population was concentrated in Asia. This chapter analyzes the demography of the African labor force in the coming decades using the latest United Nations population projections. We show that, by 2050, Africa will be the only region in the world with a growing working-age population and will be the only region in which the ratio of dependents to working-age population is falling. These dramatic differences are the result of Africa's later and slower fertility decline, with fertility still high in many African countries. Being the only region with a growing working-age population may create opportunities for investment and economic growth in Africa. This growing working-age cohort and especially its females have more years of schooling than any previous generation. But the quality of their education still lags other regions. On the demand side, Africa needs to produce 2 million jobs per month by 2040 to keep up with the growth of the working-age population. This rate of job creation is similar to that produced in Asia during the period in which its working-age population was growing at similar rates. This remains a daunting challenge for Africa in the coming decades. The dominance of the informal sector in all African labor markets, except for a few upper-middle-income contexts, implies that formally measured unemployment rates are not likely to provide telling metrics of African success. Rather, the focus for growth and improved development outcomes has to be on formal sector job creation alongside notably stronger linkages into the informal sector than has been the case in the past.

1. INTRODUCTION

In the last fifty years the global labor market has experienced massive demographic upheaval. As shown in Lam et al. (2019), the world added over 3 billion people to the working-age population between 1970 and 2020, growing from 2.1 billion to 5.1 billion. The average annual growth rate of the world's working-age population from 1970 to 2020 was 1.75 percent, with a maximum growth rate of 2.3 percent in the 1980s. Growth at this rate is historically unprecedented. As shown in Lam (2011), historical population growth rates for the world rarely reached 0.5 percent per year before 1900, reaching 1 percent around 1950. In the last half century Asia has been, by far, the largest contributor to the growth of the world's working-age population, accounting for 2 billion of the 3 billion increase (Lam et al. 2019). Adding 3 billion people of working age to the world, with over 70 million per year being added in the 2000s, was an enormous shock to labor markets. Most of the countries with the most rapid growth, however, did not experience significant increases in unemployment during this period. Data from the International Labor Organization (ILO) indicate relatively low levels of unemployment in most Asian countries throughout this period, in spite of the rapid growth of the working-age population (ILO n.d.).

Large demographic challenges continue for global labor markets, but the nature of those challenges is rapidly changing. As we will show in this chapter, growth of the working-age population in Asia will soon be negative, an enormous change from the situation of just one or two decades ago. Sub-Saharan Africa, on the other hand, will experience rapid growth of its working-age population, comparable in percentage terms to Asia's growth in previous decades. Over the next fifty years, sub-Saharan Africa's working-age population is projected to triple. By 2050, it will be the only major region in the world with a growing working-age population.

This chapter looks at the demographic trends in labor markets around the world in the rest of the twenty-first century. While our focus is on the coming decades, we also look back at the last seventy years to put the current demographic trends in perspective. We will also put a major focus on the demography of the labor force in sub-Saharan Africa because that is where almost all the growth of the working-age population will occur. We will put these trends in the context of the experience of other countries and regions in order to consider the ways in which Africa's experience is and is not unique. We also present trends for different African countries to clarify the extent to which the overall African trends are shared across the region.[2]

Most population data for this chapter come from the 2022 Revision of the World Population Prospects (WPP), the official United Nations population estimates and projections, prepared by the Population Division of the UN Department of Economic and Social Affairs (United Nations, Department of Economic and Social Affairs, Population Division 2022). The 2022 revision provides estimates from 1950 to 2021 and projections from 2022 to 2100. Most of our analysis uses the UN's "Medium Variant" projections, the most widely used population projections, although we also discuss the sensitivity of these projections to alternative assumptions about fertility decline. Lam et al. (2019) provide additional details and caveats about the UN's population data and the assumptions used for the projections.[3]

Section 2 sets the backdrop with an overview of trends in total population and the working-age population from 1950 to 2100 for the world and its major regions. In section 3, the role of changes in fertility in driving these trends is provided. Alternative projections of African fertility decline are discussed. Section 4 looks at the changing age structure of global labor markets, showing the shift from a youth bulge to an older worker bulge in Africa, Asia, and Latin America, and the associated changes in dependency ratios. Section 5 looks at the rural-urban distribution of population growth, pointing out that most of the growing labor force will be concentrated in urban areas but that Africa still has a rising rural population. Section 6 discusses the demographic dividend, exploring the challenges and opportunities created by Africa's expanding working-age population. Harnessing the demographic dividend requires putting the working-age population to productive work and, in line with this, section 7 takes us from demography to the labor market. It starts on the supply side by demonstrating the rapid increases in years of education in Africa and discusses the potentially important implications for the ability to absorb millions of new young people into the labor force. It then moves to the demand side of the labor market: realizing this potential depends on the current and future demand for labor in Africa. We conclude with a discussion of the implications of these demographic and labor market changes for development policy in Africa and the rest of the world.

2. GROWTH OF THE TOTAL POPULATION AND THE WORKING-AGE POPULATION

The changing roles of Asia and Africa in shaping the world's population can be seen in the top panel of figure 8.1, which shows the estimated and projected population for Asia, sub-Saharan Africa, Latin America, and the Caribbean (henceforth, Latin America), and the rest of the world—the sum of which is the global population (the vertical line at 2021 separates the UN estimates for 1950–2021 from the UN Medium Variant projections for 2022–2100). As seen in the top panel, world population grew from 2.5 billion in 1950 to 7.8 billion in 2020 and is projected to reach a peak of 10.4 billion in 2085, falling to 10.3 billion by 2100. Asia, which grew from 1.4 billion in 1950 to 4.7 billion in 2020, is projected to peak at 5.3 billion in 2055, and is projected to have 620 million fewer people in 2100 than it had in 2020. Sub-Saharan Africa, which grew from 180 million to 1.1 billion between 1950 and 2020, is projected to add 2.3 billion between 2020 and 2100. Asia has historically accounted for 62 percent of global population growth between 1950 and 2020, while only 17 percent was in sub-Saharan Africa. These roles will be dramatically different going forward, with Asia accounting for a negative proportion of global population growth between 2020 and 2100, and Sub-Saharan Africa accounting for 93 percent of the 2.5 billion projected increase. In sum, the growth of the world population in the twenty-first century will be dominated by Africa, and sub-Saharan Africa will be the only major region with substantial population growth after 2050.

The second panel of figure 8.1 shows the working-age population for the world and major regions. We follow standard conventions of the ILO and other international agencies in using ages fifteen to sixty-four as the definition of the working-age population. The working-age population of the world is projected to grow from 5.3 billion in 2025 to 6.1 billion in 2050, with only a slight increase to 6.2 billion in 2100. The working-age population for sub-Saharan Africa is projected to increase from 700 million in 2025 to 1.3 billion in 2050 and 2.3 billion in 2100. One of the key patterns shown in the figure is that Africa will be the only region with a growing working-age population after 2050. In fact, Africa is the only region that is projected to have a larger working-age population in 2100 than in 2025.

While the trends for the working-age population are similar to those for the total population, the second panel of figure 8.1 demonstrates that the working-age population reaches a peak sooner and grows more slowly in the twenty-first century than does total population. For example, the working-age population of Asia reaches a peak in 2043, while the total population reaches a peak in 2055. The working-age population of Latin America peaks in 2042, while the total population peaks in 2056. The difference is because those sixty-five and older will be the last age group to stop growing, an important demographic phenomenon that will be discussed in section 4.

The bottom panel of figure 8.1 shows the share of the world's working-age population located in each region. Asia's share, which was over 50 percent and growing in recent decades, reached a peak at 62 percent in 2011 and has been falling since. Sub-Saharan Africa's share of the global working-age population was below 10 percent until around 2010 and is now rising rapidly, projected to reach 20 percent around 2045 and 37 percent in 2100, roughly equaling the share for Asia.

2.1 FURTHER DETAIL ON GROWTH RATES OF THE WORKING-AGE POPULATION

Clearly then, the world's working-age population experienced dramatic growth in the last half of the twentieth century, and less dramatic, Africa-centered growth will continue in the coming decades. Two measures of

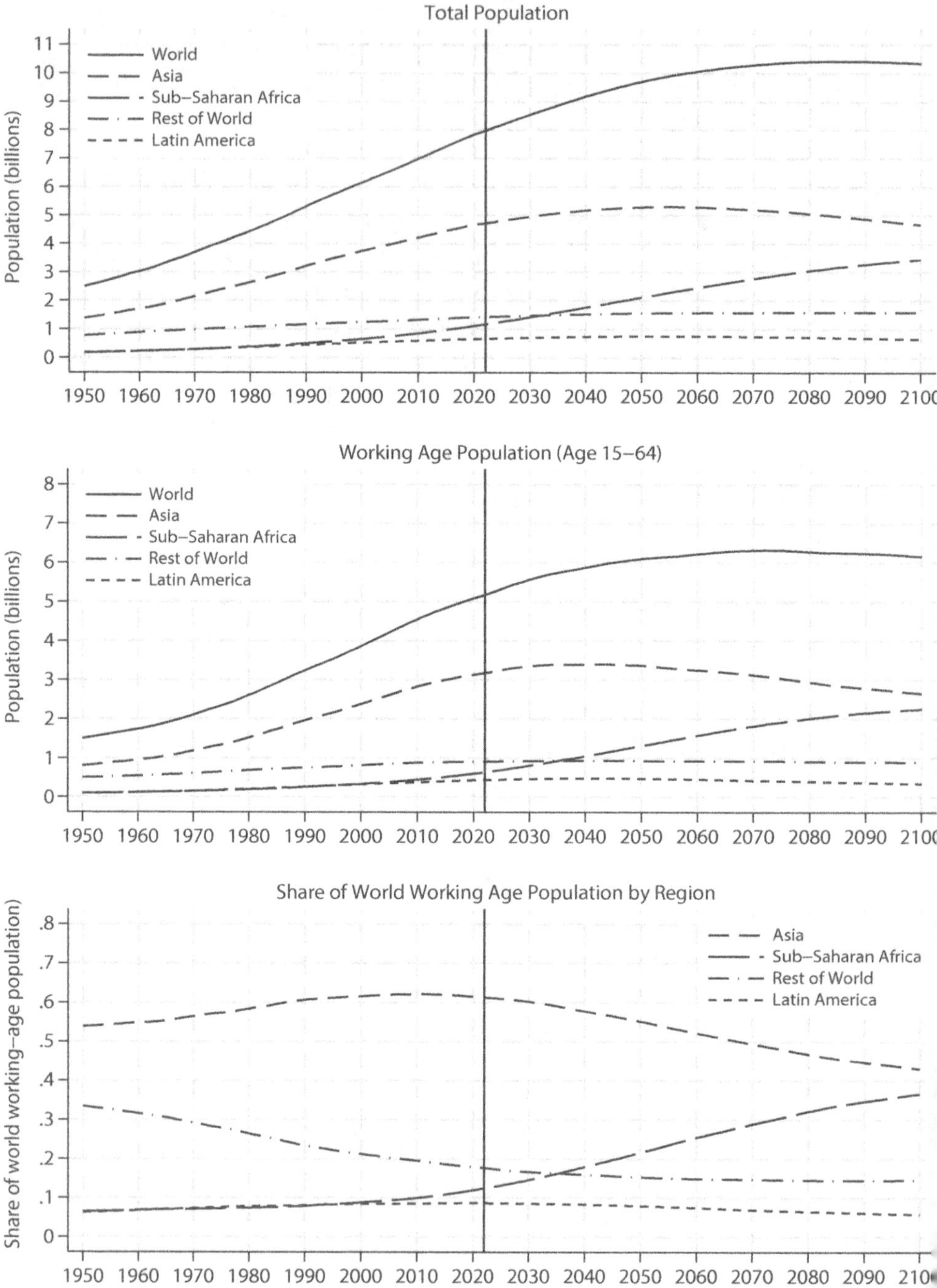

Figure 8.1 Total population, working-age population, and shares of world working-age population, 1950–2100

Source: Authors' calculations based on UN World Population Prospects 2022 (United Nations 2022): Estimates 1950–2021, Medium Variant Projections 2022–2100.

growth are helpful in thinking about the implications of this growth for global labor markets—the absolute number of people added to the working-age population each year and the rate of growth of the working-age population. The top panel of figure 8.2 shows the absolute number of people added to the working-age population each year for the world and major regions. In the 1950s, about 24 million people were added to the working-age population of the world each year. This number grew dramatically in the 1960s and 1970s, and continued climbing until it reached a peak of 73 million per year in 2005. In other words, the world would have required over 6 million new jobs each month in order to provide a job for each new addition to the working-age population. Most of these additions to the working-age population between 1960 and 2020 were in Asia. Asia peaked at an annual increase of 40 million people to the working-age population in 2005. Absolute increases in the working-age population were relatively low in the rest of the world at the end of the twentieth century. In 2000, Asia accounted for 65 percent of the 68 million people added to the world's working-age population in that year, while sub-Saharan Africa accounted for only 14 percent.

Absolute additions to the world's working-age population have dropped rapidly since the peak in 2005, although the numbers are still large. In 2025, the world's working-age population will increase by 53 million people, with 28 million added in Asia and 21 million added in sub-Saharan Africa. The annual additions will be dropping rapidly in Asia in the coming years. Sub-Saharan Africa will surpass Asia in 2028, and Asia will have zero increase in its working-age population in 2037.

Since 2010, sub-Saharan Africa has been the only region with continuing growth in the number of annual additions to the working-age population. Africa is projected to add 21 million people to the working-age population in 2025, rising to a peak of 27 million in 2050. Africa is projected to need 2 million new jobs per month by 2035 in order to provide a job for every new addition to the working-age population.

The bottom panel of figure 8.2 shows the annual rate of growth of the working-age population. For the world as a whole, the growth rate rose from 1.5 percent in the 1960s to a peak of 2.4 percent in 1970 and has been falling steadily since then. In 2025, the working-age population of the world will grow at about 1 percent per year. Asia also reached its peak growth rate in 1979, at 2.8 percent per year, followed by steady declines to a 2025 level of 0.9 percent. Latin America has followed a path similar to that of Asia, with annual growth rates near 3 percent in the 1980s,

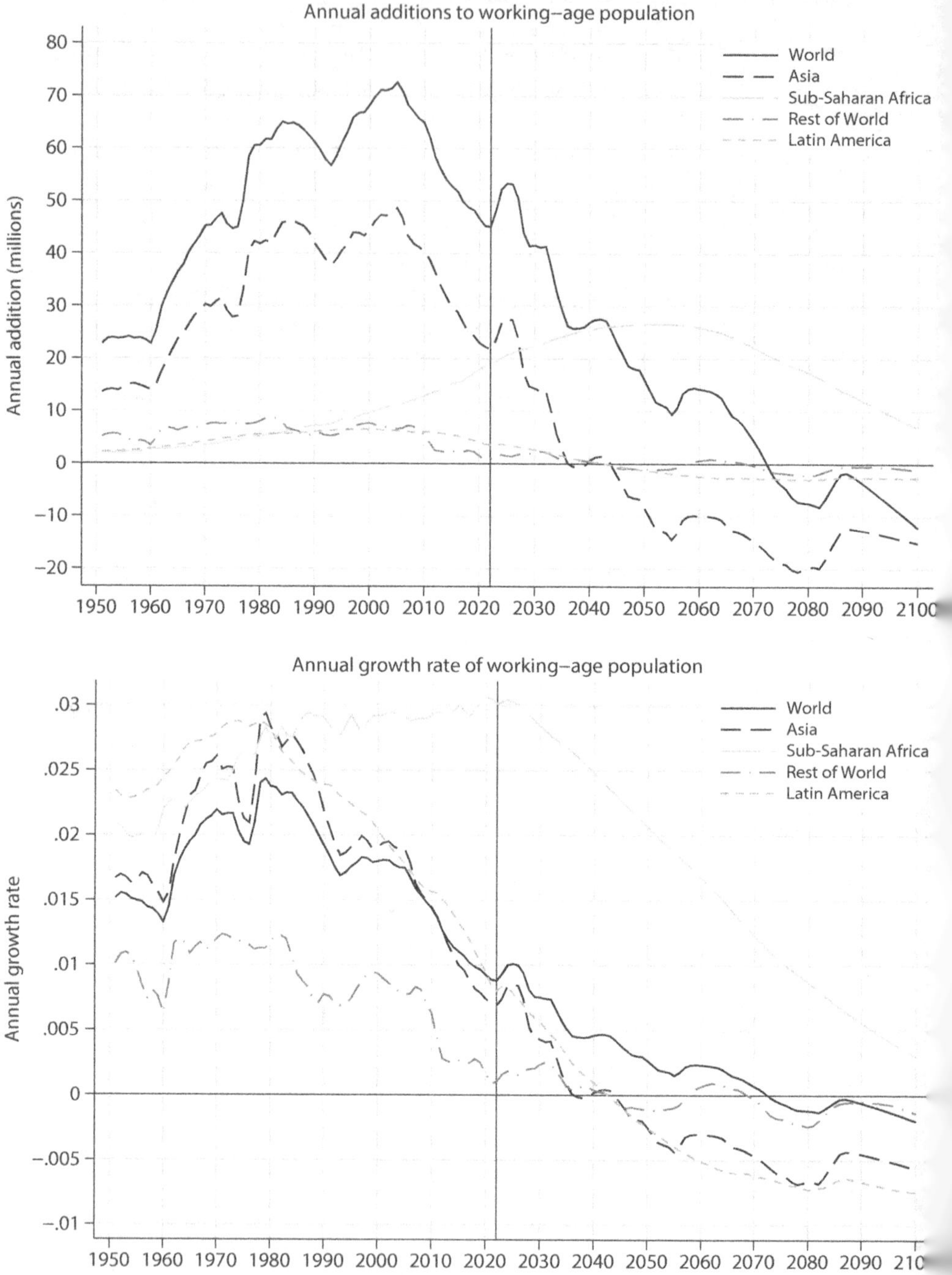

Figure 8.2 Annual additions and annual growth rate of working-age population, 1950–2100

Sources: Authors' calculations based on UN World Population Prospects 2022: Estimates 1950–2021, Medium Variant Projections 2022–2100.

followed by rapid declines to a growth rate in 2025 of around 1 percent. Sub-Saharan Africa experienced growth rates in the 1980s that were similar to those of Asia and Latin America, with an annual growth rate of 2.8 percent in 1979. The striking feature about sub-Saharan Africa in the bottom panel of figure 8.2 is that growth rates of around 3 percent per year have persisted for several decades, a contrast to the very short period of time in which Asia and Latin America experienced growth at that level. The peak annual growth rate of the working-age population in sub-Saharan Africa was 3.0 percent, reached in 2020, with the 2025 growth rate projected to be 2.9 percent. Despite Africa's dominance in the growth of the global working-age population going forward, the growth rates projected for Africa for the coming decades are below those experienced by Asia and Latin America in the 1970s and 1980s. It is important to note considerable cross-country variation in these growth rates.

2.2 COUNTRY-LEVEL VARIATION ACROSS AFRICA

The patterns shown for sub-Saharan Africa in figures 8.1 and 8.2 mask a great deal of heterogeneity across the continent. Figure 8.3 shows the decadal growth of the working-age population for 2020–2030 and 2040–2050 for a group of sub-Saharan African countries, with a group of other countries and regions shown for comparison. As can be seen in figure 8.3, Niger's working-age population will increase by 48 percent between 2020 and 2030. Uganda, Democratic Republic of Congo, Angola, and Tanzania all will increase by around 40 percent. Looking at subregions, Central Africa, East Africa, and West Africa will experience growth of their working-age populations of 35 to 40 percent between 2020 and 2030. At the lower end of these growth rates, South Africa will increase by only 13 percent and Ghana by 27 percent. The decadal growth rate of all of sub-Saharan Africa is 34 percent. This compares to 7.6 percent in Latin America and 7 percent in Asia. India's working-age population will increase by 11 percent between 2020 and 2030, Indonesia's by 9 percent, and Brazil's by 3 percent. China's working-age population is already falling and will decline by 1.6 percent over the decade.

The lower bar for each country shows the decadal growth rate for 2040–2050. It is important to note that every country will have lower growth in the 2040–2050 decade than in the 2020–2030 decade. The declines vary considerably across countries, however. Niger's working-age population is still projected to increase by 44 percent from 2040 to 2050,

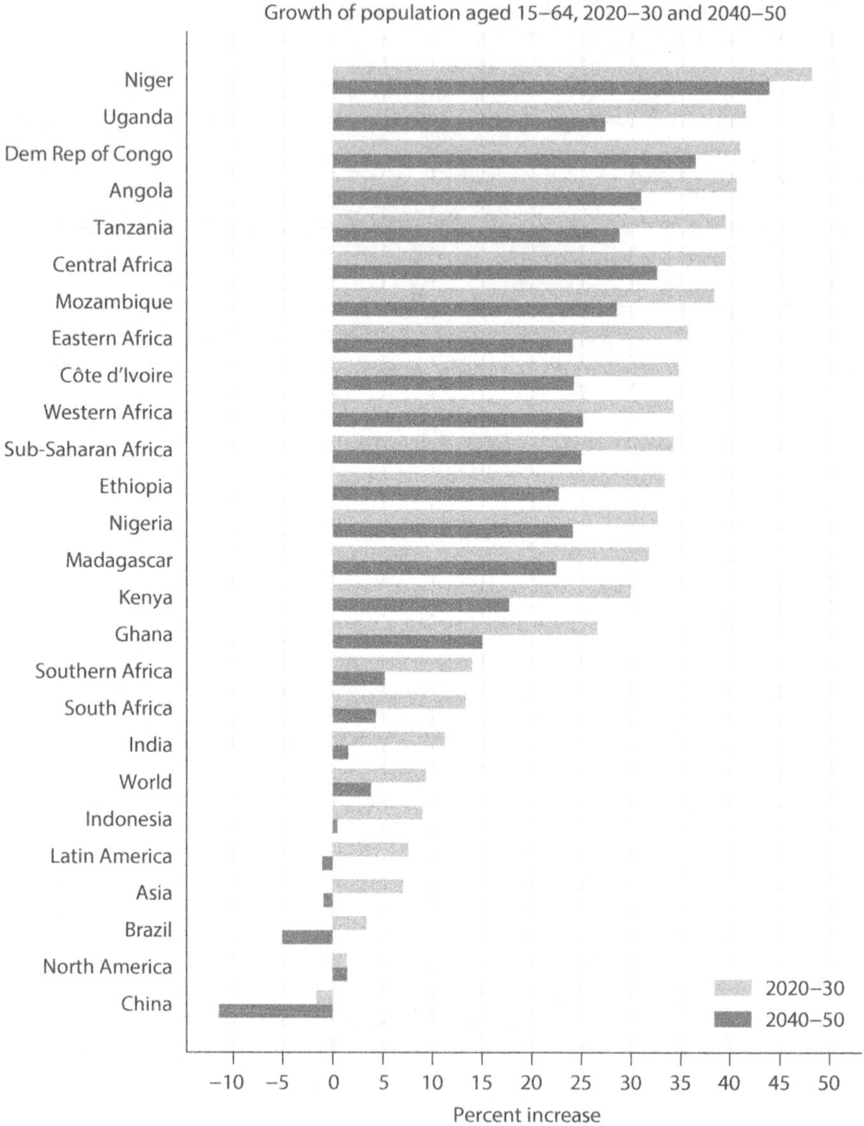

Figure 8.3 Growth of population aged 15–64 in 2020–2030 and in 2040–2050, selected African countries with comparison countries and regions

Source: Authors' calculations based on UN World Population Prospects 2022 (United Nations 2022): Medium Variant Projections 2022–2100.

only a small change from 2020 to 2030, while Uganda's decadal growth rate drops to 27 percent for 2040–2050. Ghana's working-age population is projected to increase by 15 percent for 2040–2050, while Kenya's will grow by 18 percent. By comparison, India's working-age population will only increase by 1.5 percent from 2040 to 2050, Brazil's will decline by 5 percent, and China's will decline by 11 percent. As we will discuss in section 3.1, projections of the working-age population to 2050 are not very sensitive to assumptions about the rate of fertility decline, so the patterns shown in figure 8.3 have a fairly low level of uncertainty.

3. FERTILITY RATES AND THE DEMOGRAPHIC TRANSITION

To understand the demography of the working-age population in the twenty-first century, it is important to understand the demographic processes that drove the unprecedented population growth of the last sixty years. The simple mathematics of population growth are that a population grows when the birth rate exceeds the death rate, leaving aside migration in and out of the population. The world population growth rate, which probably never exceeded 0.5 percent per year before the twentieth century, increased to around 1 percent per year in the mid-twentieth century, peaked at over 2 percent in the mid-1960s, and was back down to 1.3 percent by 2000 (Bongaarts 2009; Lam 2011). The reason for the dramatic increase in population growth is well understood by demographers. A rapid decline in death rates (especially infant and child mortality) from previously high levels caused a period of rapid population growth. A subsequent decline in birth rates then caused the rate of population growth to decline (Bongaarts 2009; Lam 2011; Lee 2003). Demographers use the term "demographic transition" to describe this fundamental process that has driven population growth everywere in the world.

Understanding the demographic transition is important in understanding the demography of global labor markets in the twenty-first century. The rapid change in the relative importance of Asia versus Africa in global population growth is driven by the differences in timing and pace of mortality and fertility decline. As shown in Lam et al. (2019), mortality rates fell earlier and faster in Asia than in Africa. Asia experienced its most rapid population growth around 1970, while Africa's population growth rate peaked around 1985. More important, sub-Saharan Africa has had a later and slower decline in fertility rates.

Figure 8.4 shows the total fertility rate (TFR) for world regions and Africa subregions. The TFR is the number of births a woman would have over her lifetime if she experienced the age-specific fertility rates in a given year. A TFR of 2.1 represents replacement fertility.[4] Figure 8.4 shows the dramatic decline in fertility that has occurred since 1950. Fertility rates for Asia, Africa, and Latin America were fairly similar in 1950, with all three regions having a TFR of around 5.7 to 6.5 births per woman. For the world as a whole, the TFR fell from 4.9 births per woman in 1950 to 2.4 in 2020, a 51 percent decrease and 89 percent of the decrease required to reach replacement fertility. Asia and Latin America had even larger declines, driving the world decline, while Africa has had a considerably later and slower fertility decline.[5] In 2020, Africa's TFR was still around 4.5 births per woman, more than double the TFR in Asia and Latin America. Africa's fertility's transition is unique in three ways: (1) African fertility was somewhat higher than that in Latin America and Asia in 1950, before fertility began to fall in any of the regions; (2) Africa's fertility transition began later than in the other regions, by at least ten to twenty years; and (3) Africa's fertility has declined more slowly than in other regions. At the same time, it is important to note that Africa's TFR has been falling since around 1980.

The bottom panel in figure 8.4 shows the TFR for African subregions. The three largest regions by population—Eastern Africa, Central Africa and Western Africa—all show a similar trend of slowly declining fertility rates that are significantly higher than the rates in other world regions. The TFR for Central Africa was estimated at 5.6 in 2021. Southern Africa, 88 percent of which was South Africa as of 2020, looks quite different, with a fertility decline more similar to those of Asia and Latin America, and with a much lower TFR in recent years than the other African regions. The TFR for Southern Africa was estimated to be 2.5 in 2021. These fertility rates are the key driver of the demographic change in each African subregion, and uncertainty about future fertility decline in Africa is the key source of uncertainty in population projections for this century.

There is much literature analyzing African fertility and the potential explanations for its later and slower fertility decline relative to Asia and Latin America. Bongaarts and Casterline (2013) note that some countries may have had a stall in fertility decline. They point out that ideal family size, as reported in survey data, is higher in African countries, even when controlling for a country's stage in the demographic transition. They find evidence of unmet need for contraception in many countries, as indicated

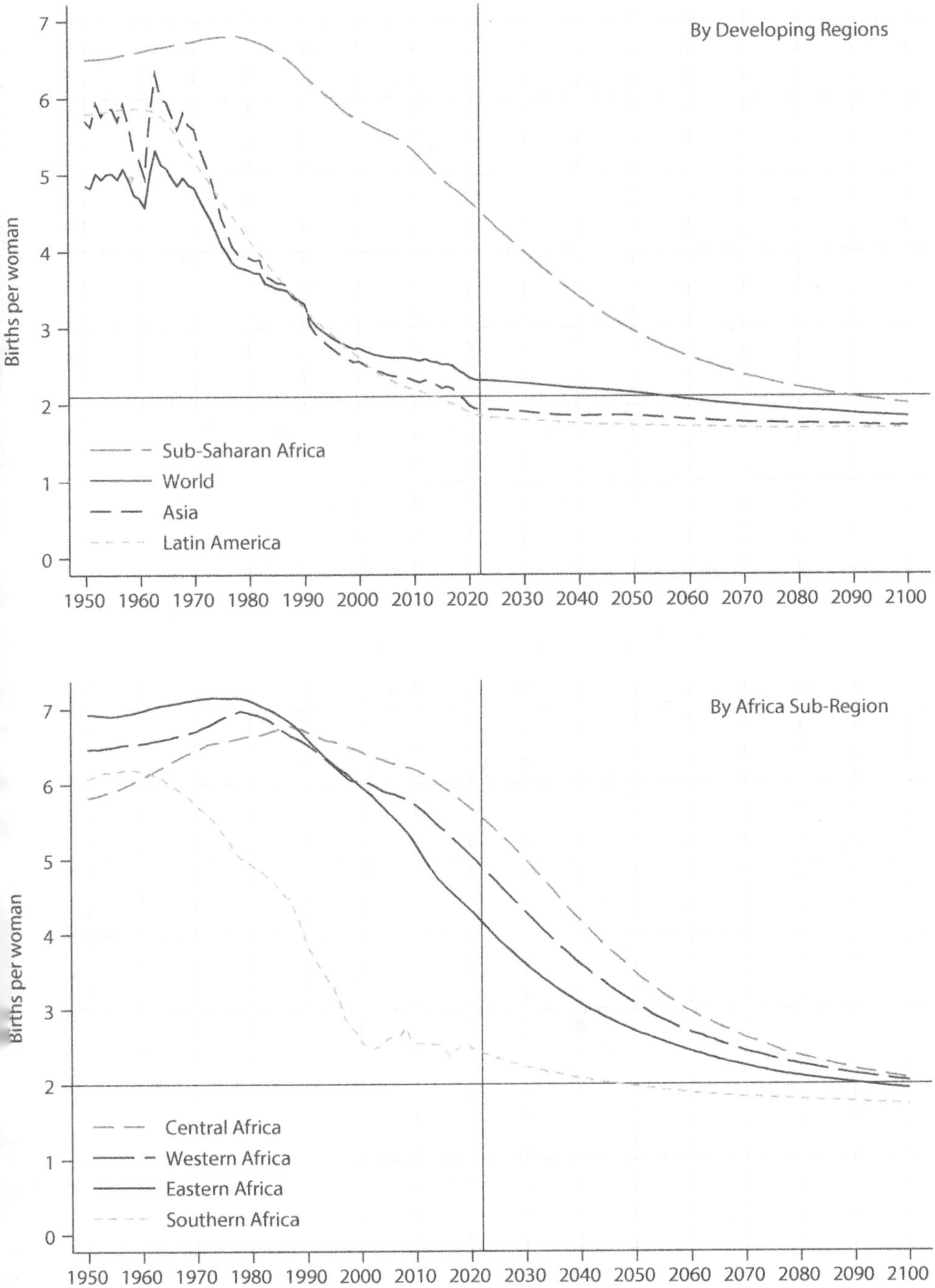

Figure 8.4 Total fertility rates by region and Africa sub-region, 1950–2100

Source: Authors' calculations based on UN World Population Prospects 2022: Estimates 1950–2021, Medium Variant Projections 2022–2100.

by a high proportion of women who report not wanting additional children but not using contraception. Singh et al. (2017) find that in both 2003 and 2014, roughly half of all African women aged fifteen to forty-nine who wanted to avoid pregnancy were using no method of conception, modern or otherwise.

Bongaarts (2017) compares the pace of fertility decline in different regions to indicators of socioeconomic development. He finds that later and slower economic development helps explain Africa's later and slower fertility decline, but he also finds evidence of a so-called African effect, in which many African countries have higher fertility than would be predicted based on social and economic variables and the estimated impact of those variables on fertility in regions outside Africa. Kebede et al. (2019) argue that one factor contributing to slow fertility decline in Africa is the disruptions in educational progress that affected women born in the 1970s and 1980s. These results suggest the pace of African fertility decline may increase as better educated cohorts enter their childbearing years.[6]

3.1 HOW WOULD FASTER FERTILITY DECLINE AFFECT AFRICA'S EMPLOYMENT CHALLENGE?

The UN's probabilistic population projections, included as part of the World Population Prospects 2022, are useful in answering several questions: How much difference would it make to projections of the working-age population if African fertility fell faster (or slower)? How large are the confidence intervals for predictions of fertility and the growth of the working-age population? How important is uncertainty about African fertility to our analysis of labor force dynamics in coming decades?

Figure 8.4 shows the total fertility rate for sub-Saharan Africa falling to roughly the replacement fertility rate of 2.1 by 2100. These UN estimates are based on a projection model that builds on the historical fertility patterns in a wide range of countries (United Nations, Department of Economic and Social Affairs, Population Division 2022). These projections play an important role in driving the projections for the growth of Africa's working-age population in the twenty-first century. The speed and magnitude of Africa's fertility decline is the main source of uncertainty in all estimates about global population in the coming decades. The 2022 UN population projections include prediction intervals based on the thousands of simulations used to create the projections. Figure 8.5 shows the projections of the total fertility rate and the size of the working-age population for sub-Saharan Africa, including the upper and lower bounds for the 80th percentile and 95th percentile prediction intervals. The top panel shows the projections for the total fertility rate. The interpretation of these prediction percentiles is, for example, that there is a 95 percent chance that the TFR for sub-Saharan Africa will be between 2.5 and 3.5 in 2050, based on the UN's probabilistic projections. There is an 80 percent chance that the TFR in 2050 will be between 2.6 and 3.3.

The bottom panel of figure 8.5 shows the range in the probabilistic projections for the working-age population of sub-Saharan Africa. A striking feature of figure 8.5 is that, even though the 95th projection interval for the TFR in 2050 has a range of more than one child per woman (±20 percent), there is much less uncertainty in the projection of the working-age population in 2050, with a range of only ±12 percent. This is because most working-age people in 2050 have already been born by 2022 and are not affected by fertility rates between 2022 and 2050. Thus, the projections of the working-age population for different regions should be interpreted with a recognition that projections for the next three decades have relatively little uncertainty.

The projected pace of fertility decline has larger effects on the working-age population as we move beyond 2050. Projections for Africa's working-age poulation in 2075 vary by 43 percent between the upper 95th percentile and the lower 95th percentile. The median projection for 2075 has a TFR of 2.3 and a working-age population of 1.9 billion in 2075, while the lower 95th percentile, corresponding to a TFR of 1.8, has 550 million fewer people in the working-age population. Faster fertility decline can clearly make a difference for the employment challenge that Africa will face in the second half of the twenty-first century. We also see in figure 8.5, however, that the nature of the employment challenge for the next three decades will be only modestly affected by the pace of fertility decline.[7]

3.2 RECENT TRENDS IN AFRICAN FERTILITY AND THEIR IMPLICATIONS FOR LABOR FORCE GROWTH

Some recent estimates of fertility in African countries provide evidence about whether African fertility may decline faster or slower than the UN estimates presented above. The best estimates of fertility for most African countries come from the Demographic and Health Surveys (DHS) and the Malaria Indicator Surveys (MIS) of the DHS Program that also collect

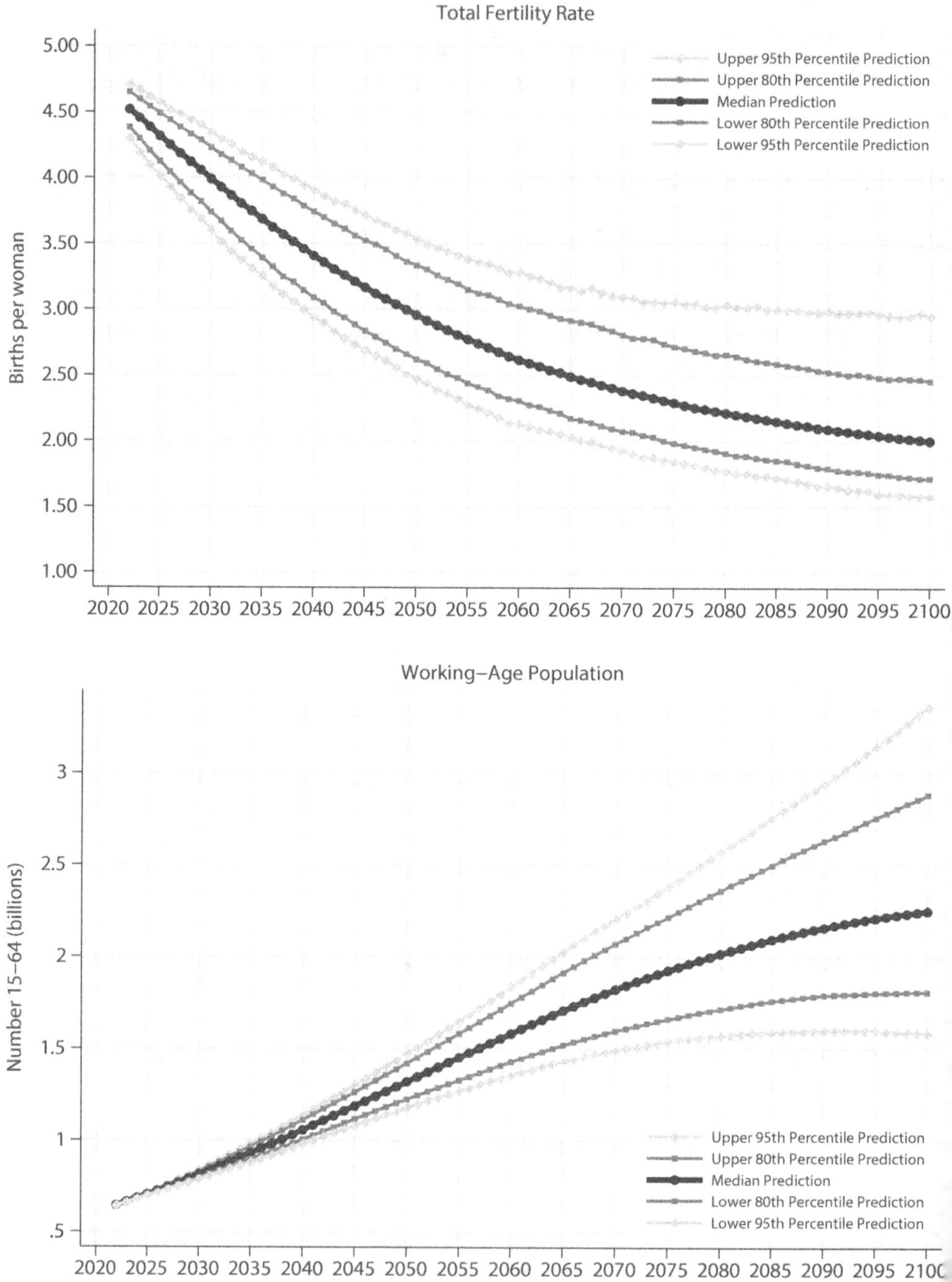

Figure 8.5 Projected total fertility rate and working-age population with prediction percentiles, sub-Saharan Africa, 2022–2100

Source: Authors' calculations based on UN World Population Prospects 2022: Median, 80th, and 95th Percentile Projections.

data on fertility. Figure 8.6 shows estimates of the total fertility rate for selected African countries that have DHS survey data from the 1980s or 1990s to recent years. The top panel shows a group of East African and Southern African countries. The bottom panel shows a group of West African countries. The solid lines show DHS/MIS data, while the dashed lines show the estimates in the 2022 UN World Population Prospects, with estimates up to 2021 and Medium Variant projections from 2022 to 2025.

As seen in the top panel of figure 8.6, there have been significant declines in the TFR in all the countries shown according to DHS estimates.[8] In Uganda, for example, the TFR in DHS surveys fell from 6.7 in 2006 to 5.0 in 2018. In Kenya, the TFR fell from 4.6 in 2008 to 3.3 in 2020. Note that the UN estimates (which are the basis for most of our analysis in this chapter) track the DHS estimates quite well. This is not surprising because the DHS data are a key source of data for the UN estimates, with the UN estimates providing a somewhat smoothed and interpolated version of the DHS estimates.[9]

The bottom panel of figure 8.6 shows the data from a number of West African countries. In this case, there is some evidence from the most recent surveys that fertility may be falling faster than projected by the UN. The most recent DHS/MIS estimates for Niger, Mali, Nigeria, and Senegal are all below the UN estimates for the same year. For example, the TFR for Nigeria fell by 0.5, from 5.3 in 2018 to 4.8 in 2021. Survey-based estimates of the TFR for a single year can be noisy (note, for example, that the TFR for Senegal went from 4.4 in 2018 to 4.7 in 2019 to 3.9 in 2020), so these recent estimates should be interpreted with caution. At the same time, these estimates do serve as a reminder that faster (or slower) decline in fertility in Africa could easily occur, with important implications for the growth of the working-age population in future decades. As previously noted, a faster pace of fertility decline over the next decade would not have much effect on the estimates we present for the working-age population over the next twenty to thirty years, but it would have a significant impact on the working-age population in the second half of the century.

Are there ways for Africa to speed up the pace of fertility decline in order to reduce the pressure on employment in the coming decades? There does not seem to be a policy consensus on this, just as there is no strong consensus among researchers about why African fertility decline has been slower than it was Asia and Latin America. While better access

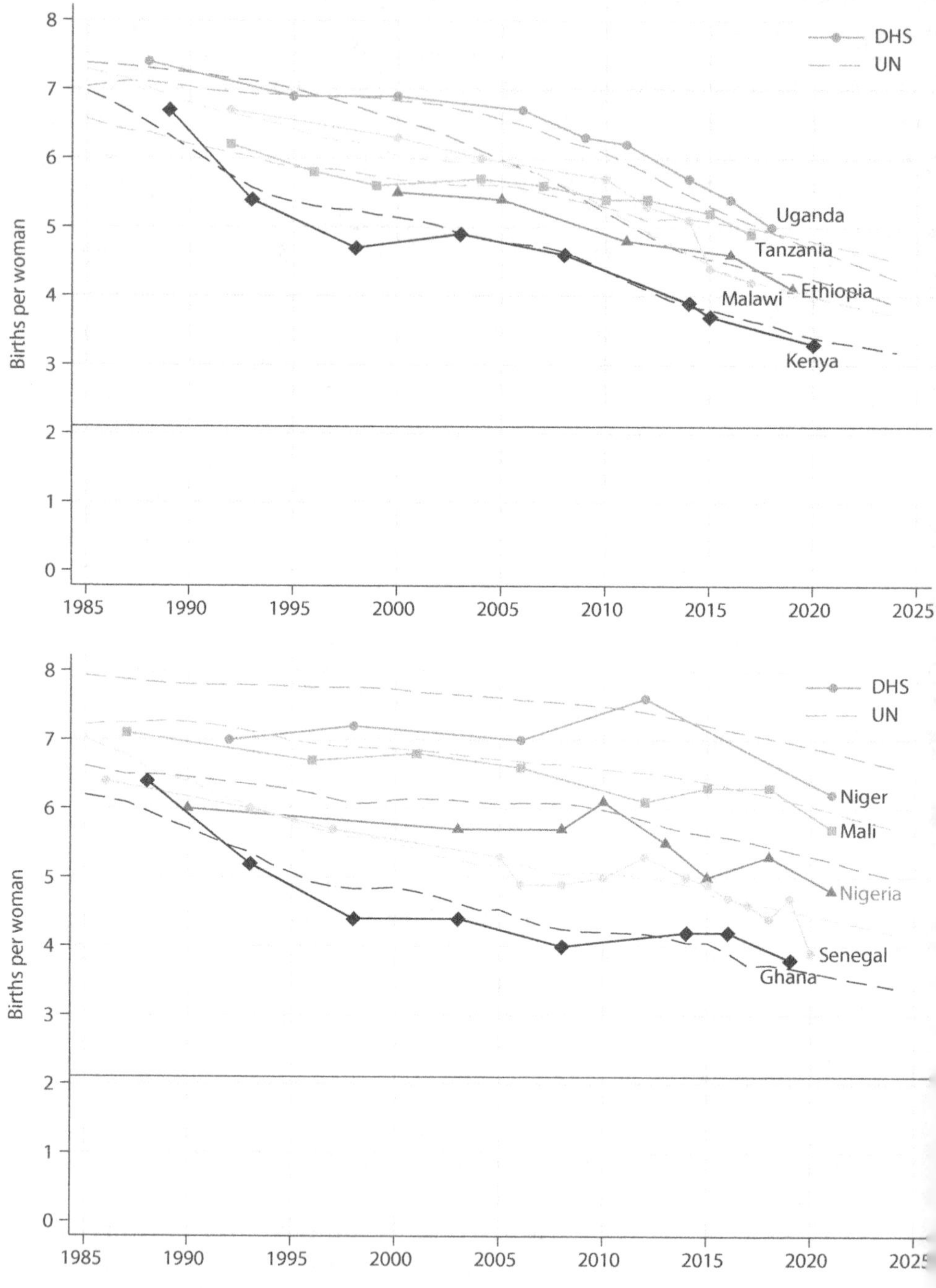

Figure 8.6 Total fertility rate for selected African countries, estimates from demographic and health surveys and estimates and projections from United Nations Population Division, 1985–2025

Source: Authors' calculations based on UN World Population Prospects 2022: Estimates 1950–2021, Medium Variant Projections 2022–2025; DHS STATCompiler (DHS 2023).

to family planning might speed up fertility decline, desired fertility continues to be high in many countries, and there have already been large investments in family planning in most countries. Bongaarts argues that Africa's higher fertility "arises largely from the link between socioeconomic indicators and desired family size rather than between desired family size and fertility," (Bongaarts 2017, 54) a pattern suggesting that increased investments in family planning per se may not speed up fertility decline. This has important implications regarding the potential interaction between job creation and fertility decline. Job creation, especially the creation of more productive, better-paying employment, may help reduce fertility, in addition to its direct effects on poverty reduction and economic growth. Combined with the substantial educational improvements that are already in place, this suggests the potential for a virtuous cycle in which improvements in employment increase the pace of fertility decline, reducing the pressure on future growth of the working-age population.

It is also important to note that family planning programs are not always a necessary condition for fertility decline. Brazil, for example, had one of the most rapid fertility declines in the world in the 1960s and 1970s, in spite of an almost total absence of family planning programs under the military government; rising levels of education, especially for women, however, appeared to have played a major role (Lam and Duryea 1999). Factors such as rising levels of education, improved employment opportunities, and declines in infant mortality may be just as important as increased access to family planning in driving African fertility decline in this century. For policymakers or international donors making the choice of whether to spend the next development dollar on family planning versus a program to enhance job creation, a strong case can be made that job creation can give immediate improvement to employment and poverty reduction while also helping drive fertility decline.

4. CHANGING AGE STRUCTURE, THE WORKING-AGE POPULATION, AND DEPENDENCY RATIOS

The rapid changes in mortality and fertility that drove the demographic changes of the last sixty years have had a dramatic impact on the age distribution of the population. The sequence of changes in age structure during the demographic transition is the same in every country, although the pace and magnitude of the changes can vary significantly. Rapid declines in infant and child mortality, the main cause of the rapid population growth of the 1960s and 1970s, first led to very young populations throughout the developing world. As fertility declined, the share of the population in the youngest age groups eventually declined, creating a movement in the age distribution, first toward young adults and then toward older age groups. There is inevitably a period in which the proportion of the population in working ages increases, creating a demographic dividend in which there is a high fraction in working wages and low fractions in both the child and elderly dependent age groups (Bloom et al. 2003; Lee and Mason 2006).

4.1 CHANGES WITHIN THE WORKING-AGE POPULATION

While it is well known that populations around the world are aging, even in Africa, less attention has been given to the aging that takes place within the working-age population. The working-age population gets older just as does the overall population, creating important changes in labor force dynamics (Lam and Leibbrandt 2013; Lam et al. 2019). Figure 8.7 shows the evolution of the age distribution of the working-age population in sub-Saharan Africa in the twenty-first century, with the total working-age population divided into ten-year age groups. The working-age population is currently highly concentrated in the youngest age groups, with the fifteen to twenty-four-year-old age group being the most prominent. This reflects the youth bulge that resulted from the rapid population growth of previous decades, which caused the population to become very young (Lee 2003; Lam 2011). As is clear in figure 8.7, however, the working-age population is rapidly aging. The size of the fifteen- to twenty-four-year-old age group is leveling off, while the older age groups will become a significantly larger share of the working-age population throughout the century.

Table 8.1 shows the age breakdown of the working-age population in 2020, 2050, and 2080 for sub-Saharan Africa, Asia, Latin America, and the rest of the world. As seen in the top panel, the fifteen- to twenty-four-year-old age group accounted for 36 percent of the region's working-age population in 2020, while the fifty-five- to sixty-four-year-old age group accounted for only 7 percent. The growth rates of the age groups across time are larger for older ages. The youngest age group will increase from 218 million to 402 million between 2020 and 2050, an 84 percent increase, while the oldest age group will almost triple, from 44 million to 124 million. Reflecting the pattern seen in figure 8.7, by 2080,

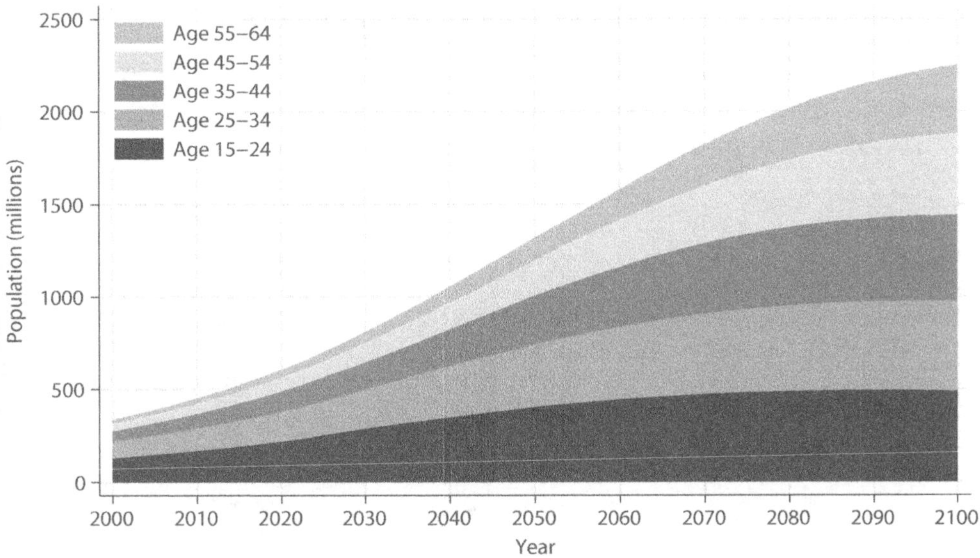

Figure 8.7 Working-age population by ten-year age groups, sub-Saharan Africa, 2000–2100

Source: Authors' calculations based on UN World Population Prospects 2022: Estimates 2000–2021, Medium Variant Projections 2022–2100.

the relative shares of the age groups will become more similar, with the youngest age group accounting for 24 percent of the working-age population, while the oldest age group will account for 14 percent.

The second panel of table 8.1 shows that Asia is already much further through the transition to an older labor force. The absolute number of fifteen- to twenty-four-year-olds and twenty-five- to thirty-four-year-olds will fall in Asia between 2020 and 2050, while there will be absolute increases in the older age groups. The five age groups will make up almost equal fractions of Asia's working-age population in 2050. All age groups will decline in absolute numbers between 2020 and 2050, with the largest declines in the youngest age groups. It is striking that the number of fifteen- to twenty-four-year-olds in Asia is projected to decline by 179 million between 2020 and 2080.

Latin America's situation is similar to that of Asia, with absolute declines in the two youngest age groups between 2020 and 2050, and declines in all age groups between 2050 and 2080. The rest of the world, meaning the world minus Asia, Latin America, and sub-Saharan Africa,

Table 8.1 Number of working-age people by age group and region in 2020, 2050, and 2080

	2020		2050		2080	
Age group	Millions	Share of total (%)	Millions	Share of total (%)	Millions	Share of total (%)
Sub-Saharan Africa						
Age 15–24	218	36	402	31	487	24
Age 25–34	159	26	337	26	463	23
Age 35–44	112	18	266	20	423	21
Age 45–54	72	12	188	14	363	18
Age 55–64	44	7	124	9	282	14
Total	606		1,318		2,018	
Asia						
Age 15–24	717	23	631	19	538	18
Age 25–34	741	24	670	20	576	20
Age 35–44	644	21	720	21	604	21
Age 45–54	593	19	675	20	602	20
Age 55–64	435	14	667	20	620	21
Total	3,129		3,364		2,941	
Latin America						
Age 15–24	108	25	90	19	73	18
Age 25–34	104	24	94	20	77	19
Age 35–44	93	21	100	21	82	20
Age 45–54	76	17	101	21	86	21
Age 55–64	58	13	95	20	89	22
Total	439		481		407	
Rest of World						
Age 15–24	175	19	176	19	171	19
Age 25–34	196	21	188	20	184	20
Age 35–44	193	21	199	21	191	21
Age 45–54	180	20	182	20	185	20
Age 55–64	171	19	188	20	186	20
Total	914		934		917	
Total Around the World						
Age 15–24	1,218	24	1,300	21	1,269	20
Age 25–34	1,200	24	1,290	21	1,300	21
Age 35–44	1,041	20	1,286	21	1,300	21
Age 45–54	921	18	1,146	19	1,237	20
Age 55–64	708	14	1,075	18	1,177	19
Total	5,088		6,096		6,283	

was already at a fairly uniform age distribution within the working-age population in 2020 and will see relatively little change in absolute numbers or relative sizes of the age groups throughout the decade.

For the world as a whole, we see once again that sub-Saharan Africa will account for more than 100 percent of the 1.2 billion increase in the world's working-age population between 2020 and 2080. The number of young workers aged fifteen to twenty-four in the world increases by only 51 million between 2020 and 2080, a stability that hides vast differences across regions. Sub-Saharan Africa's addition of 269 million fifteen- to twenty-four-year-olds over this period is almost entirely offset by the decline of 217 million fifteen- to twenty-four-year-olds in Asia, Latin America, and the rest of the world. For the world as a whole, the growth of the working-age population will be due entirely to the growth in older age groups. The youth bulge of recent decades is turning into an older worker bulge. The rising number of older workers will need to be accommodated, with no growth in the number of young workers for the world as a whole or in any of the major regions after 2050.

Another way to see the implications of this population aging for global labor markets is to look at the annual additions to the working-age population around the world. Figure 8.8 shows the annual additions to sub-Saharan Africa's working-age population, divided into the same ten-year age groups used in figure 8.7 and table 8.1. Until about 2025, the fifteen- to twenty-four-year-old age group has the largest annual increase, growing by 7.1 million per year in 2025. That addition means that the 2001–2010 birth cohort is 7.1 million larger than the 2000–2009 birth cohort, measured at the time each cohort is fifteen to twenty-four years old. The 2001–2010 birth cohort is tracked across the graph, a reminder that as we move through the century, we are following the same cohorts as they move through the age distribution. The 2001–2010 birth cohort shows up as the largest addition to the working-age population in every year, with the absolute size of the addition falling as mortality reduces the size of the cohort as it ages.

The number added at age fifteen to twenty-four reaches its historic high around 2025. The number of new fifteen- to twenty-four-year-olds being added each year is on the decline for the rest of the century and is projected to go negative by 2090. At the same time, the number of fifty-five- to sixty-four-year-olds being added each year will increase until around 2065, when the 2001–2010 birth cohort reaches that age.

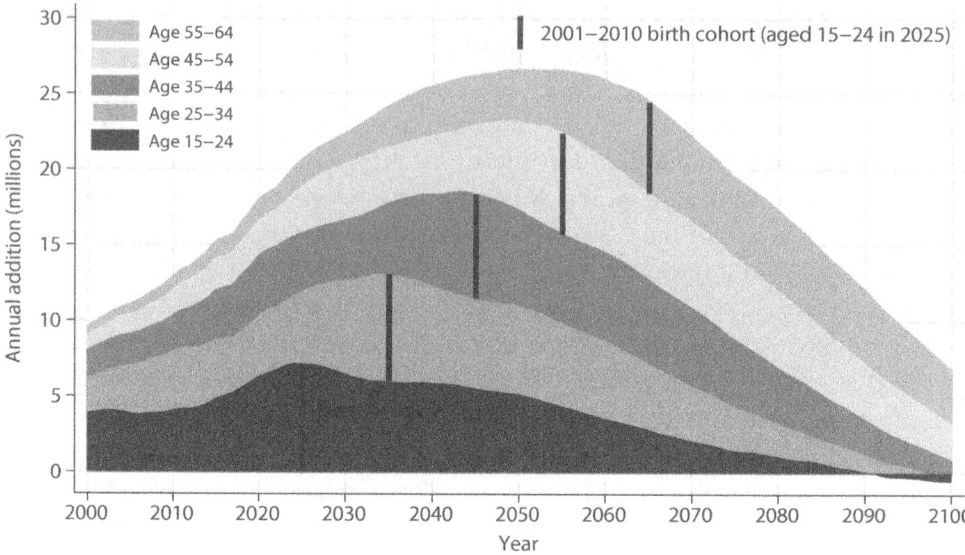

Figure 8.8 Annual additions to working-age population by ten-year age groups, sub-Saharan Africa, 2000–2100

Source: Authors' calculations based on UN World Population Prospects 2022: Estimates 2000–2021, Medium Variant Projections 2022–2100.

Table 8.2 shows the annual additions to each age group in the working-age population in 2020, 2050, and 2080 for sub-Saharan Africa, Asia, Latin America, and the rest of the world. In sub-Saharan Africa, fifteen- to twenty-four-year-olds are by far the fastest growing group in 2020, with the 6.3 million increase accounting for 35 percent of the 18.0 million increase in the working-age population. As seen in figure 8.8, the annual additions to the fifteen- to twenty-four-year-old group fall in absolute numbers in the coming decades, while the annual additions to older age groups increase. The fifty-five- to sixty-four-year-old age group, which accounted for only 8 percent of the annual additions to the working-age population in 2020, will account for 27 percent in 2050 and 31 percent in 2080. As seen in figure 8.2 and figure 8.8, 2050 is around the peak year in the number of people added each year, at 26.7 million. These are relatively evenly spread across the age distribution, with the thirty-five- to forty-four-year-old age group providing the largest number.

The second panel table 8.2 shows that, in Asia, the two youngest age groups were already shrinking in 2020. In other words, the number of

Table 8.2 Annual additions to the number of working-age people by age group and region in 2020, 2050, and 2080

	2020		2050		2080	
Age Group	Number of millions added	Share of total added (%)	Number of millions added	Share of total added (%)	Number of millions added	Share of total added (%)
Sub-Saharan Africa						
Age 15–24	6.3	35	5.2	19	1.1	6
Age 25–34	4.1	23	5.9	22	2.2	12
Age 35–44	3.9	22	6.3	24	3.6	21
Age 45–54	2.3	13	5.8	22	5.1	29
Age 55–64	1.5	8	3.5	13	5.4	31
Total	18.0		26.7		17.3	
Asia						
Age 15–24	-0.7	-3	-1.4	17	-3.1	16
Age 25–34	-0.1	0	-9.9	119	-5.1	26
Age 35–44	8.0	35	2.2	-26	-1.5	7
Age 45–54	3.7	16	0.0	0	-1.1	6
Age 55–64	12.1	53	0.8	-9	-8.9	45
Total	23.0		-8.3		-19.7	
Latin America						
Age 15–24	-0.4	-9	-0.4	33	-0.5	18
Age 25–34	0.5	13	-1.0	83	-0.6	20
Age 35–44	1.4	33	-0.2	19	-0.6	21
Age 45–54	1.1	27	-0.2	18	-0.3	12
Age 55–64	1.5	37	0.7	-53	-0.9	29
Total	4.1		-1.2		-3.0	
Rest of World						
Age 15–24	0.2	14	0.2	-18	-0.3	14
Age 25–34	-1.5	-100	-2.0	188	-0.8	37
Age 35–44	1.9	124	1.8	-174	0.4	-17
Age 45–54	-0.2	-11	0.1	-9	0.2	-11
Age 55–64	1.1	73	-1.2	113	-1.7	77
Total	1.5		-1.0		-2.2	
Total Around the World						
Age 15–24	5	12	3.5	22	-2.9	38
Age 25–34	3	6	-7.0	-44	-4.4	58
Age 35–44	15	32	10.1	63	1.9	-26
Age 45–54	7	15	5.7	36	3.9	-51
Age 55–64	16	35	3.8	23	-6.1	81
Total	47		16.0		-7.5	

jobs needed to accommodate new young workers into the labor force in Asia is already declining. The fifty-five- to sixty-four-year-old age group accounted for over half of the 23 million added to Asia's working-age population in 2020. By 2050, Asia's working-age population will shrink by 8.3 million per year, with an 11.3 million reduction in the number of workers under age thirty-five. By 2080, Asia's working-age population is projected to shrink by 20 million per year, with a decline of 9 million in the number of workers aged fifty-five to sixty-four.

In Latin America, the biggest additions to the working-age population in 2020 were in the older age groups, with a reduction in the number aged fifteen to twenty-four. Latin America's working-age population is projected to shrink by 1 million per year in 2050 and 3 million per year in 2080. The rest of the world added 1.5 million per year to the working-age population in 2020, falling to a loss of 1.2 million per year in 2050 and 2.2 million per year in 2080.

The world as a whole added 47 million per year to the working-age population in 2020, with additions from Asia somewhat larger than those in Africa. By 2050, this number falls to 16 million per year, at the same time that Africa rises to 26.7 million per year. By 2080, the world's working-age population is projected to decline by 7.5 million per year. We see once again the enormous heterogeneity across regions, however. Sub-Saharan Africa will be adding 17 million per year to its working-age population in 2080. Asia will be losing 20 million per year with Latin America and the rest of the world also losing millions each from their working-age populations.

An obvious question that arises is whether the decline in the size of the working-age population in the rest of the world help offset the millions of new potential workers being added in Africa? As seen in figure 8.2, by 2075, there will be no net additions to the working-age population of the world. If all the jobs freed up by the decline in the working-age population in other regions could be transferred to Africa, Africa's employment challenge would be met. Will capital move from Asia to Africa in response to Asia's declining working-age population? Will Africa be able to generate Asia-style employment growth in the coming decades, and will this become easier as Asia's working-age population declines? These are complex questions that go beyond the scope of this chapter but on which this book as a whole has much to say. We hope that we have made clear, however, that understanding the demography of the working-age population is critical in thinking about the dynamics of the global labor force in the rest of this century.

4.2 CHANGING DEPENDENCY RATIOS

Dependency ratios are a convenient summary measure to profile important economic implications of these changes in the age structure. Dividing the population into children (aged zero to fourteen), working age (fifteen to sixty-four), and elderly (sixty-five and older), we have three dependency ratios that are commonly used:

$$\textit{Child Dependency Ratio} = \frac{\textit{Children}}{\textit{Working Age}} = \frac{Pop(0-14)}{Pop(15-64)}$$

$$\textit{Elderly Dependency Ratio} = \frac{\textit{Elderly}}{\textit{Working Age}} = \frac{Pop(65+)}{Pop(15-64)}$$

$$\textit{Total Dependency Ratio} = \frac{\textit{Children} + \textit{Elderly}}{\textit{Working Age}} = \frac{Pop(0-14) + Pop(65+)}{Pop(15-64)}$$

Figure 8.9 shows these three dependency ratios for the world and for the three major developing regions—Asia, Latin America, and sub-Saharan Africa—from 1950 to 2100. In all three cases, Africa stands out as having some unique trends relative to the other regions. As seen in the top panel of figure 8.9, the child dependency ratio was increasing in all regions in the 1950s and 1960s but was declining by 1970 in Asia, Latin America, and the world as a whole, the result of declining fertility. In Africa, the child dependency ratio continued rising until around 1990 and has been falling since then. In 2020, the child dependency ratio was 0.78 in Africa, more than double the 0.36 child dependency ratio in Asia. In an economic interpretation, in order to generate $100 in expenditures per child, it would take $78 in taxes per working-age person in Africa but only $36 per working-age person in Asia. The child dependency ratio will be falling in Africa and in other regions throughout this century, although Africa's ratio will be substantially higher than those of other regions for several decades.

As shown in the middle panel in figure 8.9, the elderly dependency ratio has been rising in all regions since 1950 and is projected to continue rising throughout the century. This elderly dependency ratio has been much lower than the child dependency ratio since 1950, but it is rising rapidly in Asia and Latin America and is projected to surpass the child dependency ratio in those regions around 2050. Just as Africa's child

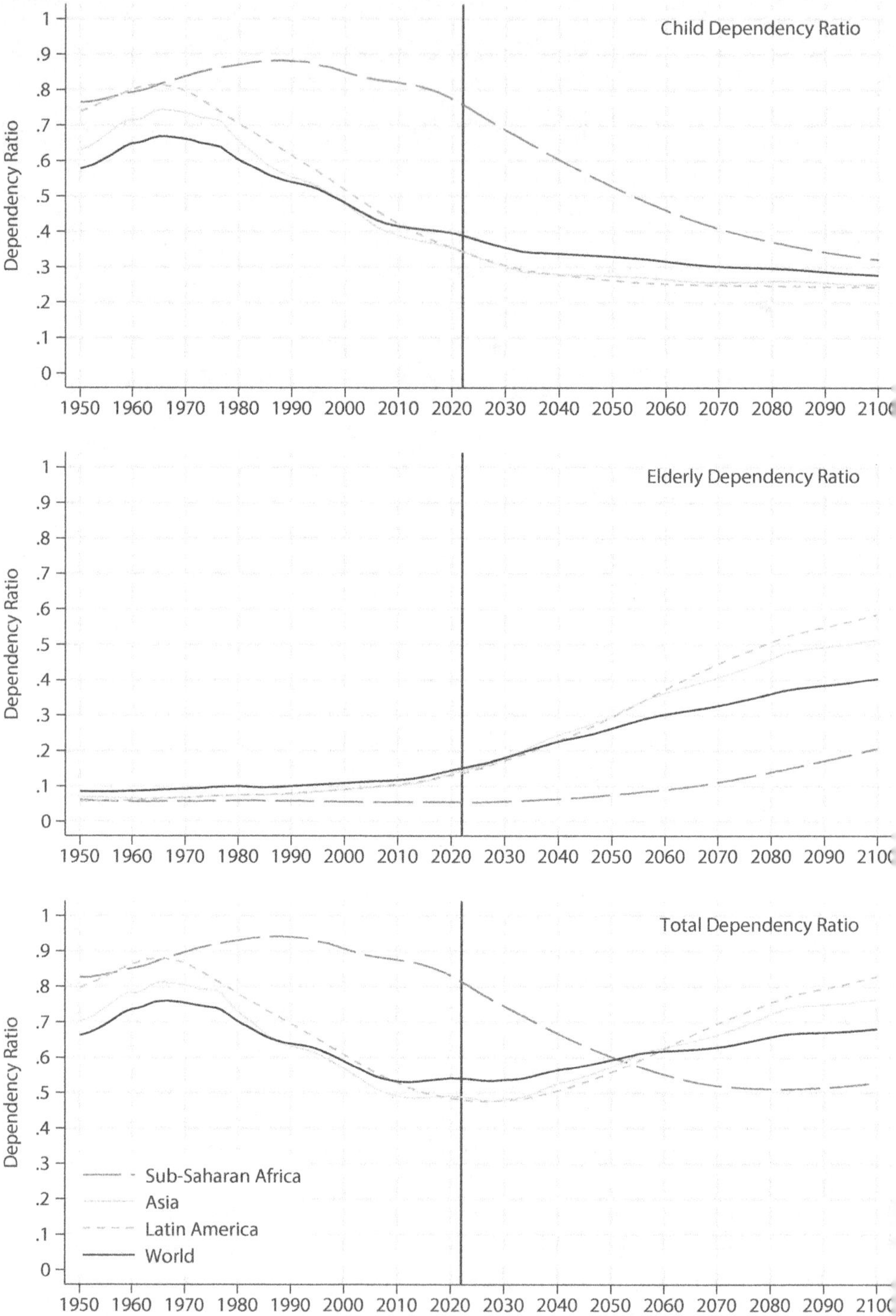

Figure 8.9 Dependency ratios by region, 1950–2100, child dependency ratio = population aged 0–14/population aged 15–64, elderly dependency ratio = population aged 65 and older/population aged 15–64, total dependency ratio = (population aged 0–14 + population aged 15–64)/population aged 15–64

Source: Authors' calculations based on UN World Population Prospects 2022: Estimates 1950–2021, Medium Variant Projections 2022–2100.

dependency ratio is currently much higher than that in other regions, its elderly dependency ratio is much lower. Africa's elderly dependency ratio in 2020 was 0.06, compared to 0.13 in Asia and Latin America. This means that generating $100 per person aged sixty-five and older would cost only $6 per working-age person in Africa, compared to $13 in Asia and Latin America. As is clear in figure 8.9, Africa's elderly dependency ratio will remain considerably below those of other regions throughout the century.

With the child and elderly dependency ratios often moving in opposite directions, it is interesting to look at the total dependency ratio, shown in the bottom panel of figure 8.9.[10] This combined dependency ratio was dominated by the much larger child dependency ratio in all regions from 1950 to 2000; as a result, it was rising until around 1970 outside Africa and was rising until around 1990 in Africa. The elderly dependency ratio begins to play a much stronger role after 2000, with a rapidly rising elderly dependency ratio pulling up the overall dependency ratio in spite of the fall in the child dependency ratio.

The total dependency ratio will be rising in the coming decades in Asia, Latin America, and the world as a whole, while it will still be falling for most of the century in Africa. Africa will experience a rapid decline in its total dependency ratio in the coming decades because of large declines in the child dependency ratio and a still low elderly dependency ratio. This is the key feature of the demographic dividend—the concentration of the population in the working ages resulting from falling fertility. By around 2055, the total dependency ratio in Africa will have fallen below the dependency ratios of Asia, Latin America, and the world as a whole, and it will continue to be below those other regions for the rest of the century.

5. THE IMPORTANCE OF URBANIZATION

Alongside these changes to the sizes and age structures of working-age and non-working-age populations, there have been substantial movements of these populations from rural to urban areas. It is important to note and take account of where populations live and where they are likely to live and work in the future.

As seen in figure 8.10, the world's urban population surpassed its rural population in 2007. The rural population is estimated to have peaked at 3.4 billion in 2020, with future population growth concentrated in urban areas. Asia's rural population peaked around 2005, with the urban

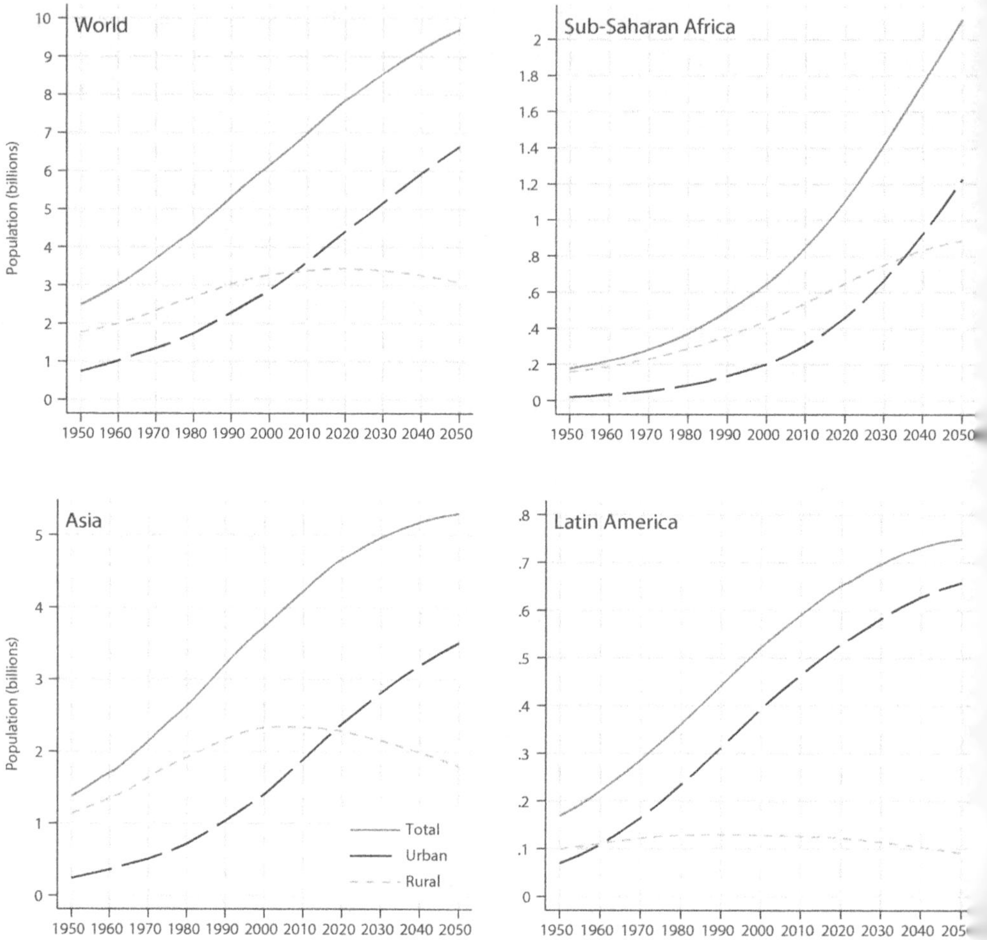

Figure 8.10 Urban and rural population by region, in billions, 1950–2050

Source: Authors' calculations. Proportion urban taken from UN World Urbanization Prospects, 2018 Revision; population totals taken from UN World Population Prospects 2022: Estimates 1950–2021, Medium Variant Projections 2022–2050.

population overtaking the rural population around 2020. Latin America has been more urban than rural since 1960 and has had a falling rural population since 1990. Compared to these regions, Africa's trends are unique. It is the only region projected to have a growing rural population going forward, with continued growth of the rural population projected to 2050. The growth of Africa's urban population is projected to be much faster than in other regions, with annual urban population growth rates of almost 4 percent projected in the coming decades, compared to less than 2 percent in Asia and about 1 percent in Latin America. Africa's urban population is projected to surpass its rural population around 2035.

As its populations increase, Africa is also becoming more urbanized at the same time as the number of Africans in rural areas is increasing, too. In 1950, the urban share of sub-Saharan Africa's population was estimated at 11 percent; it is projected to be 44 percent in 2025 and 58 percent in 2050 (United Nations, Department of Economic and Social Affairs, Population Division 2018). Urbanization occurs through two channels: rural-to-urban migration and natural increase within urban centers—the former of which receives more political attention, but both of which are likely to make significant contributions to urban growth rates (Jedwab et al. 2015).

The United Nations Population Division made projections of future urbanization around the world in its *World Urbanization Prospects, 2018 Revision* (United Nations, Department of Economic and Social Affairs, Population Division 2018). It has not updated those projections since this publication in 2018, but the data are still useful for providing a picture of the rural-urban divide in the population projections presented above. Figure 8.10 shows urban and rural population growth between 1950 and 2050 (the latest date projected by the UN) for the world, sub-Saharan Africa, Asia, and Latin America. As a cautionary note, it is important to keep in mind that comparisons of urban and rural populations between regions are complicated by the fact that the definitions of urban and rural are not consistent across countries. For example, in Nigeria, urban is defined as towns with twenty thousand inhabitants or more, while in Ethiopia, urban is defined as localities with two thousand inhabitants or more. In other countries, definitions and administrative boundaries may change over time (United Nations, Department of Economic and Social Affairs, Population Division 2018). Nonetheless, figure 8.10 is useful for comparing overall trends between and within regions.[11]

One feature of African urbanization is that it has not been closely tied to economic growth or job creation. Fox (2017) refers to Africa's experience as "urbanization without growth," pointing out that Africa's urban share has increased steadily since 1960 and its urban population has grown faster than other regions in spite of lower economic growth in many periods. Collier (2017) discusses the challenges that African cities face in providing employment, pointing out that they often lack fundamental infrastructure in electricity, roads, and transit, as well as public health and well-defined local governance. Lall et al. (2017) describes African cities as "crowded, disconnected, and thus costly," where high nominal wages discourage business but the high cost of living keeps real wages low. They also note that 60 percent of the urban population live in informal settlements, much higher than the global average, with associated challenges in providing access to basic services (Pariente 2017).

These features reduce the extent to which African cities can capture economies of agglomerations that can help produce jobs. Lall et al. (2017) argue, however, that Africa's cities can still bring economic opportunities through their concentrated geography if property rights, urban planning, and infrastructure are adequately provided. Given that Africa's urban population will be growing much faster than its rural population in the coming decades, as shown in figure 8.10, its cities will need to provide the bulk of the jobs to keep up with Africa's rapidly growing working-age population. But even up to 2050, more than 40 percent of African populations will be rural. Thus, these urbanization trends do not make the case for an exclusively urban policy focus.

6. THE DEMOGRAPHIC DIVIDEND

A discussion of the demographic dividend is very useful in linking more closely the implications of this detailed demography to the labor market and to economic development more broadly. The term "demographic dividend" is typically used to refer to the economic benefits that can result as a population shifts from a very young age structure to an age structure more concentrated in working ages because of declines in fertility (Bloom et al. 2003, Lee and Mason 2006). Bloom and Williamson (1998) argue that this was an important factor in Asia's so-called economic miracle, although similar demographic changes did not produce Asian rates of economic growth in Latin America (Bloom et al. 2003). Several mechanisms may cause the concentration of population in working ages to increase economic growth rates. One is the possible impact of lower child dependency ratios, which may increase savings rates because less income is needed to support children. Declines in fertility may also lead to higher female labor force participation, increased human capital investments for children, and increases in savings for retirement because children are less available for old-age support (Bloom et al. 2017). These changes may further accelerate economic growth.

In the simplest interpretation of the demographic dividend, dependency ratios such as those in figure 8.9 provide the key information. Asia and Latin America began to experience falling total dependency ratios beginning around 1970, with the total dependency ratio continuing to fall until around 2015 to 2020. This implies that the working-age population was steadily increasing as a percentage of the overall population, the key component of the demographic dividend. Sub-Saharan Africa began this decline in the total dependency ratio about two decades later and continues to have much higher dependency ratios than other regions. The total dependency ratios are now rising in Asia and Latin America, the result of population aging, marking a move out of the period of the demographic dividend. Africa will continue to experience a declining total dependency ratio, however, implying an increase in the share of the population in working ages, for most of this century.

The assumption that elderly dependents and child dependents are equivalent and that different ages within each of these groups are equivalent is obviously a simplification that can miss some of the important links between age structure and economic growth. An alternative approach to characterizing the demographic dividend is with National Transfer Accounts (NTAs), an approach developed by Lee and Mason (Lee and Mason 2014; Dramani and Oga 2017). The NTA approach estimates life-cycle profiles of income and consumption, looking at the gap between the two at each age and looking at how intergenerational transfers of various kinds (family, government, market) smooth these gaps. Applying this approach to sub-Saharan Africa, Dramani and Oga (2017) find that support ratios are rising in Africa but are still far lower than in Asia or Latin America—a finding consistent with the total dependency ratio.

In addition to what they call the first demographic dividend related to the increase in the proportion of the population concentrated in working ages, Lee and Mason argue that there is a second demographic dividend associated with lower fertility and population aging. The second demographic dividend results from increased investment in physical and human capital as individuals anticipate living longer and require greater savings to finance retirement (Lee and Mason 2006). Unlike the first demographic dividend, which is inevitably transitory as the population moves from a concentration in working ages to a concentration in older ages, Lee and Mason argue that the second demographic transition continues to have a positive impact even as population aging causes a decrease in the share of working ages.

As seen throughout this chapter, sub-Saharan Africa has the potential to benefit substantially from the first demographic dividend in the twenty-first century as the share of the population in working ages rises steadily. As emphasized in section 2, sub-Saharan Africa will be the only region with a rising share of its population in working ages for most of this century. This apparent demographic bonus is also a demographic challenge, however, because taking advantage of the growing working-age population requires rapid growth of new jobs across the continent (Canning et al. 2015; Cleland 2017; Cleland and Machiyama 2017; May and Turbat 2017). Africa has struggled to meet the challenges of its rapidly growing and increasingly well-educated youth population (Filmer and Fox 2014; Fox 2016; Fox et al. 2016). As shown in figure 8.7, the number of fifteen- to twenty-four-year-olds will continue to grow in sub-Saharan Africa for most of this century, creating a growing need for new entry-level jobs. In addition, the number of workers at older ages will grow at an even faster rate in the coming decades, requiring rapid expansion of jobs across the working ages. As seen in figures 8.7 and 8.8, the size of the older working-age groups will increase substantially faster than the size of the younger working-age groups in sub-Saharan Africa throughout the century, producing a much older working-age population.

Increasing women's labor force participation, linked to falling fertility, has also been cited as a mechanism through which the demographic dividend leads to increased economic growth (Bloom et al. 2009). Women's labor force participation rates in sub-Saharan Africa are currently high relative to other developing regions, with an important factor being high female participation in subsistence agriculture (Klasen 2017). With increasing urbanization, increasing proportions of women seeking employment outside subsistence agriculture will add to the need to produce new jobs in urban areas. As we will explore in section 7, however, women are much better educated than they were in the past.

Whether the twenty-first century is a demographic dividend or a demographic challenge in sub-Saharan Africa will depend on African countries' ability to produce jobs at a rate similar to the rate at which they were produced in Asia during the period in which its working-age population was growing at similar rates. This is obviously a daunting challenge. A factor potentially working in Africa's favor is that Asia and other regions are entering a period in which their working-age populations will be declining. As Africa begins to reap its demographic dividend, other regions are seeing the demographic dividend fade with population aging. The demography of the global labor force will change dramatically in the coming decades, with Africa having the potential to benefit from those changes.

7. FROM DEMOGRAPHY TO THE LABOR MARKET

7.1 THE QUALITY OF AFRICA'S LABOR SUPPLY: RISING EDUCATION LEVELS AMONG NEW LABOR FORCE COHORTS

The trends that we have unpacked in this chapter have been directed at providing a detailed picture of the size, age distribution, and location for the supply of labor in Africa and around the world. However, the ability of economies to absorb rapidly growing cohorts of labor market entrants will depend not only on the size of these cohorts but also on their characteristics. Education is one of the most important dimensions affecting the prospects and potential productivity of young workers entering the labor force, and this is our focus in this section.

It is important to recognize that the young cohorts entering labor markets in Africa in the coming decades will be the best educated cohorts in recorded history for each of the African countries. As pointed out in Lam (2011), education rose rapidly in all developing regions in the last fifty years in spite of the unprecedented growth of the school-age population. Education rose faster for women than men almost everywhere in the world, with the education gender gap narrowing or even reversing in most countries. While Africa has had more uneven progress in education in the last fifty years, the most recent decades have been a period of significant improvement in Africa, too.

Figure 8.11 shows trends in mean schooling of cohorts in four African countries—Senegal, Uganda, Guinea, and Zambia—that have recent census data that can be used to look in detail at the evolution of schooling across birth cohorts. The data are from the Integrated Public Use Microdata Series, International Program (Minnesota Population Center 2020). The horizontal axis shows the year that each birth cohort turned age twenty, roughly corresponding to the age of labor force entry. In other words, the graphs can be thought of as showing how the education of new labor force entrants has increased over time. All four countries have had significant increases in education, although Senegal and Guinea both experienced slowdowns and even reversals during the 1980s and 1990s.

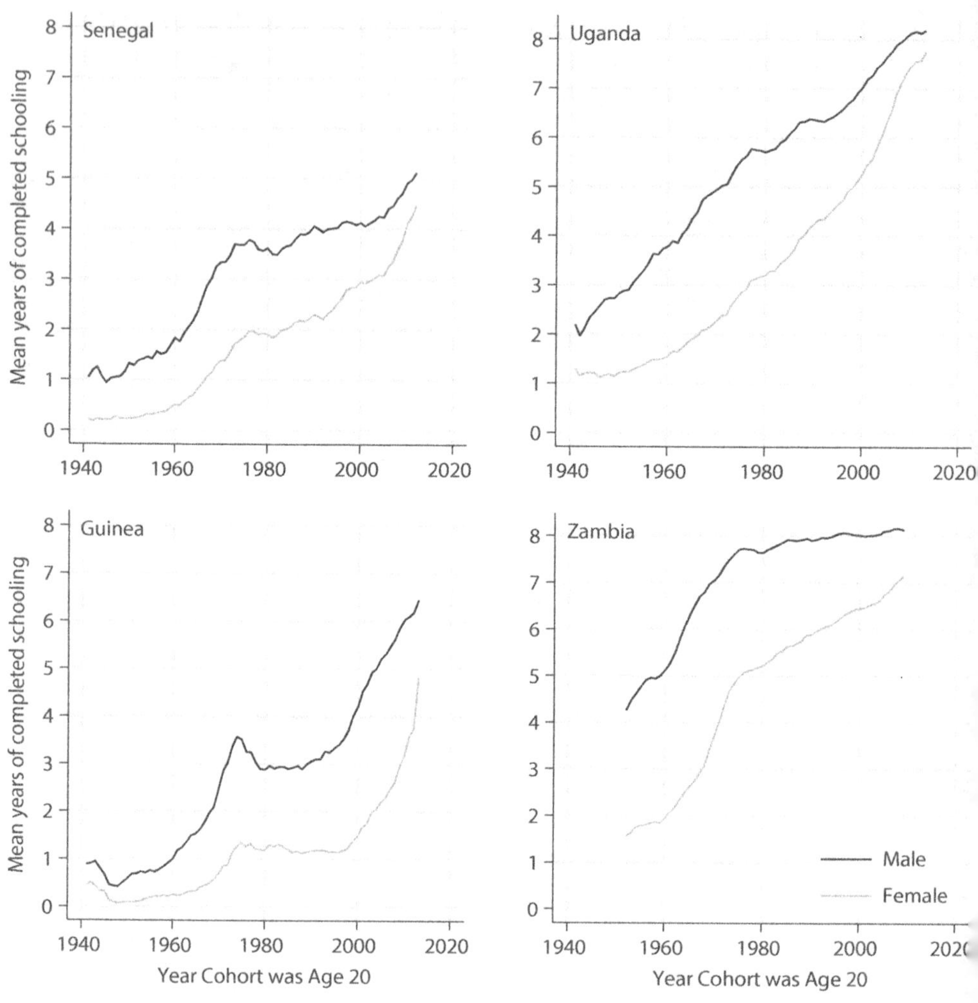

Figure 8.11 Mean years of completed schooling for cohorts at age 20, in Senegal, Uganda, Guinea, and Zambia (five-year moving averages)

Source: Authors' calculations using IPUMS-International Census Data (Minnesota Population Center 2020).

The gender gap has narrowed but not closed in all four countries, with especially rapid increases in women's schooling since the 1990s.

Recent literature on the youth in Africa suggest that these trends are true more generally across the continent (Fox and Ghandi 2021; World Bank 2018). Similar increases in schooling occurred in Asia and Latin America and may help explain why the rapid growth of cohorts entering the labor force did not lead to large increases in unemployment. The hope has been that rising levels of education for African cohorts would imply higher productivity for potential employers and increased empowerment in creating good self-employment opportunities.

It needs to be recognized, however, that the overall quality of education in Africa is still poor relative to peers in other regions, even controlling for income level (Fox and Ghandi 2021; Filmer and Fox 2014; World Bank 2018; Arias et al. 2019). This seems to be almost uniformly true across the continent. It is extremely so in the continent's resource-rich countries, which have some of the worst education outcomes even after controlling for income (de la Brière et al. 2017).

This school quality deficit is consequential. Lam and Elsayed (2022) and Fox and Ghandi (2021) review many of the labor market policy evaluations that have been undertaken in Africa. The consolidated evidence shows that the curriculum and teaching methods are not oriented toward developing noncognitive skills and employability knowledge helpful for navigating the labor market, especially in secondary and postsecondary education systems. As a result, graduating youth often do not know how to interact with potential employers to find a job or how to interact with self-employed mentors to find out how they could perform better.

7.2 THE CHANGING DEMAND FOR LABOR CONFRONTING COHORTS ENTERING THE LABOR FORCE

In an extensive review, Fox and Ghandi (2021) make several key points about the changing employment situation facing youth in Africa. On a positive note, as levels of economic development and transformation improve in Africa, youth and adult employment outcomes improve. In this regard, after controlling for income level, the outcomes in Africa are similar to those found in developing countries in other regions. They are not behind the rest of the world, except in the continent's lower-middle-income, resource-rich countries, where growth does not correlate well with improved employment and development outcomes.

Africa's labor market challenge is not only or even mostly an unemployment challenge. Open unemployment is not widespread in Africa until countries reach upper-middle-income status. Although youth unemployment is typically higher than countrywide averages, the difference is very small in the poorest countries. In this regard, too, Africa follows the pattern found in other parts of the world.

As shown by Fields et al. (2023), to be employed in these countries means creating your own job or joining with household members in farming or nonfarming activities. Particularly in Africa and South Asia, and less so in East Asia and Latin America, informal forms of economic activity remain a persistent phenomenon in spite of rapid economic growth in recent decades (Kanbur 2017). Informal employment now constitutes more than 60 percent of total global employment (ILO 2018), and in Africa, 80 percent of employment is informal (ILO 2018). Micro, small, informal, and household-run enterprises employ a large share of the workforce and provide livelihoods for the poor (La Porta and Shleifer 2014). Women are more likely to engage in precarious forms of informal work, such as contributing family/unpaid workers in the enterprises headed by the males in their households, or in poorly paid casual jobs in the informal sector (Fields et al. 2023). Rodrik (2016) argues that with premature deindustrialization, it seems likely that the trajectory toward informalization in low- and middle-income countries may be intensified in the future.

It is important to note, however, that informal economic activity takes many different forms and plays different roles. In low- and middle-income countries, it is often a place of residual employment for impoverished, marginalized, and vulnerable workers, particularly at times of economic stress and crisis. It can also act as a staging ground for household enterprises in their initial stage of growth. While the recognition of the pervasiveness of informality is crucial in twinning employment scenarios to our analysis of labor supply, it does not imply simple policy implications. It is crucial too to recognize and profile heterogeneity in informal work. (Chen 2012; De Vreyer and Roubaud 2013; Kanbur 2017).

Given that most African countries have low rates of unemployment, as conventionally measured, and have not experienced large increases in unemployment as the working-age population has grown, it is possible that these countries can continue to absorb millions of new entrants to the working-age population without an increase in unemployment rates. This could occur through continued expansion of a relatively low-productivity informal sector, including expansion of the numbers employed in agriculture. While this might mean that standard measures of unemployment do not show a dramatic increase in the coming decades, in spite of the rapid growth of the labor force, this scenario is unlikely to lead to significant economic growth or declines in poverty. A big challenge clearly is for these countries to expand formal employment at a rate that increases both the absolute size and the relative size of the formal sector. An important question that arises is whether the shrinking of the working-age population in Asia and the rest of the world help facilitate this kind of formal sector expansion? There will be particularly high growth and development returns to formal sector expansions that greatly improve linkages into and inclusion of informal enterprises. This formal-informal interface will require explicit policy attention.

8. SUMMARY AND CONCLUSIONS

The global labor market has undergone unprecedented demographic changes in the last fifty years. Three billion people were added to the working-age population of the world between 1970 and 2020, with 2 billion of those added in Asia. The world added over 60 million people every year to the working-age population from 1980 to 2010, reaching a peak of 72 million per year in 2005. The working-age population of the world grew at over 2 percent per year in the 1970s and 1980s and did not fall below 1.5 percent per year until 2010. In spite of these demographic pressures on the labor market, most countries did not experience significant increases in unemployment.

While the growth rate of the world's working-age population has declined to around 1 percent per year, there will be continued demographic pressure on global labor markets in the coming decades. The nature of these pressures has changed, however. Growth of the working-age population will be almost entirely concentrated in sub-Saharan Africa, and the working-age population in all regions will be rapidly aging.

From the perspective of sub-Saharan Africa, the projected demographic trends presented in this chapter offer both challenges and opportunities. Between 2020 and 2050, a period for which projections have relatively little uncertainty, sub-Saharan Africa's working-age population is projected to more than double, an addition of over 700 million working-age individuals. By 2035, Africa will need over 2 million jobs per month to keep up with the growth of the working-age population, up from 1.5 million per month in 2020.

While this rapid growth of Africa's working-age population creates obvious challenges for employment creation, it also represents a period of economic opportunities and shifting dynamics in the global labor force. Most African countries will have steadily rising proportions of their populations concentrated in working ages for most of this century, creating the potential for a demographic dividend that could spur economic growth. Sub-Saharan Africa will be the only major region in the world with a growing working-age population for the rest of the century. While sub-Saharan Africa will add 700 million new working-age people between 2020 and 2050, the working-age population of Asia will decline by 240 million.

The main demographic factor driving the continued growth of the working-age population in sub-Saharan Africa is the continent's later and slower fertility decline compared to regions such as Asia and Latin America. With a total fertility rate of 4.6 births per woman in 2020, Africa has fertility rates that were last seen in Asia and Latin America in the 1970s. The pace of Africa's fertility decline is the main source of uncertainty in projections of population growth in Africa and the world in this century. The UN projects that African fertility will fall steadily in the coming decades, continuing the declines of previous decades. While uncertainty in these fertility projections creates uncertainty in projections of the working-age population, they have only a modest impact on projections of the working-age population through 2050. Because most of the 2050 working-age population has already been born, the projections we have presented in this chapter through 2050 should be viewed as having only a small degree of uncertainty. Beyond 2050, the pace of Africa's fertility decline in the following decades will be an important determinant of the working-age population.

While Africa's job creation challenge in this century is daunting, it is not unprecedented. Africa's current annual growth rate of the working-age population—around 3 percent—is similar to the growth rate experienced by Asia and Latin America around 1980. While Africa is projected to add 27 million new working-age people at the peak in 2055, Asia added almost 50 million per year in the early 2000s. Thus, the demography of Africa's labor force is not exceptional in terms of the rates of growth or absolute numbers being added to the working-age population. The important difference in Africa's demography compared to Asia and Latin America, however, is that those regions experienced high rates of growth for very short periods of time, while Africa will have rapid growth of its working-age population for several decades. Outside Africa, these trends have been and will continue to be associated with rapidly rising shares of the population residing and working in urban areas. In Africa, urban population shares are rising too and, by 2050, close to 60 percent of the population will be urban. This urban share is notably lower than elsewhere, however, and in most African countries, the number of people residing in rural areas is estimated to rise going forward.

The question ultimately is whether African can turn a century in which it is the only region in the world with a growing working-age population into a period of growing employment and rapid economic growth. Moving beyond the demography, it is important to note that the education of new cohorts entering the labor force has been rapidly increasing. There continue to be issues of school quality in many African countries, with concerns that young people entering the labor force are not getting the right cognitive and noncognitive skills to meet the needs of potential employers or the challenges of productive self-employment.

Africa's labor market challenge is mostly not an unemployment challenge, at least in the traditional sense, because unemployment rates as conventionally measured are low in most countries. Informal sector employment dominates most African labor markets, functioning generally in a way that adjusts to absorb expansions in labor supply but at a cost to productivity, earnings, and support from the labor market. This generalized characterization of the informal sector understates important heterogeneities across countries in the specific configurations of the informal sector in the labor market and, particularly important, in the relationships between this sector and the formal sector. For African labor markets to reap their potential demographic dividends, the challenges ahead are to create high-productivity formal sector jobs at a rate that can keep up with the rapid growth of the working-age population and with linkages to informal sectors that are more inclusive than they have been.

NOTES

1. The authors acknowledge useful comments from participants in the Initiative for Policy Dialogue/Japan International Cooperation Agency (IPD/JICA) Conference on Employment Prospects in Developing Countries: Implications of Technological and Demographic Trends, Columbia University, January 12–13, 2023, and also further comments from Arjun Jayadev.

2. Throughout this chapter, we will often use "Africa" as a shorthand for "sub-Saharan Africa."

3. Portions of this chapter are adapted from Lam et al. (2019), which used the 2019 version of the UN population projections. All analysis in this chapter has been updated using the 2022 UN data.

4. The replacement level of fertility is slightly above two births per woman in order to account for female births that do not survive to reproductive age.

5. The sharp drop and subsequent increase for Asia and the world around 1960 is associated with Great Chinese Famine.

6. See also Casterline (2017) and Casterline and Agyei-Mensah (2017) for analyses of trends in African fertility.

7. The projections are also not very sensitive to assumptions about mortality given that death rates are relatively low in all populations between ages five and sixty-five, with plausible ranges of mortality having only modest effects on projections of the working-age population.

8. The most recent estimates for Ghana, Kenya, Malawi, Mali, Niger, Nigeria, Senegal, Tanzania, and Uganda are based on Malaria Indicator Surveys (MIS).

9. Many African countries do not have comprehensive vital statistics data that can be used to estimate annual fertility rates, so survey estimates such as those from the Demographic and Health Surveys (DHS) and Malaria Indicator Surveys (MIS) are the main source of data for those countries. These surveys are collected intermittently, as seen by the data points in figure 8.6, so many countries do not have direct data on fertility in some years.

10. It should be noted that children and the elderly may be quite different in terms of their economic impact. A one-year-old is different than a fourteen-year-old, and a sixty-five-year-old is different than a ninety-year-old. These are very simple summary measures of the dependency burden that are useful as one indicator of the economic impact of changing age structure.

11. The UN makes projections only of urban and rural populations for the total population, without breaking down the projections by age. We thus cannot break down the projected working-age population into urban and rural components.

REFERENCES

Arias Diaz, S. Omar, David Evans, and Indhira Vanessa Santos. 2019. *The Skills Balancing Act in Sub-Saharan Africa: Investing in Skills for Productivity, Inclusivity, and Adaptability*. Africa Development Forum. World Bank Group.

Bloom, David E., David Canning, Günther Fink, and Jocelyn E. Finlay. 2009. "Fertility, Female Labor Force Participation, and the Demographic Dividend." *Journal of Economic Growth* 14 (2): 79–101.

Bloom, David, David Canning, and Jaypee Sevilla. 2003. "The Demographic Dividend: A New Perspective on the Economic Consequences of Population Change." Rand Corporation.

Bloom, David E., Michael Kuhn, and Klaus Prettner. 2017. "Africa's Prospects for Enjoying a Demographic Dividend." *Journal of Demographic Economics* 83 (1): 63–76.

Bloom, David, and Jeffrey Williamson. 1998. "Demographic Transitions and Economic Miracles in Emerging Asia." *World Bank Economic Review* 12: 419–56.

Bongaarts, John. 2009. "Human Population Growth and the Demographic Transition." *Philosophical Transactions of the Royal Society of London. Series B, Biological Sciences* 364 (1532): 2985–90.

Bongaarts, John. 2017. "Africa's Unique Fertility Transition." *Population and Development Review* 43 (S1): 39–58.

Bongaarts, John, and John Casterline. 2013. "Fertility Transition: Is Sub-Saharan Africa Different?" *Population and Development Review* 38 (S1): 153–68.

Canning, David, Sangeeta Raja, and Abdo S. Yazbeck. 2015. *Africa's Demographic Transition: Dividend or Disaster?* World Bank Publications.

Casterline, John B. 2017. "Prospects for Fertility Decline in Africa." *Population and Development Review*, 43: 3–18.

Casterline, John B., and Samuel Agyei-Mensah. 2017. "Fertility Desires and the Course of Fertility Decline in Sub-Saharan Africa." *Population and Development Review* 43 (S1): 84–111.

Chen, Marty. 2012. "Mapping Size and Diversity of Informal Economy." WIEGO Technical Note 2: Mapping Informal Workers. Women in Informal Employment: Globalizing and Organizing (WIEGO) and Harvard University.

Cleland, John. 2017. "Population Growth, Employment, and Livelihoods: The Triple Challenge." *Journal of Demographic Economics* 83 (1): 51–61.

Cleland, John, and Kazuyo Machiyama. 2017. "The Challenges Posed by Demographic Change in Sub-Saharan Africa: A Concise Overview." *Population and Development Review* 43 (S1): 264–86.

Collier, Paul. 2017. "Africa's Prospective Urban Transition." *Journal of Demographic Economics* 83 (1): 3–11.

de la Brière, Bénédicte, Deon Filmer, Dena Ringold, Dominic Rohner, Karelle Samuda, and Anastasiya Denisova. 2017. *From Mines and Wells to Well-Built Minds: Turning Sub-Saharan Africa's Natural Resource Wealth into Human Capital.* World Bank Publications.

Demographic and Health Survey Program STATcompiler. Data from STATcompiler, accessed April 7, 2023, http://www.statcompiler.com.

De Vreyer, Philippe, and Francois Roubaud, eds. 2013. *Urban Labor Markets in Sub-Saharan Africa.* World Bank Publications

Dramani, Latif, and Idossou Jean-Baptiste Oga. 2017. "Understanding Demographic Dividends in Africa: The NTA Approach." *Journal of Demographic Economics* 83 (1): 85–101.

Fields, Gary S., T. H. Gindling, Kunal Sen, Michael Danquah, and Simone Schotte. 2023. *The Job Ladder: Transforming Informal Work and Livelihoods in Developing Countries.* Oxford University Press.

Filmer, Deon, and Louise Fox. 2014. *Youth Employment in Sub-Saharan Africa.* World Bank Publications.

Fox, Louise. 2016. "What Will It Take to Meet the Youth Employment Challenge in Sub-Saharan Africa?" GLM|LIC Synthesis Paper No. 2. Institute of Labor Economics (IZA), April.

Fox, Louise, and Dhruv Gandhi. 2021. "Youth Employment in Sub-Saharan Africa: Progress and Prospects." African Growth Initiative Working Paper No. 28. Brookings Institute, March.

Fox, Louise, Lemma W. Senbet, and Witness Simbanegavi. 2016. "Youth Employment in Sub-Saharan Africa: Challenges, Constraints and Opportunities." *Journal of African Economies* 25 (Suppl. 1): i3–15.

Fox, Sean. 2017. "Mortality, Migration, and Rural Transformation in Sub-Saharan Africa's Urban Transition." *Journal of Demographic Economics* 83 (1): 13–30.

International Labour Organization (ILO). 2018. World Employment Social Outlook Trends 2018. International Labour Office, Geneva.

International Labour Organization (ILO). Dataset from ILO Modelled Estimates Database, ILOSTAT, accessed April 11, 2023, https://ilostat.ilo.org/data/.

Jedwab, Remi, Luc Christiaensen, and Marina Gindelsky. 2015. "Demography, Urbanization and Development: Rural Push, Urban Pull and . . . Urban Push?" World Bank Policy Research Working Paper No. 7333. World Bank.

Kanbur, Ravi. 2017. "Informality: Causes, Consequences and Policy Responses." *Review of Development Economics* 21 (4): 939–61.

Kebede, Endale, Anne Goujon, and Wolfgang Lutz. 2019. "Stalls in Africa's Fertility Decline Partly Result from Disruptions in Female Education." *Proceedings of the National Academy of Sciences* 116 (8) 2891–96.

Klasen, Stephan. 2017, October. "What Explains Uneven Female Labor Force Participation Levels and Trends in Developing Countries?" GLM|LIC Synthesis Paper, No. 7. Institute of Labor Economics (IZA).

Lall, Somik Vinay, J. Vernon Henderson, and Anthony J. Venables. 2017. *Africa's Cities: Opening Doors to the World.* World Bank Publications.

Lam, David. 2011. "How the World Survived the Population Bomb: Lessons from 50 Years of Extraordinary Demographic History." *Demography* 48 (4): 1231–62.

Lam, David, and Suzanne Duryea. 1999. "Effects of Schooling on Fertility, Labor Supply, and Investments in Children, with Evidence from Brazil." *Journal of Human Resources* 34 (1): 160–92.

Lam, David, and Ahmed Elsayed. 2022. *Labour Markets in Low-Income Countries: Challenges and Opportunities.* Oxford University Press

Lam, David, and Murray Leibbrandt. 2013. "Global Demographic Trends and their Implications for Employment," Paper prepared for the United Nations Development Program High-Level Panel on the Post-2105 Development Agenda, April 2013

Lam, David, Murray Leibbrandt, and James Allen. 2019, November. "The Demography of the Labor Force in Sub-Saharan Africa: Challenges and Opportunities," Growth and Labour Markets in Low Income Countries Programme Synthesis Paper No. 10. Institute of Labor Economics (IZA).

La Porta, Rafael, and Andrei Shleifer. 2014. "Informality and Development." *Journal of Economic Perspectives* 28 (3): 109–26.

Lee, Ronald. 2003. "The Demographic Transition: Three Centuries of Fundamental Change." *Journal of Economic Perspectives* 17 (4): 167–90.

Lee, Ronald, and Andrew Mason. 2006. "What Is the Demographic Dividend?" *Finance and Development* 43 (3): 16.

Lee, Ronald, and Andrew Mason. 2014. "Is Low Fertility Really a Problem?: Population Aging, Dependency, and Consumption." *Science* 346 (6206): 229–34.

May, John F., and Vincent Turbat. 2017. "The Demographic Dividend in Sub-Saharan Africa: Two Issues That Need More Attention." *Journal of Demographic Economics* 83 (1): 77–84.

Minnesota Population Center. 2020, Integrated Public Use Microdata Series, International: Version 7.3. [Data set]. IPUMS. https://doi.org/10.18128/D020.V7.3.

Pariente, William. 2017. "Urbanization in Sub-Saharan Africa and the Challenge of Access to Basic Services." *Journal of Demographic Economics* 83 (1): 31–39.

Rodrik, Dani. 2016. "Premature Deindustrialization." *Journal of Economic Growth* 21 (1): 1–33.

Singh, Susheela, Akinrinola Bankole, and Jacqueline E. Darroch. 2017. "The Impact of Contraceptive Use and Abortion on Fertility in Sub-Saharan Africa: Estimates for 2003–2014." *Population and Development Review* 43 (Suppl. 1): 141–65.

United Nations, Department of Economic and Social Affairs, Population Division. 2018. World Urbanization Prospects: 2018 Revision. https://population.un.org/wup/.

United Nations, Department of Economic and Social Affairs, Population Division. 2022. World Population Prospects 2022: Methodology of the United Nations Population Estimates and Projections. UN DESA/POP/2022/TR/NO. 4. https://population.un.org/wpp/Publications/Files/WPP2022_Methodology.pdf.

World Bank. 2018. *World Development Report 2018: Learning to Realize Education's Promise*. World Bank.

CHAPTER 9

Structural Change and Employment in Sub-Saharan Africa

AN UPDATE OF RECENT TRENDS WITH MULTIPLE-SECTOR CONSIDERATIONS

Tetsuya Harada

Abstract: This chapter provides an updated analysis of structural changes in employment and labor productivity in sub-Saharan Africa, a region that is expected to experience significant labor force growth in the future. Expanding on the standard shift-share decomposition of labor productivity growth, the chapter also presents a detailed examination of sectoral performance, including various forms of the service sector, and their impact on economy-wide labor productivity. On average, labor productivity growth in sub-Saharan Africa weakened in the 2010s compared to the previous decade. Nevertheless, while the employment share in the agricultural sector continues to decline, the sector still creates the largest number of jobs, and its improvement in sectoral labor productivity contributes to economy-wide labor productivity growth. Contradicting the oft-referenced argument linking deindustrialization of the region with lower manufacturing employment, the employment share in manufacturing increased after 2000. However, its sectoral labor productivity declined in the 2010s. Negative associations between employment share growth and labor productivity decline are also observed in tradable services such as business services and finance. It is worrisome to see such relationships in sectors such as manufacturing and tradable services that could potentially drive the economy and provide quality jobs. Nontradable service sectors such as retail, wholesale, food, and restaurants absorb the largest number of nonagricultural workers. The level of labor productivity in nontradable service sectors has been low but not necessarily declining.

Keywords: employment, labor productivity, structural change, sub-Saharan Africa

1. INTRODUCTION

Employment has become a significant issue in the development of sub-Saharan Africa. The prospects for the region's population and labor force growth far exceed those of other regions. According to a recent UN estimate, the regional population of 1.13 billion as of 2021 will reach 1.76 billion in 2040 and surpass the population of East and Southeast Asia in the 2050s, and that of Central and South Asia in the 2060s. The global increase of the working-age population (aged fourteen to sixty-four) from 2010 to 2050 is expected to be around 1.5 billion. More than half of this increase (approximately 0.87 billion) is expected to take place in sub-Saharan Africa (United Nations, Department of Economic and Social Affairs, Population Division 2022). Africa's growing working-age population will thus be an engine of growth. The question is whether enough high-quality jobs can be created to accommodate this growth in the labor force.

Manufacturing has traditionally been considered as the main driver of economic development, but the recent development literature suggests that the prospects of the sector are not as bright as they used to be. Rodrik (2016) argues that "premature deindustrialization" has been observed in low- and middle-income countries in recent decades, where employment and output shares have started to decline at much lower levels of income compared to the countries that experienced industrialization in earlier decades. Felipe and Mehta (2016) report that, while the global employment and output shares of manufacturing have been relatively stable, manufacturing jobs are spread thinly, and individual countries find it difficult to sustain high levels of manufacturing employment.

The service sector has gained attention in this situation, but the extent to which it can drive employment and output growth of a country is uncertain. Ghani and O'Connell (2014) argue that the service sector can be a growth engine in low-income countries. Nayyar et al. (2021) in turn suggest that the service sector increasingly shares the benefits from international trade, scale economies, intersectoral linkages, and innovation that have been mainly held by the manufacturing sector. However, other studies such as Rodrik (2016) and Atolia et al. (2020) give a more cautious assessment of the potential of the service sector, arguing that the demand for traditional, nontradable services is constrained by income in the rest of the economy and that tradable services require a highly skilled workforce and strong fundamentals that are hardly expected at this stage in many low-income countries.

Apart from looking at the performance of individual sectors, it is also important to look at structural changes, that is, changes in labor and output across industries, to consider the future of employment and its quality in sub-Saharan Africa. For example, a large increase in productivity in one sector in the face of international competition may have only a limited effect on the country's overall productivity and employment if the labor force is simultaneously shifting to less productive industries. To analyze the contribution to aggregated labor productivity growth, a shift-share method is typically used to decompose labor productivity into a "within" component, which captures the productivity growth of individual sectors, and a "structural change" component, which captures the labor reallocation effect across different sectors. Using this method, McMillan et al. (2014) argue that the structural transformation of sub-Saharan Africa had been growth-reducing before 2000, and then the trend reversed. It is also pointed out that the labor shift from agriculture in Africa did not go toward the manufacturing activities that drove earlier Asian growth but to trade services, where productivity growth is higher than agriculture but is still sluggish (De Vries et al. 2015; Fox et al. 2017; Diao et al. 2019).

However, there are two points that previous works on structural change in employment and labor productivity in sub-Saharan Africa do not address adequately. First, previous studies focus mainly on the manufacturing sector to describe the performance of the nonagricultural sector of the economy. The service sector has often been viewed as a residual of agriculture and manufacturing. Describing individual prospects of service subsectors is not a focus of previous studies using shift-share analysis. However, characteristics such as productivity level, labor intensity, required skills, tradability, and degree of formality are diverse among different service industries, and discussing them all together is not always relevant to capturing the reality of the sector. Second, the coverage period of the previous works on structural transformation extends mainly to the early 2000s: the data that McMillan et al. (2014) use are from 1990 to 2005, while De Vries et al. (2015) work on data from 1960 to 2010, and Mensah et al. (2022) work on data from 1960 to 2015.

The 2000s are often described as a high-growth period across the African continent (5.2 percent regional growth per annum). Diao et al. (2019) have questioned the sustainability of the high-growth performance of sub-Saharan Africa, arguing that the driving force mainly comes from the demand side and is not associated with productivity growth. Therefore, it is of interest to see if there is any change of employment reallocation and productivity growth in sub-Saharan Africa in the 2010s, a period that is characterized by more modest growth (3.5 percent per year in 2010–2019), a broader penetration of information technology (IT) (Hjort and Poulsen 2019), and a low-interest environment globally.

This chapter attempts to fill the gap and present an updated picture of structural changes in employment and labor productivity in sub-Saharan Africa while also examining what has been occurring at the sector level. A shift-share method and its extended formula are employed to analyze the Economic Transformation Database (ETD) developed by the Groningen Growth and Development Centre (GGDC) and UNU-WIDER, which covers data until 2018. The shift-share method can examine the implication of patterns of employment growth across multiple sectors on economy-wide labor productivity growth, decomposing the latter into within productivity growth and the growth from structural change (labor reallocation across sectors). Its focus on labor productivity can also consider the sectoral quality of employment because sectoral labor productivity is expected to determine the level of wages in the sector, although the relationship is not always automatic. The standard formula that previous studies typically used, however, displays the within and structural change components of economy-wide productivity growth only in an aggregated manner. This chapter employs an additional formula to capture an individual sector's within and structural change contributions to better understand the performance at the sectoral level.

The result presented in this chapter shows that, on average, labor productivity growth in sub-Saharan Africa weakened in the 2010s compared with the previous decade. Nevertheless, while the share of agricultural employment continues to decline, the sector still creates the largest number of jobs, and the improvement in its sectoral labor productivity contributes heavily to economy-wide labor productivity growth. Unlike the oft-referenced argument of employment deindustrialization, the manufacturing employment share increased after 2000, but sectoral labor productivity in this area declined in the 2010s. Negative associations between employment share growth and labor productivity decline are also observed in tradable services such as business services and finance. These observations contrast with the fact that in the same nonagricultural sectors of developing Asian countries, the increase of employment share is always accompanied by productivity improvement.

It is worrisome to see such negative relationships in these sectors, which could potentially drive the economy and produce quality jobs in sub-Saharan Africa. Nontradable service sectors such as retail, wholesale, food, and restaurants absorb the largest number of nonagricultural workers. In contrast with the situation frequently described in other studies, the level of labor productivity in these sectors in the sub-Saharan region has barely been maintained.

This chapter is organized as follows. Section 2 describes the data set. Section 3 describes the general trends in sectoral employment share and productivity levels of the sub-Saharan African countries. Section 4 analyzes the employment and productivity growth of sub-Saharan African using growth decomposition analysis between within and structural change contributions to overall productivity growth performance. Section 5 presents a summary and discussion of the findings. Section 6 presents concluding remarks.

2. THE DATA

The study uses the ETD released in February 2021 by the GGDC and UNU-WIDER. The ETD is the successor to the GGDC ten-sector database, which many existing studies on structural transformation are built on. The ETD is not merely an update of the time series of an existing sectoral data set (Kruse et al. 2023) but covers more countries in its breakdown of twelve sectors based on the International Standard Industrial Classification Revision 4. The ETD contains annual employment and gross value-added data at both real and nominal prices of twelve sectors for fifty-one countries for the period 1990–2018. The list of countries and sectors covered is shown in table 9.1 and table 9.2, respectively.

Gross value-added in real and nominal prices is from National Accounts (NA) by the national statistical institutions (NSIs). Sectoral value added is compiled according to the UN system of National Accounts (UN 2008), which accounts for income from formal and informal activities (Kruse et al. 2023). Census data are used as a primary source for the benchmark level estimates for employment and are checked for reliability and replaced or supplemented by labor force survey data (de Vries et al. 2021). Employment in the ETD is defined as "all persons engaged," including all the paid employees, self-employed, and family workers aged fifteen years and older. It therefore aims to capture both formal and informal workers (de Vries et al. 2021; Kruse et al. 2023).

Table 9.1 Countries covered: GGDC/UNU-WIDER Economic Transformation Database

Developing Asia (14)	Bangladesh, Cambodia, China, India, Indonesia, Lao PDR, Malaysia, Myanmar, Nepal, Pakistan, Philippines, Sri Lanka, Thailand, Vietnam
Advanced Asia (6)	Chinese Taipei, Hong Kong (China), Israel, Japan, Korea (Republic of), Singapore
Latin America (9)	Argentina, Bolivia, Brazil, Chile, Colombia, Costa Rica, Ecuador, Mexico, Peru
Middle East and North Africa (4)	Egypt, Morocco, Tunisia, Turkey
Sub-Saharan Africa (18)	Botswana, Burkina Faso, Cameroon, Ethiopia, Ghana, Kenya, Lesotho, Malawi, Mauritius, Mozambique, Namibia, Nigeria, Rwanda, Senegal, South Africa, Tanzania, Uganda, Zambia

Source: Economic Transformation Database.

Table 9.2 Sectors covered: GGDC/UNU-WIDER Economic Transformation Database

ISICRev4 code	*ETD sector name*	*ISICRev4 description*
A	Agriculture	Agriculture, forestry, fishing
B	Mining	Mining and quarrying
C	Manufacturing	Manufacturing
D + E	Utilities	Electricity, gas, steam, and air conditioning supply; water supply; sewerage, waste management and remediation activities
F	Construction	Construction
G + I	Trade services	Wholesale and retail trade; repair of motor vehicles and motorcycles; accommodation and food service activities
H	Transport services	Transportation and storage
J + M + N	Business services	Information and communication; professional, scientific and technical activities; administrative and support service activities
K	Financial services	Financial and insurance activities
L	Real estate	Real estate activities
O + P + Q	Government services	Public administration and defense; compulsory social security; education; human health and social work activities
R + S + T + U	Other services	Arts, entertainment, and recreation; other service activities; activities of households as employers; undifferentiated goods- and services-producing activities of households for own use; activities of extraterritorial organizations and bodies

Source: Economic Transformation Database.

3. DESCRIPTIVE TRENDS

3.1 DESCRIPTIVE TRENDS FOR EMPLOYMENT AND PRODUCTIVITY

Table 9.3 lists the employment shares for the twelve sectors of the economies of the eighteen sub-Saharan African countries. These numbers are simple, unweighted averages of the eighteen countries. Agricultural employment share declined from 64.8 percent in 1990 to 45.6 percent in 2018 on average. Note, however, that the number of new entrants to the working population is growing and that the largest job creation is still taking place in the agricultural sector in the region. During 2010–2018, 57 million jobs were newly created in the eighteen countries, and 12.7 million (22 percent) of them were in the agricultural sector.

Average manufacturing employment share across the eighteen countries has also increased since the 2000s. Using the ETD, Kruse et al. (2023) argue that the deindustrialization trend has been reversed and that manufacturing is expanding in sub-Saharan Africa.

The service sector consists of trade services, transport services, business services, financial services, real estate, government services, and other services. Among these service subsectors, this chapter focuses particularly on trade services, business services, and financial services. Trade services cover wholesale and retail trade, repair of motor vehicles and motorcycles, and accommodation and food services activities. These are typically traditional services industries that are characterized as nontradable and require predominantly low-skilled labor. The informal sector often plays an important role in providing these services. The trade services provide the largest share of employment in the nonagricultural sector, and this is increasing, from 8.6 percent in 1990 to 17.4 percent in 2018.

Business services include information and communication; professional, scientific, and technical activities; and administrative and support services activities. Financial services include financial and insurance activities. In contrast to trade services, the business services and financial services subsectors are considered modern service sectors characterized by higher per capita productivity and more formalized operations, often involving medium- to high-skilled labor. The business and financial services sectors increased their employment shares, although they are still a small percentage of the total. The average employment share of business services in the eighteen countries increased from 1.3 percent in 1990 to 3.8 percent in 2018. Financial services increased from 0.3 percent in 1990 to 0.8 percent in 2010.

Table 9.3 Sectoral employment shares of sub-Saharan Africa economies

	Employment shares (%), by year			
Sector	1990	2000	2010	2018
Agriculture	64.8	61.5	53.8	45.6
Mining	1.3	0.9	0.9	1.2
Manufacturing	7.2	7.0	7.3	8.4
Utilities	0.5	0.4	0.4	0.4
Construction	3.0	3.1	3.7	4.2
Trade services	8.6	10.5	13.9	17.4
Transport services	1.6	1.9	2.5	2.9
Business services	1.3	1.7	2.9	3.8
Financial services	0.3	0.5	0.7	0.8
Real estate	0.1	0.1	0.1	0.2
Government services	6.0	6.9	7.6	8.5
Other services	5.2	5.6	6.2	6.6

Note: The percentages are simple (unweighted) averages of the eighteen sub-Saharan African countries in the ETD.
Source: Author's calculation based on the ETD.

Table 9.4 shows the relative productivity for the twelve sectors of the eighteen sub-Saharan African economies. Throughout this chapter, productivity is defined as real value-added per worker (average labor productivity). Relative productivity is the ratio of sectoral productivity to

Table 9.4 Relative productivity, by sector

	Relative productivity, by year			
Sector	1990	2000	2010	2018
Agriculture	0.4	0.4	0.4	0.4
Mining	19.1	13.7	9.2	7.8
Manufacturing	2.5	2.6	2.0	1.6
Utilities	10.8	10.7	10.8	11.3
Construction	3.2	2.8	2.0	2.1
Trade services	2.1	1.6	1.3	1.1
Transport services	3.5	3.9	3.2	2.2
Business services	16.5	11.7	5.1	3.2
Financial services	31.8	17.5	11.5	10.7
Real estate	2,290.3	603.9	238.9	101.0
Government services	4.5	3.0	2.4	2.0
Other services	1.3	0.9	0.6	0.5

Note: Relative productivity is the ratio of sectoral productivity to economy-wide productivity. The numbers are simple (unweighted) averages of the eighteen sub-Saharan African countries in the ETD.
Source: Author's calculation based on the ETD.

economy-wide productivity.[1] The relative productivity of agriculture is 0.4, which is the lowest among all the sectors for all periods. However, the relative productivity of the nonagricultural sectors is declining generally, and intersectoral productivity gaps are diminishing.

4. STRUCTURAL TRANSFORMATION IN EMPLOYMENT AND PRODUCTIVITY

4.1 METHODOLOGY

A shift-share method of labor productivity decomposition is employed to analyze the overall trend of structural transformation in sub-Saharan Africa. The shift-share method decomposes labor productivity into a within component, which captures the productivity growth of individual sectors, and a structural change component, which captures the labor reallocation effect across different sectors. The standard shift-share method, however, normally shows the within and structural change components only in an aggregated manner among different sectors, and it is not always clear what the size of the contribution of each sector is to the economy-wide productivity growth. Therefore, an additional formula is introduced to identify each individual sector's contribution to economy-wide labor productivity growth.

To start, economy-wide labor productivity of a country y at time t is given as:

$$y_t = \frac{Y_t}{E_t} = \sum_{i=1}^{N} y_{i,t}\theta_{i,t} \tag{1}$$

where

Y_t = total output
E_t = total employment of the country
$y_{i,t}$ = labor productivity of sector i at time t
$\theta_{i,t}$ = the share of employment for sector i

The economy-wide labor productivity is the weighted sum of sectoral labor productivity by sectoral labor share. Then the change of economy-wide labor productivity between the periods $t-k$ and t is expressed as follows:

$$\Delta y_t = y_t - y_{t-k} = \sum_{i=1}^{N} y_{i,t}\theta_{i,t} - \sum_{i=1}^{N} y_{i,t-k}\theta_{i,t-k}$$

$$= \sum_{i=1}^{N}(y_{i,t} - y_{i,t-k})\cdot \theta_{i,t-k} + \sum_{i=1}^{N} y_{i,t}\cdot\left(\theta_{i,t} - \theta_{i,t-k}\right) \tag{2}$$

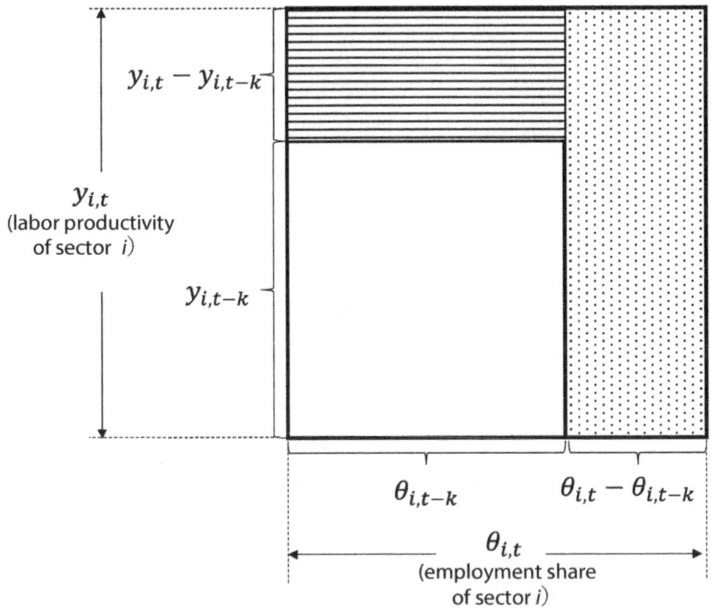

Figure 9.1 Geometric representation of labor productivity decomposition

Source: Author.

Figure 9.1 is a geometric representation of this formula. The vertical axis of the rectangle represents the level of the labor productivity of sector i, and the horizontal axis represents the employment share of sector i. The sum of the areas of rectangles with length $y_{i,t}$ and width $\theta_{i,t}$ for all the sectors ($\sum_{i=1}^{N} y_{i,t}\theta_{i,t}$) is the economy-wide productivity of a country at time t.

The difference of the sums of the areas of rectangles between two periods ($\sum_{i=1}^{N} y_{i,t}\theta_{i,t} - \sum_{i=1}^{N} y_{i,t-k}\theta_{i,t-k}$) is the growth of the economy-wide productivity. The difference of the areas of rectangles for a sector i can be divided into the horizontal line-shaded area and the dot-shaded area, as shown in figure 9.1. The horizontal line-shaded area $(y_{i,t} - y_{i,t-k}) \cdot \theta_{i,t-k}$ represents the product of the labor productivity growth of sector i between the two periods and the sectoral employment share at the initial period $t-k$. The dot-shaded area $y_{i,t} \cdot (\theta_{i,t} - \theta_{i,t-k})$ represents the growth of the sectoral employment share of sector i between the two periods multiplied by the labor productivity level of sector i at the ending period t.

4.1.1 DECOMPOSITION OF LABOR PRODUCTIVITY GROWTH (ALL SECTORS AGGREGATED)

As equation (2) shows, the change of the economy-wide productivity between the two periods is the combined sum of the horizontal line-shaded area and the dot-shaded area across all the sectors. The sum of the horizontal line-shaded area across all the sectors, $\sum_{i=1}^{N}(y_{i,t}-y_{i,t-k})\cdot\theta_{i,t-k}$, means the average growth of labor productivity weighted by each sector's employment share at the initial period $t-k$ and is called the within component of productivity growth, following McMillan et al. (2014).

The sum of the dot-shaded areas across all the sector, $\sum_{i=1}^{N} y_{i,t}\cdot(\theta_{i,t}-\theta_{i,t-k})$ captures the effect of the labor reallocation across different sectors on changes of the economy-wide labor productivity. This is the structural change component of productivity growth.

Dividing equation (2) by $y_{t-k}=\sum_{i=1}^{N} y_{i,t-k}\theta_{i,t-k}$ gives us equation (3), where the first term of the righthand side of the equation is the contribution of the within component to economy-wide productivity growth, and the second term is the structural change component:

$$\frac{\Delta y_t}{y_{t-k}}=\frac{\sum_{i=1}^{N}(y_{i,t}-y_{i,t-k})\cdot\theta_{i,t-k}}{y_{t-k}}+\frac{\sum_{i=1}^{N}y_{i,t}\cdot\left(\theta_{i,t}-\theta_{i,t-k}\right)}{y_{t-k}} \tag{3}$$

4.1.2 CONTRIBUTION OF INDIVIDUAL SECTORS

Equation (3) provides within and structural change contributions with all the sectors aggregated. Each sector's within and structural change contribution to the economy-wide productivity growth is captured using the following formula:

$$\frac{y_{i,t}\theta_{i,t}-y_{i,t-k}\theta_{i,t-k}}{y_{t-k}}=\frac{\left(y_{i,t}-y_{i,t-k}\right)\cdot\theta_{i,t-k}}{y_{t-k}}+\frac{y_{i,t}\cdot\left(\theta_{i,t}-\theta_{i,t-k}\right)}{y_{t-k}} \tag{4}$$

The first item on the right side of the equation is the contribution of the change of the labor productivity of sector i to the growth of economy-wide labor productivity. The second item on the right side of the equation is the contribution of the change of the employment share of sector i to the growth of economy-wide labor productivity. Note that the numerator of the left side of equation (4) mean the difference between the product of sectoral productivity and the sectoral employment share of periods t and $t-k$, not the difference in the sectoral labor productivity level $\Delta y_{i,t}$.

4.2 REGIONAL PERFORMANCE

Figure 9.2 uses equation (3) from section 4.1.1 to show the decomposition of economy-wide productivity growth between the within and structural change contributions for sub-Saharan Africa in the three decades 1990–2000, 2000–2010, and 2010–2018. Note that this is the simple average of eighteen countries, converted to an annualized rate. In the 1990s, labor productivity growth was mostly brought about by the within contribution, and the contribution by structural change was at a minimum. In the 2000s, the productivity growth increased to 3.46 percent annually, in which the within component was 2.62 percent and the structural change contribution was 0.84 percent.[2] In the 2010s, average productivity growth slowed down to 2.19 percent, in which the within component was 1.12 percent and the structural change component was 1.07 percent, respectively.

Note that the regional average of eighteen countries treats them equally and does not consider differences in employment, population, and

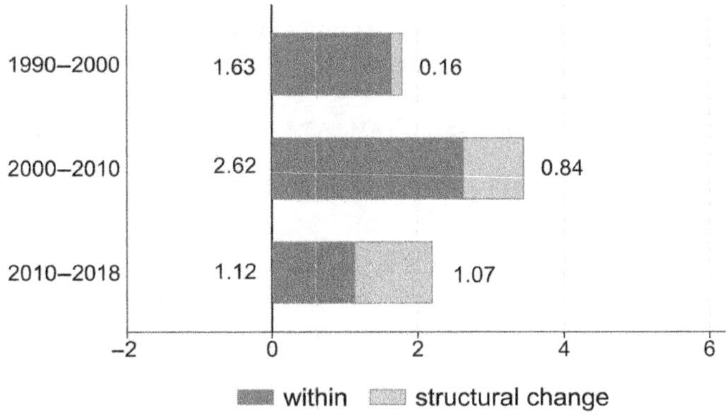

Figure 9.2 Decomposition of the economy-wide productivity growth of sub-Saharan Africa (simple average)

Source: Author's calculations using data from the Economic Transformation Database.

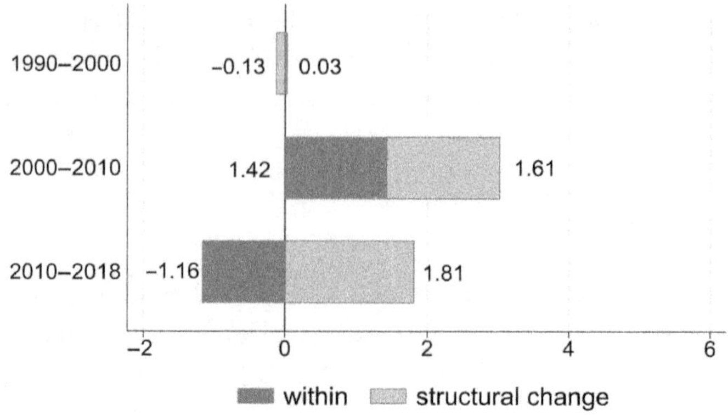

Figure 9.3 Decomposition of economy-wide productivity growth in sub-Saharan Africa (weighted average)

Source: Author's calculations using data from the Economic Transformation Database.

value-added size. Figure 9.3 shows the result when the regional average is calculated by summing the employment and output figures of the same sector across the countries using Purchasing Power Parity (PPP) exchange rates in 2015 and thereby giving more weight to larger countries. The growth of the within component turned negative in the 2010s, and the average annual growth rate in economy-wide productivity was 0.65 percent. This mainly reflects the negative within component growth of Nigeria and South Africa in the 2010s, which accounted for 34.5 percent of employment and 59.0 percent of value-added production in the region in 2018.

4.3 SECTORAL ANALYSIS

To examine the differences in how each sector contributed to economy-wide productivity growth, the first and second terms of the right side of equation (4) in section 4.1.2 are applied to each sector to identify the sectoral within and structural change contributions to overall productivity growth. Figure 9.4 gives the simple average of eighteen sub-Saharan African countries for the decomposition of sectoral within and structural change contributions to economy-wide productivity.[3] The combined sum of within and structural change contributions is the sectoral net contribution to economy-wide productivity.

The net contribution (the sum of within and structural change contributions) of the agriculture to annual economy-wide productivity growth

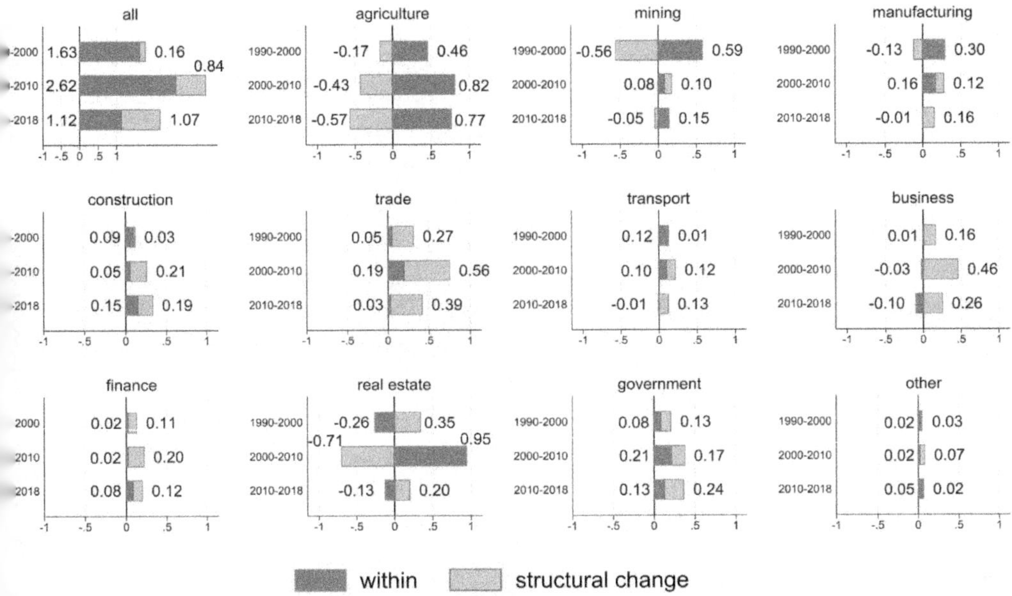

Figure 9.4 Decomposition of sectoral contribution to annual economy-wide productivity growth in sub-Saharan Africa (simple average)

Source: Author's calculations using data from the Economic Transformation Database.

Note: The utilities sector is not included in the figure for simplicity of presentation.

in each decade is 0.29 percent (1990s), 0.39 percent (2000s), and 0.20 percent (2010s). As seen in figure 9.4, agriculture is the largest contributor to the within component of the overall growth in the 2000s and the 2010s. It is partially offset by the negative structural change contribution in each decade because of the decline of the agricultural employment share. Given that the level of the agricultural labor productivity is the lowest, the fall of its employment can be interpreted as labor reallocation to other sectors with higher productivity and therefore can be viewed positively. It should be also noted that productivity improvements in the agricultural sector have enabled its positive within contribution to reach a greater scale than the negative structural change contribution, and because its employment share has remained the largest, its net contribution to economy-wide productivity growth is still significant (the second largest net contribution in the 1990s and the 2010s, after trade services, and the third in the 2000s, after trade services and business services).

The manufacturing sector's net contribution has been limited to 0.17 percent (1990s), 0.28 percent (2000s), and 0.15 percent (2010s). The sector's employment shares have turned positive since the 2000s, making its structural change contribution positive in the 2000s and 2010s. The sector's labor productivity declined in the 2010s, and its within sector contribution became negative in the most recent decade.

The trade services sector has made the largest net contribution to the economy-wide productivity growth of the region: 0.32 percent (1990s), 0.76 percent (2000s), and 0.42 percent (2010s). The main contribution comes from structural change, indicating that the sector absorbed nonagricultural employment at the highest rate during each decade. The within contribution of the sector remained positive for all the decades studied. The labor productivity growth of the sector is limited, but at least it has not fallen, while absorbing additional labor significantly. This fact can be viewed slightly more positively than the situation outlined in previous literature on African structural transformation, which often describes the nontradable service sector as a poorly performing one.

The business services sector's net contribution is 0.17 percent (1990s), 0.43 percent (2000s), and 0.15 percent (2010s). The financial services sector's net contribution is 0.13 percent (1990s), 0.22 percent (2000s) and 0.20 percent (2010s). These positive net contributions come mainly from structural change. This suggests that these two sectors increased their employment shares, which is encouraging, although the absolute level of employment shares is not yet substantial. Because the level of labor productivity of these sectors is much higher than that of traditional services sectors such as trade services, even a slight increase in their employment share makes a notable contribution to economy-wide productivity growth. The structural change contribution of both the business and trade sectors outweighed that of the manufacturing sector throughout the periods under review. Their within contributions were limited and even negative in the business services sector in the 2000s and 2010s.

The real estate sector recorded an unusually high positive within contribution (0.95 percent) and negative structural change contribution (–0.71 percent) in the 2000s. They offset each other, and the net contribution to economy-wide productivity growth is small (0.15 percent). But they nonetheless affect the composition of the total within and structural change contribution in all the sectors, making the former contribution bigger and the latter smaller. It should be noted that the decomposition methodology used in this analysis does not necessarily fit the characteristics of the real estate sector, which is therefore not the primary subject of this study. The sector's performance largely depends on the value and availability of transactions. It is not a labor-intensive industry, and its employment share is extremely low. As a result, the productivity level defined as value-added per worker is extremely high and can fluctuate substantially with a small change in the number of workers in the sector, with the within and structural contributions often offsetting each other.

The pattern of labor productivity change in the average sub-Saharan African country discussed so far contrasts sharply with that in Asia. For reference, figure 9.5 presents the average sectoral contributions to the economy-wide productivity growth of the fourteen Asian countries grouped as developing Asia in the ETD. The Asian productivity growth outpaced that of sub-Saharan Africa in every decade. The contribution of the manufacturing sector is much higher in Asia, with a strong within contribution in addition to the structural change contribution. Another notable fact is that both within and structural contributions are positive in Asia for all the sectors, except agriculture and real estate.

The next sections describe sectoral performance in relation to overall productivity, considering the heterogeneity across the countries.

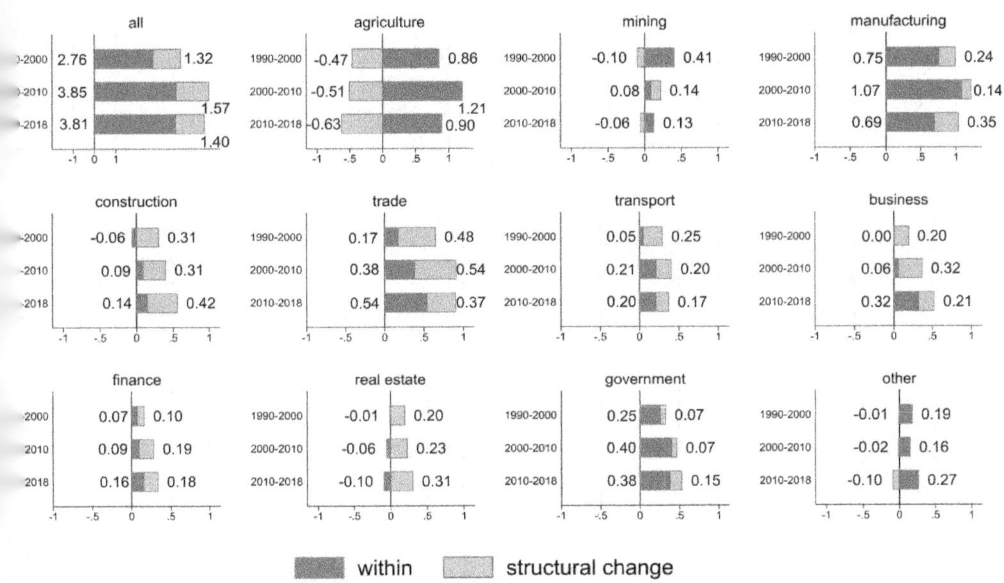

Figure 9.5 Decomposition of sectoral contribution to annual economy-wide productivity growth in developing Asia (simple average)

Source: Author's calculations using data from the Economic Transformation Database.

Note: The utilities sector is not included in the figure for simplicity of presentation.

Figure 9.6 plots the contribution of sectoral productivity growth to the economy-wide productivity growth in each country of sub-Saharan Africa. The sectoral contribution over the three decades (1990–2000, 2000–2010, and 2010–2018) are plotted indifferently to allow examination of sectoral characteristics across the periods. Figure 9.6 also draws fitted lines from the linear regression of within contributions on structural change" contributions.

Most of the dots in agriculture are on the left side of the *y*-axis, indicating that agricultural employment share declined for most of the countries across these decades. This negative structural change contribution was often associated with higher degrees of positive within contributions. Labor moving out of agriculture would lead, by itself, to improved labor productivity in the sector, particularly when the sector had been experiencing excess labor. The steep slope of the fitted line shows, however, that the sector's productivity level improved at a faster pace than that of the labor shift to nonagricultural sectors, which can be interpreted to mean that other factors, such as technological advancement, also contributed to

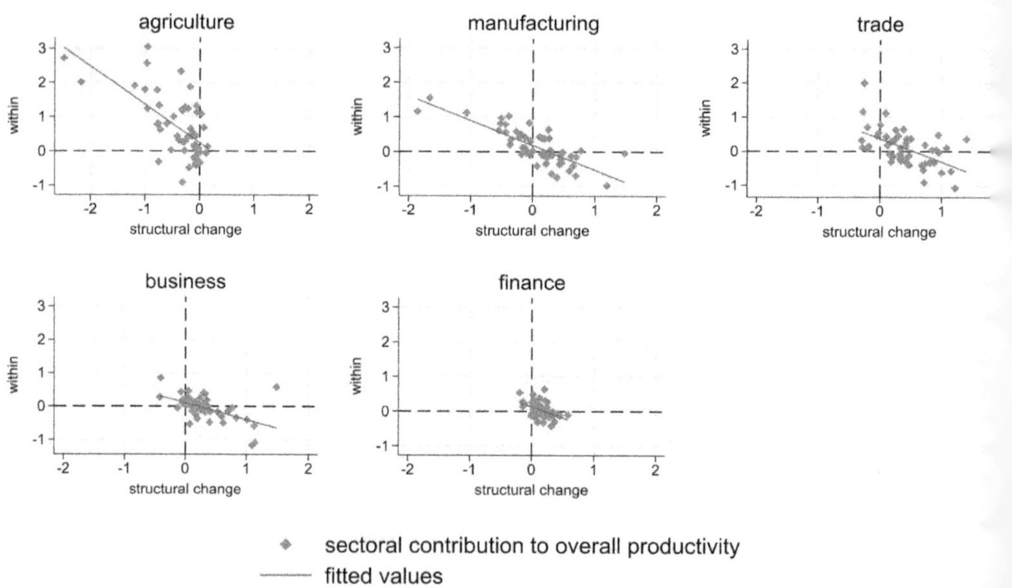

Figure 9.6 Contribution to overall productivity growth by sectors, "within" and "structural change" contributions

Source: Author's calculations using data from the Economic Transformation Database.

productivity growth in this sector. Blanco and Raurich (2022) argue that the increase in capital intensity in agriculture throughout the development process contributes to explaining the increase in agricultural labor productivity relative to nonagricultural productivity.

In the manufacturing sector across the region, the structural change contribution to overall productivity varied widely from negative to positive, depending on the country and the period. The result of the negative correlations between within and structural change contributions is straightforward. Most of the dots in the manufacturing contribution are either in quadrant 2 or 4 of figure 9.6, with few cases in quadrant 1. This means that positive labor productivity growth and employment share increases in the manufacturing sector rarely happened at the same time in sub-Saharan Africa. As discussed in Kruse et al. (2023), the share of manufacturing employment in sub-Saharan Africa did show an increasing trend since the 2000s. Manufacturing productivity on average, however, has not been associated with this trend; in fact, it has often deteriorated. Therefore, one cannot simply make a positive assessment of the increase in manufacturing employment in sub-Saharan Africa. Kruse et al. (2023) also argue that the employment increase is observed in small, unregistered firms but that their output share declines, while the employment share in registered firms declines but their output share increases. This seems to resonate with the findings of Diao et al. (2025), who argue that there is polarization among African manufacturing firms between large, capital-intensive, and productive firms without much contribution to employment creation, and small firms that absorb employment but do not increase their productivity.

In the trade services sector, the structural change contribution is positive in most cases, indicating that the sector's employment share is increasing. Among those positive structural change contributors, the within contributions are split into positive and negative with almost equal frequency. A possible explanation is that the movement of labor to the nontradable sector does not correlate with the productivity level of that sector. This would be the argument of Gollin et al. (2015), Diao et al. (2019), and Atolia et al. (2020). Urban income growth through resource exports and public expenditure expansion will therefore increase the demand for the consumption of nontradable goods and encourage the labor shift to such sectors without improving the industry's productivity.

For business and financial services, which generally represent tradable and high-productivity services, the dots are on the right side of the *y*-axis in figure 9.6, and the structural change contributions are positive. This means that these sectors are increasing their employment share. Such a structural change contribution is often associated with negative within contributions, which is similar to the performance of the manufacturing sector in sub-Saharan Africa.

4.4 COUNTRY ANALYSIS

The heterogeneity across sub-Saharan African economies can be analyzed by comparing the performance of selected countries, namely, Nigeria, Senegal, Ethiopia, and Uganda. This is not meant to make a clear and rigorous typology of African growth but rather to illustrate the dynamics that vary from country to country. Figure 9.7 shows the agricultural employment share and gross domestic product (GDP) per capita of the four countries in 1990, 2000, 2010, and 2018, enabling a comparison of the development level of these countries and the state of economic transformation from an agriculture-centered economy. Nigeria and Senegal were lower-middle-income countries in 2018; Ethiopia and Uganda were low-income countries. Nigeria increased its GDP per capita by over $900, from $1,451 in 1990 to $2,512 in 2018, while the increase in

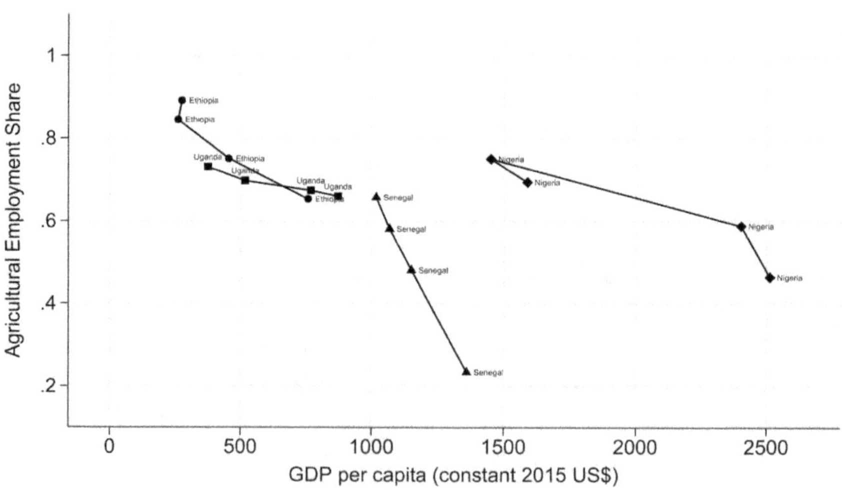

Figure 9.7 Agricultural employment share and gross domestic product (GDP) per capita of selected countries in 1990, 2000, 2010, and 2018

Source: Author's calculations using data from the Economic Transformation Database.

Senegal's GDP per capita was more limited, around $340 (from $1,016 in 1990 to $1,360 in 2018). Senegal is characterized by a large decline in the agricultural employment share, which dropped by over 40 percentage points in the ETD data.[4] During the same period, Ethiopia and Uganda started with a similar level of GDP per capita, but the pace of decline in agricultural employment share has been greater in Ethiopia and that of Uganda has been limited.

NIGERIA

Figure 9.8 shows the decomposition of sectoral contributions to the annual economy-wide productivity growth of Nigeria. The country recorded a strong overall productivity growth in the 2000s (6.07 percent), but the growth turned negative in the 2010s (-0.72 percent). Most of the within contribution in the 2000s came from the agricultural sector; the structural change contributions were mainly from trade and

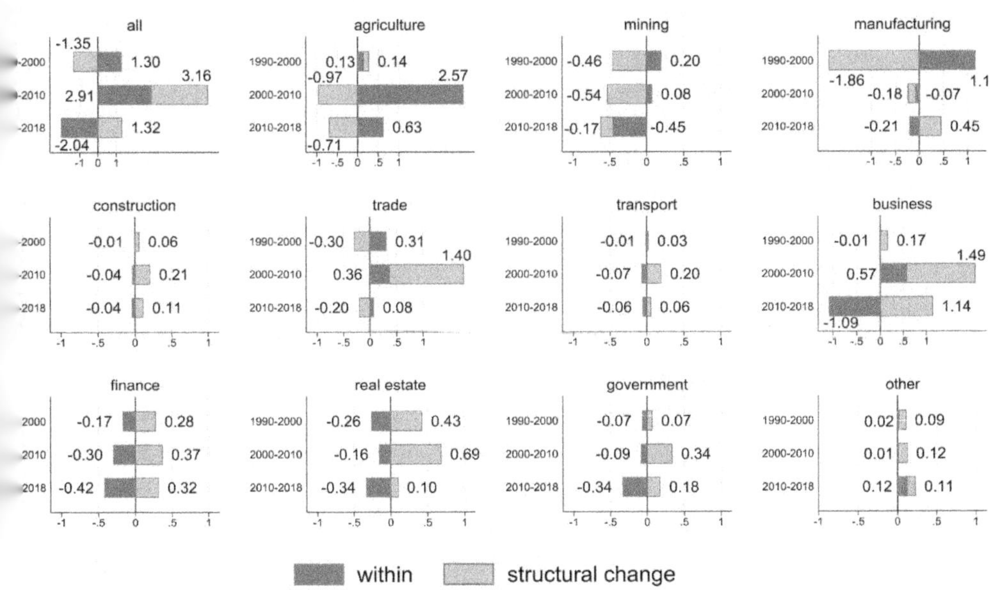

Figure 9.8 Decomposition of sectoral contribution to annual economy-wide productivity growth in Nigeria

Source: Author's calculations using data from the Economic Transformation Database.

Note: The utilities sector is not included in the figure for simplicity of presentation.

business services that expanded their employment shares in the 2000s. In the 2010s, the within growth of business and financial services was negative, which led to negative overall productivity growth during the decade. After recording significantly negative net contribution in the 1990s (–0.7 percent), the contribution of manufacturing to overall productivity growth was modest after 2000. In the 2010s, the manufacturing employment share increased but was offset by the negative within contribution.

It is an alarming sign that a country like Nigeria, a lower-middle-income country whose economic level is ahead of many other African countries, is facing negative productivity growth in multiple sectors during the expansion of the nonagricultural parts of its economy.

SENEGAL

Annual average productivity growth in Senegal has ranged from 0.53 percent (1990s) to 1.82 percent (2000s), to 0.25 percent (2010s). While the decline in agriculture's employment share has been substantial, as seen in figure 9.9, the economy-wide productivity growth has been modest in each decade in Senegal. The employment share has increased in the manufacturing sector as well as in the traditional services sector (trading services) and the modern services sector (business services), but their structural change contribution is offset by its own negative within contribution to overall productivity. As Senegal's employment data on the real estate sector is missing until 2005, its contribution to overall productivity growth cannot be calculated.

ETHIOPIA

As in figure 9.10, Ethiopia's economy-wide productivity growth was 0.18 percent (1990s), 6.07 percent (2000s), and 7.36 percent (2010s). The country recorded strong productivity growth in the 2000s and the pace accelerated in the 2010s, in contrast with the average performance of sub-Saharan African countries. The strong within contribution to economy-wide productivity growth came from the agricultural sector in the 2000s and from both the agricultural and trade sectors in the 2010s. Another notable fact about the Ethiopian structural transformation is that both within and structural change contributions of the manufacturing sector in the 2010s became positive, resulting in a net contribution of 0.66 percent from the sector. Ethiopia's manufacturing performance in the 2010s was

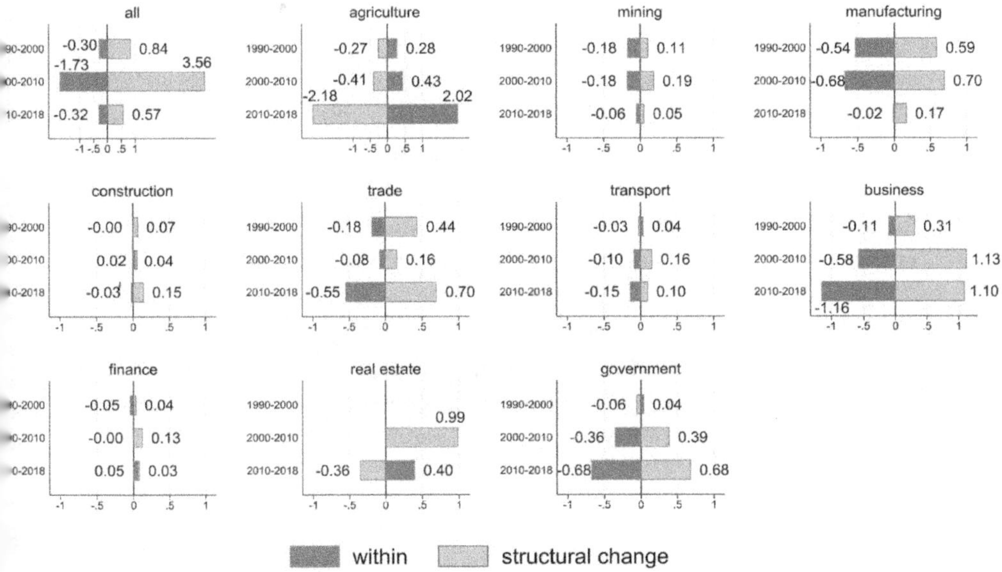

Figure 9.9 Decomposition of sectoral contribution to annual economy-wide productivity growth in Senegal

Note: The utilities sector is not included in the figure for simplicity of presentation.

Source: Author's calculations using data from the Economic Transformation Database.

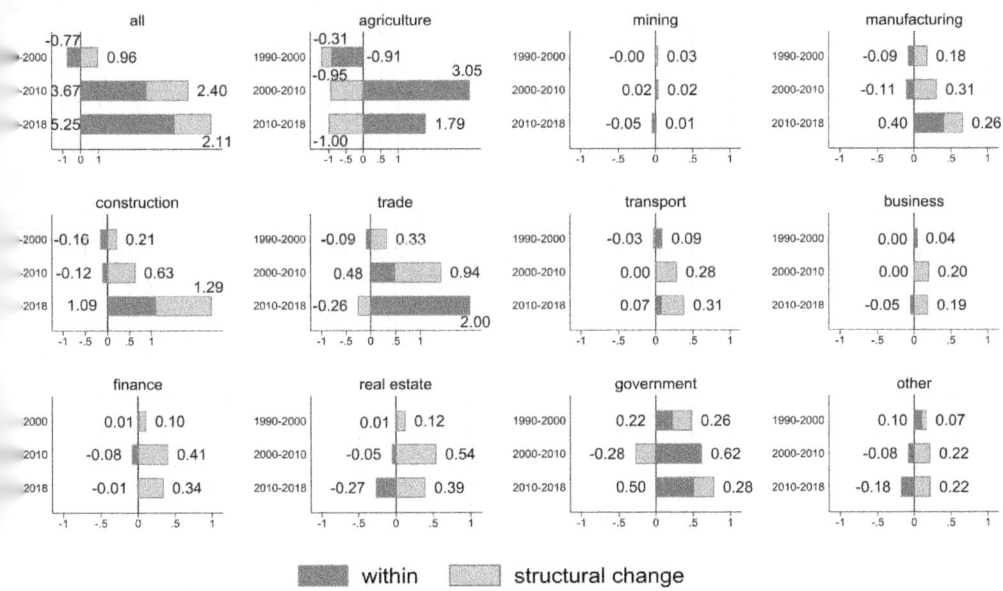

Figure 9.10 Decomposition of sectoral contribution to economy-wide productivity growth (simple average) in Ethiopia

Note: The utilities sector is not included in the figure for simplicity of presentation.

Source: Author's calculations using data from the Economic Transformation Database.

encouraging when many other countries in the region experienced negative productivity growth during the decade. This observation may require further scrutiny, however, because the analysis using Ethiopian firm data (Diao et al. 2020) provides a more reserved view. The within and structural change contributions in the construction and government sectors in the 2010s are also both positive, making the net contributions of the two sectors significant. This fact also requires careful interpretation. It is argued that the government contributed a large portion of investment in the country in the 2010s. If the contributions of the construction and government sectors are merely the results of this government-led investment, they must also be questioned in terms of fiscal sustainability.

UGANDA

In Uganda, economy-wide annual labor productivity was 4.26 percent in the 1990s, 4.76 percent in the 2000s, and then dropped significantly to 0.01 percent in the 2010s as seen in figure 9.11. The country's agricultural

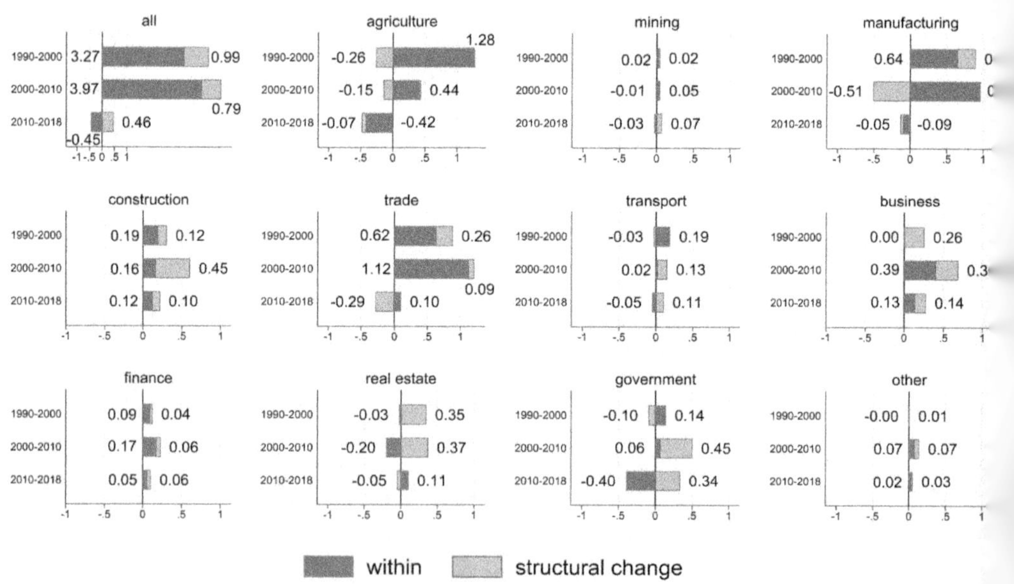

Figure 9.11 Decomposition of sectoral contribution to economy-wide productivity growth (simple average) in Uganda

Note: The utilities sector is not included in the figure for simplicity of presentation.

Source: Author's calculations using data from the Economic Transformation Database.

employment share did not diminish much in these three decades, which makes the country's growth pattern different from the other countries. Agricultural productivity growth slowed down, however, and turned negative in the 2010s. Economy-wide productivity growth in the 2000s was mainly driven by net contributions from the trade and business services sectors. Since the 2010s, the contributions of these sectors seem to have stagnated.

5. DISCUSSION

The findings from the analysis so far in this chapter are as follows. The economy-wide productivity growth slowed down in sub-Saharan Africa during the 2010s. The share of agricultural employment has continued to decline, but the sector is still the largest contributor to overall employment growth. Agricultural productivity has improved and has often made a large contribution to economy-wide productivity growth, given the sector's still significant employment share.

The manufacturing sector increased its employment share, on average, in the region after the 2000s, contradicting the oft-referenced argument linking lower manufacturing employment with deindustrialization, but labor productivity and its within contribution to economy-wide productivity growth became negative in the 2010s. Negative associations between within and structural change contributions to overall productivity are often observed in the manufacturing sector, and also at the individual country level in the region. This may relate to the argument of Diao et al. (2025), which suggests the polarization of African manufacturing firms between large, capital-intensive, and productive firms that do not contribute much to employment creation, and small firms that absorb employment, without showing much improvement in productivity. A similar trend (employment share growth with limited or negative labor productivity growth) is observed, on average, in the business services sector across the region, and in the financial services sector in some countries in the 2010s. These observations contrast with the productivity improvement that always accompanies the increase in employment share in the same nonagricultural sectors of developing Asian countries. Trends such as the penetration of information technology in the 2010s in the African region do not seem to lead to productivity improvement in these sectors. The trade services sector, which traditionally covers nontradable services such as wholesale, retail, and food and restaurants, maintained its labor productivity level, albeit barely, while absorbing the largest share of nonagricultural employment.

The heterogeneity of the performance in employment and labor productivity across sectors in sub-Saharan Africa seems to indicate the effectiveness of pursuing balanced policy interventions across multiple sectors rather than expecting a specific sector to lead, as is the case for manufacturing in Asia. For example, in many countries of the region where agriculture continues to be the dominant source of employment, even if its share is declining, policy efforts to raise labor productivity in the agricultural sector are highly conducive to economy-wide productivity growth. It is encouraging to see that traditional nontradable services industries are at least maintaining their productivity levels. The introduction of digital technologies and the strengthening of their value chains with other industries could contribute to productivity gains in the sector. While weak labor productivity growth in manufacturing and business services is a concern, the increase in employment share is a hopeful development. It would be worthwhile to consider policies to support these firms with high job creation and facilitate their investment in productivity-enhancing technology and human capital. At the economy-wide level, it may be more useful to pursue unique business opportunities that encompass multiple sectors, such as tourism, and a transition from traditional to modern agriculture that involves more service and manufacturing components.

This study has analytical limitations because it does not use detailed data on firm-level operations or country-level specific conditions. When this chapter has identified characteristics and trends in employment and productivity performance in the region, it would be useful to supplement these with more detailed country and firm data for policy discussion. In addition, the data analyzed in this chapter does not cover the period since the COVID-19 crisis. The pandemic has, of course, affected the way people work and consume, and changes in resource allocation across sectors may have taken place, such as a demand shift from in-person services to digital solutions (International Monetary Fund [IMF] 2021). However, the form and magnitude of the impact of these changes on the structural transformation of the African economy need to be carefully monitored in separate studies.

6. CONCLUSION

This chapter provides an updated analysis of structural changes in employment and labor productivity in sub-Saharan Africa, a region that is expected to experience significant labor force growth in the future. Expanding on the standard shift-share decomposition of labor productivity growth, the chapter also presents a detailed examination of sectoral performance, including various forms of the services sector and their impact on economy-wide labor productivity. On average, labor productivity growth in sub-Saharan Africa weakened in the 2010s compared to the previous decade. Nevertheless, while the employment share in the agricultural sector continues to decline, the sector still creates the largest number of jobs, and its improvement in sectoral labor productivity contributes to economy-wide labor productivity growth. Contradicting the argument associating deindustrialization with a decline in manufacturing employment, the employment share in manufacturing increased after 2000, but its sectoral labor productivity declined in the 2010s. Negative associations between employment share growth and labor productivity decline are also observed in tradable services such as business services and finance. It is worrisome to see such relationships in sectors like manufacturing and tradable services that could potentially drive the economy and provide quality jobs. Nontradable service sectors such as retail, wholesale, food, and restaurants absorb the largest number of nonagricultural workers. The level of labor productivity in the nontradable services sectors has been low but not necessarily declining.

Topics for future discussion and research thus would include supplemental analysis with more detailed country and firm data to examine further the relations between employment share growth and negative productivity growth recently observed in sub-Saharan African nonagricultural sectors and to consider productivity enhancement measures in both agricultural and nonagricultural sectors. A further update of structural change in employment and productivity considering the impact of the COVID-19 crisis would also be important.

NOTES

1. Note that careful interpretation is necessary when comparing average labor productivity across sectors. When competition is at work, what determines labor mobility between sectors is the marginal productivity of labor. The labor contribution to the value-added production of a sector also varies widely from sector to sector. For example, the relative productivity per labor is extremely high in table 9.4, but the performance of the sector depends much more on the availability and price of land transaction than on the number of workers. As shown in table 9.3, the employment share in the real estate sector is very low, ranging from 0.1 to 0.2 percent. The sector is not significant in the discussion of African employment, but it continues to be included in the analysis.

2. The annual growth rates are simple yearly averages of each decade and not a compounded annual growth rate, so that the total annual productivity growth is the sum of the annual "within" and "structural change" components.

3. The utilities sector is not included in the table for simplicity of presentation. The sector is not the focus of this chapter, and its contribution to employment and productivity growth is negligible in the context of the chapter.

4. Note that agricultural employment share figures derived from the Economic Transformation Database (ETD) do not always match those from other data sources. In the International Labour Organization (ILO) estimate, the share of agriculture in Senegal was 48.9 percent in 1991 and 30.8 percent in 2018, and the pace of the decline more modest.

REFERENCES

Abdychev, Aidar, Cristian Alonso, Emre Alper, et al. 2018. *The Future of Work in Sub-Saharan Africa.* International Monetary Fund, African Department.

Atolia, Manoj, Prakash Loungani, Milton Marquis, and Chris Papageorgiou. 2020. "Rethinking Development Policy: What Remains of Structural Transformation?" *World Development* 128: 104834.

Baccini, Leonardo, Matteo Fiorini, Bernard Hoekman, and Marco Sanfilippo. 2021. *Services, Jobs, and Economic Development in Africa.* EUI-RSC Working Paper 2021/82, Global Governance Programme—455. European University Institute, International Growth Centre.

Blanco, Cesar, and Xavier Raurich. 2022. "Agricultural Composition and Labor Productivity." *Journal of Development Economics,* 158: 102934.

Coulibaly, Brahima S., and John Page. 2021. "Addressing Youth Unemployment in Africa Through Industries Without Smokestacks: A Synthesis on Prospects, Constraints, and Policies." African Growth Initiative at Brookings, AGI Working Paper No. 36. Brookings Institution.

de Vries, Gaaitzen, Linda Arfelt, Dorothea Drees, et al. 2021. *The Economic Transformation Database: Content, Sources, and Methods.* UNU-WIDER. https://www.wider.unu.edu/node/238261

de Vries, Gaaitzen, Marcel Timmer, and Klaas de Vries. 2015. "Structural Transformation in Africa: Static Gains, Dynamic Losses." *Journal of Development Studies* 51 (6): 674–88.

Diao, Xinshen, Margaret McMillan, and Dani Rodrik. 2019. "The Recent Growth Boom in Developing Economies: A Structural-Change Perspective." In *The Palgrave Handbook of Development Economics,* edited by Machiko Nissanke and José Antonio Ocampo. Springer International.

Diao, Xinshen, Mia Ellis, Margaret McMillan, and Dani Rodrik. 2025. "Africa's Manufacturing Puzzle: Evidence from Tanzanian and Ethiopian Firms." *The World Bank Economic Review,* 39(2): 308–340

Felipe, Jesus, and Aashish Mehta. 2016. "Deindustrialization?: A Global Perspective." *Economics Letters* 149: 148–51.

Fox, Louise, Alun H. Thomas, and Cleary Haines. 2017. "Structural Transformation in Employment and Productivity: What Can Africa Hope For?" Department Paper No. 2017/002. International Monetary Fund.

Ghani, Ejaz, and Stephen D. O'Connell. 2014. *Can Service Be a Growth Escalator in Low Income Countries?* Policy Research Working Paper 6971. World Bank.

Gollin, Douglas, Remi Jedwab, and Dietrich Vollrath. 2015. "Urbanization with and without industrialization." *Journal of Economic Growth*, 21(1), 35-70

Herrendorf, Berthold, Richard Rogerson, and Ákos Valentinyi. 2014. "Growth and Structural Transformation." In *Handbook of Economic Growth*, edited by Philippe Aghion and Steven N. Durlauf. Elsevier.

Herrendorf, Berthold, Richard Rogerson, and Ákos Valentinyi. 2022. "New Evidence on Sectoral Labor Productivity: Implications for Industrialization and Development." NBER Working Paper 29834. https://doi.org/10.3386/w29834.

Hjort, Jonas, and Jonas Poulsen. 2019. "The Arrival of Fast Internet and Employment in Africa." *American Economic Review* 109 (3): 1032–79.

International Monetary Fund (IMF). 2021. "Boosting Productivity in the Aftermath of COVID-19." G-20 Background Note. International Monetary Fund.

Islam, Rizwanul. 2004. "The Nexus of Economic Growth, Employment and Poverty Reduction: An Empirical Analysis." Issues in Employment and Poverty Discussion Paper 14. International Labour Office, Recovery and Reconstruction Department.

Kapsos, Steven. 2005. "The Employment Intensity of Growth: Trends and Macroeconomic Determinants." Employment Strategy Papers 12. ILO. https://doi.org/10.1057/9780230627383_4.

Kruse, Hagen, Emmanuel Mensah, Kunal Sen, and Gaaitzen de Vries. 2023. "A Manufacturing (Re)naissance? Industrialization in the Developing World." United Nations University, UNU-WIDER. 71:439–473.

McMillan, Margaret, Dani Rodrik, and Íñigo Verduzco-Gallo. 2014. "Globalization, Structural Change, and Productivity Growth, with an Update on Africa." *World Development*, 63: 11–32.

McMillan, Margaret, and Albert Zeufack. 2022. "Labor Productivity Growth and Industrialization in Africa." *Journal of Economic Perspectives* 36 (1): 3–32.

Mensah, Emmanuel, Solomon Owusu, Neil Foster-McGregor, and Adam Szirmai. 2022. "Structural Change, Productivity Growth and Labour Market Turbulence in Sub-Saharan Africa." *Journal of African Economies* 32 (3): 1–38.

Nayyar, Gaurav, Mary Hallward-Driemeier, and Elwyn Davies. 2021. *At Your Service? The Promise of Services-Led Development.* World Bank.

Rodrik, Dani. 2016. "Premature Deindustrialization." *Journal of Economic Growth* 21 (2): 1–33.

United Nations. 2008. *System of National Accounts, 2008.* European Communities, International Monetary Fund, Organisation for Economic Co-operation and Development, United Nations, and World Bank. https://unstats.un.org/unsd/nationalaccount/docs/sna2008.pdf.

United Nations, Department of Economic and Social Affairs, Population Division. 2022. *World Population Prospects.* https://www.un.org/development/desa/pd/sites/www.un.org.development.desa.pd/files/wpp2022_summary_of_results.pdf

CHAPTER 10

Automation and Deindustrialization in the South African Manufacturing Sector

Caitlin Allen Whitehead,[1] Haroon Bhorat,[2] Robert Hill,[3] Timothy Köhler,[4] and François Steenkamp[5]

Abstract: In this chapter we examine the potential employment displacement effects of technologies related to the Fourth Industrial Revolution on the South African manufacturing sector, by observing this risk through the lens of the task-content of occupations or the routinisation hypothesis. We use network analytics to develop a manufacturing sector occupation space, which shows the occupational structure of the manufacturing sector labour force. Given the occupational structure of the sector, we identify occupations at high risk of displacement—occupations that are most at risk of being automated, computerised or digitised. Drawing on household survey data, we explore the characteristics of workers who occupy these high-risk occupations in an attempt at identifying a typology of individuals most likely to be deleteriously impacted on by these technologies. Three implications emerge: First, technology induced employment displacement is likely to jeopardise low- to medium-skill employment in the production cluster occupations, and correspondingly result in an increase in relative demand for semi- and high-skilled non-production cluster occupations. Second, the non-random distribution of high-risk occupations across the two clusters of the occupation space suggests that the skill transition to shift workers from high- to low-risk occupations is long, and in the event of substantial uptake of employment displacing technologies across the sector, technological unemployment is that much harder to mitigate. Third, the relatively high employment share associated with high-risk occupations in the production cluster indicates that the potential displacement effects resulting in technological unemployment are likely to be substantial.

JEL codes: O13; O14; O25.

Keywords: automation, employment, manufacturing, fourth industrial revolution, task content of occupations, technology; South Africa

1. INTRODUCTION AND BACKGROUND

For several centuries, the notion that "robots are coming to take our jobs" has raised fears of the displacement of workers. In 1589, Queen Elizabeth I refused to grant inventor William Lee a patent for his automated knitting machine invention because it would "ruin [my subjects] by depriving them of employment." In the early 1800s, a group of English textile artisans attempted to destroy machinery in protest of the automation of textile production (Autor 2015; Frey and Osborne 2017). In fact, the word *robot* originates from *robota*—the Slavic-language word for "work"—created by Czech writer Karel Čapek to make the purpose of machines clear. Although the principle of automation (for a machine to complete a task, a programmer must first fully understand how to perform it, then write an appropriate program so the machine can do it) has not changed throughout modern history, the cost has changed significantly. Between 1850 and 2006, the real cost of performing a standardized set of computational tasks is estimated to have fallen by at least 1.7 *trillion* fold, with most of this reduction occurring within the last thirty years (Nordhaus, 2007). These significantly lower prices have caused fears of automation regaining prominence today in response to the fourth industrial revolution because they create simple but powerful incentives for employers to substitute their relatively expensive workers with computer capital.

Technology is thus reshaping the skills needed for work. However, given that different jobs require different sets of skills, jobs face varying degrees of automation risk. As such, the labor market effects of technology are believed to be distributed unevenly across workers of varying skill sets. The dominant theory—referred to as skill-biased technological change (SBTC)—proposes that, in the last few decades, technological development has increased the demand for high-skilled workers at a rate far greater than the increase in the supply of high-skilled workers, resulting in higher returns to high-skilled jobs and in turn to higher wages. In other words, technology is biased in favor of high-skilled workers at the expense of less-skilled workers. A large body of empirical literature now exists that supports this theory, leading it to be argued as a primary cause of rising wage inequality in many countries (Acemoglu and Autor 2011; Autor and Dorn 2013).

But economists have also found that this increase in the demand for high-skilled workers (who tend to earn *high* wages) has actually been accompanied by an increase in the demand for less-skilled workers (who tend to earn *low* wages), while demand for those in the *middle* of the wage distribution has stagnated or declined. Such polarization does not align with the predictions of the SBTC theory, but it does align with an alternative theory that distinguishes between skills (an endowment of capabilities for performing tasks) and tasks (an activity that produces output). Autor et al.'s (2003) routinization hypothesis proposes that technological development has concurrently decreased the demand for workers with routine job task content (tasks that follow explicit rules that can be accomplished by machines and are thus substitutable for technology) and increased the demand for workers with nonroutine job task content (tasks that are not sufficiently well understood to be specified in computer code and are thus complementary to technology). Routine jobs tend to be concentrated in the *middle* of the wage distribution, while nonroutine jobs tend to be concentrated at the *bottom* (and they tend to be more manual in nature while requiring situational adaptability, such as truck driving through traffic or janitorial work) and at the *top* (and they tend to be more cognitive in nature and include several professional and managerial occupations). The evidence globally largely supports this theory, with many empirical studies highlighting a relative rise in routine-intensive employment and fall in nonroutine employment from the 1980s onward (Autor et al. 2003; Goos and Manning 2007; Acemoglu and Autor 2011; Autor, 2015; Frey and Osborne 2017; Lo Bello et al. 2019; Lewandowski et al. 2019, 2020).

The labor market effects of technology may be felt more severely, however, in developing countries. There is evidence of a negative correlation between the routine-intensity of jobs and levels of economic development; in other words, poorer countries tend to have a greater share of routine jobs (Aedo et al. 2013; Lo Bello et al. 2019; Lewandowski et al. 2020). This is not necessarily unexpected, considering labor markets in developing countries are generally very different compared to those in developed countries in terms of their sectoral and occupational compositions. Since the late eighteenth century, developing country labor markets have largely relied on manufacturing as a central driver for economic development. Because routine jobs tend to be concentrated in manufacturing, many developing countries are faced with a significant risk of automation-induced job loss. South Africa is not excluded from this narrative. Since the 1980s, the country has arguably shown several signs of ongoing premature deindustrialization considering its lower-than-expected manufacturing employment share and given its level of economic development, combined with a significant fall in this share over time (Andreoni and Tregenna 2021). Premature deindustrialization is a key factor locking many middle-income countries in a trap of stagnant growth—a trap from which it may be more and more difficult to escape when also faced with routine-intense jobs in the sector. If South Africa wishes to escape this trap, automation risk, as a potentially binding constraint to manufacturing-led growth, needs to be addressed.

In our analysis in this chapter, we analyze the potential employment displacement effects of technologies related to automation in the manufacturing sector of a semi-industrialized developing economy, South Africa. We do so through the lens of the task content of occupations in the labor market, following Autor et al. (2003) and the subsequent literature. First, through the application of network analytics, we examine the occupational structure of the manufacturing sector labor market. Second, given this occupational structure, additional measures of task content are used to identify which manufacturing sector occupations are at high risk of employment displacement effects. Third, by drawing on representative household survey data, we explore the characteristics of workers who occupy these high-risk occupations in an attempt to identify a typology of individuals most likely to be deleteriously affected by these technologies. By doing so, we provide a quantitative description of the distribution of automation risk within South Africa's manufacturing sector, which can be used by policymakers to target relevant and appropriate interventions.

2. METHODOLOGY

In this section, we discuss the methodologies used to construct the occupation space, which gives us a sense of the occupational structure of the manufacturing sector labor market in South Africa, as well as the method used to compute the routine task indexes (RTIs), which are used to identify the occupations that are at high risk of employment displacement effects arising from automation and other fourth industrial revolution (4IR) technologies.

2.1 OCCUPATIONAL RELATEDNESS AND THE OCCUPATION SPACE: DEPICTING THE OCCUPATIONAL STRUCTURE OF THE MANUFACTURING SECTOR LABOR MARKET

We use the concept of occupational relatedness and network analytics to depict the occupational structure of the labor market serving South Africa's manufacturing sector. To generate occupational relatedness indexes, we follow the method applied by Mealy et al. (2018).[6] Using data on the task content of occupations, we measure the relatedness between occupations, with occupations being deemed closely related if they have a large overlap in tasks, whereas unrelated occupations have few overlapping tasks. By calculating the degree of relatedness between occupations, we can depict the occupational structure of the manufacturing sector labor market using a network mapping called the occupational space.

The strength of this approach to viewing the occupational structure of the manufacturing sector lies in its ability to depict the relationships between occupations in a single snapshot, which in turn enables one to view clearly the connections between occupations in a way that is intuitive. In identifying prominent clusters of occupations within these networks, it is possible to gain insight into how work trends, such as risk of automation, are spread among occupations in the manufacturing sector. For instance, we superimpose an occupation level measure of routine task intensity (detailed in section 4.2) onto the occupation space and thus obtain a graphical depiction of the extent to which the risk of automation is spread across the manufacturing sector labor market.

The relatedness between occupations, which determines the structure of the occupation space, is calculated by generating occupation-by-occupation pair proximity measures. Our proximity measure is a continuous measure derived from data on both the level and importance of each task to each occupation—an average importance score.[7] To ensure that only tasks that are relatively important for a given occupation are used to generate proximity measures for the occupation-by-occupation matrix, we use a modified version of what Mealy et al. (2018) call the Relative Importance Indicator (RII). The RII, akin to Balassa's (1965) revealed comparative advantage (RCA) index, can be interpreted as the importance of a task for a given occupation relative to its overall importance for all occupations. Only tasks for which the RII is ≥ 1 are considered because these are flagged as being relatively important for a given occupation.[8] The relatedness between occupations is based on the proximity measure, which calculates the pairwise conditional probability of two occupations performing the same tasks. With this information, proximity measures are calculated for each pair of occupations and transformed into a proximity matrix. This collection of all proximities forms the basis for building the manufacturing sector occupation space. To build the occupational space network analysis is applied to the symmetric proximity matrix. The result is a set of *x*- and *y*-coordinates that are used to plot the occupational space network map. The formalization of the RII, the calculation of the proximity between occupations, and the approach to building an occupation space for the manufacturing sector in South Africa can be found in Allen Whitehead et al. (2021).

The interpretation of the occupational space network map is as follows: each node represents an occupation, with the lines connecting them, or edges, representing the degree of commonality in tasks between the pair of connected occupations.[9] Shorter lines indicate greater proximity in tasks. The size of the nodes is derived from the employment share of each respective occupation within the manufacturing sector. Nodes can be shaded according to occupation-level characteristics, such as the degree of risk to automation specific to a given occupation—the measure for which is discussed in the next subsection.

2.2 THE ROUTINE TASK INDEX (RTI)—MEASURING THE RISK OF EMPLOYMENT DISPLACEMENT

We generate an occupation-level routine task index (RTI) measure to capture an occupation's risk of suffering employment displacement effects driven by automation and other 4IR technologies. The RTI is based on the notion that tasks that are more routine in nature are more likely to be replicated by a machine, computerized, or digitized. Thus, occupations that are more routine in task content are at greater risk of employment displacement effects (Goos et al. 2014).

The RTI is constructed by bringing together four intermediate indicators that capture the task content of occupations. These include routine cognitive, routine manual, nonroutine cognitive analytical, and nonroutine cognitive personal task indicators. These intermediate indicators are formed by grouping measures present in the Occupational Information Network (O*NET) database—discussed in section 3.1—together according to definitions put forward by Acemoglu and Autor (2011). The measures range across a variety of tasks that could be affected by various 4IR technologies including, but not limited to, mechanization and automation.[10] For example, an occupation where the tasks of establishing and maintaining personal relationships and being creative are important is less likely to be digitized by technologies such as artificial intelligence (AI). Detailing of the approach used to bring together these measures from the Work Activities and Work Context data in O*NET can be found in Allen Whitehead et al (2021).

Our chosen RTI is based on the formulation put forward by Lewandowski et al. (2020), which we augment by drawing on Acemoglu and Autor (2011). The Lewandowski et al. (2020) formulation includes measures of the intermediate indicators controlling for routine cognitive, nonroutine cognitive analytical, and nonroutine cognitive personal tasks. However, given the importance of routine manual tasks in some of the more physical manufacturing occupations, and the potential for the exclusion of such tasks to mischaracterize the routineness of some occupations in the sector, we include a measure for routine manual tasks as defined by Acemoglu and Autor (2011). We define our RTI in the following way in equation (1):

$$RTI_i = \ln\left(\frac{r_{cognitive,i} + r_{manual,i}}{2}\right) - \ln\left(\frac{nr_{analytical,i} + nr_{personal,i}}{2}\right) \tag{1}$$

where $r_{cognitive,i}$, $r_{manual,i}$, $nr_{analytical,i}$ and $nr_{personal,i}$ are the level of routine cognitive, routine manual, non-routine cognitive analytical, and nonroutine cognitive personal tasks required for occupation *i*, respectively. The formulation of the RTI is then normalized to lie between 0 and 1, where a value of 0 indicates that a particular occupation is completely nonroutine, while a value of 1 indicates that an occupation is completely routine.

Following the method suggested by Lewandowski et al. (2020), we subdivide our RTI into three mutually exclusive categories in order to categorize an occupation's risk of displacement. Occupations with RTI values equal to or lower than the 25th percentile, between the 25th and 75th percentile (exclusive), and above the 75th percentile, of the RTI distribution, are classified as nonroutine, intermediate, and routine, respectively. Based on the routinization hypothesis, we can think of routine occupations as being at risk of displacement, while those that are nonroutine are at low risk of displacement. Those occupations classified as intermediate in their routineness are classified as intermediate in their risk of displacement.

3. DATA

The analysis draws on two data sets. First, occupation-level task content data is obtained from the O*NET data set. Second, labor market data on South Africa's manufacturing sector is taken from the Post-Apartheid Labour Market Series, Version 3.3.1 (PALMS v3.3.1) data set. This section discusses these data sets and how they are used in conjunction with one another.

3.1 O*NET DATA SET: TASK CONTENT DATA AT THE OCCUPATION LEVEL

O*NET data, as discussed in section 2.1, are used to compute measures of relatedness between occupations that are used to inform the network depiction of the occupational structure of the manufacturing sector labor market—the occupation space. As alluded to in section 2.2, these data are used to compute occupation-level RTIs that measure the potential risk of employment displacement driven by automation and other 4IR technologies.

The O*NET data set is drawn from a US survey of a comprehensive set of occupational descriptors based on labor market demands, such as work activities, abilities, and work context (O*NET 2020). Almost one thousand standardized occupations are included in the database, which is compiled based on input from a wide range of employees in each occupation, and moderated by a set of occupational analysts. The analysis in this section uses the O*NET 25.0 database from August 2020.

The O*NET occupation descriptors used in this analysis include work activities, abilities, and work context modules, with the work activities module containing data on tasks performed at the occupation level. While all three modules are used to compute the RTI, only work activities are used to measure occupational relatedness. Work activities are generalized statements based on the aggregation of a set of 19,450 detailed task statements. The analysis uses generalized work activities, which are comprised of forty-one unique work activities in the data, and include activities such as handling and moving objects; inspecting equipment, structures, or material; and thinking creatively. The abilities database consists of twenty different abilities, which include elements such as oral comprehension, written comprehension, and deductive reasoning. The O*NET data has occupation-level information on both the level and importance for each of the work activities and abilities.[11] There are also twenty alternative types of work context and for each of these a set of values (or context categories). For example, values for face-to-face discussions range from 1 = never to 5 = every day. Each of these values is assigned a frequency. If a specific work context element has five values, each value is assigned a frequency based on the share of people that reported that value. These frequencies sum to 100.

One obvious concern with using O*NET data is the applicability of the descriptors to developing country labor markets, such as South Africa. While these labor market data are drawn from the US economy, work by Hardy et al. (2018) has shown that they are acceptable for use in a developing country context.

3.2 PALMS DATA SET: LABOR FORCE SURVEY DATA

The PALMS data set, developed by Kerr et al. (2019), is a harmonized series of South African labor force survey data for the years 1994 through 2019. The original data for the series are based on nationally representative cross-sectional labor force surveys conducted by Statistics South Africa, which comprise three survey instruments: the October Household Surveys (1994–1999), Labour Force Surveys (2000–2007), and Quarterly Labour Force Surveys (2008 to the present).

The analysis is restricted to the period corresponding with the use of the Quarterly Labour Force Survey, which has a sample size of approximately thirty thousand dwellings and seventy thousand individuals. To deal with issues of seasonality and unexpected shocks, we average the data across the four quarters of 2018. To align the analysis with the manufacturing sector labor market, we restrict the sample to wage earners in the formal sector aged between fifteen and sixty-four. PALMS contains individual-level characteristics, which allows one to assess the characteristics of workers in occupations at high risk of displacement as a result of automation and other 4IR technologies.

3.3 LINKING DATA SETS—CROSSWALKS

The data set used in the analysis is compiled by combining the O*NET database of scores for work activities, abilities, and work context with the PALMS database. This process is undertaken by using a set of crosswalks that bridge the gap between the two different occupation nomenclatures, namely, the eight-digit Standard Occupational Classifications 2010 (O*NET-SOC10) used in the O*NET data, and the four-digit

International Standard Classification of Occupations (ISCO-88) used in PALMS. These crosswalks are a combination of those obtained from both O*NET and the Institute for Structural Research (IBS 2016; O*NET 2020). The merging of O*NET and PALMS data sets was successful with a 94 percent match when considering ISCO-88 occupations codes at the four-digit level. Occupations are dropped where O*NET data is missing, resulting in a list of 339 occupations. An adjustment is made to some of the occupation labels to account for differences in PALMS ISCO-88 four-digit occupation labels and those used in the crosswalks; however, this makes no material difference to the analysis.

4. TECHNOLOGY AND LABOR MARKET CHANGE: THE CASE OF THE MANUFACTURING SECTOR

In this section, we present our results according to the three research questions we identified earlier. Specifically, we begin by discussing the overall occupational structure of the South African manufacturing sector. We then progress to discussing the overall risk of automation in the manufacturing sector and identifying which occupations and subsectors are most at risk of automation in the South African context. Finally, we identify the demographic characteristics of individuals who are most at risk of displacement as a result of automation technologies in the South African context.

4.1 THE OCCUPATIONAL STRUCTURE OF THE MANUFACTURING SECTOR LABOR MARKET

In this section, we present an overview of the South African manufacturing sector's occupation space. The occupation space represents a network of occupations structured according to the relatedness of tasks and work activities performed across all sets of occupations. Figure 10.1 shows this occupational network, where each occupation is represented by a node. Pairs of occupations (nodes) are joined by an edge, the length of which is determined by the similarity of the work activities (aggregation of tasks) performed by two connected applications. The closer together two occupations are, and hence the shorter the length of the edge connecting them, the more similar two occupations are in terms of their underlying work activities. Each node in figure 10.1 is shaded according to the one-digit occupation code within which the individual occupation falls.

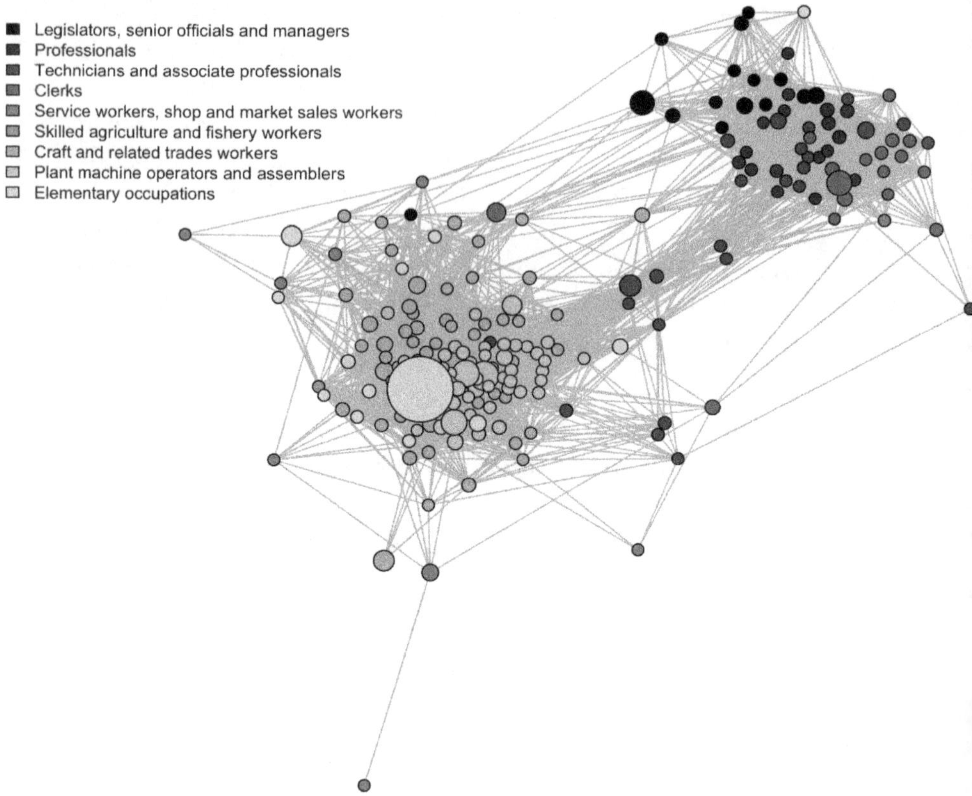

Figure 10.1 The manufacturing sector occupation space

Source: Authors' calculations from Post-Apartheid Labour Market Series, Version 3.3 (PALMS v3.3) (Kerr, Lam, and Wittenberg, 2019) and Occupational Information Network (O*NET, 2020).

Note: The four-digit occupation, represented by a node in the map, falls within a one-digit occupation grouping based on the mode value of one-digit occupation categories within a three-digit occupation. Node size is proportional to overall share of manufacturing employment in a given occupation.

The occupation space for South Africa's manufacturing sector is dumbbell-shaped overall. Two clear clusters of occupations cluster at either end of a relatively sparse center. This is suggestive of a polarized occupational structure within the manufacturing sector. We see that occupations generally classified as requiring lower levels of skills (e.g., craft and related workers, plant machine operators and assemblers, and elementary occupations) are clustered to the left of the occupation space, while occupations generally classified as requiring higher levels of skills (e.g., technicians and associate professionals, professionals, legislators, senior officials, and managers) are clustered to the right.

Note that this structure of the occupational space aligns strongly with a dichotomy between production-focused and non-production-focused jobs. Jobs that are focused on production processes are clustered on the left of the occupational space, while jobs that are not focused on production are clustered on the right of the occupation space. Given that this structure is driven by the task content of jobs, it is clear that there are stark differences in the task content of production jobs compared to non-production jobs. This suggests that the ability to shift between these two types of employment is limited because there are likely to be few overlaps in tasks and competencies between a worker in a production-focused occupation and a worker in a non-production-focused occupation.

This result could be of particular interest when considering whether individuals who are displaced by automation technologies may be able to find alternative employment in lower-risk occupations. To investigate this further, the following section elaborates on the risk profile of occupations within the South African manufacturing sector and aims to profile the risk of automation within manufacturing and its constituent subsectors over the past decade.

4.2 MANUFACTURING SECTOR OCCUPATIONS AT RISK

The occupational structure of the manufacturing sector provides insight into the types and relatedness of tasks that are required for workers employed in manufacturing jobs. However, we have not yet explored the interplay of occupation structure with risk of automation. In this section, we use the RTI described in section 2.2 to gain a better understanding of the risk of automation in the manufacturing sector over the past decade.

We begin by plotting the overall shares of manufacturing employment in routine, intermediate, and nonroutine occupations over time. These results are shown in figure 10.2. A key result from this plot is that the share of routine—and thus at-risk—employment has steadily decreased from approximately one in three employees to one in four employees over the period 2010 to 2018. This decrease in routine employment has been coupled with an increase in intermediate employment and a very slight increase in nonroutine employment. While this result may seem positive at face value, it is key to understand that a decrease in the share of at-risk manufacturing employment is not necessarily positive: this decrease in

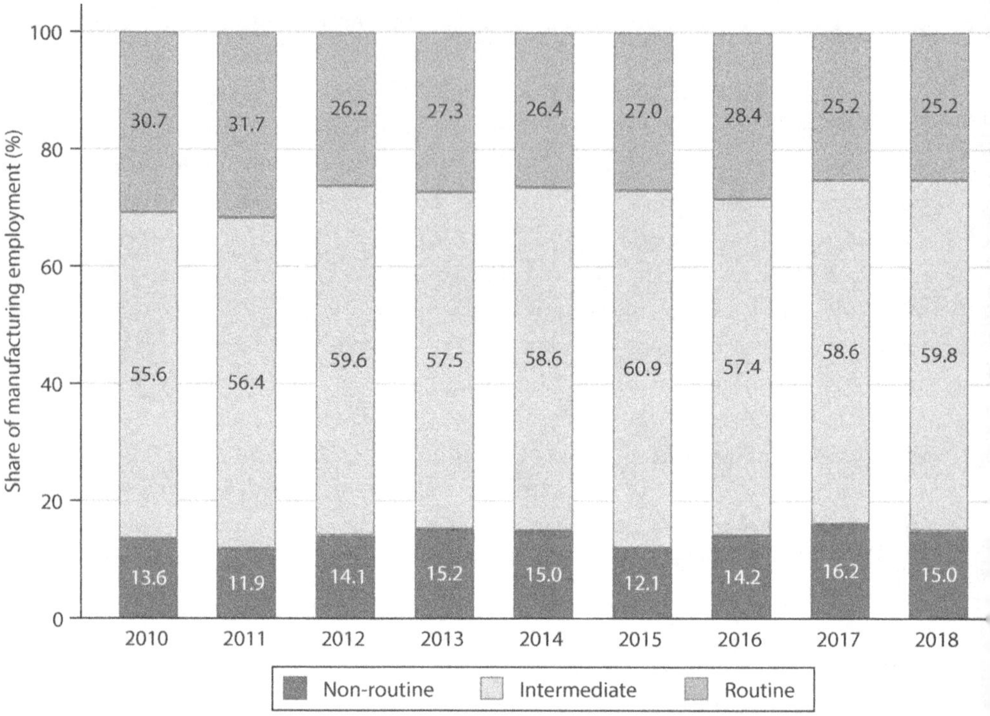

Figure 10.2 Employment shares at risk of displacement in the manufacturing sector, 2010–2018

Source: Authors' calculations from PALMS v3.3 (Kerr, Lam, and Wittenberg, 2019) and O*NET (2020).

Note: Occupations with a Routine Task Index (RTI) below the 25th percentile of the RTI distribution are classified as nonroutine, those above the 75th percentile as routine, and those in between as intermediate.

at-risk employment share could be a result of layoffs that are concentrated among workers in routine occupations.

When we further disaggregate the employment shares across the manufacturing subsector (shown in figure 10.3), we can see that this pattern of decreasing routine employment share is common across nearly all manufacturing subsectors. The only exception is in the basic and fabricated metals subsector, where the share of at-risk employment actually increased. This result is in line with the findings of Allen Whitehead et al. (2021) in their analysis of the manufacturing, engineering, and related services sector,[12] where the metals subsector was found to have increased the overall share of routine occupation employment over the period 2010 to 2018. Allen Whitehead et al. (2021) point out that this increase in the

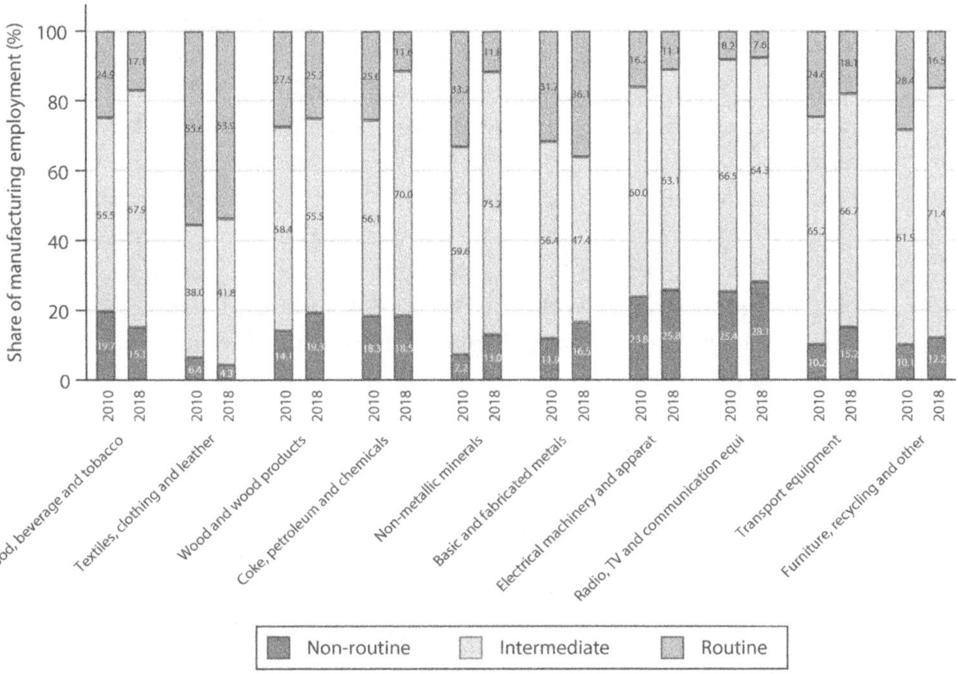

Figure 10.3 Employment shares at risk of displacement in the manufacturing sector, by subsector, 2010–2018

Source: Authors' calculations from PALMS v3.3 (Kerr, Lam, and Wittenberg, 2019) and O*NET (2020).

Note: Occupations with an RTI below the 25th percentile of the RTI distribution are classified as nonroutine, those above the 75th percentile as routine, and those in between as intermediate.

share of routine employment coupled with an increase in the number of at-risk employees could lead to much larger and more severe job shedding in the future because a practice of retaining at-risk employment in the current period may save jobs now; however, when the production processes develop and require automation in the future, the act of retaining at-risk employment will lead to larger-scale job losses at the point of automation technology adoption in the future.

This analysis also reveals some interesting subsector-specific results. First, the textiles, clothing, and leather subsector shows the largest proportion of at-risk employment of any subsector in manufacturing. Over half of all employees in the textiles subsector are employed in routine occupations, thus placing this subsector at particularly high risk of employment displacement by automation technologies. Second, three subsectors have shown large decreases in the share of at-risk employment, namely, food, beverage, and tobacco; coke, petroleum, and chemicals; and nonmetallic minerals. These three subsectors have seen large scale drop-offs in the share of routine employment, which is suggestive of potentially large impacts of automation displacement effects over the period from 2010 to 2018. Finally, it is worth noting that the electrical machinery and apparatus as well as the radio, TV, and communication equipment subsectors show the highest (and growing) proportion of nonroutine employment, coupled with the lowest share of routine employment, potentially suggesting widespread automation having taken place in these sectors prior to the period of analysis.

To truly understand the employment dynamics of the manufacturing sector in this period, it is necessary to consider changes in employment share along with the absolute changes in employment numbers. Consistent with the results presented by Allen Whitehead et al. (2021), the metals subsector has increased the overall number of at-risk employees between 2010 and 2018, even while overall employment in this sector has contracted. This suggests that there is likely to be a long-term buildup of at-risk employment over time that may culminate in large-scale employment losses at the point when automation technologies are adopted in the metals subsector. We further note that the food, beverage, and tobacco; coke, petroleum, and chemicals; and nonmetallic minerals subsectors have all seen large decreases in the number of employees at risk of automation while simultaneously expanding overall employment in the sector. This suggests that there are shifts in employment structure within these subsectors, with employment shifting from routine to intermediate and nonroutine occupations over time.

When considering the shift in total manufacturing employment numbers presented in table 10.1, it is clear that, while total manufacturing employment decreased by approximately 61,000 over the period from 2010 to 2018, at-risk employment decreased by nearly twice this number, at 102,000 employees. Taken together, these results tell an interesting story: the number of workers employed in occupations at high risk of automation has decreased over the past ten years, effectively shrinking the number of routine occupation employees by 21.35 percent. This is coupled with a growth in intermediate and nonroutine occupation employees of 3.27 and 5.95 percent, respectively. Overall employment in the manufacturing sector has also decreased over this period, by nearly 4 percent.

Table 10.1 Total and at-risk manufacturing employment changes by subsector, 2010–2018

	Total employment				At risk employment			
	2010	2018	Absolute change	Percentage change	2010	2018	Absolute change	Percentage change
Food, beverage, and tobacco	283,378	316,524	33,146	11.70	70,483	54,023	–16,460	–23.35
Textiles, clothing, and leather	183,019	185,465	2,445	1.34	101,819	99,892	–1,928	–1.89
Wood and wood products	195,679	150,205	–45,475	–23.24	53,809	37,782	–16,027	–29.78
Coke, petroleum, and chemicals	204,736	226,059	21,323	10.42	52,448	26,174	–26,275	–50.10
Nonmetallic minerals	93,446	99,812	6,366	6.81	30,986	11,792	–19,195	–61.95
Basic and fabricated metals	350,796	321,158	–29,637	–8.45	111,253	115,797	4,545	4.08
Electrical machinery and apparatus	18,460	16,348	–2,112	–11.44	2,987	1,813	–1,174	–39.30
Radio, TV, and communication equipment	23,063	19,855	–3,208	–13.91	1,880	1,513	–367	–19.52
Transport equipment	132,641	98,557	–34,084	–25.70	32,693	17,843	–14,850	–45.42
Furniture, recycling, and other	75,921	65,764	–10,157	–13.38	21,547	10,840	–10,707	–49.69
Total	**1,561,139**	**1,499,747**	**–61,392**	**–3.93**	**479,905**	**377,469**	**–102,436**	**–21.35**

Source: Authors' calculations from Post-Apartheid Labour Market Series, Version 3.3.1 (PALMS v3.3.1) (Kerr, Lam, and Wittenberg 2019) and Occupational Information Network (O*NET; 2020).

Notes: 1. Figures may not add exactly to totals in final column because of rounding. 2. Subsectors defined according to standard two-digit SIC codes for South African manufacturing. 3. At-risk employment defined to be those individuals employed in an occupation with a routine task index (RTI) above the 75th percentile of the RTI distribution.

This disproportionate change in the at-risk employment population relative to manufacturing as a whole suggests a disproportionate shedding of jobs among those workers employed in routine jobs, while the adoption of new machinery has necessitated the hiring of individuals in nonroutine occupations instead. The overall employment effect of such a shift could be mitigated if workers were easily able to shift between routine and nonroutine jobs. However, this is unlikely to be the case.

Figure 10.4 presents the manufacturing occupation space, with nodes colored by the average RTI value by occupation. A dichotomy arises

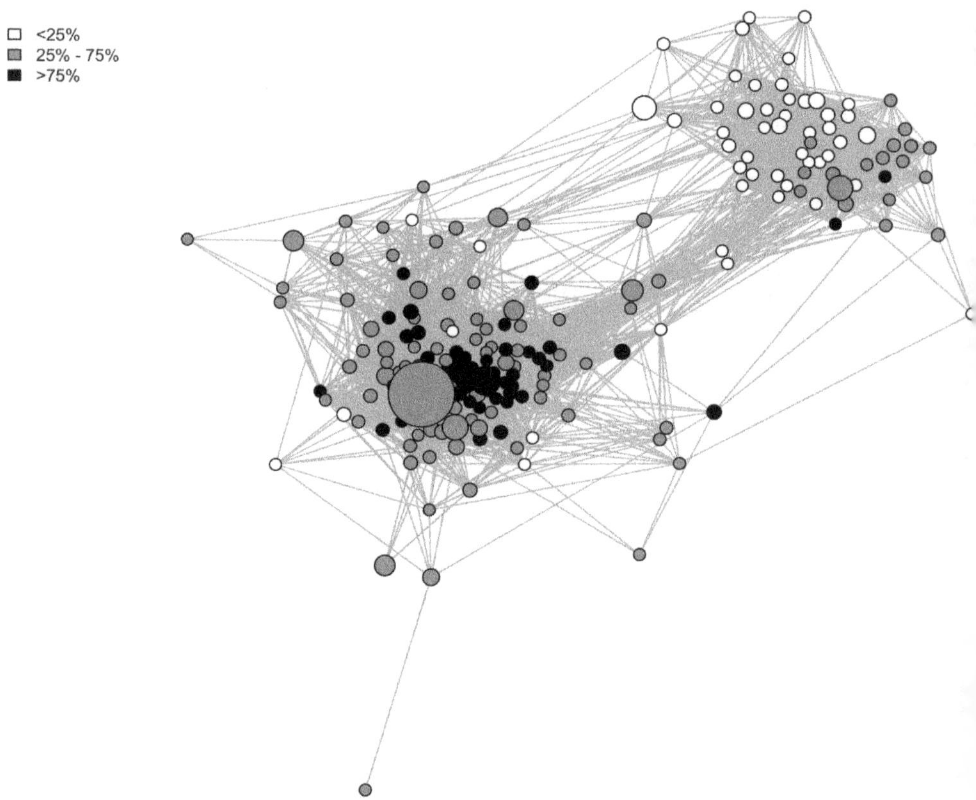

Figure 10.4 The manufacturing sector occupation space—routine task intensity

Source: Authors' calculations from PALMS v3.3 (Kerr, Lam, and Wittenberg, 2019) and O*NET (2020).

Notes: 1. Occupations with a value of the RTI equal to or lower than the 25th percentile of the RTI distribution are classified as nonroutine or low risk and shaded in white. 2. Occupations with an RTI between the 25th and 75th percentile (exclusive) of the RTI distribution are classified as intermediate or medium risk and shaded in grey. 3. Occupations with an RTI above the 75th percentile of the RTI distribution are classified as routine or high risk and shaded in black. 4. Node size is proportional to overall share of manufacturing employment in a given occupation.

immediately between the two ends of the occupation space: occupations on the bottom-left side of the space (production jobs) are at high risk of automation, while occupations on the top-right side of the space (nonproduction jobs) are generally at low risk of automation. This is evident from the generally high RTI values among production jobs and generally low RTI values among nonproduction jobs. Given this polarization of the occupation space, it is highly unlikely that the workers displaced from routine jobs will have found new employment in a low-risk nonproduction job because the distance between nodes is too far for the switch to be feasible without large-scale retraining. As a result, it is likely that the decrease in the number of routine manufacturing jobs between 2010 and 2018 has led to large-scale displacement of workers into unemployment, and there has been little if any redeployment of displaced workers into new occupations given the large differences in tasks required in more nonroutine occupations.

Overall, we see that South Africa's manufacturing sector is indeed experiencing the effects of automation and that there are employment displacement effects arising as a result. Decreases in the overall share of at-risk employment between 2010 and 2018 has been shown to be driven primarily by disproportionate decreases in the absolute number of employees in routine occupations. While there have been increases in the number of employees in intermediate and nonroutine occupations, it is unlikely that employment dynamics have seen employees shift between these two types of job: Given the polarized shape of the occupation space, it is much more likely that those individuals displaced from highly routine production jobs have been displaced out of employment completely. In the following section, we aim to take this analysis further and identify the characteristics of the individual employees who are most at risk of displacement from automation technologies and thus better understand the dynamics of South Africa's manufacturing sector and how automation could affect socioeconomic outcomes such as inequality.

4.3 CHARACTERISTICS OF MER SECTOR OCCUPATIONS AT RISK OF AUTOMATION TECHNOLOGIES—DESCRIPTIVE ANALYSIS

In this section, we aim to get a better understanding of the types of individuals who are employed in occupations that we have flagged as being at risk of automation in the previous sections. Given South Africa's history of high socioeconomic inequality, it is critical to understand the interplay between inclusive economic growth and the impact of automation.

Among other concerns, it is important to understand these outcomes because they may give a type of advance warning to policymakers regarding those who are likely to become more economically vulnerable as a result of automation technologies in the future.

In table 10.2 we present, as a preliminary analysis, a set of basic descriptive statistics that highlight the difference between employees in nonroutine, intermediate, and routine occupation employment between 2010 and 2018. In general, the demographic makeup of each type of employment has not changed significantly over the period from 2010 to 2018. There is a redistribution of employment along racial lines in the intermediate-risk group: the proportion of white employees has halved between 2010 and 2018, while the proportion of African employees in intermediate-risk occupations has increased by 13 percentage points. At the same time, there has been a significant increase in the proportion of unionized employment within the intermediate-risk group. This increase in unionization also appears for the routine and nonroutine employment groups; however, the change is not statistically significant. Although not strongly significant, there has been a general uptick in the education

Table 10.2 Demographic characteristics of manufacturing sector occupations by risk of displacement, 2010–2018

	Nonroutine		Intermediate		Routine		Ratio (routine to nonroutine)	
	2010	2018	2010	2018	2010	2018	2010	2018
Age	39.33	39.13	37.43	37.37	37.71	37.98	0.96	0.97
Male	0.71	0.70	0.64	0.68	0.74	0.75	1.05	1.07
African	0.29	0.38	0.55	0.68 ***	0.69	0.75	2.36***	2.01***
Colored	0.16	0.12	0.22	0.16	0.19	0.16	1.21	1.32
Indian	0.07	0.07	0.05	0.06	0.08	0.04	1.06	0.55
White	0.48	0.44	0.18	0.09 ***	0.04	0.05	0.09***	0.12***
Years of education	12.86	13.45*	10.77	11.12	10.09	10.53 *	0.78***	0.78***
Hours per week	40.52	42.19	42.73	42.84	42.70	43.54	1.05**	1.03
Union	0.25	0.31	0.35	0.44 **	0.40	0.43	1.57***	1.39**

Source: Authors' calculations from PALMS v3.3.1 (Kerr, Lam, and Wittenberg 2019) and O*NET (2020).

Notes: 1. Occupations with an RTI below the 25th percentile of the RTI distribution are classified as nonroutine (low risk), those above the 75th percentile as routine (high), and those in between as intermediate. 2. *** $p < 0.01$, ** $p < 0.05$, * $p < 0.1$ 3. Stars in the first three panels of the table denote the significance of a t-test on the equality of mean descriptive statistics between 2010 and 2018 within a given category of occupation (nonroutine, intermediate, or routine). Stars in the final panel of the table (ratio, routine to nonroutine) represent whether the value of the chosen descriptive statistic for individuals in routine occupations is statistically significantly different from the value of the descriptive statistic for individuals in nonroutine occupations—that is, whether the ratio is statistically significantly different from 1.

levels of employees across all risk groups, a result that is in line with overall increases in education levels among South African employees in the post-apartheid period (van der Berg and Gustafsson 2019).

The last column of table 10.2 specifically compares the characteristics of those in routine employment to those in nonroutine employment in both 2010 and 2018. These results are particularly useful because they show the relative shift in employment patterns between routine and nonroutine employment over the period. We see that, in 2010, routine employment was significantly more concentrated among African individuals, those with lower levels of education, and unionized workers, while white individuals were significantly more represented among nonroutine occupations than routine occupations. While these figures have ameliorated slightly between 2010 and 2018, it is still clear than African individuals, those who are unionized, and those with lower levels of education are disproportionately overrepresented among those employed in routine occupations.

A particularly striking finding from table 10.2 is the education gap that exists between routine and nonroutine employees. The presence of this education gap is supported by the results in figure 10.5, which plots the average educational attainment of employees across each occupation risk category from 2010 to 2018. A striking finding is that individuals employed in routine and intermediate occupations have, on average, an incomplete secondary qualification, and the level of educational attainment is generally not significantly different between these two occupation groups. However, those individuals employed in nonroutine occupations have significantly higher educational attainment—they have completed secondary education, on average. This result suggests that there are large returns to be had from completing a secondary education in terms of protecting yourself from automation risk because there is then a higher likelihood of being able to access employment in a nonroutine occupation.

This could be a key consideration for policymakers because encouraging an increase in educational attainment may make it easier for workers to transition into nonroutine occupations and save themselves from displacement as a result of automation. Research has shown that there are likely to be large skill gaps in the manufacturing sector, and indeed the attainment of an educational qualification is insufficient to ensure that employees are in possession of the requisite skills to complete a job (Allen Whitehead et al. 2022). It seems, however, that an increase in educational attainment may be sufficient as an initial signal for workers to indicate

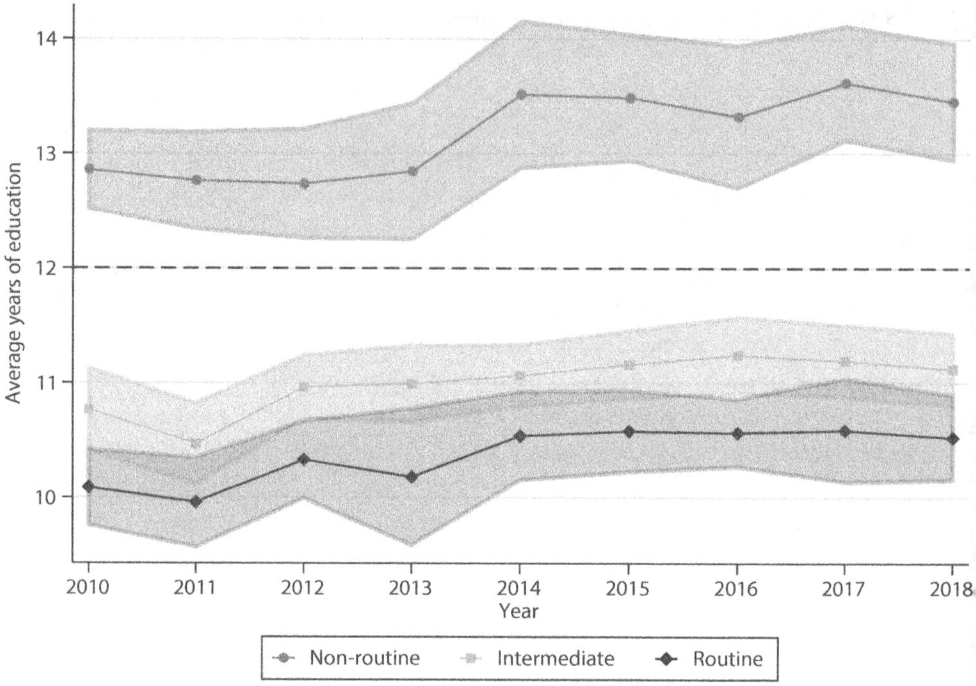

Figure 10.5 Average education level of manufacturing sector employees by occupation risk category, 2010–2018

Source: Authors' calculations from PALMS v3.3 (Kerr, Lam, and Wittenberg, 2019) and O*NET (2020).

Notes: 1. Occupations with an RTI below the 25th percentile of the RTI distribution are classified as nonroutine, those above the 75th percentile as routine, and those in between as intermediate. 2. Dashed horizontal line indicates a completed secondary education. 3. Colored bands around point estimates indicate 95 percent confidence intervals for the estimate.

that they can adapt to new types of occupations and thus protect themselves from losing their jobs in the future.

Several demographic characteristics observed above intersect heavily in the South African labor market, and thus it is not clear which of these characteristics is driving risk of displacement from automation. Understanding the partial effects of various demographic and socioeconomic indicators on risk of displacement is important for policymakers to target interventions correctly and thus mitigate the effects of future automation. As a result, we ran a probit regression model of several individual characteristics on a binary indicator of automation risk to separate the impact of certain individual- and firm-level characteristics.

The average marginal effects of our preferred probit regression model are presented in figure 10.6. This model classified individuals as being at risk of employment displacement if they were employed in an occupation classified as routine (i.e., above the 75th percentile of the RTI distribution) and not at risk of displacement otherwise. We check the robustness of these results by rerunning the model with a different classification of risk[13] as well as by using a continuous specification of the RTI as the dependent variable; however, our results remain consistent across all specifications.[14]

Certain key results emerge from the regression results. First, men, African individuals, and those who are unmarried are more likely to be employed in occupations at risk of displacement by automation technologies than their counterparts. In particular, white individuals are the least likely to be employed in occupations at risk of displacement, all else held constant. These results are very much in line with the univariate results above.

Those who are unionized are significantly more likely to be at risk of displacement than their nonunionized counterparts. This result should be interpreted with caution, however, because there is likely a level of reverse causation at play: In particular, it is very possible that those individuals who have been most at risk of employment displacement have actually had their jobs saved through union negotiations in the past, thus leading to an overrepresentation of unionized workers in routine occupations. A concern arises as to whether unions have been overprotective of routine jobs. For example, if a union has been protecting employees in a job that could have been replaced by machines in the past, this may lead to a backlog of layoffs that could culminate in large-scale displacement when or if a firm opts to adopt automation technologies in the future.

We further note that the education gradient present in figure 10.5 remains present in figure 10.6. We note, however, that education above a completed secondary education further decreases the risk of employment displacement. We specifically note that the first point at which an individual sees a marked decrease in their risk of employment displacement, relative to an individual with no schooling, is at the point when they complete their secondary education. Hereafter, completing a tertiary qualification significantly decreases further the risk of employment displacement from automation technologies. This supports the notion that investing in the upskilling and education of workers may go a long way toward protecting them from future employment displacement.

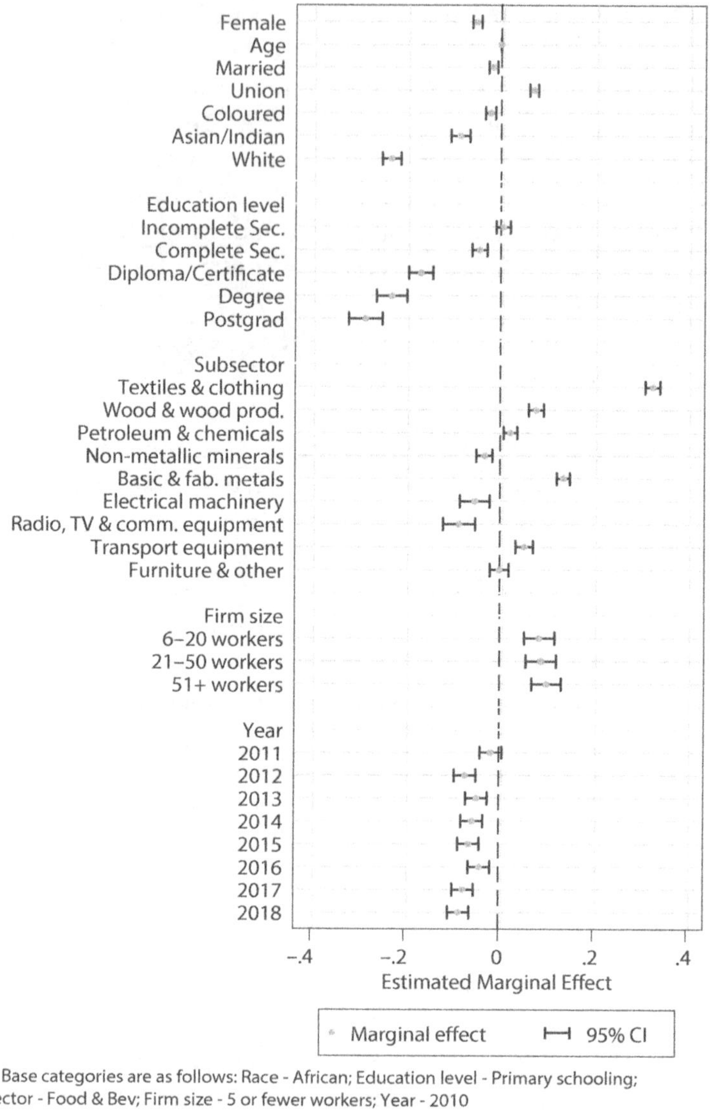

Figure 10.6 Average marginal effects on probability of being at risk of displacement

Source: Authors' calculations from PALMS v3.3 (Kerr, Lam, and Wittenberg, 2019) and O*NET (2020).

Notes: 1. Average marginal effects estimated from a probit model. 2. Base categories are as follows: gender: male; race: African; education level: primary school; subsector: food, beverage, and tobacco; firm size: five or fewer employees; year: 2010. 3. Coefficients are statistically significant at the 95 percent level if the confidence interval does not overlap the vertical red line at 0. 4. Regression estimated at the individual level.

Additional determinants of displacement risk are manufacturing subsector and firm size. Overall, the risk of displacement is heterogenous across different subsectors of the manufacturing sector. Relative to the food, beverage, and tobacco subsector, however, textiles and clothing, basic and fabricated metals, and wood and wood products have the largest increased risk of displacement. Radio, TV, and communication equipment; electrical machinery; and nonmetallic minerals have a decreased risk of displacement relative to the food, beverage, and tobacco subsector. Relative to microenterprises of between one and five employees, all larger firms have an increased risk of employment displacement from automation technologies. This is unsurprising, however, because larger firms are more likely to be able to hire more workers in production roles. What is unusual, however, is that there is no gradient of increasing risk as firm size increases. One may have expected an increasing risk gradient as firms get larger because of the increased ability to invest in the capital required for automation to take place; however, this is not the case. What this does suggest is that perhaps future automation may act to drive smaller firms out of the market in other ways. If the risk of displacement is nearly equal across firm size, then larger firms may be able to purchase automation technologies and produce goods more efficiently in the future, while smaller firms will not be able to do the same and will rely on labor instead. Given South Africa's fairly stringent labor laws and the presence of minimum wage legislation, this could lead to smaller firms being priced out of the market and thus leading to further job losses from a lack of competitiveness.

In short, we see that automation in South Africa's manufacturing sector will likely affect certain groups more than others. In particular, African individuals and those with lower levels of education, who are already considered socioeconomically vulnerable, are most likely to be at risk of displacement from automation technologies. Additonal evidence of delayed automation adoption in South Africa is also seen through the increased likelihood of unionized employees being at risk of automation. This is a precipitous position for the South African labor market because holding back and delaying automation could lead to much larger layoffs in the future. Opportunities to protect oneself from automation exist, however, and the clearest of these methods lies in education. Education itself may not provide an individual with all the required skills needed to shift into a new occupation (Allen Whitehead et al. 2022), but it is still a useful platform from which policy interventions could be built.

5. CONCLUSION

Over the past four decades, South Africa has found itself on a development path characterized by premature deindustrialization, which has likely contributed to the stagnation of economic development and low growth rates. Economists have argued that the development of a vibrant and dynamic manufacturing sector is key to encouraging economic growth in middle-income countries. With the advent of the fourth industrial revolution, however, this growth may come at the cost of routine employment—a trade-off that South Africa, with high unemployment, can ill afford. This chapter aimed to profile the South African manufacturing sector and determine to what extent automation technologies may act as a constraint to creating manufacturing-led growth for the country.

We combined representative South African labor force data with data on the task content of occupations to construct an index describing the extent to which an occupation's tasks could be classified as routine and thus to what extent the occupation could be at risk of automation. We followed a method put forward by Acemoglu and Autor (2011) to identify measures of routineness in the O*NET data and combined them into a single RTI based on a formulation proposed by Lewandowski et al. (2020). By subdividing this index into three mutually exclusive categories, we could then plot the trajectories of routine, intermediate, and nonroutine jobs over the period from 2010 to 2018 in order to better understand the role automation has played in the South African manufacturing sector.

Our key results show that the South African manufacturing sector is highly polarized in terms of occupational task content. Specifically, occupations can be grouped broadly into two categories: production-focused jobs (comprising elementary occupations, plant machine operators, and craft and related trades workers) and non-production-focused jobs (comprising technicians and associate professionals, professionals, legislators, senior officials, and managers). We find that production jobs exhibit substantially higher average RTI than nonproduction jobs, meaning that those jobs were more likely to be at risk of displacement from automation technologies than nonproduction jobs.

Over the period from 2010 to 2018, South Africa has seen a steady decrease in the number and proportion of routine manufacturing jobs, far outstripping the employment decreases in the manufacturing sector overall. These employment changes were clustered among certain manufacturing subsectors, particularly the food, beverage, and tobacco; coke, petroleum, and chemicals; and nonmetallic minerals subsectors. The decreases in routine employment over this period were coupled with increases in intermediate and nonroutine employment; given the polarized structure of the manufacturing occupation space, however, it is likely that routine job displacement was not mitigated by seeing workers reemployed in less routine occupations.

We note that workers who were most at risk of displacement as a result of automation technologies coincide with groups who may already be considered vulnerable in the labor market: specifically, African individuals and those with lower levels of education. We also note that there is a large bonus to completed secondary education in terms of protection from automation displacement risk and, as a result, it is important to encourage educational attainment as a preliminary measure to protect workers from displacement. We further note that workers may be at risk because of firm-level characteristics, such as firm size, which may lead to displacement because of competition concerns or overall proclivity to automate production processes.

In all, we find that automation technologies are likely to have significant impacts on South Africa's ability to engage in large-scale manufacturing led growth. Whether from the risk of automation threatening current jobs or from the protection of routine jobs through labor market institutions, it is clear that the adoption of automation technologies comes with employment displacement risks in the South African market. As a result, policies to protect those most vulnerable to displacement are key, and while there is no one-size-fits-all policy, it is clear that there is a need for government and industry to work hand in hand for South Africa to achieve inclusive manufacturing-led growth.

NOTES

1. Junior Research Analyst, Development Policy Research Unit, School of Economics, University of Cape Town, South Africa.

2. Director, Development Policy Research Unit, and Professor, School of Economics, University of Cape Town, South Africa.

3. Junior Research Fellow, Development Policy Research Unit, and Junior Lecturer and PhD candidate, School of Economics, University of Cape Town, South Africa.

4. Junior Research Fellow, Development Policy Research Unit, and PhD candidate, School of Economics, University of Cape Town, South Africa.

5. Senior Research Officer, Development Policy Research Unit, School of Economics, University of Cape Town, South Africa.

6. Similar approaches have been applied by Alabdulkareem et al. (2018), who explore how workplace skills drive job polarization and wage inequality, and Nedelkoska et al. (2018), who analyze whether the current wave of automation will result in technological unemployment.

7. When generating the proximity measure, we deviate from Mealy et al. (2018), whose proximity measure is based on a binary vector.

8. For example, because the "getting information" task is highly important for both biochemists and material scientists, it is highly probable that these occupations will be very similar. In contrast, because the "repairing and maintaining mechanical equipment" task is not important for human resources specialists but is very important for maintenance workers, there is a low probability that these occupations are related.

9. For example, biochemists and material scientists conduct similar tasks and are thus measured as related, while maintenance workers and human resources specialists conduct disparate tasks and are thus measured as unrelated.

10. A full list of the Occupational Information Network (O*NET) components used to define each intermediate indicator, per these definitions, is provided in table A10.1.1 in the appendix for this chapter.

11. For example, while the ability of information ordering is very important for both mechanical engineers and file clerks, engineers are required to have a higher level of information ordering, while the level of information ordering required of file clerks is average.

12. The manufacturing, engineering, and related services (MER) sector is an analytic construction of those subsectors of the manufacturing sector that are covered by the Manufacturing, Engineering and Related Services Sector Education and Training Authority (MerSETA). Overall, this sector accounts for approximately half of the broader South African manufacturing sector.

13. This alternative classification of risk is informed by Frey and Osbourne (2017), where an RTI cutoff value of 0.7 was applied unilaterally such that all individuals employed in occupations with RTI values above 0.7 were classified as at risk, while all those employed in occupations with an RTI below 0.7 were considered not at risk.

14. The interested reader is referred to table A10.1.2 in the appendix to this chapter for the full specification of each of our models.

REFERENCES

Acemoglu, D., and D. Autor. 2011. "Skills, Tasks and Technologies: Implications for Employment and Earnings." In *Handbook of Labor Economics*, Vol. 4, edited by David Card and Orley Ashenfelter. Elsevier.

Aedo, C., J. Hentschel, J. Luque, and M. Moreno. 2013. "From Occupations to Embedded Skills: A Cross-Country Comparison." World Bank Policy Research Working Paper No. 6560, The World Bank.

Alabdulkareem, A., M. R. Frank, L. Sun, B. AlShebli, C. Hidlago, and I. Rahwan. 2018. "Unpacking the Polarisation of Workplace Skills. *Science Advances* 4 (7): eaao6030.

Allen Whitehead, C., H. Bhorat, R. Hill, T. Köhler, and F. Steenkamp. 2021. "The Potential Employment Implications of the Fourth Industrial Revolution Technologies: The Case of the Manufacturing, Engineering and Related Services Sector." DPRU Working Paper 202106. Development Policy Research Unit, Cape Town (South Africa).

Allen Whitehead, C., H. Bhorat, R. Hill, T. Köhler, and F. Steenkamp, F. 2022. "Expansion and Diversification in the MER Sector: Results from an Enterprise Survey." DPRU Working Paper 202203. Development Policy Research Unit, Cape Town (South Africa).

Andreoni, A., and F. Tregenna. 2021. "The Middle-Income Trap and Premature Deindustrialization in South Africa." In *Structural Transformation in South Africa: The Challenges of Inclusive Industrial Development in a Middle-Income Country*, eded by A. Andreoni, P. Mondliwa, S. Roberts, and F. Tregenna. Oxford University Press. https://doi.org/10.1093/oso/9780192894311.003.0011.

Autor, D. H. 2015. "Why Are There Still So Many Jobs? The History and Future of Workplace Automation." *Journal of Economic Perspectives* 29 (3): 3–30.

Autor, D. H., and D. Dorn. 2013. "The Growth of Low-Skill Service Jobs and the Polarization of the US Labor Market." *American Economic Review* 103 (5): 1553–97.

Autor, D. H., F. Levy, and R. J. Murnane. 2003. "The Skill Content of Recent Technological Change: An Empirical Exploration." *Quarterly Journal of Economics* 118 (4): 1279–1333.

Balassa, B. 1965. "Trade Liberalisation and 'Revealed' Comparative Advantage." *The Manchester School* 33 (2): 99–123.

Frey, C. B., and M. A. Osborne. 2017. "The Future of Employment: How Susceptible Are Jobs to Computerisation?" *Technological Forecasting and Social Change* 114: 254–80.

Goos, M., and A. Manning. 2007. "Lousy and Lovely Jobs: The Rising Polarization of Work in Britain." *Review of Economics and Statistics* 89 (1): 118–33.

Goos, M., A. Manning, and A. Salomons. 2014. "Explaining Job Polarization: Routine-Biased Technological Change and Offshoring." *American Economic Review* 104 (8): 2509–26.

Hardy, W., P. Lewandowski, A. Park, and D. Yang. 2018. "The Global Distribution of Routine and Non-Routine Work." Institute for Structural Research Working Paper, No. 5. Institute for Structural Research.

Institute for Structural Research (IBS). 2016. *Occupation Classification Crosswalks—from ONET*-SOC to ISCO.* Dataset from IBS. https://ibs.org.pl/en/resources /occupation-classifications-crosswalks-from-onet-soc-to-isco/.

Kerr, A., D. Lam, and M. Wittenberg. 2019. Post-Apartheid Labour Market Series. Version 3.3.1 . DataFirst: University of Cape Town.

Lewandowski, P., A. Park, W. Hardy, and D. Yang. 2019. "Technology, Skills, and Globalization: Explaining International Differences in Routine and Nonroutine Work Using Survey Data." Discussion Paper No. 12339, Institute of Labor Economics: Bon.

Lewandowski, P., A. Park, and S. Schotte. 2020. "The Global Distribution of Routine and Nonroutine Work." WIDER Working Paper 2020/75. United Nations University World Institute for Development Economics (UNU-WIDER).

Lo Bello, S., M. L. Sanchez Puerta, and H. Winkler. 2019. "From Ghana to America: The Skill Content of Jobs and Economic Development." Jobs Working Paper Issue no. 23, World Bank.

Mealy, P., R. M. del Río-Chanona, and J. D. Farmer. 2018. "What You Do at Work Matters: New Lenses on Labour." Oxford Martin School. http://dx.doi.org/10.2139/ssrn.3143064.

Nedelkoska, L., D. Diodato, and F. Neffke. 2018. "Is Our Human Capital General Enough to Withstand the Current Wave of Technological Change?" CID Working Paper No. 93. Centre for International Development, Harvard University.

Nordhaus, W. D. 2007. "Two Centuries of Productivity Growth in Computing." *Journal of Economic History* 67 (1): 128–59.

Occupational Information Network (O*NET). 2020. O*NET OnLine. [Data set]. https://www.onetonline.org.

van der Berg, S., and M. Gustafsson. 2019. "Educational Outcomes in Post-Apartheid South Africa: Signs of Progress Despite Great Inequality." In *South African Schooling: The Enigma of Inequality*, edited by Nic Spaull and Jonathan D. Jansen. Springer. https://link.springer.com/book/10.1007/978-3-030-18811-5.

APPENDIX 10.1

Table A10.1.1 Definition of intermediate indicators for RTI construction

Intermediate indicator	O*NET elements
Routine cognitive	• 4.C.3.b.7 Importance of repeating the same tasks • 4.C.3.b.4 Importance of being exact or accurate • 4.C.3.b.8 Structured versus unstructured work (scored in reverse)
Routine manual	• 4.C.3.d.3 Pace determined by speed of equipment • 4.A.3.a.3 Controlling machines and processes • 4.C.2.d.1.i Spend time making repetitive motions
Nonroutine cognitive analytical	• 4.A.2.a.4 Analyzing data/information • 4.A.2.b.2 Thinking creatively • 4.A.4.a.1 Interpreting information for others
Nonroutine cognitive personal	• 4.A.4.a.4 Establishing and maintaining personal relationships • 4.A.4.b.4 Guiding, directing, and motivating subordinates • 4.A.4.b.5 Coaching/developing others

Source: Reproduced from Acemoglu and Autor (2011).

Table A10.1.2 Regression output, various specifications

	(1)	(2)	(3)
	Probit marginal effects (Lewandowski, Park, and Schotte 2020)	Probit marginal effects (Frey and Osborne 2017)	Ordinary Least Square (OLS) on continuous RTI
Female	−0.052***	−0.052***	0.003***
	(0.005)	(0.004)	(0.001)
Age	−0.001**	−0.001***	−0.000***
	(0.000)	(0.000)	(0.000)
Married	−0.017***	−0.036***	−0.009***
	(0.005)	(0.004)	(0.001)
Union	0.070***	0.037***	0.014***
	(0.005)	(0.004)	(0.001)
Race (African as base)			
Colored	−0.022***	−0.062***	−0.012***
	(0.006)	(0.004)	(0.001)
Indian	−0.086***	−0.162***	−0.039***
	(0.010)	(0.007)	(0.002)
White	−0.232***	−0.235***	−0.079***
	(0.010)	(0.005)	(0.002)
Education level (primary education as base)			
Incomplete secondary	0.005	−0.032***	−0.004***
	(0.008)	(0.005)	(0.001)
Complete secondary	−0.045***	−0.161***	−0.028***
	(0.008)	(0.006)	(0.001)
Diploma/certificate	−0.169***	−0.374***	−0.075***
	(0.013)	(0.017)	(0.003)
Degree	−0.230***	−0.612***	−0.146***
	(0.016)	(0.024)	(0.005)
Postgraduate degree	−0.286***	−0.788***	−0.173***
	(0.018)	(0.028)	(0.006)
Manufacturing subsector (food, beverage and tobacco as base)			
Textiles, clothing, and leather	0.326***	0.067***	0.058***
	(0.008)	(0.006)	(0.001)
Wood and wood products	0.077***	0.019***	0.010***
	(0.008)	(0.007)	(0.002)
Coke, petroleum, and chemicals	0.022***	−0.016**	0.004***
	(0.007)	(0.007)	(0.001)
Nonmetallic minerals	−0.033***	0.027***	0.007***
	(0.009)	(0.008)	(0.002)
Basic and fabricated metals	0.135***	−0.001	0.006***
	(0.007)	(0.006)	(0.001)

(continued)

Table A10.1.2 (*continued*)

	(1)	(2)	(3)
	Probit marginal effects (Lewandowski, Park, and Schotte 2020)	Probit marginal effects (Frey and Osborne 2017)	Ordinary Least Square (OLS) on continuous RTI
Electrical machinery and apparatus	−0.053***	−0.112***	−0.018***
	(0.016)	(0.019)	(0.003)
Radio, TV, and communication equipment	−0.086***	−0.182***	−0.031***
	(0.017)	(0.024)	(0.004)
Transport equipment	0.052***	0.015**	0.007***
	(0.009)	(0.007)	(0.001)
Furniture, recycling, and other	−0.001	0.011	0.006***
	(0.010)	(0.009)	(0.002)
Firm size (5 or less as base)			
6–20 workers	0.085***	0.097***	0.025***
	(0.017)	(0.019)	(0.004)
21–50 workers	0.088***	0.112***	0.028***
	(0.016)	(0.019)	(0.004)
51 or more workers	0.100***	0.117***	0.031***
	(0.016)	(0.018)	(0.004)
Year (2010 as base)			
2011	−0.017	0.008	0.003*
	(0.012)	(0.010)	(0.002)
2012	−0.072***	−0.007	−0.001
	(0.012)	(0.009)	(0.002)
2013	−0.047***	−0.000	0.002
	(0.012)	(0.010)	(0.002)
2014	−0.057***	0.015	0.004*
	(0.012)	(0.010)	(0.002)
2015	−0.064***	0.022**	0.006***
	(0.011)	(0.009)	(0.002)
2016	−0.041***	0.015	0.004**
	(0.012)	(0.010)	(0.002)
2017	−0.075***	0.012	0.002
	(0.012)	(0.010)	(0.002)
2018	−0.085***	0.016	0.003
	(0.011)	(0.010)	(0.002)
Constant			0.761***
			(0.004)
Observations	50,234	50,234	50,234

Source: Authors' calculations from PALMS v3.3.1 (Kerr, Lam, and Wittenberg 2019) and O*NET (2020).

Notes: 1. *** $p < 0.01$, ** $p < 0.05$, * $p < 0.1$. 2. Regressions (1) and (2) are average marginal effects estimated from underlying probit model.

CHAPTER 11

Minerals, Energy-Intensive Industries, and Development

THE GREEN TRANSITION AND EMPLOYMENT IN SOUTHERN AFRICA

Antonio Andreoni* and Simon Roberts**

* Centre for Sustainable Structural Transformation, Department of Economics, SOAS University of London and SARChI Industrial Development, University of Johannesburg

**CCRED, Department of Economics, University of Johannesburg and Centre for Sustainable Structural Transformation, Department of Economics, SOAS University of London

Abstract: Countries in southern Africa could leverage their renewable energy potential and mineral endowments to establish a new *developmental energy-mineral complex.* Upstream and downstream linkages can be exploited for the greening of the energy sector to drive domestic industrialization and generate employment. However, the employment potential—both in terms of quantity and quality of employment—depends on several factors: (1) the extent to which minerals extraction is linked to downstream minerals processing and incorporation in the manufacturing of renewable technologies machinery and equipment, (2) the extent to which part of the global and domestic demand for renewable technologies is captured domestically by developing upstream industries producing and servicing such technologies and infrastructures, and (3) the linkage connecting renewable energy to downstream green hydrogen and energy-intensive industries. Development opportunities can turn into development traps if such green transitions are not governed and regulated through a strategic approach aligned to industrial policy and regulatory reforms. Failure to develop and nurture mineral-energy-industry linkages and related technology capabilities could result in a new exploitative green minerals regime, reproducing patterns of dependent economic growth without structural transformation and broad-based industrialization. With a focus on South Africa—a country facing multiple challenges in transitioning away from carbon-intensive industry while addressing extremely high levels of unemployment—this chapter focuses on the employment implications of such green transitions depending on the approach to developing linkages for sustainable structural transformation and the implications for rethinking the role of the state.

1. INTRODUCTION

Climate change requires rapid, major, and systemic economic changes at the local, national, regional, and global levels. These changes need to happen particularly in the energy sector and energy-intensive industries, including steel, chemicals, and cement but also in other key sectors such as food and transport. The green transition in southern Africa opens several windows of opportunities for sustainable structural transformation and employment generation, although challenges persist.

The acceleration in the diffusion of renewable technologies—solar, wind, and also electric vehicle (EV) technology—has created new demands for the extraction and processing of minerals. Lithium, nickel, cobalt, manganese, and graphite are crucial to battery performance, longevity, and energy density. Rare earth elements (REEs) are essential for permanent magnets that are vital for wind turbines and EV motors. Electricity networks need a huge amount of copper and aluminum, with copper being a cornerstone for all electricity-related technologies (IEA 2022a). The production of lithium and cobalt may increase by 500 percent by 2050 to meet clean energy demand alone. The bottom line is that clean energy technologies and related infrastructures require more minerals (World Bank 2023).

Countries in southern Africa could leverage mineral endowments, given the global demand pull, to establish a new *developmental energy-mineral complex*.[1] Upstream and downstream linkages can be exploited for the greening of the energy sector to drive domestic industrialization and generate employment. However, the employment potential—both in terms of quantity and quality of employment—depends on several factors: (1) the extent to which minerals extraction is linked to downstream minerals processing and incorporation in the manufacturing of renewable technologies machinery and equipment, (2) the extent to which part of the global and domestic demand for renewable technologies is captured domestically by developing upstream industries producing and servicing such technologies and infrastructures, and (3) the linkages connecting renewable energy to downstream green hydrogen and energy-intensive industries.

In countries like South Africa and Namibia, renewable energy can fuel domestic green hydrogen production competitively given their solar irradiation and wind. In turn, green hydrogen can be used further downstream to transform difficult-to-abate sectors—chemicals, steel, and cement in particular—currently fueled mainly with coal in South Africa, or as a major source of new export in countries like Namibia, where industrial sectors are currently underdeveloped. The greening of these difficult-to-abate industries is becoming a precondition for exporting to global markets where advanced industrial economies are using their regulatory power to accelerate green transition while protecting their domestic industries.

Global demand for green hydrogen is attracting multibillion-dollar investments and could also create further upstream and downstream linkages with another critical mineral—platinum—a necessary component in the electrodes of fuel cell engines. South Africa is the world's largest platinum group metal (PGM) producer (PGMs include platinum, palladium, rhodium, and other metals) and produces more than twice as much as all other countries on Earth combined (Russia being the second). As this example shows, upstream and downstream linkages running vertically and horizontally between energy, minerals, and industrial sectors can be leveraged to create new employment and spur diffusion of green technologies.

Development opportunities can turn into development traps, however, if such green transitions are not governed and regulated through a strategic approach aligned to industrial policy and regulatory reforms. Failure to develop and nurture mineral-energy-industry linkages and related technology capabilities could result in a new exploitative green minerals regime, reproducing patterns of dependent economic growth without structural transformation and broad-based industrialization.

This chapter builds on ongoing fieldwork and research and focuses on the employment implications of such green transitions depending on the approach to developing linkages from renewable energy, upstream and downstream; key challenges in locating the transition in the context of structural transformation; and the implications for rethinking the role of the state. The chapter will examine these issues through the position of South Africa. South Africa faces multiple challenges in transitioning away from carbon-intensive industry while addressing extremely high levels of unemployment (Andreoni et al. 2021). Hence, it is an ideal case study to analyze this set of issues.

2. GREEN JOBS: A STRUCTURAL TRANSFORMATION PERSPECTIVE FOR AFRICA

In 2015, during the UN Climate Change Conference (COP21), 193 countries agreed on a set of shared ambitions and goals that came to be known as the Paris Agreement. In the period between the Paris Agreement and the COVID-19 pandemic, from 2015 to 2019, countries have been facing the challenge of decoupling carbon dioxide (CO_2) emissions from economic growth and, even more critically, from jobs creation. The pandemic shock has also affected the job market dramatically, and the retention and creation of new jobs has gained even more centrality in policy agendas. Governments have become increasingly aware of the fact that environmental and social sustainability need to go hand-in-hand; hence, economies need to keep creating jobs while they need to decarbonize. The political and social support for the Paris Agreement, especially in developing economies, require coupling environmental sustainability with and social sustainability. Within this discussion, the possibility of a new wave of so-called green jobs in renewable energy and other green-related sectors has captured governments' attention.

From a global perspective, the most recent reports by the International Labor Organization (ILO) and the International Renewable Energy Agency (IRENA) (ILO and IRENA 2022) as well as the International Energy Agency (IEA; 2022b) suggest that there are plenty of emerging opportunities for coupling decarbonization with employment creation in the new green sectors. However, investments and long-term financial commitments are needed to capture these green jobs opportunities and restructure economies, starting from their energy systems. The energy sector accounts for at least one-third of all the emissions globally, with the share being much higher in countries depending on coal to generate electricity. Generating electricity efficiently from renewable energy plays a systemic role in decoupling because all economic sectors rely on electricity generation. Emissions in the industrial sector are also highly concentrated within so-called energy-intensive industries. Specifically, iron and steel, chemicals and plastics, and cement account for more than 50 percent of all industrial emissions.

Countries across the African continent are among the most in need of capturing these windows of opportunities for sustainable structural transformation, industrial development, and green jobs creation. Unemployment in major African economies remains extremely high, with South Africa being a striking example of how difficult it has been to expand and sustain good-quality employment generation (Andreoni et al. 2021). These are also the countries where the energy sector needs to transform the most to become more sustainable and, even more critically, to sustain a growing population and drive the much-needed productive transformation of the continent. Again, South Africa is a striking example of a country whose energy system—and its dramatic collapse over the last few years—has constrained the structural transformation of the economy and job creation. It is also an energy system whose dependence on coal has the potential to jeopardize the competitiveness of downstream industries, including access to international markets.

While the green transition in Africa could provide a solution to a set of interlocked challenges and transformation gaps—productive transformation, energy system development, and job creation—in most cases, the relationships between these challenges and gaps has been approached and framed within a quite narrow perspective, starting with the definition of "green jobs." Green jobs have largely been seen as new jobs associated directly with the renewable sector—solar and wind—and a few closely related upstream industries and downstream activities, including services. Jobs associated with the production of lithium batteries or EVs are other examples of green jobs, although many of these jobs are far from occurring in large numbers on the African continent, where many of these medium-high technologies are imported. The quality of green jobs that are more likely to emerge in the short to medium term in downstream service activities has been also questioned. For example, solar panel maintenance does not generate enough good-quality jobs, as the experience of South Africa and Brazil show (Hochstetler 2020).

Even when the creation of green jobs has been framed within a value chain perspective, in value chains like solar panels or batteries, studies and policies have mainly looked at direct green job formation. The potential for indirect jobs formation through unlocking complementary developments mediated by linkages in other parallel upstream and downstream industries has been largely unrecognized. For example, several

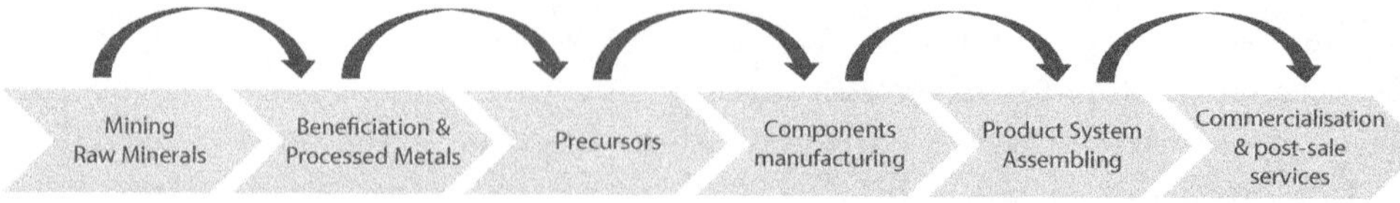

Figure 11.1 Windows of opportunities and green jobs from a linear global value chain (GVC) perspective

Source: Authors.

African countries, such as South Africa, Morocco, and the Democratic Republic of the Congo (DRC), have started targeting the opportunities from critical minerals with a focus on specific value chain (VC) upgrading steps, primarily processing of minerals and production of precursors (figure 11.1). In doing so, they have looked at the direct job creation potential. Productive and related employment opportunities in adjacent upstream and downstream industries mediated through linkages formation have remained largely unexplored.

Capturing both direct green jobs along value chains, and indirect green job formation across the economy through linkages calls for a *structural transformation perspective*. From this perspective, green jobs arise from a dynamic process of employment expansion and local production linkages development spanning different sectors, each with their different shades of brown and green relating to their associated greenhouse gas emissions. Indeed, the structural transformation process captured in figure 11.2 portrays a more complex and organic dynamic in which economies do not jump directly into a green future; on the contrary, each country explores different potential pathways for diversification and deep industrial restructuring of the economy.

Returning to our example of critical minerals, a structural transformation perspective does not simply point to the importance of increasing the local share of downstream mineral processing, for example, in producing precursors for batteries production; it also points to the ways in which processing downstream entails transformation in the parallel chemical sector. In turn, the transformation of the latter can unlock opportunities in other closely complementary but dissimilar sectors (e.g., agriculture through fertilizers). Focusing on these opportunities arising from linkages and multiple interdependencies across sectors also allows identification of potential bottlenecks, such as the risks of putting unsustainable pressure on certain scarce resources, for example, water.

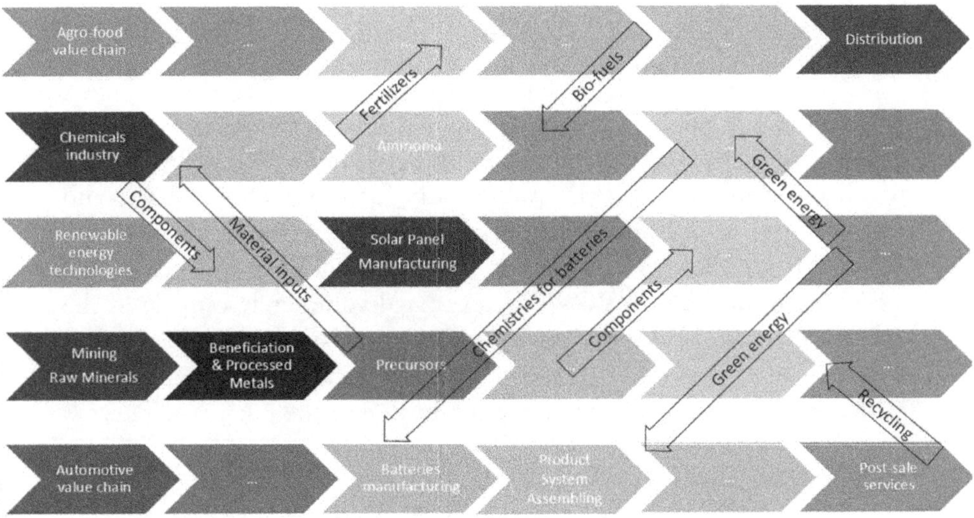

Figure 11.2 Windows of opportunities and green jobs from a structural transformation perspective

Source: Authors.

Additional structural transformation pathways highlighted in figure 11.2 are discussed in the following sections with a focus on South Africa and specific sets of industries. Notwithstanding this country and industry focus, the structural transformation perspective advanced here has implications for ways in which governments define green jobs and develop policies to seize the green windows of opportunities across broader southern Africa and the African continent.

3. MINERALS, RENEWABLE ENERGY TECHNOLOGIES, AND LINKAGE DEVELOPMENT FOR EMPLOYMENT

In this section, we first explore windows of opportunities for both direct and indirect jobs formation arising from minerals extraction, downstream mineral processing, and manufacturing machinery and equipment required for renewable technologies. We then focus on the extent to which part of the global and domestic demand for renewable technologies can be captured domestically by developing upstream industries producing and servicing such technologies and infrastructures.

3.1 FROM CRITICAL MINERALS TO MINING EQUIPMENT: DOWNSTREAM INDUSTRIES AND EMPLOYMENT DEVELOPMENT

South Africa is the country on the continent where some of the most well-known windows of green opportunities—namely, the development of a lithium-ion battery (LIB) value chain for sustainable mobility and just transition—are rapidly materializing. This is the result of South Africa's critical mineral endowment, its strategic place in the region, and its related value chains. PGMs are exported completely outside of the African continent. From South Africa's export basket to other African countries of critical minerals shown in figure 11.3, we can see that seven minerals account for 80 percent of total value of the portfolio. There is

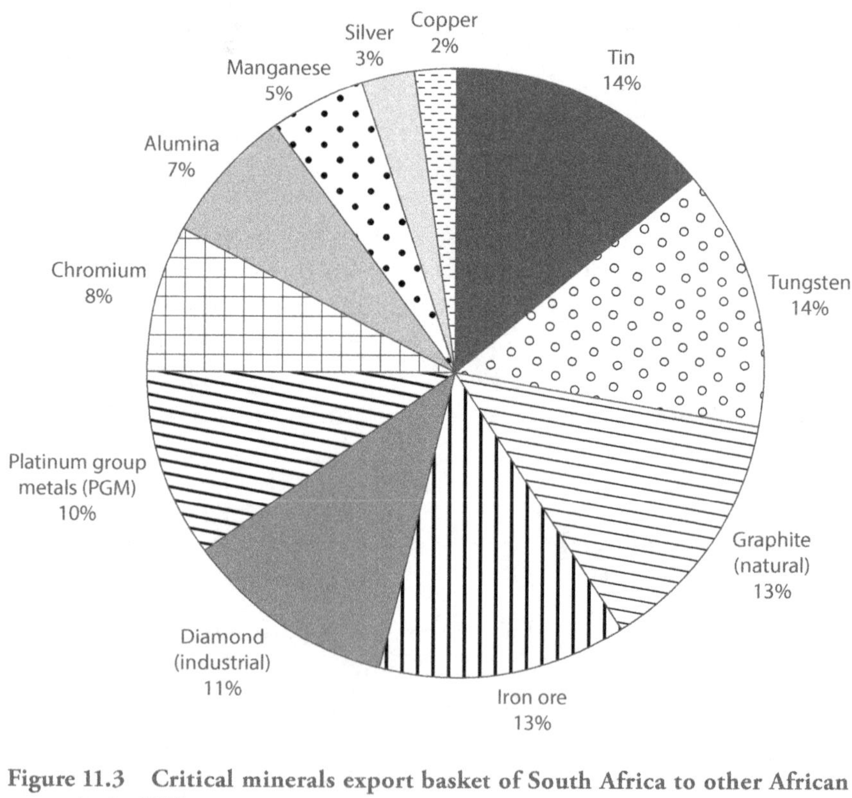

Figure 11.3 Critical minerals export basket of South Africa to other African countries in 2021

Source: Authors based on UN Comtrade.

a significant export of tin (16 percent), tungsten (21 percent), graphite (24 percent), and iron ore (13 percent) in the total continental export of minerals by South Africa. As the network analysis in Andreoni and Avenyo (2023b reveals, South Africa is not only an exporter on the continent but also a significant importer of critical minerals. This is the result of the presence of large multinational companies, which use South Africa as their base for southern and eastern Africa operations, but it is also because South Africa has developed significant mineral-processing capacity.

Given its central role in the Southern African Development Community (SADC) region, there is potential for regional industrial integration of these minerals, notably through the implementation of the SADC Industrialization Strategy and Roadmap 2015–2063, and the recent implementation of the African Continental Free Trade Agreement (AfCFTA). Among SADC minerals are graphite (Mozambique and Tanzania), nickel (Botswana and Zimbabwe), titanium (Mozambique and Madagascar), among others.

A Trade & Industrial Policy Strategies (TIPS) and United Nations Industrial Development Organization (UNIDO) (2021) report points out:

"Mining of multiple LIB-relevant minerals, such as manganese, iron ore, nickel, and titanium, is already underway in South Africa and the region. Mineral beneficiation for battery production, while limited, is also present in the country with existing pockets of excellence in manganese and aluminum, and interesting developments in lithium, nickel, and titanium. Importantly, battery manufacturing (using imported cells) and battery refurbishing (second-life batteries) is a booming opportunity, with many firms operating in this space, leveraging unique expertise and intellectual property, notably in the development of battery management systems."

In contrast, cell manufacturing, while being explored at the research and development (R&D) level, is yet to be proven commercially viable in the country. The development of recycling is also still in its early days. The bottom line is that, while pockets of technological capabilities and productive opportunities exist in South Africa, the value chain is still emerging and remains disarticulated, with different levels of development along the chain. Outside South Africa, domestic technological capabilities in the mining value chain are limited to some extraction activities and processing of concentrates; however, high-value downstream activities such as manufacturing of batteries are almost nonexistent.

The development of the LIB value chain can follow at least four pathways: (1) battery manufacturing, (2) mineral refining, (3) cell manufacturing, and (4) battery recycling. Each can be integrated over time. The TIPS-UNIDO study noted that developing battery manufacturing and mineral refining is ready for scale-up, while cell manufacturing and recycling could be explored in the medium to long term, provided they prove to be economically sustainable.

These industrial and technological development pathways are dependent, however, on the developmental governance of critical minerals, that is, the extent to which governments are not captured by particular interests and can and will negotiate mineral rights conditions as part of a domestic industrial policy for structural transformation. In this respect, the introduction of conditionalities on localization, technology sources, and complementary investments are essential (Andreoni and Roberts 2022).

The promotion of domestic productive capabilities also has to account for the fact that critical mineral-based industries are dominated by a few global giants. China is the dominant player in manufacturing LIBs, with three-quarters of production capacity. Panasonic and Contemporary Amperex Technology Limited (CATL) are the leading manufacturers of LIBs, while the cell manufacturing market is dominated by LG Chem, BYD Auto, and Panasonic. The supply of cathodes, anodes, separators, electrolytes, and electrolyte salts is concentrated in a few countries (China, Japan, South Korea, the United States) and a limited number of firms. If we look at patents related to climate change mitigation in transport and LIBs in particular, the landscape is heavily dominated by a few countries: the United States, Japan, Germany, South Korea, France, China, and the United Kingdom (TIPS and UNIDO 2021).

There are other, more viable routes, however, for diversification. South Africa could leverage its large PGM resources to develop forward linkages in a number of emerging sectors and become an exporter of value-added technologies based on its natural resources. Almost all the fuel cells sold up to 2024 used platinum as a catalyst, with smaller amounts of ruthenium. Fuel cells can be deployed in portable power generation, stationary power generation, and power for transportation (DMR 2013). Fuel cell technology is a pollution-free electricity generation technology. South Africa could develop several stages of the fuel cell value chain by evolving the catalytic converters industry for the automotive sector and its current capacity for coating of PGMs. Given the transition in the automotive sector, companies involved in the production of auto catalysts could repurpose their capabilities to enter the fuel cell value chain, with positive implications in terms of job retention and sustainability. A related route to diversification and industrial innovation can be found in the related mining equipment sector. South Africa is already a leader in mining equipment technologies. Retaining such a leadership position requires investing in new mining solutions—such as the one integrating fuel cell technologies into mining equipment.

The impact of the COVID-19 crisis across different geographies has put new pressure on traditional global mining supply chain structures, which are concentrated around a few equipment vendors from the United States, Europe, Japan, and China. Mining companies have been actively exploring alternative and broader sources of supply to reduce reliance on a small number of overseas vendors (Andreoni, Lee, and Torreggiani 2021). On the one hand, this opens up opportunities for local or regional companies with the right level of technology and production capabilities to enter such value chains. On the other hand, foreign multinationals supplying mining equipment and other critical inputs to mining houses might decide to relocate part of their production activities closer to their clients' operations through subsidiaries or collaborative partnerships with local companies. The South African mining equipment sector is well positioned to seize both these opportunities in the domestic and regional mining markets.

Mining equipment production and services are today the most relevant and technologically advanced segments of the broader special-purpose machinery industry in South Africa (Andreoni and Torreggiani 2020). The mining machinery and equipment sector represents the largest contributor to employment, turnover, and exports of the special-purpose machinery industry, and it also stands out with respect to total plant, property, equipment (PPE) and intangible assets, expenditures in R&D, royalties and patent rights, and staff training.

According to South African Revenue Service (SARS) data for companies registered in South Africa, in 2017, companies producing equipment and machines for mining, quarrying, and construction contributed more than 67 percent of the total employment in the special-purpose machinery sector (that is, around 39,000 employees), and around three-quarters of its total turnover (75 percent) and exports (79 percent). Production of machines for mining, quarrying, and construction generated around USD 1.8 billion of turnover and USD 0.6 billion of exports in 2017. The development of a mining equipment ecosystem in the Gauteng province—two-thirds of the employment and turnover are concentrated there—has driven processes of technological capabilities development and diffusion. This subsector also makes a heavy contribution to the total noncurrent assets (70 percent) and spending in capabilities development undertaken in the specialized machinery and equipment industry, as proxied by expenditures in R&D (55 percent), royalties and patent rights (77 percent), and spending in staff training (88 percent) (figure 39 in Andreoni and Torreggiani 2020, based on SARS data).

The proximity to the mines and the demand for customized and niche technology solutions well suited for the peculiar geological conditions of South Africa have been critical drivers of learning. The local companies have built global competitiveness with developed production and services operations across major extractive industries and countries, actively engaging in the technological race in the global mining value chain. Although a number of these companies are large by local standards, they are still significantly smaller than the leading multinationals operating in South Africa. Their expertise and competencies are particularly advanced and at the global frontier only in specific product segments (e.g., deep mining and related areas).

Local content requirement policies have been combined with measures to increase the participation of Black-owned businesses (Vilakazi and Bosiu 2021). These have had very limited effects because they have not been linked to industrial development plans based on a detailed assessment of the products and services to target for local manufacturing (as proposed by Andreoni and Torregiani 2021). Such an assessment would require a thorough analysis of the product and services to target, and the extent to which these products and services meet quantity, quality, and price competitiveness parameters. This measure could be complemented by local content policy reform that would increase companies' compliance with local procurement and content requirements while promoting export. Domestic companies could be given the opportunity to contribute to increasing domestic value addition either by increasing the local content of their products and services in the domestic market or by increasing the value of their products and services in the international export market. In a nutshell, companies would be allowed to import more of the products they need, to the extent that they also increase the local content value of the exported products.

This policy could appeal to several international original equipment manufacturers (OEMs), with or without a local footprint, as well as domestic OEMs who are affected by the local content requirements in their production expansion and price competitiveness. International OEMs willing to invest in South Africa would now have a new development pathway. They would be allowed to increase their imports from their global supply chain for a number of products and services to the extent that they link local companies to their exclusive global supply chains and allow them to export internationally. By doing so, local companies would have enormous export market opportunities and could potentially become the main suppliers of international OEMs in other major mining countries, such as Australia, Canada, Russia, and Brazil.

The international OEMs could also integrate the local company into their exclusive supply chains, thus 'powering' the local company. Of course, a limited number of domestic companies might be technologically and operationally ready to seize this opportunity. The development potential and growth, however, would be extremely significant. This measure would also create some competitive pressure in domestic backward industries. Local OEMs would have some alternative ways to reach local content requirements, that is, by increasing their exports instead of accepting uncompetitive prices.

Within this more flexible, local content requirement regime, specific green conditionalities could also be introduced to incentivize the adoption of those green technologies (e.g., fuel cells) and digital solutions (e.g., predictive maintenance) that would reduce emissions and waste while increasing employment, improving working conditions, and adding to overall domestic value. Increasing the domestic footprint of the mineral sector—especially in the critical minerals segments—and related mining equipment industry can have significant implications for employment in South Africa and the broader continent.

Foreign capital investments for the exploration of minerals have been significant in Africa and have created substantial employment in the African mining sector over the last two decades. Despite lower employment numbers since 2014, two-digit manufacturing data from UNIDO show a steady overall increase in employment in the production of minerals and metals in Africa over time. Trends in employment created in the mining sector differ across different regions of the continent, with a concentration of employment in the minerals and metals sector in North Africa, followed by southern Africa. The Central Africa region has the least employment concentration in mining and minerals sector on the continent. It is anticipated that, with the global aim of transitioning to clean energy, more employment opportunities may be created in resource-rich countries (Andreoni and Avenyo 2023a).

3.2 RENEWABLE TECHNOLOGIES INVESTMENTS: UPSTREAM INDUSTRIES AND EMPLOYMENT GENERATION

Over the past two decades, investment in renewable energy has grown rapidly around the world. Of the USD 2.8 trillion invested globally between 2000 and 2020, however, only 2 percent went to Africa (around USD 60 billion), despite the continent's enormous potential to generate energy from renewable sources. In Africa, investment in renewables picked up in the 2010s, driven by structured renewable energy procurement programs. These include feed-in tariff schemes and auctions supported by development finance institutions and multilateral development banks.

Investment remained concentrated in a few regions and countries. The southern Africa region attracted USD 22.4 billion, over 40 percent of total flows over the decade, and was concentrated in South Africa. Thanks to its Renewable Energy Independent Power Producer Procurement Programme (REIPPPP) (Andreoni et al. 2022), South Africa took in 85 percent of the region's investment between 2010 and 2020. Solar photovoltaic (PV) and thermal projects accounted for 60 percent (USD 13.5 billion) of that investment, followed by wind at 35 percent (USD 7.8 billion) (IRENA and AfDB 2022). In North Africa, over the 2010s, investment totaled USD 17.5 billion and was concentrated in Morocco (USD 9.5 billion) and Egypt (USD 8.2 billion). Investment was concentrated in solar (PV and thermal) (67.5 percent) and wind (32 percent).

The impact of foreign direct investment (FDI) on employment generation remains limited. Aggregating capital investment in renewable energy-related industry clusters (environmental technology, information and communication technology [ICT] and electronics, industrial, transport equipment) in Africa, the data show that more than half of the jobs that have been created between 2003 and 2018 by capital investments are in transport and ICT and electronics. Other sectors like industry and environmental technology follow, with smaller shares of jobs created.

Nonetheless, the employment generation potential from renewable technologies is rising globally. A first important attempt to estimate empirically some of the direct effects on jobs comes from work by the ILO and IRENA (2022). In their analysis of the evolution of global renewable energy employment by technology, there were over 12 million new jobs created between 2012 and 2021, with only one-third coming from the solar photovoltaic industry (figure 11.4). Among the top three contributing sectors is the bioenergy sector, including liquid biofuels, solid biomass, and biogas, accounting for another 3.4 million jobs globally, while the hydropower sector alone has created 2.37 million jobs. Wind energy has shown a relatively more modest contribution to job creation, partially because of the relatively limited diffusion of the technology and its capital intensity. Solar heating/cooling, geothermal energy, concentrated solar power, heat pumps, and green waste management are among the other sectors in which over 1 million jobs were created (figure 11.4).

The potential for jobs creation depends on the technology, its diffusion, and its value chain structure. For example, in their study of the solar PV industry, IEA (2022a) estimated that the solar PV industry could create 1,300 manufacturing jobs for each gigawatt of production capacity. To meet the IEA Net Zero by 2050 demand growth, the solar PV manufacturing sector needs to nearly double the number of jobs globally by 2030. These jobs will be differently distributed along the PV value chains and related sectors, for example, those involving the manufacture

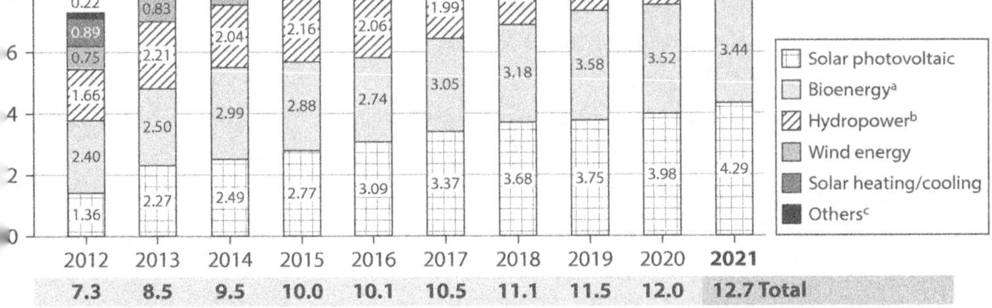

Figure 11.4 Evolution of global renewable energy employment by technology (in millions), 2012–2021Source: International Renewable Energy Agency (IRENA) and International Labor Organization (ILO) (2022).

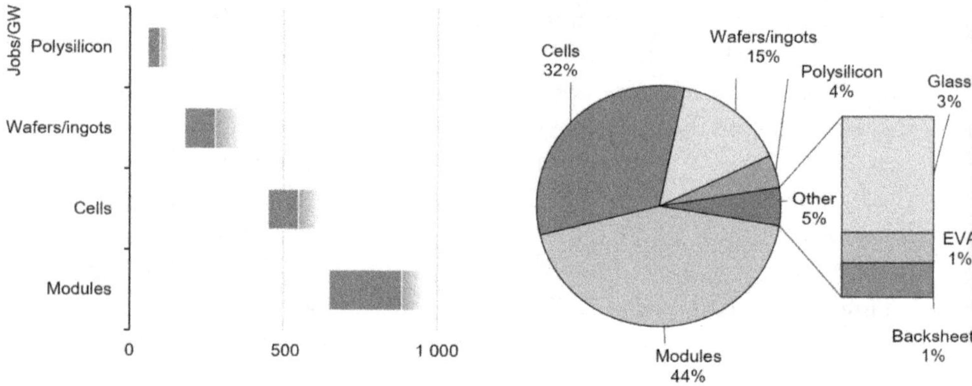

Figure 11.5 Solar photovoltaic (PV) sector: jobs per GW of manufacturing capacity and share of jobs per supply chain segment

Source: International Energy Agency (IEA) 2021.

of components such as glass, ethylene-vinyl acetate (EVA), back sheets, inverters, and mounting systems. These indirect jobs have been estimated to number around another quarter million, to be added to the direct jobs. Thin-film module manufacturing, which is less job intensive than crystalline silicon (c-Si) technology, creates only around 200 jobs per gigawatt because it entails fewer production steps, and they are mostly automatized (figure 11.5).

As highlighted in figure 11.5, the most job-intensive segments along the PV supply chain are module production (requiring 600–900 jobs) and cell manufacturing (450 to 650 jobs). Their manufacturing involves multiple steps, including in assembly and quality control, that are less prone to automation. Over the last decade, however, job automation and automated guided vehicles reduced the job intensity potential of solar PV manufacturing, especially in countries such as China, where solar PV has been produced in large capital-intensity and highly automated manufacturing plants (between 10 and 20 GW of energy generation capacity). According to IEA, for smaller manufacturing facilities that cannot realize the same economy-of-scale benefits, labor requirements could increase up to nearly 60 percent.

The job creation potential depends on the extent to which the countries investing in PV manufacturing can link into global value chains (GVCs)/markets and link back into their local production systems (Andreoni and Tregenna 2020). The degree of engagement in technology development also affects the extent to which created jobs are skills intensive. PV manufacturing requires a diversity of workers, including production engineers, material handlers, and assemblers. Because of the current geographical concentration of the solar PV supply chain, most skilled personnel are based in China and Southeast Asia. In many countries, these new skills need to be created and training scaled up so that job opportunities materialize in the local production system. Demand pull for PV technologies is also central in encouraging investments and skills development, and public procurement has become an important policy tool for the green transition.

The potential for green energy generation in South Africa through solar technologies (and wind) is immense. The country's solar energy potential is estimated to be around 500,000 MW, which is more than ten times the country's current energy capacity. South Africa's inability to ensure a reliable electricity supply to the economy has without doubt been an important contributor to its low economic growth and inability to create jobs and economic opportunities for its citizens—its structural transformation (Andreoni et al. 2021). South Africa is also a disproportionate contributor to climate change, and its power generation is largely based on coal. Therefore, an accelerated electricity sector transition toward massive upscaling of solar power generation is the key to South Africa's sustained economic recovery.

The prolonged energy crisis resulting in load shedding has stimulated a much-needed acceleration in the regulatory framework in South Africa and the opening to investments in green power generation. From 2021, reforms have been announced to allow a license exemption for independent power generation projects of up to 100 MW. It is also expected that regulations will allow firms to sell excess power to unrelated parties and to give excess electricity to the grid at a fee.

With the upscaling of green power generation, South Africa is also looking to unlock structural transformation opportunities in critical provinces. In South Africa, coal production and energy generation is concentrated in the Mpumalanga province. The province faces a multitude of socioeconomic and environmental challenges, including high levels of unemployment, inequality, and poverty as pressure mounts to transition away from a coal-based economy. The Mpumalanga provincial government has been proactive in exploring opportunities to transition the region to a labor-absorbing, green-focused economy, hence creating a positive reinforcing loop between green transition and job creation.

The government is focusing on repurposing land on ultimately decommissioned mines and coal-fired stations to pivot to renewable energy production and utilizing the existing transmission assets in the region. Alongside repurposing opportunities, the government is also interested in specific investment opportunities in the agricultural sector, where large numbers of the population work. Sector-specific opportunities include renewable energy applications, regenerative agriculture, controlled environment agriculture, smart farming/precision agriculture, and agricultural waste management. The Mpumalanga Green Cluster Agency was created to capture such opportunities and coordinate efforts between businesses, government, academia, and civil society toward a just transition. By supporting these stakeholders, the agency aims to facilitate more investment and stimulate job creation in Mpumalanga's green economy.

4. GREEN HYDROGEN FOR INDUSTRY AND EMPLOYMENT

Greening the hard-to-abate industries is becoming a precondition for exporting into global markets, where advanced industrial economies are using their regulatory power to accelerate the green transition while protecting their domestic industries. Measures such as the European Union Carbon Border Adjustment Mechanism (CBAM) seek to reduce global emissions but may undermine African industrial development and exports (African Climate Foundation and Firoz Lalji Foundation 2023) without the appropriate measures to support industrialization and employment in African countries. The extent of employment creation depends on the linkages being realized. To assess the different trajectories, we consider two of the most important hard-to-abate industries in South Africa: steel and chemicals. We draw on different types of research to assess the broad employment scenarios from steel linkages to metal products, and from green ammonia to fertilizers with linkages to agriculture.

Decarbonizing the hard-to-abate industries of steel and basic chemicals is a key part of the green industrial transformation required globally (IEA 2021; Griffiths et al. 2021). How this happens will have major implications for employment in middle income countries, especially those like South Africa, in which these industries are well developed on a foundation of cheap fossil fuel energy. The wider employment effects also depend on the linkages of the heavy industries producing key intermediate products and diversified manufacturing. At one extreme, the changes could lead to (further) deindustrialization. At the other, the advantages in terms of renewable energy provide an opportunity to place their decarbonization at the center of an employment-generating green structural transformation to realize diversified industrialization.

Historical industrial policies in South Africa built internationally competitive industries around large-scale, previously state-owned national champions. These did not become the basis for wider industrialization, however, as a result of the industrial policies followed and the market power of the lead companies (Andreoni, Kaziboni, and Roberts 2021; Black and Roberts 2009; Mondliwa et al. 2021).

The pivot to green hydrogen for these industries to decarbonize requires industrial, energy, and regulatory policies. The design of these policies will influence not only the changes in the upstream industries but also the terms on which they are supplied to downstream sectors, with implications for downstream competitiveness.

4.1 STEEL TO METAL PRODUCTS

The South African steel industry is dominated by ArcelorMittal South Africa (AMSA), which was formerly the state-owned Iscor. AMSA has the only flat steel mills in sub-Saharan Africa, with a large integrated blast oxygen furnace mill inland operating at a scale exceeding South African demand; thus, there are substantial exports. It also owns a more modern electric arc furnace mini-mill on the coast at Saldanha, which was built for export. High electricity prices, constrained generation, and weakened iron ore linkages has meant that the Saldanha plant was mothballed in 2020.

South Africa's industry is underpinned by low-cost, high-quality iron ore (ideal for the direct reduction of iron ore [DRI] method for green steel) and cheap energy; coking coal used as a reductant is imported and is relatively expensive. Changing to the use of hydrogen for steelmaking means replacing coking coal as a reductant, to reduce high-quality iron ore to sponge iron by extracting the oxygen. The iron is then processed into steel, typically through the use of electricity in electric arc furnaces or coal in blast furnaces.

The carbon intensity of the process, along with the potential of renewable energy and green hydrogen, means steel has been identified as a lead industry for green hydrogen in South Africa and around the world (Department of Trade, Industry and Competition, DTIC, 2023). South Africa is one of the most attractive international locations to make green steel, including for European export, given the renewable energy potential, existing industry base, high-quality iron ore, and available infrastructure (Trollip et al. 2022).

As green steel standards are adopted and enforced, including for steel in diversified manufactured products, the competitiveness of steel production around the world will depend on the costs of renewable energy and green hydrogen. Technological developments and reductions in renewable energy costs mean that it is expected that near-zero emission steel should approach the cost of high-emission steel, in the most favorable locations, by 2030. For example, India, one of the world's largest DRI steel producers, has targeted bringing the cost of green hydrogen down to $1.50/kg and to reach 5 million tonnes per annum of green hydrogen capacity by 2030, which would place it among the cheapest green hydrogen (GH2) producers worldwide.[2] Australia is targeting a GH2 price of $2.00/kg by 2030, while Chile's roadmap will make it the cheapest GH2 producer on the planet, at less than $1.50/kg, by 2030. To translate renewable energy into low-cost GH2 requires linked policies for investment, transmission, and production.

The benefits of lower renewable energy costs in countries with huge potential for solar and wind energy may be countered by subsidies in the United States and the European Union. Based on GH2 costs in 2022, which, at around $6.00/kg, are around three times that of alternatives, it has been estimated that a 30 percent higher green steel cost for European steel producers would need to be either compensated through subsidies or balanced by the application of carbon taxes on noncompliant steel, or a combination of the two (Meldrum et al. 2023). The global restructuring of the steel industry under decarbonization is thus going to depend on the combination of GH2 costs, coordinated policies for local industry competitiveness, international carbon duties, and subsidies. The investment and production decisions are being made by multinational companies, which are optimizing their operations across regions in response to the prevailing government policies. The United States and the European Union are pressing ahead with support for their industries under the guise of green new deals.

South Africa had among the lowest quartile costs in steel production in the 2000s, based on iron ore, coal, and historic industrial policy support. The industry was competitive and exported into European markets. As of 2019, approximately 5,000 jobs in basic iron and steel industries were accompanied by the direct formal employment of 228,000 in tin downstream fabricated metals and machinery industries (or 21 percent of total manufacturing employment; Zalk 2021).

Employment in downstream industries has been undermined, however, by a combination of monopolistic conduct by AMSA and a failure of appropriate policies—including skills and technology—for the manufacture of metal products and machinery (Andreoni et al. 2021). While steel recorded substantial net exports (around half of production when the plants operated at capacity), downstream industries have maintained substantial net trade deficits. AMSA priced steel to local buyers at import parity prices, some 50 percent higher than AMSA earned on exported steel (Black and Roberts 2009). Discriminatory pricing to local customers meant prices even higher than delivered to customers in Europe (Roberts 2008).

Realizing the potential for relatively low-cost green steel in South Africa requires a set of linked policies. The global move to renewable energy and green hydrogen for steelmaking is an opportunity for South Africa as green hydrogen replaces coking coal as a reductant, together with the advantages of abundant high-quality iron ore and existing infrastructure. However, the employment trajectory in the green transition will depend on the linkages to green downstream steel-using sectors.

The danger of the dominant steel firm dictating the policy agenda, coupled with the international incentives and border taxes, means it is likely that green steel will be exported in primary form. This will have fundamental consequences for employment. The plans being developed by AMSA in South Africa over 2021 and 2022, subsequently abandoned, were for exports of primary sponge steel to Europe and other markets—not to ensure that South African manufacturing had competitive green inputs. This lacuna is also evident in the approach to renewable energy—competitive green electricity is essential for diversified manufacturing, and not only in energy-intensive heavy industries. Provision of renewable energy to diverse customers requires the transmission infrastructure to match investments in energy generation. The South African government has delayed making the changes required.

The international concentration of the steel industry in a few countries and a few large companies makes strategic engagement with the leading multinational businesses even more important. The top five countries produce 75 percent of the world's steel, with China alone accounting for 50 percent. The top five steel companies are ArcelorMittal, three Chinese companies (Baowu Group, Ansteel Group, and Shagang Group), and Nippon Steel of Japan. The industry is represented and organized by the International Iron & Steel Institute, and government and industry have come together in the Organisation for Economic Co-operation and Development (OECD) Steel Committee.

The alignment of industry interests in the European Union and the United States and the failure of the South African government to respond to the opportunities mean that the green steel pivot in South Africa is likely to serve the green industrial transformation in Europe, with exports of commodity sponge steel from the renewable energy endowment and enclave GH2. It will avoid the steel industry closing, with the loss of additional jobs in the thousands, but it does not realize the industrialization potential across southern Africa from the wind, solar, and mineral endowment, with employment potential in the hundreds of thousands.

4.2 FERTILIZERS

Nitrogenous fertilizers account for around two-thirds of all fertilizers and are produced from ammonia, generally using natural gas. Their production is an important source of emissions that must be mitigated: production of ammonia from fossil fuels is nearly twice as emissions-intensive as crude steel production and four times as intensive as cement production in direct emissions (Chung et al. 2023, citing IEA 2021). Seventy percent of ammonia is used for fertilizers consumed by agriculture. Fertilizer supply and pricing are key factors for agriculture and food security, which faces major challenges of adaptation to climate change. The industry is also a substantial employer.

Green hydrogen to green ammonia for fertilizer links renewable energy to agriculture (Figure 11.6) and is the second most important positive tipping point, after electric vehicles, identified for a breakthrough in a study by Meldrum et al. (2023). As of 2022, three green ammonia projects were already operational around the world, and the first commercial-scale facility came online in 2024. Green ammonia can also act as a transport medium for hydrogen, and GH2 can be utilized as a fuel for electricity generation and powering large vehicles such as ships (Jones 2022; IEA 2021).

South Africa is a substantial net importer of ammonia and of fertilizer, in contrast to steel. Agriculture across southern Africa is faced with fertilizer prices that are substantially above world prices. Given transport costs, this means that fertilizer prices have been some 50 to 100 percent higher than world prices for benchmark products and that the business case

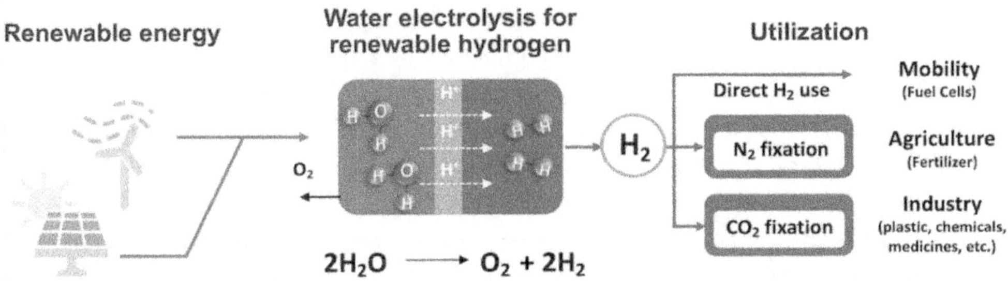

Figure 11.6 Green Hydrogen (GH2) transition opportunities and utilization in the chemicals sector

Source: Phillips (2022).

for green fertilizer is even stronger in South Africa, all else being equal. However, there are parallels with steel because the country faces a choice between investments in export enclaves of green ammonia to supply the rest of the world or production of green ammonia for fertilizer for local usage. By replacing high-priced imports, the shift to green ammonia and fertilizer at scale could reduce prices across southern Africa and improve food security. An additional parallel with steel is that a single company, Sasol, is the only producer of ammonia in southern Africa.

Sasol was built under state ownership on a coal–to–liquid fuels technology, which is extremely emissions intensive. This was to produce petrol, diesel, and kerosene. Sasol's Secunda operation is the largest single source of CO_2 in the world. Ammonia is produced by Sasol as a by-product from the coal–to–liquid fuels process and from natural gas as a feedstock. Decarbonization by Sasol is thus an existential challenge for the company. Green hydrogen is central to its transition, with the question being not if, but when and how.

The choices around green ammonia and links to fertilizer represent critical policy challenges about how the green transition happens and who benefits, with the impacts on employment and livelihoods in agriculture perhaps directly affecting a greater number of people than any other change in the green transition. This is a challenge for industrial policy and the regulatory regime that has facilitated Sasol's growth while enabling the company to retain its entrenched and vertically integrated position (Mondliwa and Roberts 2019).

Sasol had planned to transition its flagship Sasolburg plant as early as 2023 to act as the company's green hydrogen production base (Creamer

2021), however, as of 2024 this was yet to be implemented. Sasol's transition is aided by plans to develop a green hydrogen special economic zone supported by local and international funders such as the German government. These ventures include ammonia in the proposed Boegoebaai special economic zone in the Northern Cape province (Sasol 2022). The Boegoebaai development is similar to the Namibian investments located along the southwest coast of the continent, which offers the highest yielding wind and solar renewable energy potential (IEA 2021). The Namibia and Boegoebaii investments plan to produce GH2 and ammonia at scale for export, with green ammonia being used to replace heavy fuel oil as shipping fuel (Department of Trade, Industry and Competition, DTIC, 2023). This large-scale development aims to support 40 GW of electrolyzer capacity by 2050.

The economic case for green ammonia for fertilizer in southern Africa depends on the costs of the alternative. International ammonia costs have averaged $300/tonne from 2011 to 2020 (Meldrum et al. 2023). With the energy price spikes in 2021 and 2022 associated with Russia's invasion of Ukraine, prices increased to $1,000/tonne. Green ammonia was produced at around $700/ton in 2022, with the first utility project at scale under construction at Neom (in Saudi Arabia) expected to have substantially lower costs. Costs of green ammonia were projected to be $500/tonne in 2025 in planned exporting locations such as Namibia and Brazil, with a GH2 price of $2.20/kg, although projects have been delayed. The costs were predicted to fall by a further 20 to 30 percent by 2030-35. This means that a carbon tax of $100/ton would increase prices of ammonia from natural gas to parity with green ammonia in 2030.[3] By 2030-35, green ammonia from locations where renewable energy costs are low should be competitive in international markets.

When the relative prices in southern Africa are accounted for, green ammonia is competitive already in the region. South Africa is a net importer of ammonia and of fertilizers, and prices have been more than $200/tonne above international prices on an ongoing basis (figure 11.7). Prices in Zambia have been even further above world prices (apart from when the government subsidized fertilizer for farmers, as in March to June 2022). The case for local green fertilizer production is much stronger than for exports. Exporting countries of green ammonia must also subtract transport costs to supply international markets, reducing the net returns from these sales.

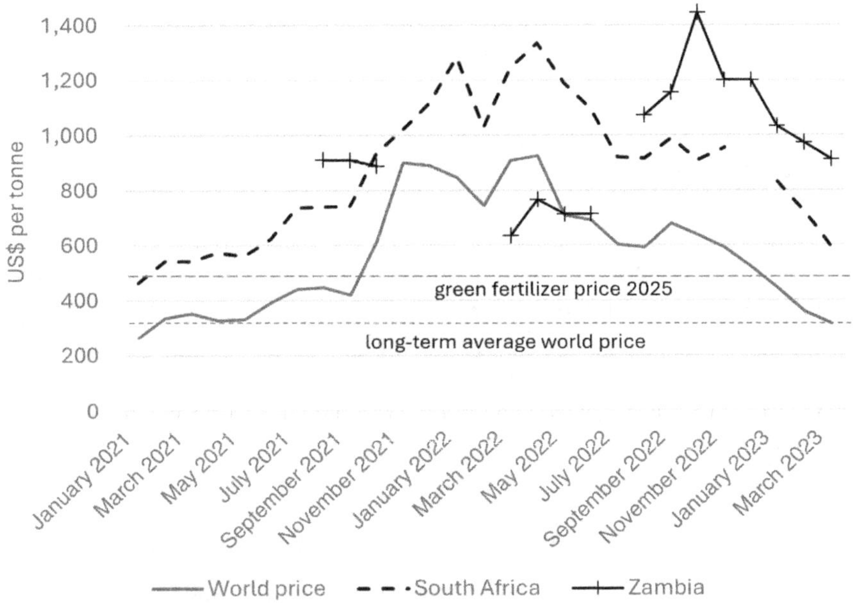

Figure 11.7 Urea fertilizer prices

Source: World price is from the World Bank. Eastern European and South African prices are from Grain SA.

It should not be a choice between a green fertilizer industry for southern Africa and an export enclave of green ammonia for international markets. The outcomes depend, however, on the major investment decisions made by the large companies.

Sasol's interests are to transform their operations, with maximum government support, in a way that ensures the best returns. The best returns depend on maintaining their dominant position in basic chemicals, including ammonia. This position has been entrenched by previous state support, rights to feedstock including coal and natural gas, and infrastructure provisions such as pipelines. The South African government has failed to use industrial policy, and regulatory and competition policy tools to discipline Sasol's exercise of market power from its entrenched dominant position (Mondliwa and Roberts 2019).

The opportunities represented by GH2 and fertilizer demand can mean investments by competing green ammonia and fertilizer producers with huge gains for agriculture across southern Africa. South Africa has had three large-scale producers of ammonia-based fertilizer and explosives. One fertilizer producer closed operations; the second is dependent on Sasol and imports for its ammonia. Green ammonia represents the potential for a diverse set of producers once again.

Sasol paints a picture of being too big to fail while it lobbies the government for favorable treatment, but its inherent advantages in the production and technology base means it is already at an advantage when it comes to investing in renewable energy and green hydrogen production. The risks from carbon taxes means it has to do so. It has realized huge windfall profits from high energy prices because of the Russian invasion of Ukraine. For competitive regional pricing and linkages to agriculture, it is essential that green industrial and energy policies support rival producers as well as Sasol.

5. CONCLUSIONS: THE ROLE OF THE STATE AND POLICY DIRECTIONS

The complex challenges posed by the green transition highlighted in this chapter in the context of South Africa—specifically the need to coordinate several structural interdependencies and opportunities while avoiding development traps—call for a renewed emphasis on the role of the state. The cases presented highlight how capturing green windows of opportunities, especially in terms of job creation, requires a focus on structural transformation. We have stressed how the necessary holistic approach to policymaking must be grounded in an understanding of both direct green job opportunities, and indirect employment generation dynamics in adjacent sectors of the economy. Job creation opportunities are nested along different sectoral value chains and linkages cutting across sectors. These opportunities can be unlocked only if linkages with minerals extraction and processing are developed and the traps of enclave development are avoided with strategic policy interventions.

Within this sustainable structural transformation perspective, it becomes clear how seizing and capturing green windows of opportunities require the strategic integration of different policies. For example, we have emphasized the importance of integrating policy for critical minerals with specific local content requirements and green conditionalities in the mining equipment industry, where large employment opportunities exist in South Africa. In another example, we have seen how aligning energy policy and industrial policy is essential for unlocking opportunities from green hydrogen to chemical and steel industries, with cascade effects along several downstream industries. The transformation of the energy-mineral complex, particularly central for South Africa, also requires integrating electricity regulation and industrial policy to plan, direct, and coordinate investments in critical infrastructure in grids, pipelines, and storage.

Market-shaping competition and regulatory rules are critical to create a viable and predictable business environment in the context of technological change and to avoid capture of the industry by the largest firms. The rules need to foster optimal levels of competition in sectors characterized by economies of scale and network effects and thus are prone to concentration. Developmental finance is also essential given the long-term nature of these investments and the need to combine multiple developmental goals. This implies that the state must play a dynamic industry-shaping role, influencing value creation and capture through regulatory rules and industrial policies.

Making these green transformations real in South Africa and across the African continent cannot be achieved realistically by compromising on the inclusiveness of these industrial transformations. The green transformation needs to be politically sustainable. Mainstreaming job creation is key to achieving such political sustainability. Strictly defined, green jobs are far too few to support a coalition for much-needed greening. Our structural transformation perspective provides some insights on how to mainstream job creation and broaden the horizon to create politically feasible pathways for change.

NOTES

1. The concept of energy-mineral complex was originally introduced by Fine and Rustomjee (1996).
2. See the National Green Hydrogen Mission of India at https://mnre.gov.in/en/national-green-hydrogen-mission/.
3. A carbon tax of $100 increases the cost of fossil fuel ammonia by close to $200/ton. Around 0.2 tons of hydrogen is required for 1 ton of ammonia. For example, the NEOM facility is going to produce 1.2 million tonnes per annum of ammonia from 220th tonnes per annum of green hydrogen (ACWA 2023).

REFERENCES

ACWA Power Company. 2023. *ACWA Power Company Earnings Call Presentation for the Fiscal Year Ended 31 December 2022*. ACWA Power Company. https://www

.acwapower.com/media/341900/acwa-power_12m2022-earnings-call_presentation_v4_20230302.pdf).

African Climate Foundation and Firoz Lalji Foundation. 2023. "Implications for African Countries of a Carbon Border Adjustment Mechanism in the EU." African Climate Foundation. https://africanclimatefoundation.org/news_and_analysis/implications-for-african-countries-of-a-carbon-border-adjustment-mechanism-in-africa/

Andreoni, A., and E. Avenyo. 2023a. "Critical Minerals and Routes to Diversification in Africa: Linkages, Pulling Dynamics and Opportunities in Medium and High-Tech Supply Chains." Background paper commissioned by the UNCTAD secretariat for the 2023 edition of the *Economic Development in Africa Report*, August 2023a. United Nations Trade and Development.

Andreoni, A., and E. K. Avenyo. "Critical Minerals and Routes to Diversification in Africa: Opportunities for Diversification into Batteries and Fuel Cells and Mining Equipment Technologies—The Case of South Africa." Background paper commissioned by the UNCTAD secretariat for the 2023 edition of the *Economic Development in Africa Report*, August 2023b. United Nations Trade and Development.

Andreoni, A., J. Bell, and S. Roberts. 2023. "Green Hydrogen for Sustainable (Re) Industrialisation in South Africa: Industrial Policy for Hard-to-Abate Industries and Linkages Development." CCRED Working Paper 2023/8. Centre for Competition, Regulation and Economic Development (CCRED).

Andreoni, A., K. Creamer, M. Mazzucato, G. Steyn. 2022. "How Can South Africa Advance a New Energy Paradigm? A Mission-oriented Approach to Megaprojects." *Oxford Review of Economic Policy* 38(2): 237–59.

Andreoni, A., L. Kaziboni, and S. Roberts. 2021. "Metals, Machinery, and Mining Equipment Industries in South Africa: The Relationship Between Power, Governance, and Technological Capabilities." In *Structural Transformation in South Africa: The Challenges of Inclusive Industrial Development in a Middle-Income Country*, edited by A. Andreoni, P. Mondliwa, S. Roberts, and F. Tregenna. Oxford University Press.

Andreoni, A., K. Lee, and S. Torreggiani. 2021. "GVCs, 'In-Out-In' Industrialization, and the Global Patterns of Sectoral Value Addition." In *Structural Transformation in South Africa: The Challenges of Inclusive Industrial Development in a Middle-Income Country.*, edited by A. Andreoni, P. Mondliwa, S. Roberts, and F. Tregenna. Oxford University Press

Andreoni, A., P. Mondliwa, S. Roberts, and F. Tregenna. 2021. *Structural Transformation in South Africa: The Challenges of Inclusive Industrial Development in a Middle-Income Country.* Oxford University Press.

Andreoni, A., and S. Roberts. 2022. *Geopolitics of Critical Minerals in Renewable Energy Supply Chains: Assessing Conditionalities on the Use of Technology, Market Capture and the Implications for Africa.* The African Climate Foundation. https://africanclimatefoundation.org/research-article/geopolitics-of-critical-minerals-in-renewable-energy-supply-chains/.

Andreoni, A., and S. Torreggiani. 2020. "Mining Equipment Industry in South Africa: Global Context, Industrial Ecosystem, and Pathways for Feasible Sectoral Reform." CCRED Report for Masterplan. CCRED Working Paper 2020/3. Centre for Competition, Regulation and Economic Development (CCRED).

Andreoni, A., and F. Tregenna. 2020. "Escaping the Middle-Income Technology Trap: A Comparative Analysis of Industrial Policies in China, Brazil and South Africa." *Structural Change and Economic Dynamics* 54: 324–40.

Avenyo, E. K., and F. Tregenna. 2022. "Greening Manufacturing: Technology Intensity and Carbon Dioxide Emissions in Developing Countries." *Applied Energy* 324: 119726.

Black, A., and S. Roberts. 2009. "The Evolution and Impact of Industrial and Competition Policies." In *South African Economy Policy Under Democracy*, edited by J. Aron, B. Kahn, and G. Kingdon. Oxford University Press.

Chung, C., J. Kim, B. K. Sovacool, S. Griffiths, M. Bazilian, and M. Yang. 2023. "Decarbonizing the Chemical Industry: A Systematic Review of Sociotechnical Systems, Technological Innovations, and Policy Options." *Energy Research & Social Science* 96: 102

Creamer, T. 2021. "Sasol Aims to Begin Producing Green Hydrogen in Sasolburg from 2023. *Engineering News*. https://www.engineeringnews.co.za/article/sasol-aims-to-begin-producing-green-hydrogen-in-sasolburg-from-2023-2021-11-22/rep_id:4136.

Department of Mineral Resources (DMR). 2013. *Fuel Cells and the Future Role of South Africa Through Its Platinum Resources*. Report R99/2013. Department of Mineral Resources, South Africa.

Department of Trade, Industry and Competition (DTIC). 2023. *Green Hydrogen Commercialisation Strategy for South Africa: Full Report*. https://www.idc.co.za/wp-content/uploads/2023/11/GHCS-Full-Report-17Oct23-Public-Submission.pdf.

Fine, B., and Z. Rustomjee. 1996. *The Political Economy of South Africa: From Minerals-Energy Complex to Industrialisation*. Witwatersrand University Press.

Griffiths, S., B. K. Sovacool, J. Kim, M. Bazilian, and J. M. Uratani. 2021. "Industrial Decarbonization via Hydrogen: A Critical and Systematic Review of Developments, Socio-Technical Systems and Policy Options." *Energy Research & Social Science* 80: 102208.

Hochstetler, K. 2020. *Political Economies of Energy Transition. Wind and Solar Power in Brazil and South Africa*. Cambridge University Press.

International Energy Agency (IEA). 2021. "Ammonia Technology Roadmap." International Energy Agency. https://www.iea.org/reports/ammonia-technology-roadmap

International Energy Agency (IEA). 2022a. *Special Report on Solar PV Global Supply Chains*. International Energy Agency. https://iea.blob.core.windows.net/assets/2d18437f-211d-4504-beeb-570c4d139e25/SpecialReportonSolarPVGlobalSupplyChains.pdf.

International Energy Agency (IEA). 2022b. *World Energy Employment Report*. International Energy Agency. https://www.iea.org/reports/world-energy-employment

International Labor Organization (ILO) and International Renewable Energy Agency (IRENA). 2022. *Renewable Energy and Jobs: Annual Review 2022*. International Labor Organization. https://www.ilo.org/global/publications/books/WCMS_856649/lang--en/index.htm.

IRENA and AfDB. 2022. *Renewable Energy Market Analysis: Africa and Its Regions*. International Renewable Energy Agency and African Development Bank, Abu Dhabi and Abidjan. https://www.irena.org/publications/2022/Jan/Renewable-Energy-Market-Analysis-Africa.

Jones, N. 2022. "From Fertilizer to Fuel: Can 'Green' Ammonia Be a Climate Fix?" Yale Environment 360, Yale School of the Environment. https://e360.yale.edu/features/from-fertilizer-to-fuel-can-green-ammonia-be-a-climate-fix.

Meldrum, M., L. Pinnell, K. Brennan, M. Romani, S. Sharpe, and T. Lenton. 2023. *The Breakthrough Effect: How to Trigger a Cascade of Tipping Points to Accelerate the Net Zero Transition.* Systemiq, University of Exeter, and Bezos Earth Fund. https://www.systemiq.earth/wp-content/uploads/2023/01/The-Breakthrough-Effect.pdf.

Mondliwa, P., S. Goga, and S. Roberts. 2021. "Competition, Productive Capabilities and Structural Transformation in South Africa." *European Journal of Development Research* 33: 253–74.

Mondliwa, P., and S. Roberts. 2019. "From a Developmental to a Regulatory State? Sasol and the Conundrum of Continued State Support." *International Review of Applied Economics* 33 (1): 11–29.

Phillips, A., 2022. "Green Hydrogen Production for Fuel Cells and Fertilizers." https://itaintmagic.riken.jp/hot-off-the-press/green-hydrogen-production-for-fuel-cells-and-fertilizers/.

Roberts, S. 2008. "Assessing Excessive Pricing—the Case of Flat Steel in South Africa." *Journal of Competition Law and Economics* 4 (3): 871–91.

Sasol. 2022. "Sasol and ITOCHU Announcing Memorandum of Understanding (MoU) on Green Hydrogen and Ammonia." Sasol. https://www.sasol.com/media-centre/media-releases/sasol-and-itochu-announcing-memorandum-understanding-mou-green-hydrogen-and-ammonia.

Trade & Industrial Policy Strategies (TIPS) and United Nations Industrial Development Organization (UNIDO). 2021. "Opportunities to Develop Lithium-Ion Battery Value Chain in South Africa." Trade & Industrial Policy Strategies, South Africa. https://www.tips.org.za/images/Battery_Manufacturing_value_chain_study_main_report_March_2021.pdf.

Trollip, H., B. McCall, and C. Bataille. 2022. "How Green Primary Iron Production in South Africa Could Help Global Decarbonization." *Climate Policy* 22 (2): 236–47.

Vilakazi, T., and T. Bosiu. 2021. "Black Economic Empowerment, Barriers to Entry, and Economic Transformation in South Africa." In *Structural Transformation in South Africa: The Challenges of Inclusive Industrial Development in a Middle-Income Country*, edited by A. Andreoni, P. Mondliwa, S. Roberts, and F. Tregenna. Oxford University Press.

World Bank. 2023. *Minerals for Climate Action: The Mineral Intensity of the Clean Energy Transition.* World Bank. https://openknowledge.worldbank.org/entities/publication/4dd08d0c-ab51-4955-a464-35a95201a5eb

Zalk, N. (2021) "Structural Change in South Africa: A Historical Sectoral Perspective" In *Structural Transformation in South Africa: The Challenges of Inclusive Industrial Development in a Middle-Income Country*, edited by A. Andreoni, P. Mondliwa, S. Roberts, and F. Tregenna. Oxford University Press

ABOUT THE CONTRIBUTORS

AKBAR NOMAN is an economist with wide-ranging experience of policy analysis and formulation in a variety of developing and transition economies, having worked extensively for the World Bank, the IMF as well as other international organizations and at senior levels of government. He taught at SIPA, Columbia University from 2005–2025 and is a Senior Fellow at the Initiative for Policy Dialogue. He has, for over two decades, run the Advanced Graduate Workshop for PhD students in Manchester, England, and Bangalore, India. His other academic appointments have been at Oxford University and the Institute of Development Studies at the University of Sussex.

EDUARDO ÓSCAR ÁLVAREZ is a lawyer specializing in labor law, having obtained his degree from the University of Buenos Aires. He has served as a national labor judge and general prosecutor before the National Court of Labor Appeals. He teaches graduate and postgraduate courses at various national and foreign universities. He has also authored monographs and publications on individual and collective labor law.

ANTONIO ANDREONI is professor of development economics at the Department of Economics of the School of Oriental and African Studies (SOAS) at the University of London and codirector of the Centre for Sustainable Structural Transformation (CSST). He is also Distinguished Visiting Professor at the South African Research Chair in Industrial Development, University of Johannesburg. Andreoni is an internationally renowned expert on inclusive and sustainable structural transformation, with a focus on green industrialization and industrial policy. He has published extensively in top journals including *World Development*, *Cambridge Journal of Economics*, *Development and Change*,

Technovation, *Energy Policy*, and *Oxford Review of Economic Policy*. His books include *Structural Transformation in South Africa* (Oxford University Press, 2021). For over fifteen years Andreoni has advised several international organizations—including United Nations Industrial Development Organization (UNIDO), UN Trade and Development (UNCTAD), International Labor Organization (ILO), United Nations Development Programme (UNDP), United Nations Economic Commission for Africa (UNECA), World Bank, Organisation for Economic Co-operation and Development (OECD)—and national governments in industrial policymaking.

KARISHMA BANGA is an assistant professor in digital economy at King's College London, and the digital trade policy adviser at the Commonwealth Businesswomen's Network, United Kingdom. Her ongoing research examines Industry 4.0, digital trade negotiations, and global value chains (GVCs), with a focus on their development implications. She has led and collaborated on a range of projects on digital economy with international and multilateral organizations, such as the United Nations Economic Commission for Africa (UNECA), Commonwealth Secretariat, UN Trade and Development (UNCTAD), the African Union, and the World Trade Organization (WTO). Prior to joining King's College, Banga held research positions at the Institute of Development Studies (Brighton), the International Economic Development Group at the Overseas Development Institute (ODI) (London), and the Centre for Trade and Economic Integration (Geneva). She has a PhD in development economics from the University of Manchester and an MPhil in economics from the University of Cambridge.

AMIT BASOLE is a professor of economics and head, Centre for Sustainable Employment at Azim Premji University, Bengaluru. He is the lead author of the *State of Working India* report.

HAROON BHORAT is a professor of economics and director of the Development Policy Research Unit at the University of Cape Town, and one of the most cited South African economists globally. His work has been hugely influential in policymaking in the areas of poverty, inequality, and labor market issues in South Africa. He is a nonresident senior fellow at the Brookings Institution and at UNU-WIDER and a research fellow at IZA; he was a Cornell University research fellow and studied at the Massachusetts Institute of Technology. He is currently a member of the Steering Committee of the International Economic Association (IEA), and he was a member on the advisory board of the United

Nations Development Programme's (UNDP) 2019 and 2020 and 2024 Human Development Reports. He sat on the World Bank's advisory board of the Commission on Global Poverty. Bhorat is an adviser to President Ramaphosa, serving on his Presidential Economic Advisory Council (PEAC). He also served as an economic adviser to two past ministers of finance and previous presidents Mbeki and Motlanthe.

NANCY H. CHAU is a professor of economics at the Charles H. Dyson School of Applied Economics and Management at Cornell University. Her areas of expertise are international economics, development economics, and regional economics. She received a PhD in economics from the Johns Hopkins University. Chau was awarded the Alexander von Humboldt Research Fellowship, and the first T. W. Schultz Award of the International Agricultural Economics Association. Her publications appeared in *Economic Journal*, *International Economic Review*, *Journal of Development Economics*, *Journal of Economic Growth*, *Journal of Economic Theory*, *Journal of Labor Economics*, *Journal of Law and Economics*, *Journal of Public Economics*, *Journal of Public Economic Theory*, and the *World Bank Economic Review*.

ZICO DASGUPTA is an assistant professor of economics at Azim Premji University, Bengaluru. His research focuses on issues of growth and distribution, monetary economics, and macroeconomic policies.

ALEJANDRO RAÚL FERRARI is a lawyer. He also serves as a union adviser and professor of labor law at the University of Buenos Aires. He also provides counsel to the Minister of Labor, Employment, and Social Security.

TETSUYA HARADA is a principal research fellow at the Japan International Cooperation Agency (JICA) Ogata Sadako Research Institute for Peace and Development, the research arm of JICA. He has extensive experience working with JICA, the World Bank, and Japan Bank for International Cooperation (JBIC) on economic infrastructure projects, policy-based loans, and corporate lending, primarily in Southeast Asia and sub-Saharan Africa. He has focused on macroeconomic monitoring and financial risk management for lending programs. At the Ogata Research Institute, Harada has published several journal articles on impact evaluations of donor-funded community development projects. He has been advancing research on structural transformation and leading studies on corridor development in Africa and the socioeconomic impact of a major bridge project in India. He has also contributed a series of Japanese newspaper articles on sovereign debt issues in developing countries. Harada holds a master of public administration from Columbia University in the United States and a master of economics from Hosei University in Japan.

ROBERT HILL is a junior research fellow at the Development Policy Research Unit and a PhD candidate at the University of Cape Town (UCT). His research focuses on the impact of curriculum change on prosocial behaviours, academic intervention, and throughput in the economics discipline. His expertise includes labor economics, education, and behavioral economics, all with a focus on econometric application. He holds a master in communications in applied economics from UCT. Hill is actively involved in both research pursuits and teaching for the School of Economics at UCT. He has taught courses ranging from introductory microeconomics to honors-level mathematics and labor economics courses. Hill was also involved in the rollout of the CORE Curriculum at UCT in 2019, leading the development of the game theory, experimental economics, and labor market sections of the curriculum.

ARJUN JAYADEV is a professor of economics and the director at the School of Arts and Sciences at Azim Premji University (APU), Bangalore. He is a senior economist at the Institute for New Economic Thinking. He has also worked as an associate professor of economics at the University of Massachusetts, Boston; as a fellow at Roosevelt Institute, New York; and as a research fellow at the Columbia University Committee on Global Thought, New York. His research interests are economics and development, with a focus across multiple areas such as macroeconomics (especially issues of debt, balance sheets, the political economy of finance and central banking, and macroeconomic policy choices), income distribution and inequality (classical approaches to distribution, and group-based inequalities), intellectual property, and the economics of power. He has won numerous awards for his research.

RAVI KANBUR researches and teaches in development economics, public economics, and economic theory at Cornell University. He has served on the senior staff of the World Bank, including as chief economist for Africa. He has also published in the leading economics journals, including *Journal of Political Economy*, *American Economic Review*, *Review of Economic Studies*, *Journal of Economic Theory*, and *Economic Journal*. The positions he has held include cochair of the Food Systems Economics Commission, chair of the Board of United Nations University/World Institute for Development Economics Research (UNU/

WIDER), member of the Organisation for Economic Co-operation and Development (OECD) High Level Expert Group on the Measurement of Economic Performance, president of the Human Development and Capability Association, president of the Society for the Study of Economic Inequality, member of the High Level Advisory Council of the Climate Justice Dialogue, cochair of the Scientific Council of the International Panel on Social Progress, and member of the Core Group of the Commission on Global Poverty.

TIMOTHY KÖHLER is a junior research fellow at the Development Policy Research Unit and a recent PhD graduate from the University of Cape Town. As an applied development microeconomist, his research centers around the socioeconomic causes and consequences of poverty and inequality in lower-income countries, and South Africa in particular, focusing on the roles of labor markets, social protection policy, education, and health care. He earned his undergraduate, honor's, and master's degrees from Stellenbosch University. He previously worked as a research assistant for the Research on Socio-Economic Policy (RESEP) unit in Stellenbosch University's Department of Economics, which he remains affiliated with, and as a research intern in the South African Reserve Bank. He regularly conducts policy-relevant research for several South African government departments such as the presidency, national treasury, and the department of employment and labour, and for multilateral organizations such as the World Bank and the United Nations.

DAVID LAM is professor emeritus in the Department of Economics and research professor emeritus in the Population Studies Center at the University of Michigan. He served as director of the University of Michigan's Institute for Social Research from 2015 to 2021. He is honorary professor of economics at the University of Cape Town and a research associate at the National Bureau of Economic Research (NBER). He has worked extensively in Brazil and South Africa, where his research analyzes links between education, labor markets, and income inequality. He has served as president of the Population Association of America and on the council of the International Union for the Scientific Study of Population (IUSSP). He was a member of the Committee on Population of the US National Academy of Sciences and has served as an adviser or consultant to the World Bank, the US National Institutes of Health, the UN Population Division, and the United Nations Development Program (UNDP).

MURRAY LEIBBRANDT holds the University of Cape Town (UCT) Research Chair in Poverty and Inequality Research within the Southern Africa Labour and Development Research Unit (SALDRU) at the University of Cape Town. He is the director for the African Research Universities Alliance African Centre of Excellence for Inequality Research, a visiting professor at Yale University, and a nonresident senior research fellow at UNU-WIDER. He has served as the pro-vice-chancellor, Poverty and Inequality, at the University of Cape Town; DSD/NRF National Research Chair of Poverty and Inequality Research; a member of the executive committee of the International Economic Association; president of the African Econometric Society; and president of the Economic Society of South Africa. Currently he is one of the principal investigators of Health and Aging in Africa: Longitudinal Studies in South Africa (HAALSA) and has served as one of the principal investigators for South Africa's National Income Dynamics Study. He was a member of President Nelson Mandela's Presidential Labour Market Commission and a member of Deputy President Cyril Ramaphosa's Panel of Experts on the National Minimum Wage.

CLAUDIO OMAR MORONI is a lawyer, holding a degree from the University of Buenos Aires. He has served as the Minister of Labor, Employment, and Social Security. He has also held the positions of director of the Federal Administration of Public Revenues and executive director of the National Administration of Social Security. He chaired the 110th International Labor Conference of the International Labor Organization in 2022.

RYOSUKE NAKATA is chief economist of the Japan International Cooperation Agency (JICA) at the time of publication. Throughout his career at JICA, he worked mostly in the field of macroeconomic analysis of partner countries as well as in the field of concessional loan operations in Asian countries. Positions he held include chief representative of JICA USA office, senior adviser of the Credit Risk and Environmental Review Department, deputy director general of the South East Asia Department, and deputy director general of the Economic Infrastructure Development Department. In addition to the various positions at JICA, he has held lectures on macroeconomic development and policies in various universities, including the National Graduate Institute for Policy Studies (GRIPS), Saitama University, and Nagoya University. He holds an MA in economics from the Graduate School of Cornell University.

ÖZLEM ONARAN is professor of economics at the University of Greenwich; the codirector of the Institute of Political Economy, Governance, Finance and Accountability; and associate head of the School of Accounting, Finance and Economics for Research. She has done extensive research on issues of inequalities, growth, employment, fiscal policy, the green economy, the care economy, and gender. She has directed research projects for the UN International Labour Organisation (ILO), UN Trade and Development (UNCTAD), ESRC Rebuilding Macroeconomics, International Trade Union Confederation (ITUC), the Institute for New Economic Thinking, the Foundation of European Progressive Studies, the Vienna Chamber of Labour, the Austrian Science Foundation, and Unions21. She is a member of the Council of the Progressive Economy Forum, Scientific Committee of the Foundation of European Progressive Studies, Scientific Advisory Board of Hans Boeckler Foundation, Policy Advisory Group of the Women's Budget Group, and Coordinating Committee of the Research Network Macroeconomics and Macroeconomic Policies, and a research associate at the Political Economy Research Institute of the University of Massachusetts, Amherst. She has more than ninety articles in books and leading peer reviewed journals such as *Cambridge Journal of Economics*, *Feminist Economics*, *World Development*, *Environment and Planning A*, *Socio-Economic Review*, *Development and Change*, *Public Choice*, *Economic Inquiry*, *European Journal of Industrial Relations*, *International Review of Applied Economics*, *Structural Change and Economic Dynamics*, *Eastern European Economics*, and *Review of Political Economy*.

CEM OYVAT is an associate professor in economics at the University of Greenwich in the School of Accounting, Finance and Economics and the Centre of Political Economy, Governance, Finance and Accountability (PEGFA). He received his PhD in economics from the University of Massachusetts, Amherst. His research interests include income distribution, agrarian structures and land inequality, urbanization, the informal sector, gender economics, the care economy, wage-led growth, conflict economics, and the impact of globalization on distribution. He has published articles in *World Development*, *Cambridge Journal of Regions, Economy and Society*, *Feminist Economics*, *Electoral Studies*, *Metroeconomica*, and *Structural Change and Economic Dynamics*, among others.

SIDRA REHMAN is an economist in the International Monetary Fund's (IMF) European Department covering Ukraine. Before that, Rehman was at the Middle East and Central Asia Department, where her responsibilities included country assignments on Saudi Arabia, Qatar, Yemen, and Djibouti as well as analytical areas related to debt, climate change, fragile states, and inclusive growth. In addition, she has worked in the IMF's Research Department and the Asia Pacific Department, where her focus was on structural reforms, trade, and the impact of automation. Before joining the IMF, Rehman worked at the World Bank and the World Trade Organization (WTO). Her main research interests lie in development economics with a focus on growth, trade, and human capital issues. She holds a PhD and an MPA from Columbia University, and a BSc from Lahore University of Management Sciences.

SIMON ROBERTS is a professor of economics at the University of Johannesburg, where he founded the Centre for Competition, Regulation and Economic Development (CCRED), and a research professor at the Centre for Sustainable Structural Transformation, School of Oriental and African Studies. From 2022, Roberts has been building an African Market Observatory on food and agriculture markets in the context of climate change. Simon has been an economics director at the UK Competition and Markets Authority (2019 to 2020) and the chief economist and manager of the Policy & Research Division at the Competition Commission of South Africa from 2006 to 2012. Roberts has been closely involved in the development of competition regimes across Africa. He has testified as an expert witness in a number of major cases in South Africa.

DIEGO SCHLESER holds a degree in economics from the University of Buenos Aires. He currently serves as the Undersecretary of Planning, Studies, and Statistics at the Ministry of Labor, Employment, and Social Security. In addition, he is a professor of the Diploma Program in Labor Studies at the Labor and Development Training and Research Center of the University of San Martín. His research expertise lies in the field of labor economics and social and labor policies.

VIDHYA SOUNDARARAJAN is a research director at the Centre for Advanced Financial Research and Learning (CAFRAL) and an assistant professor of economics at the Indian Institute of Technology, Bombay. She is an applied microeconomist, with a focus on studying the effects of various economic shocks (financial, trade, regulatory) on firm behavior, performance, and productivity. Her recent research examines the impact of import competition on contract labor, informality, and firm performance, as well as the effects of employment protection laws on informality. Her work has been published in journals such as the *Journal of Development Economics*, *European Economic Review*, and *Journal of Economic Behavior and Organization*. She was previously a faculty member at the Indian Institute of Management, Bangalore; has held various consulting positions with the World Bank; and is a core committee member of the Society for Economics Research in India. She earned her PhD in applied economics from Cornell University in 2016.

FRANÇOIS STEENKAMP is a senior research officer at the Development Policy Research Unit at the University of Cape Town (UCT). Steenkamp has a PhD from UCT, that was focused on South African export patterns and the developmental implications of these export patterns. He also holds a master's degree in economics from the University of KwaZulu Natal. He spent time working as a lecturer at the UCT School of Economics, where he taught international trade and macroeconomics. His research interests include the dynamics and patterns of trade, international economics, labor economics, economic development, structural transformation, and economic complexity.

JOSEPH E. STIGLITZ is an American economist and a professor at Columbia University. He is also the chief economist of the Roosevelt Institute. He is the recipient of the Nobel Memorial Prize in Economic Sciences (2001); the John Bates Clark Medal (1979); the 2018 Sydney Peace Prize; the XXXV Catalonia International Prize (2023); and numerous honorary doctorates, including from Harvard, Oxford, and Cambridge. He was a lead author of the 1995 *Report of the Intergovernmental Panel on Climate Change*, which received the 2007 Nobel Peace Prize. Stiglitz is a former senior vice president and chief economist at the World Bank and a former member and chair of the (US president's) Council of Economic Advisers. In 2000, Stiglitz founded the Initiative for Policy Dialogue, a think tank on international development based at Columbia University. He has been a member of the Columbia faculty since 2001 and received that university's highest academic rank (university professor) in 2003. In 2011, Stiglitz was named by *Time* magazine as one of the one hundred most influential people in the world. He is the author of numerous books, including several bestsellers. His most recent titles are *The Road to Freedom: Economics and the Good Society*; *People, Power, and Profits*; *Rewriting the Rules of the European Economy*; *Globalization and Its Discontents Revisited*; *The Euro*; and *Rewriting the Rules of the American Economy.*

PABLO ARNALDO TOPET is a lawyer. He currently serves as a professor of labor law and social security at the University of Buenos Aires. Before that, he held the position of National Director of Labor Relations at the Ministry of Labor, Employment, and Social Security. He has also worked as an external consultant for the International Labor Organization (ILO), specifically in the area of freedom of association.

DAVID TRAJTEMBERG holds a degree in economics from the University of Buenos Aires. He is a professor and researcher at the National University of La Matanza. He serves as the director of Studies and Statistics on Labor Relations at the Ministry of Labor, Employment, and Social Security. His research interests center predominantly around labor economics and labor relations.

AGUSTIN VELASQUEZ is an economist at the Strategy, Policy, and Review Department and simultaneously holds country assignment responsibilities for Tanzania in the African Department. Before these responsibilities, he was an economist for the Concessional Financing Division in the Finance Department, and country economist for Bahrain in the Middle East and Central Asia Department. Prior to joining the International Monetary Fund (IMF), he worked at the Employment Policy Department of the International Labor Organization (ILO). In his previous roles, he covered topics related to structural reforms, labor market institutions, and the impact of international trade on labor market outcomes. He holds a PhD and an MA in international economics from the Graduate Institute of International and Development Studies, an MSc in applied labor economics for development from the University of Torino and Sciences Po, and a BA in economics from the University of Buenos Aires.

CAITLIN ALLEN WHITEHEAD is currently a group measurement specialist for Allan & Gill Gray Philanthropies. She was previously a junior researcher at the Development Policy Research Unit at the University of Cape Town (UCT). She has also worked as a junior researcher for J-PAL Africa doing data analysis and as a junior researcher for the Economics of Tobacco Control Project at UCT. Whitehead graduated with a master of commerce in applied economics from UCT in 2018. She held a Vice Chancellors Scholarship throughout her undergraduate studies at Nelson Mandela University and was an Allan Gray Orbis Foundation Fellow.

INDEX

GPSR Authorized Representative: Easy Access System Europe, Mustamäe tee 50, 10621 Tallinn, Estonia, gpsr.requests@easproject.com

www.ingramcontent.com/pod-product-compliance
Lightning Source LLC
Jackson TN
JSHW022226220226
98413JS00018B/263/J
9780231220330